MOON

MONTANA

JUDY JEWELL & W. C. McRAE

35

MONTANA

D A

S   T   A   T   E   S

Havre

Fort Belknap
Indian
Reservation

2

Malta

Fort   Peck

Indian   Reservation

Culbertson

2

191

Glasgow

Wolf Point

Missouri   River

Charles M Russell
National Wildlife
Refuge

UL Bend
NWR

13

Sidney

200

Charles M
Russell NWR

Missouri

River

Fort
Peck Lake

Circle

Jordan

200

Glendive

94

Lewistown

59

River

191

87

12

Miles City

12

Baker

Harlowton

Roundup

NORTH   DAKOTA

12

3

Yellowstone

94

59

Billings

90

Hardin

Crow

Indian

Reservation

Bighorn
Canyon
National
Recreation
Area

Northern
Cheyenne
Indian
Reservation

Custer

National

Forest

Broadus

212

212

310

Bighorn

14A

Sheridan

Shoshone

14A

WYOMING

National

ational Forest

14   16   20

14

Forest

90

120

16
20

25

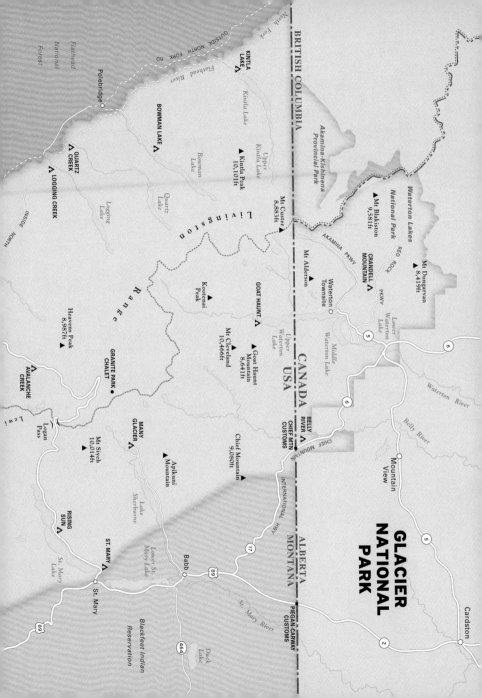

GLACIER NATIONAL PARK

BRITISH COLUMBIA

CANADA
USA

ALBERTA
MONTANA

Flathead National Forest

Polebridge

OUTSIDE NORTH FORK RD

North Fork

Flathead River

Kintla Lake

▲ KINTLA LAKE

▲ BOWMAN LAKE

Bowman Lake

Upper Kintla Lake

▲ Kintla Peak 10,101ft

QUARTZ CREEK ▲

LOGGING CREEK ▲

Logging Lake

Quartz Lake

INSIDE NORTH

Livingston

Range

Mt Custer 8,883ft ▲

Akamina-Kishinena Provincial Park

Waterton Lakes National Park

▲ Mt Blakiston 9,581ft

▲ Mt Dungarvan 8,419ft

RED ROCK PKWY

AKAMINA PKWY

CRANDELL MOUNTAIN ▲

Mt Alderson ▲

Waterton Townsite

Upper Waterton Lake

Lower Waterton Lake

Middle Waterton Lake

Kootenai Peak ▲

GOAT HAUNT ▲

Heavens Peak 8,987ft ▲

GRANITE PARK CHALET ●

Mt Cleveland 10,466ft ▲

Goat Haunt Mountain 8,641ft ▲

AVALANCHE CREEK ▲

Lewi

Logan Pass

MANY GLACIER ▲

Mt Siyeh 10,014ft ▲

Apikuni Mountain ▲

Chief Mountain 9,080ft ▲

CHIEF MTN CUSTOMS

BELLY RIVER

CHIEF MOUNTAIN

INTERNATIONAL HWY

Waterton River

Belly River

Mountain View

Cardston

RISING SUN ▲

ST. MARY ▲

St. Mary

St. Mary Lake

Lake Sherburne

Lower St. Mary Lake

Babb

Blackfeet Indian Reservation

Duck Lake

St. Mary River

PIEGAN-CARWAY CUSTOMS

Contents

DISCOVER
Montana

There is a grandness to Montana that surpasses mere size and encompasses something more of the spirit. With its soaring Rocky Mountain peaks rising above high plains carved by mighty rivers, Montana seems a place of legend, a marvel of vastness, wilderness, and epic history at the very crown of the continent. One might even say that Montana is more than a state—Montana is a state of mind.

For such a remote place, Montana has been a traveler's destination for centuries. During summers, Native American hunting parties journeyed into Montana, returning to their mountain homes with stories of a rich, mysterious land full of buffalo and holy sites. Cattle drivers, following the seasons northward, summered in Montana and returned south with tales of abundant game, endless grasslands, and high adventure. Immigrant farmers and ranchers were drawn to the expanses of Montana and brought the newcomer's conviction of fresh beginnings and wry aspirations. Nowadays, Montana attracts writers and artists who find in the state a "sense of place" both nurturing and challenging to the people who endure here.

Clockwise from top left: on the trail to Avalanche Lake in Glacier National Park; cows near Jordan; backpacking in Montana; red barn on a Montana ranch; cross-country skiing; elk.

Montana is often described as if it were two states—an eastern prairie and a western mountain range—but more than a common government links these regions. A visitor first notices the space: A sense of monumentality unites Montana, whether it's the glaciated peaks of the west or the eroded badlands of the east. It's called Big Sky Country; out here nature limbers up, stretches past the horizons, and takes up room.

But as much as space, the people define Montana. Today's Montanans derive from many strains: immigrant farmer, sheepherder, Native American, miner, logger, shopkeeper, rancher. They were all people who came to a hard land and stayed, making from Montana a living only of sorts, but always a home. Montanans are self-reliant and quick to see humor, with personalities so expansive that so few really do fill the state.

History is not very old here. Montanans are still experiencing their past, not as Western history, but as Western ethic. We invite you to experience this: Stop to investigate Montana's towns and cities, its streams and parks. Follow a hunch, dawdle along a side road. The land fairly explodes with small epiphanies of beauty. Take the long way around to a spot where a moment of history can be relived, where a lazy picnic can be shared, or where the obscure and the out-of-the-way can be found for its own sake.

Clockwise from top left: goats in Glacier National Park; the World Museum of Mining in Butte; one of Glacier National Park's red buses; rams on the road near Sula.

Planning Your Trip

Where to Go

Missoula and Northwestern Montana

Missoula is a friendly student-oriented city that's home to the University of Montana, legions of writers, and a dynamic arts community. To the south, the narrow **Bitterroot Valley** is a recreational wonderland. The Bitterroot River is renowned for trout fishing. Overlooking the rugged **Mission Mountains,** the **National Bison Range** preserves a wild herd of the American bison, hunted nearly to extinction in other parts of the West. **Flathead Lake** is one of the state's most popular destinations. This is an ideal place for a quiet vacation of water sports and fishing. **Bigfork,** on the lake's east side, is one of the artsiest small towns in Montana, with some of the best restaurants in the state. **Whitefish** sits at the

base of the large destination ski resort **Whitefish Mountain Resort.** The two combine to create a lively recreational scene, both in winter and summer.

Glacier National Park

The single most scenic destination in Montana, this park protects a wilderness of lakes, towering glacier-scarred peaks, and fragile alpine meadows. **Lake McDonald** glimmers at the base of the fantastically carved peaks. You'd be hard-pressed to find a more scenic drive in North America than **Going-to-the-Sun Road,** which climbs from the lake to cross the Continental Divide. **Waterton Lakes National Park,** adjoining Glacier Park in Canada, continues this wonderful mountain and lake scenery. It's the

Going-to-the-Sun Road in Glacier National Park

backcountry that makes Glacier Park so thrilling. Be sure to get out of the car and explore.

Butte, Helena, and Southwestern Montana

This is the region of Montana's first gold rush and its early mining history. Ghost towns such as **Bannack** and **Virginia City** tell the fascinating story of vigilantes and the early gold-mining frontier. **Helena,** the state capital, is a gold camp that managed to evolve into an endearing small city filled with fantastic period architecture. **Butte,** once known as the "Richest Hill on Earth," has more history per square inch than anywhere else in Montana. For recreation and beauty it's hard to beat the **Big Hole Valley,** and there's history at the **Big Hole Battlefield,** where Chief Joseph and his Nez Perce held off the U.S. cavalry. **Dillon** is a charming town at the center of a huge ranching valley. Fishing is excellent, and there's marvelous wildlife viewing at **Red Rock Lakes,** home to rare trumpeter swans.

The Missouri Headwaters

In this mountainous region, all roads lead to **Yellowstone National Park.** Three of the park's entrances are in Montana. Be sure to stop and spend time in **Bozeman,** a lively university town filled with art galleries and great restaurants. **Livingston** is another well-preserved town that's been transformed by its community of famous, cutting-edge visual and literary artists.

Big Sky, the state's most upscale ski resort, and the ski area at **Red Lodge** make this a great winter destination. In summer, hikers take to the mountains in **Absaroka-Beartooth Wilderness,** which boasts Montana's highest peaks and oddities, including grasshopper glaciers. Anglers come from around the world to toss a fly in the fabled trout waters of the **Madison, Gallatin, and Yellowstone Rivers.**

Billings and Southeastern Montana

One absolute must-see in this part of the state is the **Little Bighorn Battlefield National Monument.** The clash of Custer's troops with the warriors of the Sioux and Cheyenne Nations is one of those defining moments in history, and the battlefield is one of the West's most haunted headstones at the Little Bighorn Battlefield National Monument

places. Miles City's **Range Riders Museum** is one of the state's best community museums. East of Billings, **Pompey's Pillar** is a sandstone bluff with carvings made by members of the Lewis and Clark Expedition over 200 years ago. It's a mandatory stop for fans of the Corps of Discovery. The **Bighorn River,** in the Crow Reservation, is one of Montana's best trout-fishing rivers. You don't have to be an angler to be amazed by the river's mighty **Bighorn Canyon** and the **Yellowtail Dam.**

The Judith Basin and Central Montana

Rolling prairies and isolated mountain ranges make this one of Montana's most lovely, low-key destinations. **Lewistown** is a friendly spot with a beautiful old downtown little changed since the 1910s. In mid-August, the state's premier cowboy poetry event is held here. **Harlowton** is another well-preserved railroad town along the Musselshell River, and Highway 12, one of the most scenic routes across the state. The **Charles M. Bair Family Museum** in Martinsdale preserves an eclectic, fascinating collection of art and antiques in a rambling ranch home—sort of a Little Versailles on the Prairie. **White Sulphur Springs** offers hot springs cures and

mineral baths, and just down the valley the wild **Smith River** entices white-water rafters and anglers to explore a remote river canyon.

The Big Open and Northeastern Montana

As its name indicates, this part of Montana is full of wide-open spaces. If you're looking for unadulterated Western experience, stop in little towns such as **Malta** or **Jordan** for an eyeful of cattle ranching culture.

If you're passing through on a summer weekend, check to see if there's a **rodeo** in the area. The **Wolf Point Wild Horse Stampede** is one of the state's most famous. Massive **Fort Peck Dam** is one of the world's largest, backing up the Missouri River for 150 miles. Surrounding it is the **C. M. Russell National Wildlife Refuge,** the largest in the contiguous United States and home to a wealth of **fossils** (these are some of the richest dinosaur digs in the world). Migratory birds make stopovers at **Medicine Lake,** a series of prairie wetlands in extreme northeast Montana. **Fort Union Trading Post National Historic Site,** near the confluence of the Missouri and Yellowstone Rivers, is a wonderful re-creation of an 1840s fur-trading fort.

The Hi-Line and North-Central Montana

This mostly flat agricultural area brushes up against the front range of the Rocky Mountains. Great Falls is home to the **Lewis and Clark National Historic Trail Interpretive Center,** which retells the story of the Corps of Discovery's 1804-1806 journey from St. Louis to the Pacific and back. Also in Great Falls, the **C. M. Russell Museum** preserves a large collection of this amazing artist's works. Havre's raucous pioneer days are revealed in the **Havre Historical Underground Tours,** which show the businesses and communities that thrived below the city's streets in the 1890s. Near Choteau, **Egg Mountain** contains outcrops of fossilized dinosaur eggs. View these egg fossils at the **Old Trail Museum** and schedule a tour of a dino dig at the **Two Medicine Dinosaur Center.** Just west of Choteau, the **Rocky Mountain Front** rears up, a beautiful and remote area where the prairie meets the mountains.

When to Go

Most travelers come to Montana in the **summertime,** when it's easy to get around and towns are busy with events such as rodeos, **powwows,** and **arts fairs.** Even at the peak of the summer season, crowds usually aren't a big problem. Even if there are a lot of tourists, there's even more Montana.

Skiers, both downhill and cross-country, should definitely consider traveling here in the **winter.** Of course, that's when the **ski towns** are in full swing, but there are many pleasures to be had from a quiet winter visit on cross-country skis or snowshoes to Glacier National Park.

Make note that **fall** is **hunting season** and that during the spring and early summer, many mountain roads and trails will still be blocked by snow.

Remember that Montana is a big state—it takes a good two days just to drive across it on the interstate—and allow yourself ample time to explore. A week will give you a good amount of time either to touch on a few areas of the state or to really explore one region.

winter in Glacier National Park

Montana's Best Road Trip

Montana is a big state, but for those who don't mind doing some driving, it's possible (indeed, exhilarating) to do a wide-ranging tour. Expect this Tour de Montana to take the better part of two weeks; if you keep to our schedule, you'll complete this tour in nine days, but even so, you'll feel rushed. If you really want to explore any particular area, add more time.

Day 1

Start your trip in **Missoula,** northwestern Montana's cultural hub and an easy place to land. Spend the morning exploring downtown and walking along the Clark Fork River, which cuts right through downtown and is bordered by trails. When you're ready to move on, head north up the **Mission Valley,** home of the Flathead Reservation to **Flathead Lake,** the largest freshwater lake in the West. Stop for a late lunch in bustling **Bigfork,** 100 miles from Missoula, then continue another 32 miles to **Whitefish,** the region's recreational capital, for dinner and lodging.

Day 2

Eat a hearty breakfast at the Buffalo Cafe in Whitefish, then head 32 miles east to begin a tour of **Glacier National Park.** Your best bet (at least during the summer) is to drive through the park on the **Going-to-the-Sun Road.** Even a relatively deliberate drive along this 50-mile-long road can take all day, so plan to either spend at least one night in a park lodge or in the eastside border town of **St. Mary.**

Day 3

From Glacier National Park's eastern edge just south of St. Mary, you can see the striking Rocky Mountain Front as you travel south along Highway 89. It's about 140 miles from St. Mary to **Great Falls,** where visits to the **Lewis and Clark National Historic Trail Interpretive Center** and the **C. M. Russell Museum** will easily fill a day. Dive into another sort of Montana culture with an evening visit to the **Sip 'N' Dip,** where bar-goers are visited by mermaids.

the Madison River in Yellowstone

Day 4

From Great Falls, it's just over 100 miles east on Highway 87 to **Lewistown,** which is small enough to give you the flavor of eastern Montana life. Lewistown is surrounded by places to hike, fish, or explore (including ghost towns and the Missouri River badlands). It's another 125 miles to **Billings,** where you can get a taste "big" city life in the Big Sky state. Spend the night (there's a vibrant bar and brewpub scene here).

Day 5

The next morning drive about 60 miles southeast from Billings on I-90 to the **Little Bighorn Battlefield National Monument,** where General Custer, along with many others, died. Head back to I-90 and venture west; at Laurel turn south on Highway 310 for about 10 miles, then southwest on Highway 212 for about 30 miles to **Red Lodge** (about 120 miles from the battlefield), at the base of the **Beartooth Highway.** Spend the night in Red Lodge, where there are plenty of restaurants and a good brewpub.

Day 6

Plan to spend a day driving the winding **Beartooth** Highway up to **Yellowstone National Park,** where you can stay as long as you like and never run out of places to explore. Though it's only 120 miles from Red Lodge to Gardiner via the Beartooth Highway (Highway 212), it's an all-day drive. When it's time to leave Yellowstone, ease your transition by staying about 25 miles north of the park at **Chico Hot Springs.**

Day 7

After a morning soak and breakfast, travel north on Highway 89 for 25 miles to **Livingston,** which is a quirky hybrid of old and new West, with atmospheric old bars and high-end art galleries sharing Main Street. Just 26 miles west of Livingston on I-90 is **Bozeman,** home of **Montana State University** and the **Museum of the Rockies** (a dinosaur lover's must-see).

Continue on I-90 west as far as **Three Forks** (30 miles west of Bozeman), where at the Missouri headwaters, Lewis and Clark had to make some tough travel-planning choices. (As do you—if you're running short on time, take I-90 west 173 miles back to Missoula.) Tiny Three Forks has a lovely state park at the headwaters, and an equally lovely old inn, the **Sacajawea Hotel.**

Livingston

Rare is the Montana traveler who leaves the state without having seen any wildlife. And although it's impossible to guarantee that you'll see particular animals in specific locations, there are a number of areas around the state where a patient visitor is likely to be rewarded with a glimpse of wildlife.

YELLOWSTONE NATIONAL PARK

Yellowstone is famous for its wildlife: The Lamar Valley is the best place for an early-morning **wolf-viewing; elk** are commonly seen around the Mammoth Lodge; **bison** roam throughout much of the northern and western parts of the park, including the area near West Yellowstone, where lucky visitors will also see **moose.**

GLACIER NATIONAL PARK

Visitors to Glacier National Park will quickly learn about bears. Both **black bears** and **grizzlies** roam around Glacier; they're both best viewed from a distance with the aid of binoculars or a spotting scope. **Mountain goats** are frequently spotted around Logan Pass.

bear in Glacier National Park

NATIONAL BISON RANGE

The National Bison Range's large herd of **bison** is usually visible from one of the loop drives; **bighorn sheep, pronghorns, elk, deer,** and **mountain goats** also live here.

CHARLES M. RUSSELL NATIONAL WILDLIFE REFUGE

The prairies and badlands at the Charles M. Russell National Wildlife Refuge are home to a wide range of native species, including **mule deer, elk,** **bighorn sheep, pronghorn, sage grouse, burrowing owls,** and more.

PINE BUTTE SWAMP PRESERVE

Near Choteau, the Pine Butte Swamp Preserve provides wetland habitat for over 150 species of birds as well as **bighorn sheep, elk, mule deer, moose, mountain lions,** and **black and grizzly bears.** This is one of the only places on the plains that supports grizzlies. Nearby **Freezout Lake** is a prime bird-watching area, especially in the fall when snow geese and tundra swans stop by.

Day 8

To continue an exploration of Montana's heritage, head south 62 miles on Highway 87 to **Virginia and Nevada Cities,** where frontier-era buildings have been preserved, and there's a visceral sense of the ruggedness of gold-rush towns. For a true ghost town that's remarkably well preserved, don't miss **Bannack,** just south of Highway 278, west of Dillon and about 80 miles from Virginia City, on the edge of the expansive **Big Hole Valley.** For the night's lodgings, you could backtrack 25 miles to Dillon or continue 30 miles to the Big Hole town of Jackson, where **Jackson Hot Springs** is full of Western spirit.

Day 9

Follow Highways 278 and 43 west over Chief Joseph Pass, and stop along Highway 43 about 30 miles west of Jackson to visit the **Big Hole National Battlefield,** where the Nez Perce, fleeing their Oregon homeland, were attacked by the U.S. Army.

Once you reach the **Bitterroot Valley,** it's an easy drive (about 100 miles north along Highway 93) back to Missoula.

Following Lewis and Clark

When Lewis and Clark led the Corps of Discovery across Montana, they had little idea what they'd find there. They hoped for an easy passage from the upper Missouri River to the Columbia River; they knew they would encounter Native Americans, and in fact were counting on help from the local tribes. They knew they'd see all sorts of unfamiliar flora and fauna, and they were trained to document and preserve these species. But they found geography that was much more convoluted than they'd imagined, Native Americans who provided more help than they'd thought would be needed, and a richness of plant and animal life that is reflected in almost every journal entry.

Lewis and Clark took five months—from April 25, 1805, to September 10, 1805—to cross Montana, but you'll probably want to do it in a week or so. And while you may not need to report your discoveries to the president, as Lewis and Clark did, you'll surely return home with plenty to share with family and friends.

Day 1

Start, as they did, in the eastern part of the state, along the Missouri River at **Fort Union,** a fascinating re-creation of an 1840s frontier trading post at the confluence of the Missouri and Yellowstone Rivers, and head west along Highway 2, following the Missouri to **Fort Peck,** about 120 miles west of the North Dakota line. Spend the first night at Fort Peck, with its enormous

Fort Union

reservoir, dinosaur museum, and 1930s New Deal architecture, including a well-preserved hotel from the town's dam-building heyday.

Day 2

West and north of Fort Peck, Highway 2 follows the **Milk River,** named by Meriwether Lewis for the color of its water. From Fort Peck to Havre is about 160 miles, then it's another 50 miles south on Highway 87 to Loma, where you'll rejoin the Missouri and head about 25 miles south to **Fort Benton.** The trip from Loma to Fort Benton can either be on back roads or on Highway 87. A real highlight of a Lewis and Clark pilgrimage is to take a boat trip through the wild and scenic stretch of the Missouri where the corps saw "seens of visionary inchantment." Spend the night in Fort Benton.

Day 3

The great waterfalls of the Missouri meant many days of portaging for the corps members; for travelers, **Great Falls,** 36 miles southwest of Fort Benton via Highway 87, is the site of the excellent **Lewis and Clark National Historic Trail Interpretive Center.** Plan to spend the morning here.

Missouri Headwaters State Park

From Great Falls, it's 90 miles south on I-15 to **Helena.** East of town are the **Upper Missouri Lakes,** formed by a series of dams. Behind Holter Dam are the "remarkable clifts" that Lewis called **Gates of the Mountains,** which modern travelers can visit on guided boat tours. Helena is a good place to spend a night.

Day 4

From Helena, continue some 66 miles upstream (southeast on Highway 287) through Townsend to **Three Forks,** where the Madison, Jefferson, and Gallatin Rivers merge to form the Missouri. Perched on a bluff at **Missouri Headwaters State Park,** you'll realize how difficult it was for the explorers to pick the correct stream to follow to the Continental Divide. (It was the Jefferson.)

The easiest way up the Jefferson now is to take I-90 about 30 miles west of Three Forks to Whitehall, then turn south and travel another 30 miles on Highway 41 to Twin Bridges. About 15 miles southwest of Twin Bridges, on Highway 41, you'll see **Beaverhead Rock,** the landform that told Sacagawea that she was near the place where she'd grown up. Another 15 miles down Highway 41 is **Dillon,** a good base for exploring this part of the state.

Soak It Up: Hot Springs of Montana

Hot water gurgles up all over the state, and it's exploited to one degree or another by a wide variety of resorts, from the rustic to the chic. Be sure to bring a swimsuit—these aren't clothing-optional spots! A breakneck tour of the state's hot springs can be done in a few days, but chances are you'd rather relax and make this into a weeklong trip.

NORTHWESTERN MONTANA

- **Hot Springs:** This little town is pretty down-home, so don't look for luxury. Stay at the **Symes Hot Springs Hotel,** swim in the outdoor pool, and bathe in an old-fashioned tub filled with sulfurous water. Be sure to wander over to **Big Medicine Hot Springs** for a soak.

- **Quinn's Hot Springs Resort:** The outdoor pool here is popular with families. Call ahead if you want to stay here; the cabins are popular.

- **Lolo Hot Springs Resort:** At this large Bitterroot Valley resort you can think of Lewis and Clark and their crew cleaning up here after months on the road.

- **Lost Trail Hot Springs:** At the southern end of the Bitterroot Valley, pretty much in the middle of nowhere, relax in the outdoor pool, indoor hot tub and saunas, lodge, cabins, and campground.

SOUTHWESTERN MONTANA

- **Jackson Hot Springs Lodge:** The main thing going in the Big Hole town of Jackson is the hot springs, and it's a good place to spend a night.

- **Elkhorn Hot Springs:** This woodsy spot in Polaris is as rustic as it gets, but with cabins and a lodge.

- **Fairmont Hot Springs:** Stay at this large resort near Anaconda if you like the more luxurious (and crowded) style.

- **Boulder Hot Springs:** On I-15 between

soaking at Norris Hot Springs

Butte and Helena, this huge and partially reno-vated old hotel has a nice outdoor pool and indoor plunges.

CENTRAL MONTANA

- **Spa Hot Springs Motel:** In the town of White Sulphur Springs, this motel has an outdoor swimming pool and indoor soaking pool.

SOUTH-CENTRAL MONTANA

- **Chico Hot Springs:** The state's crown jewel of hot springs is home of a huge outdoor pool, a cool old lodge, and tons of atmosphere. Plan to stay here in the Paradise Valley for at least one night.

- **Bozeman Hot Springs:** Just west of town, these hot springs are a busy place with several pools.

- **Norris Hot Springs:** The charming wood-plank-lined pool here is filled with the "water of the gods." Hit Norris on a Saturday night for live music.

Day 5

If you want to muddle around in the southwestern corner of the state for as long as the corps did, you really couldn't find a lovelier place. A side trip along southwestern Montana's back roads (try Highway 324, which joins I-15 about 20 miles south of Dillon) will take you to Horse Prairie Valley, where the corps met a band of Shoshone whose chief turned out to be Sacagawea's brother, and to **Lemhi Pass** and the Continental Divide.

A more expeditious, but still highly scenic, route from Dillon follows the southern rim of the Big Hole Valley (I-15 south to Hwy. 278, then west on Hwy. 43 at Wisdom) 100 miles to the Bitterroot Valley. The Corps of Discovery struggled in the mountains here and ultimately headed north down the Bitterroot River to leave the area west of **Lolo** (present-day Highway 12). As you head north on Highway 93 through the 100-mile-long Bitterroot Valley, don't miss **Travelers' Rest,** south of Lolo, and the newly discovered corps latrine, which provides rare physical evidence (don't worry, it's not *that* graphic) of the explorers' visit.

Exploring Glacier National Park

For many visitors, a trip to Glacier National Park means a drive along the Going-to-the-Sun Road and not much more. Although this drive is spectacular, and a number of good hikes can be accessed from it, there are several other sections of the park that deserve a visit. Rather than dashing across the "Crown of the Continent," plan to spend the better part of a week exploring.

Day 1

Enter the park at **West Glacier** and find a campsite within a couple of miles of the entrance at Apgar or Fish Creek Campground (Fish Creek is about 2.5 miles north of Apgar; sites can be reserved in advance at Fish Creek). Orient yourself at the visitor information center near **Apgar** and hike from Fish Creek along the shoreline of **Lake McDonald.** Later in the day, rent a canoe or kayak at the Apgar dock and paddle on Lake McDonald. Stay up just late enough to catch an evening ranger talk at your campground.

Day 2

Drive 25 miles up Camas Creek Road and the

near Polebridge

Best Outdoor Recreation

- **Easy Mountain Biking:** The Hiawatha Mountain Bike Trail is just off I-90 at the state's far western edge. Ride 15 miles down a gentle grade over old railroad trestles and through long tunnels. Pay for a shuttle back to your car.

- **Mountain Biking:** The Whitefish Trail will get you out of town and onto looped mountain bike trails. If you need more of an adrenaline rush, head up to Whitefish Mountain and ride the lift up to careen downhill on your bike.

- **Road Biking:** In Great Falls, the River's Edge Trail is a dedicated bike path along the Missouri River. A classic Montana group ride is the Tour of the Swan River Valley, held on a late May weekend every year since 1970.

- **Hiking:** Glacier National Park is one of the best places in the country for spectacular backpacking trips, but it's equally good for day hiking. The scenery around the Continental Divide at Logan Pass is stunningly beautiful; Many Glacier is another good base with lots of trails.

- **Fishing:** There's good fishing all over Montana, but no place is as devoted to fly-fishing as the town of Ennis, situated right on the most productive stretch of the Madison River. Unless it's Fort Smith, just below the Yellowtail Dam, where a mountain river meets the prairies with stunning results.

- **Horseback Riding:** There are guest ranches across the state, but some of the best are near the Crazy Mountains near Harlowton in central Montana and along the Rocky Mountain Front, near Choteau and Augusta.

- **Rafting:** The Flathead River flows strong and fast in the area to the west of Glacier National Park. Sign on with an outfitter to float its Middle Fork. But the central part of the state offers its own adventures, particularly the Smith River near White Sulphur Springs, with a four- to six-day trip through a wilderness canyon.

- **Canoeing:** Follow in the paddle strokes of Lewis and Clark through the Upper Missouri River Breaks National Monument northeast of Fort Benton.

- **Swimming:** It takes a while to warm up in the summer, but Flathead Lake is a good place to

canoeing the gentle waters of an eastern Montana river

take a dip. The huge hot-springs pool at Chico Hot Springs is inviting year-round.

- **Downhill Skiing:** Big Sky, which is now the continent's largest ski resort, can't be beat for amount and variety of terrain.

- **Cross-Country Skiing:** The Izaak Walton Inn is known for its network of groomed cross-country ski trails and its accommodations in an old railroad hotel. Bonus: It's easy to make day trips to ski in Glacier National Park.

- **Motorcycle Touring:** Fire up the Harley! The Beartooth Highway is exhilarating in any vehicle, but especially so on a motorcycle.

- **Rockhounding:** Moss agates in the Yellowstone valley, garnets at Red Rock Mine west of Virginia City, and sapphires west of Philipsburg are just a few of the rockhounding opportunities in Montana.

- **Dinosaur Digging:** Paleontologists from the Two Medicine Dinosaur Center in the little Rocky Mountain Front town of Bynum will teach you the basics of digging and take you out into the field to search for bones.

Outside North Fork Road to the laid-back and off-the-grid hamlet of **Polebridge,** where you can pick up cinnamon rolls and muffins to fuel your adventures. From Polebridge, it's a six-mile drive along a bumpy dirt road to stunningly beautiful **Bowman Lake,** where you'll escape the crowds you may have found at Lake McDonald. (Most passenger cars can make this trip, but skip it if your car is low-slung or precious to you; trailers and big RVs aren't advised.) At the lake, take a swim or paddle (rentals are available in Polebridge) or hike the lakeshore. When you're able to tear yourself away, return to your previous night's campground.

Day 3

Break camp and head east along the **Going-to-the-Sun Road.** Although the park itself is always open, the 50-mile-long Going-to-the-Sun Road is not fully open to traffic until plowing is completed, usually sometime in June (the road closes in September, and the central section is always limited to vehicles less than 21 feet long).

Take your time on this drive. Hike past thundering falls to the glacial **Avalanche Lake** (four miles round-trip); the trailhead is about 15 miles

Logan Pass

from Apgar. Skip Logan Pass for now but take another short hike about 10 miles east of the pass at Sun Point. Continue east to camp at **Rising Sun** (37 miles from Apgar) or **St. Mary** (50 miles, reservations available).

Day 4

Backtrack from your campsite to the Continental Divide and visit **Logan Pass** (about 20 miles west of St. Mary); it's easiest to park here early in the morning, so don't dawdle. Hike up to the **Hidden Lake Overlook,** then head back to the parking lot. Grab your lunch and cross the road to hike the **Highline Trail.** The first part of the trail has some scary parts; hang onto the cable when the trail narrows and you'll be fine! You probably won't want to hike the 7.6 miles to the **Granite Park Chalet** unless you have one of the coveted bunks there, but even a short out-and-back along this relatively level trail will give you an eyeful.

Day 5

Break camp, and from St. Mary, at the eastern end of the Going-to-the-Sun Road, turn north and drive nine miles to the turnoff at Babb. Head west 12 miles to **Many Glacier,** one of the most spectacular areas of the park. The campground here is popular, so try to reserve a site in advance (available by 2016). If you're ready for a night under a roof, the Swiss-style lodge here is our favorite of Glacier's hotels. Once settled, take the two-part boat ride to the far end of **Lake Josephine** and hike about four miles up to view **Grinnell Glacier.**

Day 6

If it's time to pack up and go home, you can easily head east from the town of **St. Mary.** To get back to the West Glacier area, head south on Highways 89 and 49 to East Glacier (stop to peek inside the grand lodge here) and catch Highway 2 around the southern edge of the park back to West Glacier. From Many Glacier, it's about 125 miles, and the route is much faster than retracing the Going-to-the-Sun Road.

Missoula and Northwestern Montana

Highlights

Most riders catch a shuttle for the return trip (page 44).

★ **St. Ignatius Mission:** Built in 1854, the St. Ignatius Mission was the second Catholic mission in Montana. Inside the more modern (1891) brick church, lovely murals painted by the mission cook very sweetly illustrate scenes from the Bible (page 61).

★ **National Bison Range:** Obviously bison are the main attraction, but come prepared to see bighorn sheep, pronghorn, elk, mule deer, white-tailed deer, and mountain goats as well. Even if all the animals are in hiding, the land, the sky, and the light are beautiful here (page 62).

★ **Jewel Basin Hiking Area:** Unlike in many wilderness areas, the trails here are relatively easy to reach and suitable for day hikes. Lakes stud the basin; the meadows are strewn with Indian paintbrush, bear grass, fireweed, and spring daisies; and there are great views of Flathead Lake (page 72).

★ **Conrad Mansion:** This 1895 Kalispell mansion is considered one of the best examples of late-19th-century Pacific Northwest architecture (page 83).

★ **Summer at Whitefish Mountain:** Even in summer, a gondola travels up and down Whitefish Mountain. But if you really want to take time to examine the wildflowers—and in late summer, pick huckleberries—hike the Danny On Trail from the base of the ski area to the top of the gondola. If that's too tame, walk an elevated boardwalk through the treetops or ride a mountain bike (page 95).

★ **University of Montana:** Proclaimed by *Rolling Stone Magazine* as the "most beautiful campus in America," the U of M, with its grassy oval beneath steep mountain slopes, is indeed a lovely place to explore (page 32).

★ **Hiawatha Mountain Bike Trail:** This 15-mile trail along a former railroad runs gently downhill from its start at Lookout Pass, and passes over trestles and through tunnels.

F or many visitors, the state's north-west corner is archetypal Montana; these beautiful lakes and soaring mountain peaks are what you came here for. Not only is it the gateway to Glacier National Park, but there are fishing areas, hiking trails, and public campgrounds galore, particularly in the national forests. This area is a recreationalist's dream come true.

However, as you explore, you'll find you're not alone. The late 1990s and early 2000s saw burgeoning growth in this region, particularly in the Flathead Valley, so be prepared to share this corner of Montana with quite a few others.

Northwestern Montana's topography is characterized by a series of forested mountain ranges (the Cabinets, Missions, Bitterroots, Flatheads, Salish, Whitefish, Purcells, and Swans), running generally northwest to southeast, and the valleys that separate them. Although this is a mountainous area, it's not particularly high by Montana standards; Montana's lowest spot (1,892 feet) is where the Clark Fork River enters Idaho near Troy in the state's northwest corner.

PLANNING YOUR TIME

Travelers entering the region from the west on I-90 should consider spending part of a day on the **Hiawatha Mountain Bike Trail,** at the far western edge of the state, just off I-90. Otherwise, Missoula makes a good formal jumping-off spot for a tour of northwest Montana. Plan to spend a couple of nights here, with one day devoted to both sightseeing and informal hanging-out in this pleasant town. It's also possible to spend a full day touring the Bitterroot Valley, returning to Missoula for the night.

Once you've had your fill of Missoula, head north into the Mission Valley. If you're in luck, it'll be powwow time on the Flathead Reservation, but if not, there's plenty of Native American history and culture in towns such as St. Ignatius. Plan to devote an early morning or an evening around sunset to watching wildlife at the **National Bison Range.** If birds are more your thing, check out the wetlands at the **Ninepipe Refuge.** The **Mission Mountains** have many good hiking trails and lovely lakes, but be sure to get a

---

Previous: bridge over the Clark Fork River near downtown Missoula; on the Flathead Reservation.
Above: Libby, known for its large population of bald eagles.

Missoula and Northwestern Montana

CANADA

Kootenai
National
Forest

Eureka

Glacier

BLACKFEET

INDIAN

RESERVATION

National

Kootenai
Falls

Flathead

Park

Troy

93

BIG
MOUNTAIN

89

Libby

National

SUMMER
AT WHITEFISH ★
MOUNTAIN

Cabinet

2

Forest

Whitefish

2

Mountain

CONRAD
MANSION

Columbia
Falls

Heron

Wilderness

Kalispell

JEWEL BASIN
HIKING AREA
★

Noxon

Kootenai

Lolo

National

National

Flathead NF

Bob

Trout
Creek

Forest

Forest

35

Swan
Lake

Lolo
National
Forest

Flathead
Lake

SEE
"FLATHEAD LAKE"
MAP

Marshall

Thompson
Falls

Thompson
River SF

28

Polson

83

Condon

Lookout Pass

90

Plains

FLATHEAD INDIAN

Ronan

Wilderness

HIAWATHA
MOUNTAIN
BIKE TRAIL

St. Regis

Paradise

RESERVATION

ST. IGNATIUS
MISSION

135

200

St. Ignatius

Superior

NATIONAL
BISON RANGE

Seeley Lake

Lolo

93

Area

National

200

IDAHO

Forest

Missoula

UNIVERSITY
OF MONTANA

Lolo

90

93

12

SEE
"BITTERROOT
VALLEY"
MAP

Stevensville

1

Hamilton

38

0   20 mi

1

0   20 km

Darby

MONTANA

473   93

43

15

© AVALON TRAVEL

tribal recreation permit at any local store before setting out into the wilderness here.

Even with some lingering along the way, Polson is an easy day's drive from Missoula, and this town at the foot of Flathead Lake makes a good overnight base. It's also the best place to find a boat tour of Flathead Lake.

For those who want a slower pace and the simplest, least glitzy spa experience imaginable, take a detour to the tiny town of **Hot Springs** and spend the day checking out various plunges and pools. It's most relaxing if you just stay here for the night.

At the northern edge of Flathead Lake, **Bigfork** is as bustling as Hot Springs is laidback. Remember, this is bustling in Montana terms—it'll never be New York. This is the place to remember where you put that extra wad of cash because it's easy to be tempted by shopping and restaurants. But even on a budget, Bigfork is still entertaining, with plenty of inexpensive camping and free hiking nearby. The **Jewel Basin** is a good place for a day hike in these parts.

In **Kalispell** you can stock up on supplies for a trip into nearby Glacier National Park. Although it seems at first glance to be an entirely utilitarian town, Kalispell's **Conrad Mansion** and **Hockaday Museum of Art** are both worth visiting.

Just a few miles north, **Whitefish** is more of an upscale party and resort town. With **Whitefish Mountain** loaded with snow in the winter and huckleberries in the summer, this is a place for recreation. It's worth noting that Amtrak stops in Whitefish, making it possible to ride the train to a ski vacation.

If you only have one day in the area, chances are you'll be heading either across I-90 or along Highway 93. Either way, you're bound to spend time in Missoula; if that's not quite enough to fill your day, either make a short Lewis and Clark pilgrimage to **Travelers' Rest** in the Bitterroot Valley, perhaps combined with a trip to **Lolo Hot Springs** or a hike to **Peterson Lake,** or head north into the Mission Valley for a hike in the **Mission Mountain Tribal Wilderness Area.**

Missoula

Missoula, tucked in a fertile valley and filled with students, loggers, truck drivers, and writers, is the hub of western Montana. The Missoula Valley has always been a crossroads, first for Native Americans, then for European settlers, and nowadays for Montana's major highways. It remains a great focus and jumping-off point for the traveler.

The city (pop. 70,000, elev. 3,205 feet) takes its sense of confluence seriously. Practically within the city limits, the Clark Fork is joined by the Blackfoot and Bitterroot Rivers and several smaller streams. As home to the University of Montana, Missoula is a center of learning and one of the state's major cultural centers; it has preserved much of its historic architectural character and offers good restaurants and a full-bodied nightlife.

Missoula's nickname, the Garden City, is apt. As a locale, it's about as temperate, fertile, and hospitable as possible in Montana.

But Missoula is more than a picturesque university town. The university and artistic population are notoriously bohemian and political, while the working core of the city is, in Montana terms, decidedly blue-collar. Depending on the perspective, Missoula is either a working-class town with a radical university imposed on it or a liberal-arts college town infiltrated by the proletariat. But the juxtaposition works: Scratch a logger and find a poet.

For a traveler, Missoula is an agreeable home base for excursions into the wonders of western Montana. However, for a visitor with a little time and a taste for artistic and

Missoula

To Rocky Mountain Elk Foundation, Airport, and Smokejumper's Center
To I-90

HICKORY ST

To Town and Country Shopping Center and Good Food Store

COTTONWOOD ST

McCormick Park

Clark

MAY ST W

RED LION INN

McCORMICK ST

RIVER ST

CREGG LN

S 3RD ST W
S 2ND ST W
S 1ST ST W

S ORANGE ST

W BROADWAY ST

OWEN ST

N ORANGE ST

CHESTNUT ST

S 6TH ST W
S 5TH ST W

HAZEL ST S

BROOKS ST

MYRTLE ST

BERNICE'S BAKERY
LE PETIT OUTRE
S 4TH ST W

THE SILK ROAD ★
HOB NOB CAFE ▼

MILWAUKEE ROAD DEPOT
CAROUSEL FOR MISSOULA ★
MONTE DOLACK GALLERY ★
TAMARACK BREWING CO.

BIGA PIZZA ▼
BADLANDER/ MISSOULA CLUB ▼
RHINO ▼

THE SHACK ▼

COUNTY COURTHOUSE

WOODY ST

VERNE ST

S HIGGINS ST

BIG DIPPER

CIAO MAMBO

Fork

DOWNTOWN

To Fort Missoula, Caffe Dolce, and Bitterroot Valley

GERALD AVE

RONALD AVE

HILDA AVE

HELEN AVE

ARTHUR AVE

MAURICE AVE

Kim Williams Trail

Bess Reed Park

S CLAY ST

HOLIDAY INN MISSOULA DOWNTOWN AT THE PARK ●
SCOTTY'S TABLE ▼

TOP HAT
BIRD'S NEST ▼
RED BIRD ▼

RYMAN ST

HIGGINS BLOCK
OXFORD CLUB
BUTTERFLY HERBS ▼
PLONK ★
N HIGGINS ST 93

WORDEN'S MARKET ▼
BREAK ESPRESSO ▼

IRON HORSE BREW PUB ▼

THE DEPOT ▼

NORTHERN PACIFIC DEPOT ●

VISITOR CENTER
FACT AND FICTION ★
MISSOULA MERCANTILE BUILDING

UNION CLUB
N PATTEE ST
MISSOULA ART MUSEUM ★

POST OFFICE

WASHINGTON ST

TRAIL HEAD ★
PEARL CAFE ▼

E FRONT ST
E MAIN ST
E BROADWAY ST

N ADAMS ST

N PINE ST

Toole Park

Kiwanis Park

Madison Bridge

DOUBLETREE HOTEL MISSOULA/ EDGEWATER/ FINN AND PORTERS ●

N PATTEE ST

JEFFERSON ST

Madison Park

Rankin Park

River

GOLDSMITH'S INN ●

MOTEL 6 MISSOULA UNIVERSITY ●

MADISON ST

N 2ND ST E

90

Foot Bridge

Jacobs Island Park

CAMPUS INN ●

THUNDERBIRD MOTEL ●

COMFORT INN ●

MADISON ST

90

Blossom's B&B ●

W GREENOUGH DR

To Hell Gate Pass

VINE ST

VAN BUREN ST

POPLAR ST

MONROE ST

Greenough Park

To Rattlesnake Drive and Rattlesnake National Recreation Area

UNIVERSITY OF MONTANA ✚

CAMPUS DR

EDDY ST

STEPHENS AVE

UNIVERSITY DISTRICT

0   200 m
0   200 yds

© AVALON TRAVEL

political ferment, Missoula can become addictive. The city's saloons and salons are filled with testimonials of those who planned to pass through but have yet to leave.

HISTORY

With five valleys nearly converging here, it's no surprise that the area has long been used as a thoroughfare. Salish people from the Bitterroot and Mission Valleys traveled through Hell Gate Canyon to reach buffalo hunting grounds east of the mountains. They were regularly attacked by the Blackfeet as they entered the canyon, thus giving the passage a formidable reputation. In fact, *Missoula* is from a Salish word that has been variously translated as "by the cold chilling waters," "river of awe," or simply an exclamation of surprise and horror.

Early European settlers seemed to agree. As the story goes, French trappers were horrified when they came across the remains of all the Salish who never made it through the canyon, and called it *Porte de l'Enfer,* which became Hell Gate in English.

The first Easterners on record to explore the Missoula area were Meriwether Lewis and a brigade of his men on their return trip from the Pacific. Lewis and his group camped at the confluence of the Rattlesnake and Clark Fork Rivers in July 1806 and headed through Hell Gate Canyon without incident.

Missoula's growth was spurred by the arrival of the Northern Pacific Railway in 1883. Timber was also important to the town's development. In 1886, A. B. Hammond built what was reputedly the world's largest lumber mill at Bonner, seven miles east of Missoula. It produced timbers for railroads and mines as well as construction lumber.

When other Montana cities vied for the state capital and prison, Missoula alone attempted to land the university. It was established as the University of Montana in Missoula in 1895. Since then it has become a major cultural force, as well as one of the city's major employers.

SIGHTS

Most of Missoula's historic downtown is located on the north side of the Clark Fork, though the south side of Higgins Avenue, across the river, has become known as the "Hip Strip." The historic residential areas are south of the river, near the university.

Downtown

The old business district was located near the river, along the Mullan Road (now Front Street), where C. P. Higgins and Frank Worden built a sawmill, flour mill, and store along the banks of the Clark Fork. Most of the wooden buildings burned in 1884, and when the city rebuilt, the influence of the incoming Northern Pacific Railway pulled the downtown northward from the Clark Fork along Higgins Avenue.

Many historic buildings remain. The **Missoula Mercantile Building,** at the corner of Front and Higgins, was built between 1882 and 1891. The Merc, as it was known, was established in 1866 and stayed the city's primary mercantile establishment for more than a century. Note the cast-iron facade along Higgins Avenue.

North on Higgins is the **Higgins Block** (1889), containing well-preserved late-19th-century commercial architecture. On the corner, beneath a prominent cupola, is a gingerbread bank in the Queen Anne style. Farther along the same block are other old stores, now housing trendy businesses. One vintage interior worth visiting, **Butterfly Herbs,** has an espresso bar in the back.

The **County Courthouse** (200 W. Broadway) was constructed in 1910. This large, three-story edifice is noteworthy for its murals. These scenes from Montana history were painted by Edgar Paxson, who was called *Cot-lo-see* (He Who Sees Everything) by admiring Native Americans.

Missoula's two **train stations** are imposing and handsome. The **Northern Pacific Depot** was built in 1889 at the north end of Higgins Avenue. Missoula's bustling

Farmer's Market takes place in the park in front of the depot on Saturday mornings and Tuesday evenings in summer—the market is a great spot for people-watching and loading up on coffee, baked goods, and the local bounty of fruit and vegetables. The Spanish-style **Milwaukee Road Depot** was built in 1910 under the Higgins Avenue Bridge on the south side of the Clark Fork. Neither station is in operation as a rail depot.

Carousel for Missoula

A major source of civic pride is the **Carousel for Missoula** (406/549-8382, http://carousel-formissoula.com, 11am-7pm daily June-Aug., 11am-5:30pm daily Sept.-May, $2.25 adult, $0.75 child), which stands in Caras Park near the river just west of the Higgins Bridge. All the horses were hand-carved—making this the first hand-carved carousel assembled in the United States since the 1930s—and each horse has a highly personal, sometimes touching, story associated with it. The fundraising, carving, and construction process really hit a community chord, and almost any local will regale you with stories about the carousel and the meanings of each horse. Next to the carousel, the fantastic **Dragon Hollow**

playground was also built by community volunteers.

Missoula Art Museum

The **Missoula Art Museum** (335 N. Pattee, 406/728-0447, www.missoulaartmuseum.org, 10am-5pm Tues.-Sat., free) has a fine home in the city's old Carnegie Library. The museum houses an excellent small permanent collection featuring some top-notch Montana artists and displays traveling art exhibits.

★ University of Montana

The **University of Montana** (406/243-0211, www.umt.edu) is on the south side of the Clark Fork, at the mouth of the river's Hell Gate Canyon. A green and leafy campus built around a central oval, it's a very pleasant place to explore, as is the university district, an area of grand and historic old homes.

The university, established by the Montana Legislature in 1895, has developed into an academically broad-based institution with a strong liberal-arts emphasis. Its schools of journalism and forestry are nationally recognized, as is its graduate program in creative writing.

The earliest remaining building on campus

University of Montana campus

is the **University Hall,** built in 1899. Besides containing the university president's office, the building's central tower houses a carillon. At noon each day, students are serenaded by a 15-minute recital of bell music.

Behind University Hall is **Mansfield Library,** named for one of Montana's former senators, Mike Mansfield, and his wife, Maureen. Across a grassy mall from the library is the **University Center** (UC), a modern three-story building constructed around a central atrium. It's a good place to hang out and watch student behavior. At the second-floor food court, a wide variety of quick and inexpensive food is available. On the ground floor is the **UC Bookstore** (406/243-4921), a good all-purpose bookstore and art-supply source.

One of the university's newer additions is the **Montana Theatre** (406/243-4581), which houses two stages for live theater.

For a bird's-eye, or rather a mountain-goat's-eye, view of the university and the city, climb up Mt. Sentinel to the university's big red-and-white M. It's a 40-minute hike from the trailhead at the north end of the UC parking lot.

The University District

One of Missoula's most pleasant neighborhoods, the university district contains some interesting architectural specimens. Some of the old homes have been turned into fraternity or sorority houses, but others remain private homes. None are open to the public, but a stroll or drive through the area is a pleasant way to learn that Missoula took its early-20th-century affluence seriously. The grandest homes face Gerald Avenue, parallel to and one block east of South Higgins. See especially the neoclassical mansion at 1005 Gerald (built 1902-1903), once the home of John R. Toole, a prominent early Montana politician and industrialist, and the university president's house at 1325 Gerald, built around 1930.

South of the university, Missoula's **Vietnam Veterans' Memorial** is in a rose garden at Brooks and Franklin.

Rocky Mountain Elk Foundation

Hunters and other wildlife enthusiasts will want to stop by the **Rocky Mountain Elk Foundation** (5705 Grant Creek Rd., 406/523-4500, www.rmef.org, 8am-6pm Mon.-Fri., 9am-6pm Sat.-Sun. May-Dec., 8am-5pm Mon.-Fri., 10am-5pm Sat. Jan.-Apr., free). The large display area has a mix of wildlife art and mounted animals, including some truly impressive elk. There's also a theater with wildlife films, a gift shop, and a nature trail. The elk foundation is a nonprofit organization, mostly composed of hunters concerned with wildlife habitat conservation. Along with their conservation work, they are strong proponents of responsible hunting and publish a good free brochure of tips for hunters.

Fort Missoula

When Chief Joseph and the Nez Perce retreated across Montana in 1877, Missoula citizens asked the federal government for protection from them, and Fort Missoula was hastily established just southwest of town. During World War II the fort was used as a detention center for Italian workers, including merchant sailors, World's Fair employees, and the crew of an Italian luxury liner seized in the Panama Canal.

Two original buildings (a stone powder magazine and an officers' quarters) remain from the 1877 fort site and are now part of the **Fort Missoula Historical Museum** (406/728-3476, www.fortmissoulamuseum.org, 10am-5pm Mon.-Sat., noon-5pm Sun. Memorial Day-Labor Day, noon-5pm Tues.-Sun. Labor Day-Memorial Day, $3 adult, $2 senior, $1 student), which contains exhibits of local history. Other buildings of interest have been relocated to the fort, including an old church, a schoolhouse, and a Forest Service lookout tower. The wide boulevards, green lawns, and white military buildings now evoke a real sense of history. To get there, take Highway 93 south to Reserve Street, turn right, and follow signs at the junction with South Avenue.

The Unusual Evolution of Fort Missoula

Fort Missoula was built in 1877 in response to the flight of the Nez Perce from their homeland and settlers' fear of the increasingly recalcitrant Flathead. However, the threat of Native American attack never really materialized, and troops at the fort saw real action only once, at the Battle of the Big Hole. There, troops from Fort Missoula attempted an ambush of Chief Joseph's retreating Nez Perce and were disastrously defeated.

Thereafter, the story of Fort Missoula ceases to sound much like that of an embattled frontier outpost and begins to take on more curious dimensions. In 1888 the Twenty-fifth Infantry Corps, an all-African American regiment under the authority of Caucasian officers, was garrisoned at the fort. In 1896 bicycle enthusiast Lieutenant James Moss established the Twenty-fifth Infantry Bicycle Corps, which sought to test the potential of the bicycle as a military conveyance. The lieutenant, in comparing the bicycle to the horse, reasoned that the bike "doesn't require as much care. It needs no forage; it moves much faster over fair roads, it is not as conspicuous. . . . It is noiseless and raises but little dust."

In order to prove to General Nelson Miles that the bicycle was a viable means of troop transport, Moss and 20 men left Missoula on bicycles the following year, bound for St. Louis—1,900 miles overland. The trip, made on mud trails and sandy paths, took only 41 days. The army higher-ups were not impressed, however, and the Bicycle Corps returned to Missoula by train.

During World War I the fort served as an army training center, and during the Depression it was the regional headquarters for the Civilian Conservation Corps. During World War II, 1,200 Italian sailors and 650 American men of Japanese descent were detained at the fort, and following the war it served as a prison for court-martialed military personnel.

Fort Missoula was closed as a military post in 1947. The fort presently houses government offices and a historical museum. Its grounds are used for such benign events as dog shows.

Smokejumpers Center

Undeniably unique to Missoula and a source of pride to natives is the Forest Service **Smokejumpers Center** (5765 W. Broadway, 406/329-4934, 8:30am-5pm Mon.-Fri. Memorial Day-Labor Day, free). Here, firefighters are trained in the science of fighting forest fires as well as the art of parachuting into forest wildfires. The center features exhibits, films, a diorama, and a tour of the parachuting base. The center is a half mile west of the Missoula International Airport, south of Highway 93.

RECREATION
Hiking

Many of the in-town hikes are on paths shared by bicyclists. A casual walker can just wander down to the river and pick up the paths that run on either bank in the downtown area. Heading east, the **Kim Williams Trail** follows the south bank of the Clark Fork out of town.

For those who want more of a challenge, head over to the university and follow the zigzag trail up Mt. Sentinel to the M. It takes about 40 minutes, and a little huffing and puffing, to get there, but on a clear day there are great views of Missoula and Hell Gate Canyon.

Head north from I-90 on Van Buren, which quickly becomes Rattlesnake Drive, and travel about four miles to the **Rattlesnake National Recreation Area and Wilderness.** Here you'll find as much of a wilderness hike as you're likely to in any city. Missoula's outdoor stores sell trail maps.

The best hiking is outside of town; seven wilderness areas lie within 100 miles of Missoula.

Bicycling

Missoula is a great place to travel by bike, and bicycle tourists should definitely stop by the **Adventure Cycling Association** headquarters (150 E. Pine, 406/721-1776, www.adventurecycling.org). They distribute a small bicycle-touring map of Missoula as well as a host of other maps for routes stretching across the nation. Two major bike routes cross in Missoula: the north-south **Great Parks Route** and the east-west **Transamerica Route.** Adventure Cycling also operates bicycle tours and is a clearinghouse for information on cycle touring. There's always the opportunity for casual or obsessive bike talk at their offices.

The **Rattlesnake National Recreation Area,** a corridor through the Rattlesnake Wilderness, is a mountain biker's dream, but be sure to avoid cycling in the adjacent wilderness area; maps are available at local outdoor stores.

Mt. Sentinel's summit can be reached by riding south on Pattee Canyon Drive to the unmarked, gated Crazy Canyon Road and climbing to the top of the 5,158-foot peak. A less strenuous fat-tire ride is on the path along the Clark Fork, perhaps venturing east

Glacial Lake Missoula

Glacial ice dammed the Clark Fork River in northern Idaho approximately 15,000 years ago, forming Glacial Lake Missoula, which filled the valleys of western Montana. Riverwater ultimately floated the ice dam like an ice cube in a glass of water, and the lake drained with spectacular force, coursing across eastern Washington and forming the Columbia River Gorge. The ice dam on the Clark Fork settled back down into the riverbed and once again plugged the outlet. The lake filled again, drained again, and was reformed at least 41 times over the course of about 2,500 years. Each cycle was shorter, and the lake didn't fill as deep. The record of these successive fillings and drainings can still be seen as a series of faint, perfectly horizontal lines on the sides of Mt. Jumbo and Mt. Sentinel above Missoula.

of downtown into the **Kim Williams Nature Area,** named for the late National Public Radio commentator whose voice represented all things Missoulian to many listeners across the country.

Rent a bike at **Missoula Bicycle Works** (708 S. Higgins Ave., 406/721-6525, www.missoulabicycleworks.com).

Fishing

Fishing in Missoula can be as unpremeditated as throwing a line into the Clark Fork from a bridge in the middle of town. The Clark Fork, which was horribly polluted until cleanup measures were taken in the 1970s, is now home to trout.

Excellent fishing spots abound within an hour's drive of town. The **Clark Fork, Blackfoot,** and **Bitterroot Rivers** harbor rainbow, brown, cutthroat, and bull trout. Like the Clark Fork, the Blackfoot has had some environmental hurdles to overcome in recent years, but it has largely rebounded. **Rock Creek** is reached by traveling 26 miles east of Missoula on I-90 to exit 126. Rock Creek has been designated a blue-ribbon trout stream, although it is not necessarily an easy stream to fish. Catch-and-release fishing is enforced along the middle stretch of the creek, and fishing with bait is prohibited, except by children.

Campsites along Rock Creek range from **Ekstrom's Stage Station** (406/825-3183), a full-service tent and RV campground (complete with flush toilets, hot showers, a store, and swimming pool) 0.5 mile from I-90 on Rock Creek Road, to **Siria** (www.fs.usda.gov/lolo) a small bare-bones Forest Service campground with no drinking water, 29 bumpy miles up Rock Creek Road.

For fishing supplies, stop by **Kingfisher Fly Shop** (926 E. Broadway, 406/721-6141) or **Grizzly Hackle** (215 W. Front, 406/721-8996). Both shops run guide services; daylong trips start at about $450.

Kayaking

The many rivers of western Montana offer wonderful opportunities for kayak and raft trips. Actually, you don't even need to leave downtown Missoula to play in a kayak; check out the "play wave" that has been constructed in the Clark Fork River just downstream of the Higgins Avenue Bridge by Caras Park.

The friendly and experienced **10,000 Waves Raft and Kayak Adventures** (8080 W. Riverside Dr., 406/549-6670 or 800/537-8315, www.10000-waves.com) is one of the best of the local outfitters and offers trips on the Bitterroot, Blackfoot, and Clark Fork through both Hell Gate Canyon and Alberton Gorge. Trips are available on regular inflatable rafts, hard-shell or inflatable kayaks, or "sit-on-tops." Raft trips are the least expensive, and run around $70 for a half-day excursion; full-day trips, which include lunch, begin at $85. A variety of kayak lessons and clinics are also offered.

With headquarters west of Missoula in Alberton, **Zoo Town Surfers** (5077 Old Hwy. 10, Alberton, 406/370-4436, www.zootown-surfers.com) offers trips down the Alberton Gorge ($55 half day, $75 full day) as well as raft trips and paddling lessons in other local rivers and stand-up paddle trips on lakes in the Swan and Bitterroot Valleys.

Skiing

Montana Snowbowl (406/549-9777, www.montanasnowbowl.com) has more than 30 runs, reaching up to three miles long, and a 2,600-foot vertical drop. It's about 12 miles out of town, reached by taking the Reserve Street exit from I-90 and driving north on Grant Creek Road to Snowbowl Road. Lift tickets at Snowbowl are $45 for adults, $19 for children, with student, senior, and half-day rates available. Both skis and snowboards can be rented, and lessons are available.

In the Garnet Range, east of Missoula, the **Garnet Resource Area** (406/329-3914, $5 adult) is a Bureau of Land Management (BLM)-operated ghost mining town with 55 miles of cross-country ski and snowmobile trails. From State Highway 200, about 30 miles east of Missoula, turn south between mile markers 22 and 23. Or follow I-90 to Bearmouth 26 miles and turn north five miles on Highway 10 to Bear Gulch Road. Follow the signs for Garnet.

Closer to town, there's challenging cross-country skiing up Pattee Canyon, and the **Rattlesnake National Recreation Area**

The Clark Fork River is flanked by trails on its path through downtown Missoula.

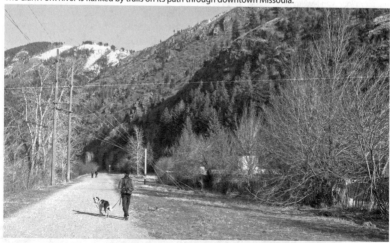

and **Wilderness** (RNRAW) has miles of trails; many are suitable for skiing. Consult the RNRAW map, available at outdoors stores, for possibilities.

Golfing

Nine-hole public golf courses include the **Highlands Golf Club** (102 Ben Hogan Dr., 406/728-7360), and the course on the **University of Montana** campus (406/728-8629). **Larchmont Golf Course** (3200 Old Fort Rd., 406/721-4416) has 18 holes. The area's top 18-hole course is **Canyon River Golf Club** (1268 Bandmann Trail, 406/721-0222, http://canyonrivergolfclub.com) on a beautiful stretch of land overlooking the Clark Fork just east of Missoula.

Swimming

Missoula is a good place to get some exercise after a long car trip. The university's indoor **Grizzly Pool** (406/243-2763) has regularly scheduled public hours and is a good option for lap swimmers. An indoor water park at **McCormick Park** (600 Cregg Ln., 406/721-7275), at the west end of the Orange Street Bridge, has two waterslides and places for both lap swimmers and water play. Splash Montana, at **Playfair** (3001 Bancroft, 406/542-9283, Memorial Day-Labor Day), behind Sentinel High School, is an outdoor pool with features for both kids and adults.

NIGHTLIFE

Nowhere does Missoula's unique mix of population become more apparent than in its many bustling watering holes. Some bars are of interest because of their historic character; others because of the characters they attract. Remember that bar life in Montana is primarily social in nature. Bars are where people meet up. There is no stigma attached to not drinking alcohol. Even if you don't care for a drink, go along for the friendly welcome. Be prepared, however, for lots of unrepentant gambling and a certain loss of ambience to the chattering of electronic gaming devices.

The downtown area is chockablock with curious old bars. The **Missoula Club** (139 W. Main, 406/728-3740) is a peanut-shells-on-the-floor, grill-in-the-back sports bar with fixtures unchanged since the 1940s. Don't attempt to resist their grilled hamburgers. They are, in their simplicity, the stuff of legend.

Also legendary, but for different reasons, is the **Oxford Club** at Pine and North Higgins. Although not always edifying, it has character by the bottleful and a certain attraction for writers. Watch the creative writing students who eye the bar's sullen denizens, waiting for epiphanies.

More standard youthful hangouts are the **Rhino** (158 Ryman, 406/721-6061); the **Badlander** (208 Ryman, 406/549-0235), with dancing a couple of nights a week; and the **Top Hat** (134 W. Front, 406/728-9865). The latter offers live music (blues, swing, funk) in an atmosphere heavy with Missoula's peculiar indolent funkiness. The **Union Club** (208 E. Main, 406/728-7980) is another popular downtown spot for live music. If you want to go out and sample Missoula nightlife but aren't into the bar scene, go to **Break Espresso** (432 N. Higgins, 406/728-7300), a coffee shop that stays open late and is a magnet for caffeine-propelled studying and hanging out.

BREWPUBS

The main thing to remember about visiting a Montana brewpub is this: go early. By law, brewpubs (i.e., places that brew on the premises) must close by 8pm or 9pm. Several Missoula establishments get around this restriction by brewing off-site. The brew scene in Missoula is both intense and abundant, with reportedly the second-greatest concentration of brewpubs per capita in the country. For a full listing of Missoula's brewpubs, go to http://montanabrewers.org/breweries.

If you'd like to explore Missoula's top brewpubs (and distillers) but don't want to drive (your car), consider **Thirst Gear** (http://thirstgear.com), a bike trolley tour that lets up to 15 revelers pedal around to some of the city's top drinking destinations. The tour takes place on a custom-built bike trolley and is captained by a (sober) tour guide who is in charge of guiding the vehicle through traffic. The tour lasts three hours and costs $20 per seat; reservations are required. Summer weekends are very busy, so reserve well in advance for those dates. Tours begin at 201 E. Front St.; participants must be 21 and older.

Some of Montana's best beer is poured at the **Kettlehouse** (313 N. 1st St. W., 406/728-1660, noon-9pm Mon.-Sat.); their Double Haul IPA and Cold Smoke Scotch Ale are featured at a number of bars and restaurants around the state. Kettlehouse is sold in environmentally friendly cans at **Worden's Market** (451 N. Higgins, 406/549-1293, 8am-11pm Mon.-Thurs., 8am-midnight Fri.-Sat., 8am-10pm Sun.), a great place to buy beer and wine in downtown Missoula.

The German-style beers from **Bayern Brewing** (1507 Montana St., 406/721-1482, noon-8pm daily) are available at the Bayern tasting room and in grocery stores around the state. Look for the great bottle labels illustrated by local artist Monte Dolack.

The **Flathead Lake Brewing Company** (424 N. Higgins, 406/542-3847, 3pm-12:30am Sun.-Thurs., 11am-2am Fri.-Sat.) is exempt from the 8pm curfew because it doesn't brew on-site; it's more properly called a "microbrew bar," featuring beers from Flathead Lake Brewing in Bigfork.

Another offshoot of a Flathead Lake-area brewery is **Tamarack Brewing Company** (231 W. Front St., 406/830-3113, 11am-midnight daily). This two-level pub is noisier downstairs, and a bit more refined up, where there is also a restaurant. During the winter, try the seasonal Old 'Stache Whiskey Barrel Porter, aged in old Jim Beam barrels.

Despite its name, the popular **Iron Horse Brew Pub** (501 N. Higgins, 406/728-8866, 11am-2am daily) is really more of a typical college-town bar. Upstairs, the focus is more on cocktails than beer, and downstairs, the beer special may well be Pabst. The food here is pretty good.

EVENTS

Summertime Saturday mornings (and Tuesday evenings) bring the **Farmer's Market** to the Circle Square, at the northern end of Higgins Avenue next to the old Northern Pacific rail depot.

A Native American **powwow** (www.umt.edu/kyiyo/powwow.htm, $5) is held annually, usually in mid-April, in the university field house.

Each May, Missoula hosts an excellent **wildlife film festival** (406/728-9380, www.wildlifefilms.org).

The 221-mile bicycle **Tour of Swan River Valley** is an annual springtime event, usually held in late May. Register well in advance for the TOSRV ride; this popular two-day ride is sponsored by **Missoulians on Bicycles** (406/250-7728, www.missoulabike.com).

The **Missoula Marathon** (www.missoulamarathon.org), held in mid-July, has grown into a major event—in fact, it's now a qualifier for the Boston Marathon and has been named *Runner's World Magazine*'s top marathon in the United States.

The **Western Montana Fair and Rodeo** (www.westernmontanafair.com) is held in Missoula during the third week of August. It's time to take in a rodeo, a delectable Montalado (a Montana-style enchilada), the llama pavilion, and perhaps a few carnival rides.

SHOPPING

For many travelers, Missoula will either be one of the first or one of the last places visited in Montana. Missoula's shops offer the visitor either a last chance to stock up on vital comestibles and to drink that final espresso, or the first opportunity in days to assuage deprivations incurred farther inland.

Butterfly Herbs (232 N. Higgins, 406/728-8780, www.butterflyherbs.com) offers tea, coffee, herbs, spices, soaps, and in fact a little of everything. The storefront is a well-preserved specimen from the end of the 19th century. The back of the store is a good espresso bar and café.

Local artist Monte Dolack's whimsical nature-oriented paintings, posters, and cards have gained a wide following. A visit to the **Monte Dolack Gallery** (139 West Front, 406/549-3248) is worth the time.

The **Bird's Nest** (219 N. Higgins, 406/721-1125) is a center for new and secondhand regional books, and **Fact and Fiction** (220 N. Higgins, 406/721-2881) is a good general bookstore.

Because of Missoula's access to the outdoors, recreation stores are important to the visitor. A good source of equipment, for both sale and rent, is the **Trail Head** (221 E. Front St., 406/543-6966). The staff are usually able to offer good advice on local trails and conditions.

Find genuinely fashionable women's clothing at **Nolita** (531 N. Higgins, 406/728-6556).

ACCOMMODATIONS

Because Missoula is a real crossroads, a great number and variety of lodgings are available. Unless there's a big football game, graduation, or some other major event going on at the university, you'll have little trouble finding something. There are many inexpensive and somewhat marginal motels along Broadway near downtown Missoula; be forewarned that many of these can be the sites of weekend parties. Also, no matter where you stay, bring earplugs; trains do run through town.

$50-100

On the east end of downtown, the **Motel 6 Missoula University** (630 E. Broadway, 406/549-2387, www.motel6missoula.com, $65-75) has been updated, allows pets, and offers an outdoor pool. It's just across Broadway from one of the town's top hotels and restaurants (the DoubleTree), and it's an easy walk to downtown, the university, or the riverside paths. Just east, the **Campus Inn** (744 E. Broadway, 406/549-5134 or 800/232-8013, www.campusinnmissoula.com, $85-110) is reasonably well-maintained but not fancy. Just to the east is the **Thunderbird Motel** (1009 E. Broadway, 406/543-7251 or 800/952-2500, $70-85 and up), another good bet for visitors who aren't looking for frills.

On the Highway 93 strip south of downtown, the standard **Super 8 Brooks Street** (3901 Brooks, 406/251-2255, $75-89) is a good launching pad for trips to the Bitterroot Valley.

Over $100

The sprawling **Red Lion Inn** (700 W. Broadway, 406/728-3300 or 800/733-5466, www.redlion.com, $109-129) is in a good location near downtown; it has a pool, a hot tub, a restaurant, and a meeting room. Rates include a good continental breakfast; pets are allowed.

The university district and downtown also have some of Missoula's nicest and most expensive lodgings. The ★ **DoubleTree Hotel Missoula/Edgewater** (100 Madison St., 406/728-3100, www.missoulaedgewater.doubletree.com, $139-155) is right on the Clark Fork across from the university. This is a generally quiet place to stay (though very popular during football weekends), with a good restaurant and a pool.

The **Comfort Inn** (1021 E. Broadway, 406/549-7600, $119-144) is a relatively good deal for this close-to-the-university neighborhood, with new comfortable rooms. Pet-friendly.

Right downtown and also on the river is the ★ **Holiday Inn Missoula Downtown at the Park** (200 S. Pattee, 406/721-8550 or 800/315-2621, $129-147). Although the hotel is very comfortable and offers an indoor pool, hot tub, sauna, and fitness center, its main asset is its great location. Pets are permitted with a $20 fee, and there's great dog-walking right out the door.

Once the home of the university's second president, **Goldsmith's Inn** (809 E. Front, 406/728-1585 or 866/666-9945, www.goldsmithsinn.com, $124-169) was relocated to the north bank of the Clark Fork and renovated to its original 1911 splendor. Of the seven rooms, four are suites with private sitting areas (one suite has a private deck and hot tub) and three are queen rooms. All rooms have private bathrooms and include breakfast.

The historic **Gibson Mansion B&B** (823 39th St., 406/251-1345 or 866/251-1345, www. gibsonmansion.com, $120-229), designed by the architect responsible for the Missoula County Courthouse and the Daly Mansion in the Bitterroot Valley, is located in a residential neighborhood about 1.5 miles from the university. It makes a very comfortable Missoula home base, with sumptuous breakfasts.

★ **Blossom's B&B** (1114 Poplar St., 406/721-4690, www.blossomsbnb.com, $110-195), a Prairie-style arts and crafts home located in the Lower Rattlesnake neighborhood with easy access to trails and not too far from downtown and the university, is that rare find—a dog-friendly B&B. The owners try to use organic foods as much as possible in the breakfasts, and the refrigerator is stocked with complimentary beer and wine.

Out at I-90 exit 101 (Reserve St.) are almost all of Missoula's recently built hotels. Trouble is, these often massive lodging complexes are a long way from the sights and experiences that attracted you to Missoula in the first place. However, if you're just blowing through on the freeway, by all means pull in at this exit—unless it's homecoming weekend, you should be able to find a room without reservations. Of the more than half dozen lodgings clustered here, a good place to land with a car full of road-weary kids is the **C'mon Inn** (2775 Expo Pkwy., 406/543-4600 or 888/989-5569, www.cmoninn.com, $129-145), an attractive log-design motel with an indoor pool, waterfall, rustic decor lounge area, hot tubs, an exercise room, and a popular Ping-Pong table. At the business-class end of the scale, the **Staybridge Suites** (120 Expressway, 406/830-3900, $143-167), offers posh suite-style rooms, an indoor pool, fitness center, and a business center.

Although its airport location is far from central, the **Wingate Inn** (5252 Airway Blvd., 406/541-8000, www.wingatemissoula.com, $109-144) is popular with families because of the two waterslides that empty into its relatively large indoor pool.

Campgrounds

Missoula's private campgrounds are all close to I-90. The sprawling **Missoula KOA** (3450 Tina Ave., 406/549-0881 or 800/562-5366, www.missoulakoa.com, all year, $43-47 RV, $32-42 tent, $68-80 cabin), complete with swimming pool and hot tub, is off I-90 at exit 101 (Reserve Street). **Jim and Mary's RV Park** (9800 Hwy. 93 N., 406/549-4416, www. jimandmarys.com, all year, $40 RV) is a Good Sam campground with no tent sites; it's on the way out of town toward the Flathead Valley and Glacier National Park. **Yogi Bear's Jellystone Park Camp** (9900 Jellystone Ave., 406/543-9400 or 800/318-9644, www. jellystonemt.com, May-Oct., $40-45 RV, $33 tent, $64 cabin) is off I-90's exit 96 and has big pull-through sites, a pool, a good play area, and a Yogi Bear theme.

The **Department of Fish, Wildlife, and Parks** (406/542-5500, http://fwp.mt.gov) operates a couple of campgrounds a little farther from town. **Chief Looking Glass** (May-Nov., $12) is a popular fishing access area with campsites on the Bitterroot River 14 miles south of Missoula on Highway 93 (to milepost 77), then one mile east on the county road. **Beavertail Hill State Park** (May-Nov., $15 Montana residents, $23 nonresidents) is 0.25 mile south of the Beavertail Hill exit off I-90 (milepost 130, 26 miles southeast of Missoula).

FOOD

There are reasons to linger over Missoula's abundance of good restaurants. For the traveler coming to Missoula from the east, this may be the first good salad seen in days. For the traveler heading into eastern Montana, Missoula may be the last place to enjoy a choice beyond fast food and steak. Every franchise imaginable is found along the Highway 93 strip. However, for those with a hankering for something local, Missoula shouldn't disappoint.

Casual Meals

From downtown motels, it's an easy walk across the Higgins Avenue Bridge for a morning muffin and coffee at **Bernice's Bakery** (190 S. 3rd St. W., 406/728-1358, www.bernicesbakerymt.com, 6am-8pm daily). By your second visit (which may be for a lunchtime sandwich), you'll feel like a local at this homey spot. Only a block away, **Le Petit Outre** (129 S. 4th St. W., 406/543-3311, www.lepetitoutre.com, 7am-6pm Mon.-Fri., 8am-5pm Sat.) has only a couple of tables out front for seating, but offers a wonderful selection of brioche, panini, and European-style breads to go.

If it's juice and coffee that you're after, **Butterfly Herbs** (232 N. Higgins, 406/728-8780, www.butterflyherbs.com, 7am-7pm daily) houses a juice and espresso bar in an impressive old downtown storefront. It's also a good place to buy tea and herbs in bulk.

★ **The Shack Cafe** (222 W. Main, 406/549-9903, www.theshackcafe.com, 7am-3pm Mon.-Thurs., 7am-9pm Fri-Sun., breakfast and lunch $5-12, dinner $9-22) has been one of Missoula's favorite breakfast and lunch stops since the 1950s. It's going stronger than ever and is now open for dinner on weekends.

The retro-hip **Hob Nob Cafe** (531 S. Higgins Ave., 406/542-3188, www.hobnobhiggins.com, 7am-4pm Mon.-Fri., 8am-4pm Sat.-Sun., $6-8) is a good place for a big breakfast among friendly Missoulians. The food is largely organically grown and the breads homemade.

For a rollicking Italian American atmosphere that's popular with families, **Ciao Mambo** (541 S. Higgins, 406/543-0377, 5pm-10pm Mon.-Sat., 5pm-9pm Sun. summer, 5pm-9pm Sun.-Thurs., 5am-10pm Fri.-Sat. winter, $10-19) can't be beat. No reservations are accepted, so expect to stand in line for a while before settling in with a giant plate of spicy spaghetti arrabiata.

One of the biggest draws on the South Higgins "Hip Strip" is the fabulous ★ **Big Dipper** (631 S. Higgins, 406/543-5722, noon-10:30pm, $2-5), home of Montana's best ice cream. Although you could go the choc-van-straw route, this is the place to branch out and taste cardamom or Irish whiskey ice cream.

Missoula's best pizza and a bustling mix of students and locals can be found at **Biga Pizza** (241 W. Main St., 406/728-2579, www.bigapizza.com, 11am-3pm and 5pm-9:30pm Mon.-Thurs., 11am-3pm and 5pm-10pm Fri., 5pm-10pm Sat., sandwich $9, pizza $12-18), where the ingredients are locally grown when possible, leading to some innovative (and delicious) pizzas, such as fennel marmalade with bacon and gouda cheese, and great salads.

At **Caffe Dolce** (500 Brooks, 406/830-3055, http://caffedolce.com, 7am-9pm Mon.-Thurs., 7am-10pm Fri., 8am-9pm Sat., 8am-4pm Sun., lunch $7-15, dinner $12-30), find a bit of sunny Italian spirit in Missoula. The food here is excellent, and the atmosphere classy but casual. Grilled sandwiches and good salads anchor the lunch menu; pizza, authentically Italian pastas, and entrées such as a pork shank confit are featured at dinner. Don't leave without some house-made gelato.

If you're hungry, thirsty, or looking to gamble away your money any time of the day or night, the **Oxford Club** (337 N. Higgins, 406/549-0117, 24 hours, $4-13) is there to serve you. Although not for the fainthearted or the easily appalled, the Ox is a Missoula fixture. Late at night, this is local color at its most opaque.

The **Good Food Store** (1600 S. 3rd St. W., 406/541-3663, 7am-10pm daily) is Missoula's best source for natural and health foods. The deli here is an excellent place to stock up for a picnic.

Fine Dining

A handful of restaurants on Higgins, none more than a couple of blocks from the river, offer great dinners. At ★ **Scotty's Table** (131 S. Higgins, 406/549-2790, http://scottystable.net, 11am-2:30pm Tues.-Fri., brunch 9am-2pm Sat.-Sun, dinner 5pm-10pm nightly, entrées $24-33), in the basement of the historic Wilma Theater, a casual bistro-style ambience complements the rather sophisticated fresh seasonal food. Here you'll find innovative twists on standard dishes and sauces, such as ravioli stuffed with braised lamb and date chutney or farro risotto served with candied lemons, walnuts, and garlic-parsley butter.

Another outstanding restaurant, ★ **Red Bird** (111 N. Higgins, 406/549-2906, http://redbirdrestaurant.com, 5pm-9:30pm Tues.-Sat., dinner entrées $24-32, wine bar $10-22, dinner reservations recommended), is right downtown tucked off the main lobby of the historic Florence Hotel. It also uses local ingredients whenever possible and buys whole animals to make tasty cured meats and sausages in-house. The food is great, and the restaurant's architecture is stunning. Even if you're not up for a full-production dinner, stop in at the restaurant's wine bar and have a snack or a light dinner.

Somewhere between a wine bar and a fine-dining restaurant, ★ **Plonk** (322 N. Higgins Ave., 406/926-1791, http://plonkwine.com, 4pm-midnight Sun.-Mon., 11:30am-midnight Tues.-Sat., $10-35) offers a superlative selection of wines by the glass plus a temping menu of small plates, such as Dungeness crab empanadas and harissa-rubbed beef tenderloin skewers, in addition to full main courses such as grilled local pork chops with hazelnut pesto and grilled peaches. This handsome dining room in a downtown historic storefront is a very happening scene.

Eat tapas from around the world at **The Silk Road** (515 S. Higgins, 406/541-0752, www.silkroadcatering.com, 5pm-10pm nightly, $6-11). The mix can be a little odd—you can choose from wiener schnitzel, carne asada, Chinese meatballs, and an Ethiopian BBQ wrap—but the food is generally good and the place is quite popular.

Also delightful is the **Pearl Café** (211 E. Front St., 406/541-0231, http://pearlcafe.us, 5pm-10pm Mon.-Sat., $20-37), a sophisticated white-tablecloth restaurant with a gentle French influence on such dishes as duckling with pomegranate cherry sauce and rabbit baked in red wine mushroom sauce with crispy polenta.

Ask any local where to find Missoula's top

steaks, and the answer will be **The Depot** (201 Railroad St. W., 406/728-7007, www.depotmissoula.com, 5:30pm-10pm daily, $11-39), an atmospheric rail depot with excellent beef, seafood, chicken, and such specialties as a free-range veal chop.

INFORMATION

The **Missoula Convention and Visitors Bureau** (101 E. Main St., 406/532-3250 or 800/526-3465, www.missoulacvb.org) has racks brimming with brochures on Missoula and the surrounding area and a helpful website.

The regional **U.S. Forest Service** office (200 E. Broadway, 406/329-3511) sells national forest maps. This is also a good place for general information on hiking and camping in national forests.

The regional office of the **Department of Fish, Wildlife, and Parks** (3201 Spurgin Rd., 406/542-5500, http://fwp.mt.gov) is a source of advice on fishing and hunting and can provide a list of public campgrounds.

The **public library** (406/721-2665) is at 301 E. Main Street. What you don't find on their shelves may well be in the stacks of the **university library** (406/243-6860). Of particular interest there is the Mansfield Collection, located on the third level down. U.S. Senator Mike Mansfield left his papers to the University of Montana, and they're housed here along with a great collection of regional history.

Listen to **Montana Public Radio** at 89.1 or 91.7 FM.

SERVICES

The **police station** (406/523-4777) is at 435 Ryman.

The main Missoula **post office** (406/329-2200) is at 1100 W. Kent, but the downtown **Hell Gate Station** (200 E. Broadway, 406/329-2222) may prove to be more convenient.

St. Patrick's Hospital (500 W. Broadway, 406/543-7271) is right downtown.

The **First Interstate Bank** (101 E. Front,

406/721-4200) is the main bank in town and the place to go to exchange foreign currency.

GETTING THERE AND AROUND
Air
Missoula International Airport (MSO) (5225 Hwy. 10 W., 406/728-4381, www.fly-missoula.com) is just northwest of town. Alaska, Allegiant, Frontier, United, and Delta Airlines fly into Missoula. **Shuttle service** (406/543-9416) is available from the airport into town, and many hotels provide shuttles. Alamo, Hertz, Budget, National, Enterprise, and Avis all have rental cars at the airport. Nearby (with service to the airport), find Thrifty and Dollar.

Bus
Greyhound buses (1660 W. Broadway, 406/549-2339, www.greyhound.com) run three times daily along the interstate. **Flathead Transport** offers bus service between Missoula, Polson, Kalispell, and Whitefish; ticketing is through Greyhound.

Mountain Line Transit (406/721-3333, www.mountainline.com, Mon.-Sat. until early evening, $1) operates the city buses, which are all equipped with bike racks. Most buses leave from the downtown transit center, behind the courthouse on East Pine between Ryman and Woody Streets. There's a nice indoor waiting area stocked with bus schedules and served by a Break Espresso outlet.

Taxi
Taxi service is provided by **Yellow Cab** (406/543-6644) and **Green Taxi** (406/728-8294), which uses hybrid vehicles.

The Lower Clark Fork

Forest-rimmed, hilly, and as wild as an interstate ever gets, I-90 follows the Clark Fork and St. Regis Rivers most of the way between the Idaho border and Missoula. From the state line east to Frenchtown, just west of Missoula, I-90 follows the Mullan Road, built by John Mullan and his crew in the 1860s as a military road from Fort Benton to Walla Walla, Washington.

It's easy to rush through this western edge of Montana, and in truth there aren't that many ways to penetrate this densely forested mountainous region. But a bike ride along the Hiawatha Trail, a dip in the pools at Quinn's Hot Springs, or a sighting of mountain sheep outside Thompson Falls may prove to be a highlight of a trip to Montana.

ALONG I-90
The Idaho-Montana border straddles the crest of the Bitterroot Mountains at the 4,710-feet-high **Lookout Pass** (I-90 exit 0), where the

Lookout Pass Ski Resort offers skiing in winter and in summer serves as an outfitter for bicyclists taking the Hiawatha Mountain Bike Trail.

Continuing east into Montana, pull off I-90 at **Haugan** (exit 16) to visit the much-hyped **World Famous 50,000 Silver Dollar Bar** (406/678-4242 or 800/531-1968), a bar that sits at the center of a dining, gift shop, lodging, and casino complex. At the least, you'll want to poke your head into the bar to see all those silver dollars.

St. Regis, at exit 34, is where the St. Regis River flows into the Clark Fork (like De Borgia to the west, St. Regis was named for the Jesuit missionary St. Regis De Borgia). After the rivers join, the Clark Fork turns sharply to the north. Highway 135 follows it along 20 miles of lovely riverscapes to Highway 200 near village of Paradise.

Superior, at exit 47, was a mining boomtown. Gold was discovered on a stream called Cayuse Creek in 1869, and over the next year, 10,000 people swarmed to the mining camp. In some areas, such as the now ghost town of Louisville, Chinese miners moved into the abandoned shacks and gleaned the remaining gold. Mining booms came intermittently over the next few decades but pretty much ended in 1910, when a huge forest fire destroyed the Keystone Mine and most everything else for miles around.

Alberton, at exit 75, is alongside a notorious gorge in the Clark Fork River and was originally a railroad town. It was a division point for the Milwaukee Road, whose depot has been restored and is visible from I-90.

★ Hiawatha Mountain Bike Trail

A rails-to-trails project converted 15 miles of Chicago, Milwaukee, and St. Paul Railroad track, tunnel, and trestle into the exhilarating **Hiawatha Mountain Bike Trail** (208/744-1301, www.ridethehiawatha.com, late May-early Oct., trail pass $10 adults, $6 children 6-13, free under 6). The centerpiece of the trail is the 8,771-foot Taft Tunnel, built in 1909 and cut through solid rock from the Montana side of Lookout Pass (the East Portal) through to Idaho (the West Portal). After emerging in Idaho, the track winds down through another eight tunnels and over nine wooden trestles before reaching the valley floor at the village of Pearson.

Bikers need headlights to traverse the trail, and hikers will want to bring along strong flashlights. Be prepared to get a little wet and chilly in the tunnel. Even though the grade never exceeds 1.7 percent, vertigo-inducing trestles stand along sheer cliffs and over steep rocky canyons. Whether you're on foot or on a bike, you'll have your heart in your mouth on several occasions.

To reach the beginning of the trail and Taft Tunnel, take exit 5 (Taft Area) from I-90. Turn south and follow Rainy Creek Road for two miles, and take the road toward East Portal at the Y junction. The parking area is immediately ahead, and just beyond is the gate to the tunnel.

A shuttle service ferries cyclists from the trail's end at Pearson back up to the West Portal (both on the Idaho side, Fri.-Sun. only). From here, you traverse the Taft Tunnel once again to return to the car park at the East Portal. Plan a full day for this trip, and reserve a spot on the shuttle in advance by calling the **Lookout Pass Ski Resort** (208/744-1301, $9 adults, $6 children). Mountain bike rentals are available at the ski area (exit 0 from I-90) for $30-36; you can also rent a tagalong bike or a trailer for kids.

Other Recreation

Recreation at Lookout Pass, on the Montana-Idaho border, turns from biking to skiing in the winter, when an average of 400 inches of generally powdery snow falls at the **Lookout Pass Ski Resort** (208/744-1301, www.ski-lookout.com). Lookout has a small downhill ski area (with free lessons for kids!) with good cross-country trails. Adult lift tickets cost $38-40 for a full day, $35 after 12:30pm. Many special rates are available for seniors, college students, military, and juniors; kids under six are free.

Alberton Gorge (or Cyr Canyon) is a 20-mile stretch of white water on the Clark Fork River. There are plenty of fishing-access sites along the Clark Fork that can be used to put in and take out boats. It's an especially challenging run when the river is high; only experienced paddlers should attempt it before August. Even when the water level drops, it's not a trip for beginners, although Missoula-based **Lewis and Clark Trail Adventures** (406/728-7609 or 800/366-6246, www.trailadventures.com, half-day trip $55 adults, $45 children; full day with lunch $75 adults, $60 children) runs regular raft trips through Alberton Gorge. This outfitter also offers other rafting and hiking trips along the Lewis and Clark Trail; see the website for details. Another good rafting tour operator is **10,000 Waves** (406/549-6670 or 800/537-8315, www.10000-waves.

The Mullan Road

It took John Mullan and his crew from 1858 until 1862 to build a military wagon road from Fort Benton to Walla Walla, Washington. This was a particularly vital stretch of road because Fort Benton marked the farthest point that steamboats could travel up the Missouri River, and Walla Walla provided access to the Columbia River. His route has held up well; I-90 follows its course from Deer Lodge to the Idaho line.

Mullan also has the distinction of having written the first travel guide to Montana. In 1865 he authored the *Miners' and Travelers' Guide to Oregon, Washington, Idaho, Montana, Wyoming and Colorado*. As may be expected, the Montana portion follows the Mullan Road.

Clark Fork for brown, cutthroat, rainbow, and bull trout.

Accommodations

Most eastbound I-90 travelers press on to Missoula once they cross into the state, but there are several quite passable lodgings along the interstate.

Down the road from Lookout, there is a string of small towns with (mostly) small unremarkable motels. Part of the **World Famous 50,000 Silver Dollar Bar** complex is the **Silver Inn** (exit 16, 406/678-4242 or 800/531-1968, www.50000silverdollar.com, $79-89) with simple, clean rooms.

The highway-side but still quite woodsy **Black Diamond Guest Ranch** (121 E. Frontage Rd., 406/678-4000, www.blackdiamondguestranch.com, cabins $75 double) has lodging in 100-year-old cabins (rustic, but with bathrooms and basic kitchens), a campground for tents ($10) and RVs ($16-37), plus camping in large canvas-walled tents ($50 for up to 6 persons, showers extra). Trail rides start at $40 per hour. Pets are permitted.

In St. Regis, the **Super 8** (exit 33, 406/649-2422, $69-84) is a reliable spot that permits pets. From St. Regis, follow Highway 135 20 miles northeast along the Clark Fork

com, half-day trip $70 adults, $50 children 5-12; full day $85 adults, $65 children); both trips include lunch. In addition to trips through Alberton Gorge, 10,000 Waves offers guided raft and kayak trips along the Blackfoot River and through Missoula's Hell Gate Canyon.

Those who aren't tempted by the white water may choose to fish this section of the

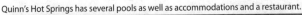

Quinn's Hot Springs has several pools as well as accommodations and a restaurant.

to find ★ **Quinn's Hot Springs Resort** (190 Quinn's Canyon Rd., 406/826-3150 or 888/646-9287, www.quinnshotsprings.com), in a woodsy area three miles south of Highway 200. This venerable resort has a clutch of attractive standard cabins ($165-225 for up to four, some are pet-friendly), luxury cabins ($235-295 double), suites ($270, sleeps five), a lodge ($135-145 adults only), and a good restaurant in a wooded glade. The temperature of the outdoor swimming pool is adjusted according to the weather; day use for walk-in guests is $10 weekday/$11 weekend per person (included for guests in lodging fee); children must be at least three years old and potty trained.

Back on I-90, in Superior, the **Budget Host Big Sky Motel** (exit 47, 406/822-4831 or 800/283-4678, www.bigskymotel.net, $69-83) has spacious rooms and is a good bet for a pleasant stay.

Camping

Several **Lolo National Forest campgrounds** (www.fs.usda.gov/lolo) are convenient to I-90. **Cabin City** Forest Service campground (Memorial Day-Labor Day, $7) is a little more than two miles off I-90 at exit 22, just east of De Borgia. Unless you hit a busy weekend, it's relatively peaceful. The campsites are set in a lodgepole pine forest, and there's a 0.75-mile nature hike down to Twelvemile Creek.

The **Slowey** (mid-May-late Sept., $10) campground is between exits 37 and 43. **Quartz Flat** (mid-May-late Sept., $10) is at the rest stop east of Superior, near mile marker 58. It's convenient but exposed to I-90's lights and noise.

THOMPSON FALLS

David Thompson, who established his Saleesh House here in 1809, is the namesake of Thompson Falls (pop. 1,345, elev. 2,463 feet). Thompson, an English-born explorer, astronomer, and geographer for both the Hudson's Bay and North West Companies, traveled down the Kootenai River from Canada

Camels in the Rockies

Camels in the Rockies? Well, why not? They're strong, they don't drink too much . . . so thought the U.S. Army in the 1860s, when some innovative military man began importing camels to use as pack animals. Although perhaps more efficient than the customary mules, camels weren't so easy to boss around. Apparently they were harder to recognize, too; several of the camels on the Mullan Road were shot after being mistaken for moose.

and into Montana in 1807. Over the next few years he set up trading posts along the Kootenai and Clark Fork Rivers and became the first European to travel the entire length of the Columbia River, which he mapped from mouth to source. Thompson spoke several Native American languages and won the trust and respect of local tribes.

The falls here were dammed in 1916, backing up a two-mile-long reservoir behind the dam. There are two more dams downstream from this one, making the Clark Fork more like a lake than a river for much of its course from Thompson Falls to the Idaho state line.

Sights

Island Park, across the footbridge at the foot of Gallatin Street, is a day-use park that's closed to automobiles. The island straddles two separate areas of the eponymous falls in the Clark Fork (both dammed), and it's full of bluffs and rocky rises and is a good place to hike around and watch birds, including the ospreys nesting on the bridge, and also salmon climbing up a fish ladder.

The **Old Jail Museum** (109 S. Madison St., 406/827-4002, noon-4pm Mon.-Fri. mid-May-Labor Day, $3 adults 18 and older, free 17 and younger) is indeed housed in the old jail, behind the police station.

About 10 miles east of Thompson Falls, the Clark Fork River trenches through a series of Precambrian shale deposits (cousins to the formations in Glacier National Park), resulting in cliffs up to 1,000 feet rising above the river, which are prime habitat for bighorn sheep. Amid this striking landscape, the **KooKooSint Mountain Sheep Viewing Area** is a roadside pullout with several informative signs. (*KooKooSint* is the name given to David Thompson by the local Native Americans. It means "Man Who Looks at Stars.") Bighorn sheep were eaten by the Flathead and by Thompson, who found them a welcome addition to his sparse winter diet. You're most likely to see sheep here in the spring, when they're at lower elevations eating the new grass, or during late November or December, when they descend to feed in the valleys and mate. Open south-facing slopes provide a winter habitat. The lambs are born in early May on the high ridges, and the sheep summer in the mountains. Mountain sheep have spongy hooves with hard edges to lend traction and support, allowing them to traverse steep slopes easily and quickly.

Recreation

Several looped hiking trails lead to small lakes in the Lolo National Forest north of Thompson Falls. Reach the **Four Lakes Creek** trailhead by driving north on Thompson River Road (which intersects Highway 200 five miles east of town) about six miles, turn left onto the West Fork Thompson River Road, and follow it, bearing left as it becomes Four Lakes Creek Road (Forest Service Road 7669), some eight miles to the trailhead. A Lolo National Forest map will detail the trails.

Fishing access to the Thompson River is easy; the road runs along it almost the entire way from Highway 200 north to Highway 2. Expect to pull mostly rainbow trout, and perhaps some brown trout, from the stretch near Highway 200.

Accommodations

Only one motel is in Thompson Falls itself; the others are about a mile west, where Highway 200 bridges the Clark Fork.

The **Falls Motel** (112 Gallatin, 406/827-3559 or 800/521-2184, www.thompson-fallslodging.com, $70-150) is a friendly place downtown and near good strolling on Thompson Falls Island. This basic and well-maintained motel has a hot tub in a pleasant little solarium; dogs are permitted for a $10 fee. West of town above the bridge and set back from the highway, the spacious **Rimrock Lodge** (4946 Hwy. 200, 406/827-3536, http://rimrocklodgemontana.com, $85-115) has good views of the Clark Fork River, a popular restaurant and lounge, and a bowling alley. Ask at the desk about the nature trail looping the motel grounds. Pets are permitted.

More riverfront lodgings are on the west side of the bridge over the Clark Fork. Here you'll find the attractive **Riverfront Motel and Cabins** (4907 Hwy. 200, 406/827-3460, www.riverfrontlodging.com, $85-95, $125-140 cabins for up to 4 persons), which also has spaces for RVs ($25).

Camping

Thompson Falls State Park (406/752-5501, http://fwp.mt.gov/parks, May-Sept., $15-23) is a mile west of Thompson Falls, just off Highway 200 on the Clark Fork. The riverside spots have running water but no other amenities. **Copper King** and **Clark Memorial** (www.fs.usda.gov/lolo, late May-late Sept., $5) are Forest Service campgrounds with no running water located up Thompson River Road (catch this road five miles east of town). Copper King is four miles off Highway 200; Clark Memorial is another 1.5 miles up the road.

Food

The **Rimrock Lodge** (406/427-3536, 6am-9pm daily, $8-15) has good river views, steaks and seafood, and if you get bored, you can opt for some bowling. Downtown, the **Thompson Grill** (611 Main St., 406/827-4900, 7:30am-9pm Mon.-Sat., $6-25) is a popular spot for burgers and good milk shakes. On Friday and Saturday nights, dinners are fancier and more leisurely. **Minnie's**

Montana Cafe (921 Main St., 406/827-3747, 7am-9pm Mon.-Sat., 7am-8pm Sun., $7-18) is a classic small-town diner, with tasty American fare prepared home-style.

NORTH OF THOMPSON FALLS ON HIGHWAY 200

Highway 200 runs along the Clark Fork River north and west of Thompson Falls to the Idaho border; thanks to the 190-foot-high Noxon Dam, for a large part of this stretch the river is known as Noxon Reservoir. The towns of **Trout Creek** and **Noxon** each have a few places to stay.

If you're in the mood to drive back roads, **Vermillion Falls** is 12 miles from Trout Creek on Vermillion River Road. A couple of miles farther along the road, find **Willow Creek Campground,** a small, free, and primitive (no water) Forest Service campground.

In Trout Creek, the **Lakeside Motel** (2957 Hwy. 200, 406/827-4458, www.lakeside-resort-motels.com, $85-115) has motel rooms and cabins. **North Shore Campground** (www.fs.usda.gov/kootenai, mid-Apr.-Nov., $7) is on Noxon Reservoir about two miles west of Trout Creek.

Although Noxon has a couple of budget motels, for something beyond a bed and a ceiling, try the ★ **Bighorn Lodge B&B** (406/847-4676 or 888/347-8477, www.bighornlodgemontana.com, $150-175). In addition to comfortable rooms and full breakfasts, the folks at the Bighorn provide guests with canoes, kayaks, and bikes, and can arrange guided horseback rides and fishing trips.

The Bitterroot Valley

Probably nowhere else in Montana provides such a diverse and satisfying unity of attractions as the Bitterroot Valley. First of all, let's make it clear that the Bitterroot is stunningly beautiful. The Bitterroot River, flanked by groves of cottonwood, winds through a wide fertile valley of farms and pastureland. The heavily wooded humped arch of the west-lying Bitterroot Mountains rears back to reveal precipitous canyons and jagged peaks. The Sapphire Range to the east is characterized by relatively low forested peaks. Historic, quiet old towns slumber in a purposeful way: There are comings and goings, but not much commotion.

Opportunities for recreation are almost limitless. The Bitterroot River provides great fishing, and the streams flowing out of the Sapphire Mountains have better fishing than the Bitterroot drainages, which debouch from alpine lakes in rounded valleys scooped out by glaciers, then fall quickly through narrow canyons gashed through the resistant mylonite rock. The Bitterroot National Forest offers thousands of acres of wilderness, with more than 1,600 miles of maintained trails to dramatic peaks, pristine lakes, and wildlife viewing. Across the valley to the east the Sapphire Range offers gem hunting and more wildlife habitat. Proximity to Missoula lends sophistication to the services in the Bitterroot, but suburban sprawl also engulfs the lower valley with residential subdivisions.

HISTORY

The Flathead came to the Bitterroot from the west, and although they took regular trips to the plains to hunt buffalo, they made ample use of the valley's roots, huckleberries, and fish.

In 1805 Lewis and Clark passed down the Bitterroot Valley from the south, over Lost Trail Pass. The Corps of Discovery had already crossed the Continental Divide at Lemhi only to discover that although the Salmon River in Idaho flowed into the Columbia drainage, it did so as the aptly named "River of No Return." The Salmon was

The Bitterroot Valley

© AVALON TRAVEL

the corps returned up the Bitterroot to cross over Gibbons Pass into the Big Hole.

Lewis is responsible for the name of the plant that gives this valley its name. While local Native Americans found the roots of the bitterroot both tasty and fortifying, Lewis pronounced it bitter and nauseating. His name now identifies the plant in Latin: *Lewisia rediviva*.

The Bitterroot Valley, with its fertile bottomland and protected climate, attracted farmers from the beginning. The discovery of gold in nearby valleys and the establishment of mining boomtowns created a demand for foodstuffs. As farmers moved into the area, they began to pressure the government to remove the Flathead from the valley, and in 1872 James Garfield, who later became the 20th U.S. president, was sent to transfer them north to the Mission Valley.

Five years later the Nez Perce passed through the Bitterroot on their tragic flight across the Northwest. Under the leadership of Chief Joseph, the band of about 700 people and nearly 2,000 horses traveled from Idaho down Lolo Creek and up the Bitterroot toward Crow country, fleeing the army infantry. Chief Joseph vowed to the army and the Bitterroot settlers to march peaceably through the settled areas of the Bitterroot in return for unmolested passage. The offer was not accepted officially, and the Nez Perce simply skirted a hastily constructed barricade at Fort Fizzle and proceeded up the Bitterroot. No shots were fired as they passed through the valley. Once they had made it over the Continental Divide in the Big Hole, however, Col. John Gibbon and 183 men ambushed the Nez Perce at the Battle of the Big Hole.

Agriculture

Farming really took hold in the Bitterroot after the Northern Pacific extended a spur line to Hamilton. One of the largest enterprises in the valley was Marcus Daly's Bitterroot Stock Farm. The copper magnate from Butte preferred the Bitterroot as a summer home, and he built a magnificent mansion on his

hopelessly impassable. The corps climbed up into Montana again, this time to follow the Bitterroot down to the area near Lolo Creek, where they established a favorite camping spot called Travelers' Rest. From here the corps followed Lolo Creek up and over Lolo Pass, and down more hospitable drainages to the Columbia. The following year they retraced their trail to Travelers' Rest. Clark and half

26,000-acre holding. Considering the fact that Daly modeled his farm on an Irish manor, it's no surprise that racehorses were the most noted of the farm's products.

In the early years of the 20th century the Bitterroot was home to an elaborate irrigation scheme that turned the valley into a huge apple orchard. The Big Ditch, as it was functionally named, provided water to the eastside benchland, which was divided into subdivisions of 10 acres each. At the height of apple euphoria, 22,000 acres of the Bitterroot were in fruit production. The soil and climate didn't quite live up to the exaggerated promises of the developers, and by the 1950s apple production had ceased to be a significant element of the area's economy.

While agriculture remains important in the Bitterroot, much of the farmland in the lower valley has now been subdivided into small "ranchettes." This part of the valley has largely been converted into a bedroom community of Missoula.

RECREATION

The Bitterroot National Forest contains 1.6 million acres, with nearly 750,000 of these protected as wilderness. Forest Service roads provide entrance for mountain bikers or off-road vehicle enthusiasts, while 950 miles of maintained trails give hikers access to some of the most tortured geology and pristine landscapes in the Rockies.

Fishing

All the larger streams that feed into the Bitterroot River harbor rainbow, cutthroat, and brook trout, and some of the higher lakes in the Bitterroots, such as the Big Creek Lakes, are known for good fishing.

For the angler, though, the real news is the Bitterroot. The river seems largely untainted by the effects of a century's worth of forestry, farming, suburban sprawl, and irrigation. In fact, even in the busy heart of the valley, the cottonwoods and willows that line the shore shield the angler from the realities of Bitterroot development. The trout here are both numerous and large. Rainbows and browns fill the majority of creeks, but cutthroat and the elusive bull are also apprehended. The lower part of the river near Missoula is where the lunkers are most likely lurking (and, rumor has it, largemouth bass), while farther south, up Connor way, is where the trout are thickest.

The state has established 10 fishing-access sites on the river, and there's also easy access

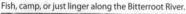
Fish, camp, or just linger along the Bitterroot River.

How Archaeologists Located Travelers' Rest

Before his great journey, Meriwether Lewis studied all the things an explorer must know, including a little bit of doctoring. His physician mentor was Dr. Benjamin Rush, who gave Lewis a stash of pills to use as a cure-all. Dr. Rush's Thunderbolts were essentially very strong mercury-laced purgatives.

While at Travelers' Rest, a couple of the Corps of Discovery members fell ill (the journals report, "Goodrich and McNeal are both very unwell with the pox which they contracted last winter with the Chinook women") and were administered the pills. They presumably spent a good bit of their time at the camp latrine, relieving themselves of whatever had ailed them, along with a good dose of mercury. When archaeologists surveyed the area in 2002, they noted a trenchlike depression in the ground. They assayed the soil in and around the trench for mercury, which was present in the trench but not in surrounding areas.

Researchers also located the corps' camp kitchen, situated as military protocol would have it, 300 feet from the latrine. Here, using equipment that detects geological disruptions, archaeologists found changes in the magnetic properties of the soil. They also found fire-cracked rocks and traces of charcoal that would have resulted from large military-style cooking fires rather than the smaller fires used by the Native Americans who frequented the area.

Travelers' Rest has become one of the few sites in Montana with physical proof of Lewis and Clark's visit.

from bridges. At no place is the Bitterroot far from the road, although remember to ask for permission before crossing private land. Boat rentals are available in Hamilton, and organized float and fishing trips are offered by the region's many outfitters.

THE LOWER BITTERROOT

From **Hamilton** (pop. About 4,500, elev. 3,600 feet) north to Missoula, the Bitterroot passes through the towns of **Corvallis, Victor, Stevensville, Florence,** and **Lolo.** Excluding the lodges of typically nomadic Native Americans, this part of the valley is the oldest continuously inhabited area in Montana, and it shows. Interesting old Victorian farmhouses are scattered among the fields, and isolated apple trees from once substantial orchards can still be seen in meadows. Main streets have changed little since they were built. Despite the crags of the Bitterroot Range rising to the west, here the Bitterroot feels lived-in and comfortable.

The visitor should leave Highway 93 as soon as possible (at Florence at the Missoula

end and at Hamilton from the south) and instead take the East Side Highway, MT 269. While 93 is undeniably a faster road, it's also very busy. The East Side Highway affords the best views of the Bitterroots and goes through the pretty towns of Corvallis and Stevensville.

Travelers' Rest State Park

Although it had long been known that the Corps of Discovery camped in the Bitterroot Valley near present-day Lolo during their westward trip in 1805 and the following spring on their way east, the exact location of this campground was a matter of some speculation. In 2002, archaeologists were able to pin down the precise location of **Travelers' Rest** (Hwy. 12, 406/273-4253, www.travelersrest.org, 8am-8pm daily June-Aug., 9am-6pm daily Apr.-May and Sept.-Oct., 9am-4pm Mon.-Fri., noon-4pm Sat. Nov.-March, $5 per vehicle non-Montana residents, visitors center typically closes one hour before the park itself), and the site was quickly developed as a state park. Although the area really just looks like a grassy field in a pretty rural setting, it is poignant to think of the Corps of Discovery resting here.

When they left this camp on July 2, 1806, Lewis and Clark parted ways, with Lewis and his small crew heading through Hell Gate Pass and into Blackfoot territory, and Clark and his group heading back to the Beaverhead, where their boats had been left the previous year, and down the Yellowstone River. The groups planned to meet up at the mouth of the Yellowstone but had no way of knowing whether that would actually happen.

St. Mary's Mission and Fort Owen

In 1841 St. Mary's Mission was founded in the Bitterroot Valley after repeated requests for Catholicism from the Flathead and Nez Perce of the area. Father Pierre-Jean De Smet, the missionary dispatched to found St. Mary's, was also Montana's first agriculturalist. He planted oats, wheat, and potatoes at the mission. This was probably also an initial attempt to make the Native Americans into farmers. Troubles arose between the missionaries and the Flathead, and in 1850 St. Mary's was sold to John Owen, who turned it into a trading post.

St. Mary's Mission (4th St., Stevensville, 406/777-5734, www.saintmarysmission.org, 10am-5pm Tues.-Sat. mid-Apr.-mid-Oct., tours $5) at Stevensville was rebuilt in 1866 by Father Anthony Ravalli out of the original hewn logs of the 1841 structure. The interior of the one-room chapel, with its wood-burning stove and wainscoting, is pretty much as Father Ravalli left it. Also on the grounds are the mission pharmacy, Father Ravalli's cabin, and a graveyard. While Father Ravalli's grave is meant to be the draw here, more curious is the sign indicating INDIAN GRAVES before an open field.

What's left of **Fort Owen** (Hwy. 269, Stevensville, 406/273-4253, http://stateparks.mt.gov/fort-owen, $5 per vehicle for nonresidents) is just east of Highway 93 between the highway and the town of Stevensville cutoff (follow signs for Fort Owen State Park). The original 1850 structure evolved from the log palisade of a frontier trader into an adobe-brick fortress with turrets and walkways after Owen became the federal Indian agent to the Flathead. Of the original buildings, one barracks remains and serves as a museum with interpretive exhibits.

Daly Mansion

Marcus Daly bought his Bitterroot Stock Farm in 1889 and built the **Marcus Daly Mansion** (406/363-6004, www.dalymansion.org, 10am-5pm daily Apr.-mid-Oct., $9 adults, $8 seniors, $6 youth 6-17) in 1897. After his death, the house was enlarged in 1910 to its present Georgian revival splendor. Built primarily as a summer home for the Daly family, Riverside, as the mansion was known, looks over the Bitterroot Valley to the rugged peaks in Blodgett Canyon that vie with the Bitterroots for splendor. The house remained in private hands until 1987, when it was acquired by the state.

Riverside is probably the most beautiful estate in Montana. A tree-lined boulevard leads to 50 acres of grounds, which contain an arboretum of specimen trees, a swimming pool, a playhouse, and a tennis court. The 24,213-square-foot mansion contains 42 rooms, 24 of which are bedrooms and 15 are baths. Some of the original furniture and most of the old fixtures remain. The grounds alone are worth a strolling tour.

The mansion is four miles south of Corvallis and two miles north of Hamilton on MT 269. After leaving the highway, follow a boulevard about one mile until you reach the grounds.

Daly's most famous racehorse was Tammany. In keeping with the Daly tradition, Tammany did not simply have a stable, but a brick edifice called Tammany Castle. To see what upscale horses lived in at the end of the 19th century, go one mile east of Hamilton on MT 269, and look to the south about 100 yards. The stable is not open to the public.

A Bit About the Bitterroot

While the bitterroot lily, Montana's state flower, grows throughout most of the western part of the state, the Bitterroot Valley is, unsurprisingly, a good place to plan a sighting.

Legend holds that the plant sprang from the tears of a Flathead mother whose family was starving. The sun, hearing the mother's sorrow, sent a bird as a messenger to turn her tears into a plant whose roots were nutritious (albeit as bitter as the mother's sorrow) but whose beauty would reflect the devotion of the grieving woman.

The roots of these beautiful light-pink flowers were a staple of the Native American diet. They were eaten fresh in season and also dried for use in the winter or when traveling. The Flathead boiled or steamed the roots, then mixed them with berries, marrow, or meat. Although the snow-white meat of the roots can be bitter to the point of causing nausea, the Flathead found that if they were gathered before flowering, or dried sufficiently, the bitterness was much reduced.

Elaborate rituals accompanied the bitterroot's harvest. Among the Flathead, one old woman led other female gatherers out in the search. When the party reached the first bitterroot, the leader would stick her elk-horn digger at the base of the plant. After the others planted their diggers, a prayer was offered, and the first plant was uprooted. Only after the prayer was offered was the season open; to dig before the ceremony was to invite a small harvest. The following day the first root was given to the chief, and a daylong feast ensued.

Hamilton

Hamilton is unique because it didn't just spring up as opportunity (or the railroad) allowed. Rather, it sprang fully formed from the brow of copper magnate Marcus Daly, who, after designing his model Irish manor, decided to establish a model town nearby. In 1890 Daly brought in planners who laid down a city complete with free plots for churches, ready-designed banks, shops, schools, and rather glorious homes. As a result, Hamilton wears its age gracefully. Stop to picnic or let the kids loose in one of its parks. An easy stop for either activity is a small playground only one block west of Highway 93 on Bedford, two blocks south of Main. There's a more substantial park where Madison Street bumps up against the Bitterroot River.

Hamilton contains several handsome old homes and public buildings. The **Ravalli County Museum and Historical Society** (205 Bedford St., 406/363-3338, http://brvhs-museum.org, 10am-4pm Tues., Wed., and Fri., 9am-8pm Thurs., 9am-1pm Sat., $3) is housed in the Old Ravalli County Court House, built in 1900. This stone-and-brick landmark bears a resemblance to the University of Montana's Main Hall. The museum has a good collection of Flathead artifacts, pioneer-era memorabilia, and an exhibit on wood ticks. Like the courthouse, the **City Hall** (175 S. 3rd) is on the National Register of Historic Places.

Hiking

Any creek worth mentioning in the Bitterroots has a trail up it, and nearly all are worth considering for a hike. But if you have only a day to spend in the lower Bitterroots, consider one of the following.

A largely overlooked long day hike (or unstressful overnight trip) that's close to Missoula leads up the Sweeney Creek drainage to **Peterson Lake.** Forest Service roads (turn west on Forest Service Road 1315 two miles south of Florence) will take the hiker most of the way up the canyon wall to a trailhead. After a couple of miles of easy traversing, the trail drops to alpine lakes, with the car having done most of the climbing.

The **Kootenai Creek Trail** stays pretty close to this rushing creek as it heads up a narrow canyon to a series of lakes. Although the lakes are nine miles up the trail, shorter hikes along the creek are good day-hike options. Find the trailhead at the end of Kootenai Creek Road, which heads west from Highway

93 about a mile north of the Stevensville junction.

A popular ascent of intermediate challenge involves climbing **St. Mary's Peak.** Again, this hike boasts a trailhead midway up the mountain, and one of the great views that the peak affords is onto the local lookout tower. From Highway 93, go two miles south of the Stevensville turnoff. A brown sign promising St. Mary's Peak points up the switchbacks of Forest Service Road 739. The trailhead is about 10 miles from the highway, and it's a 4.5-mile hike to the lookout.

Between Victor and Hamilton, at the crossroads hamlet of Corvallis, turn west to reach the **Mill Creek** trail. It's about three miles in along a great path to a waterfall; if you want to make a backpacking trip out of it, keep going for another 11 miles to a high mountain lake. This trail was damaged by the 2000 fires but has had lots of work since then.

Also damaged by the massive 2000 Bitterroot fires was the trail up lovely Blodgett Canyon, west of Hamilton. It's now a good place to see wildlife and regenerating plantlife. Hike the 1.5-mile (one-way) **Blodgett Overlook Trail** for an overview. There are also good views of the valley on the drive to the trailhead. From Hamilton, head west on Main Street to Blodgett Creek Road (Forest Rd. 736), then turn left onto Forest Road 735; the trailhead is about five miles from town. To hike up the canyon itself, follow Blodgett Camp Road and make a right onto Forest Road 746; follow the trail 1.5 miles to a nice pool or eight miles to Blodgett Lake.

The **Lee Metcalf National Wildlife Refuge** is a good place for short hikes along the Bitterroot River. This riverside refuge is full of ospreys, eagles, and whatever migrating birds need a place to spend the night. White-tailed deer and coyotes also live here. In the summer, after nesting season, a two-mile loop trail is open through the refuge. Two shorter trails are open year-round, and picnics are encouraged. From the East Side Highway (Hwy. 269), watch for the binocular signs indicating a sanctioned wildlife-viewing area, either just south of Florence or just north of Stevensville.

Other Recreation

Take a dip in the big outdoor pool at **Lolo Hot Springs Resort** (38500 W Hwy. 12, 406/273-2290, www.lolohotsprings.com 10am-10pm Mon.-Thurs., 10am-midnight Fri.-Sun. in summer, 10-am-9pm Sun.-Thurs., 10am-midnight Fri.-Sat. winter, $7 adults, $6 seniors 55 and over, $5 children 12 and under), on Highway 12 about 12 miles northeast of the state line, or about 25 miles west of Highway 93. Lewis and Clark camped and bathed here. Nowadays, these hot springs are popular with skiers returning from a long day in cross-country heaven at Lolo Pass.

A paved **bike path** between Lolo and Florence parallels Highway 93 and is a grand alternative to cycling on the busy highway.

There are **public golf courses** in Stevensville and Hamilton. The **Whitetail Golf Course** (406/777-3636), just north of Stevensville on Wildfowl Lane, has nine holes; the **Hamilton Golf Club** (406/363-4251), on Golf Course Road southeast of town, has an 18-hole course.

Cross-country skiing is pretty much the order of the season after snowfall and is as casual as just parking the car and putting on your skis. All of the Bitterroot canyons are good bets, and they are even more pleasant covered with snow, as they tend to be pretty rocky and rugged in summer. The real treasure for cross-country skiers, though, is Lolo Pass. Snow simply dumps along the pass all winter, but the Highway Department keeps the road open. Lolo Pass is 37 miles east of Lolo on Highway 12. It's very popular, but it's still possible to strike out and get away from the crowds.

Outfitters

Highway 93 has nearly as many fly shops as mini-marts, and store personnel will, in the way of cagey anglers, offer a few tips. In Florence, the **River Otter Fly Shop** (5516 Old Hwy. 93, Florence, 406/273-4858 or

866/800-4858, www.riverotterflyfishing. com) can set you up with equipment and a guide. **Chuck Stranahan's Flies & Guides** (109 Main St., Hamilton, 406/363-4197, www. chuck-stranahan.com) offers similar services just east of the Highway 93-First Street intersection in Hamilton.

Accommodations

Toward the north end of the valley, a little ways off Highway 93 in downtown Stevensville, the old community hospital has been turned into the attractive ★ **Stevensville Hotel** (107 E. 3rd St., 406/777-3087 or 888/816-2875, www. stevensvillehotel.com, $90-150). The rooms are decorated with antique furniture and art from the owners' travels in the South Pacific (they spent many years living and traveling on their sailboat). A sister property, the newly constructed **Fifth Street Motel** (105 E. 5th St., same contact as above, $65-90) is a couple of blocks from the main hotel and includes rooms with kitchens. Pets are permitted in a few rooms here.

Hamilton has the largest choice of motels in the Bitterroot Valley, where the best choice for budget lodging is the **City Center Motel** (415 W. Main St., 406/363-1651, www. remlcsportsmanslodging.com, $65-85), at the quiet end of Main Street. Pets can be accommodated here, and some rooms can have full kitchens.

The **Motel 6 Hamilton Inn** (409 1st St., 406/363-2142, $56-86) offers clean, standard rooms. If you're looking for a lodging with an adjacent casino and restaurant, head to the **TownHouse Inn** (1113 N. 1st St., 406/363-6600 or 800/442-4667, www.townhouse-innhamilton.com, $69-99). The pet-friendly **Bitterroot River Inn and Convention Center** (139 Bitterroot Plaza Dr., 406/375-2525 or 877/274-8274, www.bitterrootriver-inn.com, $119-149) is the newest lodging in Hamilton, and has all the standard amenities, including an indoor pool, hot tub, sauna, and fitness room. It's at the north end of town and just a short walk from the river.

For a different twist in lodging, consider staying at the rustic **Lolo Hot Springs Resort** (38500 Hwy. 12 W., 406/273-2294 or 877/541-5117, www.lolohotsprings.com, $40 and up economy cabins, $90 and up deluxe cabins, $16 tents, $24 RVs), which is 25 miles up Highway 12 along Lolo Creek. The economy cabins don't have bathrooms or sheets, and the deluxe cabins are only comparatively so. The adjacent **Lodge at Lolo Hot Springs** (38600 Hwy. 12 W., 406/273-2201,

The Stevensville Hotel used to be the local hospital.

www.lololodge.com, $89-149 and up) is more up-to-date; accommodations are in comfortable log lodges or more modest motel rooms with log furniture but without phones (or reliable cell or TV service).

A well-run Bitterroot Valley B&B is **Deer Crossing B&B** (396 Hayes Creek Rd., 406/363-2232 or 800/763-2232, www.deercrossingmontana.com, $100-149), south of Hamilton. Rooms are in a large log house or one of two cabins; dogs are permitted with advance notice, and there's room for traveling horses as well.

Camping

The U.S. Forest Service maintains several campsites in the Bitterroots. Most require a fair amount of determination to make use of. Some are essentially trailheads into Bitterroot canyons, and others demand long dusty drives on county roads. Still, some are handy enough for the more casual traveler to consider.

Lolo Creek Campground (www.fs.usda.gov/lolo, late May-Sept., $10) is 15 miles west of Lolo on Highway 12, and for the angler, right on Lolo Creek. An even more enticing fishing and camping site is the state's **Chief Looking Glass Fishing-Access Site** (http://fwp.mt.gov, May-Nov., $12), which is a developed campsite as well. Look for the fishing-access sign on Highway 93 at milepost 77, about midway between Lolo and Stevensville. Then turn east one mile to the river.

Charles Waters (www.fs.usda.gov/bitterroot, Apr.-Oct., $10) is a developed site at the trailhead up Bass Creek, with access to hiking up the canyon and fishing in the stream. Watch for the Forest Service sign for Bass Creek Trail four miles south of Florence or four miles north of Stevensville on Highway 93. It's about three miles in to the campsite.

There are more amenities at some of the area's private campgrounds. One of the best, **Angler's Roost** (406/363-1268, $18 tent, $30 RV full hookup), is three miles south of Hamilton on the river and caters especially to anglers.

Food

Some Missoulians claim that their city's best restaurant is actually in Lolo: ★ **Lolo Creek Steakhouse** (6600 Hwy. 12, 406/273-2622, 5pm-9pm Mon.-Thurs., 5pm-10pm Fri.-Sat., 4:30pm-9pm Sun., $12-40, reservations not accepted) is at the very northern edge of the Bitterroot Valley, practically in the Missoula suburbs. Be prepared to wait for a while to be seated, admiring the beautiful log building, which was constructed with 135- to 150-year-old logs, many felled and bucked by the restaurant's original owner. The steaks are cooked over an open-pit wood fire, and those who haven't been dreaming of the perfect Montana steak can satisfy themselves with fish, chicken, or pork.

Glen's Cafe (157 Long Ave., Florence, 406/273-2534, 9am-3pm daily, lunch $5-11), a little log building right on Highway 93, is known for its extraordinary pastries. Not that the rest of the menu is lacking (Glen's raises its own beef), but the pies are reckoned to be the best in the area.

Although there are a few cafés in downtown Stevensville, the most notable business serves beer: the **Blacksmith Brewing Company** (114 Main St., 406/777-0680, http://blacksmithbrewing.com, 2pm-8pm Sun.-Thurs., noon-8pm Fri.-Sat.). A local barbecue joint brings food in on Thursday and Saturday evenings, and there's often live music on Wednesday and Saturday. It's a fun place to hang out and drink some good beer.

In Victor, eat your beef at the **Victor Steakhouse** (2426 Meridian Rd., 406/642-3300, 11am-8pm daily, $8-20). Atmosphere is provided by the mounted animal heads observing you devour the steaks. Also in Victor, **Cowboy Troy's** (2356 Hwy. 93 N., 406/642-3380, www.cowboytroys.com, $11-16) has the area's best thin-crust pizza.

The Bitterroot's best burgers are in Hamilton at down-home **Nap's** (220 N. 2nd St., 406/363-0136, 11am-8pm Mon.-Sat., 11am-4pm Sun., $5-16). Steak and chicken platters are also available. At ★ **The Spice of Life** (163 S. 2nd St., 406/363-4433, 11am-2pm

Mon.-Fri. and 5pm-9pm Tues.-Sat., $9-27), you'll find good salads, an eclectic dinner menu with often-spicy Caribbean, Thai, Japanese, and Italian influences, and a homey bistro setting.

Bradley O's (1831 Hwy. 93 S., 406/375-1110, 4:30pm-9pm Wed.-Sun, $11-30), six miles south of Hamilton, is the sort of restaurant that the Bitterroot does best: steak (certified Angus) and seafood in a simple setting.

Taste some good local beer at **Bitterroot Brewing** (101 Marcus St., 406/363-7468, 11:30am-8pm Mon.-Sat., 11:30am-8pm Sun., $2-10). Tasty English-style ales and pub food such as fish tacos are the specialty at this friendly microbrewery across the railroad tracks and behind the Safeway.

Information and Services

The **Bitterroot Valley Chamber of Commerce** (105 E. Main St., 406/363-2400, http://bitterrootchamber.com) is just east of the stoplight in Hamilton.

The **Bitterroot National Forest Headquarters** (1801 N. 1st St., 406/363-7100, www.fs.usda.gov/bitterroot) is in Hamilton. The **Stevensville Ranger District Office** (406/777-5461) is at 88 Main Street.

Hamilton also supports a good general bookstore, **Chapter One** (252 Main St., 406/363-5220), a friendly place that serves as a de facto community center.

The **Marcus Daly Memorial Hospital** (406/363-2211) is at 1200 Westwood Drive in Hamilton.

THE UPPER BITTERROOT

The Bitterroot Valley narrows upstream from Hamilton, and the character of the countryside changes as it passes **Darby, Lake Como,** and **Sula**. The river flows faster here, and the mountains encroach. With rocky ramparts closing in, the Bitterroot ceases to be a broad valley dotted with farms and subdivisions and becomes a wooded canyon. People scramble for logging jobs or work for the Forest Service or at the local Job Corps center. For the traveler, recreation is the draw in the upper Bitterroot.

Darby marks the southern edge of old Lake Missoula, which existed in the bad old days when the entire Missoula Valley system was alternately underwater or drained as the ice age saw necessary. At **Connor,** just south of Darby, the Bitterroot River divides into the West Fork and the East Fork. The highway also divides. Highway 93 follows the East Fork up Lost Trail Pass over the Continental Divide south into Idaho or east into the Big Hole Valley. The West Fork proceeds up Highway 473 into deep canyons, first along a paved road, then along an improved road to Painted Rocks Lake.

At **Sula** on Highway 93, the East Fork opens onto pastureland—a last reprise of the Bitterroot Valley before it disappears into the heights of the Continental Divide.

History

Lewis and Clark straggled off Lost Trail Pass in September 1805 after being foiled on their way to the Columbia by the chasms of the Salmon River. They crept back into Montana via the Bitterroot and almost immediately met a lodge of Flathead. At present-day Sula, the Corps of Discovery found 400 Flathead and 500 horses encamped and quickly made friends. Remember the landscape; the enormous painting in the Montana House of Representatives in Helena depicts this meeting.

The valley at the junction of the East Fork and Camp Creek later became known as Ross's Hole. Alexander Ross was a Canadian trapper who nearly died of cold here with his family in 1824.

The Nez Perce passed through Ross's Hole in 1877 on their way to the Battle of the Big Hole, just over the Continental Divide. While the tribal leaders felt they had escaped the pursuing army, others, with "medicine powers," began to foresee the coming ambush. By this time, the army force, under the command of General Gibbon, had caught up with the fleeing Native Americans, who unwisely had taken a break from their flight from Idaho once they had reached Montana.

Recreation

The upper Bitterroot has reserved some of the best recreation for those willing to drive the extra miles to get there. You can grow hoarse talking about the hiking possibilities in the Bitterroot Range, but probably the most astonishing ascent of the entire range is the climb up **Trapper Peak.** At 10,157 feet it's the highest mountain in the Bitterroots, but it's only a moderately difficult eight-mile round-trip day hike. The trailhead is reached by following West Fork Road, MT 473, at Connor. Once you pass the Trapper Peak Civilian Jobs Corps Center, go almost seven miles to the signs pointing to the Trapper Peak trailhead. Switchbacks take you most of the way up the back of the mountain, but there's enough slogging left to satisfy more energetic hikers. If you do only one ascent in the Bitterroots, this should be it.

If a day on the mountain isn't possible for you, then enjoy the other end of Trapper Peak at **Lake Como.** This lake just west of Darby is nestled in a valley rimmed by the most unrestrained peaks in the Bitterroots. It should be no surprise that other people know of Lake Como (the Italian Lake Como is its namesake and chief rival in beauty), and don't expect to be the only camper at the lake. There's good trout fishing but too many speedboats to make it a bucolic getaway. There's an easy eight-mile loop trail around the lake. Watch for Lake Como signs five miles north of Darby.

Just across the road from Lost Trail Hot Springs, **Nee-Me-Poo Trail** traces the route of the Nez Perce on their 1877 flight from the U.S. Army. This section of the trail heads uphill through an open ponderosa pine forest past views down the Bitterroot Valley to Gibbons Pass, six miles from the road. It's a pleasant hike with a day pack filled with trail mix and water, but it's hard to hike this route without imagining what it would be like to walk it with family, friends, coworkers, and

neighbors of all ages, pursued by the U.S. Army.

A good West Fork hike starts from the Sam Billings Campground and sticks pretty close to aptly named **Boulder Creek** for the four-mile trip to Boulder Lake.

Painted Rocks Lake is a reservoir on the West Fork of the Bitterroot that receives a lot fewer visitors than Lake Como and offers better fishing, although irrigation usually draws it down during the late summer and fall. There are Native American pictographs on the rocks to the west of the lake. Painted Rocks Lake is 23 miles southwest of the junction of Highways 473 and 93. South of the lake, down West Fork Road, the still-standing Alta Ranger Station was the nation's first ranger station.

Upstream, south of Darby, the Bitterroot becomes a stream with fast action. The river is never far out of sight, and access is easy if you maintain the courtesy of asking permission to cross private property. One fishing-access site warrants mention: The **Hannon Memorial Fishing Access Site** at Connor allows the angler to fish both the East and the West Forks of the Bitterroot as they converge. Camping is allowed.

Stop by **Lost Trail Hot Springs** (406/821-3574, www.losttrailhotsprings.com, 8am-9pm Sun.-Thurs., 8am-10pm Fri.-Sat. mid-June-Labor Day, noon-9pm Fri., 8am-9pm Sat.-Sun. the rest of the year, $7.25 adults, $6.25 seniors, $5.25 children), seven miles south of Sula, for a swim in the large, pleasantly warm pool; indoors there's a hot tub and sauna. The cabins here make a good local base.

Lost Trail Powder Mountain (406/821-3211, www.losttrail.com, Thurs.-Sun. Dec.-Apr., $40 adults, $30 children, $5 one ride) straddles the Idaho-Montana border on Highway 93. Although it's a relatively small ski area with lots of intermediate runs, a few double chairlifts, and a vertical drop of only 1,200 feet, there's usually good powder here.

Accommodations

Darby is a rough-hewn little town that seems

only a few steps from its early logging days. Although there are some swanky houses on the edges of town, in-town motels are pretty simple.

To stay in miniature log cabins, go to the **Travellers Rest Cabins** (601 N. Main St., 406/821-3282, $72-89); each cabin has a single and a double bed; there are also RV sites ($32) available. The 1940s-era **Mountain Spirit Inn** (308 S. Main St., 406/821-3405 or 800/820-2554, $65-88) has been nicely fixed up.

The owners of **The Darby B&B** (4485 Thorning Loop, 406/821-0076, www.thedarbybedandbreakfast.com, $115-190), five miles south of town, run a "green" B&B, with organic foods and body products, environmentally friendly cleaning supplies, and a commitment to recycling. Three of the five bedrooms in this 1970s-era house have private baths; two rooms, which can be a suite, share a bath.

Although it's far from fancy, the **Lost Trail Hot Springs Resort** (8321 Hwy. 93 S., 406/821-3574, www.losttrailhotsprings.com, $76-86 lodge room doubles, $92-140 cabins double occupancy, larger lodge rooms and cabins available), in Sula, is a fun place to take in the Montana spirit in a beautiful forested setting. Along with the hot mineral water and an on-site bar and restaurant, there are easy-access recreational opportunities such as mountain biking, hiking, cross-country skiing, horseback riding, and fishing. Pets are accepted with a fairly stiff fee and stringent requirements. Lost Trail Hot Springs is six miles south of Sula on Highway 93, and six miles north of Lost Trail Pass.

Resorts and Luxury Cabins

If you don't want to stay in a motel on Darby's Main Street or pitch your tent in a Forest Service campground, head a few miles up the West Fork Road to one of Montana's most exclusive resorts, owned by the former CEO of Intel. Perched above the valley, the **Triple Creek Guest Ranch** (5551 West Fork Rd., 406/821-4600 or 800/654-2943, www.

triplecreekranch.com, $950-1,350 per couple in a one-bedroom cabin per night includes all meals, house wine, and ranch activities; two- and three-bedroom cabins available) offers accommodations in luxurious cabins and houses, gourmet meals, and fine wine. There are hot tubs aplenty, a well-kept heated swimming pool, tennis courts, horseback riding, fishing (all gear provided), and hiking trails heading out from the ranch property. Many guests come here to sample the various activities rather than concentrate strictly on fishing or riding, and an activities director helps them plan their days. Those who can't quite leave their work (and with these high-powered guests, that's pretty common) should note that, although there's no cell phone coverage here, there are phones in the room and Wi-Fi in the lodge. Although no minimum stay is imposed, there's enough to keep most people busy for nearly a week. The Triple Creek, which is the only Montana destination included in the ultra-prestigious *Relais & Chateaux*, is very much geared toward couples and is an adults-only place; no children under 16 are allowed.

Rye Creek Lodge (458 Rye Creek Rd., 406/821-3366 or 888/821-3366, www.ryecreeklodge.com, $275-350) is a luxury cabin resort south of Darby set in 120 acres. Each cabin has a private hot tub, a kitchen, and laundry facilities; most have two bedrooms; three-bedroom cabins available. Activities include trail riding, wilderness hiking, world-class fly-fishing, fly-casting lessons, white-water rafting, and ATV rides.

Camping

The Forest Service maintains several campgrounds in the **upper Bitterroot** (www.fs.usda.gov/bitterroot, late May-late Sept.), mostly off the beaten path. A couple are handy for casual campers who don't want to get too far off the highway. **Indian Trees** ($10) is six miles south of Sula, right next to Lost Trail Hot Springs at a location where Flathead women once spiked ponderosa pines to extract sap, which was used as a sweetener.

Lewis and Clark camped at **Spring Gulch** ($12), and so can you. The campground is right on the East Fork River, five miles north of Sula on Highway 93. Right behind the **Sula Store** (7060 Hwy. 93 S., 406/821-3364, www.bitterroot-montana.com, $15 tent, $20-25 RV, $45-85 cabin) are campsites and cabins (complete with bedding, but the cheapest require a short walk to the bathhouse) at the beginning of the canyon leading from Ross's Hole.

There are several Forest Service campgrounds up the West Fork Road; **Sam Billings** is a lovely free spot (no water) near the Boulder Creek trailhead, and there's another campground past Painted Rocks Lake at Alta ($8).

Food

There are a few cafés in Darby, and the country store in Sula has a small restaurant. The best bet for good food (prime rib, pasta, barbecue) and a fun atmosphere is the **Naughty Moose** (5390 Hwy. 93 S., Conner, 406/821-9955, 4pm-9pm daily, $10-26), located nine miles south of Darby near the West Fork turnoff.

Information

Bitterroot National Forest **ranger stations** can be found in **Sula** (7338 Hwy. 93 S., 406/821-3201) and **Darby** (712 N. Main, 406/821-3913).

Flathead Reservation and Mission Valley

The Flathead Reservation measures about 65 by 35 miles east to west and is managed by the Confederated Salish and Kootenai Tribes (www.cskt.org), with headquarters at Pablo. Of about 7,000 tribal members, some 4,500 live on or near the reservation. The Flathead population is centered at Arlee; most of the Kootenai tribal members live near Elmo.

The Mission Mountains Tribal Wilderness is the first place in the United States where a Native American nation has designated tribal lands as a wilderness preserve. It covers the west side of the range's peaks; to the east it's the Flathead National Forest, with access from Highway 83 in the Swan Valley. Any hiking or camping in the Mission Mountains Tribal Wilderness requires a tribal conservation permit, available at many local stores. A three-day conservation permit costs $10 ($16 includes camping stamp); if you intend to fish on tribal land, which includes the southern half of Flathead Lake, get the three-day combined-use/fishing permit, which is $17 for Montana residents and $46 for nonresidents.

HISTORY

Salish-speaking Native Americans originally lived near the Pacific Coast, where most Salish-speakers still reside. Legend has it that an argument developed as to whether flying ducks quacked with their wings or with their bills. The ones who voted for the wings ended up moving to the Bitterroot Valley and eventually became known as the Flathead Salish. When they arrived in the Bitterroot Valley, the Pend d'Oreille who were living there moved north, apparently as a gesture of friendliness, to the area around present-day Paradise and Plains.

The 1855 Hell Gate Treaty formed the Flathead Reservation, but Victor, head chief of the Salish, refused to move his people from their home in the Bitterroot Valley. However, in 1872, Arlee, a Flathead war chief, did sign the reservation treaty, gaining him recognition from the U.S. government as head chief of the Flathead tribe and forcing most of the tribal members to move north to the reservation in Jocko-Mission Valley.

In 1887, the Dawes Act allotted parcels of reservation land to Native American individuals in an effort to make them understand the concept of owning the land. Unallotted land was often dealt to the U.S. government and then thrown open to nonnative homesteaders. The Dawes Act was repealed in 1934, when tribal rather than individual identity was emphasized in the Tribal Reorganization Act. Under these provisions, the Confederated Salish and Kootenai Tribes were incorporated. By that time, much of the land within the confines of the Flathead Reservation was owned by non-Indians, as it remains today.

ST. IGNATIUS AND VICINITY

St. Ignatius is a reservation town at the feet of some stunningly jagged peaks. It's home to the **Salish Cultural Committee** (406/745-4572) and a longhouse, located near the St. Ignatius Mission, used by the tribe for spiritual and ceremonial events. There's a full day's worth of sightseeing in the vicinity of St. Ignatius.

★ St. Ignatius Mission

In 1854 St. Ignatius became the site of the second Catholic mission in Montana. Father Adrian Hoecken, a Jesuit priest, originally established the mission in Idaho, but it was moved to the Mission Valley at the behest of the Pend d'Oreille. A boys' school, a mill, and a press (which printed a dictionary of the Pend d'Oreille language) eventually grew up around the mission.

One of the Jesuits' original log buildings, a chapel that doubled as living quarters for the priests, still stands beside the brick church, which was built in 1891. The church deserves as much of a look as the wooden chapel; there are striking murals inside, painted by Brother Joseph Carignano, the mission cook. While these murals may not initially impress those who compare them to those at St. Paul's Cathedral or Chartres, they clearly succeeded in illustrating the life of Jesus and in imparting biblical stories to the flock. The mission is open 9am-7pm daily summer, 9am-5pm daily winter; Sunday mass is still held weekly at 9:15am. Good Friday and Easter services at the mission church have developed into a uniquely Flathead Catholic ceremony.

Much of the Flathead Reservation is on a high prairie.

★ National Bison Range

The **National Bison Range** (406/644-2211, http://bisonrange.fws.gov, 9am-5pm daily summer, 10am-2pm Mon.-Fri. winter, $5 per vehicle) has two driving tours, and it's worth taking a couple of hours to go on the long one. Stop in at the visitors center and find out where the herds have been spotted recently. Bison are the main attraction, but expect to see bighorn sheep, pronghorn, elk, mule deer, white-tailed deer, and mountain goats as well. Even if all the animals are in hiding, the land, the sky, and the light are beautiful here.

The National Bison Range was established in 1908 in response to concern that the buffalo had been slaughtered to the point of extinction. Part of the original herd was purchased from the Conrad family of Kalispell, who were early buffalo ranchers. The animals are now flourishing here, and a bison roundup is held in early October at the Bison Range.

The Bison Range is on a parcel of land carved from the Flathead Reservation by Highway 212 near Moiese. If you're approaching from Highway 93, catch Highway 212 between St. Ignatius and Ronan. If you're on Highway 200, there's a turnoff to Highway 212 near Dixon. From the north, turn off Highway 93 at St. Ignatius.

If there's no time for a tour, at least be sure to keep your eyes peeled as you drive Highway 93 north of Ravalli. Sometimes the bison come down off their mountain to water just a hundred yards or so from the highway.

Garden of One Thousand Buddhas

South of St. Ignatius, just north Arlee, find the **Garden of One Thousand Buddhas** (34756 White Coyote Rd., 406/726-0217, www.ewambuddhagarden.org, 8am-8pm daily summer, 9am-dark winter) at a Tibetan Buddhist retreat center. The gleaming white Buddha statues line up against a scenic mountain backdrop. Tibetan phrases are throughout the garden; they're translated into eight languages, including Salish.

Recreation

To explore the **Mission Mountains Tribal Wilderness,** first pick up a $10 tribal recreation permit, available at the Mountain View Cenex in St. Ignatius and other local stores. A map of the Flathead National Forest or the Flathead Reservation is another essential.

St. Mary's Lake is less than 10 miles from St. Ignatius on St. Mary's Lake Road. (Find the road just southeast of the mission and follow it as it turns into a fairly bumpy, dusty gravel road, turns left, and heads into the hills.) There are several places to pitch a tent around the lake, and it's worth taking along fishing gear and a tribal fishing permit; there are some lunker trout around here. Just over a mile up the road is the first of the **Twin Lakes,** which are a little more isolated and quieter than St. Mary's. No motorboats are allowed on the Twin Lakes; St. Mary's does permit them.

Events

Arlee, 15 miles south of St. Ignatius on Highway 93, is the site of the **Fourth of July Powwow,** held annually by the Confederated Salish and Kootenai Tribes. Expect to see both traditional and fancy dancing to the accompaniment of amazing drumming. Groups of drummers, as well as individual dancers, compete for prize money. In another area of the powwow, the sounds of hand drums signal stick games, which are ritualistic and high-stakes gambling competitions. For those not up to the complications and $100 ante of a stick game, poker and blackjack games are set up in small shacks. Admission is free, non-Indians are welcome, and drugs and alcohol are strictly prohibited.

Accommodations

The **Sunset Motel** (333 Mountain View, St. Ignatius, 406/745-3900, $75) is a simple but comfortable motel just above Highway 93 in St. Ignatius. Pets are allowed here.

Up against the Mission Mountains, the **Cheff Guest Ranch** (4274 Eagle Pass Rd.,

406/644-2557, www.cheffguestranch.com) offers accommodations on a working cattle and horse ranch outside of Charlo. Weeklong packages ($900 per person in guest rooms, $1,100 in cabins, both based on double occupancy) include all meals, lodging, and horseback riding. A couple of cabins are equipped with kitchens and can be rented by the night ($165). Cheff's also runs pack trips and short horseback rides ($50 for two hours).

RONAN AND VICINITY

Ronan was named for Peter Ronan, an Indian agent. The area around Ronan was part of the Flathead Reservation until 1910.

Pablo, five miles north of Ronan, is the headquarters of the Confederated Salish and Kootenai Tribes and home of **Salish-Kootenai College** (406/275-4800, www.skc.edu), which offers programs in general studies, Native American studies, nursing, and a range of human services and vocational fields.

Ninepipe National Wildlife Refuge

This wetland waterfowl refuge is north of the National Bison Range between Highways 93 and 212. The large reservoir and many smaller lakes are rimmed with marshlands, making it difficult to hike from many of the roadside viewing points. The best views are generally from the road that goes along the northern edge of the reservoir off Highway 212. The many pothole lakes around the refuge were dug out as glaciers moved across the land some 12,000 years ago.

Ninepipe is in the path of a major migratory flyway in the Rocky Mountain Trench. Prime bird-watching occurs in September. Canada geese, mergansers, mallards, redheads, great blue herons, grebes, double-crested cormorants, American wigeons, pintails, whistling swans, California gulls, ring-billed gulls, pheasants, bald eagles, and American avocets are some of the birds you might spot here.

Check at the headquarters of the National Bison Range for information on the birds and regulations. A tribal fishing permit is required before throwing a line into the reservoir. No hunting is permitted on the refuge, and it is closed during waterfowl-hunting season (in the fall) and nesting season (March through mid-July).

Pablo National Wildlife Refuge, off Highway 93 about 12 miles north of the Ninepipe Refuge, is a similar waterfowl sanctuary and governed by similar regulations.

Ninepipes Museum of Early Montana

In the motel complex adjacent to the wildlife refuge, the **Ninepipes Museum of Early Montana** (69316 Hwy. 93, 406/644-3435, www.ninepipesmuseum.org, 10am-4:30pm Mon.-Sat. Apr.-Oct., $5 adults, $4 students, $2.50 children 6-12) celebrates the history and culture of the Flathead Reservation and the early history of all of Montana.

The People's Center

The tribal museum and gift shop known as **The People's Center** (406/883-5544, www.peoplescenter.org, 9am-5pm Mon.-Sat. June-Sept., 9am-5pm Mon.-Fri. Oct.-May, $5 adults, $3 seniors and students), located in Pablo, also runs educational programs led by tribal members.

Arts and Entertainment

The **Red Poppy** (1 Eisenhower St. SW, Ronan, noon-6pm Mon.-Sat.) is a fine arts and cultural center across from True Value in Ronan. Along with art, music, and movement classes, the Red Poppy hosts an occasional concert. The gallery displays and sells works from over 130 regional artists.

Accommodations and Food

The **Ninepipes Lodge** (41000 N. Hwy. 93, 406/644-2588, www.ninepipeslodge.com, $80) is the area's most attractive motel. It's across from the bird refuge five miles south of Ronan. The lodge dining room, the

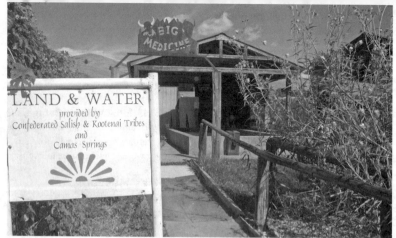

Big Medicine Hot Springs is a sweet place for a soak.

Allentown Restaurant (11am-9pm daily, $14-28) is known as much for its beautiful views (and taxidermy) as its American-style food.

HOT SPRINGS AND VICINITY

The western part of the Flathead Reservation has a couple of commercial hot springs in and around the very modest and unresortlike town of Hot Springs. Several massage therapists have practices in town, so it's easy to get *very* relaxed here.

Locals mix with day-trippers up from Missoula at **Big Medicine Hot Springs** (406/741-5140, $5), where the outdoor pools on the northeast edge of town were developed by a member of the Confederated Salish and Kootenai Tribes. Camping ($5-20) and cabins ($25) are available in case you get too relaxed

The Symes Hot Springs Hotel is the biggest hotel in the town of Hot Springs.

to leave. Another tribal member-run site is **Rose's Plunge,** at the Camas Recreation Center.

If you do want to spend the night within an easy sniff of the waters, **Symes Hot Springs Hotel and Mineral Baths** (104 Wall St., 406/741-2361 or 888/305-3106, www.syme-shotsprings.com, pool use only $7 adults, $4.50 children 12 and under, rooms $55-133) has rather basic rooms with bathtubs plumbed with the local sulfurous brew; there are also newer outdoor soaking and swimming pools. This downtown Hot Springs hotel is a mix between an old-fashioned therapeutic spa and a New Age retreat.

Economy rooms are equipped with a toilet and sink off the bedroom; to bathe you go downstairs to a long row of huge claw-foot tubs, each enclosed in its own wooden cubicle, and draw yourself a bath. Showers are also available, and more expensive rooms ($69 and up) have their own tubs. If you're here for the real treatment, there's a massage therapist on-site.

Another Hot Springs original is **Alameda's Hot Springs Retreat** (308 N. Springs St., 406/741-2283, www.alame-dashotsprings.com, $65-110), which has hot tubs, massages, and rooms (all with private toilet but some with shared shower facilities) in an old-fashioned motel. Pets are allowed both here and at Symes.

Flathead Lake

When western Montanans go away for a weekend, there's a pretty good chance they're headed to Flathead Lake. At 28 miles long, 7-8 miles wide, and more than 300 feet deep, it's the largest natural freshwater lake west of the Mississippi. The lakeshore is dotted with campgrounds and summer cabins, many owned by the same families for years.

Flathead Lake fills a trench carved by glaciers during the Pleistocene Epoch. A terminal moraine at the foot of the lake divides the Flathead Valley from the Mission Valley to the south.

Three upper forks of the Flathead River join above Kalispell to pour into Flathead Lake. The North Fork originates in southeastern British Columbia, the Middle Fork

Flathead Lake

Flathead Lake

Kalispell
CONRAD MANSION
JEWEL BASIN HIKING AREA
93
Flathead River
82
83
0   5 mi
0   5 km
Somers
Big Fork
WAYFARER
Lakeside
Woods Bay
Swan River
BLACKTAIL MTN AND BLACKTAIL CROSS-COUNTRY SKI AREA
WEST SHORE SRA
Flathead
Lake Mary Ronan
Rollins
35
YELLOW BAY
Dayton
Lake
To Hot Springs
Wild Horse Island
28   Elmo
Big Arm
BIG ARM
SAFE HARBOR MARSH PRESERVE
FINLEY POINT
Polson
93
To Missoula
© AVALON TRAVEL

Lake, where the lower Flathead River drains from the lake and flows toward its junction with the Clark Fork around Paradise. Highway 93 takes a turn here and becomes an east-west road for its extremely busy run through Polson. It's the seat of Lake County and the business center of Flathead Lake and the upper Mission Valley.

Parks

There's plenty of public shoreline, and several parks make appealing sitting, swimming, fishing, or boat-launching spots: **Boettcher Park** is toward the eastern edge of town, **Sacajawea Park** is right downtown off Kootenai Avenue, and **Riverside Park** is on the east end of the bridge over the river.

Lake Cruises

Lake cruises on the *KwaTaqNuk Shadow* (406/883-3636, www.kwataqnuk.com, late June-Aug., $15 per person, children 5 and under free; $40 family) run three times daily during the summer, leaving from the KwaTaqNuk Resort marina at 1, 4, and 7:30pm. Inquire about dinner cruises on Wednesday and Sunday ($30).

Polson-Flathead Historical Museum

The **Polson-Flathead Historical Museum** (704 Main St., 406/883-3049, www.polson-flatheadmuseum.org, 10am-5pm Mon.-Sat., 10am-3pm Sun., Memorial Day-Labor Day, $5 adults, $2.50 seniors, children under 12 free) is a dark jumbled place that houses a stuffed steer named Rudolf, a Lewis and Clark puppet display, and a 7.5-foot sturgeon caught in Flathead Lake in 1955 and reputed to have been the Flathead Monster.

Miracle of America Museum

The **Miracle of America Museum** (58176 Hwy. 93, 406/883-6804, www.miracleofamericamuseum.org, 8am-8pm daily Memorial Day-Sept.; 8am-5pm Mon.-Sat., 1:30pm-5pm Sun. Oct.-late May; $6 adults, $2 children 2-12) is marked by a large log towboat

rises in the northern part of the Bob Marshall Wilderness (near the southern edge of Glacier National Park), and the South Fork flows from the southeastern region of the Bob Marshall Wilderness via Hungry Horse Reservoir.

Fruit orchards are established all along the eastern shore of the lake. Although they're subject to periodic killing frosts, Flathead Lake's cherry trees are productive enough to supply farm stands and roadside vendors around the region.

POLSON

Polson (pop. 4,600, elev. 2,938 feet) is tucked into a glacial moraine at the foot of Flathead

The Flathead Lake Monster

Is there a monster lurking deep in Flathead Lake? Sightings have been reported for well over 100 years, and in 1955 it was even reported to have been caught. Although the creature in question turned out to be a 7.5-foot, 181-pound white sturgeon, it is preserved in the Polson-Flathead Historical Museum.

The capture of the sturgeon did not put an end to monster sightings. Read detailed incident reports at www.monsterwatch.itgo.com.

in the parking lot. Inside this sprawling and big-hearted "Smithsonian of the West," the intrepid museumgoer will find a unique homage to cleanliness: a collection of antique vacuum cleaners. Music lovers will thrill to the sound of the violano, a coin-operated violin-piano combination; the State Fiddlers' Hall of Fame is also housed here. There's simply *a lot* of everything here, from old motorcycles to vintage tractor seats.

Safe Harbor Marsh Preserve

The **Nature Conservancy** (406/443-0303) maintains a bird refuge north of Polson at **Safe Harbor Marsh.** Reach it by turning off Highway 93 just north of town onto Rocky Point Road. More than 130 species of birds and waterfowl have been observed here.

Recreation

All manner of watercraft, including sea kayaks and canoes, can be rented from **Absolute Water Sports** (406/883-3900) at the KwaTaqNuk Resort marina.

The lower Flathead River, considered to be Montana's warmest river, has spectacular badlands scenery and some thrilling rapids just below Kerr Dam. The **Buffalo Rapids** are a challenging stretch of white water for experienced rafters. Those with less-than-expert white-water skills should get on the river at

the Buffalo Bridge, about 10 miles below Kerr Dam, or sign on with the **Flathead Raft Company** (50362 Hwy. 93 N., 406/883-5838 or 800/654-4359, www.flatheadraftco.com, half-day trips $45 adults, $39 seniors, $35 children 8-12), which has a branch at Riverside Park in Polson that operates tours of the lower Flathead River, including Buffalo Rapids. The raft company also offers white-water kayak instruction and trips and sea kayak tours of Flathead Lake (half day $79 adults, $69 children 8-12).

The scenic 27-hole **Polson Bay Golf Course** (111 Bay View Dr., 406/883-8230, http://polsonbaygolf.com, $49 for 18 holes) is east of downtown on the lake side of Highway 93.

Because the southern half of Flathead Lake is on the Flathead Reservation, **anglers** need a tribal permit, which can be purchased at Zimmer Tackle in Pablo or at the tribal office (406 6th Ave. E.) or Wal-Mart in Polson. Although the number of kokanee salmon in the lake has decreased sharply in recent years, there are still lake trout (many topping 20 pounds), whitefish, and some cutthroat trout throughout the lake, as well as largemouth bass and perch in warm shallow spots, such as Polson Bay. Fishing Flathead Lake requires some thought about water depth and temperature—the big guys live deep. Although the lower Flathead River doesn't have much in the way of trout, there are plenty of big pike.

Entertainment

The former golf course clubhouse is now the John Dowdall Theatre, home to the **Port Polson Players** (406/883-9212, www.portpolsonplayers.com), a summer theater troupe that's been active since 1976. The season starts in July, with three plays produced each summer at 8pm Wednesday through Saturday evenings and at 2pm Sunday.

Accommodations

A good budget choice is **Bayview Inn** (406/883-3120 or 800/237-2965, www.bayview-inn.com, $65-115), with great views of

Flathead Lake and the Mission Mountains. Since it's right on the highway, there can be a bit of road noise. Pets are welcome here. The large **Best Western KwaTaqNuk Resort** (406/883-3636 or 800/882-6363, www.kwataqnuk.com, $170-186), a casino and hotel owned by the Confederated Salish and Kootenai Tribes, is the only real lakeside hotel in town, and it's the nicest of the few hotels in Polson. The KwaTaqNuk has both indoor and outdoor pools adjacent to the marina.

Port Polson Inn (502 Hwy. 93, 406/883-5385 or 800/654-0682, www.portpolsoninn. com, $130-300), just across the road from the lake, has indoor and outdoor hot tubs, an exercise room and sauna, kitchenettes, and free continental breakfast. It's not a fancy place, but it has a good location and is well kept up.

Swan Hill B&B (39407 Kings Point Rd., 406/883-1450, www.swanhillbedandbreakfast.com, $125-280) is worth considering. Set on 12 acres outside of town, amenities include an indoor pool and sauna, exercise room, kayaks and a paddleboat, a dock on the lake, and hiking trails. If you're not the chummy B&B sort, stay in the Flathead Lake cabin, which is a short walk from the B&B and has a full kitchen. A minimum stay of two nights is required.

Camping

RV campers may want to check out the **Polson KOA** (200 Irvine Flats Rd., 406/883-2151 or 800/562-2130, www.polsonkoa.com, RV with hookups $44-56, cabin with bath $175), about a half-mile north of the bridge, just west of Highway 93. If you want to camp close to Polson and you'd like a nice setting with some amenities, this is the place to be. Farther north of town you'll find lakeside state parks.

Food

For smoked meats and barbecue, the **East Shore Smoke House** (35103 Hwy. 35, 406/887-2096, www.eastshoresmokehouse. com, 11:30am-9pm Sun.-Thurs., 11:30am-10pm Fri.-Sat. Memorial Day-Labor Day, closes 1 hour earlier in off season, $10-28) offers steak-house fare, plus salmon, trout and pasta, in a rustic dining room with deck seating in good weather.

A good place that won't bust the budget is **Hot Spot Thai** (50440 Hwy. 93, 406/883-4444, www.hotspotthai.com, 11:30am-2:30pm and 5pm-8pm daily, $10-15). They have a deck with lake (and highway) views.

Down by the lake at Boettcher Park, the **Boardwalk Outdoor Cafe** (30 Country

Rent a kayak and explore Flathead Lake.

Club Shores, 406/339-1024, 11am-8pm daily mid-May-Aug., closed on rainy days, about $5) is a local institution where, during the summer months, you can eat fish-and-chips or a burger at an outside table (no indoor seating).

A few miles out of town, but worth the drive, **Finley Point Grill** (35 S. Shore Rd., mile marker 6 on Hwy. 35, 406/887-2020, 4pm-9pm Mon.-Fri., 11:30am-9pm Sat., 10am-8pm Sun., $12-25) uses locally sourced ingredients in their fairly standard American-style menu. Pizza is also popular here.

Both beer drinkers and soda lovers should go a few blocks out of their way to find **Glacier Brewing Co.** (6 10th Ave. E., 406/883-2595, www.glacierbrewing.com, noon-8pm daily). In addition to microbrews such as Port Polson Pilsner and Slurry Bomber Stout, Glacier brews up a fine root beer and a good (though extrasweet) cherry cream soda. Although food is not served, you can bring in your own picnic.

Information and Services

St. Joseph Medical Center (6 13th Ave. E., 406/883-5680) has 24-hour emergency service. The **post office** is at 219 1st Street East.

The **Polson Chamber of Commerce** (406/883-5969, www.polsonchamber.com) has an office at 418 Main Street.

The **public library** (2 1st Ave. E., 406/883-8225) has several cases of books on Montana, a good variety of magazines, and lovely views onto Flathead Lake.

WEST SIDE OF FLATHEAD LAKE

While driving along this side of Flathead Lake, you have a good view across the water to the Mission Mountains. There's more of an open feeling to this side of the lake than the east side—off to the west the rolling Salish Mountains mellow the light and lend a glow to the surrounding land and sky.

Wild Horse Island State Park

There are indeed wild horses on this island

near the Big Arm of Flathead Lake. There's also a thriving herd of bighorn sheep and a wealth of birdlife, including ospreys, bald eagles, red-tailed hawks, and Canada geese. The island exists because its rock base resisted the plowing action of the glacier that scooped out Flathead Lake. It was used as a sort of safe house for the local Flathead and Pend d'Oreille horses when Blackfeet came on raids.

Private concerns took over the island for many years, but it became a state park in 1977, and in 1983 the Bureau of Land Management began turning horses loose there. In 1940 two bighorn sheep were transplanted there as a tourist attraction; the herd now numbers about 200.

Wild Horse Island (406/849-5256, http://stateparks.mt.gov/wild-horse-island) is a day-use park; camping and fires (including camp stoves) are prohibited, and there are still some private landholdings to avoid. You'll need a boat to get here (available at Flathead Boat Company, 50230 Hwy 93 S., Polson, 406/883-0999, www.flatheadlakemarina.com).

Big Arm State Recreation Area

Big Arm State Recreation Area (406/849-5626 summer, 406/752-5501, http://stateparks.mt.gov/big-arm or http://montanastateparks.reserveamerica.com, day use year-round, $5 per vehicle non-Montanans, $15-23 camping, $45-55 yurt) is 14 miles north of Polson on Highway 93. This campground has showers, a rarity in the public campgrounds of Montana. It's a good spot if you want to swim or boat, but the campsites are packed close together, making it a little uncomfortable for just plain camping. Don't expect to find peace and solitude here, but it's a lovely lakeside spot, so it's understandable that families flock here.

Dayton

The **Mission Mountain Winery** (82420 Hwy. 93, 406/849-5524, www.missionmountainwinery.com, 10am-5pm daily May-Oct.) has vineyards, a winery, and a tasting room in Dayton. The quality of Mission Mountain's wines has improved in recent years, and it's worth stopping in for a taste of Monster Red, a merlot-cabernet blend.

Lake Mary Ronan

Six miles off Highway 93 near Dayton, **Lake Mary Ronan** is a popular place to fish, especially for kokanee salmon, which flourish here as they used to in Flathead Lake. Because the lake is not on reservation land, only a state fishing permit is needed. There are several fairly rustic resorts on the lake, all with cabins, tent and RV camping, boat rentals, and restaurants, and all able to accommodate pets in at least a few cabins. Come here to kick back, *not* to be catered to and pampered (unless you import your own pamperer).

Lake Mary Ronan Resort (406/849-5483 or 888/845-7702, www.lakemaryronanlodge. com, $65-175 cabins, $10 tents, $25-30 RVs), eight miles from Highway 93 near the end of the lake road, has cabins and a trailer home with bedding and kitchens (but no cooking gear) and a few campsites.

Camp Tuffit (48629 Camp Tuffit Rd., 406/849-5220, www.camptuffit.com, $30-69) has the venerable feel of your aunt's backyard: very pretty, well manicured, with green grass and Adirondack chairs. Most accommodations are in extremely simple rustic housekeeping cabins (you use the common bathhouse), but there are a few larger, somewhat more modern houses. Boat rentals are available. Although there isn't really any tent camping here, there are a few RV spaces.

Lake Mary Ronan State Park (406/849-5082, http://stateparks.mt.gov/lake-mary-ronan, May-Sept., $5 day use per vehicle non-Montanans), a very nice campground near Mountain Meadows Resort, is the lake's best bet for tent campers ($15-23).

Rollins

So you picked up a bottle of wine in Dayton. Now stop at **M & S Meats** in Rollins (86755 Hwy. 93 S., 406/844-3414, www.msmeats.com, 7am-7pm Mon.-Thurs., 7am-8:30pm Fri.-Sat., shorter hours during winter) for some buffalo jerky or other meat products to add to your Montana gift basket. If you'd rather not tote around M & S's renowned ham and sausages, they'll ship their products to you.

West Shore State Recreation Area

Between Rollins and Lakeside on Highway 93, **West Shore State Recreation Area**

bighorn sheep on Wild Horse Island

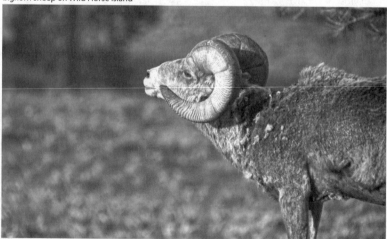

(406/844-3044, http://stateparks.mt.gov/west-shore or http://montanastateparks.reserveamerica.com, day use year-round, $5 per vehicle non-Montanans, $15-23 camping) is another state campground on Flathead Lake. The campsites are set among trees, which provide screening from the nearby highway.

Lakeside

Despite the name of this town, most of the lake access is tied up by private landowners. Fortunately, **Volunteer Park** (Adams St. at Hwy. 93) is a city park where there's easy, free access to a swimming beach and dock. Just across the highway, **Lakeside Ski and Sports** (7212 Hwy. 93, 403/844-2188, 8:30am-6pm daily, $20-25) rents paddleboards, kayaks, and wakeboards in the summer and skis in the winter.

Cruise Flathead Lake with **Far West Boat Tours** (Lakeside Marina, 406/844-2628, www.flatheadlakeboattour.com, 1pm Tues.-Sun., 7pm Sun., Tues., Wed., $20 adults, $10 children 6-12). Tours are just under two hours and travel south along the lakeshore before looping back to the marina.

One of Montana's newest ski resorts, **Blacktail Mountain** (406/844-0999, www.blacktailmountain.com, 9:30am-4:30pm Wed.-Sat. approximately late Nov.-Apr., $38 adults, $26 teens, $17 children 8-12) is 14 miles west of Lakeside on Blacktail Road. With three chairlifts (no high-speed quads) serving 24 runs and few crowds, it's a nice low-key place with terrain that's accommodating to beginning and intermediate skiers and boarders. Unlike most ski areas, the lodge and parking areas are at the top of the mountain, meaning that skiers can hit the slopes right away in the morning, rather than starting the day in a lift line. Half-day rates and a variety of special deals are available, as are rentals and lessons.

Blacktail Cross-Country Ski Area (www.blacktailmountain.com) is off Blacktail Road about eight miles from Lakeside. The trails range from easy to difficult and are at an elevation of about 5,500 feet, which means a fairly long skiing season and a chance to get above the clouds. If you have two vehicles, park one at the lower parking lot and use it to shuttle back to the upper lot at the end of your ski tour. Only upper lot parking is necessary if you plan to ski the easiest (and the only groomed) trail of the network. Do not ski on the road: There is logging truck traffic on it, even in winter.

If you want to spend a week in Lakeside, consider staying at **Flathead Lake Suites** (829 Angel Point Rd., 406/844-2204 or 800/214-2204, www.angelpoint.com, $800-1,200 per week per couple). Located on a peninsula jutting out into Flathead Lake with 312 feet of shoreline, the three units (a chalet and two condos) each come with complete kitchen, dining and sitting area, large two-room baths, and private entrances. Guests have full run of the extensive property, including a dock, fishing platform, canoe, rowboat, patio, barbecue area, beach pavilion, and gazebo.

Stop for breakfast or lunch at **Farmhouse** (306 Stoner Loop, 406/844-0610, www.farmhouselakeside.com, 8am-2pm Tues.-Sun., $7-12), a locavore's delight. The BLT is made with local bacon, arugula, fried green tomato, and sweet onion relish served on focaccia. Although ingredients are pure as possible, there's room for doughnuts on the menu.

Just off Highway 93, **Tamarack Brewing** (105 Blacktail Rd., 406/844-0244, www.tamarackbrewing.com, 11am-midnight daily, $7-12) serves microbrews and good food. Grab a spot on the creekside patio and sip a Yard Sale ale.

Somers

Somers Bay is a good place to paddle a canoe. The water here is relatively shallow and warmer than the rest of the lake, and the lakeshore is dotted with old wharves and buildings, islands, and birds (keep an eye out for ospreys diving into the lake).

A relatively flat 10-mile-long **rails-to-trails bike path** starts in Somers and heads west to the town of Kila, on Highway 2 west of Kalispell. Along the way it passes a wild-life area.

The tidy modern kitchenette cabins at **Somers Bay Log Cabins** (5496 Hwy. 93 S., 406/857-3881 or 888/443-3881, www.somers-baycabins.com, $149-209 with lower off-season rates) are just south of town, across the highway from the lake.

The most upscale hotel in the area is the **Best Western Plus Flathead Lake** (4824 Hwy. 93 S., 406/857-2400 or 888-226-1003, www.bestwesternflatheadlake.com, $229) north of town at the junction of Highways 93 and 82. It's within easy striking distance of Kalispell and Flathead Lake destinations, including Bigfork. Highway 82 will put you on the back route to Glacier National Park, bypassing Kalispell's often-heavy traffic.

The place to go for breakfast and lunch is the **Somers Bay Cafe** (47 Somers Rd., 406/857-2660, www.somersbay.com, 7am-2pm daily, $4-9) with classic bacon-and-egg breakfasts and lunchtime sandwiches, wraps, and burgers. The café is in a 1905 bank building and has a very pleasant vintage atmosphere.

EAST SIDE OF FLATHEAD LAKE

Except for the touristy town of Bigfork at the northeastern edge, the east side of Flathead Lake is even less developed than the west side. Toward the southern end of the lake, cherry orchards are both a business and an attraction around Flathead Lake. Cherries are usually harvested beginning the third week of July.

The University of Montana runs the **Flathead Lake Biological Station** (406/982-3301, www.umt.edu/flbs) at Yellow Bay. Limnology, the study of the life of lakes, ponds, and streams, especially research on water quality and plankton, is a major focus here. Summer classes in freshwater biology and ecology are offered for credit and for audit. If your interest is more casual, drop by the station. Students are often pleased to discuss their research, and there are newsletters and bulletin boards to browse.

Camping

The campgrounds off Highway 35 can be quite pleasant during off-peak times, and crowded and noisy during summer weekends. The forested **Finley Point State Park** (406/887-2715, http://stateparks.mt.gov/finley-point, reservations at http://montanastateparks.reserveamerica.com, May-Sept., $15-28) is at the south end of the lake, four miles off Highway 35 on cherry-tree-studded Finley Point. In addition to regular camping sites, most with electricity, there are a few sites with boat slips. **Yellow Bay State Park** (406/982-3304, http://stateparks.mt.gov/yellow-bay, May-Sept., $15-23) and campground has only five campsites; it's right next to the University of Montana's Biological Station.

BIGFORK

Bigfork (population 4,300) is situated on a bay where the Swan River empties into Flathead Lake. It's an exceptionally lovely site that's turned into an upscale resort community. Certainly no other town in northwestern Montana is so devoted to art galleries, fine restaurants, high-end boutiques—and real estate offices.

Summer is theater season in Bigfork, with its accompanying tour buses and crowds. If the prospect of crowded sidewalks seems a little daunting, consider visiting Bigfork in the off-season, when it's more pleasant to wander through the galleries and bookshops.

Bigfork was founded in 1902, about the time the hydroelectric plant at the mouth of the Swan River was built to supply electricity for Kalispell. The electric company is still here, and the bridge is the best place to stand and ponder how it works. (Water from the Swan River is diverted to a higher level, and then dropped through turbines to generate power.)

★ Jewel Basin Hiking Area

The **Jewel Basin Hiking Area** has been set aside as an easily reached wilderness-like area with wildflower meadows and trout-filled lakes. There are 35 miles of trails that make day-hike loops or longer backpack trips. To get there from Bigfork, take Echo Lake Road off Highway 83. (It can also be reached from the west side of Hungry Horse Reservoir.) Pick up an extremely helpful map at Forest Service offices in Bigfork, Hungry Horse, or Kalispell.

Hikes take you through wildflower meadows and thickets of subalpine fir. Climbing in from the west, you'll first have expansive views of the Flathead Valley and Lake, then pass over a ridge and realize that Jewel Basin is indeed a basin. It's hard to say which are the jewels—the lakes that stud the basin or the Indian paintbrush, bear grass, fireweed, and showy daisies strewn throughout the meadows. Some of the lakes are stocked with trout.

Other Recreation

Base Camp Bigfork (8525 Hwy. 35, 406/871-9733, www.basecampbigfork.com), five miles out of town, rents kayaks ($35-50 half day), mountain bikes ($40), and paddleboards ($40) and provides shuttles and guided tours, including dogsled tours ($155-175 half day) in the winter.

Rent a ski boat, pontoon, or personal watercraft from **Wild Wave** (180 Vista Ln.,

406/844-2400, www.wildwaverentals.com, half-day rates $195-595) at the Marina Cay Resort. Also at the Marina Cay dock, find **A Able Fishing Charters** (406/257-5214, http://aablefishing.com, $350 half day for 1-2 people). Without the fishing, they'll take four people on a half-day tour of Flathead Lake for $400.

Boat tours of Flathead Lake leave from right in town, where **Pointer Scenic Cruises** (452 Grand Dr., 406/837-5817, May-Nov.) is headquartered. They run charters, so call to arrange a trip, which could include a stop at Wild Horse Island.

Fly fishers should stop by **Bigfork Anglers** (405 Bridge St., 406/837-3675, www.bigfork-anglers.com, hours vary Apr.-Oct.), a guide-run fly shop, to stock up on fishing gear or arrange a guided trip on the local waters, including the Flathead and Swan Rivers.

Right in town, the two-mile **Swan River Nature Trail** offers a bit of peace and quiet to those who'd rather hike or mountain bike while their traveling companions shop in downtown Bigfork. Catch the trail near the corner of Grand and Electric Avenues.

Rent a bike from **Mountain Mike's** (417

Cruise Flathead Lake from Bigfork.

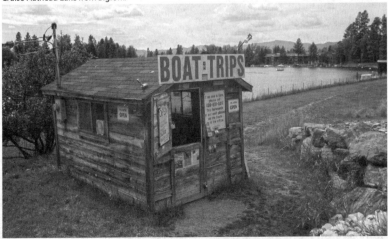

Bridge St., 406/837-2453)—Mike can also tell you where to ride or even take you on a guided bike tour.

Some of the state's wildest water is found in the mile or so of the Swan River immediately before the Bigfork dam. Kayakers love it, but it's not for the inexperienced.

In keeping with its role as a resort village, Bigfork has one of the best golf courses in the West. The 27-hole **Eagle Bend Golf Club** (279 Eagle Bend Dr., 406/837-3700, www.eaglebendgolfclub.com, high season greens fee $110, reserve well in advance), just off Holt Drive west of Highway 35, has received high ratings from *Golf Digest* magazine and from Montana golfers. Eagle Bend also houses the **Montana Athletic Club** (850 Holt Dr., 406/837-2582, www.montanaathleticclub.com, 5am-9pm Mon.-Fri., 8am-6pm Sat.-Sun., guest pass $12), which includes fitness classes, racquetball, squash, aerobics, an indoor pool, and a weight room.

Entertainment and Events

Bigfork is known throughout the state for its summer theater productions: The **Bigfork Summer Playhouse** (526 Electric Ave., 406/837-4886, www.bigforksummerplayhouse.com, 8pm most Mon.-Sat., 2pm some Sun., mid-May-early Sept., weekend $28) has mounted plays here since the 1960s, usually classic Broadway musicals such as *West Side Story* and the occasional comedy. Check the website for ticket discounts. Along with the town's lovely setting the theater is largely what fueled Bigfork's growth as a tourist destination.

Bigfork makes a big deal of holidays. Christmas brings lots of lights and conifer boughs, then there's Easter, cherry blossoms in early May, a white-water festival in mid-May, the playhouse's opening night on the Fourth of July, and the Festival of the Arts in early August—it's hard to arrive in Bigfork when there's not *something* going on.

Galleries and Shops

Several arts-and-crafts galleries are in downtown Bigfork. The **Bigfork Museum of Art and History** (525 Electric Ave., 406/837-6927, http://bigforkmuseum.org, 11am-5pm Mon.-Sat.) shares a building with the public library. Upstairs are exhibits on Bigfork history, while the main floor is a sales gallery for local artists and craftspeople. **Art Fusion** (471 Electric Ave., 406/837-3526, www.bigforkartfusion.com, 10am-5:30pm Mon.-Thurs., 10am-6pm Fri.-Sat., 11am-5pm Sun.), which shows the work of some of the state's top artists, is always worth a stop.

Bayside Gallery (482 Electric Ave., 406/837-5335, www.rieckesbaysidegallery.com, 11am-5pm daily), across from the Bigfork Inn, features the Western and wildlife art of Gary Riecke.

Bay Books and Prints (350 Grand Ave., 406/837-4646, 10am-5pm Mon.-Thurs., 10am-8pm Fri.-Sat., 1pm-4pm Sun.) specializes in books on Montana. Charlie Russell and Lewis and Clark buffs will find it especially hard to leave without a book or two. Most of the books are used, with a good selection of rare and out-of-print titles.

Accommodations

Lodging is expensive in Bigfork (although during the spring, fall, and winter, prices can drop by nearly 50 percent at many options). The town is a little too highfalutin to have a good selection of budget motels. In fact, the only place that comes close to fitting that bill is the **Timbers Motel** (8540 Hwy. 35, 406/837-6200 or 800/821-4546, www.timbersmotel.com, $100-110), slightly outside of Bigfork proper, above Bigfork Bay and Highway 35. There's a pool, sauna, and outdoor hot tub; pets are welcome with a $10 fee. The setting, back off the highway among trees, is rather snug and comfortable. Open May-September only.

Marina Cay (180 Vista Ln., 406/837-5861, www.marinacay.com, rooms $110 and up, condos $169-469) is a large complex right on the bay that contains the majority of the rooms available in Bigfork. Facilities include several restaurants and bars, a marina with boat rentals and other recreational outings, lounge-side pool, and a couple of hot tubs. The majority of the units are one- and two-bedroom condos with full kitchens, though several luxury level town houses are available.

For a more intimate place to stay right in the heart of downtown Bigfork, the **Swan River Inn** (360 Grand Ave., 406/837-2328, www.swanriverinn.com, $195-395), up a flight of stairs from a restaurant, has comfortable and carefully decorated B&B suites overlooking Bigfork Bay.

Right on the edge of town, where the Swan River flows into Bigfork Bay, the ★ **Bridge Street Cottages** (309 Bridge St., 406/837-2785 or 888/264-4974, www.bridgestreetcottages.com, studios $195-325) are just close enough to town, but not smack-dab in the middle of it. Most are one-bedroom cottages with full kitchens, but there are also a few studios with refrigerators and coffeemakers. These cottages are good places to stay if you want to settle in for a while; weekly and monthly rates are available.

Five miles south of town in Woods Bay, the **Mountain Lake Lodge** (1950 Sylvan Dr., 406/837-3800 or 877/823-4923, www.mountainlakelodge.com, $189-285) is a classy lodge-style motel with spacious rooms, an outdoor pool, and great views. Dining options include a pub and steak house.

A few miles south of town, just across the road from the lake in Woods Bay, the **Islander Inn** (39 Orchard Ln., 406/837-5472, http://sleepeatdrink.com, $159-179) has accommodations in bungalows, each one named after a different island—from Bali to Zanzibar to Wild Horse—and decorated in the style of that place. These colorful cottages have basic cooking facilities (most have microwaves and refrigerators, while a couple have full kitchens), and well-behaved dogs are allowed in some units with a stiff deposit and $25 nightly surcharge. It's right across the road from the Raven, a popular bar and restaurant.

Guest Ranches

One of Montana's most famous and exclusive guest ranches, ★ **Averill's Flathead Lake Lodge** (150 Flathead Lodge Rd., 406/837-4391, www.flatheadlakelodge.com, $3,696 per week per adult) is a well-established full-service dude ranch with all meals and activities included open mid-June-September. The ranch is right on the shores of Flathead Lake, just south of Bigfork, so if you're looking for a family ranch vacation that mixes swimming, fishing, tennis, and kayaking with the traditional horseback riding and campfire sing-alongs, this is it. Children and teens have lower rates.

Camping

Save an easy $100 by making **Wayfarers State Park** (406/837-4196, http://stateparks. mt.gov/wayfarers, reservations at http:// montanastateparks.reserveamerica.com, May-Sept., $15-23) your base in Bigfork. This campground is just across Highway 35 from the main road into town. Because there are only 30 sites here, plan your arrival strategically, especially on holiday weekends.

Food

You can eat very well in Bigfork; people drive for miles to dine here. Dinner reservations are mandatory at most restaurants. Many are closed in the winter.

The **Garden Bar** (451 Electric Ave., 406/837-9914, 11am-2am daily, $8-12) is a casual place to drop in for a beer and a burger. The bar is chatty and friendly, and the tables out back provide a quiet place to sit and read in the afternoon.

The **Bigfork Inn** (604 Electric Ave., 406/837-6680, http://bigforkinn.com, dinner from 5pm nightly, $10-28) is one of Bigfork's originals, the place that put Bigfork on the culinary map several decades ago. Open for dinner only, the menu is eclectic, with steaks, pasta, two types of schnitzel, and a showcase duck with local bing cherry and red currant sauce.

Another well-regarded dinner restaurant in downtown Bigfork is **Showthyme!** (548 Electric Ave., 406/837-0707, www.showthyme.

com, 5pm-9pm Tues.-Sat., $18-29), housed in an old brick bank building next door to the Bigfork Playhouse. Food here is subtle, refined, and often innovative. Vegetarian and pasta dishes are also featured, and there's outside seating in good weather.

★ **When in Rome** (8270 Hwy. 35, 406/837-6664, www.wheninromebigfork. com, 11am-9pm Wed.-Mon., $12-24), in a strip mall up on the highway above Bigfork, is an authentic Mediterranean eatery that's casual in style but delivers high-quality pasta and pizza. Choices range from full-flavored pasta alla puttanesca to tangy veal saltimbocca to the self-style Best Pizza Ever (it did win second place in the Western Division of the International Pizza Competition held in Las Vegas): a white pizza with pepperoni, roasted red peppers, red onions, gorgonzola cheese, and garlic.

Head about five miles south of town to find **The Raven** (39 Orchard Ln., 406/837-2836, http://sleepeatdrink.com/the-raven-restaurant, 11am-10pm daily, $10-15), a lakeside restaurant with a great deck and a sort of Jimmy Buffet parrot-head appeal. The decor is Caribbean, and dinner specialties come from around the world; choose between Baja tacos and locally sourced yak meat loaf. In the same area, find the taproom at **Flathead Lake Brewing Co.** (26008 E. Lake Shore Rte., 406/837-0353, http://flatheadlakebrewing.

It's easy to find good food, including good ice cream, in Bigfork.

com, noon-8pm daily). In Bigfork proper, Flathead Lake Brewing has opened a brewhouse at 116 Holt Drive.

Information

The **chamber of commerce** (8155 Hwy. 35, 406/837-5888, www.bigfork.org) is next to the Lakehills Shopping Center.

The Swan and Blackfoot Valleys

The Swan Valley is not as large and broad as the valleys to the west, but with two rivers and many lakes, the Swan Range shooting out to the east, and the Mission Mountains stacking up high in the southwest, it is quite beautiful. Being between the Bob Marshall and Mission Mountains Wilderness Areas, it is a popular vacation spot for Montanans, but it doesn't draw the crowds that you'll find around Flathead Lake, Bigfork, or Glacier National Park.

Even an amateur geologist can pick out the signs of the glaciers that formed the Swan Valley. Drive down Highway 83 and look up at the jagged peaks and high cirques of the Mission and Swan Ranges. Notice the distinctive pothole lakes southeast of Salmon Lake. And the big lakes—Seeley, Salmon, Alva, Placid, and Inez—all were created when glaciers melted some 10,000 years ago.

Wildlife viewing is a special attraction of the Swan Valley and its many lakes. Although a canoe is probably the best vehicle for nature watching around the lakes and rivers here, keep your eyes open while you're driving or biking Highway 83; there are several designated wildlife-viewing areas, mostly featuring waterbirds.

Recreation

The lakes and easy access to mountains and wilderness are the main recreational attractions of the Swan Valley, but there's more here than boating, fishing, hiking, hunting, and horseback riding.

Highway 83 through the Swan River Valley is the stage for a popular bicycle tour held every May. The two-day **Tour of the Swan River Valley** (TOSRV West, www.missoulabike.org) starts in Missoula, heads up the Swan Valley, and comes back down through the Mission Valley. Even with summer traffic, Highway 83 is a good cycling road with plenty of rest stops and campsites.

The Swan Valley has surprisingly good cross-country skiing in the winter. It's high enough to have snow when it's raining in nearby Missoula.

SWAN LAKE

The **Swan River National Wildlife Refuge** is a nesting area for bald eagles, blue herons, and other birds. Canada geese, whistling swans, and mallards winter here. Other animals that can be spotted in this marsh, grassland, and river habitat include elk, moose, deer, beavers, river otters, muskrats, and grizzly and black bears. The refuge is on the Swan River in the northern part of the Swan Valley, near the town of Swan Lake.

Accommodations

These lodgings are actually quite close to Bigfork, and are good laid-back alternatives to staying in that more expensive town. The attractive ★ **Laughing Horse Lodge** (71284 Hwy. 83, 406/886-2080, www.laughinghorselodge.com, $118-128 and up) has newer log cabin-style units furnished with massive log beds (but with no telephones, alarm clocks, or TVs) as well as a freestanding two-bedroom cabin ($495 for three nights). The lodge is run as a dog-friendly B&B, and rates include a good breakfast. The restaurant here is worth a stop, even if you're not sleeping over, and kayaks and bikes are available for rent.

Up a steep rutted road from Highway 83 north of Swan Lake are the **Swan Lake Cabins** (406/837-1137 or 888/837-1557, http://swanlakecabins.com, $149-249, two-night minimum), with recently constructed, nicely detailed log cabins. The cabins, tucked into the woods, all come with propane grills and comfy porch swings; breakfast is included with most rentals. Dogs are allowed.

Camping

At the north end of Swan Lake, the **Swan Lake Campground** (406/837-7500, reservations at 877/444-6677 or www.recreation.gov, www.fs.usda.gov/flathead, mid-May-Sept., $15) includes a Forest Service campground on the east side of the highway and a day-use area with a swimming beach and a boat launch on the west side. **Point Pleasant State Forest Campground** (406/754-2301, June-Oct.) is a small, free campground seven miles south of Swan Lake.

HOLLAND LAKE AND CONDON

All of the Swan Valley is lovely, but perhaps no single spot captures the essence of this narrow, lake-filled valley flanked by sawtooth peaks as well as Holland Lake. In addition, the lake is graced with a charming old-fashioned resort that has played home to generations of visitors.

Recreation

Holland Lake is the trailhead for a popular trail into the **Bob Marshall Wilderness Area.** It's about 10 miles from road's end to the wilderness boundary, and most people entering this way go around Upper Holland Lake and up over Gordon Pass toward the South Fork of the Flathead River.

Across Highway 83 from Holland Lake, several roads lead west from Condon toward the **Mission Mountains Wilderness Area.** The Lindbergh Lake road leads to a small campground (free, no water) and several trailheads. Lindbergh Lake is named for Charles Lindbergh, who camped here not long after his transatlantic flight. Hikers should pick up either a Flathead National Forest map (south half) or a more detailed Mission Mountains Wilderness map. Both are available at the ranger station in Bigfork. Be aware that the Mission Mountains are home to some grizzly bears.

Accommodations and Food

★ **Holland Lake Lodge** (1947 Holland Lake Lodge Rd., 406/754-2282 or 877/925-6343, www.hollandlakelodge.com, open mid-May-Oct., $290 lodge room, $320 cabin) is four miles off the highway at the end of Holland Lake Road. It's a down-home woodsy place, with rooms in the main lodge or in cabins scattered along the lakefront, all with a veneer of charm and rustic comfort that only decades

Holland Lake Lodge

of history can produce. Meals in the restaurant are very good, especially in high season. The dining room (8:30am-9:45am, noon-2pm, 5:45pm-8:45pm, $15-32) is open to the public, and it's well worth a visit. During the high summer, when a professional chef is in residence, the dinners are particularly inspired and feature both steaks and more continental fare like roast duck.

During the high summer, lodge rates include lodging, all meals, and a daily hourlong canoe or kayak rental. The per-person rates go down if you pack more than two people into the rooms, and children are given a substantial discount.

The **Swan Valley Centre Cabins** (milepost 42 on Hwy. 83, 406/754-2397 or 866/754-2397, $85-115) are fairly rustic, but a good deal. Each of the three cabins is equipped with a kitchen and, for that ultimate backwoods touch, a TV with no reception. (Well, they're TV/DVD combos, and the on-site general store will lend you movies to watch.)

Camping

Holland Lake (406/837-7500, www.fs.usda. gov/flathead, reservations at 877/444-6677 or www.recreation.gov, mid-May-Sept., $15) is the site of one of the prettiest, and sometimes one of the most crowded, Forest Service campgrounds in the area. It's south of Condon and east of Highway 83 on Holland Lake Road. The lake contains whitefish, cutthroat and rainbow trout, and a few bull trout and kokanee salmon.

Holland Lake is a popular departure point for horse trips into the Bob Marshall Wilderness Area, and in addition to the regular Forest Service campground **Owl Creek Packers' Camp** is a small campground for horse packers, charging a few dollars for a corral fee. At the road's end there are short hiking trails for the casual day hiker as well as trails leading into the Bob Marshall Wilderness Area. The hike in to Holland Falls is not difficult (three miles round-trip).

BOB MARSHALL WILDERNESS AREA

In 1964 the **Bob Marshall Wilderness Area** was created when 950,000 acres were set aside; in 1978 the Scapegoat Wilderness was added to the south and the Great Bear Wilderness to the north of the Bob Marshall. The three contiguous areas include 1.5 million acres, falling roughly east of the Swan Valley. The designated wilderness areas are heavily used during the summer and fall. Backpacking and horse packing are the main summer activities, while hunting predominates in the fall, starting in mid-September.

The Chinese Wall is an impressive and popular destination in the "Bob." To the west the earth's crust has thrust upward and forced the eastern part to slide underneath it for a distance of about 20 miles. Haystack Mountain provides a good view of the Chinese Wall from the west.

Great Northern Mountain (8,705 feet) is the highest spot in the Great Bear Wilderness. The Middle Fork of the Flathead runs through the Great Bear.

Access to the Wilderness

Napa Point Road starts near the headquarters of the Swan River State Forest and provides access to the **Inspiration Pass** trailhead. It's a challenging but fairly lightly used trail. Sup Creek Campground near the trailhead is a good place to spend the night before embarking on the full-day hike to Sunburst Lake.

Smith Creek Pass also receives less traffic than many of the other trails that lead into the wilderness. To reach the trailhead, take Falls Creek Road (across from the Condon Work Center on Highway 83) four miles to Smith Creek Road. Make a sharp right and drive another mile to the trailhead. The climb up the west side of the pass is not easy, and coming down the east side can be even tougher.

Gordon Pass, starting from Holland Lake, is well maintained and heavily used by horse packers and hikers. Big Salmon Lake is a popular destination. Trails come at it from every direction, but the shortest route is from Holland Lake.

Pyramid Pass, with a trailhead near Seeley Lake, leads to the headwaters of the South Fork of the Flathead River, which starts as Danaher Creek deep in the Bob and flows toward the southern tip of Hungry Horse Reservoir. Reach the trailhead by taking Cottonwood Lakes Road (just north of the town of Seeley Lake) to Morrell Road (No. 467). Turn left on Morrell Road and travel six miles to Pyramid Pass Road (No. 4381, Upper Trail Creek Road). Turn right and drive six miles to the trailhead. Pyramid Pass is a steep climb and receives medium to heavy use by backpackers and horse packers.

From the south, reach the **North Fork of the Blackfoot** trailhead by taking Highway 200 to five miles east of Ovando and turning up the North Fork of Blackfoot Road. Drive four miles to North Fork Trailhead Road, and take it seven miles to the trailhead. It's a fairly heavily used trail, with both foot and horse traffic.

Many outfitters run trips into the Bob; horse-packing guides from the **Seven Lazy P** (406/466-2044, www.sevenlazyp.com), based in Choteau, have excellent reputations.

SEELEY LAKE AND VICINITY

Seeley Lake is the only place in the Swan Valley with full services. Because of the many moderately priced motels and comfortable, long-established lodges and resorts, Seeley Lake has a long tradition of hosting summer family reunions and weddings. With the lake's water recreation and access to hiking, good restaurants, golf, and just plain relaxation, there's something for everyone to do here.

Clearwater Canoe Trail

The **Clearwater Canoe Trail** is really a floating and hiking loop trail. There's a three-mile canoe segment from an access point off Highway 83 four miles north of the town of Seeley Lake, then a one-mile hike back to the put-in spot. The meandering Clearwater River

is a good place to watch birds. Keep an eye out for loons, which nest here and in neighboring lakes. (During the loons' May-mid-June nesting period, it's important to stay well away from the nests, especially while fishing on the lakes.) Canoe rentals are available at the nearby **Tamaracks Resort** (3481 Hwy. 83 N., 406/677-2433 or 800/447-7216, www. tamaracks.com).

Other Recreation

Morrell Lake and **Morrell Falls** are on a national recreation trail north of Seeley Lake via Cottonwood Lakes Road to the east of Highway 83. It's an easy two-mile hike in to the falls (actually a 100-foot-tall lower fall topped by a series of smaller falls and cascades). **Morrell Mountain Lookout** is about 18 miles from the highway via Cottonwood Lakes Road (follow it for nine miles) and Road 4365 (follow it for another nine miles). It's a rough drive in a passenger car, and it's wise to check with the **ranger station** (406/677-2233) for current road conditions. The lookout has views of the Mission Mountains, the Swan Range, and the Blackfoot and Clearwater Valleys.

The **Mission Mountains Wilderness Area** falls on the eastern part of the mountains' divide; the western part is the Mission Mountains Tribal Wilderness managed by the Confederated Salish and Kootenai Tribes. The wilderness managed by the Forest Service has about 45 miles of trails. There are several trails into the Mission Mountains Wilderness Area: Glacier Creek, Cold Lakes, Piper Creek, Fatty Creek, Beaver Creek, Lindbergh Lake, Jim Lakes, Hemlock Creek, Meadow Lake, and Elk Point. Maps of the Mission Mountains Wilderness or the southern half of the Flathead National Forest are available at the ranger station in Bigfork.

Seeley Lake is a good place to **fish** for bass, and it's also stocked with rainbow trout. To the south, Salmon Lake has rainbow and cutthroat trout and kokanee salmon.

Seeley Lake gets pretty snowy in the winter. Most local lodgings are proud to point out that you can ski or snowmobile from your door into a million acres of wilderness. Find an extensive network of groomed **cross-country ski trails** one mile east of Seeley Lake, up Morrell Creek Road. These trail loops double as **mountain bike trails** in the summer.

Accommodations
$50-100

The friendly **Seeley Lake Motor Lodge** (3206 Hwy. 83 N. 406/677-2335, www.seeleylakemotorlodge.com, $85-95) is one of the better deals on Seeley Lake, located convenient to recreation and to services in the little town center.

North of the town of Seeley Lake, on the lake, the **Montana Pines Motel** (mile marker 16 on Hwy. 83, 406/677-2778, www.montanapinesmotel.com, $75-140) is a motel complex built on the original town site of Seeley. The Elkhorn Restaurant is adjacent to the motel, right near the highway.

OVER $100

The most attractive and upscale resort in the Seeley-Swan area is the ★ **Double Arrow Resort** (933 Golf View Dr., 406/677-2777 or 800/468-0777, www.doublearrowresort.com, $155-800), a gem of a Swan Valley hideout. The lodge and cabins sit on a bluff overlooking a stream and a meadow filled alternately with golfers and browsing deer; the old lodge and dining room, built in the 1930s, are extremely welcoming and idyllic; you'll want to curl up with a book or watch the sunset from the veranda. The food here is also top-notch. Choose from a room in the lodge, a homey cabin, or a larger log lodge that'll sleep up to eight. Breakfast and use of a large indoor pool, hot tub, and tennis courts are included. None of the rooms have a TV or telephone.

The Double Arrow is also a good base for recreation. The nine-hole course is a real beauty, shaded by ponderosa pines and cleaved by a chattering stream. The resort offers a full range of horseback activities, as well as mountain bike, canoe, and fishing gear

rentals. In winter the Double Arrow is the center of a series of cross-country trails and also rents snowmobiles; you can even arrange for horse-drawn sleigh rides.

The rustic log cabins at the **Lodges on Seeley Lake** (Boy Scout Road, 406/677-2376 or 800/900-9016, www.lodgesonseeleylake.com, $159-300), just west of Seeley Lake town site, were favorites of local writer Norman Maclean. These 1930s-era cabins have been joined by a handful of modern ones, and there's a central lodge with games and easy chairs. Cabins all have fireplaces as well as full kitchen and bathroom facilities, and canoes, rowboats, and bikes are available for guests' use. A second property, called **Eagle Port Lodge,** offers five large, newly built suites ($164-185) in a turreted structure four miles to the east; these lodgings all come with full kitchens and fireplaces.

On the north shores of Seeley Lake is **Tamaracks Resort** (3481 Hwy. 83 N., 406/677-2433 or 800/447-7216, www.tamaracks.com, $155-450). The resort consists of a central lodge and lakefront cabins with kitchens (the least-expensive cabins sleep 2; the top-of-the-line cabin sleeps 10). The resort is right on Seeley Lake, and canoes, fishing boats, and mountain bikes are available for rent. There's also an area for RV and tent campers ($35).

Camping

There are three national forest campgrounds around Seeley Lake: **Big Larch** (406/677-2233, www.fs.usda.gov/lolo, mid-May-mid-Nov., $10) is closest to the highway on the east side of the lake; **River Point** and **Seeley Lake** (both Memorial Day-Labor Day, $10) are farther around the southern and western sides of the lake, respectively. Several miles south of Seeley Lake, the state park campgrounds (406/677-6804, http://stateparks.mt.gov/placid-lake or http://montanastateparks.reserveamerica.com, $15-28, some sites have electricity) at **Placid Lake** (May-Nov.) and **Salmon Lake** (May-Sept.) are often less crowded than their northern counterparts.

Food

In these parts, the **Seasons Restaurant at Double Arrow Resort** (933 Golf View Dr., 406/677-2777, www.doublearrowresort.com, 7am-9pm daily, $22-35), two miles south of Seeley Lake, is the best place to eat. The menu specializes in continental cuisine, featuring dishes such as elk medallions with a morel mushroom sauce. It's a pleasure to eat here, and not just because the food is good; the dining room, overlooking the Seeley Valley, is beautiful and the service top-notch.

For a good hand-cut steak, delicious potatoes, and authentic Montana atmosphere, go to **Lindey's Prime Steak House** (3129 Hwy. 83 N., 406/677-9229, 11am-10pm daily May-Sept., 11am-3pm and 5pm-9pm Thurs.-Mon. Oct.-Mar., 5pm-9pm daily Apr. 1-15, $6-30), located on the lake in the town site.

Information

Find the **chamber of commerce** (2920 Hwy. 83 N., 406/677-2880, www.seeleylakecham-ber.com) downtown across from the Chicken Coop restaurant. The **Seeley Lake Ranger Station** (3583 Hwy. 83 N., 406/677-2233) is about three miles north of town at the northern end of Seeley Lake.

BLACKFOOT VALLEY

The Blackfoot River is well-known to local anglers and floaters. It's a lovely undammed river noted for its variety of fish habitats and its 30 miles of "recreation corridor," which allow easy public access to the river. Read Norman Maclean's classic, *A River Runs Through It,* to get a feel for the place.

Blackfoot-Clearwater Wildlife Management Area

The **Blackfoot-Clearwater Wildlife Management Area,** east of Highway 83 and north of Highway 200, includes the southern part of Salmon Lake as well as the lower Clearwater River. Near the junction of the two highways the land is prairie, but the northeastern corner of the area rises into forested mountains. The entire area is closed December 1-May 15, but open to hunters and anglers at other times of the year (within the restrictions of hunting season). There are plenty of deer and elk here, as well as black bears, grouse, and waterfowl.

Garnet Ghost Town

Garnet Ghost Town (406/329-3914, www. garnetghosttown.net) is an abandoned mining town where about 30 buildings have been preserved. In the winter it's a great place for cross-country skiing, and two of the original mining cabins are available to rent December-April ($30-40). With woodstoves for heat, no plumbing, and access by ski, snowshoe, or snowmobile only, these very popular cabins are for hearty winter sports enthusiasts.

To reach Garnet, drive east of Missoula 30 miles, and turn south on Garnet Range Road located between mile markers 22 and 23. From here, it's 11 miles to the ghost town along a half-paved, half-gravel road. Though maps show a road continuing south of Garnet and meeting up with I-90 at Bearmouth, this road is very rugged and suitable only for jeeps.

Recreation

Fishing, especially for brown trout, has long been a major preoccupation in the Blackfoot Valley. Although past mining and ongoing heavy logging have deteriorated conditions, rehabilitation efforts have begun to pay off. On the Blackfoot and its tributaries, catch-and-release is required for cutthroat and bull trout (actually, you're not supposed to intentionally catch bull trout at all). For the more prevalent brown and rainbow trout, check current regulations.

The **Clearwater Bridge** is a fishing-access site on Sunset Hill Road (which intersects Highway 200 just east of Greenough Hill). Farther down Sunset Hill Road is another fishing-access site. To reach the **Scotty Brown Bridge,** turn down the gravel road seven miles east of Clearwater Junction on Highway 200. It's marked with a fishing-access site sign, and the road leads to several fishing sites.

Blackfoot River Road has two junctions with Highway 200, one just north of the McNamara Bridge (14 miles east of Missoula) and the other at the Roundup Bridge (28 miles east of Missoula). There are several fishing-access sites along this road, most with undeveloped campsites nearby.

During the winter, the recreational focus shifts to **snowmobiling.** There are more than 200 miles of groomed trails, many of them springing from a hub in the town of Lincoln.

Accommodations

The Blackfoot Valley is undeniably beautiful but no part of it is less than an hour from the abundant lodging choices in Missoula. However, one upscale resort deserves mention if you're looking for a luxury accommodations or the chance to go glamping, or glamour camping. **The Resort at Paws Up** (40060 Paws Up Rd., Greenough, 406/244-5200, www.pawsup.com, luxury tents from $1,480, homes from $1,705) is a longtime cattle operation that's been retrofitted into a very high-end guest ranch. Along with the two- to four-bedroom homes scattered around the ranch and the luxury wall tents (complete with camp butler), you'll have a chance to go on trail rides, fish the Blackfoot River, and enjoy high-end camp cooking.

Camping

Many fishing-access sites have good campgrounds. The **Johnsrud Fishing Access Site** (no camping) is about a mile off Highway 200, 11 miles east of Bonner. Continuing east on the gravel road that leads to Johnsrud will bring you to several fishing-access sites with campgrounds, including **Thibodeau, Corrick's Riverbend,** and **Ninemile Prairie.** All charge a campground fee of $15.

Food

For food in this stretch of the Blackfoot, there's a collection of truck stops at Clearwater Junction, where Highways 83 and 200 meet, although the restaurants at Seeley Lake are just 15 miles north. In Ovando, **Trixi's Antler Saloon** (4520 Hwy. 200, 406/793-5611, 10am-9pm Sun.-Thurs., 10am-10pm Fri.-Sat., $6-20) has a reputation as a *real* Montana bar, the kind with brands burned into the bar and trophies staring down from the wall. The dining room serves sandwiches, burgers, and steaks.

North of Flathead Lake

KALISPELL

Drive around northwestern Montana for a while, and by the time you pull into Kalispell (pop. 20,000, elev. 2,930 feet), you'll feel that you're in a real city. Kalispell is the commercial center for the booming "resortification" of northwestern Montana, although like too many other Montana towns, the locals seem to measure success by the length and relentlessness of suburban commercial strips.

Kalispell is on the Flathead River near where it converges with the Stillwater and Whitefish Rivers, about seven miles above Flathead Lake. It's at the upper end of the Flathead Valley, and the mountains visible to the north are part of the Whitefish Range; to the east, the Swan Range rises. Between Kalispell and Flathead Lake, the Flathead River is as convoluted as the folds of a brain.

★ Conrad Mansion

When the building of the transcontinental railroad was underway, Charles Conrad, a Fort Benton freight kingpin, got a hot tip from the head of the Great Northern Railway, Jim Hill, to move west to the Flathead area. Conrad did, and in 1891 the Great Northern arrived. Conrad prospered and became a uniquely Montanan model citizen, keeping

Kalispell

his own buffalo herd on what is now known as Buffalo Hill, just north of downtown.

The **Conrad Mansion** (330 Woodland Ave., 406/755-2166, www.conradmansion. com, 10am-5pm Wed.-Sun. May 15-May 31, 10am-5pm Tues.-Sun. June-Oct. 15, $10 adults, $9 seniors, $6 students 12-17, $4 children under 12), built in 1895, was home to members of the Conrad family for most of the next 80 years . None of the original architecture was changed during this time. When the home was donated to the city of Kalispell in 1975, the interior and exterior were renovated,

and the mansion is now considered one of the best examples of Pacific Northwest late-19th-century architecture.

Other Sights

Woodland Park (2nd St. E. north of Woodland Ave.) is a lovely city park, with rose gardens, a duck pond and lagoon, a large swimming pool, and a track. It was originally part of Charles Conrad's estate.

The **Hockaday Museum of Art** (302 2nd Ave. E., 406/755-5268, www.hockadaymuseum.org, 10am-5pm Tues.-Sat., $5 adults, $4 seniors, $2 college-age students, 18 and under free) hangs some striking and innovative contemporary art as well as more traditional Western art. Anyone who thinks that conceptual art is solely an urban phenomenon should stop in and see what's going on in the studios of Twodot and Bozeman. There's a small crafts shop in the gallery, which is housed in the old brick Carnegie Library building. The center also sponsors Arts in the Park weekend in July.

At the **Museum at Central School** (124 2nd Ave. E., 406/756-8381, www.yourmuseum.org, 10am-5pm Mon.-Fri., $5 adults, $4 seniors, 18 and under free), sometimes called "The M," historical exhibits, including a history of the Forest Service in Montana, are housed in an 1894 school building.

On Highway 2, 13 miles west of Kalispell, stop near milepost 108 to see the **Native American pictographs** on the cliffs on the north side of the road.

Recreation

The 27-hole **Buffalo Hill Golf Course** (1176 N. Main St., 406/756-4530, www.golfbuffalohill.com, $68 for 18 holes in high season) is one of northwestern Montana's most challenging greens. Also just north of town is

Northern Pines Golf Club (3230 Hwy. 93 N., 406/751-1950, www.bigmountaingolfclub. com, $65 for 18 holes in high season).

Lone Pine State Park is five miles southwest of town off Foys Lake Road (get there from Hwy. 2 via Meridian Rd.). It's set up on a hill, and hiking and biking trails lead to overlooks with a good view of Kalispell and Glacier National Park.

The large **city pool** is in the middle of **Woodland Park** (406/758-7812).

Entertainment and Events

The **Northwest Montana Fair** (406/758-5810, http://nwmtfair.com) is held at the fairgrounds in Kalispell in mid-August every year.

If you're in town during the concert season (Oct.-May), catch the **Glacier Symphony and Chorale** (406/407-7000, www.gscmusic. org), which performs at the high school auditorium; they also play a summer pops concert in Bigfork.

Accommodations

During the summer, Kalispell's lodgings fill up quickly with people on their way to and from Glacier National Park. Most chains have a presence here, as well as a host of

Conrad Mansion

somewhat scruffy budget motels; look for these on Highway 2 east of downtown. In winter, expect much lower rates, sometimes as much as half the summer rates listed here.

For inexpensive lodgings, the **Blue and White Motel** (670 E Idaho St., 406/755-4311 or 800/382-3577, www.blueandwhitemotel. com, $70 and up) has funky theme rooms east of downtown.

As budget motels go, the **Aero Inn** (1830 Hwy. 93 S., 406/755-3798 or 800/843-6114, www.aeroinn.com, $102-106) is a pretty good bet, with an indoor pool, hot tub, and sauna. Pets are permitted in smoking rooms, and there's a free continental breakfast.

The ★ **Kalispell Grand Hotel** (100 Main St., 406/755-8100 or 800/858-7422, www.kalispellgrand.com, $114-162) is a nicely renovated historic hotel right in downtown Kalispell. While the lobby and sitting areas preserve a comfortable late-19th-century glamour, the guest rooms are very nicely furnished and fully modern, with large gleaming bathrooms. Pets are accepted, and there's free parking, free continental breakfast, and afternoon cookies.

The **Red Lion Hotel Kalispell** (20 N. Main, 406/751-5050 or 800/325-4000, www. redlion.com/kalispell, $178-251) is also right downtown on the edge of a large shopping mall. The lobby here has a Western lodge look, and the rooms are spacious and well furnished.

One of Kalispell's newer hotels is the very large and extra comfortable **Hampton Inn** (1140 Hwy. 2 W., 406/755-7900 or 800/426-7866, www.kalispell.hamptoninn.com, $239-339). Facilities include a fitness center, indoor pool, and hot tub, and rates cover a rather lavish continental breakfast.

Another newer hotel, tucked behind a big-box home supply store on the leading edge of Kalispell's northern sprawl, is the surprisingly nice **Holiday Inn Express** (275 Treeline Rd., 406/755-7405, www.kalispell-HIE.com, $263-299). The rooms are trim and elegant, and the pool and exercise rooms

quite usable. There's a stiff surcharge for pets, but they are permitted.

Camping

There's not much in the way of peaceful tent camping in Kalispell, but there are a couple of RV-style campgrounds right in town: **Glacier Pines RV Campground** (120 Swan Mountain Dr., 406/752-2760, http://glacier-pines.com, year-round, $37), one mile east of Kalispell on Highway 35, and **Rocky Mountain Hi** (825 Helena Flats Rd., 406/755-9573, www.glaciercamping.com, year-round, $29-33), which is four miles east of Kalispell on Highway 2 and has some tent sites ($22) and cabins ($55-150).

A little farther from town you'll find more tent-friendly options, including **Whitefish Lake State Park** (1615 E. Lakeshore Dr., 406/862-3991, http://stateparks.mt.gov/whitefish-lake, $10-24 Montana residents, $18-34 nonresidents), just outside of Whitefish. For something more remote, go to **Ashley Lake** (406/863-5400, www.fs.usda.gov/flathead mid-May-mid-Sept., free, no water), 16 miles west of Kalispell on Highway 2, then 13 miles north on the county road that starts around milepost 105. Still farther west of Kalispell (32 miles) is the **McGregor Lake** (406/293-7773, www.fs.usda.gov/kootenai, mid-May-Labor Day, $12) Forest Service campground. Even though it's just off Highway 2, it's not a bad spot, and it has a few relatively private tent sites. Lake trout are the big fish here, but kokanee salmon, cutthroat and brook trout, and yellow perch are also caught.

Food

If a full breakfast isn't necessary, head to the **Coffee Traders** (326 W. Center St., 406/756-2326, 7am-5pm Mon.-Fri., $5-10) for espresso drinks and light breakfasts. Right downtown, ★ **Ceres Bakery** (318 Main St., 406/755-8552, 7am-6pm Mon.-Fri., 7am-3pm Sat.) makes the region's best (well, the only) artisanal bread and pastries.

An excellent spot for breakfast or lunch is ★ **Bonelli's Bistro** (38 1st Ave. E.,

Stop for a scone at Ceres Bakery in downtown Kalispell.

406/257-8669, www.bonellisbistro.com, 8am-3pm Mon.-Sat., $6-11) a fun and friendly Mediterranean spot with scrambles and quiche for breakfast and salads, wraps, paninis, and subs for lunch. The apple strudel French toast will light up your morning, and a prosciutto and fig panini may be the highlight of the rest of your day.

Another notable breakfast and lunch favorite is **Split Rock Cafe** (30 2nd St. E., 406/890-7577, 8am-9pm Tues.-Sat., 8am-2pm Sun.-Mon., $7-10, dinner $11-21), with good traditional and not so traditional breakfasts (roast turkey eggs Benedict) served morning and at lunch, plus good burgers, salads, and sandwiches such as a pesto BLT. In the evening, along with the entrées, there are a number of small plates—try the duck quesadillas.

If you're staying downtown, **Norm's News** (34 Main St., 406/756-5466, 9am-7pm Mon.-Sat., 10am-5pm Sun., $6 burgers) is a place to stop in and join the group of retired gentlemen who gather at this well-loved Kalispell institution. Norm's is a combination newsstand, candy store, and soda fountain and a good place for a burger and shake.

Another good place for a shake or ice cream cone is **Sweet Peaks** (343 Main St., 406/257-1102, www.sweetpeaksicecream. com), the local's favorite ice cream shop, with locations in Whitefish, Bigfork, and Missoula as well as downtown Kalispell.

Kalispell's most renowned tavern, **Moose's Saloon** (173 N. Main St., 406/755-2338, http://moosessaloon.com, 11am-2am daily, under $10), is a place to spend an evening throwing peanut shells on the floor while drinking beer and listening to local musicians. Legend has it that this is where Evel Knievel came up with the idea to blast across Hell Gate Canyon on his motorcycle. Pizza is the food of choice at Moose's.

Find an outstanding selection of craft beers at **Hop's Downtown Grill** (121 Main St., 406/755-7687, www.hopsmontana.com, 5pm-9pm Mon.-Thurs., 5pm-10pm Fri.-Sat., $14-25). The food, which is high-end pub grub (such as a wild boar burger with jalapeño cheddar and bacon), is good. Wine drinkers aren't ignored; there are good wines available by the glass.

Kalispell Brewing Company (412 Main St., 406/756-2739, www.kalispellbrewing. com, noon-8pm Tues.-Sun.) is the local craft brewery, with a brewery and tasting room housed in a 100-year-old downtown building. Fill your growler with award-winning Snowslip Stout, an oatmeal stout.

Information

The **visitors center** is downtown (15 Depot Loop, 406/758-2800, www.discoverkalispell. com). The **Flathead National Forest Headquarters** (650 Wolfpack Way, 406/758-5200) has a variety of pamphlets and flyers, and a few books for sale.

Services

The **Kalispell Regional Medical Center** (310 Sunnyview Ln., 406/752-5111) is the biggest and most complete hospital in this part of Montana. It's off Highway 93 just north of downtown.

Getting There and Around

Glacier Park International Airport (4170 Hwy. 2 E., 406/257-5994, www.iflyglacier.com), eight miles northeast of Kalispell on Highway 2, is served by United, Delta, Alaska/Horizon, and Allegiant Air.

At the airport you'll find **Avis** (406/257-2727 or 800/331-1212), **Budget** (406/755-7500 or 800/527-0700), **Hertz** (406/758-2220 or 800/654-3131), and **National** (406/257-7144 or 800/227-7368). **Dollar, Enterprise,** and **Thrifty** are all near the airport. Call **Glacier Taxi** (406/250-3603) for a cab. **Wild**

Horse Limo (406/756-2290 or 800/841-2391, www.wildhorselimo.com) will take you to your hotel or to Glacier National Park (about $150-200).

Amtrak serves Whitefish, just 14 miles north, along the *Empire Builder* line that links Portland and Seattle with Chicago.

WHITEFISH AND VICINITY

Whitefish (pop. 6,650) calls itself the "recreation capital of Montana." It's a likely enough claim, what with the town's 3,033-foot setting

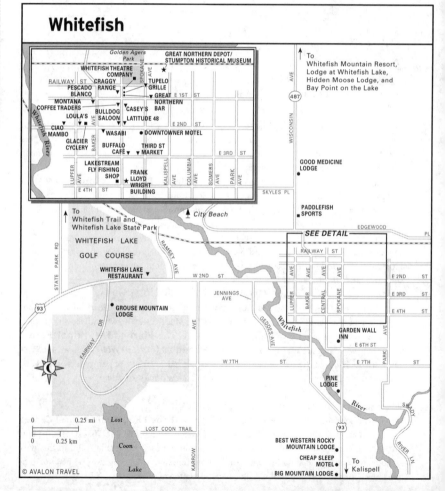

at the base of a major ski mountain some 40 miles from Glacier National Park. To orient yourself in Whitefish, it may help to realize that Highway 93, usually a north-south road, turns to the west as it passes through town.

Success as a tourist destination has brought changes to this town that pulled tree stumps out of its muddy city streets for so long that it earned the nickname "Stumptown." Whitefish Mountain (formerly known as Big Mountain) has become a major ski area, and many of those skiers are returning for summertime visits or to start their own businesses here.

Sights

Most people come here for the proximity to Whitefish Mountain Resort and Glacier National Park. In fact, that's why most of the local people ended up here. It's the sort of place a skier or avid outdoors person moves to.

Surprisingly enough, Whitefish has a **Frank Lloyd Wright building,** but only the most fervid architectural buff would find it particularly interesting. It's on Central Avenue between 3rd and 4th Streets and looks like any old one-story modern office building, currently housing insurance offices and opticians.

The historic and handsome **Great Northern Depot** is styled along the same lines as the Glacier Park chalet hotels. It is currently used by Burlington Northern Santa Fe and Amtrak, and also houses the **Stumptown Historical Museum** (500 Depot St., 406/862-0067, www.stumptown-historicalsociety.org, 10am-4pm Mon.-Sat., free). It's definitely worth a stop for a browse.

Recreation

Hike or mountain bike the **Whitefish Trail** (www.whitefishlegacy.org), a 26-mile trail system accessed by seven trailheads, all near town. This community project is still under development, and trails are being planned and constructed to connect town with nearby natural areas. From downtown, head west on Highway 93 toward Whitefish Lake State Park to the well-signed Lion Mountain trailhead.

Several hiking trails originate from various points around Tally Lake, about 20 miles west of town via Highway 93 and Forest Service Road 113. From the Tally Lake campground, the **Tally Lake Overlook** is a 1.2-mile hike. The **Boney Gulch Trail** is a steep three-mile trail. Its trailhead is on Road 913 about three miles from the campground. For the less driven hiker, the **Stove Pipe Canyon Trail**

The Great Northern Depot serves Amtrak and also houses a historical museum.

is just one mile long and goes into a canyon that is true to its name. This trail starts off Road 2924 on the west side of the lake.

Another good place to hike in the summer is Whitefish Mountain (see the *Whitefish Mountain Resort* section).

The Forest Service irregularly maintains cross-country ski trails at **Round Meadows** (www.fs.usda.gov/recarea/flathead) about 10 miles northwest of town. Take Highway 93 north to Star Meadows Road. A trail map is available on the forest's website or from the ranger station in Whitefish. The elevation here is relatively low (approximately 3,300 feet), and good skiing is generally limited to late December through early March. Once the snow melts, mountain bikers take to the trails here.

Dogsledding is another winter sport to consider if you want a day away from the skis. **Dog Sled Adventures** (406/881-2275, www. dogsledadventuresmont.com, $90 adult, $45 children 12 and under) operates out of Olney about 20 miles north of Whitefish. A typical tour is an hour and a half and travels "at the speed of dog" for about 12 miles through the Stillwater State Forest.

Glacier Cyclery (326 E. 2nd St., 406/862-6446, www.glaciercyclery.com, 9am-6pm Mon.-Fri., 9am-5pm Sat. summer, open at 10am in winter) rents bikes and trailers and serves as a staging area for bicycle tourists, who can arrange to have their bikes shipped to the store in advance of bike trips in the area. The staff can provide you with a bike map of the area and suggest rides; they also sell Flathead National Forest maps with good mountain-bike roads highlighted. During the summer, Glacier Cyclery stables a fleet of mountain bikes on Big Mountain.

Swim in Whitefish Lake at **City Beach** (head north from downtown on Baker, left on Edgewood Dr.) or **Whitefish Lake State Park** (head west on Hwy. 93, $5 for day use). Canoe and paddleboat rentals are available at City Beach.

Whitefish Lake Golf Course (1200 Hwy. 93, 406/862-4000, www.golfwhitefish.

Bike or hike the Whitefish Trail.

com, $62 for 18 holes) is one of the best in the state. This country club-like 36-hole course is on Highway 93 West, across from the Grouse Mountain Lodge. Drive north to fish in **Upper Stillwater Lake,** off Highway 93 just north of Olney. The lake is known for its large northern pike along with whitefish and cutthroat and brook trout. There's a small un-developed lakeside campground.

For fishing gear or guided fishing trips, call or stop by **Lakestream Fly Fishing Shop** (334 Central Ave., 406/862-1298, www. lakestream.com, 9am-6pm daily).

Paddlefish Sports (105 Wisconsin Ave., 406/260-7733, 10am-6pm daily) rents stand-up paddleboards ($20 for two hours) and cruiser bikes ($10 all day).

Entertainment

Although it may seem that Whitefish is wholly devoted to outdoor recreation, there are several artists and other culture ma-vens in town. The **Whitefish Theatre Company** (1 Central Ave., 406/862-5371, www.whitefishtheatreco.org) is housed in an attractive arts center and draws enough support to produce plays almost year-round. The arts center also hosts concerts, mostly featuring indie and roots musicians.

Accommodations

Most of Whitefish's accommodations are either along the long, busy Highway 93 strip south of town (also called Spokane Avenue) or up at the Whitefish Mountain Resort. Quality is quite high, as are prices; be sure to reserve early. Summer high-season rates are listed here; there's usually a significant reduction in the off-season.

UNDER $150

One of the few inexpensive lodging deals in Whitefish is the **Cheap Sleep Motel** (6400 Hwy. 93 S., 406/862-5515 or 800/862-3711, www.cheapsleepmotel.com, $97-114) which is pretty much what its name promises, but also includes an outdoor pool, fridges, and accepts pets. Rooms are basic but clean and pleasant.

Another good value is the **Pine Lodge** (920 Spokane St., 406/862-7600 or 800/305-7463, www.thepinelodge.com, $143-159), an attractive motel with a fairly large indoor-outdoor pool (a swimming channel connects the two pools), hot tub, exercise room, and some rooms with kitchenettes and fireplaces.

The **Downtowner Motel** (224 Spokane Ave., 406/862-2535, www.downtownermotel.cc, $130) is the only lodging in the heart of downtown Whitefish and has an outdoor hot tub, a sauna, and a pretty good exercise room. The motel isn't deluxe, but it's a short walk from good restaurants, shops, and bars.

OVER $150

Best Western Rocky Mountain Lodge (6510 Hwy. 93 S., 406/862-2569 or 800/862-2569, www.rockymtnlodge.com, $181-220) is one of the newer Whitefish accommodations, with a grand lobby, continental breakfast, pool, hot tub, exercise room, and guest laundry. Available are attractive minisuites

with fireplace, whirlpool tub, microwave, refrigerator, and wet bar.

Big Mountain Lodge (6390 Hwy. 93 S., 406/862-4020 or 800/888-4479, www.bigmountainlodgewhitefish.com, $169), on the highway strip south of town, is notable for its pleasant rooms, indoor pool with a 90-foot waterslide, and two outdoor hot tubs.

The ★ **Good Medicine Lodge** (537 Wisconsin Ave., 406/862-5488 or 800/860-5488, www.goodmedicinelodge.com, $190-305) is especially attractive—a cross between a small inn and a B&B. While a big breakfast buffet and evening appetizers and drinks are provided and there are pleasant common rooms, the atmosphere is low-key, and you don't feel as if you need to whisper as you pad around. Rooms have vaulted wooden ceilings, upscale-rustic decor, and great views. Some rooms are wheelchair accessible, all rooms have telephones, and there's a hot tub and a guest laundry. The lodge is located in an older residential neighborhood on the way to Whitefish Mountain.

On the road to Whitefish Mountain, **Hidden Moose Lodge** (1735 E. Lakeshore Dr., 406/862-6516 or 888/733-6667, www.hiddenmooselodge.com, $169-249) is an attractive newer log lodge with B&B accommodations in upscale Western-themed rooms. Each room or suite is equipped with a TV and DVD player, telephone, refrigerator, and deck. The common areas, including the great room and an outdoor deck and hot tub, are all striking and good places to hang out and enjoy the complimentary evening drink.

For comfort in a conveniently located, historic, and beautifully restored home, the ★ **Garden Wall Inn** (504 Spokane Ave., 406/862-3440 or 888/530-1700, www.gardenwallinn.com, $155-215) is a good choice. The home was built in the 1920s, with strong arts-and-crafts influences; fabrics, tiles, wall coverings, and art have been carefully selected to evoke the era. Most of the furniture is native to 1920s Montana, which lends a specifically regional atmosphere to the graciously decorated rooms. Modern considerations haven't been neglected, however, and all rooms have private baths. A four-person suite is available for $315. Both the owner and the innkeeper have trained as professional chefs, and the breakfasts are renowned. The innkeepers are also avid outdoors people and will help plan excursions.

If you're heading to Montana hoping to stay in your own log cabin, then consider the **North Forty Resort** (3765 Hwy. 40 W., 406/862-7740 or 800/775-1740, www.north-fortyresort.com, $219-289) between Whitefish and Columbia Falls, making it a good base for trips to Glacier National Park. The 22 recently constructed deluxe cabins are set in a quiet pine-shaded grove, and all have full kitchens, baths, and fireplaces. The furniture is hand-crafted in Montana. All cabins sleep at least five, and some sleep up to eight. Hot tubs and a sauna are also available. Pets are allowed in some cabins.

The Grouse Mountain Lodge (1205 Hwy. 93 W., 406/862-3000 or 800/321-8822, www.grousemountainlodge.com, $229-269) is a large recreation, convention, lodging, and restaurant complex across from Whitefish Lake Golf Course. Guests have access to a pool, a sauna, hot tubs, tennis courts, and rooms looking out onto a golf course rather than a highway.

Right on the lake, the **Lodge at Whitefish Lake** (1380 Wisconsin Ave., 406/863-4000, www.lodgeatwhitefishlake.com, two-night minimum stay in high season, $279-378) is perhaps Whitefish's most upscale lodging, a very handsome stone and timber lodge with a variety of room types, a spa, marina, outdoor pool, bar, and restaurant. The majority of the rooms in the lodge itself are studio suites ($334-378), with a fireplace, balcony, and efficiency kitchen, while standard hotel rooms ($279-368) are in a separate structure, the Viking Lodge. Two- and three-room condos are also available.

To rent a condo on Whitefish Lake, call **Bay Point on the Lake** (300 Bay Point Dr., 406/862-2331 or 800/327-2108, www.baypoint.org, $214 and up, two-night minimum). Rates for these comfortable and quiet lodgings vary seasonally, and there are eight different room configurations with three different luxury levels available, so it's best to call and discuss your needs. For a vacation home rental, contact **Five Star Rentals & Property Management** (406/862-5994, www.five-starrentals.com).

Guest Ranches

At the **Bar W Guest Ranch** (2875 Hwy. 93 W., 406/863-9099 or 866/828-2900, www.the-barw.com) you'll feel a little removed from the town of Whitefish, even though it's less than 10 miles away. Here you'll be immersed in the Western life, with plenty of horseback riding, which is the ranch's main attraction. The majority of guests are here for one of the multiday all-inclusive packages (two day, three night $907-1,215 per adult, double occupancy; five day, six night $1,815-2,430 per adult, double occupancy), though individual rooms are sometimes open on a B&B basis ($95-275 double; three-night minimum). A variety of packages are offered, including the "Cowgirl Up" women's weeks; the ranch's B&B rate does not include riding or meals other than breakfast.

Camping

Whitefish Lake State Park (406/862-3991, http://stateparks.mt.gov/whitefish-lake, May-Sept., $15-18) is about two miles west of town off Highway 93. Pick this as your place to stay if you're after convenience, if you want to spend some time near civilization, if you want to eat out or shop in Whitefish, or if you want a handy launching spot for a trip to Glacier National Park. Be aware that trains run right by this campground throughout the night. There's a boat launch and a swimming beach popular with local kids. The campground has running water, flush toilets, and showers.

Out of town, **Tally Lake** (800/416-6992, www.fs.usda.gov/flathead, Memorial Day-Labor Day, $15) has a Forest Service campground six miles west of Whitefish on Highway 93, then 15 miles west on Forest Service Road 113.

Food

BREAKFAST AND CASUAL MEALS

Whitefish is a great place to eat breakfast. The ★ **Buffalo Cafe** (514 3rd St. E., 406/862-2833, www.buffalocafewhitefish.com, 7am-2pm and 5pm-9pm Mon.-Sat., 8am-2pm Sun., $5-10 for breakfast and lunch, $11-18 dinner) is populated with an easy mix of locals and tourists. The breakfast menu features about half a dozen variations on huevos rancheros and at least as many omelets, and it's all really yummy! For dinner, choose from burgers, Southwestern specialties, or grilled meat and fish.

Another good breakfast spot is **Loula's** (300 2nd St. E., 406/862-5614, 7am-4pm daily and 5pm-9pm Thurs.-Sun. summer, 7am-3pm daily and 5pm-9pm Thurs.-Sun. winter, $6-10, dinner $12-22), which is also beloved for its berry pies. Dinners focus on comfort foods, including meat loaf and potpie.

Stand in line at **Montana Coffee Traders** (110 Central Ave., 406/862-7667, 7am-6pm Mon.-Sat., 8am-3pm Sun.) and you'll learn all the local news. The coffee and pastries are as good as the gossip.

Third St. Market (244 Spokane Ave., 406/862-5054, www.thirdstreetmarket.com, 8:30am-7pm Mon.-Sat.) is the local health-food store. Many of the towns in this part of Montana have small health-food boutiques, but this one is more of a complete food store and community rendezvous than most.

AMERICAN FARE

The ★ **Great Northern Bar and Grill** (27 Central Ave., 406/862-2816, www.greatnorthernbar.com, 11am-2am daily, $7-16) is a friendly, low-key bar with sports on the TV in the front, sandwiches and burgers served at the tables in the back, and a party on the side patio. It's open for lunch and dinner, and usually has live music several nights a week.

The **Bulldog Saloon** (144 Central Ave., 406/862-5601, www.fart-slobber.com, 11am-11pm daily for food; bar open until 2am daily, $6-8) is a good bar to hang out in and maybe munch a burger. **Casey's** (101 Central Ave., 406/862-8150, www.caseyswhitefish.com, 11am-2am daily, $10-15), a casino bar, is housed in Whitefish's oldest building. It was built in 1903, when Whitefish was a rollicking railroad town, and after a day on the slopes, many still find it an excellent place to rollick. For something more of this century and a little more refined, the **Craggy Range** (10 Central Ave., 406/862-7550, www.thecraggyrange.com, kitchen open 11:30am-10pm

The Great Northern Bar and Grill is a Whitefish classic.

daily, entrées $14-24) has standard bar food and good pasta and dinner entrées.

ETHNIC AND REGIONAL FOOD

The ★ **Tupelo Grille** (17 Central Ave., 406/862-6136, www.tupelogrille.com, 5pm-10pm daily, $16-42) is a local favorite. It focuses on Southern specialties, such as shrimp and grits, and Cajun food. Don't miss dessert here; the bread pudding deserves all the raves it gets.

Expect to wait in line at the casual and noisy **Ciao Mambo** (234 E. 2nd St., 406/863-9600, www.ciaomambo.com, 5pm-10pm Mon.-Sat., 5pm-9pm Sun., $11-19); this popular, reasonably priced restaurant has a brassy New York Italian atmosphere, delicious food in that same tradition, and a wine list worthy of *Wine Spectator*'s notice. For real entertainment, eat at the bar that surrounds the kitchen area.

Another great choice is, believe it or not, a sushi restaurant. **Wasabi** (419 E. 2nd St., 406/863-9283, http://wasabimt.com, 5pm-9pm Mon.-Sat., $8-25, reservations recommended) has delicious fresh fish and a soothing, elegant atmosphere.

Check out **Pescado Blanco** (235 1st St., 406/862-5285, www.pescadoblanco.com, 5pm-9pm nightly, $11-22) for Mexican dinners that veer well away from cheesy Mexican-American platefuls served at most Montana Mexican restaurants. Here you'll find something more like Montana-Mexican fusion, such as elk chorizo tacos.

FINE DINING

★ **Latitude 48** (147 Central Ave., 406/863-2323, www.latitude48bistro.com, 5pm-9pm Tues.-Sat., $13-29) is a swank temple to fine cuisine, with steaks, fresh seafood, handmade traditional pastas, wood-fired pizzas, roasted chicken, and other Mediterranean fare in a handsome dining room of red brick and dark leather. In addition to the main courses, there's a good small-plate menu designed for sharing. Many of these small plates ($7-13) are also available downstairs in the stylish **The**

Pescado Blanco is the place for Mexican food in Whitefish.

Red Room, which is as close as to a nightclub as you'll find in Whitefish.

For fine dining with true Western character, it's hard to beat the ★ **Whitefish Lake Restaurant** at Whitefish Lake Golf Club (1200 Hwy. 93, 406/862-5285, www.whitefishlakerestaurant.com, 11am-9:30pm daily, $21-40, reservations recommended) in the course's log-built clubhouse from 1937. The restaurant is wonderfully atmospheric with superb steaks and prime rib, fresh fish and seafood, and meaty temptations such as rack of lamb with pinot noir dried tart cherry demi-glace and roast duckling with blackberry vin blanc. Or just come for a drink and an appetizer and enjoy the ambience.

Information and Services

The **Whitefish Convention and Visitors Bureau** (307 Spokane Ave., 406/862-3548, www.explorewhitefish.com, 9am-5pm Mon.-Fri.) dispenses an array of brochures and maps.

The local bookstore, **Bookworks** (244

Spokane Ave., 406/862-4980, 10am-6pm Mon.-Sat., 11am-3pm Sun.), is an excellent place to pick up regional literature, field guides, or a good novel to read on your road trip.

Getting There and Around

Amtrak stops at the **North Central Avenue Depot** (406/862-2268, www.amtrak.com) on its way across the top of the country. The *Empire Builder* runs between Chicago and Seattle or Portland and stops in Whitefish daily. The eastbound train comes through around 4:30am, the westbound at approximately 10:45am.

Flathead Valley Eagle Transit (406/758-5728, https://flathead.mt.gov/eagle) runs between Missoula and Whitefish.

Car rentals are available at **Budget Rent-a-Car** (803 Spokane Ave., 406/862-8170).

WHITEFISH MOUNTAIN RESORT

Whitefish Mountain Resort (406/862-1900 or 800/858-3930, www.skiwhitefish.com) is one of Montana's top-ranked and most popular ski resorts in winter, and in summer it offers a bevy of family-friendly recreation options and relatively inexpensive lodging. The location could not be more perfect—just an hour from Glacier National Park, moments from forested hiking and biking trails, and just down the hill in Whitefish is lake swimming and water sports in Whitefish Lake, plus the gustatory pleasures of the city's dining scene.

However, the resort itself is like a village: An entire community has built up around the ski area, with several hotels and condominiums, a number of restaurants, a grocery store, a day care center, and ski shops. It's a great place to find yourself at the end of a busy day of outdoor adventure.

★ Summer at Whitefish Mountain

In summer, the lifts and other recreational facilities at Whitefish Mountain are open mid-June-Labor Day daily, and Friday, Saturday, and Sunday through September.

For hikers, the **Danny On Trail** leads from the main resort parking lot 3.8 miles up to the summit of Big Mountain. There are plenty of huckleberries on the trail late in the summer, and spur trails offer wildflower meadows and vistas of the Flathead Valley. If you'd prefer to ride the lifts to the top and begin your hike there, simply take the **gondola** (10am-5:30pm, $13 adults, $9 seniors and children 7-18, 6 and under free) and you have the choice of hiking or riding back down. Thrifty folks will appreciate the free ride down on the lift that's available to those who make the hike up. The entire trail is usually clear of snow from July through mid-September.

Mountain biking is a big summer activity at Whitefish Mountain. Bikes are available for rent at the resort, and there are 20 miles of single-track trails on the mountain. An all-day lift ticket for a person and a bike costs $32; a two-hour ticket is $22.

Perhaps the coolest summer activity on the mountain is the three-hour **Walk in the Treetops** (10am, 1:30pm daily, reservations suggested, $49), which starts with a shuttle or one-mile bike ride, then segues into a naturalist-led hike through the forest canopy on a boardwalk suspended up to 60 feet above the ground. Though walking across a fairly narrow plank suspended far above ground sounds like some terrifying character-building exercise, the solid cable-rigged railings and the securely tied safety harness on each participant make this adventure accessible to all but the most acrophobic. After a few minutes of getting used to the height, the treetops begin to seem like a great place to view not only the nearby lakes and mountains, but also a wide variety of birdlife, such as western tanagers, red-tailed and kestrel hawks, pine grosbeaks, and kinglets. Squirrels, pine martins, moose, deer, and coyotes may also be spotted. Due to the size of harnesses, participants must be at least 54 inches tall and have a waist of 42 inches or smaller.

There's even more adventure on the resort's

zipline tours. Six separate ziplines extend above the valley, one is over a mile long, another is over 300 feet high. There are two different tour packages, one with five ($79 July-Labor Day) and one with seven ($84 July-Labor Day) zip tours, with discounts in the shoulder season. The tours are open to riders of all ages who are at least 54 inches tall and between 60 and 230 pounds. Reservations strongly suggested; there are 15 tours offered daily, but each is open only to a dozen people at a time.

For high-speed thrills, the resort's **alpine slide** offers a bobsled-like experience to adrenaline seekers ($8 per ride). The course drops 281 feet along its 1,605 foot length; children under 8 ride free but must share a sled with an adult.

Winter at Whitefish Mountain

With about 300 inches of snow a year, 14 lifts (including three high-speed quads and, in 2014-2015, a new fixed triple) serving over 100 trails, and the pleasant Amtrak-accessible town of Whitefish at the bottom of the hill, it's easy to see why people come from all over to for **Whitefish Mountain skiing** (early Dec.-early Apr., $71 adults, $60 seniors, $63 youth 13-18, $37 ages 7-12). The elevation at the summit is 7,000 feet, the base is at 4,600 feet, the vertical drop is 2,300 feet, and there are lights for night skiing ($20 for everyone). Ski and board rentals are available, as are lessons for the entire family.

Accommodations

If you plan to stay at Whitefish Mountain Resort, you'll pay for the convenience of skiing to and from your door, but there are frequent deals, especially for groups. The lodges at Whitefish Mountain are also open in summer, and rates are generally about 25 percent lower than the high-season winter prices listed here.

Many, but not all, of the accommodations on the mountain are run by the ski area; for this broad selection of rooms and condos, the easiest way to arrange for lodgings is to call Whitefish Mountain's **central reservation number** (800/858-4152) and discuss your needs with the reservations clerk, or check the options at the **website** (http://skiwhitefish.com). Of the lodgings offered by the ski area, **Hibernation House** ($100) is the economy choice, especially if you're traveling on your own or with one other person. This is a bed-and-breakfast hotel; breakfast is included in the rates. There are a number of condo options in other buildings at the resort, all with kitchens and fireplaces (and many with two bedrooms) running about $200-300 for one bedroom per night for studios; hotel-style rooms are also available ($140 double and up) as are a range of private homes with indoor pools and hot tubs.

The mountain's upscale hotel isn't handled by the ski area's central reservations. ★ **Kandahar Lodge** (3824 Big Mountain Rd., 406/862-6098, www.kandaharlodge.com, $159-239, open June-Oct. and early Dec.-mid-Apr.) is Whitefish Mountain's fanciest, with an excellent restaurant and alpine lodge decor; suites with kitchens are available. The Kandahar is a ski-in lodge; there's a short walk and a little downhill ski to get to the lift in the morning.

About three miles down the hill from the lift area is **Ptarmigan Village** (3000 Big Mountain Rd., 406/862-3594 or 800/552-3952, www.ptarmiganvillage.com, $140-500), with studio condos, indoor and outdoor pools, hot tubs, and a sauna. This is a good pick if you don't fancy being right in the hub of the ski area; it's in a woodsy setting and is much less bustling than the area up the mountain. It's operated independently of the ski area.

Food

The best dining is at **Cafe Kandahar** (406/862-6247, www.cafekandahar.com, 5:30pm-9:30pm daily, $26-42, five-course tasting menu $70, dinner reservations recommended) for serious cuisine with French and Mediterranean influences. The atmosphere is far more casual at the **Hellroaring Saloon & Eatery** (406/862-6364, www.

hellroaringsaloon.com, 11am-11pm daily during ski season, 5pm-9pm Tues.-Sun. summer, $8-24), in the chalet at the base of the lifts, with good Southwestern-influenced food and a lively bar.

COLUMBIA FALLS

Columbia Falls (pop. 4,800, elev. 2,960 feet) is a handy jumping-off point for both Hungry Horse Reservoir and Glacier National Park. There are several motels and enough stores to do some last-minute stocking up before heading into the mountains.

There are no falls in Columbia Falls. When it was time to name the town, *Columbia* was the initial choice. Since that name had already been taken, *Falls* was tacked on just because it sounded good.

Recreation

Test the 10 slides and hot tub at **Big Sky Waterpark** (7211 Hwy. 2 E., 406/892-5025, www.bigskywp.com, 11am-7pm daily Memorial Day-Labor Day, $25 adults and teens over 48 inches, $20 children under 48 inches and seniors), at the junction of Highways 2 and 20.

The **Meadow Lake Resort** (100 St. Andrews Dr., 406/892-8700, www.meadowlake.com, greens fees $68) has an 18-hole golf course open to the public.

Accommodations

Glacier Inn Motel (1401 2nd Ave. E., 406/892-4341, www.glacierinnmotel.com, $100) is a simple but clean and convenient family-run motel.

The basic **Western Inn & Campground** (7285 Hwy. 2 E., 406/892-7686, www.glacierparkmotelandcampground.com, $127-175), at the junction of Highways 2 and 206, has several amenities, including free continental breakfast in the summer, miniature golf, and a play area. Some rooms have full kitchens; there's also a campground with camping cabins ($75), tepees and wall tents ($55), and tenting and RV sites ($45). Pets are permitted.

One of the finest B&Bs in these parts is ★ **Bad Rock Country Bed & Breakfast** (406/892-2829 or 888/892-2829, www.badrock.com, $185-395), just south of Columbia Falls off Highway 206. In addition to the rooms in the main house (including a two-room family suite), behind the house are three modern, stylishly simple log cabin suites and a guest house and apartment (no kitchens), constructed with squared logs and filled with rustic pine furniture and gas fireplaces. All rooms have private baths and queen or king beds; breakfast is ample and delicious, and the hospitality is top-notch. The B&B is set in a 30-acre meadow with views onto the mountains leading to Glacier Park; from the hot tub the lighted runs of Whitefish Mountain are visible at night.

North of town, just past the Blankenship turnoff to the North Fork area of Glacier Park, **Moss Mountain Inn** (4655 North Fork Rd., 406/387-4605, www.mossmountaininn.com, June-Sept., $150-190) is a showcase for sustainability and good organic food, much of it grown in the B&B's garden. The small inn has four suites decorated with Caribbean and Indonesian art and a spacious solarium. **Meadow Lake Resort** (100 St. Andrews Dr., 406/892-8700 or 800/321-4653, www.meadowlake.com, $229-300), which includes a small hotel, condominiums, and resort homes, borders an 18-hole championship golf course. There are tennis courts, a fitness center, an outdoor swimming pool, and a year-round outdoor hot tub on the grounds. During the winter the resort runs a shuttle to and from the Whitefish Mountain ski area. The restaurant here is one of the area's best.

Camping

The Forest Service's **Big Creek Campground** (www.fs.usda.gov/flathead, $12) is 21 miles north of Columbia Falls on Road 210, where Big Creek runs into the North Fork of the Flathead River. During the summer it's one of the quieter spots around, as well as one of the least expensive.

Food

If you're passing through town and need a jolt of caffeine and a little food to get to Glacier National Park, stop at **Montana Coffee Traders** (30 9th St. W., 406/892-7696, 6am-4pm daily, $5-10), right on Highway 2 in downtown Columbia Falls. You'll find good breakfasts, lunches, baked goods, and espresso drinks.

Another good lunch spot is the **Palette Cafe** (734 9th St. W., 406/897-2019, 10am-3pm Mon.-Fri., $6-9), with excellent salads, soups, panini, and rice bowls. Shockingly for this neck of the woods, healthy eaters can choose to add kale to almost every dish.

Dine on "Rocky Mountain fare with an Italian flare" at **Three Forks Grille** (729 Nucleus Ave., 406/892-2900, 5pm-9pm daily, $10-25, reservations recommended), a surprisingly good restaurant that'll make you consider pausing on your way to Glacier Park. It's easy to eat cheap here … the burgers are good and entrées such as a brined and grilled pork chop with marsala sauce, mushrooms, and pickled huckleberries are reasonably priced.

The **Back Room at the Nite Owl** (522 9th St. W., 406/892-3131 or 406/892-9944, 5am-11pm, dinner 4pm-9pm daily, $7-20) is a casual bar, café, and dinner house complex that serves really good pizza, chicken, and ribs. It doesn't look like much, but ponder the always-full parking lot and rest assured that this is the best inexpensive food in Columbia Falls.

Information and Services

The **Columbia Falls Chamber of Commerce** (233 13th St. E., 406/892-2072, www.columbiafallschamber.com) can provide you with more information on the area.

HUNGRY HORSE

During the severe winter of 1900, two draft horses used for logging in the area, Tex and Jerry, wandered off. When they were found about a month later, they were all scraggly and hungry. Thus the name of the town.

The huckleberry is the culinary specialty of Hungry Horse. The **Huckleberry Patch** (8858 Hwy. 2 E., 406/387-5000, www.huckleberrypatch.com, 7am-10pm daily May-Oct., 11am-6pm daily Nov.-Apr.) is a convenient place to load up on gifts of huckleberry preserves and to toss down a slice of huckleberry pie or a huckleberry milk shake in the café. It's also easy enough to pick your own berries. They start ripening around mid-July, and almost any trip off Highway 2 into the hills will lead to good picking—but watch out for bears; they feast on berries to prepare for hibernation.

Sights

Fans of dam technology will want to tour the visitors information center at the **Hungry Horse Dam** (406/387-5241, 9am-4pm Wed.-Sun. June-Aug., free) four miles south of town. The 564-foot-high concrete dam holds back the 34-mile-long Hungry Horse Reservoir, filled by the South Fork of the Flathead River.

A road circles the reservoir and provides access to trails into the surrounding national forest and wilderness areas. Jewel Basin Hiking Area lies to the west of the reservoir, the Great Bear Wilderness is to the east, and the Bob Marshall Wilderness is to the south. Great Northern Mountain, east of the reservoir, rises to an elevation of 8,720 feet. The South Fork of the Flathead River flows into the southern end of the reservoir. You'll see guest ranches around the reservoir, and there's no dearth of public campgrounds.

Don't want to ogle the dam? How about visiting the **House of Mystery** (7800 Hwy. 2 E., 406/892-1210, www.montanavortex.com, 10am-6pm daily Apr.-mid-Oct., $9 adults, $6.50 children 6-12), where the laws of physics go awry, or the **A-Mazing Ventures Fun Center** (406/387-5902, www.amazingfuncenter.com, 9:30am-dark daily Memorial Day-Labor Day), with a giant maze, bumper boats, and other family-friendly activities. Check the website for the rather complex entry prices.

Great Bear Wilderness Area

The Great Bear Wilderness Area comprises

285,771 acres just south of Glacier National Park, north of the Bob Marshall, on the west side of the Continental Divide. An airstrip at Schafer Meadows is an unusual feature of this wilderness area, and it's possible to fly in; call **Red Eagle Aviation** (406/755-2376, about $425 one-way) for details.

Trailheads from the Spotted Bear Ranger Station lead to Lodgepole Creek and the Spotted Bear River. Just about every trail in the wilderness complex will go into the valley of the South Fork of the Flathead River. The headwaters of the Middle Fork of the Flathead River are in the Great Bear Wilderness.

Accommodations

The least expensive lodging you'll find in this area is at the **Crooked Tree Motel** (8688 Hwy. 2 E., 406/387-5531, $80-145). Some rooms have kitchenettes, and there's also an indoor pool and RV park.

Between Hungry Horse and Coram, find the **Tamarack Lodge** (406/387-4420 or 877/387-4420, www.historictamaracklodge. com, $125-320), where the log lodge dates back to 1907. Rooms are also available in cabins and a motel.

Even though its name is a little odd, the **Mini Golden Inns Motel** (8955 Hwy. 2 E., 406/387-4313 or 800/891-6464, www.hungry-horselodging.com, $118-147) is a surprisingly pleasant place to stay along this busy highway, with many wheelchair-accessible rooms and some kitchenettes. Pets are allowed.

Located 55 miles south of Highway 2, the **Spotted Bear Ranch** (406/270-5235, www. spottedbear.com) is an upscale lodge catering mostly to anglers and hunters. A three-day fishing vacation here costs $2,300 per person, including all meals and guide service.

Camping

There are eight **Forest Service campgrounds** (406/387-3800, www.fs.usda. gov/flathead, $10-15) around Hungry Horse Reservoir. Check with the Forest Service on the piped-water status of these campgrounds; service cutbacks eliminated water, but it's been restored to some closer-in campgrounds.

Lost Johnny Camp is eight miles down Road 895 from Hungry Horse; **Lost Johnny Point** is one mile farther. **Lid Creek** is 15 miles from Hungry Horse; **Lakeview** is 24 miles; **Handkerchief Lake** is 35 miles from Hungry Horse on Road 895, then another two miles on Road 897. There's a trail from Handkerchief Lake up to the Jewel Basin Hiking Area. **Spotted Bear** is at the south end of the reservoir, 55 miles from Martin City on Road 38 (and about the same distance from Hungry Horse). **Murray Bay** and **Emery Bay** are along the east side of the reservoir. Emery Bay is the closest spot to Martin City; it's seven miles down Road 38.

Information

The *Hungry Horse News* (www.hungry-horsenews.com) is the newspaper of record in these parts, definitely worth picking up if you want to read a weekly paper loaded with stories of mountain lions in the streets, bear maulings and bee stings in Glacier Park, as well as numerous DUI violations.

The Northwestern Corner

The Kootenai (KOOT-nee) National Forest is the defining physical feature of this far corner of the state. It has a Pacific quality, and its lush, forested hillsides are drained by the Kootenai, the Clark Fork, and a host of smaller rivers and streams. Even in Montana this is considered remote country—beautiful, off-the-beaten path landscapes beyond the well-trod routes of most tourists.

BULL RIVER ROAD AND THE CABINET MOUNTAINS WILDERNESS

Bull River Road (Highway 56) runs from Highway 200 (just west of Noxon) to Troy. The Bull River and several lakes are along the road, and the Cabinet Mountains Wilderness is just to the east. Fishing is good in the river (but not spectacular in Bull Lake, which does not feed the river). Native American history records that Bull Lake was formed when a landslide blocked a stream and destroyed a camp. There is still some evidence of such a slide at the foot of the lake.

There's a good chance that wildlife will be somewhere along this road almost any time you drive it. You'll probably see deer, and there are also plenty of elk and moose in the area.

Highway 56 was a Native American trail; it was also used by smugglers bringing Chinese laborers down from Canada to work on the construction of the Northern Pacific Railway.

Ross Creek Cedar Grove

This grove of old-growth western red cedar is like an open-air cathedral, a remarkable spot for a short hike. The forest here is a Pacific rainforest, which is a little unusual for Montana. It gets 50 inches of rain a year, so don't be surprised if you take the mile-long nature hike in a shower. The raised boardwalk trail on parts of the interpretive hike protects

the forest floor and makes it easy to hike in the rain. There are trails up the Middle Fork and the South Fork of Ross Creek starting from the parking lot of the cedar grove. Bring your cross-country skis here in the winter for a lovely easy tour through the big trees. Ross Creek Cedar Grove is about five miles off Highway 56 just south of Bull Lake (17 miles north of Highway 200).

Cabinet Mountains Wilderness

In the Kootenai National Forest, the Cabinet Mountains Wilderness comprises nearly 95,000 acres. It can be reached from Highway 56 or Highway 200. Snowshoe Peak is the high point in the wilderness at 8,738 feet. There is good hiking here, and some rock climbing on the peaks.

To reach the four-mile-long trail to **St. Paul Lake,** a 4,715-foot-high lake in a cirque beneath St. Paul Peak, go up East Fork Road off Bull River Road. About one mile up East Fork Road is a Forest Service sign noting directions and distances to several trailheads. The St. Paul Lake trailhead is four miles from this point, up a gravel road that's easy to drive in a passenger car until the final short descent to the trailhead, which requires some caution. The trail passes through some old-growth western red cedar and western hemlock before it reaches the lake.

Camping

The **Bull River Campground** (406/295-4693, www.fs.usda.gov/kootenai, mid-Apr.-Nov., $10) is situated by the Cabinet Mountains where Bull River runs into the Clark Fork.

There's also camping on the road to the Ross Creek Cedar Grove. **Bad Medicine Campground** (406/295-4693, www.fs.usda.gov/kootenai, Apr.-Nov., $10) is two miles off Highway 56 overlooking Bull Lake. There is a boat launch at this cedar-scented site.

TROY AND VICINITY

At 1,892 feet, Troy is the lowest point in Montana. It's an unprepossessing town of about 950 on the west bank of the Kootenai River, which flows northwest from Troy into Idaho. The Purcell Mountains to the north of Troy were completely blanketed by ice age glaciers, which ground the mountains into soft peaks. To the south, glaciers carved valleys and cirques in the Cabinet Mountains but did not cover them so completely as to smooth them out.

There's not much to delay the tourist in Troy, aside from gas stations, a couple of eateries, and a **historical museum** (406/295-1064) with erratic hours. It's found in a former railway building in the midst of a small park at the corner of Highway 2 and St. Regis Haul Road.

Nine miles northwest of Troy on Highway 2, Forest Road 508 (aka the Yaak River Road) leads up the Yaak River Valley 29 miles to the tiny community of Yaak. This is very remote country, known to those few who frequent it simply as "The Yaak." The Yaak has gained a certain literary fame thanks to writer Rick Bass, whose *Winter Notes* and *The Book of Yaak* chronicle snow, woodcutting, and isolation.

It would be a shame to drive all the way up to Yaak and not stop in at the **Dirty Shame Saloon** (29453 Yaak River Rd., 406/295-5100, hours vary according to business and other factors, but open every evening), where local color is abundant.

Recreation

Pulpit Mountain Trail, a national recreation trail, is a five-mile (one-way) hike just north of Troy. It passes an old fire lookout on Pulpit Mountain and has good views of the Cabinet Mountains. The easiest way to walk the trail is to start from the trailhead on Lynx Creek Road and hike to where the trail comes out on Rabbit Creek Road.

To reach the **Northwest Peak Scenic Area,** turn up Pete Creek Road just west of Yaak. This is an isolated area of the state, and it's rare to see many other hikers on the trails. One of the more popular trails leads to Northwest Peak. It's a two-mile hike to the peak, which has grand views and a deserted lookout. Call the **Troy ranger station** (406/295-4693) for trail information.

Camping

Yaak River Campground (406/295-4693, www.fs.usda.gov/kootenai, $10), seven miles west of Troy on Highway 2, is a good entrance or exit campground to the state. There are plenty of paths down to the river. There are several other Forest Service campgrounds in the area. Head up the Yaak River to **Yaak Falls Campground** (free, no water) set by a cascade eight miles up from Highway 2. **Whitetail Campground** ($7) is on a quiet stretch of the Yaak River; it's a good place for a swim. **Pete Creek** ($7) is an exceptionally pretty campground set on a bluff above Pete Creek, just west of the town of Yaak.

Information

The **ranger station** (12858 Hwy. 2, 406/295-4693, 7am-4:30pm Mon.-Fri.) is on the west edge of town.

LIBBY

Libby (pop. 2,700, elev. 2,066 feet) spills along the Kootenai River Valley, with the Cabinet Mountains to the south, the Purcell Mountains to the northwest, and the Salish Mountains to the northeast. It's a pleasant mountain town, with good lodgings and choices for dining, but by no means a tourist town. However, it's easy to spend a day or two in the area, especially if you're hiking, fishing, or—in the autumn—watching the local eagles.

History

Canadian explorer David Thompson's reconnoitering in 1808 resulted in a small influx of fur traders during the first half of the 1800s, but little development occurred until gold was found in 1865. A mining town was thrown up by Libby Creek in the 1880s, and it moved to wherever the gold seemed to be. Libby ended up in its present location when the railroad came through in 1892.

Mining continued until 1990, when W. R. Grace and Co. shut down its vermiculite mining and processing operation in Libby. Mixed in with the vermiculite was a mineral called tremolite, a rare and toxic form of asbestos. Tragically, the miners and many townspeople have suffered from the effects of asbestos poisoning. Many have died from asbestos-related cancers, and even more became ill. Even though W. R. Grace and Co. *and* the U.S. government knew about the asbestos, until 1999 nothing was done to stop the dust that contaminated the town. Since then, the Environmental Protection Agency has carried out a massive cleanup, removing contaminated soil from all over town, including the school athletic field. The cleanup efforts are ongoing, but now focus on small, isolated areas of contamination.

Sights

The **Heritage Museum** (1367 Hwy. 2 S., 406/293-7521, www.libbyheritagemuseum. org, 10am-5pm Mon.-Sat., 1pm-5pm Sun., June-Aug., free) is a large polygonal log building with a dark interior filled with display cases brimming with Libby's old musical instruments (including two ukelins, one pianoette, two mandolin harps, and the sheet music for "Let Me Call You Sweetheart"), household implements, and logging equipment. There are special displays on the region's wildlife, logging, and mining.

If you're out to relive Libby's history, it may be more profitable to pan for gold. Gold was discovered in Libby Creek in 1865 and was mined fairly intensively around the end of the 19th century. There's still some gold there, though. The original dredging equipment got only 85-90 percent of what gold was in the creek. What's left is most likely to be found near the bottom of gravel piles left by early miners. The Forest Service has an area set aside for gold panning on Libby Creek; it's important not to search outside the designated area because mining claims are staked close by.

Libby is known as the City of Eagles for its large population of bald eagles.

To reach the **Libby Creek Gold Panning Area** (406/293-7773, www.fs.usda.gov/kootenai), turn from Highway 2 onto Bear Creek Road (seven miles south of Libby) and drive 18 miles to the small parking area beside Libby Creek. (Or take Libby Creek Road, 12 miles down Highway 2 from Libby, and follow it just over 10 miles to the panning zone.) Howard Lake Campground is one mile south of the gold-panning area. If you tire of prospecting, follow Libby Creek Road (the road that goes west at the Howard Lake junction) to its end and take an easy two-mile round-trip hike along Libby Creek past an old miner's cabin.

For a look at the dramatic, cascading, 200-foot-high **Kootenai Falls** from the highway, there's a turnout on Highway 2 about five miles west of Libby. This is one of the few waterfalls on a major Northwest river that hasn't had its power harnessed for electrical generators. A quarter-mile trail leads from the casual campground by the highway pullout, across a bridge over the railroad tracks, and down to viewpoints of the cascades. Continue west on the trail to a swinging footbridge downstream from the falls. Bighorn sheep are often seen just east of here grazing on the cliffs across the river.

Recreation

The 23-mile **Skyline National Recreation Trail** (406/293-7773, www.fs.usda.gov/kootenai) starts at the west fork of Quartz Creek, northwest of Libby, and ends in the Yaak Valley. It's a good place for an overnight backpacking trip, with lots of camping spots and wildlife.

The Kootenai River is popular with rafters and canoeists. The Canoe Gulch Ranger Station on Highway 37 is a good put-in spot, and boats can be taken out in town just below the California Avenue Bridge. The trip is a little too challenging for inexperienced river runners, and it's important to remember that Kootenai Falls, five miles downstream from Libby, are not passable.

There are large rainbow trout living below Libby Dam (a 33-pound trout was caught here), but those who fish this part of the Kootenai River should pay close attention to the water level; release of water from the dam can cause quick rises. Fishing is best when the water level drops. For water-release schedules, call **Libby Dam's River Discharge Information** (406/293-3421). **Kootenai Anglers** (13546 N. Hwy. 37, 406/293-7578, www.montana-flyfishing.com) is the local fly shop and guide service.

Stone Hill, near Lake Koocanusa on Highway 37, is a very popular rock-climbing area, especially in the spring. More than 200 routes are accessible from the roadside near the Libby Dam visitors center.

The downhill ski area at 5,952-foot **Turner Mountain** (406/293-4317, www.skiturner.com, Fri.-Sun. and holidays, $37 adult, $30 over age 61, college student, or military with ID, $25 teen, $20 ages 7-12), 22 miles up Pipe Creek Road from Libby, has a 2,100-foot vertical drop on trails that are generally ungroomed and mostly for expert skiers (60

percent are black diamond runs) and one double chairlift.

There are groomed **cross-country ski trails** at **Bear Creek** (go seven miles south of Libby on Hwy. 2, then right onto Bear Creek Rd. 278 for about 2.5 miles) and **Flatiron Mountain** (22 miles out Pipe Creek Rd. to Rainbow Lake Rd.). Few of the logging roads around Libby are plowed in the winter. Stop by the ranger station to find out which roads have been set aside for skiers. Snowmobilers should check with the Forest Service to see which roads are designated for snowmobile use.

Events

Logger Days (406/293-8585, www.loggerdays.org) are held in late June every year. Libby's **Nordicfest** (406/293-6430, www.libbynordicfest.org), held the second weekend of September, features Scandinavian food, crafts, music, and dancing.

Accommodations and Camping

A host of inexpensive motels line Highway 2 in Libby. **Venture Motor Inn** (443 Hwy. 2 W., 406/293-7711 or 800/221-0166, www.venture-innlibby.com, $107) is the nicest place to stay in town. It has a heated pool, hot tub, and restaurant, and just out back is Fireman's Park, a good place for a morning walk. Another good bet is the **Sandman Motel** (688 Hwy. 2 W., 406/293-8831, www.sandmanmotel.us, $55), set back off the road just a bit. It has an outdoor hot tub and some rooms with microwaves and refrigerators. Pets are permitted at all of these motels.

There's no pool at the **Caboose Motel** (714 W. 9th St., 406/293-6201 or 800/627-0206, www.mtwilderness.com, $65) but everything else you might need.

Camp in **Fireman's Park** ($10), behind the Libby Chamber of Commerce building. It's a bit too much in the thick of things for tent camping, and there are no hookups, but the convenience and the price are enticing. There are several public campgrounds on Lake Koocanusa, not far from town.

Food

Expect hearty American food from Libby's restaurants, and you won't be disappointed. For breakfast be sure to stop by **The Last Straw Cafe** (30890 Hwy. 2 W., 406/293-4000, 8am-4pm Tues.-Fri., 8am-2pm Sun.-Mon., $3-10), where breakfast specials might include a pork chop and the soups are good. The Last Straw is open occasionally for special dinners featuring ethnic cuisine.

The **Red Dog Saloon and Pizza** (406/293-8347, 3pm-11pm daily, pizza $12-18) is seven miles up Pipe Creek Road from Libby, on the way to Turner Mountain. It's a little ways off the main drag, but haven't you been craving some really good pizza? It's a friendly local hangout for both food and drinks.

Information and Services

Visitor information is proffered on Highway 2 near the Venture Inn at the **Libby Chamber of Commerce** (406/293-4167, www.libby-chamber.org) or the **Kootenai National Forest Headquarters** (1101 Hwy. 2 W., 406/293-6211). Another ranger station is at **Canoe Gulch,** 13 miles north of Libby on Highway 37, near Libby Dam.

Saint John's Lutheran Hospital is at 350 Louisiana Avenue (406/293-0100).

Getting There and Around

Amtrak (100 Mineral Ave., 800/872-7245) stops ever so briefly in Libby; the eastbound train comes through at 2:30am, the westbound at midnight, and the station is generally unstaffed.

LAKE KOOCANUSA

Ninety-mile-long Lake Koocanusa, framed by the Purcell and Salish Mountains, was formed in 1972 when the Libby Dam backed up the Kootenai River from just above Libby all the way north into Canada.

Libby Dam now provides hydroelectric power to much of the Northwest and stores water in Lake Koocanusa to prevent flooding downstream. Water is released from the dam to supply the 17 dams downstream on the Columbia River. The dam is a straight-axis, concrete gravity dam: It holds back Lake Koocanusa by its own weight. The Libby Dam has an attractive **visitors center** (406/293-5577, 9:30am-6pm June-Sept.), 17 miles north of Libby; free guided tours (10am, noon, 2pm, and 4pm Memorial Day-Labor Day, bring

Montana's highest and longest bridge spans Lake Koocanusa near Rexford.

ID) of the dam and powerhouse are offered. There's also a boat launch and picnic area.

Paved roads circle a good portion of Lake Koocanusa. Highway 37 runs along the east side; Forest Service Road 228 follows the western shore. Cross the lake on Montana's highest and longest bridge, just south of Rexford.

The name Koocanusa, derived from Kootenai, Canada, and USA, was coined by a resident of Rexford, a town largely flooded by the lake. Part of the town simply picked up and moved to higher ground, a grand tradition among dam-flooded sites.

Recreation

There is good fishing around Libby Dam, most notably for kokanee salmon. **Bald eagles** are onto this one too and can be spotted here in the fall, swooping down for spawning kokanee. Late October through mid-November is the peak season for eagle viewing. Arrive early in the morning and you may see 40 or 50 eagles just downstream from the dam.

Just up the road from the visitors center is a trail (approximately two miles) to **Alexander Mountain,** continuing on 1.5 miles to **Fleetwood Point.** The short trail to **Little North Falls** (off Road 228) is wheelchair accessible.

Camping

Campsites are abundant around Lake Koocanusa—there are over 40 campgrounds (www.fs.usda.gov/kootenai). On the west side, six miles above Libby Dam, is **McGillivray,** a large Forest Service campground and recreation area ($10). There's a boat launch and a swimming area on the lake at McGillivray, but they can only be used when the lake is filled with water, generally any time after early July. If McGillivray is too crowded, check the sign at the entrance for smaller and less developed campgrounds in the area. It's possible to reserve a campsite in advance at **Rexford Beach Campground** (800/280-2267, www.reserveusa.com, $9).

Information

The **Canoe Gulch Ranger Station** (Hwy. 37 just south of junction with Rd. 228, 406/293-7773 or 406/293-5758 for a recording) has information on recreation around Lake Koocanusa.

EUREKA

Eureka (pop. 1,100, elev. 2,577 feet) is located on the Tobacco River, so named because that was a crop grown by the area's Kootenai people (though some sources contend that missionaries attempted to grow tobacco here and that the name comes from their failed efforts). It's a scenically dramatic spot, with the Rocky Mountains rising to 9,000 feet directly behind the town. The Canadian border is just 7 miles north; the **port of Roosville** (406/889-3865) is open 24 hours daily.

The Tobacco Valley, Plains, and the Paradise Valley all claim the title of "banana belt of Montana." Farming supplements timber around Eureka; in fact, coming in from the big timber country to the west, Eureka looks strikingly agricultural.

Sights

Downtown Eureka, though not large or flashy, is quite appealing, with a core of vintage buildings now transformed into shops and cafés. It's easy to while away an hour or two exploring Dewey Avenue (the main street) or strolling along the two-mile Riverwalk.

Eureka doesn't just have the standard small-town historical museum; rather it has the full-blown **Tobacco Valley Historical Village** near the south end of downtown (4 Dewey Ave., 406/297-7654, 1pm-5pm daily Memorial Day-Labor Day). Most of the buildings there were salvaged from the original town of Rexford (now drowned by Lake Koocanusa). The old Rexford general store now houses a museum, which boasts, among the old books and papers, an ancient permanent-wave machine for hair. Another oddity here is larch balls, which form when larch trees drop their needles into a stream and the currents and eddies form the needles into a ball.

Murphy Lake, 14 miles southeast of Eureka on Highway 93, is home to a loon population as well as a host of other animals, including horned grebes, bald eagles, herons, ospreys, white-tailed and mule deer, and beavers. Be sure to respect the privacy of nesting loons, which are protected during nesting season by boating restrictions on the southern end of the lake.

Recreation

Ten Lakes Scenic Area is adjacent to the Canadian border near Eureka and has been nominated for wilderness-area designation. To reach the Ten Lakes area, turn off Highway 93 at Grave Creek (about 10 miles south of Eureka) and follow the road for 30 miles, almost to its end. Several hiking trails start at the end of the road (just beyond Little Therriault Lake) and lead to many of the lakes in the area.

Paradise and Bluebird Lakes are the closest, about two miles in, with an elevation gain of about 1,000 feet. A pamphlet with a rough trail map is available at the Murphy Lake Ranger Station south of Eureka. Pick up a map of the Kootenai National Forest for clearer detail.

In the winter, Grave Creek Road and several spur roads are groomed for cross-country skiing and snowmobiling. To access 4.5 miles of easy snowmobile-free cross-country skiing, park at the **Birch Creek Recreation Area** adjacent to the Murphy Lake Ranger Station.

Golf at the **Wilderness Club** (1885 Sophie Lake Rd., 406/889-6501, www.thewilderness-club.com, $60-110 for 18 holes). The resort also has accommodations in upscale cabins ($190-250) with stay-and-play specials.

Accommodations

On the north edge of town, **Ksanka Inn** (Hwy. 93 and Hwy. 37, 406/296-3127, www.ksankainn.com, $68) has a convenience store and a Subway restaurant as well as a motel.

For attractive log cabin accommodations, **Riverstone Family Lodge** (6370 Hwy. 93 N., 866/345-0026, www.riverstonefamily-lodge.com, $109-159) offers recently built duplex cabins in a pretty setting about five miles north of town.

Camping

North of Eureka, the Ten Lakes Scenic Area has two campgrounds, **Big Therriault Lake** and **Little Therriault Lake** (www.fs.usda.gov/kootenai, $5). To the south, camp at **Murphy Lake** ($7).

Food

Heaven's Peak (355 Hwy. 93 N., 406/297-3504, 8:30am-7pm Mon.-Sat., 10am-6pm Sun.) is a friendly natural foods store. Stop in at the very popular **Cafe Jax** (207 Dewey Ave., 406/297-9084, 7am-3pm Mon.-Sat., 8am-3pm Sun., $6-10) for a hearty breakfast or a milk shake. A popular bar and restaurant is **Trappers Saloon** (6040 Hwy. 93 N., 406/889-3400, 11am-2am daily, $6-17) with burgers, steaks, and cold brews just north of town.

Information and Services

The **Eureka Ranger Station** (949 Hwy. 93, 406/296-7188, 7:30am-4:30pm Mon.-Sat.) is on the north edge of town. There's also a ranger station south of Eureka at **Murphy Lake** (406/882-4835, 7:30am-4:30pm Mon.-Sat.).

Glacier National Park

Highlights

Road, and if you ride the park shuttle, you'll really get to ogle the details of the marvelously engineered road through a showcase of geology. Plus the road gives you access to great hiking trails (page 125).

★ **Logan Pass:** Take the park shuttle bus to this pass, the high point of the Going-to-the-Sun Road, and avoid the parking nightmare. Drop by the visitors center here, join a naturalist hike, and enjoy the alpine scenery (page 131).

★ **Highline Trail:** After a visit to Logan Pass, spend a few hours on this trail, with its above-the-timberline views and chattering marmots. Go as far as you'd like, then turn around and return the way you came. If you walk far enough, you can hook up with other trails and construct a fine backpacking trip (page 132).

★ **Glacier Park Lodge:** Like all the park's lodges, Glacier Park Lodge has a spectacular lobby, and it's not necessary to book a room here in order to visit and enjoy the architecture (page 136).

★ **Grinnell Glacier Overlook:** Quick! See a glacier while you still have a chance. Take a day hike from Many Glacier to reach Grinnell Glacier (page 141).

★ **Upper Waterton Lake:** Don't neglect a visit to Waterton Lakes National Park in Canada, just north of the border. Take a boat ride on Upper Waterton Lake to reach prime hiking trails. It's also okay just to ride the boat and never hike a step (page 144).

★ **Cross-Country Skiing Around the Izaak Walton Inn:** The Izaak Walton Inn is a great spot any time of year, but it's especially magical as a wintertime base for cross-country skiing (page 117).

★ **Going-to-the-Sun Road:** It's hard to visit Glacier without traveling the Going-to-the-Sun

G lacier National Park contains more than 1,500 square miles of extraordinarily scenic wilderness. Towering glacier-pocked summits bend over mirrorlike lakes. Wildlife, including bears, mountain goats, moose, and ptarmigans,

inhabits the park's thick forests, streamsides, and rocky promontories. Easily one of the most spectacular drives in the country is Going-to-the-Sun Road, which climbs from lakes and forest up the face of the Rockies to a fragile alpine meadow almost 7,000 feet above sea level.

Glacier is a park for the outdoor-minded; as much as possible, you'll want to leave the car behind. More than 700 miles of hiking trails link backcountry peaks and lakes. In winter the park's roads double as cross-country ski trails.

You'll have to do some hiking to stand on a glacier. There are now only 25 in the park, down from about 150 in 1850 and 50 in 1968. Go now; these glaciers are shrinking rapidly and projected to be gone within the next few decades.untain

Sometimes called the "Crown of the Continent" for their staggeringly rugged skyline, Glacier and its Canadian cousin Waterton Lakes National Park form one of the crown jewels of the national park system.

PLANNING YOUR TIME

It takes several days even to begin to skim the surface of Glacier National Park, but in reality many people have only a day to spend here. If that's the case, structure yours around a drive or shuttle ride on the spectacular **Going-to-the-Sun Road,** but be sure to get out of the car for at least one hike (if you stop at Logan Pass, you can hike in an alpine meadow or take a jaunt on the Highline Trail) and to visit the Lake McDonald Lodge.

With a few more days to play around here, you can explore the several distinctive areas of the park: the isolation and big lakes up the North Fork; the forests around Lake McDonald; the comparative spareness of the east side; the incredible closeness of the mountains, the glaciers, and—sometimes—the bears at Many Glacier; and the distinctly

---

Previous: Many Glacier Hotel, on the shore of Swiftcurrent Lake; mountain goats grazing at Logan Pass.
Above: Lake McDonald.

Glacier National Park

BLACKTAIL

Whitefish Lake

BIG MOUNTAIN

Whitefish Range

Kalispell

Whitefish River

Whitefish

Lakeside

Somers

Flathead River

Columbia Falls

Big Creek

Camas Rd

Flathead Lake

Bigfork

Hungry Horse

Apgar

West Glacier

Lake McDonald

Fish Creek

North Fork Rd

Big Creek

Lake McDonald

Going-to-the-Sun Road

Flathead National Forest

Hungry Horse Reservoir

Swan Range

Mt Jackson 10,052ft

Lewis Range

Mt Logan 9,239ft

Continental

Triple Divide Peak

Cross-Country Skiing Around the Izaak Walton Inn

Essex

Middle Fork Flathead River

Glacier National Park

Mt Stimson 10,142ft

Flathead Range

Divide

Elk Mountain

Two Medicine Lake

Rising Wolf Mountain

Cut Bank

Devil Creek

Two Medicine

Great Bear

Wilderness

Marias Pass

Lower Two Medicine Lake

Glacier Park Lodge

East Glacier

Lewis and Clark National Forest

0
5 km
0
5 mi

© AVALON TRAVEL

Canadian flavor of Waterton Lakes. Add another day or two and head along the southern edge of the park for a visit to the Izaak Walton Inn in Essex. In fact, if you choose to make a winter pilgrimage to Glacier, the Izaak Walton makes a cozy base for several days of cross-country skiing in and around the park.

Longer visits almost invariably mean more hiking, perhaps including a backpacking trip. Visitors who plan far in advance (or those lucky last-minute few) may be able to arrange a stay in one of Glacier's backcountry chalets.

Entrance Points

The two main park entrances are at Apgar (near West Glacier) on the western edge, and St. Mary on the east. These points are linked by Going-to-the-Sun Road. On the western edge north of Apgar is the Polebridge entrance, which provides access to Bowman Lake and trails in the park's remote northwestern corner.

Other entrances on the eastern edge of the park, Two Medicine and Many Glacier, have roads that dip just a short way into the park. Highways 49 and 89 form the main north-south road on the eastern edge of the park; about four miles north of the town of East Glacier, a short road leads from this highway in to Two Medicine Lake. The road to Many Glacier splits off Highway 89 at the town of Babb and travels nine miles to its terminus near the Swiftcurrent Motor Inn. Continue north on Highway 89 to cross the border into Canada and visit Waterton Lakes National Park.

ACCOMMODATIONS

The enormous lodges built by the Great Northern Railway still stand at East Glacier, Waterton, and Many Glacier, and they have become near trademarks for the park. These old lodges, along with the Swiss chalet-style Lake McDonald Lodge, are tremendously evocative and charming, but rooms aren't cheap, and for the money the amenities aren't great. That said, you simply must stay in at least one of these old landmarks. (But don't

try to bring a dog along; no pets are allowed in park lodgings.)

There are good campsites at each entry to the park and at lakeside recreation areas. Motels abound just outside the park boundaries, particularly near the west entrance.

In the backcountry, the Sperry and Granite Park Chalets are accessible only by trail and require reservations far in advance.

BACKCOUNTRY TRAVEL

Although most travelers stick to scenic drives and day hikes, Glacier's backcountry makes up over 95 percent of the park, and many visitors come back year after year to explore these remote trails. In fact, backcountry travel has increased in recent years, causing environmental impacts that have necessitated more regulations.

Prepare well for such an outing; you'll need a backcountry permit allowing you to camp at designated **backcountry campgrounds** (backcountry information line 406/888-7857 mid-Mar.-Oct., $5 per person per night, $2.50 youth 8-15, plus $30 per trip reservation fee, reservations accepted starting Apr. 16). During the initial planning stages of a backpacking trip, be sure to visit the park website. Here you'll find a backcountry application and detailed strategies for getting a permit for your ideal trip, a map detailing all backcountry campgrounds and noting which sites can be reserved, and lots of good information about backcountry safety.

Although waiting until you're at the park to get a permit will save you the $30 reservation fee, it may severely limit your choices of where you can camp. Backcountry permits are available at the following locations:

- **Apgar Backcountry Permit Center** (daily May-Oct.; during off-season, permits are available at Park Headquarters on weekdays and at the Apgar Visitor Center on weekends)

- **St. Mary Visitor Center** (daily late May-mid-Sept.)

- **Many Glacier and Two Medicine**

Glacier's Plants and Animals

mountain goats near Logan Pass

Glacier National Park rises from a high-plains ecosystem on the east to alpine tundra along the Continental Divide and back down to Pacific forests, all within 25 miles. It's an amazingly concentrated venue for viewing many of Montana's wide-ranging animals and plants.

PLANTS

Plants, more than animals, reflect the quick-changing and numerous ecosystems in the park. Skirting Lake McDonald and other westside lakes are forests of red cedar, Douglas fir, and hemlock. Watch for skunk cabbages and bracken ferns in marshy lowlands. Farther up mountain slopes are extensive stands of lodgepole and deciduous cone-bearing larch, indicating an ongoing history of forest fires.

Along the Continental Divide are expanses of alpine tundra. The midsummer wildflower display, including lemon-yellow glacier lilies, dark blue gentians, pink heathers, and the greenish white spires of bear grass, is spectacular. Examine rocky outcrops for colorful lichens.

The east side of the park is much drier, with aspen commingling with the dominating conifers. Wildflowers include red and white geraniums, Indian paintbrush, gaillardia, and pasqueflowers.

ANIMALS

Grizzly bears are the most talked-about animal in the park, but they are much less numerous than the smaller black bears. Both species deserve respect. Recognize grizzly bears by the huge shoulder muscles, which form a substantial hump just behind the neck. Generally a mottled brown color, grizzlies also have a dish-shaped face. Black bears aren't always black but are often brown or cinnamon-colored. At 200 pounds, they are one-third the size of their grizzly brethren.

Mountain goats haunt the peaks and escarpments of Glacier Park. Near Logan Pass, they gather at natural salt licks in the cliffs above the road. Bighorn sheep, a few wolves, white-tailed deer, and moose are other large residents. Near streams, watch for beavers and river otters. Hoary marmots frequent hiking trails, and ground squirrels nose into pant legs and lunch bags at every picnic area.

Ospreys and bald eagles are the park's principal birds of prey. Watch for water ouzels, or "dippers," near streams; they're not drowning themselves, but diving and bouncing around underwater looking for food. A hatch of ptarmigans sauntering across the road often brings traffic to a halt.

Ranger Stations (daily late May-mid-Sept.)

• **Polebridge Ranger Station** (daily early June-mid-Sept.)

• **Waterton Lakes National Park Visitor Reception Centre** (daily early June-mid-Sept., payment by credit card only—no cash). Waterton staff are only authorized to issue trips that start at Chief Mountain or Goat Haunt.

Most hikers visit the backcountry in July and August; depending on the amount of snowfall the previous winter, even early July hikers can expect to encounter snow on the trails or dangerous high-water stream crossings.

A guide service, **Glacier Guides** (406/387-5555 or 800/521-7238, www.glacierguides.com), is permitted to lead trips in Glacier's backcountry.

INFORMATION

Glacier National Park (406/888-7800, www.nps.gov/glac, 7-day pass $30 per vehicle, $20 winter, $25 for motorcyclists, $15 winter, $15 for hikers and bikers, $10 winter, $60 annual pass for Glacier, $80 Interagency Annual Pass good for most federal recreation sites) is open daily year-round, but most park services only operate from late May through September. There is a separate fee for Canada's **Waterton Lakes National Park** (403/859-5133, www.pc.gc.ca/pn-np/ab/waterton, C$7.80 per day adult, C$6.80 senior, C$3.90 youth 6-16, C$19.60 family).

The park service distributes a free *Vacation Planner* at the park gates and neighboring tourist centers; it's also posted on the park's website. It contains a good overview of current information on rates, programs, recreation, and services.

Three different companies operate the lodging within the park. For reservations at Lake McDonald Lodge, the Many Glacier Hotel, Rising Sun Motor Inn, Swiftcurrent Motor Inn, and the Village Inn at Apgar, contact **Glacier National Park Lodges/**

Xanterra (303/297-3175 or 855/733-4522, www.glaciernationalparklodges.com). **Glacier Park Inc.** (406/892-2525,www.glacierparkinc.com) operates Glacier Park Lodge in East Glacier and the Prince of Wales Hotel in Waterton as well as a few other lodgings in and around the park. Sperry and Granite Park Chalets are operated by **Belton Chalets** (888/345-2649, www.sperrychalet.com, www.graniteparkchalet.com).

Classes

The **Glacier Institute** (406/755-1211, www.glacierinstitute.org) offers workshops focusing on many aspects of natural history as well as outdoor skills, including fly-fishing, photography, and journaling.

For spur-of-the-moment education about the park, take a hike with a ranger: Several hikes of varying intensity are offered daily in each area of the park during the summer.

GETTING THERE

Kalispell offers the closest airline service to the park. **Amtrak's** *Empire Builder* (800/872-7245, www.amtrak.com) provides train service, with daily stops at East Glacier (summer only), Belton (West Glacier), and Essex, on Highway 2 near the southern tip of the park.

Intercity bus lines can get you as close as Whitefish on the west and Great Falls to the east.

From Kalispell, you can also arrange a shuttle to the park by contacting **Airport Shuttle Service** (406/752-2842) or **Glacier Taxi** (406/250-3603) or **Wild Horse Limousine** (406/756-2290 or 800/841-2391, www.wildhorselimo.com, $165 to Apgar; transport to other park destinations is available). Rental cars are available in Kalispell, Whitefish, and Great Falls.

GETTING AROUND

The highest reaches of the spectacular road through the park, the Going-to-the-Sun Road, are closed by snow during the winter months, and spring and fall are devoted to road repair.

The road is generally open from mid-June to late September. Be sure to gas up before entering the park; there are no gas stations in the park. Highway 2, which skirts the southern border of the park, is open year-round, as is the Outside North Fork Road leading to Polebridge.

Park Shuttle

The park operates a free shuttle bus along the Going-to-the-Sun Road (buses every 30-60 minutes 7am-7pm July 1-early Sept.). Although you are still allowed to drive along the road, be aware that parking is often tight at trailheads, especially at Logan Pass, making the shuttle a great option if you're out for sightseeing or hiking. Buses run from hubs at the Apgar and St. Mary Visitor Centers up to Logan Pass.

Until 2017, Going-to-the-Sun Road will be the site of extensive and ongoing road repairs (it's a high-elevation road built during the era of Model T Fords, and it needs lots of attention). The shuttle is a way to avoid some of the construction hassle as well as the environmental impact of heavy auto traffic.

Commercial Van Tours

The park's 1930s-era red rolltop buses, operated by Xanterra, take visitors on tours of the park with stops at all of Glacier's lodges and inns. In nice weather the canvas tops roll back to create a sort of convertible. A variety of **tours** (303/297-2757 or 855/733-4522, www.glaciernationalparklodges.com, $30-90 adult depending on duration and distance) are offered. These buses are favorites of many longtime parkgoers, and drivers usually provide lively commentary.

Glacier Park Inc. runs van shuttles on the park's east side, connecting the St. Mary Lodge (or, by special request, the St. Mary Visitor Center, with access to the free Going-to-the-Sun Road shuttle) with Many Glacier, Two Medicine, East Glacier, and Waterton. These are not free—it's $15 from Many Glacier to St. Mary.

Xanterra operates similar shuttles; one is between the St. Mary Visitor Center and Many Glacier ($10), and the other runs from the West Glacier train station to Lake McDonald Lodge ($5).

From East Glacier, **Sun Tours** (406/226-9220 or 800/786-9220, www.glaciersuntours.com, $35-75) offers interpretive tours of the park from a Native American perspective. Tours highlight Blackfeet culture and history and how they relate to the park's natural features.

Vehicle Restrictions

Because Going-to-the-Sun Road is narrow and tortuous by modern standards, there is a limit on the size of vehicles allowed between Avalanche Campground on the western side of the Continental Divide and Sun Point to the east. All vehicles (including towed campers) must measure less than 21 feet in length and less than 8 feet in width (including mirrors). Vehicles taller than 10 feet may have trouble traveling westbound from Logan Pass to the Loop because of rock overhangs.

Bicycles are not allowed on Going-to-the-Sun Road between Apgar and Sprague Creek Campgrounds from 11am to 4pm between June 15 and Labor Day. During these same hours, bikes are prohibited from the eastbound (uphill) lane between Logan Creek and Logan Pass. Contact the National Park Service for other cycling restrictions.

Boating

All boats brought into the park are required to have permits ($10 for 7-day motorized permit, $40 for annual motorized permit, free for non-motorized boats), which are issued after park staff check for invasive species. Permits are available at park headquarters in West Glacier, at the St. Mary Visitor Center, and at ranger stations in Many Glacier and Two Medicine.

PETS

Although pets are permitted on leashes in park campgrounds and parking areas, they are not allowed on the trails, in the backcountry, or in any park buildings. They must not be left unattended.

West Glacier and the Flathead River Middle Fork

The Middle Fork of the Flathead River runs out of the Bob Marshall and Great Bear Wilderness Areas and along the southwest border of the park to West Glacier. Along the edge of the park, the tiny town of **Essex** is home to a classic old hotel.

SIGHTS

Splurge on a **helicopter ride** over the park. **Glacier Helitours** (12205 Hwy. 2 E., West Glacier, 406/387-4141, www.glacierhelitours. net), across the highway from the Vista Motel, is a reliable operator. Both half-hour and one-hour tours are offered, and prices depend on the number of people taking the flight (with a maximum of six per flight). For two, a half-hour flight is $250 per person; for six, the price drops to $125 per person.

Head about 35 miles southeast on Highway 2 to visit the **goat lick,** a mineral-laden cliff that provides goats with salt. A parking area near milepost 182 vents onto a short trail to the overlook. Spring is the big mineral-licking season; evenings in early June are certain to keep visitors entranced with billy, nanny, and kid goats. Binoculars help.

The relatively gentle **Marias Pass** marks the Continental Divide on Highway 2, between Essex and East Glacier. Salish tribes living west of the Continental Divide traditionally traveled over this pass on yearly trips to hunt buffalo. After the Blackfeet moved to prairies east of the park in the late 1700s, they consolidated their hold over the entire area; Marias Pass became the scene of bloody battles when Salish hunting parties encountered Blackfeet warriors.

When James J. Hill was planning the route

Moose News

There's never any doubt when you've seen a moose. With its big rack, its long legs, and its sheer size, the moose is one of North America's most distinctive animals. No matter how comical it may look, nor how much it makes you think of Bullwinkle, a moose, which stands about six feet high at the shoulder and weighs about a thousand pounds, is not to be taken lightly.

The word *moose* comes from the animal's Algonquian name, which means "twig-eater." And that's what you'll usually see them doing, because it takes a big bundle of twigs to satisfy a moose's hunger. During the summer they more often browse for food underwater and can be seen standing in marshes or shallow lakes, dipping their faces in and out of the water. You may also see a moose taking a swim across a lake. Curiously, moose do not have teeth in the front of their upper jaw; they use their thick sturdy tongues and lips to pull the leaves from a branch, then crush the food with their six pairs each of premolars and molars.

Because of the way a moose's eyes are set toward the sides of its head, the animal has a rather large blind spot to its front. This is most likely why it has the reputation of being nearsighted. Its eyes move independently (one can roll forward while the other goes back) . . . go ahead, try doing that yourself!

Only male moose have antlers. Also, bull moose have light brown hair above the eyes and black faces, while a cow moose's face is uniformly light brown.

Moose live across western Montana and are commonly seen in the North Fork area of Glacier National Park and just outside of West Yellowstone.

No matter how adorable or goofy a moose looks, remember that it's a wild animal, and a very large wild animal at that. They have the reputation of being fearless and unpredictable. Males can be particularly aggressive, and females are very protective of their young.

of the Great Northern Railway, he heard rumors of a "lost" pass over the Continental Divide. In the winter of 1889, railroad surveyor John J. Stevens found Marias Pass and deemed it navigable by rail.

RECREATION
Hiking
Most of the hikes in this part of Glacier are long backpacking trips on little-used trails into wild country. Animals, including bears, abound in these woods and stream bottoms. Glacier National Park maps show trails along every creek. Those planning to hike in the area should seek up-to-date trail information and permits, which are required for overnight hikes, from the backcountry permit station at Apgar.

A couple of shorter hikes originate at the unstaffed Walton Ranger Station, near Essex. Hike to **Ole Creek** and follow the trail as far as you like. The same trailhead provides access to the **Scalplock Lookout,** four unrelentingly steep miles to great views.

Leave the highway about two miles east of the goat lick to find a trail into the Great Bear Wilderness Area.

Rafting
Several white-water companies are based in West Glacier. Float trips on the Middle Fork of the Flathead account for most of their scheduled outings, though arrangements can be made to float the South Fork (in the Bob Marshall Wilderness Area) or the North Fork (in the northwest corner of the park). Half-day and full-day trips along the lower stretch of the Middle Fork are good family floats, with great scenery and some white water. The river's upper stretch is a wild four- to six-day trip (around $175-200 per person per day for a guided fully outfitted adventure).

Glacier Raft Co. (406/888-5454 or 800/235-6781, www.glacierraftco.com) gets good recommendations from local folks. It and other operators such as **Glacier Guides** (406/387-5555 or 800/521-7238, www.glacierguides.com); **Great Northern Resort**

(406/387-5340 or 800/735- 7897, www.greatnorthernresort.com); **Wild River Adventures** (406/387-9453, www.riverwild.com) offer similar trips and prices. Daylong floats run $89-125; half days are $52-80. Each of these companies will provide longer trips, with the option of adding hikes and horseback rides to the river run.

The Middle Fork is a Wild and Scenic River, and this official designation is particularly apt in its upper reaches in the Bob Marshall and Great Bear Wilderness Areas. It's possible to fly in to float this wilderness river; the Schaefer Meadows airstrip is near the river in the Bob Marshall.

The wilderness stretches of the river are not easy, and they can be dangerous for novices. Even the lower reaches are better floated in a raft or kayak than a canoe, and anyone with questionable skills should sign on with an outfitter. Early summer is the best time to float the Middle Fork; water levels are high, but not at flood stage, and some of the chill has gone out of the air.

Fishing
The stretch of the Middle Fork of the Flathead paralleling Highway 2 isn't a particularly noteworthy fishing stream, but its upper reaches in the Great Bear Wilderness are loaded with trout. These aren't official fishing waters of the national park, so a Montana fishing license is required. The raft companies serve double duty as fishing guides.

Golfing
Glacier View Golf Club (406/888-5471, $32) is just north of Highway 2 at West Glacier. It's a public 18-hole course looking onto the mountains.

★ Cross-Country Skiing Around the Izaak Walton Inn
More than 20 miles of beautifully groomed cross-country ski trails surround the **Izaak Walton Inn in Essex** ($10 adults, $5 children 12 and under, free to hotel guests), and though most of them are geared toward novice

or intermediate skiers, a few runs are studded with face-plant opportunities, even for good skiers. If there's fresh powder, leave the trails for a while and practice making graceful turns down the sides of Dickey Bowl. (It's right behind the trail system.) Most trails are also okay for snowshoers.

It's worth venturing away from the inn's trail system into Glacier National Park for at least one day of skiing there. Head to Marias Pass for excellent skiing at the Continental Divide; it's as gentle as a major pass can be, with terrain suitable for beginners and intermediates. Skiers who'd rather not go it alone can sign up at the Izaak Walton for a guided tour. Après-ski at the Izaak Walton means a visit to the inn's sauna, then hanging out in the lobby to watch the trains go by. There's usually enough snow for skiing from Thanksgiving through mid-April.

ACCOMMODATIONS

Most of the motels around West Glacier are small, family-run places. It's no surprise that they fill up quickly during the summer. The lodgings in Apgar Village, at the park's west entrance, are just a couple of miles from West Glacier.

$50-100

West Glacier Motel and Cabins (200 Going-to-the-Sun Rd., 406/888-5662, www. westglacier.com, rooms $90-114, cabins $196-279) is just off Highway 2 in the cluster of businesses near the park entrance. Its woodsy location on the Flathead River provides easy access to fishing and float trips. Rooms have a budget ambience, if not price.

Several of the RV resorts in the area have accommodations in cabins or yurts; see the *Camping* section.

Over $100

The Swiss-style ★ **Belton Chalet** (406/888-5000 or 888/235-8665, www.beltonchalet. com, $160-350) was built in 1910 when the park opened, closed for years, and renovated and reopened in 2000. The rooms still have an old-fashioned charm, which means no TVs or phones; one modern touch is the addition of spa services, quite nice after a night on the train or a day of hiking. It's also home to the best restaurant in the area. A three-bedroom cottage ($325) or a lovely two-bedroom adobe house ($350) is great for larger groups. This is where early park visitors debarked from the train, and Amtrak still stops here daily.

The Belton Chalet, just outside the park entrance in West Glacier, has the area's best food and lodging.

During the winter season, from early October to late May, only cottage and adobe house rentals are available ($105-250).

The view from the **Vista Motel** (12340 U.S. Hwy. 2 E., 406/888-5311 or 800/837-7101, www.glaciervistamotel.com, mid-May- Sept., $100-165) is grand. Perched on a bluff overlooking Highway 2 and the peaks of Glacier, this is a hard one to miss on the drive in from Kalispell. The view *is* the best thing about this place (the Vista is showing its now-considerable age), and that, plus convenience, friendliness, and a heated pool, makes it a good bet.

The **Great Northern Resort** (406/387-5340 or 800/735-7897, www.greatnorthernresort.com, May-mid-Oct., $295-415) offers several chalet-style cabins, each containing a kitchenette, fireplace, and barbecue and one to three bedrooms. The owners also operate a white-water raft outfitting service and can arrange horseback riding and fishing trips. During spring and fall, rates drop to as low as $99; in peak summer season a three-night stay is required.

Also run by an outfitting company, the newly built, ecofriendly **Glacier Guides Lodge** (120 Highline Blvd., West Glacier, 406/387-5555 or 800/521-7238, May-mid-Oct.,

$193) is in a quiet spot near the park entrance. Pets are allowed in some rooms with advance notice.

Thirty miles southeast of West Glacier in the tiny town of Essex, the ★ **Izaak Walton Inn** (406/888-5700, www.izaakwaltoninn.com, lodge rooms $159-259, cabins $189-239, train cars $249-259) is a Montana classic. The hotel was built by the Great Northern in 1939 to house railroad workers. (Essex was, and still is, an important railroad post; it's where extra engines are added to help trains over Marias Pass.) It's now popular with railroad buffs and cross-country skiers.

Amtrak's *Empire Builder* stops a stone's throw from the half-timbered hotel, and groomed ski trails run for miles. In summer the lodge is occupied by park visitors, hikers, anglers (this isn't called the Izaak Walton for nothing), and mountain bikers. Even if you don't have time or the inclination to head into the wilderness, the Izaak Walton has atmosphere to spare. Rooms in the lodge during high season (June 16-Sept. 15 and Dec. 16-March 31) are fairly rustic, but all have private baths. The Izaak Walton has also renovated some cabooses and a locomotive as one-of-a-kind lodgings. The cabooses sleep four and

The Izaak Walton Inn is a vintage railroad workers' hotel.

have kitchenettes (which can save you some money on restaurant meals if you're willing to schlep groceries to Essex). Cabins offer another alternative to groups. Don't expect a luxury hotel; none of the rooms have TVs, radios, or telephones; cell service is basically nonexistent; and caboose guests must be able to squeeze around some tight spots and climb into bunks. (Be sure to ask about the cancellation policy; it's extremely strict.) If you arrive via Amtrak, the Izaak Walton also has cars for rent. Most guests eat at the lodge restaurant.

Camping

All of West Glacier's campgrounds are private RV enterprises. You can find a Forest Service campground, **Big Creek** (406/387-3800, www.fs.usda.gov/flathead, $13), about 20 miles northwest of town, at the north end of Camas Creek Road. There are also many campsites in Glacier Park itself, though these fill up quickly during the summer.

Lake Five Resort (540 Belton Stage Rd., 406/387-5601, www.lakefiveresort.com, RV site $50-55, tepees $63, cabins $83-253) is a little way north of Highway 2. It's a pleasant Montana-style lakeside resort complete with cabins, boat rentals, and lake swimming. The season runs mid-May through mid-September.

North American RV Park and Campground (10640 Hwy. 2 E., 406/387-5800 or 800/704-4266, www.northamerican-rvpark.com, mid-Apr.-mid-Sept., RV $44), between Coram and West Glacier, rents a few clean and cozy yurts ($40-50) and small camping cabins ($60); for both of these options, bring your own bedding and be prepared to trek to the bathhouse.

Tent campers and RVers alike find the **West Glacier KOA** (355 Half Moon Flats Rd., 406/387-5341 or 800/562-3313, www.westglacierkoa.com, tent $38, RV $55-90, cabin $90-395) to be handy (two miles west of the park entrance), well-equipped, and large. Even bigger and closer to the park, **Glacier**

Campground (12070 Hwy. 2 W., 406/387-5689, tent $25, RV $30-35, cabin $40-60) is noted for its evening barbecues and a generally high activity level on the sprawling forested campground. The season for both the KOA and Glacier Campground runs May through September.

FOOD

Stop in for a good meal in a lovely atmosphere at the Belton Chalet's ★ **Grill Dining Room** (406/888-5000, www.beltonchalet.com, 5pm-10pm daily mid-May-early Oct., 3pm-8pm Fri.-Sat. and 10am-2pm Sun. early Dec.-March, $21-36). Here you can dine on bacon-wrapped buffalo meat loaf. Lighter meals (that same tasty meat loaf, made into a sandwich, about $12) and a variety of microbrews are available from the adjoining **Belton Taproom.** Sit outside and order off either menu to enjoy the view of the Belton's gardens. Be prepared to wait at this popular restaurant (reservations taken for parties of six or more).

The food at the **Izaak Walton Inn** (406/888-5700, www.izaakwaltoninn.com, 7am-8pm daily, dinner $23-30) is satisfying after a day of cross-country skiing, with entrées such as herb-roasted pheasant with huckleberry compote. The dining room looks right out onto the tracks, and railroad workers mix with Essex neighbors, railroad buffs, and cross-country skiers in the dining room.

The setting of the **Backwoods Bistro** (10270 Hwy. 2 W., 406/250-9993, 8am-2pm Wed.-Sun., 5pm-9pm Fri.-Sat., June-early Sept., dinner $10-13), a campground pavilion, can't get much more casual, but it's worth stopping by for a weekend evening dinner of fried chicken or jambalaya. Brunch trends healthy; you can even get a breakfast salad!

GETTING THERE AND AROUND

Amtrak's *Empire Builder* (800/872-7245, www.amtrak.com) stops daily at West

Glacier's Belton Station (9:53pm westbound and 5:16am eastbound) and Essex Station (9:11pm westbound and 5:55am eastbound).

Car rentals are available at **Glacier Highland Resort** (406/863-1213), just across from the depot.

North Fork of the Flathead River

The northwestern border of Glacier National Park is formed by the North Fork of the Flathead River. Roads inside and outside the park run up the valley to the small settlement of Polebridge: the all-dirt inside road, open only in summer, is especially spectacular in a scary way. Since early in the park's history, the hamlet of **Polebridge** has been a quiet neighbor just outside Glacier's boundary. Many residents have fought development that would bring them fully into the tourist hubbub. There's no electricity running up the North Fork, which means dark nights and excellent stargazing, with a decent chance of seeing the Northern Lights.

Don't look for naturalist-led day hikes or bus tours of this northwest corner of Glacier; it's the park's least developed valley, although perhaps also its most threatened,

with tentative stabs at road building, logging, dams, mineral exploration, and general development in the non-national park areas of the North Fork. You'll see ample evidence of fire here, too; in 2003 fires in this area burned for three months and there's now a good picture of the succession of plant growth, with both scars and regrowth visible.

SIGHTS
McGee Meadow

Five miles up Camas Creek Road from Apgar, McGee Meadow is a marshy magnet for wildlife. Moose are particularly fond of such boggy areas and may be spotted by quiet evening visitors. The road here is relatively high and exposed, yielding good views of the park's mountains. To the west there are a couple of hiking trails from Camas Creek Road into

trail near McGee Meadow

the Apgar Mountains. Howe Ridge is to the east, and ridge runners must hike up from the Inside North Fork Road; the trail past shallow Howe Lake crosses moose and beaver habitat.

Bowman Lake

Bowman Lake is one of the park's prettiest and least visited. (There's a reason for this—it's at the end of a six-mile-long, rough, narrow dirt road.) Long and thin and surrounded by mountains, this is a good spot for photography and reflection. Hiking trails start at the Bowman Lake Campground and head seven miles along the lakeshore to the head of the lake (then up to Brown Pass and other trails), or up into the mountains that come right down to the lake. The Bowman Lake Campground is usually pretty uncrowded; RVs are not recommended, and it's important to follow bear-country precautions.

RECREATION
Hiking

A flat seven-mile trail edges Bowman Lake's northwest shore and is a good up-and-back walk for a family. Extend the trip by continuing past the lake on a relatively gentle creek-side climb to **Brown Pass.** (It's another seven miles between the backcountry campground at the head of Bowman Lake and the Brown Pass campground.) From the pass, hikers can cross the divide and continue east to Goat Haunt, on Waterton Lake, or take the high road back west to Kintla Lake.

Or try this variation: Start at **Kintla Lake,** hike 32 miles east to Goat Haunt, and then head south to a terminus at Logan Pass. Cut this trip shorter by taking the boat from Goat Haunt up to Waterton. The country between Upper Kintla Lake and Brown Pass is phenomenal, and one of the places a hiker is most likely to see black bears or grizzlies. The Hole-in-the-Wall Campground, one mile west of the Continental Divide along this trail, may be the park's finest and is certainly one of the remotest.

The six-mile trail to **Numa Lookout** starts at Bowman Lake campground and, after level lakeside stretch, climbs nearly 3,000 feet to the lookout. It's a good place to walk slowly with an eye out for wildlife and good views of Bowman Lake and the Livingston Range.

Bowman Lake

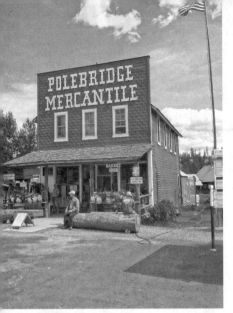

Polebridge Mercantile

Another long day hike or overnight trip starting at Bowman Lake is the 13-mile loop to **Quartz Lake**.

Fishing and Boating

Fish the lakes up the North Fork for magnificent scenery and an occasional cutthroat trout. Most anglers take to boats on Bowman Lake, which is open to motorboats with engines below 10 horsepower; no motorized boats are allowed in Kintla Lake. Both of these lakes are ideal for canoeing and flat-water kayaking—they're long, with miles of animal-sheltering shoreline to explore. Rent a canoe ($79), inflatable kayak ($59), or paddleboard ($39, and quite fun to paddle on the lakes) in Polebridge at **North Fork Recreation** (406/888-9853 summer, 406/253-3374 winter).

Cross-Country Skiing

The broad North Fork Valley is just as beautiful, and even more isolated, when it's covered with snow. Skiing is generally good here because cold temperatures keep the snow powdery. Two ski trails start at the Polebridge Ranger Station: one, suitable for beginners, heads three miles north to Big Prairie; the other follows the six-mile-long unplowed road to Bowman Lake. Stop in at the ranger station before heading out; they'll tell you whether it's safe to ski onto the lake.

ACCOMMODATIONS AND FOOD

In terms of food and lodging, the North Fork's only options are in Polebridge, a cluster of buildings in a meadow lacking proper streets or addresses. Polebridge is 25 miles north of Apgar.

The ★ **North Fork Hostel and Square Peg Ranch** (406/888-5241 or 406/253-4321, www.nfhostel.com, $20 tent camping, $25 dorm bed, $50-55 cabin or tepee, $100 log home) is a great place for a budget traveler or anyone with a relaxed sense of sociability. Lights and kitchen appliances are powered by propane, woodstoves provide the heat, guests come prepared with sleeping bags and food, and the outhouse is plastered with reading material. The **Polebridge Mercantile** (406/888-5105) is the center of activity in town, indeed in the whole North Fork. Its **bakery** is known for its pastries, especially the giant bear claws. The Merc also has a few rental cabins ($89-119); although they have stoves and coolers, don't expect running water or plumbing.

During the summer, the café next to the mercantile is worth a stop for its conviviality and good food. The **Northern Lights** (406/888-9963, 11am-2pm and 4pm-11pm daily Memorial Day-mid-Sept, $10-21) pours beer as well as coffee and is a comfortable Polebridge hangout, with occasional live music: It's the only restaurant in town, which means it can get crowded—in midsummer, come prepared for a wait.

The accommodations at **Polebridge Ranch Cabins** (8855 North Fork Rd., 406/662-1552, www.polebridgeranchcabins.

com, $90-175), several miles south of the Mercantile and Polebridge central, are somewhat less rustic than other local cabins; each cabin has a bathroom and generators provide electricity. A café/tavern is next door.

Camping

Bowman Lake Campground ($15 in summer, $10 primitive camping mid-Sept.-Nov., no reservations) is the largest and most popular in the North Fork. Hiking trails wander off in all directions, including an easy one along the lakeshore. The campground at **Kintla Lake** ($15 summer, $10 primitive camping in May and mid-Sept.-Nov., no reservations) is small, with only 13 sites and fewer trails to choose from, but equally desirable. Both of these campgrounds are fairly developed national park campgrounds, although they don't have the parking-lot quality of those in the more traveled areas of Glacier.

Other roadside campgrounds a notch down in development are **Big Creek** (406/387-3800, www.fs.usda.gov/flathead, $13), a Forest Service campground on the Outside North Fork Road near the Camas Creek entrance to the park, and **Logging Creek** and **Quartz Creek,** Glacier National Park campgrounds (July-Nov., $10) on Inside North Fork Road between Apgar and Polebridge. These are primitive campgrounds; bring your own water.

INFORMATION

The periodically staffed **Polebridge Ranger Station** is right near the no-longer-pole-constructed bridge over the North Fork. Stop here for backcountry permits, trail information, or a chat about the local wolf packs.

the Northern Lights café

GETTING THERE AND AROUND

Drive in from the park on Camas Creek or Inside North Fork roads; the Inside North Fork is rougher, but there are some campgrounds along it. The Camas Creek Road is paved for about 12 miles, and good gravel beyond that. From Columbia Falls, the Outside North Fork Road, with good views of the Livingston Range, leads to Polebridge. Blankenship Road connects the Outside North Fork Road with West Glacier. In the winter, Outside North Fork Road and Blankenship Road are plowed.

Lake McDonald Valley

Lake McDonald Valley has all the earmarks of glacial action; it's long, straight, and U-shaped. The lush forests surrounding the lake are characteristic of the Pacific Northwest. Western red cedar and western hemlock form the climax forest; Douglas fir, larch, pine, and spruce add diversity. Hiking trails in the area take in everything from damp old-growth forests to gushing waterfalls to alpine meadows.

SIGHTS
Apgar

Just inside the park entrance at West Glacier, Apgar Village greets travelers with a visitor information center, gift shops, motels, a campground, cafés, and lovely Lake McDonald. The National Park Service purchased much of the town in 1930, but part of it is still privately owned.

★ Going-to-the-Sun Road

It took practically 20 years to build this road; when it opened for travel in 1933, it was an instant hit. The road, which starts its 52-mile run over the spine of the Rockies at Apgar, is a spectacular drive, even when clogged with traffic. Glacier may be a hiker's park at heart, but for those without the capacity or the time for trail walking, the Going-to-the-Sun Road provides a good view of the park's muscles and bones. The free park shuttle allows motorists to actually enjoy the views rather than concentrating on the road. Note that vehicles longer than 21 feet or wider than 8 feet are prohibited on the road past Avalanche Campground.

The Park's Early Days

Under pressure from the railroads, miners, and settlers, the Blackfeet sold the eastern slope of what is now Glacier National Park in 1895 for $1.5 million, thus opening up the area for business. Copper mining was a bust here, as was oil exploration. Tourism—amply advertised by the Great Northern Railway, which in 1891 completed its service through Marias Pass just south of the park—was left as the area's economic mainstay. Conservationists, in league with powerful railroad interests, sought to establish the area as a national park. In 1910 President Taft signed the bill creating Glacier National Park.

Between 1910 and 1917 the Great Northern spent $1.5 million developing tourist facilities. It built a series of huge lodges, chalets, and tent camps, each a day's horseback ride away. The Great Northern's recommended itinerary of hikes, fishing, and trail rides required a full week to "do" the park.

This leisurely, genteel, and recreation-oriented era was challenged in 1933 when the Civilian Conservation Corps finished the Going-to-the-Sun Road, thus introducing the automobile to Glacier. The volume and pace of traffic in the park increased: In 1925 only 40,000 people visited Glacier; 210,000 visitors traveled through in 1936, many simply to experience the Going-to-the-Sun Road. The old Great Northern facilities fell into disuse, and strip towns grew up on the outskirts of the park to service the needs of motorists. Fragile ecosystems in the park began to deteriorate under the weight of increased traffic. Tourism in Glacier reached a nadir during the late 1960s, when a survey found that the average tourist spent only 25 hours in the park.

Glacier Park's backcountry is still not on the typical tourist's itinerary, and many people still zoom over Going-to-the-Sun Road on a cross-country road-trip blitz. But increased environmental awareness since the 1970s has multiplied the number of people who linger among Glacier's unique topography and wildlife haunts.

From Lake McDonald the road follows McDonald Creek to the east and slightly uphill. The grade increases after Logan Creek, and it becomes genuinely steep as it approaches the Loop, a big switchback that brings the road under the Garden Wall, which it follows to the Continental Divide at Logan Pass. Approaching the pass from the west, it's easy to follow the changes in vegetation and geology: The coniferous forests near Lake McDonald give way to shrubs and scattered pines.

Dark slatelike rocks near the head of Lake McDonald, originally laid down under seawater, are the oldest on the west side of the park. Up the Going-to-the-Sun Road, greenish mudstone of the Appekunny Formation developed in shallower water. Farther east and higher, the red rocks of the Grinnell Formation were originally mudflats and turned red when exposure to the air oxidized their ferrous minerals.

Once the road really begins climbing, it moves into the Empire Formation, grayish-green rocks deposited underwater, and then to the Helena (Siyeh) limestone, which comes into view near the Loop. The Helena Formation is dotted with stromatolites, cabbagelike fossil traces of blue-green algae.

Lake McDonald

In 1895 an early homesteader, George Snyder, built a small hotel by Lake McDonald, 15 years before the area became a national park. John Lewis, a Columbia Falls furrier, took over Snyder's hotel, built the present lodge in 1914, and decorated it with hunting trophies (most of which still stare down from timbered beams and balconies). The artist Charlie Russell had a cabin nearby, and it has long been rumored that the pictographs around the lodge's fireplace are his work.

One needn't be a hotel guest to lounge in the **Lake McDonald Lodge** lobby or in the chairs overlooking the lake, and it's a comfortable stop after a day of hiking.

Lake McDonald—10 miles long, a mile wide, and more than 400 feet deep—has long

Lake McDonald

been the territory of tourist **cruise boats** (406/257-2426, www.glacierparkboats.com, 11am, 1:30pm, 3pm, 5:30pm, and 7pm daily late May-Labor Day, $16.25 adults, $8 children), and you can still board a tour boat at the dock behind Lake McDonald Lodge. Tours are an hour long; the evening tour is especially popular, and sunsets can be phenomenal.

Evening programs by park naturalists are scheduled nightly at Lake McDonald Lodge, Apgar Campground, and Fish Creek Campground. These are usually quite interesting, and they're free.

RECREATION
Hiking

A trail starting at Fish Creek Campground follows a ridge along the **west bank of Lake McDonald,** eventually looping around the muddy head of the lake and ending up at the lodge. It's 6.7 miles from the campground to the lodge; a mile-long walk from the campground goes to **Rocky Point,** yielding good views of the lake and the mountains. This area was scorched by the huge 2003 fires; witness the forest succession now taking place.

A trailhead across the road from Lake McDonald Lodge is the starting point for a couple of good day hikes as well as a variety of longer trips. Paths branch off the main trail to shallow **Fish Lake** (6 miles round-trip), the **Mt. Brown Lookout** (a steep, arduous 10-mile round-trip), and **Snyder Lake** (4.5 miles in to a campground beside an emerald lake nestled in the mountains).

The main trail from this trailhead continues up to **Sperry Chalet** (6.4 miles one-way, with a 3,432-foot elevation gain) or three steep miles farther to **Lake Ellen Wilson** or, on another spur, to **Sperry Glacier** (7 steep miles from Sperry Chalet). The trail continues on another 10 miles from Lake Ellen Wilson (which has a backcountry campground) over Gunsight Pass and returns to Going-to-the-Sun Road at the Jackson Glacier viewpoint, five miles east of Logan Pass. From this point, it's another long day's hike over Piegan Pass and down the other side of the Continental Divide to the Many Glacier Hotel.

One of the park's easiest and most popular hikes takes in the western red cedar and hemlock forest near Avalanche Campground. The 0.7-mile-long, wheelchair-accessible **Trail of the Cedars** follows a boardwalk over the floor of the old-growth forest, past Avalanche Gorge, and returns via the campground. It's a splendid trail, even with crowds; solitude seekers will like it even better in the winter, when cross-country skiers may share the trail with moose.

The trail to **Avalanche Lake** starts near Avalanche Campground and the Trail of the Cedars and follows Avalanche Creek two miles through forest to the lake. Waterfalls draining Sperry Glacier tumble over the 1,500-foot wall, which encloses a cirque, and pour the glacial water into Avalanche Lake.

Bicycling

Because of heavy traffic and slim shoulders, bicycle travel along Going-to-the-Sun Road is restricted during the busy summer months. From June 15 to Labor Day, bikes are prohibited on the road between Apgar and Sprague Creek Campground, and eastbound between Logan Creek and Logan Pass, 11am-4pm. Logan Creek, at the base of the Loop, is about 10 miles from Sprague Creek Campground and about 6 miles from Avalanche Campground. Between Apgar and Logan Creek the road stays in the McDonald Creek Valley, climbing some but not dramatically.

Avalanche Lake

Shortly after it crosses Logan Creek, the road really takes off uphill. Expect the ride between Logan Creek and Logan Pass to take three hours.

Cyclists who'd rather not dodge the cars on Going-to-the-Sun Road can bike the paved trail between Apgar and the park entrance. Also starting in Apgar, Camas Creek Road heads up toward the North Fork area, and it is paved for the first 12 miles.

Boating and Fishing

Rent kayaks ($15-18 per hour), paddleboards ($10), canoes ($18), rowboats ($18) or motorboats ($25) at the Apgar dock. Rowboats and small motorboats are also available for rent at the Lake McDonald dock.

No license is needed to fish in the park, and Lake McDonald is known mostly for its lake trout population; check at the boat docks for fishing regulations.

Horseback Riding

Swan Mountain Outfitters (406/387-4405 or 877/888-5557, www.swanmountainoutfitters.com) runs horseback rides in the park. Day rides leave from corrals at **Apgar** (406/888-5010) and **Lake McDonald** (across the road from the lodge, 406/888-5121) and range from a $45 one-hour amble through the forest to a $175 daylong ride to Sperry Chalet. Multiday pack trips are also available. Call for specific destinations and departure times.

Cross-Country Skiing

In the winter, Going-to-the-Sun Road is plowed to the head of Lake McDonald. From the parking area there, it's possible to ski as far up the road as stamina permits. The skiing is technically easy, and there's usually some wildlife around. Ski about two miles up the main road and turn left to view **McDonald Falls;** continue upstream for another mile to visit the **Sacred Dancing Cascades.** From the parking area, **Avalanche Creek** is an 11.6-mile round-trip.

For a longer trip (about 12 miles), ski up Camas Creek Road, take a right at McGee

Meadow, and return on the **Inside North Fork Road.** A final detour through the Fish Creek Campground to **Rocky Point** adds a couple of miles and a good view of Lake McDonald.

ACCOMMODATIONS

The least expensive rooms in the area are in the woods alongside McDonald Creek at the **Apgar Village Lodge** (406/888-5484, www.westglacier.com, mid-May-Sept., $95-309), with older motel rooms (the cheapest ones without TVs, Internet, or alarm clocks) starting at $95 and rustic cabins starting at $120. Larger cabins can sleep up to six adults.

Also in Apgar Village, the **Village Inn** (406/888-5431 or 855/733-4522, www.glaciernationalparklodges.com, late May-mid-Sept., $150-260) is, like Lake McDonald Lodge, operated by Xanterra. The lakeside motel rooms are adequate, and the porches overlooking Lake McDonald are perfect places to sit with morning coffee. Families may opt for a two-bedroom suite that sleeps six ($260).

Lake McDonald Lodge (406/888-5431 or 855/733-4522, www.glaciernationalparklodges.com, late May-late Sept., $135-329, reservations required) is perhaps the most charming of Glacier's lodges. It retains rugged, hunting-lodge touches, such as grizzly bear hides draped over the balcony railings, animal heads posted on massive timbered columns above the lobby, and a walk-in fireplace bordered by pictographs (rumored to have been drawn by Charlie Russell). The rooms aren't as comfortable as the lobby, however, and they're pretty spendy. Tiny dorm rooms with a shared bath are cheaper ($85). The adjacent 1950s-era **Motel Lake McDonald** (406/892-2525, www.glacierparkinc.com, June-Sept., $149) is under different management.

Hike seven miles from Logan Pass along the Highline Trail to the backcountry ★ **Granite Park Chalet** (888/345-2649, www.graniteparkchalet.com, July-mid-Sept., $97 first person, $78 each additional person in room, $20 optional linen fee; reserve well in advance), built in 1914 and perched on an igneous outcropping at the north end of the Garden Wall. Four trails lead to the chalet; the most popular is the stunningly beautiful, nearly level Highline Trail, which follows the base of the Garden Wall from Logan Pass. (Hikers with a fear of heights should note that in some places the Highline Trail hugs the edge of a cliff.) Other trails come in from the Loop on Going-to-the-Sun Road (a steep four miles), over Swiftcurrent Pass from Many Glacier (eight miles), and from Goat Haunt at the head of Waterton Lake (an approximately 23-mile backpacking trip via the northern extension of the Highline Trail).

Hikers generally bring their own sleeping bags, food, and water, although it is possible to rent bedding and purchase premade meals—be sure to do this via the website in advance of your trip. In lieu of electricity, there's a propane stove and a few propane lights. Guests may use the kitchen area to prepare their own food, and though there's no running water, guests are provided with filtered water to drink. Reservations for this popular chalet open at the end of October for the following summer season.

With a gorgeous setting and classic rustic mountain architecture, ★ **Sperry Chalet** (406/387-5654 or 888/345-2649, www.sperrychalet.com, mid-July-early Sept., $201 for one person, $141 for each additional person in room, includes meals, reservations essential), perched on a rocky ledge 6,560 feet above sea level that's popular with the local mountain goats, offers full-service backcountry lodging midway on a trail between Lake McDonald Lodge and Logan Pass; it's a 6.7-mile hike from Lake McDonald Lodge. Accommodations are rustic, with no heat, electricity, or running water, but come with three meals a day. Bedding is also provided, so there's no need to pack in a sleeping bag. Reservations must be made well in advance.

Camping

The **Apgar Campground** (early May-mid-Oct., $20; Apr. and late Oct., primitive camping $10; winter camping free with park pass) is the park's largest and most bustling, although sites are laid out to provide a reasonable amount of privacy. Depending on how you look at it, it's either conveniently or annoyingly close to Apgar Village. Lake McDonald is a short walk away.

Just slightly off the beaten path, **Fish Creek Campground** (877/444-6777, www.recreation.gov, June-Labor Day, $23, reservations

The Village Inn is located right on Lake McDonald in Apgar.

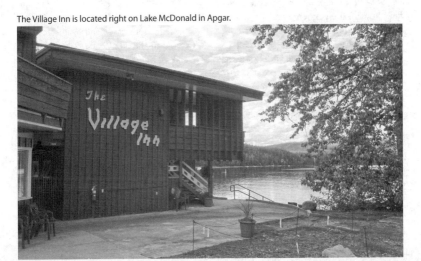

available) is a triple-looped jumble of trailers perched just above the northwestern shore of Lake McDonald. Fish Creek, which is just off Camas Creek Road, is a handy base for day trips around the Lake McDonald area and up the North Fork of the Flathead River. It's one of the few park campgrounds with showers (albeit very few).

Sprague Creek Campground (early May-mid-Sept., $20), on Going-to-the-Sun Road about a mile west of Lake McDonald Lodge, is appealing to some because of its small size and by not permitting towed RVs, but it's actually less private and secluded than Apgar or Fish Creek. It is, however, a handy jumping-off point for bicyclists heading up the Going-to-the-Sun Road.

Avalanche Campground (late June-early Sept., $20) is well situated for hikers; the short Trail of the Cedars and the somewhat longer trail to Avalanche Lake start here. The park shuttle bus stops across the road from the campground.

FOOD

The well-detailed **Russell's Fireside Dining Room** (Lake McDonald Lodge, 303/297-3175, 6:30am-10am, 11:30am-2pm, and 5pm-9:30pm daily late May-late Sept., dinner $12-30, no reservations accepted) has a faux-hunting-lodge theme that strongly influences the dinner menu (think wild game). Even if you just stop in for a bowl of chili or a salad, the ambience and the view (more than the passably decent food) make it worth a visit. If the dining room seems to be just too expensive or too much of a production, the lodge's cozy **Lucke's Lounge** (406/892-2525,

11:30am-11pm, under $10) is a good bet for a buffalo burger and a beer.

Across from the lodge, **Jammer Joe's Grill and Pizzeria** (11am-9pm mid-June-early Sept., $6-15) serves good beer and tolerable food that's less expensive than the lodge dining room.

Don't turn up your nose at **Eddie's Cafe** (Apgar, 406/888-5361, http://eddiescafegifts.com, 7am-10pm daily early June-mid-Sept., dinner $13-20); it's a good place to pick up lunch (sack lunches $9) before heading out on a hike. Desserts and ice cream are especially tempting here.

Camp stores at Apgar and the Lake McDonald Lodge complex stock essential groceries.

INFORMATION

The **Apgar Visitor Center** (406/888-7800), a new building adjacent to the Apgar Transit Center, has park rangers on duty 8am-6pm (shorter hours during the spring and fall, weekends during the winter) to answer questions and suggest hikes; pick up backcountry permits at the nearby **permit office** (406/888-7857, 7am-4:30pm).

GETTING THERE AND AROUND

Park shuttles depart from the Apgar Transit Center (7am-7pm, free), and head east along the Going-to-the-Sun Road to Logan Pass. At Logan Pass riders can transfer to the St. Mary Valley Route to continue along the Going-to-the-Sun Road. Although these are not interpretive tours, shuttle rides provide a great way to get to and from hiking trails.

Logan Pass to St. Mary

From the Highline Trail at Logan Pass to Two Dog Flats around St. Mary Lake, the scenery on the east face of Glacier National Park is just as spectacular as, and more exposed than, that on the west side of the Continental Divide. Geology is suddenly lucid as red Grinnell rocks and the green rocks of the Appekunny Formation glow in the morning light bouncing off St. Mary Lake.

East of the pass, drying winds blow across stands of aspen and cottonwoods to the plains, which rapidly replace the mountains a few miles east of St. Mary.

SIGHTS
★ Logan Pass

At 6,680 feet, Logan Pass is an alpine-arctic tundra environment. Just uphill from the visitors center, tiny wildflowers poke up through the July snow, the native grasses are stunningly green, and the glacier-cut mountains are close at hand. In a landscape so big, it's a surprise when your eye is drawn to tiny wildflowers, but they're captivating for their toughness. The nodding yellow glacier lily,

which often pokes up through the snow, is emblematic of Logan Pass.

Even though the landscape here is shaped by a harsh climate, it's not able to withstand flower-picking or trampling by hordes of hikers. To learn more about alpine ecology, stop in for a naturalist's talk at the Logan Pass visitors center. Talks occur throughout the day from early June through Labor Day. The visitors center stays open as long as the road is passable, usually from June through September.

Logan Pass is the most popular destination in the park, and the parking lot can fill up by mid-morning and stay full well into the afternoon. If you plan to visit mid-day, seriously consider riding the shuttle.

St. Mary Lake

Even nonhikers will want to stop at the **Sun Point** trailhead and walk a few yards to the "peak finder." Of the nine peaks visible from Sun Point, **Going-to-the-Sun Mountain** stands out at 9,942 feet. The mountain, whose name was taken for the road, recalls Napi, the

You may find yourself hiking in the clouds at Logan Pass.

Blackfoot Old Man, who left his home in the sun to help the Blackfeet. Once he had finished his work on earth, he returned home via this mountain.

Boat tours (406/257-2426, www.glacier-parkboats.com, 10am, noon, 2pm, and 4pm daily, late June-Labor Day, 1.5-hour cruise $24.25 adults, $12 children) of St. Mary Lake set out several times a day from the dock across from the Rising Sun complex. The 6:30pm sunset cruise is popular, but unlike the daytime rides it doesn't have the option of hopping off the boat for a short walk to Baring Falls. Passengers on the 10am and 2pm boats can enjoy an optional two-hour (3-mile round-trip) walk to St. Mary Falls with a park naturalist and return later.

HIKES AROUND LOGAN PASS
Hidden Lake Overlook

Glacier's most popular trail is the boardwalk from Logan Pass to Hidden Lake Overlook, a three-mile round-trip hike through delicate alpine meadows, home to marmots, ptarmigans, and mountain goats. The weather can be blustery up here, even in midsummer, and the 500-foot climb to more than 7,000 feet above sea level can be surprisingly fatiguing. If you have a little extra energy, keep hiking just a little ways beyond the overlook for more spectacular views. The trail continues down to the lake, but that adds 3 miles to the round-trip, and a 780-foot descent to—and climb from—the lake.

★ Highline Trail

For a fairly level trail that goes on for miles, the Highline Trail can't be beat. It's the main route to Granite Park Chalet (7.6 miles), and it can be frustratingly crowded, but the above-timberline views, bear-grass meadows, and chattering marmots are absorbing enough to eclipse the other hikers. (Do note that there are some high ledges to traverse here; people hiking with young children and those with a fear of heights might want to give this trail a pass.)

HIKES AROUND ST. MARY LAKE
Sun Point

Walk out to Sun Point for a view of St. Mary Lake and the surrounding mountains. For visitors who aren't up to a long backcountry hike, Sun Point is a good place to stretch your legs without exhausting yourself and get a dramatic view of the scenery. This was the site of

Hidden Lake Overlook

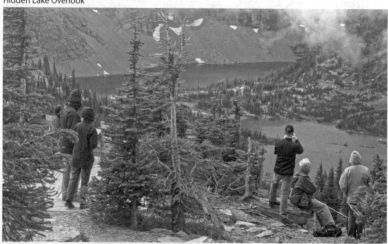

would expect, persevering hikers are rewarded with great views and a delicate alpine environment. After passing alpine larch trees and wildflower meadows at Preston Park, the Siyeh Bend cutoff trail heads back to Going-to-the-Sun Road, making this a 12-mile hike. (Actually, most people do this hike in the opposite direction, which is easier uphill, but yields less-spectacular views.)

St. Mary Falls

No matter which route you choose to get to St. Mary Falls, you'll be rewarded by seeing this three-step cascade. One option is to ride the St. Mary Lake tour boat and hop off for the three-mile (mostly level) round-trip hike. If you don't want to pay the boat fare, hike from the St. Mary Falls trailhead (1.6 miles round-trip, 260 feet elevation loss) or the St. Mary Falls shuttle stop (2.4 miles round-trip, 260-foot drop). Parking can be tight, so consider the shuttle.

Gunsight Lake

An eight-mile hike to Gunsight Lake starts at the Jackson Glacier Overlook west of St. Mary Lake on Going-to-the-Sun Road. There's a campground and spectacular scenery at Gunsight Lake; Gunsight Pass is another *steep* two miles up the trail. From the pass, the trail drops down to Lake Ellen Wilson and Sperry Chalet, and ultimately reaches the road again at Lake McDonald Lodge. The whole 18-mile Gunsight Pass route takes most hikers two days. Besides the inevitable switchbacks and vistas, expect to see mountain goats along this trail.

OTHER RECREATION
Boating and Fishing

Although boats are permitted on St. Mary Lake, there's no place to rent them. All boats brought into the park have permits ($10 for 7-day motorized permit, $40 for annual motorized permit, free for nonmotorized boats), which are issued after park staff check for invasive species. Permits are available at park headquarters in West Glacier, at the St. Mary

Catch the spectacular Highline Trail at Logan Pass.

the most elaborate of the Glacier's chalets; it fell into disuse and was dismantled in the late 1940s once Going-to-the-Sun Road became the focus of trips to the park. From Sun Point the trail skirts the lakeshore for less than a mile to **Baring Falls.** Access this trail from the Sunrift Gorge pullout; the shuttle stops there.

Sunrift Gorge

Sunrift Gorge is on Baring Creek just above the falls; cap off the Sun Point walk by taking the spur trail and climbing to the gorge. Or, follow the lead of most gorge viewers and park in the Sunrift Gorge pullout and walk 50 yards up the path to the narrow chasm, formed not by erosion but by a vertical slip of the rock.

Siyeh Pass and Preston Park

Those in search of a *real* hike will want to continue past Sunrift Gorge to Siyeh Pass and Preston Park. This is no easy amble; the trail shoots up once it leaves Baring Creek, and Siyeh is Glacier's highest pass. As one

Bear Grass

Bear grass covers the slopes of Glacier National Park in July and August. Not every summer brings a bumper crop, however, and that has less to do with the weather than it does with the plant's life cycle. An individual bear grass plant blooms only once every seven years. Some years the torchlike stalks are abundant; other years there's a mere scattering.

Bear grass, which is relatively resistant to fire, is often the first plant to grow after a fire, sprouting from rhizomes just below the surface of the ground. Like many other native plants, it needs periodic burns to produce strong new growth.

Native Americans used the long, tough leaves of the plant (a member of the lily family) for trading, especially with Pacific Coast tribes, who wove the leaves into clothing and watertight baskets. Some tribes also roasted and ate the root.

Although bears don't eat bear grass, elk and mountain goats do.

Bear grass is a highlight of Glacier's summer wildflower display.

Visitor Center, and at ranger stations in Many Glacier and Two Medicine.

Anglers generally prefer boat fishing to bank fishing on St. Mary Lake, which is not really known for good fishing but does have some whitefish, rainbow, and brook trout. Hikers are rewarded by better fishing at Red Eagle Lake, south of the eastside park entrance, or at Gunsight Lake.

Cross-Country Skiing

Loop trails around **Red Eagle Valley,** near the eastern park entrance, offer several miles of skiing for beginning and intermediate skiers. For those who want more of a challenge, the trail to Red Eagle Lake is a 14-mile round-trip along Red Eagle Creek.

ACCOMMODATIONS

Rising Sun Motor Inn (303/297-3175 or 855/733-4522, www.glaciernationalpark-lodges.com, June-mid-Sept., $135-145) near St. Mary Lake has uninspiring but comfortable motel rooms and cabins (most are pretty small) without amenities such as TVs, telephones, and air-conditioning. The view from the front porch makes up for the nondescript interiors.

At the St. Mary crossroads, the **St. Mary Lodge and Resort** (406/892-2525, www.glacierparkinc.com, June-Sept., $119-440) includes the newer Great Bear Lodge as well as the older St. Mary Lodge motel buildings and several circa-1937 cabins. The views don't suffer for being just outside the park boundaries, and the accommodations are every bit as comfortable as, and a touch cheaper than, those inside the park. Most, but not all, rooms have TVs, though reception may be limited. The on-site restaurant is pretty good.

Camping

The **Rising Sun Campground** (late June-mid-Sept., $20) has some shade (necessary in this part of the park) and good views. It's just across the road from St. Mary Lake (try to get a spot away from the road ... some are rather close); a hiking trail heads five miles up Rose

Creek to Otokomi Lake, and there are pay showers in the nearby cabin complex. This area of the park is often frequented by bears, so don't leave food out!

Just inside the park boundary, the **St. Mary Campground** (800/365-2267, www.recreation.gov, late May-late Sept., $23; Apr.-late May and late Sept.-Oct., primitive camping $10; Nov.-Mar., no fee) is about twice as large as Rising Sun but not so well positioned for boaters and hikers. A path connects the campground to the visitors center, where there's a shuttle stop. It's possible to reserve a site in advance here, and the campground has showers. Winds can be strong in this area of the park.

There's a **KOA** (105 West Shore, St. Mary, 406/732-4122 or 800/562-1504, www.goglacier.com, mid-May-Sept., $35 tent, $48-65 RV, $100-700 cabins) in St. Mary with tent sites tucked among riverside trees. "Cabins" range from walled tents to deluxe lodges.

FOOD

Hungry travelers should note that between Lake McDonald and St. Mary, Rising Sun is the only place to buy food. Fortunately the **Two Dog Flats Grill** (406/892-2525, 6:30am-10am, 11:30am-2pm, and 5pm-9:30pm daily mid-June-late Sept., $12-22) serves decent café breakfasts, lunches, and dinners. Burgers (including bison burgers and veggie burgers) are good, as are the salads.

It's worth heading out of the park to dine in St. Mary. One good bet is the casual ★ **Park Cafe** (3147 Hwy. 89, 406/732-9300, www.parkcafe.us, 7am-10pm daily June-late Sept., dinners $10-20, no alcohol), where the hip, friendly staff serve good burgers, sandwiches, and dinner specials at the junction of Highway 89 and Going-to-the-Sun Road. Don't leave without a slice of huckleberry pie.

Up the road, between St. Mary and Babb, it's hard to miss the brightly painted ★ **Two Sisters Cafe** (3600 Hwy. 89 N., 406/732-5535, www.twosistersofmontana.com, 11am-10pm daily June-Sept., $11-24), a fun and funky place with good food, including some of the best burgers (ask for the red burger) and sweet-potato fries you'll find anywhere. Margaritas make the sometimes-long wait pass more quickly.

The **Snowgoose Grille** (406/732-4431, 7am-9pm daily mid-May-Sept., dinner entrées $12-28) at St. Mary Lodge is more elegant than the other places in the area and features good salads and pasta dishes, buffalo rib eye, and other entrées that occasionally transcend the expected steak, trout, and chicken dishes.

The Park Cafe is a favorite place to eat in the town of St. Mary.

INFORMATION

Rangers at the **Logan Pass Visitor Center** (9am-7pm late June-Labor Day, 9:30am-4pm Labor Day-late Sept.) keep the fireplace stoked on chilly days and dispense maps, backcountry permits, and advice. More-detailed maps and books on the park's trails, geology, and history are available from the **Glacier Natural History Association** shop here. The **St. Mary Visitor Center** (8am-7pm late June-mid-Aug., 8am-5pm late May-June and mid-Aug-early Oct.) and the **St. Mary Backcountry Office** (7am-4:30pm late May-mid-Sept.) are just inside the eastern park entrance.

GETTING THERE AND AROUND

Free **park shuttles** (every 40-60 minutes, 7am-7pm) leave from the St. Mary Visitor Center to Logan Pass. Glacier Park Inc. runs van shuttles on the park's east side, connecting the St. Mary Lodge (or, by special request, the St. Mary Visitor Center, with access to the free Going-to-the-Sun Road shuttle) with Many Glacier, Two Medicine, East Glacier, and Waterton. These are not free—it's $15 from Many Glacier to St. Mary. Xanterra operates a similar shuttle between the St. Mary Visitor Center and Many Glacier ($10).

East Glacier and Vicinity

Although East Glacier is not the best base for a several-day tour of the park, it is a handy entrance point for travelers from the east. Camp or hike at nearby Two Medicine Lakes, with all the scenery and far less company than you'll find at Many Glacier or Lake McDonald.

There's more of a Native American presence here than in many other areas of the park. Even though most of East Glacier is controlled by non-Indians, it is within the Blackfeet Reservation boundaries and part of an area that is historically and culturally important to the Blackfeet.

For the Native American angle on the park, join one of the interpretive tours of the park featuring Blackfeet guides run by **Sun Tours** (406/226-9220 or 800/786-9220, www.glaciersuntours.com, $35-75).

THE LAND

The Lewis Overthrust came to a halt just west of present-day East Glacier, and its leading edge is visible at Running Eagle Falls near Lower Two Medicine Lake. The hard Precambrian rock of the Lewis Formation rolled on top of a younger, softer shale, which has worn away to form the gentler hilly landscapes east of the overthrust.

Glaciers dug out the bottoms of the three Two Medicine Lakes (upper, middle, and lower). Moraines formed dams, allowing water to fill the troughs. Two Medicine Valley is surrounded by peaks, many adorned with waterfalls and hanging valleys.

EAST GLACIER
★ Glacier Park Lodge

Glacier Park Lodge is a spectacular building, with huge Douglas fir timbers forming the Ionic columns in the Greek revival lobby. Early park visitors typically pulled in on the train from the east and disembarked at East Glacier to spend a night at the lodge before saddling up to ride the circuit of backcountry chalets and tent camps in the company of a guide. For a hearty evocation of such a trip, read Mary Roberts Rinehart's *Through Glacier Park in 1915*. Once Going-to-the-Sun Road was built, auto travel supplanted both the train and the horse, and the spotlight was off the massive lodge, which lies slightly outside the park boundaries and several miles from the closest hiking trails, which are in the Two Medicine area.

TWO MEDICINE

Two Medicine boasts some of the park's most spectacular scenery, but it's a ways from the Going-to-the-Sun Road and is often overlooked.

A glacier gouged **Lower Two Medicine Lake** at the foot of purplish red Rising Wolf Mountain (elev. 9,505 feet). Backcountry chalets built by the Great Northern were the first stop on a horseback circuit popular in the pre-automobile days. One such wooden chalet remains as the Two Medicine camp store.

Boat tours (406/257-2426, www.glacierparkboats.com) of Lower Two Medicine Lake leave the dock at 10:30am and 1pm, 3pm, and 5pm daily early June-early September; staring in July, a 9am trip is added. The 45-minute tour costs $12.25 for adults and $6 for children.

RECREATION
Hiking

It's a short walk from the well-marked bridge over Two Medicine Creek through some conifers and across a rocky creek side to **Running Eagle Falls** (Trick Falls). When there's plenty of water, it appears to be like any other waterfall. The trick comes when water volume decreases late in the summer and water spouts from a hole beneath the main shelf of the falls. Look at the rim of the falls for the fault line marking the eastern edge of the Lewis Overthrust. Running Eagle, or Pitamakan, was a Blackfoot woman who reportedly led warriors over Cut Bank Pass on raids against Flathead and Kootenai tribes to the west.

For a full day's hike, **Upper Two Medicine Lake** is five miles from the Two Medicine Campground. The trail runs along the south shore of Lower Two Medicine Lake. To shorten the hike, catch the tour boat to the head of the lake.

Hike eight miles up the valley of Cut Bank Creek to **Triple Divide Pass.** The trail starts at the Cut Bank campground and, after a hike and a final scramble from cairn to cairn, reaches the spot where Atlantic,

Pacific, and Hudson Bay Creeks issue from the Continental Divide.

Boating

Canoes, kayaks, and rowboats rent for $15-18 per hour at the boat dock on Lower Two Medicine Lake. Although motorboats are permitted, speed is limited to 10 miles per hour.

Fishing

Pick up a tribal permit at the lodge or the Two Medicine camp store to fish the Two Medicine River or Lower Two Medicine Lake. Once inside the park boundaries, stop by any visitors center or ranger station and get park fishing regulations (no license is necessary). Brook and rainbow trout lurk in Lower Two Medicine Lake and Cut Bank Creek.

Golfing

The nine holes of the **Glacier Park Lodge Golf Course** (406/892-2525, late May-Sept. $20 for nine holes) span Highway 49 just north of the lodge.

Cross-Country Skiing

Once the snow starts piling up in late December, it's easy to strap on skis at the Two Medicine Road junction with Highway 49 and glide along Two Medicine Lake. On nice days it's an easy day trip; on windy day (common in this area), it can be challenging. Strong skiers can make the 10-mile round-trip to Running Eagle Falls.

ACCOMMODATIONS
Under $50

Step upstairs from the 1920s log **Brownie's Market** (406/226-4426, www.brownieshostel. com, May-Sept., $19 dorm bed, $29-49 private room) to find a charmingly decrepit youth hostel with sloping linoleum floors and lots of old photos and books in the sleeping rooms.

Backpackers Inn (29 Dawson Ave., 406/226-9392, May-Sept., $15 dorm bed, $40 private cabin) also offers dorm accommodations (bring your own sleeping bag) in cabins behind Serrano's Mexican Restaurant (across from the Amtrak depot). The cabins face onto a pleasant grassy yard.

$50-100

Several small motels house guests in detached cabinlike units. All of these places provide the basics, but none are fancy. **East Glacier Motel** (1107 Hwy. 49, 406/226-5593, www. eastglacier.com, June-Aug., $95 motel rooms, $70-90 cabins, $125 bungalow) has cheery motel rooms (some with kitchens), simple cabins, and a bungalow with a full kitchen (two-night minimum). **Mountain Pine Motel** (406/226-4403, May-Sept., $80-100) is another well-kept but older family-run motel with a friendly, helpful owner. It's set back from the road beneath tall trees. At **Jacobson's Cottages** (1204 Hwy. 49, 406/226-4422, mid-May-Sept., $80-105) conventionally shaped units are tucked behind the A-frame office, and the proprietor will pick you up at the Amtrak stop. Cabins at **Sears Motel** (1023 Hwy. 49, 406/226-4432, www.searsmotel.com, mid-May-Sept., $69-84) are somewhat funky, but the place is run by very friendly folks who also maintain a tent and RV campground and run a rental car business. Ask in advance and they'll pick you up at the train depot.

There's a secluded feeling to the cabins at **Bison Creek Ranch,** two miles west of town on Highway 2 (between mileposts 207 and 208, 406/226-4482 or 888/226-4482, www. bisoncreekranch.com, May-Sept., $84-132 including breakfast). Larger A-frame cabins have kitchens, and there's also a family-style restaurant (5pm-9pm daily) on-site.

Over $100

Even if you stay elsewhere, plan to check out the impressive lobby and common rooms at **Glacier Park Lodge** (406/892-2525, www. glacierparkinc.com, late May-Sept., $161-480). There's a heated pool out the back door.

Bear Creek Guest Ranch (Hwy. 2, mile marker 192, 406/226-4489, www.bearcreek-guestranch.com, $189 includes breakfast) is 17 miles west of East Glacier via Highway 2.

It's a long-established guest ranch; horseback riding is available.

Camping

Camp on **Two Medicine Lake** (late May-late Sept., $20; late Sept.-Oct., primitive camping $10), 12 miles from East Glacier via Highway 49. During the peak summer season, campfire presentations by park naturalists and Blackfeet tribal members are held most evenings at 8pm.

Head west of East Glacier on Highway 2 to reach Forest Service campgrounds, which often have empty spaces when the national park campgrounds are full. **Summit Campground** (www.fs.usda.gov/lewis-clark, $10), near the rest area at Marias Pass, is 12 miles from East Glacier. **Devil Creek Campground** (www.fs.usda.gov/flat-head, $12) is another six miles southwest on Highway 2.

FOOD

★ **Serrano's Mexican Restaurant** (29 Dawson Ave., 406/226-9392, 5pm-10pm nightly mid-May-Sept., $6-18) has good Mexican food and margaritas that taste extra-special after a long hike. Another good spot is **Luna's** (1112 Hwy. 49, 406/226-4433, 7am-9pm daily June-Sept., dinner $8-18), a bright and friendly café with good burgers (including buffalo burgers and salmon burgers … aka "grizzly bait"), fish tacos, Indian tacos, and, of course, huckleberry pie. Luna's is also a good place for a hearty pre-hike breakfast.

Next door to Brownie's Market and the hostel is the **Whistle Stop Restaurant** (1024 Hwy. 49, 406/226-9292, 6:30am-9pm daily, $8-13) with great breakfasts (huckleberry French toast) and creative dinner specials such as Cuban potpie.

The **Great Northern Dining Room** (406/892-2525, 6:30am-10am, 11am-3pm, and 5pm-9:30pm daily, late May-Sept., dinner $12-33), the Western-themed Glacier Park Lodge dining room has mediocre steak and seafood specialties.

INFORMATION AND SERVICES

There's no Glacier National Park visitors center in East Glacier, but the **information desk** at the lodge is staffed by generally helpful people. The **ranger station** at Two Medicine Lake (7am-5pm daily late May-mid-Sept.) has more specific information on nearby hiking trails; backcountry permits are available here until 4:30pm daily.

The **post office** is east of Highway 2, behind the Glacier Park Trading Company. A **laundry** and **showers** are two blocks south at the Y Lazy R RV Park behind the Exxon station.

GETTING THERE AND AROUND

Amtrak stops at the East Glacier Park station during the summer. The westbound train comes through in the evening; eastbound service is midmorning daily. From September through May the train stops in Browning rather than East Glacier; check exact dates and times with **Amtrak** (800/872-7245, www.amtrak.com).

Glacier Park Inc. runs **van shuttles** on the park's east side, connecting the St. Mary Lodge (or, by special request, the St. Mary Visitor Center, with access to the free Going-to-the-Sun Road shuttle) with Many Glacier, Two Medicine, East Glacier, and Waterton. These are not free—it's $15 from Many Glacier to St. Mary.

Xanterra operates similar shuttles; one is between the St. Mary Visitor Center and Many Glacier ($10), and the other runs from the West Glacier train station to Lake McDonald Lodge ($5).

Car rentals are available at the **Sears Motel** (406/226-9293).

Many Glacier

Aside from the Going-to-the-Sun Road, this is the most popular and the most spectacular area of Glacier National Park. The mountains are *right there,* with the knife-edge-thin Garden Wall as a backdrop to the southwest, and a glacier but a day hike away. Many Glacier is spectacular enough to warrant a quick detour just for a snooze on the hotel veranda, but it also makes a good base for several days' worth of hiking, canoeing, and bicycle or horseback riding.

THE LAND

Head up any of the numerous valleys converging on the hotel, and on the way to high cirques and glaciers, observe all four of Glacier's geologic formations. Tan Altyn limestone is exposed in the hotel parking lot. Climb through the green layers of Appekunny mudstone, look for mud cracks and ripple marks in the red Grinnell mud, then scale the buff-colored Helena (or Siyeh) Formation, where large stromatolites abound. High on the Garden Wall, the Purcell diabase is a dark 100-foot-tall layer of igneous rock that shot up through the mud and limestone until it spread into a yielding gap in the sedimentary layers. The molten intrusion seared the adjacent limestone layers, turning them to marble.

Just east of Many Glacier is the edge of the Lewis Overthrust. Chief Mountain, visible from the road between Babb and Waterton Lakes National Park, is the far eastern outpost of the overthrust of Precambrian rock and the leading edge of the Rocky Mountains. Younger Cretaceous shales, buried by older rocks in most of Glacier Park, take over the valley floor just east of the mountains.

Glaciers filled Swiftcurrent Valley and left their trademark U-shaped valleys running down from the peaks and converging in Many Glacier Valley. Valley floors here are striped with moraines and dotted with glacial lakes, which get colder and more milky-blue as they

Many Glacier Region

near their glacial sources. Cirques tucked into the face of the Garden Wall were the starting points for many glaciers, and the Grinnell and Gem Glaciers still creep across the shady flank of the arête.

SIGHTS
Park Tours

An eight-hour **Red Bus tour** (303/297-3175 or 855/733-4522, www.glaciernationalpark-lodges.com, $80) leaves Many Glacier Hotel every day at 9am and heads to St. Mary and westward across Going-to-the-Sun Road. Lunch (not included) is at Lake McDonald Lodge, and the return trip retraces the route.

Boat Tours

Scenic cruises of **Swiftcurrent Lake** and **Lake Josephine** leave the hotel boat dock several times daily (406/257-2426, www.gla-cierparkboats.com). Grinnell Glacier, only partially visible from the hotel, comes into view as the boat crosses Lake Josephine. The one-hour tour is $24.25 for adults and $12 for children. The trip involves a short but fairly steep hike between the two lakes. It's easy to hop off the boat for a hike or a picnic at Lake Josephine and then catch another boat back to the hotel.

SHORT HIKES
Swiftcurrent Lake

Of the many hikes in the Many Glacier area, the one around Swiftcurrent Lake is the simplest, if the least spectacular. It's a good evening stroll from the lodge or campground—2.5 miles of flat lakeside terrain. The trail occasionally breaks out of the trees for views of the Garden Wall and nearby mountains. Pick up a nature guide at the official trailhead, the picnic area halfway between the lodge and the campground.

Grinnell Lake

Another easy walk combines a boat trip to the far end of Lake Josephine with a 1.5-mile round-trip hike to Grinnell Lake, a milky aquamarine lake full of icy water and glacial flour from Grinnell Glacier.

DAY HIKES
★ Grinnell Glacier Overlook

Park naturalists lead several different hikes each day in Many Glacier Valley. Although it's perfectly okay to hike to the Grinnell Glacier overlook on your own, hikers with an interest in geology should try to catch the naturalist-led hike to view this glacier. In combination with a boat shuttle across Swiftcurrent Lake and Lake Josephine ($24.25), the all-day hike is eight miles round-trip with a 1,600-foot elevation gain. (Forgo the boat rides and it becomes 11 miles.) Grinnell Glacier reached its peak size during a sort of miniature ice age in the 1800s. Melting since then has left two smaller glaciers: The Salamander clings high on the Garden Wall; Grinnell Glacier proper is below and to the left. Climate change has enlarged the iceberg-laden lake beneath the glacier, making it particularly hazardous to walk onto the glacial ice.

Iceberg Lake

Watch out for bears on the trail to Iceberg Lake, an aptly named glacial lake 4.7 miles from the trailhead in the Swiftcurrent parking lot. The trail crosses alpine meadows before

tour boat traversing Swiftcurrent Lake

dropping into a cirque holding the milky blue lake. Mountain goats, marmots, and an occasional bear share this path with myriad hikers.

Ptarmigan Falls and Ptarmigan Lake

The trip to **Ptarmigan Falls** (2.6 miles) and **Ptarmigan Lake** (4.3 miles) also starts in the Swiftcurrent parking area. The waterfalls and flower-strewn meadows make up for the steepness of the trail. Hikers reaching the lake with boundless energy should go another mile to the 183-foot-long **Ptarmigan Tunnel,** which emerges onto the north face of the Ptarmigan Wall, looking out to the Belly River country.

LONGER HIKES

For an extended jaunt, start at the camp store parking lot and head up Swiftcurrent Creek past **Red Rock Falls** (1.8 miles), cross the Continental Divide at **Swiftcurrent Pass** (6.6 miles), and join up with the **Highline Trail** on the other side. It's eight miles from the trailhead in the camp store parking lot to the Granite Park Chalet (and campground) and another eight miles from the chalet to Logan Pass.

Start at the hotel, pass Lake Josephine and Grinnell Lake, and skirt Mt. Siyeh and Going-to-the-Sun Mountain on the 12-mile route across **Piegan Pass** to **Going-to-the-Sun Road.** Geology, wildflower meadows, waterfalls, mountain goats, and big views are highlights of this hike. There are no backcountry campgrounds along this trail.

OTHER RECREATION
Boating

Rent a canoe, kayak, or rowboat ($15-18 per hour) at the boat dock behind the hotel. Determined boaters will heft their vessels 0.25 mile over the moraine separating Swiftcurrent Lake and Lake Josephine. The isolation and views from Lake Josephine are worth the portage.

Motorboats, except for the tour boats, are prohibited on Swiftcurrent Lake and Lake Josephine but are allowed on larger Lake Sherburne.

Fishing

There are trout in Swiftcurrent Lake, but they're not always eager to swallow a hook. Both Lake Josephine and Grinnell Lake are home to brook trout; it's worth the extra hike to Grinnell Lake for both the beautiful turquoise waters and the fish. For a change from the trout, head down to Sherburne Lake for northern pike.

Horseback Riding

The **corral** (406/732-4203, www.swanmountainoutfitters.com) behind the Many Glacier Hotel parking lot is the starting point for several regularly scheduled guided horseback rides. All-day rides (about $175) leave each morning to Poia Lake. Shorter rides ($45-68) leave several times a day for Grinnell Lake, Lake Josephine, or Cracker Flats.

ACCOMMODATIONS

Three separate accommodations (two motels and a set of cabins) are grouped together at **Swiftcurrent Motor Inn and Cabins** (303/297-3175 or 855/733-4522, www.glaciernationalparklodges.com, mid-June-mid-Sept., $89-155), near a major trailhead about a mile downhill from Many Glacier Lodge. The cabins are especially popular with families; although the less-expensive cabins lack toilets and kitchens, they evoke pleasant hazy memories of some idealized summer camp or the perfect 1962 family vacation. Please note that the Pinetop Motor Inn facilities are among the park's least desirable.

The ★ **Many Glacier Hotel** (406/892-2525, early June-late Sept., $165-259), a 214-room Swiss-style chalet perched on the shores of Swiftcurrent Lake, has the loveliest setting in the park, with stunning views from the lobby windows. Geology comes right down to meet you here, and wildlife is often spotted on the slopes across the lake. If you plan to spend a significant amount of time in your room, splurge on the lake view: The view is what makes this place; the rooms themselves evoke 1970s dorm rooms, and the walls are thin.

Camping

No reservations are accepted for the **Many Glacier Campground** (late May-late Sept., $20-23; late Sept.-Oct., primitive camping $10), so campers need to grab a spot early in the day; it's often full shortly after noon. Half of the sites are expected to be available by reservation in 2016 (reservations 877/444-6777, www.recreation.gov). Pay showers are available at the **Swiftcurrent Camp Store**, near the campground.

FOOD

The **Ptarmigan Dining Room** (6:30am-10am, 11am-2pm, and 5pm-9:30pm daily early June-late Sept., dinner $15-30) at the Many Glacier Hotel has great views, a continental Swiss-inspired theme, and thoroughly average food. It's the same meat and fish dispensed to other Glacier Park hotels, but here it's sauced and stuffed rather than grilled or breaded and fried. The adjacent bar (11:30am-10pm) is an okay place for a light meal.

In the Swiftcurrent Motor Inn, you'll find the **Swiftcurrent Restaurant** (6:30am-9:30am, 11:30am-2pm, and 5pm-10pm, $7-15),

a pretty good casual pizza and pasta place with Montana microbrews, and a camp store.

INFORMATION AND SERVICES

Rangers dispense trail information and back-country permits from their station near the campground. Find general trail information and specifics on bus tours and hotel activities at the information desk in the **Many Glacier Hotel** lobby.

The most coveted of all services for campers—**showers** and a **Laundry facility**—are in the Swiftcurrent cabin complex. Purchase shower tokens at the camp store.

GETTING THERE AND AROUND

Many Glacier is 12 miles west of Babb, a cross-roads town on the Blackfeet Reservation nine miles north of St. Mary. Travelers relying on public transportation can catch a shuttle at St. Mary to the Many Glacier Hotel and vice versa.

Glacier Park Inc. runs **van shuttles** on the park's east side, connecting Many Glacier with other sites on the east side of the park, These are not free—it's $15 from Many Glacier to St. Mary. Xanterra operates a similar shuttle between the St. Mary Visitor Center and Many Glacier ($10).

Waterton Lakes National Park

Just across the Canadian border from Glacier is **Waterton Lakes National Park** (403/859-2224, www.pc.gc.ca/ pn-np/ab/waterton, day pass C$7.80 adult, C$6.80 senior, C$3.90 youth 6-16). Although a much smaller park (it covers only 203 square miles), it's worth visiting for spectacular scenery and a distinctly Canadian flavor. The views from Waterton are outstanding—both the look down glacier-dug Waterton Lake and the view of the prairies meeting the mountains. The two parks are known collectively as the Waterton-Glacier

International Peace Park, but they are managed separately with separate entry fees.

There's actually a town in Waterton Park, with a handful of year-round residents, several private summer cottages, and a small tourist strip on the Cameron Creek delta. Development has been kept pretty much in check, though; there are no soaring condominium towers and no McDonald's.

All prices quoted for Waterton are in Canadian dollars. Alberta's area code is 403.

As with most of the eastern slopes of the

Rockies, the wind can be persistent and strong in Waterton.

SIGHTS
★ Upper Waterton Lake

The *International* (403/859-2362, www.watertoncruise.com, early May-early Oct., C$43 adult, C$22 teen, C$14 child) has cruised 500-foot-deep glacier-dug Upper Waterton Lake since the Prince of Wales Hotel opened in 1927. The two-hour round-trip boat ride from the Waterton marina to Goat Haunt, Montana, at the southern end of the lake departs several times daily. From the boat you'll get good views of tower cliffs, waterfalls, and one mountain after another. From Memorial Day through mid-September, hikers can hop off at Goat Haunt (provided they have the passport required to cross the international border), explore the trails there, and take a later boat back to Waterton.

Other Sights

Cameron Falls drops from a hanging valley, where a small glacier came in from the side and was swallowed up by the large Waterton Valley glacier. Find the falls right in town, on Evergreen Avenue.

A paddle-wheeled boat submerged in Emerald Bay beneath the Prince of Wales Hotel can be seen through the clear water. It holds a particular fascination for **divers.**

Take the nine-mile-long **Red Rock Canyon Parkway** from town to the canyon. At road's end there's a short self-guided walk around the canyon and a picnic area; it's a 20-minute amble to Blakiston Falls.

A **bison paddock** north of the park entrance corrals a small herd of buffalo. There's a quite pretty driving tour through the paddock, which is more interesting than it sounds.

RECREATION
Hiking

Walkers and bicyclists share the **Townsite Trail,** a two-mile tour that you can catch along the lakefront in the town site and take to Cameron Falls. Take off from the park information center and follow the trail up the **Bear's Hump,** a hard rock protrusion that stopped the advance of the huge glacier that filled Waterton Valley during the last ice age. From the top of the hump, you'll have a great view of the lakes and town below. It's less than a mile to the top of the ridge, but the climb is steep and views are often accompanied by stiff winds.

Waterton Lakes National Park

Waterton Lakes National Park

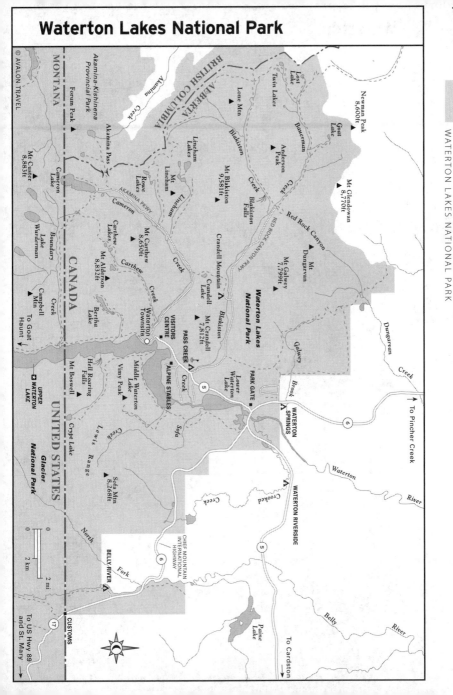

© AVALON TRAVEL

Waterton

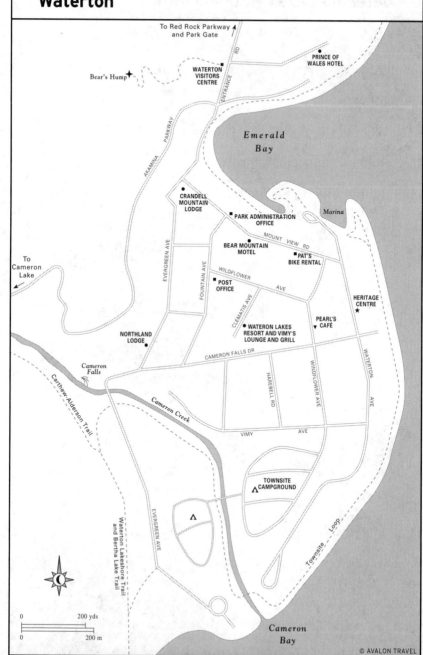

To Red Rock Parkway
and Park Gate

WATERTON
VISITORS
CENTRE

Bear's Hump

PRINCE OF
WALES HOTEL

ENTRANCE RD

Emerald
Bay

AKAMINA PARKWAY

CRANDELL
MOUNTAIN
LODGE

PARK ADMINISTRATION
OFFICE

Marina

MOUNT VIEW RD

BEAR MOUNTAIN
MOTEL

PAT'S
BIKE RENTAL

To
Cameron
Lake

EVERGREEN AVE

FOUNTAIN AVE

WILDFLOWER

POST
OFFICE

AVE

CLEMATIS AVE

HERITAGE
CENTRE

PEARL'S
CAFÉ

NORTHLAND
LODGE

WATERON LAKES
RESORT AND VIMY'S
LOUNGE AND GRILL

WATERTON AVE

Cameron
Falls

CAMERON FALLS DR

Carthew-Alderson Trail

Cameron Creek

HAREBELL RD

WINDFLOWER AVE

VIMY

AVE

Waterton Lakeshore Trail
and Bertha Lake Trail

EVERGREEN AVE

TOWNSITE
CAMPGROUND

Townsite Loop

0   200 yds
0   200 m

Cameron
Bay

© AVALON TRAVEL

The **Bertha Lake Trail** is a 3.5-mile tromp starting at the town site and heading through montane and subalpine forests to a high cirque lake. Waterton is known for its variety of wildflowers, and they're particularly well-displayed along this trail. For hikers who are not up to the seven-mile round-trip, **Bertha Falls** is just under two miles up the same trail.

Take the tour boat to **Goat Haunt** at the south end of Upper Waterton Lake and from there hike one mile to Rainbow Falls and back, or take off on foot back to the Waterton town site. There's an eight-mile trail up the west side of the lake, although the trail passes mostly through lodgepole pine, Engelmann spruce, and some aspen and birch trees with only a few views over the lake.

Catch a **water shuttle** (403/859-2362, www.watertoncruise.com, mid-May-early Oct., C$21 adults, C$10.50, C$9 children 4-12) to Crypt Landing for the 5.4-mile hike to **Crypt Lake.** On the way to the lake, hikers pass several waterfalls, sidle along steep trails, creep through a natural tunnel, and climb 3,000 feet. This is a hike to challenge both muscles and nerves. It's rather scarier than most day hikes, but when you get to the lake, you're up there with the mountain goats.

Backcountry Trips

Before setting out on an overnight trek, get a **backcountry camping permit** (403/859-5133, C$9.80 per night) and trail information from the park information center or administrative office. Reservations are available for wilderness campsites. A nonrefundable reservation fee (C$11.70) is charged, plus a modification fee for any additional changes to your itinerary. Reservations for backcountry trips may be made 90 days in advance beginning April 1 of each year.

A good two-day trip is the 19-mile **Tamarack Tour** toward the northwestern end of the park. Start on the Rowes Lake trail from the trailhead on the Akamina Parkway, and follow it north and west past tiny Lone Lake, Twin Lakes, and Lost Lake to the Snowshoe

Trail, which follows Bauerman Creek to the Red Rock Parkway.

Fishing

There's a C$9.80 fee for a seven-day Canadian National Park fishing permit. Purchase one at the park information center or administrative office if you plan to go after the trout, northern pike, or whitefish of the Waterton lakes.

Bicycling

The **Townsite Trail** is perfect for an easy bike ride; for more of a challenge, pedal up the hill to the Prince of Wales Hotel for tea or out Red Rock Canyon Parkway; ride carefully on the narrow roads and be prepared for stiff winds. The four-mile **Kootenai Brown Trail** links town with the campground and other visitor facilities; it's separated from the road and good for less experienced cyclists. **Pat's** (403/859-2266) rents mountain bikes at the corner of Mountain View Road and Windflower Avenue.

Golfing

The stunning and recently restored 18-hole **Waterton Lakes Golf Course** (403/859-2114, www.golfwaterton.com, C$59) is on the Red Rock Canyon Parkway just north of Highway 5.

Horseback Riding

Trail rides leave every hour on the hour from **Alpine Stables** (403/859-2462, www.alpinestables.com), just past the edge of town on the golf course road. Hour-long rides cost C$38; daylong rides are C$150.

ACCOMMODATIONS

At the 1960s-era **Bear Mountain Motel** (208 Mount View Rd., 403/859-2366, www.bearmountainmotel.com, C$105-225), some rooms have kitchenettes, but none have telephones. Rooms are small and simple, but it's the only place in this price range in town.

The grand **Prince of Wales Hotel** (406/892-2525 or 403/236-3400, www.glacierparkinc.com, mid-June-mid-Sept.,

C$239-799), built by the Great Northern Railway in 1926 as a stopover for tour buses shuttling between Glacier National Park and Jasper, Alberta, is perched on a bluff over town. It's run as part of the Glacier Park Inc. hotel system and has a British Isles theme overlaid on the Glacier Park hotel chassis. Big wingback chairs look out from the lobby over Upper Waterton Lake; take advantage of this grand view even if you don't stay here. Top-end rooms also have an awe-inspiring view onto the lake; many other rooms are cramped.

The **Northland Lodge** (408 Evergreen Ave., 403/859-2353, C$149-194) is a well-run B&B housed in a 1929 lodge. It's built on a mountain slope just a short walk from Cameron Falls.

Crandell Mountain Lodge (102 Mount View Rd., 403/859-2288 or 866/859-2288, www.crandellmountainlodge.com, open year-round, C$140-220) has 13 country inn-style rooms, including a couple of suites with kitchens.

Waterton Lakes Resort (101 Clematis Ave., 403/859-2150 or 888/985-6343, www. watertonlakeslodge.com, May-Oct., C$199-244) offers accommodations in separate lodges that cluster around a central court-yard. Hotel guests are free to use the health club next door, and there's a good restaurant in the lobby. Some rooms have kitchenettes.

Camping

The wind-tossed **Townsite Campground** (877/737-3783, www.pccamping.ca, late Apr.-mid-Oct., C$28-39) is of the parking-lot variety, but many of the 238 sites are close to the lake, and there are showers. It's immediately south of downtown, near the Bertha Lake trailhead and the Falls Theatre on Windflower Drive. Reservations are available.

Belly River Campground (mid-May-mid-Sept., C$16) is a cheaper, but not necessarily more appealing, alternative off Chief Mountain International Highway just north of the international border. It's away from the lakes and can be hot. The **Crandell**

Mountain Campground (mid-May-early Sept., C$22) is a pleasant, though sometimes crowded, spot five miles from town on the Red Rock Canyon Parkway.

FOOD

The dining room at the **Prince of Wales** (403/859-2231, 6:30am-10am, 11am-3pm, and 5pm-9:30pm daily, dinner C$22-35) puts a British Isles twist on the standard Glacier Park hotel menu: They serve Irish stew at lunch, and dinners include British Columbia salmon. There's also a quite charming ★ **tearoom** here, serving scones and other pastries 2pm-4pm. Full high tea costs C$30.

Pearl's Cafe (305 Windflower Ave., 403/859-2498, 7am-4pm daily, C$10-13) serves up good breakfasts and lunches, with a hiker-friendly vibe. Stuffed French toast is a specialty. **Vimy's Ridge Lounge & Grill** (in the Waterton Lakes Resort, 101 Clematis Ave., 403/859-2150 or 888/985-6343, www. watertonlakeslodge.com, 7:30am-10pm daily mid-May-Sept., 11am-10pm Mon.-Fri., 7:30am-10pm Sat.-Sun. Oct.-mid-May, C$15-36) is the village's fine-dining restaurant, with good views and pasta, steaks, and seafood, plus such old-fashioned dishes as beef Wellington.

INFORMATION AND SERVICES

Just across from the Prince of Wales Hotel, the **Park Information Centre** (403/859-2445) is open from mid-May through mid-October. The **park administration office** (403/859-2224) is open year-round on Mountain View Road. The in-town **Heritage Centre** (117 Waterton Ave., 403/859-2267, mid-May-mid-Sept.) is run by the Waterton Natural History Association. The friendly staff will help plan hikes, meals, and motel stays. A small historical museum and a bookshop operate out of the same Waterton Avenue building.

Free interpretive programs are presented each evening in the **Falls Theatre** across from Cameron Falls and in the theater at

Crandell Campground. Programs focus on both history and nature studies and usually include slides or a movie.

For **ambulance services,** call 403/859-2636. Reach the **fire department** at 403/859-2113. The **police station** (403/859-2244) is at the corner of Waterton Avenue and Cameron Falls Drive.

Most businesses will accept U.S. dollars at the current exchange rate, but dispensing foreign currency in change is restricted. Find bank machines and money exchange at the **Tamarack Village Square** (403/859-2378).

GETTING THERE AND AROUND

The Chief Mountain International Highway (Highway 17) connects Glacier and Waterton National Parks, but both the highway and the customs stations along it close down mid-September to mid-May, forcing drivers to head north from Montana on Highway 89 to Cardston, then west on Highway 5 to Waterton.

Citizens of Canada and the United States will need a passport to cross the border and proof of sufficient funds to finance your trip.

Butte, Helena, and Southwestern Montana

S outhwestern Montana is rich in almost every meaning of the word. Early prospectors discovered some of the richest gold deposits ever along the flanks of the Rocky Mountains here. Beginning at Bannack in 1862, then in Virginia

City, and then in almost every ravine throughout the area, prospectors found mineral wealth. Gold camps sprang up, the easily panned gold played out, and the settlement moved on.

This early colorful era of Montana's mining history ended when silver replaced gold as the mineral of choice. Silver demanded mills and smelters for extraction, which required costly investment. Soon the ripsnorting life of the prospector was replaced by a corporate payroll, and panning for gold in a lonely stream was traded for a shift underground with a crew of workers.

Whereas the early transitory life of the placer miner left few monuments, corporate mining from the 1880s to the 1930s built cities of worldwide influence. During the 1880s, Butte, "the richest hill on earth," was the largest silver producer in the world.

The boom that fed this early growth has largely turned bust. Nowadays, residents measure their wealth in the majestic beauty of the mountains, the free-flowing rivers filled with trout, and the potent culture of old cities and towns whose rich culinary heritage is still keenly observed.

Some of the best recreation in the state is here. The Jefferson River and its tributaries provide blue-ribbon trout fishing and enormous national forests provide unparalleled camping, hiking, and wildlife-viewing opportunities: The Beaverhead-Deerlodge National Forest alone is larger than many Atlantic states.

PLANNING YOUR TIME

For those interested in the history of the Old West, southwestern Montana is an incredibly rich destination; if you're interested in the history of the gold rush, Native Americans, or frontier ranch life, you could easily spend a week here. That the region is also rich in hot springs, mountain recreation, and fishing just makes the living a bit easier.

Previous: hay bales in the Big Hole area; the Montana State Capitol in Helena. **Above:** old mine in Butte.

Highlights

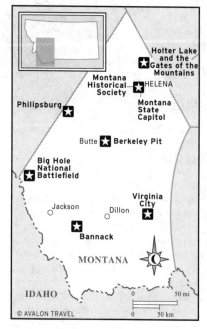

many ghost towns are also worth visiting (page 168).

★ **Big Hole National Battlefield:** In 1877, rather than move onto a reservation, Chief Joseph's band of Nez Perce fled their home. When they paused to rest in the Big Hole, they were ambushed by the U.S. Army. The battlefield is a moving place to visit in a beautiful setting (page 171).

★ **Bannack:** The remains of this well-preserved ghost town commemorate the rich 1862 gold strike on Grasshopper Creek, the scene of some of Montana's most violent early history (page 179).

★ **Virginia City:** Here original and restored buildings from the 1860s and 1870s have been more or less in use ever since they were built; today it's a "working ghost town" (page 185).

★ **Montana State Capitol:** This imposing structure is domed with a cupola of Butte copper. In the House Chamber hangs one of Charlie Russell's largest and most acclaimed works (page 196).

★ **Montana Historical Society:** Montana's premier museum mixes fine art, history, and changing exhibits. One of the nation's largest public collections of Charlie Russell's art is here (page 197).

★ **Holter Lake and the Gates of the Mountains:** Holter Lake is the most awe-inspiring of the three upper Missouri Lakes. Behind the dam lies the Gates of the Mountains, so named by Meriwether Lewis (page 205).

★ **Berkeley Pit:** Don't think that just because this is a giant pool of toxic water it's not worth a visit. Its vastness will give you a real sense of the scale of open-pit copper mining and how it swallowed up whole neighborhoods (page 159).

★ **Philipsburg:** Downtown Philipsburg's Victorian storefronts are colorful and well-preserved, many with original signage. The area's

The two urban destinations in this part of Montana are Helena and Butte, both legendary for the wealth that mining brought to early prospectors and to later industrialists.

Helena is a gracious small city backed up into a narrow Rocky Mountain valley. As the state capital, it deserves a couple of days' visit just to check out the capitol, the excellent **Montana Historical Society Museum,** and the amazing frontier architecture. The massive Queen Anne mansions that line the graceful old streets are evidence of the city's original wealth. A second day in the Helena area should be spent exploring the environs, either gold mine ghost towns or the boat tours through the **Gates of the Mountains,** where the first part of the Missouri River carves a canyon between sheer uplifts of limestone.

Butte, as you will discover, is another story. This scruffy, entirely fascinating mining center was once one of the West's largest cities from 1880 to 1930; then the mines closed, leaving this thriving city more an open-air museum than an actual urban center. However, there's history galore—and just wandering the streets, having drinks in venerable bars, and a long contemplation on just what an extraction economy *really* amounts to makes this one of Montana's most unique destinations. Stop by the **World Museum of Mining** to actually descend into the Orphan Girl mine or visit Chinese opium dens and brothels—now museums—to get a sense of what the Western frontier was really like. Two days in Butte will just begin to scratch the surface if you're a fan of Western history.

Downstream from Butte is **Deer Lodge,** where two completely incongruent sites are well worth a stop. The **Old Montana Prison** is an eerily beautiful structure that served as the state penitentiary from the 1890s to 1979. Tours are fascinating, and if you like the

feeling of being "in the pen," stay for a theater production on the outdoor stage. The **Grant-Kohrs Ranch National Historic Site** tells a different tale of Western history—that of an early cattle ranch founded in the 1860s.

West of Deer Lodge and the Clark Fork Valley, in the western foothills of the Flint Creek Mountains, is **Philipsburg,** a beautifully preserved mining town that's little changed since the 1890s. With a summer theater—Montana's oldest, built in 1891—good restaurants, and the excellent **Broadway Hotel** from 1890, Philipsburg is a lovely spot to spend the night. And if by now you've got the mining bug, you can drive west of town to try your luck at mining for jewels at the **Gem Mountain Sapphire Mine.**

South of Philipsburg is the **Big Hole Valley,** a scenic high valley devoted to ranching, fishing, and recreation. A highlight is the **Big Hole National Battlefield** where the Nez Perce under Chief Joseph held off the U.S. Army in 1877. History of another sort was made at **Bannack,** where Montana's first gold strike was made in 1862. Bannack went on to become the first territorial capital, and just as suddenly as it boomed came the bust. By 1890 the town was deserted, and it's now one of the West's most complete ghost towns. If all this frontier history has you feeling a bit creaky, spend the night at **Jackson Hot Springs,** where the naturally therapeutic hot mineral waters will soak out your aches and pains.

Early Montana's other big gold rush town was **Virginia City,** another territorial capital but not quite yet a ghost town. Many old businesses are still in operation, and wandering the steep streets is like wandering through an open-air museum of the mining West. Historic homes provide B&B accommodations, while vintage bars provide nightlife spice.

Butte, Helena, and Southwestern Montana

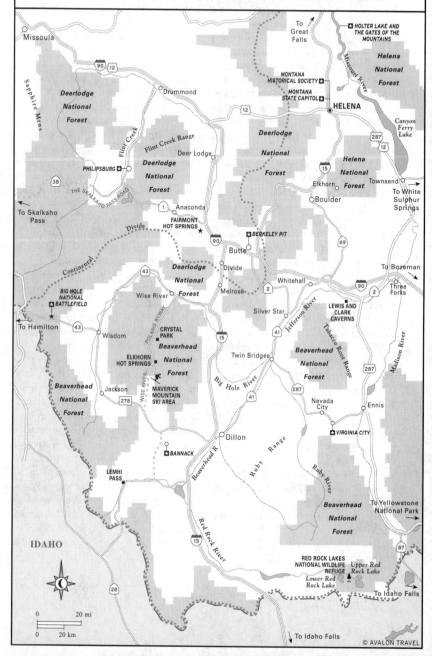

© AVALON TRAVEL

Butte

Montana's most representative city, Butte (pop. 34,000, elev. 5,755 feet) is also unique. Touted as "the richest hill on earth," Butte was the nation's largest single source of silver in the late 19th century and the largest source of copper until the 1930s.

This early and extreme wealth gave Butte a singular history and destiny. The town's politicians utterly dominated Montana government for the first 50 years of statehood. It became the state's first industrialized city, and it was also the largest until the 1960s.

Montanans from other parts of the state have always been deeply ambivalent about Butte; its political infighting, religious rivalries, hot temper, and its wealth and self-importance created a statewide atmosphere of distrust. However, many of the things that now seem typically Montanan—the can-do swagger, the spirited politics, the jocular and embracing sociality, its unspoken sense of neighborliness, even its food and drink (and the gusto and quantity in which they're consumed)—reached a zenith in the early days of Butte.

The city's greatest resource was always its people, the swirling mix of Irish, Poles, Italians, Slavs, Chinese, and others who forged the cosmopolitan collection of neighborhoods known as Butte. Nowadays, Billings makes much of being Montana's largest city and enjoys likening itself to a youthful Denver. Early in the 1900s, though, Butte had nearly as large a population tucked into a steep swale on Silverbow Creek; with its bluster and ethnic diversity, Butte was more like Chicago than any other city in the West.

Butte was a much larger, more vigorous city before the Berkeley Pit left a big hole in its center, but some of the charm and much of the history of the old city still remain: People still self-assuredly bustle, good food and drink are unquestionably an elemental part of daily life, and the old mansions and civic buildings that great wealth built still stand beside the ugly smokestacks, head frames, and piles of tailings.

SIGHTS

For a two-hour introduction to the sights and history of Butte, take the **Trolley Tour.** The tour leaves from the **chamber of commerce office** (1000 George St., 406/723-3177 or 800/735-6814, www.buttecvb.com, 10:30am, 1pm, 3pm Mon.-Sat., 10:30am and 1pm Sun. Memorial Day-Sept., $15 adults, $13 seniors, $10 students 12-17, $6 children 4-10, reservations required) and stops only at the Berkeley Pit. A fun alternative to the trolley is the more personalized **Urban Safari Tour** (842 W. Galena St., 406/723-3959, http://uptown-butteworks.com, 11am-2pm Tues.-Sun. June-Aug., $35 adults, $17.50 under 12), in which up to five passengers pile into a tricked-out golf cart with a knowledgeable guide, who will drive places that are inaccessible to the trolley.

A more active way to explore Butte's history is offered by **Old Butte Historical Adventures** (117 N. Main St., 406/498-3424, www.buttetours.info, 10am-2pm on the hour Mon.-Sat., $15 adults, $12.50 seniors, military and students with ID, $10 children under 12), offering tours of Butte's underground as well as a couple of tours exploring aboveground historic neighborhoods. Guides are knowledgeable and enthusiastic, and bring the old buildings to life. Especially wonderful is the speakeasy on the underground tour; it was

Butte from uptown

forgotten after Prohibition ended and rediscovered, in great condition, in 2004. Tours are fairly vigorous, so people with difficulty walking up and down hills and steps for an hour and a half should opt for the trolley tour.

World Museum of Mining

West of Montana Tech at the end of West Park Street, the **World Museum of Mining** (155 Museum Way, 406/723-7211, www.miningmuseum.org, 9am-6pm daily, Apr.-Oct., $8.50 adults, $7.50 seniors, $6 students 13-18, $3 children 5-12) sits on an old mining claim called the Orphan Girl. Visitors can pay extra ($17 adults, $14 seniors, $12 students 13-18, $9 children 5-12 includes museum) to don hard hats, miners' headlights, and battery belts and head 65 feet underground into the 2,700-foot-deep mine. The underground tours, which are the best part of the museum, depart at 10:30am, 12:30pm, and 3pm daily; it's a good idea to call ahead for a reservation.

Included on the grounds are a head frame, ore carts, a locomotive, and other hardware.

Butte's Mining Boom

When the first placer miners arrived near Butte in 1864, they discovered pits dug with elk antlers: Apparently Native Americans also knew of the area's gold deposits. But prospecting for gold requires water, and here, in this basin just under the crest of the Continental Divide, scarcely a stream runs. The gold camp drifted along until 1874, when the first silver claims were made. Abundant quartz in the Butte area contained an unparalleled richness in silver. The rush was on.

News of the silver strikes spread quickly, attracting miners and entrepreneurs from throughout the West. Two stand out: William Clark, a canny businessman, banker, and former miner from the Bannack gold-rush days, gained control of one of the richest mines. In 1876, Marcus Daly arrived in Butte from Colorado, sent by mining investors to scout out the mines of Butte. Both men controlled enough capital to develop the rich mineral deposits of Butte.

Silver doesn't freely occur like gold does. It must be milled out of the rock, usually quartz, in which it is suspended. This shift in method produced far-reaching

Copper mine head frames still dominate Butte's skyline.

changes in the Montana mining West. The gold camps inhabited by free-spirited prospectors quickly evolved into industrial towns dominated by the political and corporate interests of mine and smelter owners—and by organized labor.

Clark became the first of the mining kings of Butte by owning not only mines but also the supply stores, transportation systems, real estate, banks, and processing plants necessary for the development of Butte.

Daly was the first industrialist to recognize the potential of the Butte copper deposits. He bought up the now-legendary Anaconda Mine and discovered veins of nearly pure copper 100 feet across; this mine alone produced more than 50 million pounds in 1887. Before anyone else realized the value of copper—copper for electric wire was only just becoming a worthwhile commodity—Daly bought up the mines adjacent to the Anaconda. He built the city of the same name 26 miles west of Butte, where he sent copper ore to be smelted.

Besides mineral deposits and investment capital, the third component needed to make Butte boom was the railroad. The Utah and Northern reached Butte in 1881, suddenly linking Butte minerals with a world in the midst of industrialization and modernization.

The indoor museum contains mining tools, steam engines, ore samples, and an extensive archive of old photos from Butte's boom years.

In the same complex is **Hell Roarin' Gulch,** a replica of a mining camp from 1900. A millinery shop, Chinese herb store, bank, church, school, post office, and other period buildings have been faithfully reconstructed.

Montana Tech

Montana Tech, a division of the University of Montana, sits on a bench of Big Butte, the promontory just west of uptown Butte. Established in 1900, the college specializes in teaching mineral science and other professional and technical curricula.

From the ramparts of the campus are great views over the city to the Continental Divide; a statue of 19th-century copper baron Marcus Daly shares the view from the university's entrance on Park Avenue. Visit the **Mineral Museum** (Main Hall, 1300 W. Park St.,

406/496-4414, www.mbmg.mtech.edu/museum, 9am-5pm daily mid-June-mid-Sept., 9am-4pm Mon.-Fri. mid-Sept.-mid-June, free), where 1,300 mineral specimens, including a 27.5-ounce gold nugget found near Butte in 1989, are displayed. In a separate darkened room is an interesting exhibit of fluorescent minerals.

Uptown

Butte's magnificent homes and commercial and civic buildings attest to its early wealth and importance. Increasingly, vacant buildings and boarded-up windows are more the norm than the exception as the town sadly slumps into a pre-ghost town torpor. A vaguely eerie quality also comes from the **mining head frames** that stand preserved around the edges of uptown. These tall structures were used to lower miners to their underground workplaces.

Much of uptown Butte is protected as a national landmark, and many individual buildings are on the National Register of Historic Places; the chamber of commerce provides a brochure with a walking tour of historic buildings. The following are open to the public:

The **Copper King Mansion** (219 W. Granite St., 406/782-7580, www.thecopperkingmansion.com, 9am-4pm daily May-Sept., $10 adults, $5 children) was built in 1888 by William Clark at a time when he was one of the world's richest men. This three-story brick High Victorian mansion contains 30 rooms, many with frescoed ceilings, carved staircases, inlaid floors, and Tiffany windows. Clark spent $300,000 on the building and imported many craftspeople from Europe. The third floor boasts a 60-foot-long ballroom and a chapel. Immerse yourself more deeply by spending the night; the mansion is also a B&B.

Clark's son Charles was so taken by a château he visited in France that he procured the plans and had it reconstructed in Butte. Now known as the **Charles W. Clark Chateau** (321 W. Broadway, 406/490-6678, http://co.silverbow.mt.us/722/Clark-Chateau,

noon-5pm Wed.-Mon., June-mid-Sept., noon-5pm Sat.-Sun. mid-Sept.-May, $7, or $15 family), it features photos and exhibits on Butte's architectural history.

The showpiece of Butte civic architecture is the **Butte-Silver Bow Courthouse** (155 W. Granite St.), built in 1910. A lovely stained-glass dome tops the four-story rotunda, murals decorate the ceilings, and oak fixtures predominate throughout. Butte leaders spent almost twice as much on this courthouse as the state spent on the Montana capitol.

Down on Mercury Street, the **Dumas building** (45 E. Mercury St., 406/299-2702, www.thedumasbrothel.com, 11am-4pm Tues.-Sat., $10 tour) was Butte's longest-lived brothel, in operation from 1890 until 1982. It's unique in that the building was purpose-built as a brothel: The two-story brick structure, which is slowly being restored from its rather decrepit condition, still has quite a few architectural features peculiar to a house of prostitution, such as windows onto the corridors and bedrooms that the miners more appropriately called cribs. This structure is the only surviving remnant of Butte's once-thriving red-light district. The Dumas is a pretty crazy place, and it's uniquely Butte—be sure to check it out.

Also unusual is **The Mai Wah** (17 W. Mercury St., 406/723-3231, www.maiwah.org, 10am-4pm Tues.-Sat., June-Sept.; $5 adults, $3 children under 12), a museum dedicated to telling the story of Chinese miners and workers who pioneered in Butte. The Mai Wah building contained several Chinese-owned businesses; Butte's China Alley, the heart of the old Chinatown, is adjacent.

Another gem of old Butte architecture is the **Mother Lode Theater** (316 W. Park St., 406/723-3602). This magnificent theater has been refurbished and serves as Butte's performing arts center. Although the theater is not open for regular tours, art events and organizations use the facility, so try to have a look.

Head all the way to the top of Main Street to visit the open-air **Granite Mountain**

Mine Memorial (www.minememorial.org), which pays tribute to the 168 miners who died in 1917 when fire broke out in the Granite Mountain mine. The memorial features an excellent audio presentation as well as letters from the doomed miners to their families and the names of the miners who died; it's also a good place to get a panoramic view of Butte.

Overlooking Butte from the vastness of the Continental Divide is **Our Lady of the Rockies** (406/782-1221 or 800/800-5239, www.ourladyoftherockies.net, tours 10am and 2pm Mon.-Sat., 11am Sun., June-Oct., $15 adults, $13 seniors, $11 students 13-17, $7 children 5-12, $2 children 4 and under), a 90-foot statue of the Virgin Mary. Completed in 1985, the monument was the result of six years of volunteer community work, including building the access road to the site, 8,510 feet above sea level. There is a viewing point at Continental Drive and Pine. Private vehicles are not allowed on the road up to the statue; you'll need to join a tour bus group (the buses leave from the Butte Plaza Mall, 3100 Harrison Ave.).

★ Berkeley Pit

Veering from the high to the low, there's the **Berkeley Pit,** the enormous open-pit copper mine just next to uptown Butte. Because of the high costs of hard-rock underground mining, in 1955 Anaconda began stripping low-grade copper ore from the surface. Eventually the Berkeley Pit reached a depth of 1,800 feet; the gulf from side to side is more than one mile across. Mining has ceased here, and today the pit is filling with water—at 900 feet, it's Montana's deepest body of water.

It is also probably its most toxic water, percolating up as it does through abandoned mine shafts. The poisonous, acidic (pH 2.5) water is a threat to passing waterfowl: A flock of endangered trumpeter swans died in the lake one spring. However, some species of fungus and bacteria have adapted to the conditions here; indeed, some produce toxins themselves to enhance their survival and others ingest metals, which may ultimately lead to an alternative to traditional toxic cleanup methods.

If left undrained, it's estimated that the rising water will enter the Butte water table by 2020, causing further havoc. Measures have been taken to divert the flow of water into the pit, slowing the rise of the water level. A **viewing stand** (200 Shields St., 406/723-3177, March-Nov., $2) allows you to look down into the Berkeley Pit and its eerily green water (from dissolved copper and mineral salts).

The Berkeley Pit is filled with toxic water.

RECREATION

Stodden Park (Sampson and Utah Sts., 406/494-3686) has a swimming pool, picnic grounds, tennis courts, and a nine-hole golf course.

Fourteen miles north of Butte on I-15 (at the Elk Park exit) is **Sheepshead Mountain Recreation Area:** This fishing and wildlife-viewing facility is completely accessible to wheelchairs. It's a stopover for migrating waterfowl, and moose and elk are frequently sighted.

Rock climbers need only look to I-90 and **Homestake Pass,** where the Boulder Batholith's granite juts up from the interstate. Head 25 miles south on I-15, turn east at exit 99, and continue to **Humbug Spires Wilderness Study Area** to climb the 600-foot granite outcroppings or merely to hike and gawk.

NIGHTLIFE

Within a state that already has a rowdy reputation, Butte bears the sybaritic crown; in the Butte equation, bars are elemental. Remember that in Montana, you don't have to drink alcohol to go out to bars; bars are *what you do.*

A night out on the town in Butte should include a walk by the infamous, and now shuttered, **M & M** (9 N. Main St.), which from its opening in 1890 until its closing in 2014 was open 24 hours a day with the exception of a few years of closure in the early 2000s. Other classic Butte bars include the **Silver Dollar** (133 S. Main St.), **Maloney's** (112 N. Main St.), and the **Metals Sports Bar and Grill** (8 W. Park St.).

Butte's long history of brewing is upheld by the folks at **Quarry Brewing** (124 W. Broadway, 406/723-0245, www.quarrybrewing.net, 3pm-8pm Mon.-Fri., 1pm-8pm Sat., 1pm-6pm Sun.).

EVENTS

Butte's biggest annual event is **St. Patrick's Day,** when uptown is decked out with shamrocks and a big parade turns the streets into a sea of green. The parade route then heads pretty much straight through the bar doors or into any of the many restaurants serving special corned beef and cabbage.

The Fourth of July is celebrated in a similarly heady fashion, and there's always a good fireworks display. In mid-July, come for the

the popular Montana Folk Festival

excellent **Montana Folk Festival** (406/497-6464, www.montanafolkfestival.com) to hear cowboy, jazz, klezmer, blues, and world music.

Prepare for **Evel Knievel Days** (http://evelknieveldays.org, end of July) by learning all the verses to *Born to be Wild*. Expect crowds; motorcycle not required.

Another recent addition to the festival calendar is **An Rí Rá** (www.mtgaelic.org), an Irish cultural festival that focuses on music, dancing, and language, held the second weekend of August.

ACCOMMODATIONS
$50-100
In the historic center of Butte, there are a couple of pleasant older motels. The ★ **Finlen Hotel & Motor Inn** (100 E. Broadway, 406/723-5461 or 800/729-5461, www.finlen.com, $84-104) was once Butte's landmark hotel; although it's now largely taken up with offices and apartments, a couple of floors are reserved for hotel rooms. It's joined by an adjacent motor court ($72-82, allows dogs) and is central for exploring Butte's nooks and crannies.

Also within walking distance of historic sites, the **Rodeway Inn Capri** (220 N. Wyoming, 406/723-4391, www.rodewayinn.com/Butte, $58-98) is a good budget choice and allows dogs.

Those interested in staying in a grand historic home should check out the **Copper King Mansion B&B** (219 W. Granite St., 406/782-7580, www.copperkingmansion.com, $85-135). In addition to a B&B, the Copper King Mansion—William A. Clark's private Xanadu, built in 1884—also serves as a museum. In fact, travelers stay in the rooms viewed by the public during summertime museum hours. Access to the rooms is structured, so travelers should weigh potential disruptions against their need for seclusion before arranging a stay.

Over $100
Most of Butte's motels cluster around I-90 exit 127. Of these mostly chain operations,

a few stand out. The classiest hotel in town is the **Hampton Inn** (3499 Harrison Ave., 406/494-2250 or 800/426-7866, www.butte-hamptoninn.com, $143-153), with fancy linens, extracomfy beds, and an indoor pool.

Best Western Butte Plaza Inn (2900 Harrison Ave., 406/494-3500, www.bestwesternmontana.com, $107-117) offers an indoor pool, exercise room, sauna, steam room, and hot tub. The hotel is near shopping, and there's a complimentary breakfast buffet daily.

Removed from both uptown and I-90 is ★ **Toad Hall Manor B&B** (1 Green Ln., 406/494-2625 or 866/443-8623, www.toadhallmanor.com, $125-180), which takes its name and its aura from *The Wind in the Willows*. The inn (it's a cross between a small hotel and a B&B) overlooks the country club golf course and is as elegant as Butte gets these days.

If you don't mind staying a few miles out of town, consider making **Fairmont Hot Springs** (1500 Fairmont Rd., 406/797-3241 or 800/332-3272, www.fairmontmontana.com, $159-425) your base.

Camping
The **Butte KOA** (1601 Kaw Ave., 406/782-8080, mid-Apr.-Oct., $31 tent, $41-46 RV, $60 cabin) is off I-90's exit 126, two blocks north. Farther from town, find the Forest Service's **Lowland Campground** (406/494-2147, www.fs.usda.gov/bdnf) to the north of town (Elk Park exit from I-15).

FOOD
Only in Butte could one even begin to make the argument that there is a historic Montana cuisine. Its large ethnic population and intense urban character gave restaurants a prominence and an enthusiastic clientele that was unusual in frontier Montana. Butte specialties include the pasty (PAST-ee), brought over from Cornwall, England, and the pork chop sandwich. Meals in Butte were traditionally served in courses; the price of dinner included a relish tray, breadsticks, soup and salads, a pasta course, the main dish,

and dessert. This evening's worth of food and service is sometimes called eating "Old Meaderville" style, for the Meaderville Italian neighborhood that collapsed into the Berkeley Pit, fine restaurants and all. It's still the norm at many Butte restaurants.

At the ★ **Uptown Cafe** (47 E. Broadway St., 406/723-4735, www.uptowncafe.com, 11am-2pm Mon.-Fri., 5pm-10pm daily, dinner $12-30), the best of Butte tradition meets lively up-to-the-minute sauces and ingredients. The wine list is intriguing, the ambience is light and friendly, and the fare—with lots of fresh seafood, veal, and pasta on the menu, and a nice selection of homemade desserts—is superb. Early dinner specials (until 6:30pm) are a real bargain at $14.50. Most dinners are a five-course extravaganza, so come with a big appetite.

Butte's most famous restaurant is **Lydia's** (4915 Harrison Ave., 406/494-2000, www.lydiassupperclub.com, 5:30pm-9pm nightly, $20-35), which is housed in a suspiciously drab 1970s-era building out on the edge of town. Inside, the typical steaks and seafood are joined by Italian food and plenty of old-fashioned but highly creditable side dishes, served in an atmosphere of slightly dated chic. (Be sure to tour the restaurant's stained-glass windows and lamps.)

Don't count out Butte for steaks. **Casagranda's Steakhouse** (801 S. Utah St., 406/723-4141, http://casagrandassteakhouse.webs.com, 5pm-9pm Sun.-Thurs., 5pm-10pm Fri.-Sat., $13-25, reservations encouraged), housed in a historic warehouse, has become a favorite place for steak, pasta, chicken, and seafood, including sushi. Dinners include several courses, so come prepared to eat.

For something uniquely Butte, try **Pork Chop John's** (8 W. Mercury St., 406/782-0812, or 2400 Harrison Ave., 406/782-1783, www.porkchopjohns.com, 10:30am-8pm Mon.-Fri., 10:30am-6:30pm Sat., Mercury St., 10:30am-10:30pm daily Harrison Ave., $3.25). The boneless pork chop sandwich is a Butte original; order it the traditional way, with pickles, onions, and mustard, and think

of all the hungry miners who also gained satisfaction here.

Find Butte's other culinary gem, the pasty at **Joe's Pasty Shop** (1641 Grand, 406/723-9071, 6am-7pm Mon.-Fri., 6am-6pm Sat., $7); sit down and enjoy your pasty with some gravy. In uptown, **Gamer's Café** (15 W. Park, 406/723-5453, 7am-2pm Mon.-Sat. 8am-2pm Sun., $4-8), a Butte favorite for hearty meals for more than a century, also serves pasties. **Nancy's Pasty Shop** (403/782-7410, 8am-5:30pm Tues.-Fri., 8am-5pm Sat., $7.50) is near the Berkeley Pit and serves especially large and tasty pasties, as well as sandwiches and burgers.

Broadway Cafe (302 E. Broadway, 406/723-8711, 11am-9pm Mon.-Thurs., 11am-11pm Fri., noon-9pm Sat., $6-17), housed in a historic building, is a hip and friendly place for espresso, microbrews and wine, or pizza and live music. Another comfortable place to hang out is the sweet and earnest ★ **Hummingbird Cafe** (605 W. Park, 406/723-2044, http://hummingbirdbutte.com, 7:30am-4pm Mon.-Fri., 9am-4pm Sat., $4-9), which uses organic ingredients when possible in its smoothies, juices, soups, and sandwiches. This is one of the best spots in town for breakfast.

INFORMATION AND SERVICES

The **Butte Convention and Visitors Bureau** (406/723-3177 or 800/735-6814, www.buttecvb.com) is at 1000 George Street.

St. James Hospital (406/723-2500) is at 400 South Clark Street.

GETTING THERE AND AROUND

Butte's **Bert Mooney Airport** (http://butteairport.com) is served by **SkyWest.**

Also at the airport, south off Harrison Avenue, are car rental agencies: **Avis** (406/494-3131) and **Budget** (406/494-7573). **Enterprise** (3825 Harrison Ave., 406/494-1900) is near the airport.

Greyhound (800/231-2222) and **Rimrock**

Stage (800/255-7655) bus lines link Butte to other Montana cities. The bus station is located at 1324 Harrison Avenue (406/723-3287). For a cab, call **Mining City Taxi** (406/723-6511).

The Bus (406/497-6515, www.buttebus.org), as Butte's small transit system is known, runs during the daytime Monday-Friday, with a limited Saturday schedule.

163

The Upper Clark Fork River Valley

Silver Bow Creek drains the Butte Basin before charging almost 1,000 feet down a narrow channel to the wide valley below. Here the creek is renamed the Clark Fork River, and it begins to pick up the many tributaries that eventually make it one of the most important arms of the mighty Columbia.

Early settlers knew this as the Deer Lodge Valley. The state's first ranches grew up when some miners recognized that a quicker and more dependable profit could be made selling agricultural products to the booming mining towns.

Today, this open stretch of the Clark Fork River Valley is the stepping-off point for hikes in the rugged Flint Creek Range. Fishing in the revivified Clark Fork River is both popular and possible; in the not-too-distant past it was neither.

FAIRMONT HOT SPRINGS

The old **Fairmont Hot Springs spa** (1500 Fairmont Rd., 406/797-3241 or 800/332-3272, www.fairmontmontana.com, pool use $8.75 adults, $4.75 seniors, $5.75 children 10 and under), just off I-90 halfway between Butte and Anaconda, is one of the most popular family resorts and conference hotels in Montana. The hot springs here fill four pools. Two of them (one indoors, one out) are Olympic-size and heated to 90-100°F; the others run 100-105°F and are meant for soaking weary muscles. There's a separate charge to use the somewhat old-fashioned-looking waterslide; a combined pool and slide pass costs $16 for adults and $12 for kids. A challenging and well-designed 18-hole golf course ($45) is a very big draw (the "mile long, mile

high" fifth hole is one of the state's most challenging).

Fairmont is a good base for hiking and riding in the Deerlodge National Forest and Anaconda-Pintler Wilderness Area, fishing and water sports at Georgetown Lake, and skiing at Discovery Basin. Cross-country skiers love Fairmont; after a day skiing the trails around nearby Mt. Haggin, a good hot soak takes the ache out of tired muscles.

If soaking doesn't do the trick, the resort's massage therapists can provide a Swedish, salt-glow, or hot rock massage ($75 and up).

At Fairmont, a full range of rooming options includes suites and kitchenettes; double rooms start at $159. Dining is available, but neither outstanding nor inexpensive.

Some resorts with Fairmont's amenities and potential would discourage kids, but not here. This is a great place to take active children. Indeed, when schools are out, it's a bit raucous, but fun for kids. There are enough supervised activities here that harried parents might even be able to have some time to themselves.

DEER LODGE

Named for a salt lick that was popular with deer during the frontier days, Deer Lodge is the center of a vast valley full of history and recreation.

While the valley prospered as a result of its proximity to Butte and Anaconda markets, the pollution of these two industrial centers was at odds with the farms and ranches. The Works Progress Administration's 1939 *Montana: A State Guide Book* described the waters of Silver Bow Creek just above present-day Fairmont Hot Springs as "muddied with

The Grant-Kohrs Ranch

Canadian trader Richard Grant and his sons Johnny and James began trading cattle in the 1850s along the Oregon Trail in Idaho. The Grants would trade westbound pioneers one fat, healthy cow fattened on western Montana grasses for two emaciated specimens that had just crossed the plains. It didn't take long for the Grants to amass a huge holding of cattle. In 1862 Johnny Grant established a base ranch in the Deer Lodge Valley, Montana's first. When the gold rush began in the 1860s, cattlemen like the Grants were already in place to sell beef to hungry miners.

When the first influx of prospectors swooped into Bannack in 1862, some disenchanted souls decided to explore the new territory for other options. Among them was a German named Conrad Kohrs. After a stint as Bannack's butcher, he put together his own cattle herd and went off to Deer Lodge Valley. He bought Johnny Grant's ranch and never looked back. Building on Grant's base, Kohrs was the foremost rancher in Montana for almost 40 years.

Johnny Grant's 1862 log home was considered the finest house in the territory, but when Kohrs took over, he expanded both the house and the ranch; by the 1880s Kohrs was grazing cattle on over a million acres of open-range prairie and meadow across four states and southern Canada. Even after the disastrous winter of 1886, Kohrs was able to ship 8,000-10,000 cattle per year to eastern markets.

Kohrs reduced the size of the ranch in the 1910s, but the Deer Lodge holdings stayed in the family until 1972, when the National Park Service bought the ranch to preserve it as a historic monument.

the refuse of Butte mines, though in places it is intensely blue from dissolved copper salts." The Clark Fork was unable to support aquatic life until the 1960s, after 10 years of cleanup. In 1903, after cattle began dying in the fields from poisoned air, the smelter at Anaconda raised its smokestack 300 feet in order to disperse its smoke higher in the atmosphere.

Between stricter mining regulations and the decline of mining in general, the valley has returned to a degree of its former integrity. A portion of the Clark Fork by Warm Springs offers such great fishing that it is now regulated by the Department of Fish, Wildlife, and Parks.

Although Deer Lodge has several interesting places to visit, its accommodations are pretty basic. Travelers will find more lodging and dining choices in nearby Butte.

Grant-Kohrs Ranch National Historic Site

The **Grant-Kohrs Ranch National Historic Site** (316 Main St., 406/846-2070, www. nps.gov/grko, 9am-5:30pm daily Memorial

Day-Labor Day, 9am-4:30pm the rest of the year, free), the home and outbuildings of Montana's first ranch, provides a fascinating glimpse into the real life of cowboys and ranchers in the early days of Montana. The ranch is maintained as a working ranch; the old 23-room ranch house is wonderfully intact—a delightful mix of Victoriana and frontier living. The house is open for guided tours only, and no more than 12 people may tour at once. Admission is on a first-come, first-served basis.

Old Montana Prison Complex

The **Old Montana Prison** (1106 Main St., 406/846-3111, www.pcmaf.org, 8am-6pm daily, $10 adults, $9 seniors, $6 children, covers admission to all local museums) is the core of a series of contiguous historical exhibits. Montana Territory first established a penitentiary in Deer Lodge in 1871, but the disturbingly attractive buildings now open to the public were begun in the 1890s. The castellated three-story cell block of red brick was built in 1912. It contains 200 cells, each six by seven feet. W. A. Clark financed the construction of the prison theater in 1919. The oldest structure is the quarried sandstone guard wall, 24 feet high and anchored 4 feet below ground, built in 1893.

All of these structures (and others) were built by forced convict labor, a practice that was later outlawed. After a violent prison riot and investigation into the deteriorating conditions at the old prison, a new facility was built in 1979. Most of the facility is open for self-guided tours. Check out the gun ports in the shower room, the "galloping gallows" for off-premises executions, and maximum-security's Black Box. The **Montana Law Enforcement Museum** is located in the prison. Here is a memorial to officers slain in the line of duty, as well as curiosities such as Lee Harvey Oswald's handcuffs.

Resist the reaction to find all of this really creepy, and do visit the old prison. The perfectly preserved quarters and facilities tell a grim story of prison life in the recent past, but almost eerily, the handsome architecture and pleasing symmetry of the row upon row of empty cells give the prison a forlorn but intense beauty.

Also in the prison complex is the **Montana Auto Museum,** the world's second-largest antique Ford automobile collection. Edward Towe began his hobby in 1953 with the acquisition of a 1923 Ford Model-T Runabout; the collection now comprises more than 100 automobiles. Some of the standout cars are the 1931 A-400 convertible sedan, a 1957 Thunderbird, and a 1910 Willys Overland.

Other Museums

Across the street from the prison is the **Powell County Museum** (1199 Main St., 406/846-1694, 9am-5pm daily Memorial Day-Labor Day), which contains dinosaur bones, Native American tools, mining equipment, cowboy gear, and other relics of Powell County's rich

history. Nearby is **Yesterday's Playthings** (1017 Main St., 406/846-1133, 9am-5pm daily Memorial Day-Labor Day), a doll and toy museum featuring 1,000 antique dolls. The **Frontier Montana Museum** (1153 Main St., 406/846-0026, 9am-5pm Thurs.-Sat.) displays Western memorabilia, with a particular focus on guns and saloon memorabilia. Your ticket to the Old Montana Prison includes admission to all of the above museums as well; these smaller museums close down from Labor Day to Memorial Day.

Recreation

The Flint Creek Mountains rise directly west of Deer Lodge. These jagged peaks harbor many high mountain lakes linked with good hiking trails; these are also good trails to explore on mountain bikes. From the **Racetrack** Forest Service campground, a rough road continues eight miles to **Indian Meadows trailhead.** Here, a series of alpine lakes reposes beneath the 9,000-foot Twin Peaks. The lakes are high enough to be undependable as fisheries. To reach Racetrack, take I-90's Racetrack exit 11 miles south of Deer Lodge and head 11 miles west on Racetrack Road (Forest Rd. 169).

Hikes to other high mountain lakes begin at **Tin Cup Lake,** eight miles west of Deer Lodge, off Montana State Prison Road; and west of Rock Creek Lake, about 15 miles northwest of Deer Lodge on Forest Service Road 168. Consult the **Deer Lodge National Forest ranger station** (in Grant-Kohrs Ranch visitors center, 406/846-1770, www.fs.usda.gov/bdnf) and map for more information.

Information and Services

The **Powell County Chamber of Commerce** (406/846-2094, www.powell-countymontana.com) is at 1109 Main Street.

The **Powell County Memorial Hospital** (406/846-2212) is at 1101 Texas Street.

Pintler Scenic Route

Montana Highway 1 leaves the Clark Fork Valley at Anaconda to wind through high mountain valleys and past ghost towns and old mining centers. The highway plunges down to join the Clark Fork and I-90 at Drummond. This alternative to the interstate doesn't involve any extra mileage, but it does lead to plentiful scenic and historic sites, including the towns of Anaconda, known chiefly for its smelter but also for its incredible Superfund cleanup, and Philipsburg, a convivial old silver town with a wealth of century-old storefronts, private homes, and civic structures. Located in a steep draw beneath craggy peaks, "P-Burg," as Montanans call it, is one of the most picturesque towns in the state.

ANACONDA AND VICINITY

Anaconda (pop. about 9,300, elev. 5,331 feet) is the town that Marcus Daly built. As the smelter for Butte's enormous reserves of copper and zinc, Anaconda became a powerful city, nearly edging out Helena as capital of Montana.

To the industrialists who built Butte, its incredible mineral wealth was only half the equation. A *lot* of water was needed to refine the ore. Butte, situated in an arid basin near the Continental Divide, had scarcely enough water for prospectors to successfully pan for gold.

Copper King Marcus Daly decided that, rather than bring the water to the ore, he'd take the ore to a better water source so he went to the Warm Springs Creek Valley, 26 miles west of Butte, to establish a smelter.

The **Washoe Smelter,** towering on a hill above Anaconda, became the largest copper smelter in the world. The immense smokestack that rose above Anaconda became a landmark; at 585 feet high, nearly seven million bricks were used in its construction.

Anaconda was inextricably tied to the fate of Butte. When Butte stumbled, Anaconda also faltered. After years of failing business, ARCO, which had purchased Anaconda in the late 1970s, closed the Washoe Smelter in 1983.

Sights

Anaconda has preserved its historic town center. Stop by the **vistor center** (306 E. Park) for a map of historic buildings. One of the most imposing buildings is the old **City Hall** (401 E. Commercial). Constructed in 1895, it is made of local materials: pressed brick, Anaconda granite, and copper trim. City and county offices are now housed in the courthouse, along with the historical society and the **Copper Village Museum and Art Center** (406/563-2422, www.coppervillageartcenter.com), a community arts center.

The **Deer Lodge County Courthouse,** at the south end of Main Street, dominates the town. Built in 1898, it features a rotunda, a copper-clad cupola, curving staircases, and a dumbwaiter to convey books from floor to floor.

An art deco extravaganza, the **Washoe Theatre** (305 Main St., 406/563-6161) is one of Anaconda's most stellar showcases, and still a good place to catch a movie. The hammered metal-leaf decorations are almost overwhelming. The imposing **Hearst Free Library** (401 Main St.) was an 1898 gift to Anaconda from newspaper magnate William Randolph Hearst's mother, Phoebe.

Catch the 1936 **vintage bus** at the chamber of commerce (306 E. Park, 406/563-2400, $8) for a 90-minute tour of Anaconda. Tours start at 10am and 2pm Monday-Saturday, mid-May-mid-September.

The 585-foot-tall smelter stack is the world's tallest freestanding masonry structure and now marks the site of the **Anaconda Stack State Park** (Hwy. 1 at Monroe St., http://stateparks.mt.gov/anaconda-smoke-stack).

The park is pretty undeveloped; it's mainly a place to view the stack (from a distance) and a few interpretive signs.

Recreation

The biggest thing to hit Anaconda since the smelter is the Jack Nicklaus-designed **Old Works Golf Course** (406/563-5989, www.oldworks.org). Built by ARCO on a huge Superfund site, the course incorporates many historic features of the erstwhile Old Works Smelting Site, including black slag left over from mining, resulting in a strikingly attractive black and green course. This is a long tough course—seven miles from start to finish, with some exceptional holes. Greens fees are reasonable for such a high-caliber course; summer weekday rates run $50 for 18 holes.

Another former Superfund site, **Warm Springs Ponds** is an almost shockingly good place to go bird-watching or fishing (catch-and-release only). These ponds and wetlands, created from ponds built to catch mining wastes drifting downstream from Butte, are laced with 15 miles of hiking or biking trails and include nesting areas for ospreys and many songbirds. Some of the state's largest trout have been pulled from these ponds. To reach the ponds, take Exit 201 (Warm Springs) from I-90 and head east.

Mt. Haggin Wildlife Management Area offers stunning views onto local mountains and also the chance to see bashful moose and elk. Mt. Haggin is popular with cross-country skiers in winter and mountain bikers in summer. To reach Mt. Haggin, follow Highway 274 south from Anaconda 14 miles; watch for the sign for **Mule Ranch Vista.**

Accommodations

Right downtown is the **Marcus Daly Motel** (119 W. Park, 406/563-3411 or 800/535-6528, www.marcusdaly.com, $79); it's both comfortable and convenient, with an attentive owner. Special rates, including ski and golf packages, are available. The **Vagabond Lodge Motel** (1421 E. Park, 406/563-5251 or 800/231-2660, $69-92) is an attractive brick inn across from the city park and within walking distance of the golf course.

Find B&B lodgings at the **Hickory House** (218 Park, 406/563-5481, www.hickoryhouse-inn.com, $70-100), a nicely restored former rectory with a lovely garden.

Also consider staying just a few miles down the road at **Fairmont Hot Springs** (1500 Fairmont Rd., 406/797-3241 or 800/332-3272, www.fairmontmontana.com, $159-425).

Camping

Lost Creek State Park (406/287-3541, http://stateparks.mt.gov/lost-creek, May-Nov., $15 Montana resident, $23 nonresident) six miles off Highway 48, two miles east of Anaconda, is a campground in a narrow limestone canyon. A waterfall, interesting geology, and mountain goats and bighorn sheep make this a nice alternative to urban RV sites. **Big Sky RV Park** (350 Copper Sands Rd., 406/563-2967, $35) has fishing access on Warm Springs Creek and is near public parks. **Warm Springs Campground** (www.fs.usda.gov/bdnf, late June-mid-Sept., free) is in the Beaverhead-Deerlodge National Forest 11 miles northwest of town on Highway 1, then 2 miles north on Forest Service Road 170.

Food

Although Butte has many more dining options, it's possible to find both pasties and multicourse meals in Anaconda. **Wind's Pasties** (208 E. Park, 406/563-2362, www.windspasties.com, 8am-4:30pm Mon.-Fri.) offers the local version of the hearty pies, including a breakfast version.

Despite its rather grim exterior, **Barclay II Supper Club** (1300 E. Commercial, 406/563-5541, 5pm-9pm Tues.-Sun., $10-30) is Anaconda's most stylish restaurant, with excellent steaks and multicourse Italian-influenced meals.

Information and Services

The **Anaconda Chamber of Commerce** (406/563-2400, www.anacondamt.org) is at 306 East Park.

The **Community Hospital of Anaconda** (406/563-8500) is at 401 West Pennsylvania.

GEORGETOWN LAKE

Georgetown Lake, at the upper reaches of Flint Creek, is one of the state's oldest hydroelectric projects, created in 1885 when Flint Creek was dammed. The lake is incredibly popular with the locals and is visited summer and winter.

Today, the preferred pastimes at Georgetown Lake are boating, fishing, and swimming, although many people simply go there to weekend at their cabins. Unfortunately, the area's lodgepole pines have been attacked by mountain pine beetles, leaving a forest full of standing dead trees.

Discovery Ski Area

Located 20 miles west of Anaconda in the Flint Creek Range, **Discovery** (406/563-2184, www.skidiscovery.com, $42 adult, $32 senior, $21 child 12 and under) offers a vertical drop of 2,400 feet along 67 runs. Full rental facilities are available, as well as food and beverage services at the ski lodge. Discovery is known both for its ski school and for its lack of crowds. There's no lodging at the ski area, but there are some reasonably priced small places nearby; Fairmont Hot Springs Resort offers package deals combining lodging and skiing.

Accommodations

Camping is easy at Georgetown Lake, with an abundant mix of private and public campgrounds in the area. The lakeshore is dotted with **Forest Service campgrounds** (406/859-3211, www.fs.usda.gov/bdnf). **Lodgepole** (reservations available at 877/444-6777, www.recreation.gov, late May-late Sept., $13, $9 reservation fee) is along Hwy. 1 just across from Georgetown Lake; **Piney** ($15) and **Philipsburg Bay** ($15) are farther from the highway. **Flint Creek Campground** (May-Sept., free) is a primitive Forest Service campground three miles west of Georgetown Lake just off Highway 1.

Remember to bring drinking water, because there is no piped water.

Although most visitors here camp or stay in their family cabins, a couple of Georgetown Lake hotel-restaurant combinations offer good food plus access to the lake and nearby Discovery Basin skiing. **Forest Edge Inn** (789 Georgetown Lake Rd., 406/563-5323, www.forestedgeinn.com, $125-175) is a newer and very comfortable B&B.

★ PHILIPSBURG

Between Georgetown Lake and Philipsburg, Highway 1 follows Flint Creek down precipitous Flint Creek Canyon to the Philipsburg Valley. The terrain eventually becomes more hospitable to ranching, and between Philipsburg and Drummond the landscape becomes increasingly agrarian.

Whether it is the community's isolation or the integrity of its Victorian-era architecture, Philipsburg (pop. 850, elev. 5,195 feet) has recently gained a reputation as a refuge for artists. Philipsburg has an exceedingly handsome Victorian-era town center, and each year seems to see another old building brought back to life with lots of paint, loving care, and entrepreneurial pride.

Sights

Philipsburg never really changed much after 1900, and the old town has remained intact. Pick up a brochure detailing a walking tour to the town's historic buildings from the **Granite County Museum and Cultural Center** (155 S. Sansome St., 406/859-3020, www.granitecountymuseum.com, noon-4pm daily June-Aug.), a former hotel that now houses exhibits on hard-rock mining and ghost towns. This is a good place to learn about the many ghost towns in the neighborhood; ask for directions to Kirkville, Black Pine, or Red Lion.

Lots of antiques stores and cafés now line the streets. Downtown's Victorian storefronts are especially colorful and well-preserved, many with original signage. The grade school, built in 1894, is the oldest school building in Montana still in use. The local candy store,

Sweet Palace (109 E. Broadway, 406/859-3353, www.sweetpalace.com, 9am-6pm Sun.-Fri. June-Aug., 9am-5pm Sun.-Fri. Sept.-May) is loaded with both old-fashioned charm and sugar; it's a very popular stop in P-Burg.

The **Opera House Theatre** (140 S. Sansome St., 406/859-0013, www.operahousetheatre.com, Thurs.-Sun. late June-Labor Day weekend, $20 adults, $10 children 12 and under), Montana's oldest theater still in operation, built in 1891, is a source of local pride. The theater presents a three-play summer season of vaudeville and comic melodramas.

Four miles southeast of Philipsburg on a gravel road is **Granite,** whose rich mines earned it the nickname "Silver Queen." Granite boomed along with Philipsburg; $30 million of silver was mined there during the 1880s. Granite suffered more grievously when the bottom fell out of the gold market in 1893. Within hours of the mines' closing, 3,000 miners and their families reportedly descended on Philipsburg to withdraw their bank accounts and purchase one-way tickets out. The handsome Miner's Union Hall, a three-story brick structure, is one of the few buildings still standing.

Mining hasn't totally gone bust in Philipsburg. Visitors can stop by the **Sapphire Gallery** (115 E. Broadway, 406/859-3236 or 800/525-0169, www.sapphiregallery.com, 10am-6pm Sun.-Fri. summer, 10am-5pm Sun.-Fri. winter) or **Opal Mountain Gems** (204 W. Broadway, 406/859-6725, www.opalmtgems.com, 9am-7pm daily) and dig through concentrate from nearby mines for sapphires. Very nice sapphire and ruby jewelry is also in both stores.

Accommodations

Right downtown, the ★ **Broadway Hotel** (103 W. Broadway, 406/859-8000, www.broadwaymontana.com, $80-130) is a beautifully restored hotel from 1890, with nine themed rooms, all with private baths, including a suite with its own card room. Some rooms are pet-friendly; arrange this when you book your stay. If you need more space,

a two-bedroom guest cottage and a one-bedroom apartment are near the hotel ($140). A continental breakfast in the hotel's coffee bar is included. This wonderfully updated and comfortable hotel is alone worth the detour to Philipsburg!

The **Inn at Philipsburg** (915 W. Broadway, 406/859-3959, www.theinn-philipsburg.com, $50-70) also has an RV park and meeting rooms; pets are accepted.

A beautifully renovated historic church houses the unique **Sanctuary** (208 Kearney Ln., 406/859-1003, www.thesanctuarymontana.com, $79-129), which, although it's open to all travelers, is especially popular with motorcyclists ready for a chance to relax among comrades, sleep on comfy memory-foam mattresses, and soak in the hot tub.

Food

Doe Brothers (120 E. Broadway, 406/859-7677, 11am-8pm daily, $5-14) is an old-fashioned soda fountain that also serves burgers and sandwiches. For a traditional Montana evening meal of steak or prime rib, stop by **Montana John's Silver Mill Saloon** (128 E. Broadway, 406/859-7000, 4:30pm-10pm Tues.-Thurs., 11am-11pm Sat.-Sun., $9-35).

The dog-friendly **Philipsburg Brewing Company** (101 W. Broadway, 406/859-2739, www.philipsburgbrewingcompany.com, 10am-8pm daily), housed in a beautiful old building in the heart of downtown, serves prizewinning craft beers. Although they don't serve food, there are often food carts outside.

If you're in town on a night when it's open, line up for **Friday Night Pizza** (607 S. Sansome, 406/859-3000, www.fridaynightpizza.net, 4pm-9pm Thurs.-Sat., $15-22), one man's good idea that has caught on with the entire community. Find it next to the laundry.

Information

Find the **Philipsburg Chamber of Commerce** (406/859-3388, www.philipsburgmt.com) at 135 South Sansome. The **Philipsburg Ranger Station** (406/859-3211, www.fs.usda.gov/bdnf) is at 88 Business Loop.

THE SKALKAHO PASS ROAD

Six miles south of Philipsburg, Highway 38 leaves Highway 1 and winds west through the Sapphire Mountains, eventually dropping into the Bitterroot Valley at Hamilton. Travelers should consider this 50-mile drive, partly on gravel roads, for several reasons. The Skalkaho Pass Road connects two otherwise distant valleys along a route with great scenic value. On the west side of the divide the road is forested and steep, often cliff-hanging. The east half is gentler and runs along the lovely upper reaches of Rock Creek, one of Montana's premier fishing streams.

Anglers will want to leave Highway 38 for Rock Creek Road and follow it to its namesake's confluence with the Clark Fork River. The upper reaches of Rock Creek receive a lot less attention than the more developed areas closer to Missoula, but the fishing is as good.

Amateur prospectors can try their hand at sapphire mining along the banks of Rock Creek. The **Gem Mountain Sapphire Mine** (13 miles west of the junction with Hwy. 1, 406/859-4367 or 866/459-4367, www.gemmtn. com, 10am-5pm mid-May-late Sept., $20 per bucket) offers buckets of sapphire-rich gravel to process. The sapphires come in several shades (classic blue being one of the rarest) and are relatively easy to find. Buy prewashed concentrated gravel by the bucket, then sort through it to spot the gems. Staff members are happy to help—they even offer a faceting and mounting service—and the experience makes a good family outing.

West of Skalkaho Pass, 32 miles from Highway 1, **Skalkaho Falls** roars down under the highway and makes a great place to picnic. Although hiking isn't necessary to enjoy the falls, plenty of hiking trails, both formal and informal, sprout from the road. Trail 313, at the divide, is a good one to follow for a short or long hike. Head north along this trail to Dome-Shaped Mountain, home of mountain goats. The trail also passes by the **Skalkaho Game Preserve,** accessible by a rough dirt road at Skalkaho Pass. Marshes here are favorite summer habitat for elk; patient visitors may also see mule deer, coyotes, and black bears.

Skalkaho Pass Road is closed from mid-October to June. Early or late in the season, call the **state highways department** (800/226-7623, www.mdt.mt.gov) to be certain the road is open.

The Big Hole River Country

The Big Hole Valley is some of the highest and flattest land in Montana. Almost all of the farm and ranch land hovers well above 6,000 feet in wide valley swatches 15 miles across.

Lewis and Clark named the three forks of the Jefferson River Wisdom, Philanthropy, and Philosophy. In time, Wisdom River became the less abstract Big Hole River, so named by later ranchers who were impressed with the vast real estate hemmed in by towering peaks. The Big Hole River flows north, draining a huge high valley lying between the Bitterroot Mountains on the west and the Pioneer Mountains on the east. After bumping into the Anaconda Range, the river does a U-turn and flows south, picking up the east-slope drainage of the Pioneers.

For anglers and floaters, the river's the thing. Fishing in the Big Hole is superlative, and the rafting is challenging. For hunters, this is the best hunting ground for pronghorn in the state, outside of the prairies of eastern Montana. History buffs can hike the trails and war fields of the Battle of the Big Hole, where in 1877 the Nez Perce fought the U.S. Army as the band tried to flee incarceration on reservations.

To comprehend the Big Hole's allure, understand that this is still the West. Resorts haven't yet replaced ranches. You can catch trout elsewhere in Montana, but here you can share a drink and tell your fish stories to a hired hand or cowboy, not a conventioneer.

★ BIG HOLE NATIONAL BATTLEFIELD

In 1877, rather than move onto a reservation, Chief Joseph's band of Nez Perce fled their home in northeastern Oregon and Idaho to find refuge with the Crow tribe. When they paused to rest in the Big Hole, they were ambushed by the U.S. Army. The Big Hole National Battlefield, which preserves the site of the battle, is a moving place to visit in a beautiful setting.

The Nez Perce

One of the most famous Indian battles in Montana history involved a tribe that's not indigenous to the state. The Nez Perce homeland was the region where Oregon, Washington, and Idaho meet. The Nez Perce Nation was a largely peaceable confederation of loosely knit tribal units, each under a powerful chief.

By the 1850s, settlement by Easterners began to displace the Nez Perce. An 1855 treaty confined them to a reservation; because the boundaries included their traditional homeland, and because the treaty

also restricted settlement on their land, they complied.

By 1863, however, more stockmen, miners, and settlers were encroaching on Nez Perce land. A new treaty was drawn up, reducing the reservation to one-quarter of its former size. The Nez Perce chiefs whose land was still within the reservation signed the new treaty; those chiefs whose land was being taken away refused. On the pretext that the signature of any Nez Perce chief represented the commitment of the whole tribe, the U.S. government ordered the "nontreaty" Nez Perce onto the new reservation.

While both the Native Americans and the U.S. Indian Bureau dallied for several years without strict enforcement of the order, increasing pressure from settlers—especially after Custer's rout in 1876—made compliance a priority. In 1877 the U.S. Army was sent in to compel the delinquent Nez Perce onto the reservation.

At this time, a band of young warriors attacked and killed four settlers in Oregon, whom the Native Americans believed guilty of earlier murders of Nez Perce elders. Fearing harsh retaliation and foreseeing a dismal future for the tribe, five bands of the nontreaty Nez Perce—about 800 people—fled eastward

The Big Hole is surrounded by mountains.

from northeastern Oregon. After two skirmishes in Idaho, where the bands eluded the army, the Nez Perce realized they had to leave the area completely. They crossed over to Montana, intent on journeying to Crow country on the Yellowstone, where they hoped to reestablish the tribe.

The Battle of the Big Hole

Once in Montana the pace of the exodus slowed, and after pushing up the Bitterroot Valley the Nez Perce camped on the western side of the Big Hole Valley. Here they considered themselves out of reach of the army for a few days. They stopped to cut new travois poles and to ready themselves for more traveling.

The Nez Perce knew that the Washington-based army detachment was two weeks behind them. However, they didn't realize that the Seventh Infantry, under Col. John Gibbon of Fort Shaw, had moved south to ambush them. In the early morning of August 9, 1877, a Nez Perce sentry rode into the advance guard of Colonel Gibbon's forces. He was shot and killed, and the gunfire awoke the rest of the warriors. Mounting a full attack on the Nez Perce as they emerged from their tepees, the infantry killed women, children, braves, and elders indiscriminately.

Nez Perce warriors quickly took up defensive positions, and with sniper fire forced the army back onto the side hill. Both sides sustained heavy losses. The Nez Perce successfully besieged the army troops the rest of that day and night, giving their people time to strike their bivouac and flee eastward in search of Crow allies. (The Crow proved to be no allies, and the Nez Perce confronted the army yet again, in the Battle of Canyon Creek.)

The Battlefield

Hike the trails here not just for their history, but for the quiet beauty of this lush meadow flanked by mountains and a swift stream.

The **visitors center** (16425 Hwy. 43 W., 406/689-3155, www.nps.gov/biho, 9am-5pm daily Memorial Day-Labor Day, 10am-5pm the rest of the year, free) provides audiovisual displays that explain the background of the Nez Perce flight and the Big Hole battle. Exhibits include artifacts of the battle and items from the daily life of the early settlers and the Native American bands who fought here in 1877.

An extensive network of self-guided hiking trails links the sites of the battle. From the parking lot, a 1.5-mile trail leads to the site of the Nez Perce camp; a shorter trail leads to the siege area. Here, for devotees of military strategy, interpretive signs chart the development of the battle in great detail. A somewhat steeper hike leads to the site of the howitzer captured by the Nez Perce, where there are great views over the battlefield and the Big Hole Valley.

For hiking of a different magnitude, the **Nee-Me-Poo Historic Trail** (www.fs.usda.gov/npnht) passes through the Big Hole Battlefield. This 1,200-mile trail follows the route of the Nez Perce from Oregon to the Bear Paw Mountains, where the army finally apprehended the fleeing tribe.

Accommodations

There are picnic facilities at the lower parking lot along the river, but camping is not allowed. The closest services are in Wisdom, 10 miles east. **May Creek Forest Service campground** (406/689-3243, www.fs.usda.gov/bdnf, $7) is eight miles west on Highway 43.

THE BIG HOLE

Although the Big Hole River is more than 100 miles long, the term *big hole*—frontierese for a deep, wide valley—refers to the river's upper basin. Here, between Jackson and Fishtrap, is fabled ranch country, rivaling only eastern Montana for its eternal flatness and traditional Western ways. Here too is great fishing for the discriminating angler, with rushing streams full of scrappy brook trout and rare arctic grayling, a long-finned species rarely found outside of Alaska and northern

Canada. Almost all river access is through private land, so be sure to ask permission from the landowner.

Jackson

Captain Clark and his return party passed through here in 1806 and stopped at the local hot springs. Not content with just a soak, the Corps of Discovery also cooked their dinner in the 138°F water. Now, as then, this little community is known mostly for the springs.

The ★ **Jackson Hot Springs Lodge** (406/834-3151, www.jacksonhotsprings. com, $126-156), off Highway 278, operates a Western-style resort at the spot where Lewis and Clark dined. The lodge is right on Jackson's main drag and dominates the town. Even if you don't stay the night, stop for a swim ($5) or a drink at the bar. Open year-round, the lodge caters to summer anglers and tourists but really gears up for winter guests. Nearby are excellent cross-country trails, some groomed and others informal; snowmobilers also use the lodge as a center. Standard accommodations at the resort are in cabin-like motel rooms. Tent camping is allowed on the back lawn ($30). Good food (three meals a day), drink, and live music on many weekend nights are provided at the lodge. The pool is drained every Wednesday, so try to avoid visiting then if you want to swim.

A couple of **Forest Service campgrounds** (406-689-3243, www.fs.usda. gov/bdnf, early July-Labor Day, $7) are west of Jackson. **Miner Lake** is about 10 miles west of town via Forest Service Road 182, which heads off toward the Bitterroots right at the south end of town. The campground is not well-marked; look off to your left when you're 10 miles out of town and you'll find at least one of the many de facto campsites in the area. To reach the **Twin Lakes** campground, take Road 1290 west from Highway 278 about halfway between Jackson and Wisdom and travel for about 13 miles. Both campgrounds are pretty places perched on the east slopes of the Bitterroots. The lakes are great canoe spots, but motorboats are not allowed.

Wisdom

This little crossroads—more an outpost than a town—is a trading center for the cattle ranches and hay farms that stretch across the wide valley. Higher civilization is making inroads, however. As a sign of changing times, Wisdom supports watering holes for local ranch hands and a tony art gallery.

The nicest place to stay in Wisdom is

Soak in the rustic pool at the Jackson Hot Springs Lodge.

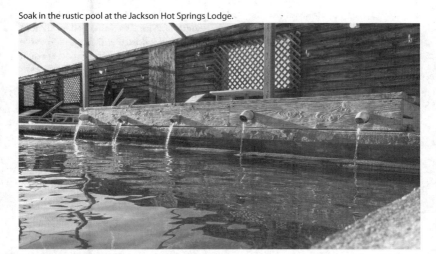

the attractive **Pioneer Mountain Lodge** (406/689-3229, http://pioneermountainlodge. com, $70), a small newer motel with kitchenettes. It's also worth considering staying down the road at Jackson Hot Springs.

Head 10 miles east of town on Road 31 to a small **campground** at the trailhead leading to Sand Lake and Lily Lake. Actually, keep going on the trail system here and you can cross the Pioneers, coming out north of Elkhorn Hot Springs.

The center of life in Wisdom revolves around its bars and restaurants. **The Crossing Bar and Grill at Fetty's** (406/689-3260, www.thecrossingbarandgrill.com, 7am-9pm summer, 8am-8pm winter, breakfast or lunch $5-11, dinners $9-25) is a local institution that's been given a new life. Bread, bagels, cinnamon rolls, and soups are all made fresh daily.

The **Antlers Saloon** (Main St., 406/689-3100) is a popular place for a drink; it's not unlike having a beer in a taxidermy shop. **Hook and Horn Trading Post** (317 Hwy. 43 W., 406/689-3272, 7am-5pm daily, www.montanahookandhorn.com) is the upscale revision of Wisdom's trading post; stop here for a coffee drink and a snack, gifts and jewelry, camping supplies, or a fishing license.

Go 28 miles west of Wisdom on Highway 43 to pick up the **Continental Divide Trail** at Chief Joseph Pass. The Bitterroot Ski Club maintains an extensive network of groomed cross-country ski trails on the north side of Highway 43 at the pass. No dogs are permitted on the groomed trails.

The **Wisdom Ranger Station** can be contacted at 406/689-3243.

Wise River

Between Wisdom and Wise River, the Big Hole Valley narrows. The river enters a canyon and picks up speed. Rainbow and brown trout begin to dominate the waters, in numbers and sizes that excite a national audience of fly fishers. There are several fishing-access sites as the river enters its canyon: good for anglers, handy for floaters, and perfect for picnickers. At the town of Wise River, the river of the same name enters the Big Hole. A designated scenic byway along Highway 484 begins here.

A couple of lakes in the Anaconda Mountains to the west are of interest to the traveling angler. **Mussigbrod Lake,** 23 miles northwest of Wisdom, has some of the best arctic grayling fishing in the Lower 48. There's also a Forest Service campground. There's another campground at **Pintler Lake,** 10 miles off Highway 43 up Pintler Creek Road. The lake offers good fishing for rainbow and cutthroat and a scenic base camp for explorations of the surrounding pine forests.

What passes on the map for a town at Wise River is in fact a couple of bars at the junction of the Big Hole and Wise Rivers. Not to sound dismissive—a couple of bars in fact *do* a town make, at least out here in fly fisher's heaven.

The **Wise River Club** (406/832-3258, www.wiseriverclub.com, restaurant open 8am-10pm daily May-Sept., 8am-8pm Sun.-Thurs., 8am-9pm Fri.-Sat. Oct.-Apr., $9-30) is a taciturn old bar full of taxidermy. It's still enough of a local's bar to be at once suspicious and friendly. The club's motel has rooms with bath down the hall for $65 and cabins for $85; there is also limited camping for RVs ($25).

South of Wise River, the road to Elkhorn Hot Springs is dotted with **Forest Service campgrounds.** Most of these spots are right on the Wise River, with good fishing access.

Outfitters and guest ranch resorts provide accommodation options for anglers. The **Complete Fly Fisher** (406/832-3175, www. completeflyfisher.com) offers guided fishing, great cooking, and lodging in cabins or lodge rooms, about $4,200 for a week. The attractive riverside **Big Hole Lodge** (406/832-3252, www.flyfishinglodge.com, $3,500 and up per person per week) offers accommodations and guided fishing trips to their angler guests.

The **Wise River Ranger Station** can be reached at 406/832-3178.

THE LOWER BIG HOLE RIVER

Downstream south from the community of Divide, the Big Hole, with great fishing up to this point, becomes a blue-ribbon trout fishery. Brown trout are both huge and abundant. Mid-June, when the salmon flies hatch, marks a frantic season for fish and fishers alike. To the misfortune of the trout, there are several good fishing-access sites between Divide and Glen.

Divide

Big Hole River floaters need to beware of a diversion dam just upstream from Divide. Here, water from the Big Hole River is pumped over the Continental Divide to Butte at a rate of five million gallons per day. In its day, the pump station was quite an engineering feat; it's on the National Register of Historic Places.

For hikers, often overlooked is the **Humbug Spires Wilderness Study Area,** a day hike into an area of geologic interest. Intense faulting has fractured granite extrusions into steep, sharp needles that resemble menhirs (prehistoric monoliths). About three miles in, the trail reaches a watershed, and there's a good view over the spiny valley. Exit I-15 at Moose Creek Road, three miles south of Divide, and turn east. Contact the **Butte BLM office** (106 N. Parkmont, Butte, 406/533-7600, www.mt.blm.gov/bdo) for a brochure and map.

The BLM runs **Divide Bridge campground** ($6, has water) along the Big Hole River near Divide.

Melrose

Near Melrose, the Big Hole leaves its steep-sided canyon and resolutely flows to its appointment with the Beaverhead River. This is a good place to leave I-15 and follow old Highway 10. From Glen, off-road enthusiasts can follow a gravel road along the Big Hole River as it trends east to the Beaverhead. It's a pretty drive, becoming dramatic as it approaches historic Beaverhead Rock from its back side.

Melrose lollygags along the old rail sidings that spawned its early growth, a town caught in the midst of a stretching exercise. This pleasant hamlet is known for its fishing; with several fishing-access sites, an attractive motel, a cabin resort, a café, and bars, it's no wonder that anglers flock here.

Head west out of Melrose up Trapper Creek (Rd. 40), then Canyon Creek (Rd. 41) to the **Lion Creek trail,** a nine-mile loop from the campground at road's end to Lion Lake and back again. From the lake, a hike up nearby Sharp Mountain will give you a pretty good chance of spotting mountain goats.

As elsewhere on the Big Hole, it's easy to find an outfitter to guide you to the fish. Guides associated with the **Sunrise Fly Shop** (406/835-3474, www.sunriseflyshop.com) offer trips on all the area's rivers.

The **Sportsman Motel** (540 N. Main St., 406/835-2141, http://sportsmanmt.com, $75-112) is a handsome log motel complex with gas barbecue grills, horse boarding (other pets are allowed too), laundry facilities, and an RV park. Two private cabins ($112), a two-bedroom log house ($250 per night, three-night minimum), and sites for tents ($15) and RVs ($27) are also available. Head 4.5 miles south of town on the frontage road to **Great Waters** (406/835-2024, www.greatwatersinn.com, $2,895 per week includes all meals and guide, shorter stays also offered), an attractive fishing resort with a guide service and a good restaurant in the lodge. Nonanglers can stay for $175 per night (includes meals). Another resort, **Canyon Creek Guest Ranch** (877/223-0970, www.canyoncreekguestranch.com, $250-350) is tucked away up in a remote area in the mountains west of town.

THE PIONEER MOUNTAINS

Surrounded on three sides by the meanderings of the Big Hole River, the Pioneer Mountains are in fact two different ranges divided down a north-south axis, linked yet separated, sort of like the underside of a coffee bean. These out-of-the-way mountains come to life in the winter; a hot springs resort and a small downhill ski area combine to bring in the locals. In the summer the hills are covered with violet-blue lupine. The Wise River drainage is popular with anglers; there are several large Forest Service campgrounds with fishing access along the river.

Highway 484 bisects the Pioneer Mountains, from Wise River in the north through Polaris to Highway 278 in the south. The Forest Service has designated this route running down the furrow of the coffee bean as the **Pioneer Mountains Scenic Byway.**

Maverick Mountain Ski Area

The legendary heavy snows of southwestern Montana are put to good use at the homey, family-oriented **Maverick Mountain Ski Area** (406/834-3454, www.skimaverick.com, Thurs.-Sun., $34 adults, $25 seniors, $21 age 12 and under), where the vertical drop is 2,020 feet, and there's only one real lift to serve the 24 runs. Maverick Lodge offers lessons, rentals, day care, and food; cross-country skiers are welcome.

Many skiers come up for the day from Dillon, but the closest lodging to Maverick is the **Grasshopper Inn** (406/834-3456, http://polarismontanavacations.com, $75), with motel rooms and a popular restaurant at the base of the slopes beside the near-ghost town of Polaris.

Elkhorn Hot Springs

The venerable resort of **Elkhorn Hot Springs** (13 miles north of Hwy. 278 on Hwy. 484, 406/834-3434 or 800/722-8978, www.elkhornhotsprings.com, $50-120) is the other popular lodging for skiers. Cross-country skiers converge here; with 25 miles of cross-country trails managed by the resort, an entire mountain range of informal trails to explore, and a good hot soak to come home to, this is near-heaven (at an elevation of 7,385 feet, literally so). In summer the hot springs are popular for hikers. There are two outdoor mineral pools plus a sauna, and it costs $7 ($5 for kids) for a swim.

Rooms are either in the lodge ($50, bathroom down the hall) or in rustic cabins scattered among the trees. The restaurant in the lodge is open for three meals a day. Cabins, with electricity and wood-burning stoves but no plumbing (an outhouse is shared with neighboring cabins), start at $80 for a double (swimming included). Don't come to Elkhorn expecting a trendy spa getaway; it's funky and remote, and with that in mind, charming and relaxing.

If you want to stop at Elkhorn for a swim and a soak but would prefer to camp out, the very pretty Forest Service **Grasshopper Campground** (406/683-3900, www.fs.usda.gov/bdnf, June-Sept., $10) is less than one mile down the road. Pick up the **Blue Creek trail** just south of the campground and head into the West Pioneers. North of Elkhorn Hot Springs are several more campgrounds and trailheads.

Crystal Park

At the Forest Service-maintained site of **Crystal Park** (406/683-3900, www.fs.usda.gov/bdnf, $5 per vehicle) four miles north of Elkhorn Hot Springs, rock hounds can dig for quartz crystals. It's a very popular spot, attracting dedicated amateur crystal miners who come with shovels and screens to sift through the dirt for quartz and amethyst. But even ill-equipped novices can scrape through the topsoil for a few minutes and come up with a small crystal or two.

The Southwestern Corner

History was quick to find this corner of Montana. High on a forgotten pass between Montana and Idaho is Sacagawea Historical Area, where the Corps of Discovery crossed the Continental Divide. Bannack State Park, Montana's best-preserved ghost town, commemorates the state's first city and first territorial capital. Red Rock Lakes National Wildlife Refuge is one of the nation's most important bird sanctuaries. It is a primary breeding ground for trumpeter swans, which were once feared extinct.

With two million acres of national forest in Beaverhead County alone, and a vast network of streams forming the Missouri's most distant headwaters, southwestern Montana has plenty of room for outdoor recreation. Yet the great fishing, hunting, and hiking opportunities in this lovely corner of Montana are blessedly free of crowds.

RED ROCK VALLEY

The Red Rock River, the Missouri's most distant headwater, drains a broad valley overlooked by the Continental Divide. This is high

country: The valley stretches out prairie-like at elevations above 6,000 feet.

Red Rock Lakes

This remote and beautiful valley, ringed with high but rounded peaks, would probably be ignored by the traveler if it weren't for Red Rock Lakes. At these marshy lakes, biologists discovered trumpeter swans, once feared extinct in the United States, in 1933.

Trumpeter swans formerly ranged over much of the continent. However, during the 19th century, hunters found a vigorous market for quill pens, powder puffs, and swan meat. As the homestead movement changed the environment of eastern Montana, with land falling to the plow and marshes being drained, swan populations plummeted. Biologists found only 66 trumpeters in 1933 at Red Rock Lakes, the last individuals of the species in the country.

The U.S. Department of the Interior established the 40,300-acre **Red Rock Lakes National Wildlife Refuge** (406/276-3536, www.fws.gov/refuge/red_rock_lakes) in 1935.

an abandoned cabin near Red Rock Lakes, in the high country of southwestern Montana

Currently about 500 trumpeters summer here; the winter population is also sizable as geothermal activity maintains ice-free water temperatures in some areas of the lakes.

Upper and Lower Red Rock Lakes are nestled beneath the 9,800-foot Centennial Mountains. This isolated corner of Montana is home to a variety of wildlife, including moose, deer, elk, pronghorn, and foxes; 232 bird species have been sighted at the lakes and the surrounding area. Fall migration can be particularly spectacular.

To reach the refuge, turn at Monida, just below the Continental Divide on I-15. The reserve is a rattly 28 miles up a gravel road. Wildlife viewing is best between May and November, which is about the only season the road is dependably passable. The reserve can also be reached in good weather from Idaho on the Red Rock Pass Road, 17 miles from West Yellowstone on Highway 87.

Recreation

Fishing is allowed in most areas of the refuge and provides good sport for trout anglers. Although their population is dwindling and a recovery plan has been implemented, arctic grayling live here. Nonmotorized boats are allowed on some areas of the lakes; the upper lake is open to boating from July 1 until the lake freezes, and the lower lake is open September 1 until freeze-up. Hunting is permitted in designated areas of the refuge for specific species.

Practicalities

This is camping country: There are two **campgrounds** ($7) at the wildlife refuge—one alongside each lake—meaning great views but also a potential mosquito assault.

The closest accommodations to the refuge are at the remote **Elk Lake Resort** (406-276-3282, www.elklakeresortmontana.com, $140 double with breakfast, $197 double with all meals), which has many options for your stay, including packages that include access to ATVs, canoes, fishing boasts, and horseback and mountain bike riding. This low-key and friendly resort is in a beautiful setting northeast of Red Rock Lakes.

Back on I-15 the closest motel to the wildlife refuge is in Lima; Dillon offers more choices.

HORSE PRAIRIE VALLEY

The Red Rock River meets Horse Prairie Creek at Clark Canyon Reservoir, and the Beaverhead River issues forth. While the reservoir is popular with local boaters and anglers, and old ranches fill the wide valley traditionally known as the Horse Prairie, travelers will want to explore the area to relive some of the most stirring moments of the Lewis and Clark Expedition.

The Shoshone were the first Montana-area natives to acquire horses. They stormed north through the upper Jefferson River drainages to threaten and finally dominate the high plains east of the Rocky Mountain front in the 1750s. The Blackfoot federation, moving south from Canada with guns obtained from the British, halted the Shoshone's expansion. The Shoshone were forced back into Idaho by the 1800s, where Lewis and Clark first encountered them.

Corps of Discovery

As the Corps of Discovery pushed up the Jefferson River in search of the Missouri headwaters, Sacagawea began to recognize landmarks of her childhood.

Recognizing the need for horses to proceed over the difficult Continental Divide that faced them, Lewis and three men went ahead to scout for the Shoshone, into whose homeland Sacagawea insisted they had entered. Lewis sighted the expedition's first Native American in Montana in the Horse Prairie Valley and continued over Lemhi Pass to encounter a Shoshone lodge near Tendoy, Idaho. After tenuous negotiations for horses, the Shoshone agreed to backtrack with Lewis and his party to meet the rest of the corps.

As the party approached, Sacagawea began to suck her fingers, a sign that she recognized her kin. A Shoshone woman broke rank and ran forward to embrace Sacagawea, recognizing her from her childhood. When Sacagawea was summoned to interpret the dialogue between the explorers and the natives, she entered the tent where the men were conversing and immediately recognized her brother Cameahwait, who had become chief of the Shoshone.

Consider for a moment what the negotiations for horses and supplies entailed. Sacagawea translated her brother's Shoshone terms into Minataree, which her husband, Charbonneau, understood. He in turn spoke French to a French-speaking member of the corps, who then translated the terms into English for Lewis and Clark. However circumlocutory, the translations worked. The corps traded for 24 horses, and on August 29, 1805, the entire party climbed over Lemhi Pass and the Continental Divide into Spanish territory.

Lemhi Pass

A drive up the steep, graveled road to Lemhi Pass (elev. 7,373 feet) is a must for any Lewis and Clark buff with a high-clearance vehicle. Turn off Highway 324 onto Lemhi Pass Road and follow the road, sometimes more rock than gravel, for about 20 miles. From the top—the Montana-Idaho border—mountains stretch to the west as far as the eye can see. A sign commemorates the Corps of Discovery's historic ascent and subsequent descent into Idaho.

Just below the crest of the pass on the Montana side, the state has established **Sacagawea Historical Area,** with picnic facilities and a small campground. Here, where a tiny spring gushes out of the rock only yards from the Continental Divide, Lewis thought he had found the "most distant fountain of the waters of the Mighty Missouri." (It's not; that distinction goes to Hellroaring Creek south of the Red Rock Lakes.) The party of four drank from the spring and stood astride it "exultingly," thankful to have lived to put a foot on each side of the "heretofore deemed endless Missouri."

Today's visitor will be unable to resist doing the same. Bring a picnic; this is an enchanting spot and you'll want to stretch your legs before bumping back down to the valley. A steep Forest Service road continues into Idaho; however, it's not advised for cars. Check with the **Salmon Ranger Station** (208/756-5200); sometimes the road is closed for logging.

Recreation

There's often good fishing for trout in **Clark Canyon Reservoir,** although the barren treeless setting and the seemingly always underfilled lake are charm-free. The 5,000-acre lake is popular with boaters from Dillon. The **Red Rock River** just above the lake is good fishing for cutthroat and rainbow.

Practicalities

Dillon is the closest center for amenities. There are several primitive campgrounds on the shores of the Clark Canyon Reservoir.

★ BANNACK

Prospectors found rich gold panning along Grasshopper Creek in 1862. Bannack sprang up in response, becoming the first real town in Montana. By the time it became the territorial capital in 1864, Bannack boasted hotels, a governor's mansion, churches, and a Masonic temple.

Montana's vigilante movement was born in Bannack. The first elected sheriff, Henry Plummer, was a smooth operator who ran a gang of road agents—deceptively called the Innocents—on the side. They preyed on miners and travelers until vigilantes prevailed and hanged more than 20 suspected outlaws.

Bannack is now a well-preserved ghost town whose remains commemorate the scene of some of Montana's most violent early history. Bannack State Park is self-guided and undeveloped; visitors are free to explore this fascinating old territorial capital at will and without threat of gift shops.

History

Prospectors gone bust in the Colorado gold

boom came north to southwestern Montana and in 1862 discovered gold at Grasshopper Diggings, about 20 miles west of Dillon. The first of the great Montana booms was on. A sign written in axle grease stood at the confluence of the Beaverhead River and Grasshopper Creek:

Tu grass Hop Per digins
30 myle
Keep the trale nex the bluffe.

By winter, a thousand ragtag adventurers, many of them refugees from the Civil War, had assembled on the banks of Grasshopper Creek. They named their camp Bannack (symptomatically misspelled) for the native Bannock tribe.

When it came to law and order, which the advent of sudden great wealth demanded, early Montanans just faked it. Henry Plummer was a veteran of the California and Nevada gold rushes, and his urbane good looks and considerable charm won the trust of Bannack (and later Virginia City) voters, who elected him sheriff.

At the same time, Plummer also secretly led a band of road agents of considerable ruthlessness. These ruffians and killers preyed on travelers, authorities, Native Americans, and anyone else who got in their way. Bannack in 1863 was the West portrayed by Hollywood: gunfights in the street, men gunning each other down over cards, strangers killing strangers for the way they looked. Especially at risk were travelers between Bannack and Virginia City; stage robberies were customary, and cold-blooded murder was frequent.

Even for the Wild West, violence in Bannack was excessive: During the first year of Plummer's stint as sheriff, the Innocents, as he called his gang, killed more than 100 men. Just as many deaths probably went unreported; in a gold camp of several thousand miners, the summer's orgy of lawless killings claimed a significant percentage of the population.

Once Grasshopper Creek froze up and panning ceased for the winter, outraged citizens decided to take the law into their own hands. A secret alliance of men formed a Vigilance Committee and codified their own set of laws and punishment (invariably death), a secret oath, and their cabalistic secret number

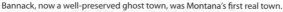

Bannack, now a well-preserved ghost town, was Montana's first real town.

3-7-77, with which they marked their victims (and which is now part of the Montana State Patrol's insignia).

The vigilantes moved quickly. In a period of two weeks, 24 of Plummer's gang were summarily hanged. Plummer's last words were "Give me a good drop."

The experience of lawlessness reinforced the need for a stronger civil authority. In 1864 the miners in Bannack and Alder Gulch sent Judge Sidney Edgerton to petition the U.S. government for territorial status, which the Senate granted and President Lincoln signed on May 26. Bannack became the first territorial capital when Edgerton convened the first legislature here; his house became the first governor's mansion.

Bannack's prominence had already begun to fade as the far richer colors of Alder Gulch attracted upward of 10,000 miners by 1864. The territorial capital followed the miners to Virginia City. Little remained of Bannack by 1890.

Bannack State Park

More than 60 structures remain standing at **Bannack State Park** (406/834-3413, www. bannack.org, 8am-dusk; $5 per vehicle, $3 bicyclist or walk-in, free to Montana residents).

The streets, homes, hotels, and civic buildings extend along Grasshopper Creek in various states of disrepair. The entire park is self-guided: Explore at will, being careful of dubious stairways and decrepit second stories. The old hotel is rumored to be the most photographed site in Montana. Other buildings of note are the governor's mansion, the Masonic hall, the jail, and the Methodist church. During the summer, hourlong guided tours of the town are offered (2pm Mon.-Fri., 10:30am and 3pm Sat.-Sun., Memorial Day-Labor Day). A separate tour (noon Sat.-Sun., Memorial Day-Labor Day) visits the otherwise restricted Hendricks Mill; one of the highlights of this tour is riding a 1931 Model AA Ford truck to the mill site. The third weekend of July is **Bannack Days** at the state park. Events include a black-powder shoot, horse and wagon rides, and a buffalo-steak barbecue.

The **park campground** (406/834-3413, www.reserveamerica.com) costs $23 per site ($15 for Montana residents) or $25 to stay in a tepee (call to reserve). To reach Bannack, turn off Highway 278 and follow a county road for three miles. From the south, Bannack can be reached from Highway 324 at Grant, 11 miles along a gravel road.

Dillon

Even if Dillon (pop. 4,200, elev. 5,057 feet) weren't the center of a vast region of broad fertile valleys filled with old ranches and rushing streams brimming with trout; even if Dillon weren't surrounded by national forests and wildlife refuges; and even if Dillon weren't close to the crossroads of Lewis and Clark, Chief Joseph, Henry Plummer, and a territory's worth of early miners and ranchers, Dillon would deserve the traveler's attention.

Dillon is an authentic old trade town that has managed to endure the recent economic malaise of the agricultural West without facing extinction or resorting to survival as a self-parody for tourists. Filled with historic architecture but kept young by the presence of students at the University of Montana-Western, Dillon is one of Montana's most bewitching small cities and makes an excellent base for day trips to the Big Hole Battlefield, the Pioneer Mountains, Bannack, and Virginia City.

SIGHTS
Historic Dillon

For a city of its size, Dillon has an unexpected array of architectural styles. Some highlights: The **Beaverhead County Courthouse,** at

Dillon

To Butte

To Twin Bridges

15

15

GUESTHOUSE INN

BEST WESTERN
PARADISE INN

FIESTA
MEXICANA

SUNDOWNER
MOTEL

RAILROAD AVE

MONTANA ST

ST

ST

HELENA ST

E CENTER ST

PAPA T'S

MELTEN
HOTEL

DILLON TRIBUNE BUILDING

BEAVERHEAD
COUNTY MUSEUM

PATAGONIA
OUTLET

SWEETWATER COFFEE

BEAVERHEAD
COUNTY COURTHOUSE

E BANNACK ST

E GLENDALE ST

VISITOR
INFORMATION
CENTER

IDAHO

WASHINGTON

BACKCOUNTRY ANGLER

ORR ST

ST

CORNELL ST

ST

PACIFIC

ATLANTIC

UNIVERSITY OF
MONTANA–WESTERN

0   400 yds

0   400 m

To Idaho

To I-15 and Barrett
Memorial Hospital

SPARKY'S GARAGE

15

© AVALON TRAVEL

Pacific and Bannack Streets, was built in 1889 and contains a four-faced Seth Thomas clock in its tower. The **Dillon Tribune Building,** at Bannack and Idaho Streets, housed Dillon's first newspaper; the 1888 facade is made entirely of pressed metal. One of the grandest of all the old hotels in Montana is the **Metlen Hotel,** built in 1897 as "one of the best, if not the best, constructed edifices in the state." A little down on its luck today, the Metlen is still an imposing monument to the era of grandiose railroad hotels.

Orr Mansion, at the south end of Idaho Street, is flanked by estates of other early entrepreneurs. William Orr was a California cattle rancher who brought his herd north

to the Beaverhead country in 1862. Success was more or less immediate, and by 1864 Orr began to build his Italianate villa.

At the **Beaverhead County Museum** (15 S. Montana St., 406/683-5027, http:beaverheadcountymuseum.org, 8am-5pm Mon.-Fri., plus 9am-5pm Sat. in the summer, $3), a towering Alaskan brown bear (mounted, of course) oversees the exhibits of Native American artifacts, early ranching curios, and mining memorabilia.

RECREATION

You can't turn around in Dillon without bumping up against great recreation opportunities. Dillon is the natural hub for the entire

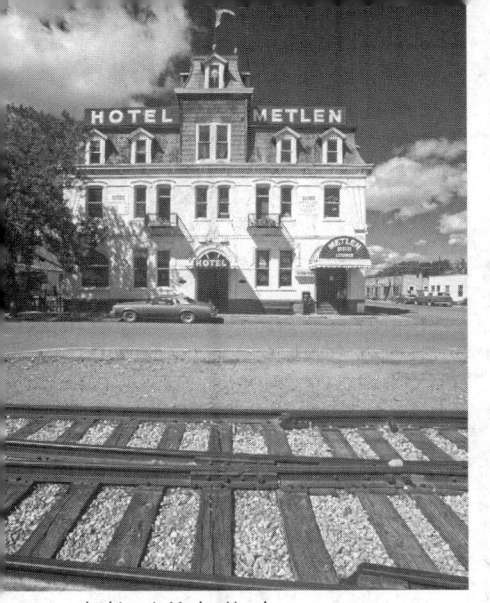
the historic Metlen Hotel

is fished best by floating; during high flows, travelers should consider enlisting the aid of outfitters. Of course, one river does not an angler's paradise make: the Ruby, Big Hole, and Red Rock Rivers, not to mention the mountain streams that feed them, are all within easy casting distance from Dillon. Don't miss Blacktail Deer Creek, just southeast of Dillon, for more leisurely, streamside fishing for brookies and cutthroat.

Hiking

With the Continental Divide arrayed around the perimeter of southwestern Montana, it's no wonder there's great hiking and camping just about everywhere that's uphill. A Beaverhead National Forest map reveals hikes in every direction, but avid hikers should try to visit a few isolated ranges.

The Snowcrest Range contains rugged and seldom-visited 10,000-foot peaks, with large populations of elk and mountain goats. The mountains divide the Ruby, Red Rock, and Blacktail Deer drainages in a remote area. The Snowcrests are about 20 miles southeast of Dillon along Blacktail Deer Creek Road. Even remoter and more rugged are the mountains at the head of **Big Sheep Creek** (turn west at the Dell exit 45 miles south of Dillon and follow signs for Big Sheep Canyon).

Between the Beaverhead Mountains (guardians of the Continental Divide) and the Tendoy Mountains, tributaries of Big Sheep Creek fan out. Trails lead up to glaciated valleys and knife-edge ridges along the Montana-Idaho border. Check with the Forest Service office in Dillon for details.

Outfitters

Guide Tim Tollett operates a fly shop, **Frontier Anglers** (680 N. Montana, 406/683-5276 or 800/228-5263, www.frontieranglers.com), and he and his crew lead fishing trips. **Backcountry Angler** (426 S. Atlantic St., 406/683-3462, www.backcountryangler.com) offers lodging, a fly shop, and guided fishing trips.

Lewis and Clark buffs may want to arrange

southwestern corner of Montana, where fishing, hiking, hunting, camping, and exploring the outdoors in general are incarnated in rich abundance.

Biking

Some of Montana's best dirt-road biking is detailed on the Great Divide Mountain Bike Route, section 2, a map published by Missoula's **Adventure Cycling** (406/721-1776 or 800/755-2453, www.adventurecycling.org). Order the map, which includes the area between Polaris in the Pioneer Mountains all the way south into Wyoming, from Adventure Cycling.

Fishing

The races and runnels that form the fabric of the Jefferson River are all legendary, highly productive fisheries. The Beaverhead River forms below Clark Canyon Dam; between here and Dillon is some of the most challenging and satisfying trout fly-fishing in Montana. Much of this fast-flowing river a tour with the **Great Divide Wildlands Institute** (406/683-4669, www.greatdivide-tours.com). This outfitter specializes in historical tours, sometimes on horseback, to sites along the Corps of Discovery's route.

For horseback rides or pack trips into the Pioneer Mountains, call **Diamond Hitch Outfitters** (406/683-5494 or 406/683-4191, www.diamondhitchoutfitters.com). Rates start at about $40 for a short trail ride; dinner rides from Dillon are $70.

SHOPPING

People come to Dillon from all over western Montana to shop at the **Patagonia Outlet** (16 S. Idaho St., 406/683-2580, 10am-6pm Mon.-Sat., 11am-5pm Sun.) for bargain-priced outdoor clothing.

ACCOMMODATIONS

The nice-for-the-price **Sundowner Motel** (500 N. Montana St., 406/683-2375 or 800/524-9746, $58), across the street from the local fertilizer plant and four blocks from downtown, has a playground, permits pets in smoking rooms, and serves free morning coffee and doughnuts.

A homey and comfortable place to stay on the edge of downtown are the rooms rented out by the **Backcountry Angler** (426 S. Atlantic St., 406/683-3462, www.backcountryangler.com, $85 single, $95 for two). Although the outfitter's fishing clients get first dibs on these suites with kitchens, there are occasional openings for the general public.

The **Best Western Paradise Inn** (650 N. Montana St., 406/683-4214, http://bestwesternmontana.com, $90-110) is relatively plush, with an indoor pool, exercise room, hot tub, and restaurant-casino on the premises. The other very comfortable conventional hotel is out by I-15: The **GuestHouse Inn** (580 Sinclair St., 406/683-3636 or 800/214-8378, www.guesthouseintl.com, $100-130) has an indoor pool and a breakfast bar.

At the **Five Rivers Lodge** (12530 Hwy. 41, 406/683-5000 or 800/378-5006, www.fiveriverslodge.com), perched above the Beaverhead River near spring-fed ponds on Highway 41, the emphasis is on fishing, although there are amenities for nonanglers. Guests stay in comfortable rooms, are fed three meals a day, and are accompanied by a guide on fishing expeditions to public streams and private spring creeks and ponds. Rates run $3,525 for five days of fishing and six nights of lodging. Shorter stays and nonfishing discounts are available.

Camping

The **Bureau of Reclamation campground** (406/683-6472, www.usbr.gov/gp, free) at Barretts, five miles south of town on the frontage road, sits right on the Beaverhead River as it leaves its canyon. Head 20 miles south of Dillon to **Clark Canyon Reservoir,** where more Bureau of Reclamation campgrounds line the shore and are conveniently, but not annoyingly, close to I-15. Right in town, the **Dillon KOA** (735 W. Park, 406/683-2749, RV $37-39, tent $25, cabin $52) has a pool, showers, and restrooms. The **Southside RV Park** (exit 62, 104 E. Poindexter St., 406/683-2244, http://southsidervpark.com, $38) has a lovely location on Blacktail Deer Creek. The campground at **Bannack State Park** (406/834-3413, www.reserveamerica.com, $23 tent site or $15 for Montana residents, $25 tepee) is also a good option.

FOOD

Start off a day in Dillon with a jolt of espresso and a homemade scone at **Sweetwater Coffee** (26 E. Bannack St., 406/683-4141, 8am-6pm Mon.-Fri., $6-8). It's also a good place to have a bite of lunch so that you don't shop the nearby Patagonia Outlet on an empty stomach.

Step up to some good Mexican food at **Fiesta Mexicana** (510 N. Montana St., 406/660-0915, 9am-10pm daily, $6-12), more commonly known as the "Taco Bus," an old school bus outfitted with a tiny kitchen that puts out some of the best meals in town. If the weather's nice, join the locals and eat at the big picnic table out front; the seating inside the bus is cramped.

Sparky's Garage (420 E. Poindexter St., 406/683-2828, http://sparkysrestaurant.com, 6:30am-9:30pm Mon.-Thurs., 7am-10pm Fri.-Sat., 7am-9pm Sun., $7-24), a popular spot for ribs, pulled pork, sweet-potato fries, and tasty corn bread, is near the university.

Papa T's (10 N. Montana St., 406/683-6432, 11am-10pm daily, $7-12) is not fancy, but it's a good solid burger and pizza joint with a devoted local following.

INFORMATION AND SERVICES

Find visitor information at the **Beaverhead Chamber of Commerce** (10 W. Reeder St., 406/683-5511, www.beaverheadchamber.org).

Barrett Memorial Hospital (406/683-1113) is at 609 Highway 91 South with a walk-in clinic staffed Monday through Saturday.

The **Dillon Ranger District,** Beaverhead-Deerlodge National Forest (406/683-3900, www.fs.usda.gov/bdnf), is at 420 Barrett Street. The **Bureau of Land Management** office (406/683-8000, www.mt.blm.gov/dfo) is at 1005 Selway Drive.

GETTING THERE

If you're flying to this neck of the woods, check fares on flights into Idaho Falls; it's less than two hours down I-15 and sometimes cheaper than flying into Montana airports.

Alder Gulch and the Ruby River Valley

In 1863, one year after the first big gold strike in Montana, a group of prospectors led by Bill Fairweather left Bannack for the Yellowstone Valley. En route they were harried by Crow warriors and turned back. After pitching camp in the Gravelly Range, the prospectors decided to pan for tobacco money. Their panning turned up rich color, and the miners realized they had discovered a major gold deposit at Alder Gulch.

They vowed to keep silent about their claims, but after they returned to Bannack, their free-spending ways drew the attention of other prospectors. When they started back to Alder Gulch, hundreds of miners followed them, each hoping to cash in on the presumed new strike. Within a year, 10,000 hopefuls lived in settlements along Alder Gulch.

★ VIRGINIA CITY

Virginia City (pop. 195, elev. 5,760 feet) is that oxymoronic anomaly, a working ghost town. Five streets of original and restored buildings from the 1860s and 1870s define the town, which led to Virginia City's designation as a

national historic landmark in 1962. But the town never died. Virginia City is still the county seat, and behind its false fronts and log-frame structures, cafés and shops serve locals and visitors year-round.

Although Bannack came first as a gold camp, Virginia City was Montana's first incorporated town; while the gold at Bannack played out quickly, mining continued at Virginia City. When the second territorial congress convened in 1865, it met at the state's population center, Virginia City, thereby elevating it to territorial capital. It remained so until 1875.

Sights

Virginia City is best thought of as an open-air museum of the early mining West. While strolling along the board sidewalks, poke into the old buildings. Those that aren't currently in business have been restored and contain artifacts of Alder Gulch's boom years. Most of the following structures lie along Wallace Street, now Highway 287. Buildings are open early May-early September.

The **Madison County Courthouse,** built in 1876, still serves as the seat of local government. The territorial offices were housed on the second floor of the **Content Corner** building. The **Montana Post Building,** with its display of printing equipment, was home to Montana's first newspaper. Within **Vigilante Barn,** the Montana vigilante movement was supposedly born.

The **Pioneer Bar** is an authentic restoration of a mining-era watering hole. The **Bale of Hay Saloon** contains period mechanical peep shows and is still a good place to get a beer and hear a bar band. At the back of the **Gypsy Arcade,** pay homage to a rare fortune-telling machine.

The **Masonic Temple,** built of cut stone, still houses lodge meetings. The **Madison County Museum** contains artifacts from the Alder Gulch mining days, including furniture, clothing, and photos, and a collection of barbed wire. The **Thompson-Hickman Memorial Museum and Library** (406/843-5346) contains the preserved clubfoot of a desperado and other vigilante mementos, as well as ore samples and mining equipment.

Other buildings have been restored to serve their original purposes, as barber shops, grocery stores, and other small businesses of an early mining camp and state capital.

A short walk south on Jackson Street leads to **Alder Gulch Discovery Monument,** which commemorates the original gold strike of 1863. North on Fairweather Street about 0.5 mile to a bluff above town is the **Boothill Cemetery.** Here are buried three road agents who were hanged by vigilantes during their brief tour of duty. Bill Fairweather was buried here until he was reinterred in a new cemetery with more law-abiding neighbors. Fairweather maintained the respect of the citizens of Alder Gulch by riding along Wallace Street scattering gold dust for children and the less fortunate. From Boothill there is also a good view of Alder Gulch.

Tour the area aboard a **1941 fire engine** (406/600-2598, 10am-6pm

Many of Virginia City's old buildings still house thriving businesses.

mid-May-mid-Sept., $8 adults, $4.50 children 12 and under, carry-on kids free); the drivers do a good job of pointing out the sights and telling colorful stories. **Stagecoach rides** (406/843-5200, www.montanacarriage.com, 10:30am-5pm Tues.-Sun. late May-early Sept., $15 adults, $12 children 7-12) are also popular; the same folks offer horseback rides in the area and pony rides in the corral for children ($32 one hour, $10 corral ride).

Montana's oldest summer-stock theater group, the **Virginia City Players** (406/843-5377 or 800/829-2969, www.virginiacityplayers.com, Memorial Day-Labor Day, $18 adults, $16 seniors and students, $10 youth 7-17), performs period melodramas and comedies at the historic **Opera House.** Near the east end of town, at the **Gilbert Brewery** (406/843-5218 or 800/829-2969, www.breweryfollies.net, 4pm and 8pm Wed.-Sun. late May-late Sept., $18), now restored as a bar, Montana's first brewery provides the stage for slightly naughty comedy shows nightly.

Getting the Gold Out

The tremendously rich gold-bearing gravels of Alder Gulch lay beneath a considerable weight of overburden. Shafts and tunnels had to be dug and the gravel hoisted out to the surface. The gravel was then shoveled into a "rocker," where water sloshed away lighter materials while the gold nuggets tumbled into baffles on the bottom of the device. If the claim was near streams, water could be diverted into sluice boxes. Dozens of miners could work along a sluice, sometimes hundreds of feet long. During the first five years of mining operations in Alder Gulch, an estimated $40 million was extracted, and by 1928 the total exceeded $100 million, with gold at $16 an ounce.

After miners removed the richest deposits of gold in Alder Gulch, more advanced technology allowed the processing of low-grade ore and tailings from early mining to extract trace deposits. The large berms of gravel at the little town of Alder reveal the debris of gold-dredging operations from the early 1900s. Although gold-seekers still pan for gold, and mines south of Virginia City produce gold and silver, the talc mines in the Ruby Range are now the area's largest operations.

Accommodations

Virginia City is a popular place to stay in the summer. If you can't find a room in town, consider staying in Ennis. The **Fairweather Inn** (315 W. Wallace St., 406/843-5377 or 855/377-6823, www.aldergulchaccommodations.com, $95 with shared bath, $120 with private bath) is a lovingly restored Victorian hotel. Rooms go fast, especially on weekends, so call ahead for reservations. It's open from mid-May to mid-September. Virginia City's B&B inns are open year-round in restored and period-furnished National Register of Historic Places homes. The **Gingerbread House and Karen's Cabins** (201 E. Idaho, 406/843-5471 or 877/424-4012, www.gingerbreadhousemontana.com, $105-155, shared baths in main house) is a tall, trim Victorian house with a couple of log cabins out back.

The **Virginia City RV Park** (406/843-5493, www.virginiacityrvpark.com, tent $25, tepee $35, RV $33-40, cabin $60-65) is just east of Virginia City.

Food

During the summer it's easy to find a bite to eat in one of the cafés along Wallace Street. **Wells Fargo Steak House** (306 W. Wallace St., 406/843-5556, http://wellsfargosteakhouse.com, 11:30am-9pm Tues.-Sun. Memorial Day-Oct., $16-34) is a classy Western-style restaurant and bar with live music on many weekend nights and the most ambitious food service in town, including many dishes such as cumin-crusted chicken with chimchurri that deviate from the steakhouse theme. Lunch here is a bit more expensive than at some of the other places in town ($10-15), but also more satisfying.

Information

Find the **Virginia City Chamber of Commerce** (406/843-5555 or 800/829-2969, www.virginiacity.com) at 211 West Wallace Street.

NEVADA CITY

Virginia City's sister city one mile downstream grew up in the boom days of placer mining in Alder Gulch. Abandoned by the 1880s, the ghost town was restored in the 1950s by Charles and Sue Bovey, the driving force behind Virginia City's renovation. The Boveys brought in period buildings from other areas of Montana, creating an outdoor museum of early mining in Montana.

During the peak summer season, a $10 admission fee ($8 youth 6-16, free for children under 6) is required to tour most of the buildings (a few are outside of the fenced-off fee area).

Try your hand at panning for gold at **River of Gold** (406/843-5247, $15). It's by the mining dredge between Virginia City and Nevada City.

In addition to restored shops and businesses, the **Alder Gulch Short Line** (800/829-2969, 10am-5pm daily summer, $10 adult round-trip, $8 ages 5-16 or over 55) runs a train between Virginia City and Nevada City. A museum at the Nevada City depot contains a collection of rolling stock and engines from the early days of railroading.

Also of interest is the **Nevada City Museum and Music Hall** (10am-6pm Mon.-Fri., $8 adults, $6 ages 5-16 or over 55), which houses an astonishing collection of old mechanical music machines. Check behind the Nevada City Hotel to glimpse the renowned two-story outhouse. During summer weekends, living history events (10am-6pm Sat.-Sun., $10 adults, $8 ages 5-16 or over 55) are staged here.

The **Nevada City Hotel and Cabins** (406/843-5377 or 855/377-6823, www.aldergulchaccommodations.com, mid-May-late Sept., $100-150) was originally a stage station from south of Twin Bridges; it was moved here and restored with an eye to modern comforts. The cabins are original miners' lodgings, now equipped with bathrooms, but still rustic. At **Just an Experience** (1570 Hwy. 287, 406/843-5402, http://justanexperience.com, $90-140), just east of town on Highway 287, rooms are either in the main house or in charming log cabins. The **Star Bakery Restaurant** (406/843-5777, 7am-7:30pm daily Memorial Day-Labor Day, $6-12) is a homey café for light meals. Although it's called a bakery, and historically sold bread to miners, it's now really a family restaurant.

RUBY RIVER VALLEY

During the 1860s and 1870s the stage route called the Vigilante Trail ran from Alder Gulch down the Ruby River to Twin Bridges, and then to Bannack or Helena. Thievery along this route led to the establishment of the vigilantes. Here too, traders and farmers began communities that would outlast the mining boom.

The Ruby River rises in the gentle peaks north of the Red Rock Lakes. Native Americans called the Ruby *Passamari* (Stinking Water) for the sulfur springs along its banks. The Ruby River, later named for the deceptive red garnets that early settlers mistook for rubies, is interred at Ruby Reservoir, where much of its flow is diverted into irrigation canals.

Nevada City is a little quieter than neighboring Virginia City.

Alder

After low-tech placer mining extracted the richest gold deposits along Alder Gulch, gold dredges were brought in to rework the displaced, lower-grade gravel. The banks of pebbles at Alder are the remains of this process.

Rock hounds who want to take a stab at finding some gems in the Ruby Valley can stop along the highway between Nevada City and Alder, where the roadside **Red Rock Mine** (406/842-5760, 9am-5pm Mon.-Sat., noon-5pm Sun. May-Sept.) offers an opportunity to sift through the gravel for garnets. A bucket of gravel, typically containing many tiny garnets, is $20.

The Northern Pacific built a branch line from Whitehall to Alder in the early 1900s to take out the dredged gold and other precious metals from the nearby hills. Today, talc mines in the Ruby Range are the area's most important mining operations. Watch for the white mounds near railroad sidings.

At Alder, a gravel road leads south seven miles to **Ruby Reservoir.** There is a free campground (no piped water) and, when the lake's not drawn down by irrigation, boating and fishing. Keep an eye out for garnets.

Right in Alder, the **Broken Arrow Lodge** (24 Fly Fisher Ln., 406/842-5437, http://brokenarrowlodge.com) is a down-home place catering to anglers and to those looking for a dude ranch vacation. Rates are quite reasonable: a three-day dude ranch vacation goes for $525 adults, $265 children, including meals.

★ **Upper Canyon Outfitters** (406/842-5884 or 800/735-6514, www.ucomontana.com) operates a guest ranch for anglers, hikers, and horseback riders, and offers fly-fishing lessons on the Ruby River. In the fall, the focus is on hunting. Basic rates (June-mid-Sept.) run $175 per person for lodge accommodations (meals included) and $275-300 for a cabin (per cabin, meals not included). A wide variety of packages are available.

Ruby Springs Lodge (2487 Hwy. 287, 406/842-5250, www.rubyspringslodge.com, $6,300-7,000 per person per week, including guided fishing), one mile north of Alder off Highway 287, is an exclusive fishing lodge catering to a small number of guests at a time. If you can't stay for a week, shorter stays are possible.

Robber's Roost

Between Alder and Sheridan, along the old stage route between Alder Gulch and Bannack, is the roadhouse and bar once known as Pete Daly's Place. This two-story log bar and dance hall was built in 1863 and became associated with Henry Plummer and his band of ne'er-do-wells. After two outlaws were lynched by vigilantes nearby, Pete's Place became known as Robber's Roost. Bullet holes in the walls attest to the character of the Alder Gulch bar scene.

A full-length porch with hitching rail opens onto the first-floor bar and gambling hall; upstairs was the dance floor. On the veranda, dancers could catch a breath of air or desperadoes could plot mayhem as the situation demanded.

Sheridan

Sheridan (pop. 650, elev. 5,079 feet) was established in 1866 as mining spread from Alder Gulch and northeast to the Tobacco Root Mountains. Sheridan grew into a prosperous trade center catering to miners and ranchers, a fact reflected in the handsome period storefronts.

The pet-friendly **Moriah Motel** (220 S. Main, 406/842-5491, www.moriahmotel.com, $75) has downtown rooms equipped with fridges and microwaves, plus a laundry room for guests' use. If you'd rather stay in an old Victorian house, the **Ruby Valley Inn B&B** (3209 Hwy. 287, 406/842-7111, www.rubyvalleyinnllc.com, $100) is comfortable and welcomes anglers and others.

There are a few local restaurants, and in nearby Twin Bridges, the Old Hotel serves gourmet dinners.

The Jefferson River Valley

At Twin Bridges the Jefferson River collects its mighty tributaries—the Big Hole, Beaverhead, and Ruby Rivers—and flows north to its appointment with the Missouri at Three Forks. For much of this 80-mile journey the Jefferson and its valley are open, wide, and relaxed, as if they too enjoy the spectacular mountain scenery rising above them. The ragged peaks of the Tobacco Root and Highland Mountains contain granite intrusions that are cousins to the mineral-rich formations near Butte.

The Jefferson's deep holes and brushy banks, which hampered Lewis and Clark's journey upriver, now excite sportspeople. Brown trout of storied size lurk in the shade of the overgrowth; river floaters, more captivated by the rugged mountain scenery than challenged by the current, enjoy the river's leisurely pace.

East of LaHood, the river drops into the Jefferson Canyon. Stop and watch for bighorn sheep along the high sheer cliffs. In a limestone formation high on the side of the canyon are the Lewis and Clark Caverns, one of the nation's largest developed cavern systems.

HISTORY

After Lewis and Clark ascended to Three Forks in 1805, their journey became a series of conjectures about which river fork, and which fork of forks, to follow to the Continental Divide. At Three Forks the Corps of Discovery chose the Jefferson. They could have saved themselves hundreds of miles of rambling in the upper Jefferson drainages if they had heeded Charbonneau's advice and traveled up Pipestone Creek near Whitehall. They would have surmounted the Continental Divide in 20 miles and found themselves in the Columbia River drainage.

Near Twin Bridges the captains chose to follow the Beaverhead River. A few miles upstream, Sacagawea recognized Beaverhead

Rock, an immense limestone outcropping rising above the river, as a landmark for her people, the Shoshone.

TWIN BRIDGES AND VICINITY

Twin Bridges slumbers near the confluence of the Ruby, Beaverhead, and Big Hole Rivers. Lewis and Clark rested here before continuing up the Beaverhead. At Three Forks the captains named the mightiest of the Missouri forks for President Jefferson. At the forks of the Jefferson, they decided to name each for the cardinal virtues of the president: Philanthropy, Philosophy, and Wisdom. Later settlers waxed less poetic, renaming the rivers the Ruby, the Beaverhead, and the Big Hole. History is silent as to whether the later generation considered these attributes of President Jefferson.

Twin Bridges is now a good base for anglers and a thoroughly pleasant place to stop for the night if you're touring this part of Montana.

For many, Twin Bridges is the object of a pilgrimage just to go to the **R. L. Winston Rod Company shop** (500 S. Main St., 406/684-5674). This company makes well-regarded fly-fishing rods.

King's Motel (307 S. Main, 406/684-5639 or 800/222-5510, www.kingsflatline.com, $80-100) is a tidy, pleasant little motel with a wide variety of cabin-style rooms ranging from single rooms with kitchenettes to units that sleep up to seven people. The owners will gladly set you up with fishing guides. (It's best to call in advance if this is what you have in mind.)

A good place for a meal in this small town is ★ **The Old Hotel** (101 E. 5th Ave., 406/684-5959, 5pm-9pm Tues.-Fri., 8am-1pm and 5pm-9pm Sat., 9am-2pm and 5pm-9pm Sun. mid-May-mid-Oct., 5pm-9pm Thurs.-Sat., 9am-2pm Sun. mid-Oct.-mid-May, dinners $20-27, dinner reservations recommended), where the owners turn out wonderful meals, often with Pacific Rim influences (one of the owners is from Hawaii), and where there's always a good veggie option. The Old Hotel also has two B&B suites for $150.

Cabin accommodations are sometimes available at **Stonefly Inn** (409 N. Main, 406/684-5648, www.thestoneflyinn.com, $1,995 for three nights lodging, two days of fishing, breakfasts and dinners), though they are often filled with the Stonefly's fishing clients who book all-inclusive trips.

East of town, **Healing Waters Fly Fishing Lodge** (270 Tuke Ln., 406/684-5960, www.hwlodge.com, Apr.-Nov., $4,325 per angler per week) is highly acclaimed for both its top-notch guides and its amenities.

Beaverhead Rock

Between Dillon and Twin Bridges is Beaverhead Rock, a landmark to settler and Native American alike. The excited Sacagawea recognized the huge outcropping and told the rest of the Corps of Discovery that they were in her homeland. Three hundred feet high, it is apparently the leading edge of land thrust eastward by mountain building to the west.

LEWIS AND CLARK CAVERNS

Leave I-90 at Three Forks or Whitehall and follow back roads through Jefferson River Canyon for a scenic loop-road alternative to the interstate. The quickening pace of the river as it cuts through walls of steeply tilted sedimentary rock makes this a popular expedition for floaters.

High on the north side of the canyon in a vein of exposed limestone on Highway 10, west of Three Forks 19 miles, or 13 miles east of Whitehall is **Lewis and Clark Caverns State Park** (406/287-3541, http://stateparks.mt.gov/lewis-and-clark-caverns, tours 9am-4:30pm May 1-June 14 and Aug. 20-Sept. 30, 9am-6:30pm June 15-Aug. 19, $10 adults, $5 children 6-11). When a ramrod of granite magma thrust up the Tobacco Root Mountains about 70 million years ago, sedimentary layers laid down hundreds of millions of years earlier rose to flank the new mountains in steeply pitched strata. In an exposed face of Madison limestone, rainwater began to erode the porous rock. Many millions of years later, water has cut 3,000-foot-long

A roadside pullout has views of historic Beaverhead Rock, an important landmark.

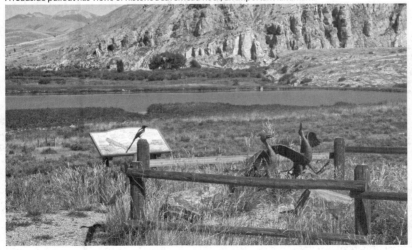

chambers and passageways 300 feet below the surface, making this the third-largest cavern in the United States.

Water carrying minute traces of minerals has stained the many stalagmites and stalactites into wonderful colors. Fanciful minds have assigned the caverns' rich abundance of exotic formations theme chambers, with such names as Granny's Kitchen and The Princess and the Frog. Tours last about two hours; visitors should be sure on their feet and ready to negotiate stairs and walk in a crouch. Take a jacket—the caverns remain at 50°F.

The caverns stand on a hilltop three miles from the highway. At the base of the hill, find a visitors center, pleasant **campground** ($15-28 nonresident, $7-20 Montana resident), and hiking trails. Light snacks are available at the small visitors center/ticket lobby at the top of the hill.

formations at Lewis and Clark Caverns

I-15: Butte to Helena

Between Helena and Butte, I-15 crosses over the Boulder Batholith, an intrusion of magma that shot up from the bowels of the earth like a piston about 70 million years ago. The formation is made largely of granite, but in places it also contains an almost incomprehensible wealth of valuable minerals. Near towns such as Clancy and Jefferson City, gold was panned, mined, and dredged. The orderly dikes of processed gravel tailings from streambeds lie like welts across the landscape.

Boulder and Basin survived the decline of Montana's mining industry by establishing a somewhat more diversified economy. As early as the 1880s, Boulder Hot Springs attracted tourists and weekenders to its spa resort. Boulder was also the trade center for ranchers in the Boulder River Valley. Basin struggled on as a rail center for local gold and silver mines until the 1940s, when the presence of uranium met the demands of a changing world. After a brief flurry of activity, these radium-rich

mines became the radon health mines that currently energize the local economy.

BOULDER AND VICINITY

Named for the large stones littering its valley, Boulder (pop. 1,200, elev. 5,158 feet) began as a stage stop between Fort Benton and Virginia City in the 1860s. Its prominence as a trading center was enhanced when the state built the Montana Home for the Feeble-Minded here in 1892. Now known as the Montana Developmental Center, the facility houses and trains developmentally disabled citizens.

Old Boulder

The town center of Boulder, with its sprawl of redbrick storefronts, retains much of the flavor of a frontier commercial center. Its most prominent landmark is the **Jefferson County Courthouse,** built in 1889. Its grand scale and gargoyles betray the German education of designer John Paulsen, who also

Miracle Cures in Montana Radon Gas Mines

In 1950 a California woman who suffered from arthritis accompanied her husband into a uranium mine near Boulder. She noted a marked relief from the constant pain to which she had grown accustomed. She related her experiences to a fellow arthritis sufferer. The friend also visited the Boulder mine, and her stay produced the same rapid recovery.

Word of the "miracle cure" soon spread, reaching an early peak when *Life* magazine sent a news team to cover the "stampede" of people arriving to seek this underground cure.

Just why the cure seems to work hasn't been adequately explained. Radon gas is a naturally occurring gas formed when radium oxidizes in the process of aging. This radioactive gas occurs in Basin-Boulder mines in levels deemed safe for miners but in concentrations considered therapeutic by the mines' many promoters. Sympathetic researchers contend that radon gas stimulates the pituitary gland to produce health-giving hormones and natural steroids, which can ease or eradicate the pain of conditions caused by hormonal dysfunction.

The recommended "cure" involves a careful regimen of contact with radon gas. Patrons are asked to spend no more than one hour at a time in the mines no more than three times per day. About 30 hours of contact with radon gas is considered to be the optimum treatment. Within the mines, there are sofas, tables, and chairs for the visitors' comfort; card games and reading are the usual pastimes.

Radon gas therapy is *not* medically accepted in the United States (the European medical establishment is less hostile to radon gas therapy), and the owners stress that the mines are open for people seeking *nonmedical* treatment. There is no guarantee of a cure.

There are, however, many moving testimonials from people who have found relief from aggravated and long-standing afflictions. The list of physical conditions for which radon gas is claimed to be efficacious grows as the number of afflicted visitors grows. Sufferers of arthritis, migraines, eczema, asthma, diabetes, and allergies have testified to the mines' healing virtues.

Three health mines operate in the area: **Free Enterprise Health Mine** (148 Depot Hill Rd., Boulder, 406/255-3383, www.radonmine.com); **Earth Angel Health Mine** (61 Earth Angel Rd., Basin, 406/225-3516, www.earthangelmine.com); **Merry Widow Health Mine** (29 Frontage Rd., Basin, 406/255-3220, www.merrywidowmine.com). Expect to pay about $5-10 for a visit.

Radon therapy is very popular; if you are considering a visit, call ahead for reservations, and don't be surprised if the facilities are all booked up. Also, don't come expecting a four-star spa; accommodations can be quite rustic.

designed the administration building for the Home for the Feeble-Minded. Both are listed on the National Register of Historic Places.

Boulder Hot Springs

One of the earliest tourist facilities in the state, **Boulder Hot Springs** (406/225-4339, www.boulderhotsprings.com, 7 adults, $5 seniors, $4 children) began in 1883 as a spa for the rich and influential in Helena and Butte. Spa options today include a swim in the 90-95°F outdoor pool, then a plunge into indoor hot and cold pools or sitting in the steam room. Over the years the lodge has been redesigned and reinterpreted in fashionable, ever more grandiose architectural vernaculars. The earliest wooden-frame hotel was replaced by a Queen Anne clapboard lodge, only to be renovated in Spanish mission style. The imposing lodge at Boulder Hot Springs is undergoing another rejuvenation, this time as a health and spiritual retreat center. Part of the huge lodge has been renovated (the rest seems to be perpetually under construction) and is open with both hotel and B&B options. Basic old-fashioned hotel rooms with bath down the hall cost $85-90; B&B rooms range from $109-139. Swimming and soaking are free to all guests. Various types of massage and other healing arts are also available, but alcohol is not. Boulder Hot Springs is three miles south of Boulder on Highway 69.

Elkhorn

The silver-mining town of Elkhorn began in the 1870s and flourished until the early 1890s, when the international silver market bottomed out. Although only the ghosts of the town remain, Elkhorn is reckoned to be one of the best-preserved mining camps in the state. Buildings of note include **Gillian Hall,** a two-story bar and dance hall, and **Fraternity Hall,** a meetinghouse built in the neoclassical style. Elkhorn is six miles south of Boulder on Highway 69, then 12 miles north on gravel Elkhorn Road. During winter the trip is best made on cross-country skis.

BASIN

Set in narrow Boulder River Canyon, Basin is an old mining town that has avoided the ghost-town destiny of many other mining camps. By luck or connivance, Basin always successfully managed to market what it has. Gold prospectors such as Granville Stuart helped found the community, but silver mines put Basin on the map during the 1880s. The town fell into a long doze after a spurt of gold mining during the 1920s, then reactivated when the uranium market developed during World War II. The radon gas present in many of the old mines is now marketed for its reputed health-giving benefits.

Basin's main street exhibits structures from more prosperous times. The **Masonic Hall** dates from the early 20th century, as does the old boardinghouse in the Sockerson Block. Watch the hillsides near Basin for old flumes and mine adits.

Support local artists with a visit to **Basin Creek Pottery and Gallery** (82 Basin St., 406/225-3218); the resident potter gets his clay from local mining sites.

If you've been hurtling down I-15 and need to stretch your legs, turn off the interstate south of Basin at the Bernice exit (exit 151) and drive a couple of miles east to the **Bear Gulch trail.** While it's not exactly wilderness, the trail through open forest and meadows is a good break from the road.

Most of the health mines provide accommodations and campgrounds for their guests. The small **Basin Canyon Campground** run by the Forest Service (406/287-3223) is five miles north of Basin on I-15, then three miles east on Forest Road 172. It's free but has no piped water. There are a couple of places to eat in town, including a pretty good pizza place.

Helena

Montana's capital city straddles one of history's richest gold strikes: Last Chance Gulch. Unlike its contemporary boomtowns, Helena (pop. 29,600, elev. 4,124 feet) managed not only to survive but to prevail through good times and bad. Like a snake swallowing its tail, Helena transformed itself from seething gold camp to trade center, then to capital city, and finally into a cultural and tourist center.

In Montana, only Butte can approach Helena in sheer historicity, but history has left Helena a richer legacy of monuments and architecture. From the elegance of the State Capitol and the Cathedral of St. Helena to the stone shacks on Reeder's Alley, the highs, lows, and middlings of the state's history each have their testimony here. Excellent museums and galleries present and preserve the best of Montana's past and present.

Helena is unbelievably well-situated for recreation. With fishing and boating on nearby lakes on the Missouri, hiking and skiing in Helena National Forest, and exploring old ghost towns and other reminders of the past always just nearby, the Helena area tempts the traveler with a rich brew of history and outdoor activity.

Helena

To Missoula

ARCHIE BRAY
FOUNDATION

Spring
Meadow
State Park

COUNTRY CLUB AVE

12

EUCLID AVE

STUART ST

FLOWERREE ST

CENTRE AVE

HAUSER

Mt. Helena ▲

MAIN ST

MONROE ST

GILBERT

HOLTER

POWER

MADISON AVE

DEARBORN AVE

HARRISON AVE

LAMPLIGHTER
MOTEL

MANSION
DISTRICT

BENTON AVE

REEDER'S ALLEY

MEDITERRANEAN GRILL
PARK AVE BAKERY

BLACKFOOT
TAP ROOM

ADAMS ST

LAWRENCE

LUCCA'S

HOLIDAY INN
ON BROADWAY

Last Chance Gulch

RIALTO

BERT &
ERNIE'S

Park Ave

SILVER STAR
STEAK CO

E 14TH ST

NEILL AVE

BREWHOUSE
BREW PUB

CARROLL COLLEGE

GETCHELL ST

CRUISE ST

WARREN ST

DOWNTOWN
HELENA

McMURRY'S

CHAMBER
OF COMMERCE

CATHEDRAL
OF ST HELENA

BARRISTER B&B

SANDERS B&B

OLD GOVERNOR'S MANSION

HOLTER MUSEUM
OF THE ARTS

GREAT NORTHERN
TOWN CENTER

BEST WESTERN GREAT
NORTHERN INN

HELENA ST

EWING ST

RODNEY ST

LYNDALE AVE

LUCCA'S

LAST CHANCE GULCH

To Lakes

DAVIS ST

BROADWAY

6TH AVE

MONTANA AVE

To Great Falls

EAST
SIDE

ROBERTS ST

11TH AVE

PROSPECT AVE

MONTANA
STATE CAPITOL

JORGENSON'S
INN

WINGATE BY
WYNDHAM

MONTANA
HISTORICAL SOCIETY

DAYS INN

15

287

RED LION
COLONIAL INN

287 12

COLONIAL DR

To
Butte

To Townsend, and
Taste of the City

0   0.25 mi

0   0.25 km

HISTORY

Helena began, as did so many other gold camps, as the cry went up, "Just one last chance before we leave." In this case, four former Confederate soldiers were panning for gold in 1864 in a narrow gulch called Prickly Pear, just below the crest of the Continental Divide. The "Four Georgians," as they were later known, found color in their pans in the draw they called Last Chance Gulch. Word spread, and the rush was on. By 1876 the town had grown to 4,000 inhabitants.

At the time, Montana was a territory lacking a cohesive center. Because of the boom-and-bust nature of its initial settlements, the focal point of Montana moved from strike to strike. The earliest territorial capital, Bannack, was almost deserted by the time the center of government moved to Virginia City. In turn, Helena attracted the territorial capital in 1875.

Helena had advantages that the other mining centers lacked. The gold, then the silver and lead, were richer in Helena than in other early settlements. Helena was midway on the stage routes between Fort Benton—the uppermost steamboat reach on the Missouri—and Virginia City and other mining areas in southwestern Montana. Newcomers quickly realized that wealth was in trade, not mining, and gravitated to Helena, the largest center of population in the territory. Trade quickly underpinned mining to support Helena's economy. Onetime miners, now important captains of industry, built huge mansions on the city's west side.

Helena continued to hold sway over the rich and powerful during the late 1890s and early years of the 1900s, as is witnessed by its elaborate architecture of the period. Be they ranchers, miners, or tradespeople, the rich from across the state hadn't "arrived" until they had engaged in the mansion-building competition that thrived on the west side of Last Chance Gulch. The concentration of wealth in Helena is legendary. In the late 1880s there were more millionaires in Helena per capita than anywhere else in the nation.

Helena has a rich architectural history.

SIGHTS
★ Montana State Capitol

The **Montana State Capitol** (1301 6th Ave., http://visit-the-capitol.mt.gov, 7am-6pm Mon.-Fri., 9am-3pm Sat.-Sun., tours on the hour 9am-2pm Mon.-Sat., May-Sept., 9am-2pm Sat. only Oct.-Apr., free) was begun in 1899. This imposing structure, domed with a cupola of Butte copper, was enlarged in 1912 by the extensions containing the present legislative wings. The statue on the dome commemorates an odd episode in Montana history. After the bruising fight for state capital between Helena and Anaconda, the Capitol Commission ran off with the books. When this statue arrived at the railroad station from a foundry in Ohio, no one knew who had ordered it, who had paid for it, or what it was meant for. The foundry's records were shortly destroyed in a fire, leaving the mysterious statue no history and no future. The builders of the capitol needed statuary for the top of its dome, and the *Goddess of Liberty* found its way to the top.

The *Goddess of Liberty* tops the dome of the Montana State Capitol.

Significant paintings and murals decorate the capitol. In the House Chamber hangs *Lewis and Clark Meeting the Flathead Indians at Ross's Hole* by Charlie Russell, one of his largest and most acclaimed works. In the lobby of the House of Representatives, six paintings by E. S. Paxson detail the state's history. For tour information, contact the **Montana Historical Society** (406/444-4789, http://mhs.mt.gov).

The Capitol Area

Known in local parlance as the East Side, the area around the capitol is directly south of the downtown area and contains many buildings of historic interest.

Probably the first thing a summer visitor should do while in Helena is take the hour-long train tour offered by **Last Chance Tours** (406/442-1023, www.lctours.com, Mon.-Sat. June 1-Sept. 15, $8 adults, $6.50 children 4-12). This open-air train tour does a quick drive-by of most of Helena's historic and scenic properties; the traveler can decide what

to explore in further depth. On the route are buildings in the capitol area, Last Chance Gulch, Reeder's Alley, the mansion district, and Carroll College. Catch the "Last Chancer," as the tour train is nicknamed, just outside the Montana Historical Society at 6th Avenue and North Roberts Street, across the street from the capitol. The tours peak in July and August with four tours a day at 11am, 1pm, 3pm, and 5:30pm; call or check the website for shoulder season departure times. This tour company also runs two-hour Segway tours ($65).

★ MONTANA HISTORICAL SOCIETY

The **Montana Historical Society** (225 N. Roberts St., 406/444-2694, http://mhs.mt.gov, 9am-5pm Mon.-Wed. and Fri.-Sat., 9am-8pm Thurs., $5 adults, $1 children, free 5pm-8pm Thurs. and 9am-5pm second Sat.), nicknamed "Montana's Museum," is Montana's premier museum, mixing fine art, an exhibit charting the state's history, and changing exhibits. Of special interest is the **MacKay Gallery of Charles M. Russell Art,** one of the nation's largest public collections of Russell's works. If Western art seems like an oxymoron to you, come marvel at the brilliant use of color and composition by this unschooled cowboy artist.

The **Montana Homeland Exhibit** tells the story of Montana, beginning with Native American prehistory and moving on through the era of settlement. Three galleries contain more than 2,000 artifacts. Other galleries change exhibits but often contain fascinating displays of frontier photographs. Of interest to historians and researchers are the library and photo archives.

OLD GOVERNOR'S MANSION

From 1913 to 1959, Montana's governor lived at the **Old Governor's Mansion** (304 N. Ewing St., 406/444-4789). Built in 1883 by a local entrepreneur, the 20-room residence is now owned by the Montana Historical Society, which has restored the ornate building to its historic splendor. **Tours** operate on the hour (noon-3pm Tues.-Sat. May-Sept., noon-3pm Sat. Oct.-Apr., $4 adults, $1 children, combo tickets with the Montana Historical Society are available).

CATHEDRAL OF ST. HELENA

The **Cathedral of St. Helena** (530 N. Ewing St., 406/442-5825, www.sthelenas.org, 9am-4:30pm except during services, free) was begun in 1908 but wasn't finished until 1924. Modeled after Cologne Cathedral, Helena's largest church dominates the skyline with its 230-foot twin spires. Its stained glass was fashioned in Germany, although the images of the Seven Sacraments seem out of a Burne-Jones pre-Raphaelite painting. Guided tours are available 1pm-3pm Tuesday-Thursday from the week after Memorial Day through Labor Day.

Last Chance Gulch

In the 1860s, Prickly Pear Creek snaked down from the mountains through a thicket of mining claims called Last Chance Gulch. As mining gave way to commerce, the gulch remained the main street; its winding path, and especially the one-claim-sized business buildings, still reflect its mining past. The old business district of Helena is still impressive, even after a 1933 earthquake destroyed some of its buildings.

Much of Last Chance Gulch is now a pedestrian mall, designed in the 1970s to make this historic main street more attractive to tourists and businesses. Have a look at the handsome storefronts—many empty—and decide if it has worked.

The extensive infrastructure of historic business buildings in Helena proves that the capital's most significant occupation was commerce, not mining. Notable buildings not to miss include the following:

The Power Block (58-62 N. Last Chance Gulch) was built in 1889; note that on the southeast corner, each of the five floors has windows grouped in corresponding numbers of panes. The **Securities Building** (101 N. Last Chance Gulch), built in 1886,

the Cathedral of St. Helena

is a Romanesque former bank with curious carved thumbprints between the first-floor arches. The **Montana Club** (24 W. 6th Ave.) was Montana's most prestigious private club: Membership was open only to millionaires. The club's present building was designed by Cass Gilbert, who designed the U.S. Supreme Court Building.

The **Atlas Building** (7-9 N. Last Chance Gulch) is one of Helena's most fanciful; on a cornice upheld by Atlas, a salamander and lizards do symbolic battle. **Reeder's Alley** (308 S. Park Ave.) is a winding series of one-room brick shanties built in the 1870s to house the mining camp's many bachelors. Today, it's a theme alley with shops, offices, and places to eat.

Visit the **Wells Fargo Bank** (350 N. Last Chance Gulch, 406/443-0136) to see the **Gold Collection,** displaying gold in many forms, from nuggets to leaves.

West-Side Mansions

Montana's grandest historic homes grace the hillside above Helena. In an area roughly

The tiny buildings in Reeder's Alley once housed miners; they're now restaurants and offices.

bounded by Stuart, Monroe, Dearborn, and Power Streets stand dozens of imposing monuments to the economic clout of their merchant, mining, or ranching owners. The mansions display a bewildering assortment of styles; Mark Twain described these Helena homes as "Queen Anne in front and Mary Ann behind." In all their opulence, these are what money could buy in Helena during the boom years of 1880-1900.

None of the old homes are regularly open for viewing, but a walk through these beautiful old neighborhoods is a must for anyone with an interest in historic homes.

Downtown Environs

Given all the beautiful architecture in Helena, it is ironic that the city's most distinctive building is the **Civic Center** (corner of Neill and Fuller), built in 1921 as the

Last Chance Gulch is a downtown pedestrian mall.

Masonic Algeria Shrine Temple. This exercise in high camp is a Moorish revival edifice with a 175-foot minaret, onion dome, and intricately modeled exterior brickwork. It now houses Helena's municipal offices and a performance hall.

Just east of downtown is the new **Great Northern Town Center** (www.gntowncenter.com), a development on 11 acres of land that was until recently unused rail yards. The development has several significant public buildings, including a new federal courthouse, plus a hotel, several restaurants, shops, a **carousel** (989 Carousel Way, 406/457-5353, www.gncarousel.com, 11am-8pm Mon., Wed.-Thurs., 11am-9pm Fri.-Sat., 11am-7pm Sun., $1.50), an outdoor exhibit documenting Lewis and Clark's journey, and **Exploration Works** (995 Carousel Way, 406/457-1800, www.explorationworks.org, 10am-5pm Tues.-Sat., 2:30pm-5pm most Mon., $9 adults, $6.50 seniors and students, $5.50 youth under 18), a kid-oriented science museum. As a modern commercial district, the Great Northern Town Center harmonizes nicely with Helena's classic Western architecture.

Overlooking Helena from the northeast is **Carroll College,** a private Catholic college with a student body of 1,400. Carroll stands on 63 acres atop a bluff still known as Capitol Hill. The site was offered for the state capitol in 1895, but the landowner wanted $7,000 for the real estate, and the frugal Capitol Commission went elsewhere.

Marysville

Seven miles north of Helena off Highway 279, this almost ghost town has just enough life left to feed passersby. The **Marysville House,** in the midst of abandoned general stores, churches, and hotels, is a bar and restaurant housed in the old train depot and is known for its ample meals.

GALLERIES
Holter Museum of the Arts

The **Holter Museum of the Arts** (12 E. Lawrence St., 406/442-6400, www.

holtermuseum.org, 10am-5:30pm Tues.-Sat., noon-4pm Sun., free) displays very good changing exhibits of contemporary art and offers workshops, readings, and a gallery store. Summer visitors should check out the auction exhibition; early in August the works are auctioned off at a big party.

Last Chance Gulch Galleries

Several private Western art galleries range along Last Chance Gulch, including **Ghost Art Gallery** (21 S. Last Chance Gulch, 406/443-4536, http://ghostartgallery.com) and the **Mountain Sage Gallery** (433 N. Last Chance Gulch, 406/457-8240).

Archie Bray Foundation

The **Archie Bray Foundation** (2915 Country Club Ave., 406/443-3502, www.archiebray.org) is a studio workshop, classroom, and gallery for ceramic artists. The brickyard and kilns of the **Western Clay Manufacturing Company** have stood just outside Helena for more than 100 years. Archie Bray, whose father began the business, was approached by local artists to use the brickyard's huge beehive kilns to fire ceramics. Bray, who was already active in the Helena arts scene, decided to dedicate a portion of the factory to the ceramic arts. In 1951 he founded the Archie Bray Foundation, now a world-famous facility for training talented young potters and a space in which resident artists can experiment and exhibit.

Visitors can watch potters in workshops, visit the permanent collection, and view works for sale in the gallery (10am-5pm Mon.-Sat. free). The old kilns and outbuildings still stand, while avant-garde ceramics, colorful and abstract, are strewn about with guileless abandon.

THE ARTS

The **Myrna Loy Center for the Performing Arts** (15 N. Ewing St., 406/442-0287, www.myrnaloycenter.org), named for the late film actress who hailed from the Helena area, is housed in the revamped 1880s jail. A performance space, gallery, and art-film theater combine to make this a jewel in Helena's cultural crown.

The **Grandstreet Theatre** (325 N. Park Ave., 406/447-1574, http://grandstreetheatre.com) is Helena's community theater. Grandstreet works closely with drama students from Carroll College and conducts a theater school for young people.

RECREATION

Hiking is as close as **Mt. Helena,** the city's 620-acre park on the west side of Last Chance Gulch. Seven trails wind up and across the mountainside; some ascend to Mt. Helena's 5,468-foot peak, and others dawdle in meadows. To reach the park, follow the ravine behind Reeder's Alley on foot or drive to the top of Adams Street behind the mansion district.

A good diversion for hot kids is **Spring Meadow Lake State Park** (2715 Country Club Dr., 406/495-3270, http://stateparks.mt.gov/spring-meadow-lake, $5 per vehicle non-Montana residents), a small lake just west of Helena off Euclid Avenue. A trail rings the lake, but the real attractions are the beaches lined with swimmers and anglers in summer.

Great Divide Ski Area (406/449-3746, www.skigd.com), 22 miles northwest of Helena near Marysville, is a ski and snowboard hill with 1,503 feet of vertical drop, five double chairlifts, about 140 trails, and reasonable rates. It's a good place to learn to ski. Adults ski for $40, seniors and students pay $30, and children grades 1-5 are $16. The season runs from mid-December to early April.

The municipal **swimming pool** (1203 N. Last Chance Gulch, 406/447-1559) is at Memorial Park. There are **tennis courts** at the park behind the Civic Center (Neill St. at Park Ave.) and at Barney Park (Cleveland St. and Hudson St.). Both parks also have picnic facilities and playgrounds.

Holter, Hauser, and Canyon Ferry Reservoirs, in the vicinity of Helena, provide excellent fishing, boating, and even windsurfing in the dammed waters of the Missouri River.

ACCOMMODATIONS

Most of Helena's hotels and motels are at the fringes of the city at busy intersections, particularly I-15 exit 293. Except at the very bottom end, chains dominate the scene; B&Bs are a good alternative.

Under $100

West of downtown, not far from Carroll College, the **Lamplighter Motel** (1006 Madison Ave., 406/442-9200, $65) offers accommodations in homey cottage units dating from the 1930s. Some are family units with full kitchens, and several are two- or three-bedroom units; prices go up according to number of people.

Jorgenson's Inn (1714 11th Ave., 406/442-1770, www.jorgensonsinn.biz, $85-130) is an older but well-maintained lodging complex with an indoor pool, exercise equipment, guest laundry, free airport shuttle, and restaurant and lounge. Rooms come in a wide variety of configurations, from economy rooms to suites; it's near the capitol.

The **Days Inn** (2001 Prospect Dr., 406/442-3280 or 800/325-2525, www.daysinn.com, $83-88) is a good basic place to stay right near the Prospect exit off I-15; it's pet-friendly.

Over $100

The ★ **Best Western Premier Great Northern Hotel** (835 Great Northern Blvd., 406/457-5500 or 800/829-4047, www.bestwesternmontana.com, $169-189) is at the center of the new Great Northern Town Center district. Rooms are very large and nicely furnished, and the hotel offers a complimentary breakfast, 24-hour business center, high-speed Internet access, an indoor pool, and fitness center. Restaurants and shopping are right out the front door.

The other good downtown hotel is the **Holiday Inn Helena** (22 N. Last Chance Gulch, 406/443-2200 or 877/859-5095, www.ihg.com, $121-177), a well-appointed hotel with an indoor pool. All of downtown Helena's restaurants, galleries, and historic architecture are just a stroll away.

The **Red Lion Colonial Hotel** (2301 Colonial Dr., 406/443-2100 or 800/422-1002, http://redlion.com/colonial, $107-170) has a small pool, hot tub, fitness room, free airport shuttle, restaurant, and lounge; it's pet-friendly.

Those who simply can't get enough of Helena's historic homes might consider spending a few nights at ★ **The Sanders Helena's Bed and Breakfast Inn** (328 N. Ewing St., 406/442-3309, www.sandersbb. com, $130-145), an impressive mansion built in 1875 by Montana's first U.S. senator. This National Registry property is amazingly well-preserved and filled with lovely furnishings, many original to the home. Even though a great deal of care is taken to preserve period authenticity, all of the seven bedrooms have private baths and Wi-Fi, and the entire mansion is air-conditioned. All of the rooms have a TV tucked away, although more in keeping with the spirit of the place are the radio alarms, each tuned to the local public radio station. Breakfasts are served in the formal dining room, a showpiece of carved oak moldings.

Just down the street is another historic inn, **The Barrister B&B** (416 N. Ewing St., 406/443-7330, http://thebarristermt. com, $122-137), an 1874 mansion located near St. Helena Cathedral. Its features include ornate fireplaces, antique stained-glass windows, and carved staircases. Modern niceties are also in evidence, including air-conditioning, TVs in rooms, all private baths, and a guest business center. The brother-sister team who run the B&B welcome dogs.

Most of Helena's newest upscale chain motels are quite a distance from the capitol and downtown, but the **Wingate by Wyndham—Helena** (2007 N. Oakes at I-15 exit 193, 406/449-3000 or 800/228-1000, www.wingatehotels.com, $109-175) is one of Helena's newer hotels, offering free continental breakfast, indoor pool, exercise center, and large, nicely furnished rooms in a spot that's not too far from the sights and restaurants you came to Helena to see.

Camping

Moose Creek Campground (406/449-5490, www.fs.usda.gov/helena, $5) is a very pleasant and popular small campground in the Helena National Forest just east of the Continental Divide. It's 10 miles west of Helena on Highway 12, then 4 miles south on Rimini Road. The Bureau of Land Management maintains a couple of campgrounds on **Canyon Ferry Lake,** about 20 miles east of town.

FOOD
Breakfast, Lunch, and Casual Meals

It makes sense in a town fueled by the business of politics that there are as many or more good choices for lunch in Helena as for dinner. Clustered in the Last Chance Gulch area are several good restaurants that serve a busy and boisterous lunch clientele. One of the busiest places at lunchtime is **Murry's** (438 N. Last Chance Gulch, 406/441-2886, www. murrystakeout.com, 8am-3pm Mon.-Fri., $5-10), a casual place with a few tables (plus outdoor seating) and good daily lunch specials that range from sweet potato lentil curry to especially tasty barbecued pork sandwiches to meatloaf and mashed potatoes.

Helena's best bakery, the **Park Avenue Bakery** (44 S. Park Ave., 406/449-8424, www. parkavenuebakery.com, 7am-6pm Mon.-Fri., 7am-4pm Sat., 8am-1pm Sun.) offers European-style pastries, real French bread, and specialty desserts. A great cheese Danish and a cup of their fine coffee induce a near out-of-Montana experience. At lunch, there is a daily-changing soup, salad, and pizza selection ($4-8).

Bert and Ernie's (361 N. Last Chance Gulch, 406/443-5680, www.bertanderniesof-helena.com, 11am-10pm daily, $12-25) serves a sandwich-dominated menu with a wide selection of beers.

For a drink in a Helena institution, go to the **Rialto** (52 N. Last Chance Gulch, 406/442-1890, 2pm-2am Mon.-Sat.). Try the burger ($7) in this venerable old bar (popular with students from Carroll College).

Helena's most famous sweets sanctuary is **Parrot Confectionery** (42 N. Last Chance Gulch, 406/442-1470, www.parrotchocolate. com, 9am-6pm Mon.-Sat.), a soda fountain and candy factory that isn't just old-fashioned but actually *old*. Try the handmade chocolates or a malted milk; the Parrot's sole feint to solid food is its renowned chili, made according to the restaurant's 80-year-old recipe ($4.50 per bowl).

American Fare

The ★ **Windbag Saloon** (19 S. Last Chance Gulch, 406/443-9669, 11am-ppm Mon.-Fri., noon-9:30pm Sat., $12-30) was a brothel named Big Dorothy's until 1973. With this colorful history and filled with namesake politicians, the Windbag is one of Helena's unique restaurants. The burgers (about $11) are the thing for lunch, with steaks, pasta, and seafood on the dinner menu.

The **Brewhouse Brew Pub and Grill** (939 Getchell St., 406/457-9390, http://atthe-brewhouse.com, 11am-10pm daily, $9-26) serves Lewis and Clark Brewery beers and ales along with good pub food. Feast on burgers, barbecue ribs, steaks, and such house special-ties as macadamia nut halibut. The brewery (previously in the basement of the pub) is now located at 1517 Dodge Avenue (406/442-5960, http://lewisandclarkbrewing.com, 2pm-8pm daily) with a taproom but no food service.

A downtown taproom worth visiting is the **Blackfoot Tap Room** (66 S. Park Ave., 406/449-3005, http://blackfootriverbrewing. com, 2pm-8pm daily), home of Blackfoot River Brewing and a popular after-work stop for downtown workers. Although they aren't permitted to sell food, free popcorn is pro-vided, perhaps washed down by a Scottish-style strong ale.

A fun and lively spot that combines an en-ergetic jazz bar atmosphere with a locovore-focused menu is ★ **Benny's Bistro** (108 E. Sixth Ave., 406/443-0105, http://bennysbistro. com, 11am-3pm Mon.-Tues., 11am-3pm and 5:30pm-9pm Wed.-Sat., $20-27), with a food selection that occupies the ground between fine dining and comfort food. Crepes are a specialty, as is beef Stroganoff and house-made gnocchi with brown butter sage sauce.

For one of Helena's most unique dining experiences, you'll need to leave town. In the old near-ghost-town of Marysville near the Great Divide Ski Area, **Marysville House** (153 Main St., Marysville, 406/443-6677, www.marysvillemontana.com, 4pm-10pm Wed.-Sun., $9-32) doesn't have a huge menu, but the 24-ounce T-bone steaks, grilled half chickens, oyster skillets, and marshmallows toasted out back for dessert at this rustic fron-tier-era bar keep locals coming back for more. Marysville is seven miles north of Helena on I-15, then nine miles west along Highway 279, and a final six miles south along the gravel road to Marysville (the route is well-signed).

Fine Dining

Tasty Northern Italian cuisine appears at **On Broadway** (106 Broadway, 406/443-1929, www.onbroadwayinhelena.com, 5:30pm-10pm Mon.-Sat., $17-43) in a light, airy, red-brick atmosphere. Another bastion of fine Italian cookery is ★ **Lucca's** (56 N. Last Chance Gulch, 406/457-8311, www.luccasital-ian.com, 5pm-9:30pm Wed.-Sun., $22-34), an intimate (just 15 tables) restaurant with excel-lent appetizers, pasta, and meats, and a care-fully chosen wine list. Roasted double-cut lamb chops are served with feta cheese and rosemary olive oil.

The **Mediterranean Grill** (42 South Park Ave., 406/495-1212, 11am-9:30pm Mon.-Sat., 10am-2pm and 5pm-9:30pm Sun., www. mediterraneangrillhelena.com, $12-27) of-fers a pan-Mediterranean menu: Excellent pasta, pizza, and Italian dishes are paired with Moroccan and Turkish specialties (the owner is Turkish).

The ★ **Silver Star Steak Company** (833 Great Northern Blvd., 406/495-0677, www. silverstarsteakco.com, 11:30am-10pm Mon.-Sat., 4pm-9pm Sun., $16-40) is at the center of the new Great Northern district. As one of Helena's most popular restaurants, you'll need reservations most evenings, but the food and atmosphere are both notable. In addition to top-quality steaks and prime rib, expect to find lamb, pasta, and seafood.

East Helena is a separate town from Helena, five minutes south on I-15. It was home to the smelter for the ores carved out of the famed Last Chance Gulch mines. Today, this workers' town is a little worse for wear, but its historic redbrick downtown is a great spot for savvy restaurateurs looking for inexpensive rent.

★ **Taste of the City** (24 W. Main, East Helena, 406/227-5552, www.tasteofthecity. org, 5pm-9pm Tues.-Sat., $20-30) offers very up-to-date food in an old bar in East Helena. Savor such dishes as pistachio-encrusted Berkshire pork tenderloin with rhubarb compote over heirloom wild rice and Rhode Island-style clam fritters with a trio of dipping sauces. The talent behind this notable restaurant is chef-owner Jeremy Mather, who previously cooked at New York City's Waldorf Astoria Hotel and worked formerly as personal chef for Paul Newman.

INFORMATION AND SERVICES

The **Helena Convention and Visitors Bureau** (406/442-4120, www.helenamt.com) is at 225 Cruse Avenue. **Downtown Helena** (www.downtownhelena.com) is another good source of information.

The **Helena National Forest Ranger Station** (406/449-5201) is at 2880 Skyway Drive. The **Department of Fish, Wildlife, and Parks** office (406/444-2535) is at 1420 East 6th Avenue.

The central **post office** (406/443-3304) is at 2300 North Harris Street. The **Lewis and Clark County Library** (406/447-1690) is at 120 South Last Chance Gulch.

St. Peter's Hospital (406/442-2480) is at 2475 Broadway.

GETTING THERE AND AROUND

Helena is served by Alaska, Delta, and United airlines. The **airport** is east on Washington

Street, or you can take the airport exit from I-15. **Salt Lake Express** (800/356-9796, www.saltlakeexpress.com) buses link Helena other cities along I-15. You'll find the **bus station** at 1415 N. Montana.

Hertz (406/449-4167), **Alamo** (406/442-1765), **Avis** (406/442-4440), and **National** (406/442-8620) rent cars at the airport. Call a **cab** at 406/449-5525.

THE UPPER MISSOURI LAKES

Southeast of Helena, and north of Townsend, three dams in rapid succession impound the Missouri. Because they are near major population centers and are served by good roads, these lakes are among the most popular and developed in Montana. Canyon Ferry, Hauser, and Holter Lakes are well trod by local anglers, boaters, and campers, but they bear up pretty well considering their heavy use.

The range of recreational options is boggling: There are 25 state, Bureau of Land Management, and Bureau of Reclamation parks on Canyon Ferry Lake alone, which makes a brief overview difficult. Contact the **Department of Fish, Wildlife, and Parks** (1420 E. 6th Ave., Helena, 406/444-2535, http://fwp.mt.gov) for more complete information.

Canyon Ferry Lake

Canyon Ferry Dam was built in the 1950s by the Bureau of Reclamation, creating the largest of the three lakes on the upper Missouri. Canyon Ferry backs up 25 miles of reservoir with almost 80 miles of shoreline. At the south end nearest Townsend, the lake is widest and the surrounding countryside rolling, gentle, and treeless. To the north the reservoir narrows and begins to flow into a steep canyon.

Although it's not as scenic as the other Missouri lakes, there is popular fishing and boating at Canyon Ferry. The lake is stocked with rainbow trout, and they are usually hungry and scrappy enough to make a lucky angler feel skilled. Most of the facilities, both public campgrounds on Hauser Lake. If the beach at **White Sandy,** seven miles northeast off I-15 on Highway 453, is full, then continue a few yards farther to **Black Sandy.**

While at Hauser Lake, try your hand at sapphire mining. The **Spokane Bar Sapphire Mine** (5360 Castles Rd., 406/227-8989, www.sapphiremine.com), 10.5 miles east of Helena via York Road, offers buckets of sapphire-laden gravel. Here the novice can wash gravel to discover highly colored sapphires as well as garnets, rubies, and gold. Buckets of gravel from the sapphire mine cost $25-100, and it's best to come equipped with a screwdriver and tweezers, essential tools of the gravel mining trade.

★ Holter Lake and the Gates of the Mountains

Holter Lake is the most awe-inspiring of the three upper Missouri Lakes. Behind the dam lies the Gates of the Mountains, so named by Meriwether Lewis:

July 19th, 1805: This evening we entered the most remarkable clifts that we have yet seen. These clifts rise from the waters edge on either side perpendicularly to the hight of 1,200 feet. Solid rock for the distance of 5¾ miles. I entered this place and was obliged to continue my rout until sometime after dark before I found a place sufficiently large to encamp my small party; from the singular appearance of this place I called it the gates of the mountains.

The Missouri cut a deep gorge through thick deposits of limestone; although the flooding of Holter Dam (built in 1913) has decreased the rush of the river through these gates, it is still a startlingly dramatic landscape of geologic and human history. Wildlife viewing, historical vignettes, geologic curiosities, and drop-dead beautiful riverscapes make this one of Montana's most compelling side trips.

Gates of the Mountains (406/458-5241, www.gatesofthemountains.com), two miles east from the Gates of the Mountains exit off I-15, offers guided open-air **riverboat tours**

Holter Lake

public and private, cluster at the northern end of the lake.

Follow Canyon Ferry Road (or Montana Avenue) east nine miles out of Helena to reach the lake. If coming north on Highway 12, turn on Highway 284 eight miles north of Winston. Rent a boat at **Yacht Basin Marina** (3555 W. Shore Rd., 406/475-3440).

On the southern end of the lake, the campgrounds thin out. The most convenient **campsites** are at Silo, seven miles north of Townsend on Highway 12, where there are both public and private campgrounds.

Hauser Lake

Built in 1908 by Montana Power, Hauser Dam is named for Samuel Hauser, an early Montanan who advocated damming the Missouri to harness electricity for regional mining enterprises. At this 3,720-acre lake, heavily used for boating and waterskiing, the fishing is okay for rainbow and brown trout, walleye, and perch.

There are two scenic, practically adjacent

(Memorial Day-Sept., $16 adult, $14 senior, $10 child) of the entire canyon. During the two-hour trip, travelers usually see bighorn sheep, mountain goats, eagles, ospreys, and deer. Guides point out Native American pictographs along the limestone cliffs. The departure schedule is complex; call or check the website for times.

Plan your day carefully, and disembark from the boat at Meriwether Picnic Area. The boat captains allow passengers to break the trip at this point. Here at the site of Lewis and Clark's 1805 camp are trails that lead up into the **Gates of the Mountains Wilderness Area,** a 28,560-acre wildlife reserve within the deep limestone canyons along the east side of the Missouri River. It was back in this remote and precipitous area that 16 young firefighters died in 1949, a tragedy that led to the writing of Norman Maclean's best-selling book *Young Men and Fire.*

If you lay over at the wilderness area, be certain to know when to expect a returning riverboat, and save your ticket stub.

The **Bungalow B&B** (2020 Hwy. 287, 406/235-4276, www.bungalowb&b.com, $125-145), Charles Power's 1911 country lodge, is now one of Montana's most historically significant bed-and-breakfasts, located near the small town of Wolf Creek in the Gates of the Mountains canyon country. Power was one of the engines of early Montana capitalism. Beginning rather humbly as a trader at Fort Benton in the 1870s, by the time of his death Powers owned 95 different corporations, controlled four square blocks of downtown Helena (including Helena's most architecturally significant, the Power Block), and was one of the state's richest people. When it came time to build a country home, Power turned to Robert Reamer, the architect who designed the Old Faithful Lodge in Yellowstone Park. For furnishings, Power turned to young interior designer Marshall Fields. Many of the original furnishings remain in the stately log lodge, which offers four guest rooms (one with private bath).

There are three public **campgrounds** (406/235-4314, $15) along Holter Lake, all on the east side. Turn south from I-15 at the Wolf Creek exit, cross Wolf Creek, then turn north (left) on Recreation Road and proceed a few miles to the bridge. Turn south on Bear Tooth Road after crossing the Missouri. Continue three miles to **Holter Lake Recreation Area.** Four miles up the same road are **Log Gulch and Departure Point Recreation Areas.**

The Missouri Headwaters

Highlights

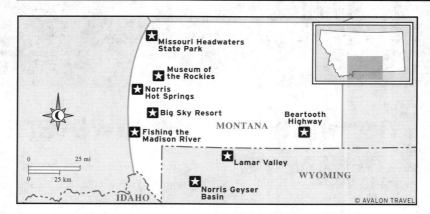

★ **Museum of the Rockies:** Home to many varied collections, this museum is best known for its dinosaur bones, including the *Tyrannosaurus rex* skull excavated in eastern Montana in 1990 (page 213).

★ **Missouri Headwaters State Park:** It's not immediately apparent which of the three braided streams is the true main stem of the river. Lewis and Clark followed the Jefferson upstream; it provided the best path west to the Continental Divide (page 223).

★ **Norris Hot Springs:** Not only is this small hot springs pool a good place to soak, it's also one of the best places around to hear live acoustic music (page 226).

★ **Fishing the Madison River:** The 50-mile stretch of the Madison River from Quake Lake north to Ennis is an almost continuous riffle. The abundant trout are eager to grab passing morsels (page 229).

★ **Big Sky Resort:** Skiers and snowboarders should try to arrange a winter trip to Big Sky—ride the tram all the way to the top of Lone Mountain, take a big gulp as you look at the drop, and point your skis downhill (page 234)!

★ **Beartooth Highway:** This 68-mile-long road climbs to 10,947 feet and crosses alpine meadows and snowfields on its run from Red Lodge to Yellowstone National Park. It'll take at least half a day to drive (page 258).

★ **Norris Geyser Basin:** This ever-changing thermal area may not be as well-known as Old Faithful, but it's far more atmospheric and a better place to hike past geysers and boiling pools (page 268).

★ **Lamar Valley:** It may not have the spectacular geothermal features found in other areas of Yellowstone National Park, but this wide valley on the stretch of road between Cooke City and Gardiner is the best place in the park to spot the famous Yellowstone wolves. The best time to see them is around dawn (page 271).

More than any other part of the state, this country of broad valleys, rugged mountains, lush ranches, and trout-laden rivers is what people expect to find in Montana—and it doesn't disappoint. From the Yellowstone

River, the longest undammed river in the Lower 48, to the Beartooth Highway, declared by the late Charles Kuralt to be one of the most spectacular drives in the United States, to the serene history-laden Missouri headwaters, this is country that cuts deep into the soul.

The Missouri headwaters, where the Jefferson, Madison, and Gallatin Rivers merge and create the Missouri, anchor the northwestern corner of this region. In the northeastern corner, the Crazy Mountains rise wildly from the plains. The Beartooth and Yellowstone Plateaus are at the southern edge. Rivers roll off south-central Montana's mountain ranges—the Beartooths, the Absarokas, the Gallatins, the Madisons, the Gravellys, and the Tobacco Roots—and course north to the Missouri.

Anglers are lured to the Madison, Gallatin, and Yellowstone Rivers by trout. People do run rivers, hunt, and mountain bike here, but the fishing draws pilgrims from around the world. The hatches of salmon flies and caddis flies are as closely watched as the seasons, and most everyone knows brown from rainbow from cutthroat.

PLANNING YOUR TIME

Bozeman has decent air service and is a good place to transition from the rest of the world to Montana. It's worth spending a night or two here, but don't make it your sole destination in this spectacular region.

The rivers draining south-central Montana run south to north, and each has a state highway running alongside it. Take at least a day to explore each of the Madison, Gallatin, and Yellowstone Rivers; the riverside highways are easily accessed from I-90 in the north, and each leads, at least eventually, to Yellowstone National Park. The **Madison River** is known for its excellent fishing, especially south of **Ennis,** which is

Previous: the Missouri Headwaters; elk in Yellowstone. **Above:** bear in Yellowstone.

The Missouri Headwaters

IDAHO

Beaverhead National Forest

Gravelly Ridge

FISHING THE MADISON RIVER

Madison River

Cameron

287

Ennis

287

Pony

To Butte

Tobacco Root Mtns

Three Forks

Lewis and Clark State Park

Norris

287

NORRIS HOT SPRINGS

32

MADISON BUFFALO JUMP

BOZEMAN HOT SPRINGS

90

MISSOURI HEADWATERS STATE PARK

Mcatee Bridge

Ennis Lake

Madison Range

BIG SKY RESORT

LONE MOUNTAIN RANCH

191

Gallatin River

Bozeman Hot Springs

Bozeman

Belgrade

MUSEUM OF THE ROCKIES

BRIDGER SKI AREA

Bridger Range

Quake Lake

32

20

Beaverhead National Forest

Hebgen Lake

Yellowstone

Continental Divide

West Yellowstone

Gallatin Range

89

Emigrant

Livingston

To Idaho Falls

Norris

NORRIS GEYSER BASIN

Yellowstone River

National

Park

Yellowstone Lake

212

LAMAR VALLEY

Silver Gate

Pray

CHICO HOT SPRINGS

MONTANA

Absaroka Range

Boulder River

Natural Bridge State Monument

McLeod

Yellowstone River

To Melville and Crazy Mountains

191

GREYCLIFF PRAIRIE DOG TOWN

Big Timber

Stillwater River

Cooke City

Beartooth Range

Nye

Fishtail

Columbus

90

16

WYOMING

(CLOSED IN WINTER)

BEARTOOTH HIGHWAY

RED LODGE SKI AREA

Roscoe

Absarokee

32

212

72

Red Lodge

310

Laurel

To Billings

310

0
15 km
15 mi

© AVALON TRAVEL

a good place to spend a night. The **Gallatin River** is a fun place for a raft trip; it runs near **Big Sky,** a huge ski resort with plenty of accommodations and good summertime hiking. The **Yellowstone River** is scenic, with legendary fishing and an almost equally legendary hot springs resort; it's a straight shot from the artsy I-90-side town of **Livingston** south along the river to the Mammoth entrance to Yellowstone Park.

Yellowstone National Park deserves at least a week on its own; it's a big park, with many diverse ecosystems. But if you only have a day, the route from Mammoth across the northern tier of the park to the town of **Cooke City** will set you up for one of the state's most spectacular drives: the **Beartooth Highway** from Cooke City to Red Lodge. The drive is not long in miles, but it takes some time and lots of focus, so it's worth planning to spend a night in Red Lodge before heading back to Bozeman.

Bozeman and Vicinity

Bozeman (pop. 39,000, elev. 4,754 feet), home of Montana State University, lies at the foot of the Gallatin Valley, with the Gallatin and Madison Ranges to the south, the Bridger Range to the northeast, the Tobacco Roots farther west, and the Big Belts way off north and west.

It's a lovely setting, and Bozeman makes the most of its physical attributes, with hiking and skiing practically out the back door. However, what makes Bozeman such a great destination for a traveler is the town. Bozeman has maintained its handsome old downtown as a business center, which makes the city seem centralized and community-focused. Add some excellent restaurants, art galleries, inexpensive lodging options, and an outgoing youthful population, and you've got Montana's most beguiling urban experience—though it's not to be mistaken for the real Montana.

SIGHTS
Historic Bozeman
One fortune seeker who passed through Bozeman in 1882 claimed it was the nicest place he'd been since St. Paul. In a letter to his sister, he told of "two churches, court house, fine large brick school, and the nicest lot of small dwelling houses all painted white with green lawns and level as a floor. There are lots of brick store buildings here.

That is something you don't see the whole length of the Yellowstone River." Many of these attractive buildings remain: To embark on a walking tour, with a foray into residential areas, start at the large brick building at Main and Rouse; it once housed city hall, but was first the opera house, with the original sign remaining over the front door for years afterward. Historic business buildings along Main Street include the **Baxter Hotel** (eat in one of the restaurants it now houses, or simply step in and admire the lobby), the **Hotel Bozeman,** the **Ellen Theatre,** and **Holy Rosary Church.** Historic homes cluster in the neighborhood between Main Street and the university, especially along Willson Avenue. The large house at Willson and College is known locally as the **Story Mansion.** It was the home of the son of Nelson Story, the first cattle rancher to drive cattle up from Texas to the Gallatin Valley, a journey that inspired Larry McMurtry's novel *Lonesome Dove.*

Sunset Hills Cemetery, immediately south of Lindley Park, is now home to John Bozeman, Nelson Story, Chet Huntley, and most of the people for whom Bozeman's buildings and streets are named. The old part of the cemetery is off to the west.

Find downloadable walking-tour brochures of the cemetery and Bozeman's historic neighborhoods at www.bozemancvb.com.

Bozeman

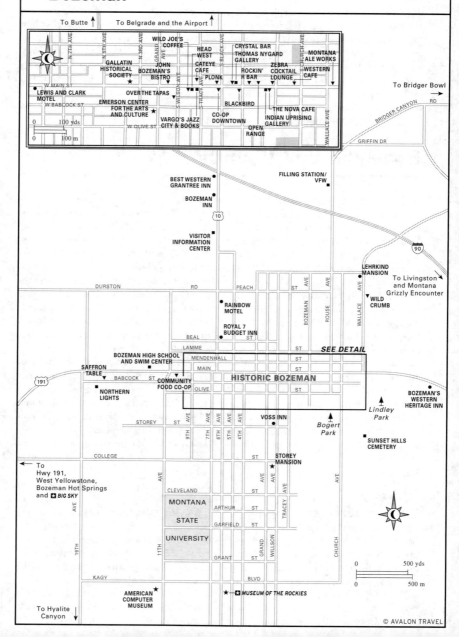

To Butte

To Belgrade and the Airport

To Bridger Bowl

WILD JOE'S COFFEE

HEAD WEST

CRYSTAL BAR

THOMAS NYGARD GALLERY

MONTANA ALE WORKS

GALLATIN HISTORICAL SOCIETY

JOHN BOZEMAN'S BISTRO

CATEYE CAFE

PLONK

ROCKIN' R BAR

ZEBRA COCKTAIL LOUNGE

WESTERN CAFE

LEWIS AND CLARK MOTEL

OVER THE TAPAS

EMERSON CENTER FOR THE ARTS AND CULTURE

BLACKBIRD

THE NOVA CAFE

INDIAN UPRISING GALLERY

VARGO'S JAZZ CITY & BOOKS

CO-OP DOWNTOWN

OPEN RANGE

W MAIN ST

W BABCOCK ST

W OLIVE ST

0   100 yds

0   100 m

BRIDGER CANYON RD

GRIFFIN DR

BEST WESTERN GRANTREE INN

FILLING STATION/ VFW

BOZEMAN INN

10

VISITOR INFORMATION CENTER

90

LEHRKIND MANSION

To Livingston and Montana Grizzly Encounter

DURSTON   RD

PEACH

BOZEMAN

ROUSE

WALLACE

WILD CRUMB

RAINBOW MOTEL

ROYAL 7 BUDGET INN

BEAL

LAMME   ST

SEE DETAIL

BOZEMAN HIGH SCHOOL AND SWIM CENTER

MENDENHALL

SAFFRON TABLE

MAIN

191

BABCOCK   ST

COMMUNITY FOOD CO-OP

HISTORIC BOZEMAN

NORTHERN LIGHTS

OLIVE

BOZEMAN'S WESTERN HERITAGE INN

STOREY

9TH

7TH

6TH

5TH

4TH

VOSS INN

Lindley Park

Bogert Park

COLLEGE

To Hwy 191, West Yellowstone, Bozeman Hot Springs and ⚡ BIG SKY

STOREY MANSION

SUNSET HILLS CEMETERY

CLEVELAND

MONTANA

ARTHUR

TRACEY

STATE

GARFIELD

11TH

UNIVERSITY

19TH

GRANT

CHURCH

KAGY

BLVD

0   500 yds

0   500 m

To Hyalite Canyon

AMERICAN COMPUTER MUSEUM

★ ⚡ MUSEUM OF THE ROCKIES

© AVALON TRAVEL

Holy Rosary Church

bones, including the *Tyrannosaurus rex* skull excavated in eastern Montana in 1990—the largest dinosaur skull ever found. The dinosaur exhibits are housed in the spacious new Siebel Dinosaur Complex. It's a good place to take the kids, and adults may want to prepare by reading Jack Horner's book *Dinosaurs Under the Big Sky* before their visit. Horner, the renowned paleontologist in charge of the museum's impressive paleontology department, was the model for the paleontologist in *Jurassic Park*.

The museum also offers a sampling of modern art, pioneer history, and astronomy. Almost as popular as the dinosaurs is the museum's planetarium, where the impressive projection system simulates flying through space. The museum's extensive photo archive includes many images of and by Native Americans. Many of these photos can be browsed on the museum's website.

During the summer months, gardeners and cooks in period dress work at the adjacent **Living History Farm.** Admission to the gardens and the 1889 farmhouse is included in museum admission.

Montana State University

Founded in 1893, **MSU** (406/994-0211, www.montana.edu) is the state's oldest university. Originally the "ag school" in the state system, it is now a haven for about 15,000 outdoorsy students with a technical bent. The university, located south and west of the city center (take 7th Avenue south from Main Street to find the campus), is dominated by unremarkable modern buildings and, except for the Museum of the Rockies at the edge of campus, isn't really much of a destination.

Museums
★ MUSEUM OF THE ROCKIES

At the southeast corner of the MSU campus is the **Museum of the Rockies** (600 W. Kagy Blvd., 406/994-2251, www.museumoftherockies.org, 8am-8pm daily Memorial Day-Labor Day, 9am-5pm Mon.-Sat., noon-5pm Sun. remainder of year, $14 adults, $13 seniors, $9.50 students 5-18, free for kids under 5). The collection is eclectic, but most people know the museum for its significant stash of dinosaur

GALLATIN PIONEER MUSEUM

Gallatin Pioneer Museum (317 W. Main St., 406/522-8122, www.pioneermuseum.org, 10am-5pm Mon.-Sat. Memorial Day-Labor Day, 11am-4pm Tues.-Sat. Labor Day-Memorial Day, $5) took over the old county jail in 1982; there are still jail cells and a gallows among the Native American artifacts, old household items, and barbed wire collections.

Other exhibits feature the story of John Bozeman, a mountain man and immigrant guide of the 1860s; his namesake trail, essentially a spur of the Oregon Trail leading to Montana's gold country, ran along what is now a section of I-90. Frequent attacks by Sioux and Cheyenne bands plagued sojourners on the Bozeman Trail. Bozeman was killed, perhaps by Blackfeet (or perhaps by a business colleague or a jealous husband), near Livingston in 1867.

bronze *Tyrannosaurus rex* statue in front of the Museum of the Rockies

AMERICAN COMPUTER MUSEUM

Lest you think that all historical museums in Montana focus on early settlers, take note of the **American Computer Museum** (2023 Stadium Dr., 406/582-1288, www.compustory.com, 10am-4pm daily June-Aug., noon-4pm Tues.-Sun. Sept.-May, donations welcome), located a block from the MSU campus. You'll not see one old kitchen utensil in this surprisingly absorbing museum. Instead, ponder computers that seem immense and confusing and realize that they are little more than 20 years old. There's also an exhibit that focuses on printing presses and includes a replica of the Gutenberg press and an actual page from the original Gutenberg Bible.

CHILDREN'S MUSEUM OF BOZEMAN

Restless children may enjoy a visit to the **Children's Museum of Bozeman** (202 S. Willson Ave., 406/522-9087, www.cmbozeman.org, 10am-5pm Mon.-Sat., $5 over age 1), where they can put on a puppet show, create huge bubbles, or visit kid-friendly exhibits about nature or history.

MONTANA GRIZZLY ENCOUNTERS

Although the Grizzly and Wolf Discovery Center in West Yellowstone is a more fully developed facility, if you can't get there and really want to see a grizzly bear on your trip to Montana, stop by **Montana Grizzly Encounters** (80 Bozeman Hill Rd., 406/586-8893, www.grizzlyencounter.com, 9am-7pm daily summer, 10am-6pm spring and fall, 10am-4pm Thurs.-Sun. winter, $7 adult, $6 seniors, $5 children 3-12). The center has rescued several bears that were bred in captivity but living pretty miserable lives. The bears' new home near Bozeman Pass (off I-90 at exit 319 between Bozeman and Livingston) provides a more natural environment while allowing visitors to watch them play, forage, and snooze.

RECREATION
Pools and Parks

The 50-yard **city pool** (1211 W. Main St., 406/587-4724, $4 adults, $3 children) is adjacent to the high school. Regular morning, noon, and evening lap swims are scheduled. **Bogert Park** (325 S. Church Ave.) has an outdoor swimming pool, an ice rink, and a summertime Saturday morning farmers market. Just south of Bogert Park, pick up the **Gallagator Linear,** a walking, running, skiing, and biking trail that runs from South Church Avenue and Story Street to 3rd Avenue and Kagy Boulevard.

Lindley Park is just on the eastern edge of downtown, on the south side of East Main Street. The Sweet Pea Festival takes over the park early each August, and it's a good spot for a picnic at other times. During the winter, it's a good place for an easy cross-country ski.

Dogs run free at **Cooper Park** (8th and Story), which has a large off-leash area.

Bozeman Hot Springs

The main pool at the suburban **Bozeman Hot Springs** (81123 Gallatin Rd., 406/586-6492, www.bozemanhotsprings.co, 6am-11pm Mon.-Thurs., 6am-sundown Fri., sundown-midnight Sat., 8am-11pm Sun., $8.50 adult, $7.50 age 5-12 and 60+, $4 age 4 and under) is large, steamy, and indoors; it's joined by a small outdoor pool, several soaking pools, a sauna, a steam room, a fitness center, and a spa. The atmosphere is homey and family-oriented rather than overly plush; Saturday nights can get crowded.

Hiking

Hyalite Canyon is about a half-hour south of town via South 19th Avenue and Hyalite Canyon Road. Drive to the end of the road to launch a five-mile hike past nearly a dozen waterfalls to Hyalite Lake, then go another two miles to reach Hyalite Peak. One drainage over from the Hyalite Lake hike, another five-mile hike leads to pretty Emerald Lake in a high cirque. Turn left off the road shortly after the youth camp at Hyalite Reservoir to reach this trailhead.

The trails in this area are well-maintained and well-signed. Many of the trails, campgrounds, and fishing-access points in Hyalite Canyon are designed to allow people of differing physical abilities to use them. The trails are rated from easiest to most difficult; one of the easy trails is a 0.5-mile paved loop from

Langohr Campground with nature trail signs in both type and braille. **Friends of Hyalite** (www.hyalite.org) helps to support the area, and this website has good trail info.

North of town, trails start at the **M Picnic Area** on Bridger Drive (head north on Rouse; it becomes Bridger Drive). If you're just up for a short hike, hike up to the "M" for a great panorama of Bozeman and Bridger Canyon. The **Bridger Foothills National Recreation Trail** starts at the M Picnic Area and continues for 21 miles to the Fairy Lake Campground. To drive to the **Fairy Lake Campground,** take Bridger Drive for 24 miles to Forest Road and go another 7 miles to the campground. From there it's a two-mile hike to **Sacagawea Peak.**

Another good view of the city and surrounding mountains comes from **Peet's Hill,** right in town at the corner of South Church and Story, across the road from the entrance to the Gallagator Linear trail. It's a short and rewarding climb up the hill.

Fishing

Although there aren't any major trout streams flowing through Bozeman, the town is close enough to the Gallatin, Yellowstone, and Madison Rivers to support several good fly shops and outfitters. Right downtown is **The Bozeman Angler** (23 E. Main St., 406/587-9111 or 800/886-9111, www.bozemanangler.com). **River's Edge** (2012 N. 7th Ave., 406/586-5373, www.theriversedge.com) and **Montana Troutfitters** (1716 W. Main St., 406/587-4707 or 800/646-7847, www.troutfitters.com) are also convenient. Any of these shops can set you up with a guide, and each shop has good information on current fishing conditions on its website.

Skiing

Big Sky and neighboring **Moonlight Basin,** one hour to the south, form the state's largest downhill ski resort; on the same mountain, find good cross-country skiing at **Lone Mountain Ranch** (406/995-4644).

Bridger Bowl (15795 Bridger Canyon Rd.,

406/587-2111 or 800/223-9609, http://bridgerbowl.com, mid-Dec.-mid-Apr., $52 adults, $18 children 6-12, $26 seniors, half-day and multiday passes available), 16 miles northeast of town up Bridger Canyon Road, is Bozeman's local nonprofit ski mountain. It's just as snowy as Big Sky, though smaller, less glitzy, and less expensive. During the ski season a free shuttle bus runs several times daily between Bridger and the Gallatin County Fairground (901 N. Black Ave.). In downtown Bozeman, a beacon atop the Baxter Hotel flashes blue when there's at least two inches of fresh snow at Bridger.

Cross-country skiers can head up Bridger Canyon to the groomed trails at **Bohart Ranch Cross Country Ski Center** (16621 Bridger Canyon Rd., 406/586-9070, www.bohartranchxcski.com, Dec.-Mar., $15 adults, $8 children 7-12, no dogs). Lessons and rentals are also available. During the summer the trails are free to use for mountain biking, hiking, and horseback riding (bring your own horse). There are also cross-country ski trails at **Hyalite Reservoir,** 18 miles south of town; **Bozeman Creek,** 5 miles south of town; and **Stone Creek,** 10 miles northeast of Bozeman. Check with the **Forest Service** (406/522-2520, www.fs.usda.gov/gallatin) for details on these trails.

Other Activities

In downtown Bozeman, **Chalet Sports** (108 W. Main St., 406/587-4595, www.chaletsportsmt.com) rents skis and bikes. **Round House Sports** (1422 W. Main St., 406/587-1258, www.roundhouse-sports.com) rents gear downtown and at Bridger Bowl.

Pick up a copy of Beartooth Maps' **Bozeman Big Sky Outdoor Recreation Map** at any bike or outdoor store; it shows routes for the area's hiking and mountain biking trails. The same publisher makes a good map showing day hikes around Bozeman.

Golf **Bridger Creek** (2710 McIlhattan Rd., 406/586-2333, www.bridgercreek.com, $33-35 for 18 holes) or **Cottonwood Hills** (8955 River Rd., 406/587-1118, www.

cottonwoodhills.com, $36-40 for 18 holes), both public courses.

NIGHTLIFE

The 1939 Works Progress Administration *Montana: A State Guide Book* characterized Bozeman as "an old and decorous town. Local ordinances prohibit dancing anywhere after midnight and in beer halls at any time. It is illegal to drink beer while standing, so all Bozeman bars are equipped with stools."

Well, things have loosened up a little bit since the 1930s. College students have a nasty habit of standing up to drink, and the electronic gaming machines now endemic in bars threaten to make bar stools obsolete.

At the **Crystal Bar** (123 E. Main St., 406/587-2888), both the decor and decorum sometimes seem a bit tenuous. This Main Street fixture was once dominated by cowboys, but now students and tourists join the mix. Crystal's rooftop terrace is surrounded by chicken wire to keep patrons from tossing beer bottles onto the sidewalk below.

The **Rockin' R** (211 E. Main St., 406/587-9355), an MSU favorite, was destroyed by a 2009 natural gas explosion that leveled part of downtown but has reopened and is once again a local favorite that's also a friendly place for a visitor to land. Head down to the corner of Main and Rouse, to the old Bozeman Hotel building, to find the **Zebra Lounge** (321 E. Main St., 406/585-8851) with cocktails and indie bands.

Head north to the **Filling Station VFW** (2005 N. Rouse Ave., 406/587-5009) for music from local and national bands, many playing alternative Western music. It's also at least a quasi-official stop for scores of Harley riders on their way to the annual Harley-Davidson Festival in Sturgis, South Dakota. Another good, and intimate, place to hear singer-songwriters is **Live from the Divide** (627 E. Peach St., http://livefromthedivide.com), just north of downtown in the redbrick Peach Street Studios; shows here are just one hour long and broadcast on KGLT, 91.9 FM.

ENTERTAINMENT AND EVENTS

The **Gallatin County Fair** is held the third week of July.

One of Bozeman's pleasant surprises is the **Intermountain Opera** (406/587-2889, www.operabozeman.org), which stages two productions a year (May and October).

Early August is a festive time in Bozeman. During the first week of the month, booths from local restaurants line up along Main Street for the Wednesday-evening **Bite of Bozeman,** a big picnic-cum-dinner party that kicks off the **Sweet Pea Festival** (406/586-4003, www.sweetpeafestival.org, first full weekend of August), a big arts festival. A parade, a run, and plenty of musical and arts events are scheduled for the festival weekend. It's a good idea to book your hotel room well in advance of this festival.

September marks the start of the season for the **Bozeman Symphony** (406/585-9774, www.bozemansymphony.org). Performances occur approximately once a month through April.

SHOPPING

There's plenty of shopping to be done on and around Main Street, with many shops focusing on Western-style interior decorating and others offering designer cowboy clothes. **Head West** (24 W. Main St., 406/587-2153, http://headwestbozeman.com, 10am-6pm Mon.-Sat., 11am-5pm Sun.) is a particularly fun place to shop for vintage snap shirts and new or broken-in boots.

Northern Lights (1716 W. Babcock St., 406/585-2090, www.northernlightstrading-company.com, 9am-7pm Mon.-Fri., 9am-6pm Sat., 10am-5pm Sun.) has equipment and clothing for hikers, climbers, campers, and cross-country skiers. The staff here can also supply recreational information, especially concerning climbing routes in Hyalite Canyon, Gallatin Canyon, and at Bozeman Pass. For a large selection of kayaks, rafts, and canoes, head a couple of miles west of town on Highway 191 to Northern Lights' other place,

The Barn (83 Rowland Rd., 406/586-6029, 10am-6pm Mon.-Fri., 9am-6pm Sat., 10am-5pm Sun.).

The shelves at **Vargo's Jazz City & Books** (6 W. Main St., 406/587-5383, 10am-6pm Mon.-Sat., 11am-5pm Sun.) are packed with new and used books on topics both mainstream and obscure; the shop is also known for its quirky postcards and large collection of vinyl. **Country Bookshelf** (28 W. Main St., 406/587-0166, 9am-7pm Mon.-Fri., 9am-6pm Sat., 10am-5pm Sun., www.countrybookshelf.com) is an exceptionally good general bookstore with many books autographed by their Montana authors.

If you need special camera supplies, stop by **F-11** (16 E. Main St., 406/586-3281, 9:30am-5:30pm Mon.-Fri., 10am-5pm Sat., www.f11photo.com). It's one of the best photo supply shops in the state, serving both film and digital photographers; many camera repairs are done in-house.

GALLERIES

A number of art galleries dot downtown Bozeman; most stay open until 8pm on the second Friday of the month, June-September, for an **Art Gallery Walk.**

The **Emerson Center for the Arts and Culture** (111 S. Grand, 406/587-9797, www.theemerson.org) houses artists, craftspeople, performers, yoga teachers, and a restaurant. Visitors can browse the studios and galleries, stop for dinner at the Emerson Grill, and attend evening performances.

A rather serious gallery with a scholarly bent is the **Thomas Nygard Gallery** (135 E. Main St., 406/586-3636, 10am-5pm Mon.-Sat.), focusing on 19th- and 20th-century American art.

Indian Uprising Gallery (308 E. Main St., 406/586-5831, 10:30am-5:30pm Mon.-Sat.) shows contemporary Native American art, largely from Plains Indian tribes. **Sundog Fine Art** (17 E. Main St., 406/431-7812, 11am-6pm Mon.-Sat.) focuses more on antique Native American, folk, and Western art.

A good contemporary gallery is **Visions**

West (34 W. Main St., 406/522-9946, 11am-6pm Mon.-Sat.), which also has a branch down the road in Livingston.

Cello (2 W. Main St., 406/522-9999, 10am-6pm Mon.-Sat., noon-4pm Sun.) focuses on "functional art," such as handcrafted furniture, fiber art, and jewelry.

ACCOMMODATIONS

Expect hotel prices to soar when the Bobcats play in town.

$50-100

A good budget choice on the 7th Avenue strip is the extraclean and well-run Royal 7 Budget Inn (310 N. 7th Ave., 406/587-3103, www.royal7inn.com, $60-75). The rooms at the Royal 7 are considerably nicer than what you'll find in other budget motels in town. In the same area, the Rainbow Motel (510 N. 7th Ave., 406/587-4201, www.rainbowmotel-bozeman.com, $50-95) has a small outdoor pool and a suite with a kitchen ($150).

Bozeman's Western Heritage Inn (1200 E. Main St., 406/586-8534 or 800/877-1094, www.westernheritageinn.com, $99-159) is a comfortable motel with spacious rooms, including some with kitchenettes, plus a fitness room, hot tub, steam room, suites with whirlpools, and free light breakfast. Pets are permitted.

A short walk from downtown, and next door to Bozeman's excellent food co-op, is the Lewis & Clark Motel (824 W. Main St., 406/586-3341 or 800/332-7666, www.lewisandclarkmotelbozeman.com, $79-129), a large complex that includes a 20-yard indoor pool, fitness center, sauna, hot tub, plus a restaurant and lounge.

Right at the I-90 exit is a bundle of motels. One locally owned place, Bozeman Inn (1235 N. 7th Ave., 406/587-3176 or 800/648-7515, www.bozemaninn.com, $65-125), has a pool and a large hot tub; pets are allowed. The adjoining restaurant, Santa Fe Red's, is popular, although better food is available downtown.

Over $100

The Voss Inn (319 S. Willson Ave., 406/587-0982, www.bozeman-vossinn.com, $115-125 single, $135-145 double), in a 120-year-old mansion on a lovely and well-situated neighborhood street, is Bozeman's premier bed-and-breakfast. The six guest rooms are furnished with antiques, and each has a private bathroom. Breakfast is served in the guest parlor or in guests' rooms, and afternoon tea is served in the parlor.

★ Lehrkind Mansion (719 N. Wallace Ave., 406/585-6932, www.bozemanbedandbreakfast.com, $189-199) is owned by former Yellowstone National Park rangers, who are full of good travel hints. The house, a fanciful antique-filled Victorian with a huge hot tub on the back deck, is joined by an old farmhouse with several more guest rooms.

East of town off I-90, Howler's Inn (3815 Jackson Creek Rd., 406/587-5229 or 888/469-5377, www.howlersinn.com, $145-205) is a little different from your average B&B—it's also a wolf sanctuary. Income from the B&B supports wolves that can't be released into the wild; they live in a three-acre fenced enclosure. The rooms are comfortable, with views of mountains and wolves, and guests may use the hot tub and sauna.

One of Bozeman's nicest conventional motels is the Best Western GranTree Inn (1325 N. 7th Ave., 406/587-5261, $170). It's a ways from downtown, but an indoor pool, hot tub, laundry room, restaurant and lounge, and an airport shuttle are all available; except during summer and football weekends, rooms run about $100.

If you need a comfortable and convenient place to stay by the freeway, the C'mon Inn (6139 E. Valley Center Rd., 406/587-3555, www.cmoninn.com, $139-209) delivers. This regional chain does it right, with great decor and a pool area that's way nicer than average.

The Gallatin Gateway Inn, a historic railroad hotel 15 miles from town in the Highway 191 hamlet of Gallatin Gateway, was closed at the time of this writing, but new owners were reportedly working toward re-opening this grand hotel.

About 10 miles west of town, the luxurious **Gallatin River Lodge** (9105 Thorpe Rd., 406/388-0148 or 888/387-0148, www.grlodge. com, $375-500, includes all meals) is located on a large ranch in the Gallatin Valley. All six suites have elegant oak Mission-style furniture. Each has a private bath containing a large whirlpool tub and shower. Add about $500 per day for guide service.

Consider renting a cottage or lodge from **Bozeman Cottage Vacation Rentals** (406/580-3223, www.bozemancottage.com, $799-1,725 per week). A variety of well-maintained houses, many located in Bozeman's close-in residential neighborhoods, are available. Nightly rentals can sometimes be arranged.

A property management company with a number of high-quality houses and apartments for short-term rentals or more extended stays is **Intermountain Property Management** (406/586-1503 or 888/871-7856, www.montanavacation.com, $800-3,400 weekly). They have listings all over south-central Montana.

Camping

Tent campers can head for one of the three **Gallatin National Forest campgrounds** (406/522-2520, www.fs.usda.gov/gallatin, mid-May-mid-Sept., $14) in Hyalite Canyon: **Langohr** is 11 miles south of town on Hyalite Canyon Road, and **Hood Creek** and **Chisholm** are another 6 and 7 miles down the same road, respectively. Reach Hyalite Canyon Road by heading south on 19th Avenue.

Convenient though rather expensive camping is available at the recently remodeled **Bozeman KOA** (81123 Gallatin Rd., 406/587-3030 or 800/562-3036, tent $29, RV $55, cabins $55), eight miles west of town on Highway 191, next door to Bozeman Hot Springs.

FOOD

Bozeman's prosperity and trendiness are reflected in its restaurants—not a bad thing for the hungry traveler. That doesn't mean that all the best meals are served in posh new cafés, but the emphasis on fresh ingredients and vivid flavors resonates even in more modest venues.

Casual Meals

At the **Western Cafe** (443 E. Main St., 406/587-0436, www.thewesterncafe.com, 6am-2pm daily, $5-10), you can experience old-time Bozeman; cinnamon rolls come out of the oven at 8am, the grill cook is quick, and there's a jackalope head mounted above the milk dispenser. In short, it's an old-fashioned Western diner with great food.

Stop by **Wild Joe's** (18 W. Main St., 406/586-1212, http://wildjoescoffee.com, 6:45am-7pm Mon.-Thurs., 6:45am-9pm Fri.-Sat., 7:45am-6pm Sun., $3-5) for coffee, tea, pastries, and weekend-evening live music. If necessary, head to the rear of the shop to a do-it-yourself bike and ski workshop, with benches and tools for fixing your ride.

Head a few blocks north of Main Street to an industrial-chic district to find **Wild Crumb** (600 N. Wallace, 406/579-3454, www. wildcrumb.com, 7am-3pm Tues.-Fri., 7:30am-2:30pm Sat.-Sun., $3-8) and its excellent artisan pastries and lunchtime sandwiches, which are premade and served on small baguettes.

★ **Cateye Café** (23 N. Tracey St., 406/587-8844, www.cateyecafe.com, 7am-2:30pm Mon.-Fri., 7am-2pm Sat.-Sun, $8-12) is a good-natured and hip spot with a strong streak of retro. All diners, kids and adults alike, are provided with toys to play with while waiting (sometimes for quite a while) for meals to come. Once a month the Cateye is open for a special four-course dinner.

Another stylish and rightly popular breakfast or lunch spot is **Nova Cafe** (312 E. Main St., 406/587-3973, www.thenovacafe.com, 7am-2pm daily, $7-13); the menu items are good takes on standards such as breakfast burritos or Belgian waffles, and the specials (lemon blackberry ricotta pancakes) are often inspired. Gluten-free baked goods are available, and food is from local sources when possible.

★ **Over the Tapas** (19 S. Willson Ave., 406/556-8282, www.overthetapas.com, 11am-9pm Mon.-Wed., 11am-9:30pm Thurs.-Sat., small plates $4-14) is a good place to while away an evening running up your tapas bill. But it's also easy to get out of here pretty cheaply; a large helping of delicious patatas bravas is only $4. At lunch, a variety of sandwiches and tacos are offered.

One of the best additions to Bozeman's restaurant scene in recent years is ★ **Blackbird Kitchen** (140 E. Main St., 406/586-0010, www.blackbirdkitchen.com, 5pm-9pm Tues.-Thurs. and Sun., 5pm-10pm Fri.-Sat., $11-28), with an informal atmosphere featuring great people-watching and an open kitchen that turns out very good wood-fired pizza. Traditional pasta and meat dishes are offered, usually with a subtle creative twist and good, fresh ingredients.

The simply but stylishly decorated **Saffron Table** (1511 W. Babcock St., 406/586-0800, www.saffrontable.com, 5pm-9:30pm Tues.-Sat., $16-26) fills what had been a gaping culinary hole in Bozeman—Indian food. Although it's not a vegetarian restaurant, about half of the menu items are meatless. If you're not sure what to order, go for the thali, which includes a good variety of vegetarian dishes.

Montana Ale Works (611 E. Main St., 406/587-7700, www.montanaaleworks.com, 4pm-11pm Mon.-Thurs., 4pm-midnight Fri.-Sun., $10-37) has a huge room full of pool tables and serves microbrews from all over the region. The menu ranges from burgers (including Kobe and bison burgers) and huge delicious salads to steak and seafood, and both the food and the wine list are way better than is common at a brewpub. It's a reliable standby.

Serious wine drinkers should head to ★ **Plonk** (29 E. Main St., 406/587-2170, http://plonkwine.com, 11:30am-2am daily summer, 11:30am-1am Tues.-Sat. and 4pm-midnight Sun.-Mon. winter, $10-28), a wine bar with a small but good lunch and dinner menu and the most studiously hip atmosphere in town. They offer a wide selection of wines by the bottle or by the glass, as well as more than 60 beers, and a surprising selection of cheeses.

The deli at the **Community Food Co-op** (44 E. Main St., 406/922-2667, https://www.

Montana Ale Works is a popular place for a beer and a good dinner in downtown Bozeman.

bozo.coop, 8am-8pm Mon.-Fri., 8:30am-8pm Sat., 8:30am-7pm Sun., and 908 W. Main St., 406/587-4039, 7:30am-9pm Mon.-Sat., 8am-9pm Sun.) serves a wide variety of vegetarian soups, salads, and casseroles. The downtown location is much smaller and more deli-oriented than the main store on West Main.

Fine Dining

Open Range (241 E. Main St., 406/404-1940, http://openrangemt.com, 5pm-midnight Mon.-Sat., $14-42) has brought a touch of rugged Western class to Main Street. The look of the dining room, from the jars of preserved lemons visible through the front windows to the sepia-toned paintings of cattle on the golden-hued walls, is as carefully curated as the menu, which is focused on steaks, including a 44-ounce porterhouse, but strays to include a good pork chop and shrimp and grits. Service is professional and friendly, and the atmosphere is not fussy.

John Bozeman's Bistro (125 W. Main St., 406/587-4100, http://johnbozemansbistro.com, 11:30am-2:30pm and 5pm-9:30pm Tues.-Sat., 9am-1pm Sun., $12-27) has risen from its American bistro ex-hippie roots to become one of Bozeman's fine-dining restaurants. The menu is global in its scope; order seafood in a Thai red curry sauce over soba noodles while your companion has shrimp gumbo. A gluten-free "super food" platter is loaded with roasted veggies and hummus.

One of Montana's best steak houses, ★ **Sir Scott's Oasis** (204 W. Main St., Manhattan, 406/284-6929, 11am-10pm Tues.-Sun., 4pm-10pm Mon., $12-25, reservations recommended), is 20 miles west of town, just off I-90 in Manhattan. Entrées, which include seafood as well as steaks and prime rib, come with a relish tray, soup, salad, potato, dessert, and coffee. The decor is about as dated as the relish tray and the option of jo-jo potatoes, but the steaks are top-notch.

Also worth a little drive is the classy yet thoroughly Western ★ **Mint Bar & Café** (27 E. Main St., Belgrade, 406/388-1100, www.mint-cafe.com, 11:30am-10pm Tues.-Sat.,

$11-35), which features hand-cut steaks, seafood, and martinis. Come by early (4pm-7pm) for happy hour appetizers. The Mint is not far from Gallatin Field, the airport serving the Bozeman area.

Gallatin River Grill (9105 Thorpe Rd., 406/388-0148, 5pm-9pm nightly, entrées $24-32, reservations recommended), in the Gallatin River Lodge south of Belgrade, serves dinner nightly in a dining room with fir floors, oak furnishings, and an early-1900s oak back bar where diners sometimes spot white-tailed deer grazing by the trout pond. The fairly short menu focuses on Western standards, expertly prepared from high-quality local meats and produce.

INFORMATION AND SERVICES

The **Bozeman Area Chamber of Commerce** (406/586-5421 or 800/228-4224, www.bozemancvb.com) is at 2000 Commerce Way, near the 19th Avenue exit from I-90.

Bozeman Deaconess Hospital (406/585-5000) is at 915 Highland Boulevard.

Find the **public library** (406/582-2400) at 626 E. Main Street. Pick up **Yellowstone Public Radio** at 102.1 FM in and around Bozeman. Good alternative tunes come out of KGLT at 91.9 FM.

GETTING THERE AND AROUND

Gallatin Field is eight miles west of town, near Belgrade. Served by Alaska/Horizon, Delta, Allegiant, Frontier, and United, flights come in from cities around the West along with Minneapolis/St. Paul, Chicago, and Atlanta.

Automobile rentals are available at the airport through **Budget Rent-A-Car** (406/388-4091 or 800/527-0700), **Alamo/National** (406/388-6694 or 800/227-7368), **Hertz** (406/388-6939 or 800/654-3131), and **Enterprise** (406/388-7240 or 800/261-7331). Shuttle service between Gallatin Field and some Bozeman hotels can be arranged by calling **Karst Stage** (406/556-3500 or

800/845-2778, www.karststage.com); **Greater Valley Taxi** (406/388-9999) will take you where you want to go. **Shuttle to Big Sky & Taxi** (406/995-4895 or 888/454-5667, www. bigskytaxi.com) is well described by its name; they'll also take you to West Yellowstone.

If you're over 21 and have a motorcycle license, you can rent a Harley from **Yellowstone Harley Davidson** (540 Alaska Frontage Rd., Belgrade, 877/388-7684, www. yellowstoneharley.com, rentals June-Sept.).

Greyhound (2345 N. 7th Ave., 406/587-3110) stops in Bozeman on its way across I-90/94. **Rimrock Trailways** (800/255-7655) provides bus service to Billings and Missoula from the same bus terminal.

Three Forks and the Madison River Valley

Even if the notion of the Missouri headwaters doesn't automatically stir your blood, a visit there probably will. There's something *big* about the place where three lively trout streams join up to make their way across the plains that gives the spirit an almost geological uplift.

All three of the Missouri's forks come straight from the mountains. The Madison Range flanks the Madison Valley to the east; to the west are the northerly glacier-cut Tobacco Root Mountains and the southerly low Gravelly Range.

The Madison River, which forms the middle fork of the Missouri, starts in Yellowstone National Park and joins with the Jefferson and the Gallatin at Three Forks. Mention of the Madison quickens the pulse of anglers across the United States; people come from all over to fish here, and the valley's several guest ranches and many campsites accommodate them.

The Madison Range has obvious current geologic activity. The eastern front is moving along a fault. A lurching move in August 1959 jacked the mountains up and dropped the valley floor. The southern end of Hebgen Lake (just west of Yellowstone National Park) rose,

Madison River Valley

the northern end dropped, and a rock slide buried campers and blocked the Madison River, forming Quake Lake.

FISHING STRATEGIES

Fish the lower Madison (north of Ennis Lake) for brown trout or the upper river for the rainbow and brown trout. The state once stocked the Madison with hatchery trout, but this practice was discontinued and, although wild populations suffered when whirling disease came along in the 1990s, they have largely recovered fairly well.

Along with the beautiful riffled water and trout come crowds. To avoid them, look for spots far from Highway 287 and fish early or late in the season. Although the high waters make most stretches of the Madison too turbulent for fly-fishing until late June, some stretches (especially inside Yellowstone Park) are okay for flies by early June, and turbulent waters don't seem to deter anglers when the salmon flies hatch around the end of June.

July and August are when the caddis hatch, and anglers flock to the upper Madison. North (downstream) of Ennis Lake, the river warms up too much for good summer fishing; try this area in the spring or fall. Fly-fishing is usually good through mid-October on most of the Madison.

Some areas of the Madison River are closed to fishing from a boat; bait fishing is prohibited along some stretches, and for a 30-mile stretch of the upper river, catch-and-release fishing is mandated. Special regulations will usually be posted at fishing-access areas, but check ahead with the Department of Fish, Wildlife, and Parks or your fishing guide.

THREE FORKS AND VICINITY

Three Forks (pop. 1,900) gets its name from the confluence of the Gallatin, Madison, and Jefferson Rivers, which occurs on a wetland plain surrounded by mountains just north of town. A large factory on the edge of town produces talc. (In mountains to the south of town, deeply buried marble deposits have further metamorphosed into talc, making this a major talc-mining area.)

Just west of Three Forks, Highway 287 follows the Jefferson River through fossil-ridden limestone that's been jostled into a tilted position. For a few miles the land is open and dry; past Lewis and Clark Caverns, the Madison River flows through a gorge of high buff-colored hills. This road, which eventually leads to Cardwell, is a pleasant alternative to the interstate.

★ Missouri Headwaters State Park

Well before Lewis and Clark camped at the site of **Missouri Headwaters State Park** (1585 Trident Rd., four miles northeast of Three Forks on Road 286, 406/285-3610, http://stateparks.mt.gov/missouri-headwaters, daylight hours, year-round, camping May-Sept., $5 day-use fee for non-Montana residents), this area where the Madison, Jefferson, and Gallatin Rivers join up to form the Missouri was well traveled. It was a disputed hunting area and the site of frequent battles between the Crow and the Blackfeet. The mountain and river bands of the Crow had regular rendezvous at the headwaters, where they'd hunt, fish, and later, trade with Europeans.

When the Corps of Discovery reached the Missouri headwaters on July 27, 1805, Lewis and Clark concluded that none of the three rivers was sufficiently larger than any other to warrant calling it the Missouri and calling the other two feeder streams. They solved this dilemma by declaring them "three noble streams" and took the opportunity to name them after the president (Jefferson), the secretary of state (Madison), and the secretary of the treasury (Gallatin). Actually, river-naming was not foremost in their minds—they were far more preoccupied with meeting the Shoshone, from whom they hoped to obtain horses.

Try to visit the headwaters early or late in the day, when the light comes in low and opens you up to some special magic held by the rivers and bluffs. Good information

Missouri Headwaters State Park

stations discuss local flora and fauna as well as Corps of Discovery history. The headwaters site includes an old hotel and log cabin from Gallatin City, built in 1864 with the somewhat deluded thought that steamboats would be able to navigate to this point. (The city did not thrive.) A small cave is painted with several faded and damaged Native American **pictographs;** follow the trail south from the main interpretive center to see it.

If bird-watching appeals to you more than steeping yourself in Lewis and Clark lore, there are herons, ospreys, Canada geese, and songbirds along the headwaters trail. Climb Lewis Rock or Fort Rock to scan the cliffs for golden eagles. Vegetation here is characteristic of the plains: prickly pear and pincushion cacti, bluebunch wheatgrass, big sagebrush, saltbush, and buckwheat brush. The headwaters area is also a popular fishing spot.

Madison Buffalo Jump State Monument

The semicircular limestone cliff at **Madison Buffalo Jump State Monument** (6990 Buffalo Jump Rd., seven miles south of Logan, 406/285-3610, http://stateparks.mt.gov/

madison-buffalo-jump, daylight hours, year-round, free for Montana residents, $5 for non-Montana residents) has changed little since Native Americans regularly drove bison over its edge. In fact, bone shards are still scattered in the dirt at the foot of the cliff, and tepee rings are clustered around the top. Buffalo jumps were commonly used before the introduction of horses; fleet-footed young men dressed in skins would lure the bison to the edge of the cliff, then somehow manage to get out of the way as the herd plunged over.

Headwaters Heritage Museum

Downtown Three Forks's **Headwaters Heritage Museum** (202 S. Main St., 406/285-4778, www.tfhistory.org, 9am-5pm Mon.-Sat., 11am-3pm Sun., June-Sept., free) has a good collection of historical photographs and an archaeological display among the exhibits.

Pony

Nestled just below the Tobacco Root Mountains about 30 miles southwest of Three Forks and six miles up a paved road from Harrison, Pony initially appears to be

Whirling Disease

In the 1990s it looked like the Madison River fishery was doomed. Trout populations were down by as much as 90 percent due to whirling disease. Although over 150 rivers in the state have been infected, the Madison has now recovered significantly from this parasitic disease, thought to have originated in Europe, where brown trout have largely developed immunity to it.

The disease is caused by a parasite that infects the head and spine of fingerling trout, causing them to swim erratically. In addition to their whirling swimming, infected fish may have a darkened tail, twisted spine, and deformed head with a shortened and twisted jaw. Although rainbow and cutthroat trout are most susceptible, the condition can affect any salmonid species.

Researchers have worked on ways to ameliorate the damage of whirling disease, including identifying resistant fish, and preventive measures have significantly helped prevent the spread of *Myxobolus cerebralis,* the protozoan spore that causes the illness. Because there is no known cure for the disease, it is important that anglers follow these precautions:

- Remove all mud and aquatic plants from your vehicle, boat, anchor, trailer and axles, waders, boots, and fishing gear *before* departing the fishing-access streams. If you've been fishing in infected streams, it may be a good idea to wash boots, waders, and fishing equipment in a bleach solution. Be sure to rinse the bleach off thoroughly so it doesn't damage the waders.

- Drain all water from your boat and equipment—including coolers, buckets, and live wells—*before* departing the fishing-access site or boat dock.

- Dry your boat and equipment between river trips.

- Don't transport fish—dead or alive—from one body of water to another.

- Don't dispose of fish entrails, skeletal parts, or other by-products in any body of water or in a garbage disposal. Put them in the garbage for disposal in a landfill.

- Don't use salmon, trout, or whitefish parts as bait.

Pony is not quite a ghost town, as evidenced by its lively bar.

a ghost town, but it actually has about 200 residents. The town is named for Tecumseh "Pony" Smith, who mined gold here in 1868. Gold, silver, and some tungsten were mined in Pony through the early part of the 20th century; an early 1990s attempt at cyanide-process gold mining netted virtually no gold. The **Pony Bar** (uptown Pony, 406/685-3386, 1pm-close Mon.-Fri., noon-close Sat.) is still doing business; stop in for a beer and a burger and see why one local remarked, "Well, there's only one Pony."

★ Norris Hot Springs

At **Norris Hot Springs** (406/685-3303, www. norrishotsprings.com, 10am-10pm Wed.-Mon. June-Aug., 4pm-10pm Thurs., Fri. and Mon., noon-10pm Sat.-Sun. Sept.-May, $7 adults, $5 seniors 65 and up, $3 children under 12), just east of Norris on Highway 84, the natural springs fill a small pool lined with wooden boards. Hot water shoots into the air and showers down onto a corner of the pool, lowering the temperature of the water from the source temperature of 120°F to about 104°F. From one side of the pool bathers can look out onto the nearby wetland, which is frequently visited by wildlife, including sandhill cranes, deer, antelope, and eagles. The

hot springs has also become a great place to hear acoustic roots music (7pm Thurs.-Sun., $2 music cover charge). A good café serves sandwiches and snacks, using mostly ingredients grown in the resort's garden. A small **campground** has spaces for a few tents ($22) and RVs ($33 with hookups).

Fishing

Fish the Missouri River and its tributaries at **Headwaters Park.** The **Drouillard Fishing-Access Site** offers entry to the Jefferson River on Highway 10 two miles west of Three Forks. The **Sappington Bridge** crosses the Jefferson on Highway 287 at Highway 10, and the **Williams Bridge** is just to the east. The Jefferson is deeper and slower than the riffly Madison, but fishing very early or late in the day will often yield brown trout as well as a host of whitefish, carp, chubs, and suckers.

Cobblestone, Grey Cliff, and **Black's Ford** fishing-access sites are on the lower Madison River between Highway 84 and the Missouri headwaters. To reach this stretch of the Madison, head south on Highway 286 (off I-90 east of Three Forks) or east from Norris on Highway 84, then north on Highway 286. The relatively warm lower Madison, while

soaking at Norris Hot Springs

popular, does not share the incredible reputation of the river's cooler upper reaches.

There are several pullouts on Highway 84 near the bridge nine miles east of Norris, and the more ambitious angler can head up the trail into Beartrap Canyon.

Other Recreation

Beartrap Canyon, a Bureau of Land Management wilderness area east of Norris, is a steep gorge cut by the Madison River. A hiking trail starts three miles down a dirt road from the **Red Mountain Campground** (about nine miles east of Norris on Highway 84) and runs seven miles up the canyon. A dam at the southern end holds back Ennis Lake; hiking is prohibited around the dam, forcing hikers to retrace their steps to leave the canyon. The trail is popular with both hikers and anglers and can get crowded on summer weekends.

Events

The lively and popular **Three Forks Rodeo** (www.threeforkrodeo.com) is held the third weekend of July. A mid-April roundup and late April high school rodeo also draw big crowds.

The second weekend of August brings **Rockin' the Rivers** (406/285-0099, www.rockintherivers.com) to town. This huge outdoor music festival draws up to 15,000 to hear performers such as Jefferson Starship, Uriah Heap, and a Lynryd Skynyrd tribute band (Bonnaroo it ain't).

Each September, Headwaters State Park is the site of the **John Colter Run** (406/587-4415), a seven-mile dash through the prickly pears commemorating Corps of Discovery member Colter's 1808 feat of survival when he was stripped naked and hunted by Blackfeet and still managed to escape. Clothing and shoes are permitted on this run.

Accommodations

Three Forks's grand ★ **Sacajawea Hotel** (5 N. Main St., 406/285-6515, www.sacajaweahotel.com, $99-209) has been a local landmark

since 1910, and in recent years has been through a succession of owners, with several extended closures and a big remodel in 2010. From the comfortable chairs on the wide front porch to the big claw-foot bathtubs in some of the rooms, the Sac has an easygoing yet refined comfort.

On a side street in downtown Three Forks, the family-run **Broken Spur Motel** (124 W. Elm, 406/285-3237 or 888/354-3048, www.brokenspurmotel.com, $75) is a comfortable but basic place with free continental breakfast.

Camping

The **Missouri Headwaters State Park campground** (1585 Trident Rd., four miles northeast of Three Forks on Rd. 286, 406/285-3610, http://stateparks.mt.gov/missouri-headwaters, May-Sept., $15 Montana resident, $23 nonresident) has brushy riverside sites and one tepee ($25 resident, $35 nonresident) perfect for those on a Lewis and Clark pilgrimage. Read their journals first if you doubt the importance of bringing mosquito repellent.

There's also a state park campground (with showers and some RV electrical hookups) at **Lewis and Clark Caverns** (19 miles west of Three Forks on Hwy. 2, 406/287-3541, http://stateparks.mt.gov/lewis-and-clark-caverns, tents $15 Montana resident or $23 nonresident, RVs $20 resident, $28 nonresident).

From Norris, about 30 miles south of Three Forks, head east on Highway 84 for nine miles to find **Red Mountain** (406/683-2337, www.blm.gov/mt, May-Nov., $8), a BLM campground near the bridge over the Madison River. For a secluded spot, try **Potosi** (about eight miles south of Pony, 406/682-4253, www.fs.usda.gov/bdnf, June-Sept., free).

Food

Pompey's Grill, the dining room at the **Sacajawea Hotel** (5 N. Main St., 406/285-6515, www.sacajaweahotel.com, 4:30pm-9pm Wed.-Sat., $17-36, half-size meals available $9-19, reservations recommended), is a classy but laid-back place with the best meals in town. The bar scene is comfortable, with a wide range of generally friendly locals and travelers. The bar is a reclaimed bridge trestle that was originally part of a bridge that spanned the Great Salt Lake. Sunday brunch is served a couple of times a month; check the website or call for the schedule.

Locals think nothing of driving for miles to eat barbecued ribs at **Willow Creek Café & Saloon** (six miles southwest of Three Forks in Willow Creek, 406/285-3698, 4pm-10pm daily summer, 4pm-9pm winter, $8-22, reservations recommended). Both the restaurant and the bar are easy spots in which to while away a couple of hours (don't expect quick service). Next door to the restaurant, the **Willow Creek Gallery** is worth a visit.

Just off I-90 at the Three Forks exit, stop at **Wheat Montana** (10778 Hwy. 287, 406/285-3614, www.wheatmontana.com, 6am-8pm daily summer, 6am-7pm daily winter, sandwiches $8-9) for anything from a muffin to a deli sandwich to a giant bucket of flour or a loaf of bread. This is one of several retail outlets for a large local wheat farm, which sells their chemical- and pesticide-free wheat nationwide.

Thanks to the fact that Montanans will go out of their way for a good charbroiled steak, Logan's **Land of Magic Dinner Club** (11060 Front St., 406/284-3794, www.landofmagicsteakhouse.com, 3pm-10pm nightly, $7-39, reservations recommended), housed in a great old log building six miles east of Three Forks, has been pulling in customers for more than 25 years. Aside from the steaks, the Land of Magic is known for its shrimp, its duck à l'orange, and its wine list. Come prepared to work your way through relish tray, salad or shrimp cocktail, potato, bread, and ice cream in addition to your entrée.

Information

The **Three Forks Chamber of Commerce** (406/285-4753, www.threeforksmontana.com) is a good resource for information about local businesses and sights. The **visitors center** is housed in a railroad caboose just around the corner from the Sacajawea Hotel.

ENNIS AND VICINITY

Ennis (pop. about 850, elev. 4,927 feet) is known for its superb fishing, for all the cowboys that come to town on the weekends, and for its lively Fourth of July rodeo and popular Hunters Feed and Wild Game Cook-Off.

Originally founded as a supply station for the gold towns of Virginia City and Nevada City shortly after gold was discovered in

Mountains rise up west of Ennis.

Alder Gulch, Ennis has survived on a newer economic mainstay of ranching. Many of the area's ranches are now owned by wealthy investors who hire real ranchers to manage and run the cattle (or buffalo, as in the case of Ted Turner's nearby ranch). Anglers flock to Ennis in the summer, when they outnumber the cowboys on Main Street.

★ Fishing the Madison River

The 50-mile stretch of the Madison River from Quake Lake (near Yellowstone Park) north to Ennis is an almost continuous riffle, and trout are eager to grab passing morsels. The Madison is also the state's most trout-dense river. This makes for good fishing for beginning fly anglers, but it also means the river can get crowded. The first 30 miles of the Madison (from Quake Lake to Varney Bridge) is a catch-and-release area, with no live bait permitted.

The state maintains several fishing-access sites on the Madison River near Ennis. **Ennis FAS** is on Highway 287 just south of Ennis; **Burnt Tree Hole** is one mile west of Ennis on Highway 287, then two miles south on the county road; **Eight Mile Fork** is four miles down the same county road; **Varney Bridge** is another six miles down the road. To reach **Valley Garden FAS,** turn north from Highway 287 onto the county road 0.25 mile south of town and travel two miles. **McAtee Bridge,** 18 miles south of Ennis, also provides access to the Madison.

Ennis Lake (Ennis Reservoir or Meadow Lake) is a silty shallow reservoir backed up by a rather small Montana Power dam on the Madison just below the lake. Because it's so shallow, Ennis Lake gets very warm during the summer. The warm water makes for pleasant swimming but causes rampant algae growth and is generally rough on fish downstream. Because of the warm water, it's best to fish the lower Madison (downstream of Ennis Lake) during the cooler weather of the spring and fall.

Floating the Madison River

Float the Madison, but take care where you go. Beartrap Canyon is for white-water experts, and the multichanneled stretch between Cameron and Ennis is tough for a novice to navigate. A popular and easy trip runs 30 miles from Quake Lake (put in at the Highway 87 bridge four miles from the lake) to the Varney Bridge in Cameron. This stretch of the river passes several campgrounds. Fishing from a boat is restricted on certain stretches of the Madison. Check the current regulations before casting a line.

Bozeman-based **Montana Whitewater** (406/995-4613 or 800/799-4465, www.montanawhitewater.com, $125) runs daylong trips on the Madison through Beartrap Canyon's big rapids. Rafters are given the option of walking around the Class IV Kitchen Sink rapids.

For a less daunting trip, rent a tube from **Christensen Rentals** (201 Madison Ave., 406/682-4748, $11/day), on the western edge of Ennis, and float a gentle stretch of river. **Meadowlark Shuttles** (406/682-4188) operates on the upper Madison River.

Other Recreation

Madison Meadows (406/682-7468, $21 for nine holes) is a public nine-hole golf course just west of town.

Many old logging roads in the hills south of Ennis are closed to motorized traffic and make good mountain-bike routes. Get the current road-closure information at the Ennis Ranger Station. The Gravellys are popular with elk hunters, but the recent road building and logging have threatened elk habitat.

September brings upland game-bird hunters to the area for Hungarian partridge and sharptail, blue, and ruffled grouse.

Events

The Fourth of July weekend **rodeo** is taken seriously here. Mid-October, on the Friday before the start of rifle hunting season, Ennis holds its **Hunters Feed and Wild Game Cook-Off.** Visitors can taste the dishes and vote for their favorites. Both the rodeo and the cook-off are known statewide as happenin' events. Contact the **chamber of commerce** (406/682-4388, www.ennischamber.com) for details.

Shopping

Many of the anglers who flock to Ennis come with nonfishing spouses. Main Street shopkeepers have taken note, and Ennis is now a fun place to while away an afternoon browsing antique and home decor shops. There are also several fly-fishing shops in town, including **Madison River Fishing Co.** (109 W. Main St., 406/682-4293 or 800/227-7127, www.mrfc.com, 7am-7pm daily), **The Tackle Shop** (127 E. Main St., 406/682-4263, www.thetackleshop.com, 7am-7pm daily), and **Trout Stalkers** (301 E. Main St., 406/581-5150, www.montanatrout.com, 7am-7pm daily). These shops can also recommend guides.

Stop by **Willie's Distillery** (312 E. Main St., 406/682-4117, http://williesdistillery.com, 10am-8pm Mon.-Sat., 10am-6pm Sun.) to take a look at the copper still and sample (or purchase) moonshine, bourbon, or chokecherry liqueur made from local ingredients.

If the fishing is off, would-be anglers can head west on Highway 287 to Twin Bridges for a shopping spree at the **R. L. Winston Rod Company,** where the extremely well-regarded rods are handcrafted.

Accommodations

$50-100

Riverside Motel (346 E. Main St., 406/682-4240, www.riversidemotel-outfitters.com, $75-165) is a good choice—it's just on the edge of downtown Ennis, next to a little riverside park. A large grassy area is used for fly casting, and a pond is stocked for kids' fishing. The units are detached, like little cabins, and the more expensive ones have kitchenettes and two or three bedrooms.

The **Fan Mountain Inn** (204 N. Main St., 406/682-5200 or 877/682-5200, www.fanmountaininn.com, $77-85) is a clean and quiet budget place on the north edge of town.

About 34 miles south of Ennis, **West Fork Cabin Camp** (1475 Hwy. 287 N., 406/682-4802 or 866/343-8267, http://wfork.com, $75-100) has housekeeping cabins and an RV campground (there are also some tent sites). It's a great location, right on the Madison,

about halfway between Ennis and West Yellowstone.

OVER $100

A couple of Ennis's nicest motels are just south of town. ★ **El Western Resort** (4787 Hwy. 287 N., 406/682-4217 or 800/831-2773, www.elwestern.com, $110-389) sits on 17 wooded acres near the river. Accommodations are in duplex log cabins, which range from simple sleeping cabins (available May-Oct.) to more luxurious lodges complete with kitchens, fireplaces, and up to four bedrooms. Right next door on Highway 287, the **Rainbow Valley Lodge** (406/682-4264 or 800/452-8254, www.rainbowvalley.com, $90-300) is the only motel in town with a pool. The rooms are large and nicely furnished in a Western style. You have a choice of one- or two-bedroom units, kitchen units, and rooms with patios overlooking the river. The Rainbow Valley is the only motel in town that does not accept pets in the rooms, although they can arrange for very reasonably priced horse boarding.

Tucked in back of the bank on Main Street, the **Ennis Homestead** (206 2nd St., 406/682-4086, www.ennishomestead.com, $795-1,295 for three nights, $1,395-2,695 per week) offers the most upscale lodgings in town on the grounds of the estate of Ennis's founders. The cabins and house in this little gated adults-only community are beautifully furnished, and all have kitchens and laundry facilities.

The area south of Ennis, near the town of Cameron, has several fishing-oriented lodges. ★ **The Old Kirby Place** (34 miles south of Ennis, west of MP 15 on Hwy. 287, 406/682-4194 or 888/875-8027, www.oldkirbyplace.com, $245 per person includes meals and beverages, three-night minimum, May-early Oct.) is noted for its log lodge and bunkhouse dating from the 1880s, its great location, and its fabulous fishing. The food is good, and local fishing guides often drop in for dinner to chat and share fish stories.

Just north of Ennis, between the Madison River and Jack Creek, the **Madison Valley Ranch** (307 Jeffers Rd., 406/682-3214 or

800/891-6158, www.madisonvalleyranch.com, $1,825-1,975 per person for three nights lodging and two days of guided fishing) is an all-inclusive fishing lodge.

Camping
Ennis Fishing-Access Site (http://fwp.mt.gov, May-Nov., $12), just out of town on the south side of the bridge, is a simple base camp for a fishing trip. Also on the edge of town, **Riverside Motel** (346 E. Main St., 406/682-4240, www.riversidemotel-outfitters.com, $29 RV) has RV sites with full hookups.

Once you get south of Cameron, there are plenty of public campgrounds. **Ruby Creek** and **Palisades** are BLM campgrounds (406/683-8300, www.blm.gov/mt, $8) just off Highway 287 about 25 miles south of Ennis.

About 34 miles south of Ennis, near the West Fork rest area, find both the **West Fork Madison** (406/682-4253, www.fs.usda.gov/bdnf, late May-mid-Sept., $8) and the **Madison River** (late May-mid-Oct., $8) Forest Service campgrounds.

Food
Ennis's restaurant of note is the ★ **Continental Divide** (47 Geyser St., 406/682-7600, 5:30pm-10pm daily May-Oct., $23-43, reservations recommended) in an unlikely location north of town near Ennis RV Village. But no fear, creative, sophisticated bistro-style meals, such as roasted elk with huckleberry demi-glace, are served here in a setting that's not too intimidating to be a real treat, and where you can find the day's fishing report posted on the front door.

In a great place to eat in town is **Bandito's** (305 E. Main St., 406/682-5552, 7:30am-11:30am and 5pm-10pm Tues.-Sun. late May-mid-Sept., $14-23), where many dishes have just a hint of Tex-Mex, such as the enchiladas made from roasted veggies and couscous wrapped in Swiss chard leaves. Banditos is part of a complex that includes the **Gravel Bar** (305 E. Main St., 406/682-5553, www.gravebarmt.com 11am-late daily year-round, $10-12), a bar and casual restaurant sharing

the same address. Summer weekends bring some good bands to the Gravel Bar.

South of Cameron, in the West Fork area, the **Grizzly Bar & Grill** (1409 Hwy. 287, Cameron, 406/682-7118, 4pm-9pm Wed.-Mon., $14-34) serves up excellent burgers and steaks and a good helping of Western atmosphere.

Information and Services
The **Ennis Chamber of Commerce** (201 E. Main St., 406/682-4388, www.ennischamber.com) is a good source of general information about Ennis and member businesses. The area around Ennis is part of the Beaverhead-Deerlodge National Forest. The local **ranger station** (just west of town at 5 Forest Service Rd., 406/682-4253, www.fs.usda.gov/bdnf) has maps and information on recreation and camping.

The **Madison Valley Hospital** (406/682-6862) is at 305 North Main Street.

CLIFF LAKE AND WADE LAKE
If you are ready to give up your cell phone and kick back in a quiet place where you may see some wildlife, try Cliff Lake and Wade Lake. These turquoise lakes are about six miles west of Highway 287 via Forest Service Road 8381 (find this road just north of where Highway 87 joins Highway 287).

The road in to the lakes passes the ghost town of Cliff Lake, crosses the "Missouri Flats," a high sagebrush prairie with abundant birdlife, and climbs to the forested lakeshores. Trumpeter swans sometimes appear here in the winter, and raptors live and nest around the lakes. Moose are also common. Wade Lake has good trout fishing.

The southern road to Cliff and Wade Lakes snakes in through humpy sagebrush and pine-covered hills from Highway 87, north of where Raynolds Pass crosses the Continental Divide into Idaho at a remarkably level 6,834 feet.

Accommodations and Food
There are three very pleasant Forest Service

campgrounds (406/682-4253, www.fs.usda.gov/bdnf, June-Oct., $12) in the area: **Wade Lake, Hilltop,** and **Cliff Point,** all near Wade Lake Resort.

The utterly charming ★ **Wade Lake Cabins** (406/682-7560, www.wadelake.com, $85-110) are simple housekeeping cabins (each with its own outdoor gas grill in addition to the more traditional kitchen setup) for rent year-round. Bathrooms are in a separate shared bathhouse. At Wade Lake, the focus is on low-impact recreation. During the summer, anglers come to fish the lakes, known for their huge rainbow and brown trout. A wood-fired hot tub is especially welcome in the winter, when the resort caters to cross-country skiers, grooming nearly 22 miles of trails. Winter visitors are especially likely to see wildlife; lots of animals winter in the area. A three-night minimum stay is required, no credit cards are accepted, and pets cannot be accommodated. Rates rise a bit in the winter, when the resort hosts will shuttle your food and gear from the road while you ski in to your cabin. Canoes and motorboats are available for rent at the lodge.

Over on the far side of Cliff Lake, about one mile from the lakeshore, **Wilderness Edge Retreat** (406/682-4611 or 866/226-7668, www.wedgeretreat.com, mid-May-mid-Oct., $75-525) has a handful of very nice new log lodges (the largest has five bedrooms) as well as the resort's original rustic cabins with refrigerators, outdoor grills, and a shared bathhouse. Dogs are permitted in the rustic cabins but must stay out of the larger houses. The resort can arrange fishing trips and horseback rides, and guests may rent small motorboats, canoes, kayaks, and mountain bikes.

QUAKE LAKE AND HEBGEN LAKE

South on Highway 287 toward Hebgen Lake, the mountains rise off the plain of the Madison Valley. Hebgen Lake is the reservoir formed by the damming of the Madison River in 1915. The lake's north side has a smattering of resorts and private campgrounds; several

public campgrounds are on the lake's less-trafficked south side.

Late on the night of August 17, 1959, the Madison River Canyon shuddered as an earthquake with a magnitude of 7.5 started a giant landslide. A 7,600-foot-high mountain collapsed into the river, burying campsites at the Rock Creek Campground and damming the Madison to form Quake Lake. Twenty-eight people were killed. A couple of large fault blocks dropped and tilted north. A huge tidal wave swept across Hebgen Lake, over Hebgen Dam (six miles away), and into the Madison River Canyon. Amazingly, Hebgen Dam held.

Dead trees now stand in Quake Lake, the Madison River is still choked with rubble, and a "ghost village" near the east end of Earthquake Lake (the official name of Quake Lake) is a jumble of buildings swept up and dropped by floodwaters. Reach the ghost village via the road across from Cabin Creek Campground.

A **visitors center** (406/682-7620, 10am-6pm daily late May-mid-Sept., $3 per vehicle) now overlooks the site of the landslide.

Recreation

The **Lee Metcalf Wilderness Area,** just north of Hebgen Lake, and the adjacent **Cabin Creek Wildlife Management Area** are crisscrossed with trails. Several trails start at the end of Beaver Creek Road, and a trail heads out from Cabin Creek Campground to the wilderness area and other trails. Consult a Gallatin National Forest map, available from the ranger stations in West Yellowstone or Ennis, before setting out.

Hebgen Lake is a popular boating and waterskiing spot. Even when the lake is iced over, fishing continues here. Brown and rainbow trout predominate and can be large. Smaller populations of cutthroat, whitefish, and arctic grayling also live in these waters. Fishing is not quite as good on Quake Lake, which was one of the Madison River's prime fishing areas before the 1959 earthquake.

Accommodations

Most Hebgen Lake establishments shut down

from late September until early May because of snowfall. When West Yellowstone is booked up or seems too hectic, this area can be a good place from which to stage trips into Yellowstone National Park. Restaurants are in short supply around Hebgen Lake; most visitors cook for themselves, eat in West Yellowstone, or hang out at the Happy Hour Bar.

Campfire Lodge Resort (155 Campfire Ln., 406/646-7258, http://campfirelodgewestyellowstone.com, late May- Sept. $80-200) is on the Madison River between Hebgen and Quake Lakes. It's a laid-back cabin resort, with rustic kitchenette cabins, an RV park ($30-40), and a few tent sites ($23-30).

Kirkwood Resort & Marina (11505 Hebgen Lake Rd., 406/646-7200, www.kirkwoodresort.com, cabins $84-139) is right on Hebgen Lake and rents cabins, tepees ($25), RV sites ($29-39), tent sites ($15-18), and boats. This resort does stay open year-round. On Highway 191, just south of where Highway 287 comes in, the **Madison Arm Resort** (406/646-9328, www.madisonarmresort.com) has log cabins ($180), larger prefab cottages ($195), an RV park ($40-43), lakefront tent sites ($30), and a marina.

Yellowstone Holiday (16990 Hebgen Lake Rd., 877/646-4242, www.yellowstoneholiday.com, Memorial Day-Labor Day, cabins $75-130) is on a flat grassy patch of land between the road and Hebgen Lake about 13 miles northwest of West Yellowstone. Although it's mainly an RV park ($50-60), there are also some cute cabins (bring your own linens, towels, and cooking utensils).

Hebgen Lake Mountain Inn (15475 Hebgen Lake Rd., 406/646-5100, www.happyhourbar.com, $125) has newer condo-style rooms with full kitchens on a bluff across the road from the lake and the sometimes boisterous **Happy Hour Bar,** owned by the same friendly folks as the inn.

★ **Parade Rest Guest Ranch** (7979 Grayling Creek Rd., West Yellowstone, 406/646-7217 or 800/753-5934, www.paraderestranch.com, mid-May-Sept., $260 per person per day, all-inclusive, lower rates for children and early-season guests) is a well-established traditional guest ranch with daily guided horseback rides and close ties to many local fishing guides. (It's best to arrange for guide service well in advance.) The ranch is near Hebgen Lake, and a short drive from Yellowstone National Park. **Firehole Ranch** (11500 Hebgen Lake Rd., 406/646-7294, www.fireholeranch.com, early June-late Sept., $6,100-6,800 per person per week double occupancy, includes meals and guided fishing) is a luxurious Orvis-endorsed fishing-oriented vacation ranch, with in-house fishing guides and a full complement of other recreational activities. Lodging is in beautiful log cabins and the gourmet meals are notable.

Camping

Cabin Creek and **Beaver Creek** Forest Service campgrounds are on the Highway 287 side of Hebgen Lake. To the east, **Rainbow Point** (on the Grayling Arm of Hebgen Lake) and **Bakers Hole** (on the Madison River above Hebgen Lake) are public campgrounds close to West Yellowstone and are often full of RVs. **Spring Creek** and **Lonesomehurst** are Forest Service campgrounds on the less-traveled south shore of Hebgen Lake. Contact the **Hebgen Lake Ranger Station** (331 Hwy. 191 N., West Yellowstone, 406/823-6961, www.fs.usda.gov/gallatin) for details. A lot of snow falls here in the winter, and virtually all of these places shut down between late September and early May; prices run $14-16.

Not far removed from camping are the several **Forest Service cabins** (406/823-6961, www.fs.usda.gov/gallatin, $30) in the Hebgen Lake area. These cabins are rustic, with outhouses and (in our experience) resident mice.

Information

The deluxe **Earthquake Lake Visitor Center** (406/682-7620, 10am-6pm daily late May-mid-Sept., $3 per vehicle) sits above Quake Lake. Stop by to see a rather dramatic film of the 1959 earthquake. The **Hebgen Lake Ranger Station** (406/823-6961) is actually on the northern edge of West Yellowstone.

Big Sky and the Gallatin Valley

Highway 191 follows the swift Gallatin River north from Yellowstone National Park through a narrow valley speckled with dude ranches and resorts. The Madison Range is west of the Gallatin Valley; the Gallatin Range rises to the east. In the rugged northern part of the Madison Range, the Spanish Peaks rise as high as 11,000 feet.

SIGHTS

Big Sky, Montana's largest ski resort, is on Lone Mountain about one hour north of West Yellowstone. The slopes of Lone Mountain have been grazed since the 1890s, and dude ranches began to spring up a few years later. When native son Chet Huntley retired from the newscasting business, he started up Big Sky Resort in what he figured was the ideal spot to blend development with the natural environment; though at the base of the lifts, the Huntley Lodge and its swarming parking lot now teeter on the edge of overwhelming nature.

Development here has not led to wide use of street addresses. Instead, businesses are located by the "village" they occupy: The Huntley Lodge and ski lifts are in the development known as Mountain Village; Meadow Village is toward the base of the mountain; the West Fork-Town Center area is in between, about 2.5 miles from Highway 191 and six miles from Mountain Village.

Soldiers Chapel commemorates Montana's native sons who died in the infantry in World War II. The log chapel is on Highway 191 near Big Sky. Sunday services are held here during the summer, and the chapel is open daily May through September.

While in Big Sky, you may hear about the **Yellowstone Club,** but unless you're one of the elite, you won't see the world's only private ski and golf community, which seems to have weathered the economic downturn and

the founders' messy divorce and made its way out of bankruptcy.

SKIING AND SNOWBOARDING
★ Big Sky Resort

Big Sky Resort (800/548-4486, 406/995-5900 snow phone, www.bigskyresort.com, $103 adults, $83 seniors 70 and up, college students with ID, and youth ages 11-17, $53 children 10 and under, or free if staying in resort lodging) is the nation's biggest and one of its best downhill ski resorts. Since it was consolidated with the former Moonlight Basin ski area, it's grown to over 5,800 skiable acres, with 300 named runs lacing three mountains (Lone Peak is the big one). An average of 400 inches of snow falls each year, and there are enough lifts, including a tram to the top of 11,166-foot Lone Peak, to keep

The Gallatin River flows right alongside Highway 191.

lines fairly short. The tram, with its two 15-passenger cars, stops just 16 feet short of the summit and opens up lots of steep terrain. (For those who deem it too steep, it's perfectly fine to get back on the tram and ride down to some nice intermediate-level slopes.) The vertical drop is an amazing 4,350 feet, and the longest runs go on for six miles (from Liberty Bowl to Mountain Mall). Just off the Ram Charger high-speed quad, a terrain park offers several rails and a half-pipe, with terrain for all levels of snowboarders. Half-day and multiday rates are also offered. Big Sky's winter season runs from late November through mid-April.

The Moonlight Basin area, on the northern face of Lone Mountain, has spectacular views and is a good place for beginners because there's plenty of gentle terrain; at the other end of the spectrum, extreme skiers and boarders hike up from the Headwaters lift to access steep chutes and gullies.

Cross-Country Skiing
LONE MOUNTAIN RANCH
Cross-country skiers and snowshoers can buy daily passes for the trail network at **Lone Mountain Ranch** (406/995-4644 or 800/514-4644, www.lonemountainranch.com, $20 adults, $10 seniors age 60-70, seniors 70 and over and children 12 and under free). The nearly 53 miles (85 km) of ski trails are groomed for both traditional and skate skiing and cross a variety of terrain with some good views of the Gallatin Valley. The grooming here is exceptionally good, and the snow quality is usually very good, making for smooth, relatively fast skiing. About 18 miles (30 km) of trails are apart from the ski trails. Unless you're visiting on a holiday or on a beautiful weekend day, it's not particularly crowded and, even though you're usually not far from the lodge, it feels like a true wilderness. Lessons and naturalist-guided tours into Yellowstone National Park are also offered. Cross-country skiing is usually possible from early December through mid-April.

OTHER CROSS-COUNTRY SKIING AND SNOWSHOEING AREAS
Cross-country skiers can also head to the **Spanish Creek Cabin** on the edge of the Lee Metcalf Wilderness Area, about 10 miles north of Big Sky. It's rented out year-round for $30 per night. Call the **Bozeman Ranger Station** (406/522-2520) for reservations.

Rent snowshoes from the Lone Mountain Ranch or **Grizzly Outfitters** (11 Lone Peak Dr., Meadow Village, 406/995-2939, www.grizzlyoutfitters.com) and head for **Moose Tracks,** a 2.2-mile dedicated snowshoe trail at Big Sky Resort starting at the base of Andesite and Lone Mountains. Find the snowshoe trail behind the Mountain Village near the base of the Swift Current Express lift.

GALLATIN RIVER RECREATION
Floating
The Gallatin is popular with white-water enthusiasts; it's a challenging river to float, with some huge rapids in the lower canyon, the 20-mile stretch between Big Sky and the mouth of Gallatin Canyon, which is the focus of outfitters' half-day raft trips. Two rafting outfitters have their headquarters on Highway 191 near Big Sky. **Montana Whitewater Raft Company** (Hwy. 191, mile marker 64, seven miles north of the Big Sky turnoff, 406/995-4613 or 800/799-4465, www.montanawhitewater.com, $55 half day, $92 full day) and **Geyser Whitewater Expeditions** (Hwy. 191 next to Buck's T-4 Lodge, 406/995-4989 or 800/914-9031, www.raftmontana.com, $58 half day, $94 full day) both run daily whitewater trips.

Fishing
Fishing access to the Gallatin River is easy: The road runs alongside it much of the way from Yellowstone to Bozeman, and there are many pullouts—de facto fishing-access sites. There's an official site at the Axtell Bridge, between Gallatin Gateway and Bozeman Hot Springs. Fish don't grow large in the cold waters of the upper Gallatin, but most anglers

pull something from the riffling waters of this stretch. The West Fork comes in near Big Sky, and the combined waters flow through a canyon with exceptionally good fishing. Fishing from a boat is prohibited on the Gallatin.

The salmon flies hatch from late June through early July on the Gallatin, but there's good fishing for brown and rainbow trout April through October. **Gallatin Riverguides** (47430 Gallatin Rd., 406/995-2290, www.montanaflyfishing.com) has a fly shop, and the guides lead fishing trips year-round. Guest ranches **Lone Mountain Ranch** (406/995-4644) and **320 Ranch** (406/995-4283 or 800/243-0320, www.320ranch.com) can set you up with a fishing guide, as will **Wild Trout Outfitters** (406/995-2975 or 800/423-4742, www.wildtroutoutfitters.com). Guide rates vary widely depending on the sort of trip that's arranged and how many anglers participate, but count on spending $325-450 for a day of private guided fishing. Costs per person go down dramatically when two or three people share a guide.

OTHER RECREATION

The summertime hiking and mountain bike trails at **Big Sky Resort** head uphill, downhill, and around the mountain. The Moonlight Basin area is particularly appealing; the steep 1.4-mile Elkhorn Trail passes through wildflower meadows to great views of the Spanish Peaks, and the Beehive Basin trail (6.6 miles round-trip) leads from the end of Beehive Basin Road to a pretty lake in a glacial cirque and good views of Lone Peak. Stop by the Moonlight Basin lodge to pick up a trail map. Hikers are advised to carry bear spray—and know how to use it.

From the Meadow Village, head west to Ousel Falls Road, turn left and continue two miles to **Ousel Falls Park** and the start of a lovely and very easy 1.7-mile round-trip hike to the falls.

Hikers flock to the **Lee Metcalf Spanish Peaks Wilderness Area** during the summer. Trails, more suitable to overnight backpacking

than to day hiking, cross the peaks. Trailheads sprout on Highway 191 between Big Sky and Bozeman; the Cascade Creek hike is especially popular, and the trail can be crowded on the weekends. The Swan Creek trail heads out of the Swan Creek campground and follows the creek 11 miles to the Gallatin Divide.

Backpackers can hike up almost any creekside trail and catch the **Gallatin Divide Trail,** which runs north-south along the divide between the Gallatin and Yellowstone Rivers from the Yellowstone National Park boundary to Hyalite Peak, just outside Bozeman. The trail passes lakes, petrified forests (don't carry out petrified wood unless you have a permit from the ranger station), and badlands; lucky hikers will see moose and possibly bears.

Big Sky Resort runs scenic lift rides ($16, $33 with bike) all summer long, transporting hikers and **mountain bikers** up Lone Mountain. A free nine-hole **disc golf course** starts behind Huntley Lodge. An additional nine holes start at the top of Andesite Mountain and wind down to the base area; pay for a scenic lift ride to the top of this course. If you can fathom the idea of renting a disc, they're available at Big Sky Sports.

The popular **Lone Peak Expedition** ($83) requires no walking: a lift, truck, and tram ferry you to the top of the mountain.

Bike rentals are available near the base of the gondola (406/995-5840) or from **Grizzly Outfitters** (Town Center, 406/995-2939, www.grizzlyoutfitters.com), where full-suspension mountain bikes rent for $45 per day.

Soar through the trees on **ziplines** at **Big Sky Resort** (406/995-5769, www.bigskyresort.com, $63-93) or **Montana Whitewater** (406/995-4613, www.montanawhitewater.com, $550-750 for 1-12 participants). The 18-hole **Big Sky Golf Course** (Meadow Village, 406/995-5780, early June-mid-Sept., $75), a scenic course along the banks of the West Fork of the Gallatin River, was designed by Arnold Palmer and is open to the public.

Jake's Horses (406/995-4630 or 800/352-5956, www.jakeshorses.com, $37 one-hour ride, $83 dinner ride) offers a wide variety of guided trail rides around Big Sky. Find the stables three miles south of Big Sky on Highway 191.

EVENTS

The **Music in the Mountains** concert series (406/995-2742, www.bigskyarts.org) brings classical, jazz, country, and blues music to the slopes on weekends in late July and early August.

ACCOMMODATIONS

There are several lodging options at Big Sky. Motel rooms, cabins, and condominiums are all available at different elevations on Lone Mountain. During the winter, a free shuttle bus runs between all of the lodging spots and the ski lifts. Room prices are somewhat fluid and can vary greatly by season and by day of the week. Additionally, each place will have different room types available. It's best to call and see what's available to fit your needs. On Highway 191, ★ **Best Western Buck's T-4 Lodge** (46625 Gallatin Rd., 406/995-4111 or 800/822-4484, www.buckst4.com, $169-225) is a very nice lodging with two large outdoor hot tubs. Pets are permitted with a $20 fee. The restaurant here is one of Big Sky's best. **Whitewater Inn** (47214 Gallatin Rd., 406/995-2333 or 800/548-4486, www.bigskyresort.com, $157-169) is on Highway 191 near Buck's. It's worth staying here if you have kids who want to use the indoor pool, which has a slightly cramped waterslide emptying into it.

Five miles south of the Big Sky turnoff on Highway 191, find the ★ **Rainbow Ranch Lodge** (42950 Gallatin Rd., 406/995-4132 or 800/937-4132, www.rainbowranchbigsky.com, $175-250) on the Gallatin River. Although the main lodge at this resort was destroyed by fire in 2008, it has been rebuilt and is beautiful. Rooms, most of which are actually suites decorated in an upscale Western style, have views of a pretty pond or decks overlooking the river. The restaurant here is one of the area's best.

On the road up Lone Peak, find the ★ **River Rock Lodge** (3080 Pine Dr.,

406/995-4455 or 800/995-4455, www.riverrocklodging.com, $169-265), with comfortably elegant lodgings, in the Meadow Village, an easy walk to several restaurants. The tasteful Western-craftsman decor has a practical note, like the handsome wool blankets and down comforters on each bed.

Many of the accommodations at the Mountain Village are owned by Big Sky Resort. Surprisingly, there's not a huge variation between winter and summer rates here. Rooms at the **Huntley Lodge** (Mountain Village, 406/995-5000 or 800/548-4486, www.bigskyresort.com, $228-240) and the adjacent **Shoshone Condominium Hotel** ($397-606) offer easy ski-in, ski-out access to the main base area. There are two swimming pools, a steam room, hot tubs, and great access to the slopes. Under the same management and also part of the Mountain Village is the rather swank **Summit at Big Sky** ($322-982), a high-rise hotel-condominium complex with a wide variety of room configurations. Big Sky Resort operates several other condo developments in the Mountain Village; the resort's website has a good schematic, and telephone reservations clerks are generally quite helpful. Lodgings in the **Moonlight Basin** area (800/548-4486, www.bigskyresort.com, $573-1,285) are also run by Big Sky Resort; here you'll find a variety of ski-in, ski-out lodgings, ranging from town houses to log cabins to penthouse suites in the lodge and houses.

Resort Property Management (406/995-4800 or 800/548-4488, www.rpmbigsky.com, $200 and up at Meadow level, $400 and up Mountain level) rents a staggering array of lodging choices, ranging from reasonably priced suites that can accommodate up to eight people to many condos and homes for nightly rental. Many of these properties have hot tubs.

Guest Ranches

★ **Lone Mountain Ranch** (750 Lone Mountain Ranch Rd., 406/995-4644 or 800/514-4644, www.lonemountainranch.com, $330-355 per adult including meals and activities, lower rates for children), halfway between the highway and the ski lifts, is a little different from the other Big Sky lodgings. Originally a working cattle ranch, it has become a great cross-country ski resort (some say the nation's best), and during the summer it's a dude ranch with special programs for anglers and for children learning to ride. Different packages are offered, but a standard summertime seven-day stay, including all meals, horseback riding, and guided hikes, costs $3,100 per person, with lower rates for teens and children. Winter rates for a week-long stay run $2,300 per person.

Another noteworthy guest ranch, the **Nine Quarter-Circle Ranch** (5000 Taylor Fork Rd., 406/995-4276, www.ninequartercircle. com) specializes in families and has plenty of children's activities. The Nine Quarter-Circle, which is near the northwest corner of Yellowstone National Park, has been in operation since 1912 and accommodates its guests in log cabins, all with private baths and woodstoves. Meals are served in the handsome central lodge. Activities include horseback riding, fishing, overnight pack trips, and square dancing. Weekly rates start at $1,926 per person double occupancy, with discounts for children.

The ★ **320 Ranch** (205 Buffalo Horn Creek, 406/995-4283 or 800/243-0320, www.320ranch.com, $180-360), another guest ranch that has been around since the beginning of the 20th century, is 12 miles south of Big Sky and 6 miles north of Yellowstone National Park. Lodging is in cabins (some with kitchenettes) or larger log houses; the most interesting is the McGill cabin, the home of Dr. Caroline McGill, Montana's first woman physician and former owner of the 320. Even if you're not sleeping at the 320, it's a good place to stop for a meal.

Camping

Spire Rock is a small Forest Service campground about 15 miles southeast of Gallatin Gateway. Other good bets are **Moose Creek Flat,** five miles north of Big Sky on Highway

191; **Swan Creek,** just north of Moose Creek Flat; and **Greek Creek,** just north of Swan Creek. On Highway 191 about eight miles south of Big Sky, **Red Cliff** is a riverside Forest Service campground about 50 yards off the highway. These campgrounds are part of the **Bozeman Ranger District of the Gallatin National Forest** (3710 Fallon St., Bozeman, 406/522-2520, www.fs.usda.gov/gallatin, mid-May-mid-Sept., $14) and can be reserved online (www.recreation.gov).

The **Bozeman Ranger District** (406/522-2520, www.fs.usda.gov/gallatin, $30) rents out a number of rustic cabins in the Gallatin National Forest, including several in the general area of Big Sky. They're generally equipped with woodstoves but have no running water, and they may require a substantial hike from road's end. For a list of cabins, call the ranger station or visit the website.

FOOD

There's no dearth of good food around Big Sky. Down on Highway 191, **Buck's T-4** (46625 Gallatin Rd., 406/995-4111, www. buckst4.com, 6pm-9pm nightly, reservations recommended, $18-39) serves some of the best dinners around. Buck's specializes in wild-game dinners; try the pan-seared red deer served with truffle risotto. A cheaper way to go is eating off the bar menu; a wild game meat loaf grilled-cheese sandwich goes for $14.

Also along the highway, **Rainbow Ranch Lodge** (42950 Gallatin Rd., 406/995-4132 or 800/937-4132, www.rainbowranchbigsky. com, 5:30pm-9pm daily mid.-Dec.-Sept., $24-55), serves some of the Gallatin Valley's best dinners. Here, you can eat pheasant roasted in rose petals or an elk steak served with bourbon peppercorn sauce.

About five miles south of Big Sky on Highway 191, the **320 Ranch** (205 Buffalo Horn Creek, 406/995-4283 or 800/243-0320, www.320ranch.com, 5:30pm-9pm nightly, $24-42) is worth a stop for expertly prepared Montana-style steak, trout, and wild-game dinners.

About halfway up the mountain, **Lone Mountain Ranch** (750 Lone Mountain Ranch Rd., 406/995-2782, www.lonemountainranch.com, 5:30pm-8:30pm daily, dinner reservations required, $20-35) serves good dining-room meals, but the real draw for those who aren't staying at the ranch are the wintertime **sleigh-ride dinners** ($98 adults, $81 children 4-12). Guests take the horse-drawn sleigh to a remote cabin, where woodstove-cooked prime rib is served family style. Reservations are required well in advance for these dinners.

For lunch or a takeout dinner, try the deli in the **Country Market** (Meadow Village, 406/995-2314, www.bigskygrocery.com). They make delicious soups, sandwiches, and salads; shop online and have groceries delivered to your condo. A Meadow Village standout is ★ **Olive B's** (151 Center Ln., 406/995-3355, www.olivebsbigsky.com, 11am-9pm Mon.-Sat., $24-38). In addition to the venison, pheasant, and beef, Olive B's offers a vegan grilled tofu with quinoa and pea shoots. Lunch is also good here, and during the summer, the patio is the place to be. Also in the Meadow Village, **Lone Peak Brewery** (48 Market Pl., 406/995-3939, http://lonepeakbrewery.com, 11:30am-9:30pm daily, $9-12) serves typical pub food (if bison quesadillas are your norm) and an oatmeal stout named "Hippie Highway."

Just up from the Meadow Village, in the Westfork area, the very casual ★ **Blue Moon Bakery** (3090 Big Pine Dr., 406/995-2305, 7am-10pm daily, $6-15) serves soups, pizzas, and large tasty sandwiches in addition to bread, bagels, and breakfast pastries. It's all homemade, and quite tasty. Right next door, the **Lotus Pad** (3090 Big Pine Dr., 406/995-2728, www.lotuspadbigsky.com, 6pm-10pm Mon.-Sat., $15-24) is a very popular Thai restaurant. It's not very large, so it's a good idea to call ahead for a reservation.

Ousel & Spur Pizza (50 Ousel Falls Rd., 406/995-7175, www.ouselandspurpizza.com, 7am-1pm and 5pm-10pm Mon.-Sat., $10-20) serves good pasta as well as pizza (try some elk sausage on your pie) in a dining room that's as fresh and hip as the food, with big windows onto Lone Peak.

Out on Highway 191 at the Big Sky turn-off, the **Bugaboo Café** (47995 Gallatin Rd., 406/995-3350, 7am-3:30pm daily, $8-14) has good food, a full bar, and a relaxed but bustling environment; it's an especially popular breakfast spot.

INFORMATION AND SERVICES

For information specifically on the downhill ski area and its lodgings, contact **Big Sky Resort** (406/995-5000 or 800/548-4486, www.bigskyresort.com). General area information is available from **Visit Big Sky** (406/995-3000 or 800/943-4111, www.visitbigskymt.com).

GETTING THERE AND AROUND

Bozeman's Gallatin Field is the closest airport.

During the ski season **Karst Stage** (406/556-3500 or 800/845-2778, www.karststage.com, $51 one-way, reservations required) runs a shuttle from the airport to Big Sky.

Another good option is **Shuttle to Big Sky & Taxi** (406/995-4895 or 888/454-5667, www.bigskytaxi.com), with competitive rates.

Skyline (406/995-6287, www.skylinebus.com) runs buses between Bozeman and Big Sky ($5) and operates a free shuttle between Big Sky's Meadow and Mountain Villages.

Livingston and the Paradise Valley

Back when passenger trains still crossed southern Montana, Livingston was the gateway to Yellowstone National Park. Parkgoers would change trains at the Livingston depot and take the rail spur to Yellowstone.

Nowadays, travelers with a little time to pass can stock up on some of the world's most coveted flies in Livingston, cast them into the Yellowstone River, soak in the hot springs at Chico, or wander out of the broad sun-filled Paradise Valley into the Absaroka-Beartooth Wilderness Area. There's really no sense in a pell-mell dash to often hectic Yellowstone when there are so many places to linger around just to the north.

LIVINGSTON

Few towns have seen the gentrification boom as much as Livingston. What was, not too long ago, a sleepy and rough-edged town with a local artist and a writer or two is now a mandatory way station on the glam tour of Montana. For lively Livingston-based fiction, read Tom McGuane's *Driving on the Rim*.

Livingston (pop. 7,130, elev. 4,490 feet), the Park County seat, is situated at the wind-tossed northern end of the Paradise Valley on the banks of the Yellowstone River. The Absaroka Range, rising up in the south, dominates the town, and the Crazy Mountains show up to the northeast. After its northerly run up from Yellowstone National Park, the Yellowstone River turns east at Livingston, where I-90/I-94 meets the river and ushers it from the state.

History

Mt. Baldy (or Mt. Livingston), southeast of Livingston in the Absaroka Range, was the site of winter vision quests by Crow braves. William Clark camped on the Yellowstone

River south of Livingston on July 15, 1806. Several days later, Crows stole his party's horses, forcing the explorers to build dugouts and bullboats.

While Bozeman quickly gained a reputation as a straitlaced town, Livingston, 26 miles east, never had any such opprobrium to live down. It's a town with a history of such Wild West legends as Calamity Jane and Kitty O'Leary, also known as Madame Bulldog, described in the Works Progress Administration's *Montana: A State Guide Book:*

> Madame Bulldog, once Kitty O'Leary, ran what was euphemistically known as a dance hall. Her joint, she said, was a decent one. Announcing that she would stand for no damfoolishness, she saved the wages of a bouncer by polishing off roughnecks herself. Her dimensions, like her sensibilities, were pachydermal; she tipped the scales at 190, stripped. And stripped she was most of the time. Calamity Jane was one of her associates for a time, but legend has it that they fell out, whereupon Madame Bulldog tossed Calamity into the street, "as easy as licking three men." When asked whether Calamity Jane really tried to fight back, one who knew both women replied succinctly, "Calamity was tougher'n hell, but she wasn't crazy!"

Sights

The **Depot Center** (200 W. Park St., 406/222-2300, www.livingstonmuseums.org, 9am-5pm Mon.-Sat., 1pm-5pm Sun., Memorial Day-Labor Day, free) is a well-curated historical, cultural, and art museum housed in the historic Northern Pacific Railway Depot. The depot was built in 1902 and resembles an Italian villa. The park next to the depot is the site of many summer festivals.

The other historical museum in town, the **Yellowstone Gateway Museum** (118 W. Chinook St., 406/222-4184, http://yellowstonegatewaymuseum.org, 10am-5pm daily Memorial Day-Sept., 10am-5pm Thurs.-Sat. Oct.-Memorial Day, $5 adults, $4 seniors) is tucked into an old schoolhouse and a 100-year-old Northern Pacific car across the tracks from downtown. (Cross the tracks at B Street or 5th Street; the museum is two blocks from the tracks.) The museum's four main exhibits focus on early explorers in Montana, Native American culture, pioneers, and transportation.

During the 1970s every eligible site in **downtown Livingston** was placed on the National Register of Historic Places. There's great pride taken in the restoration of downtown buildings to their original Western

Many buildings in downtown Livingston are on the National Register of Historic Places.

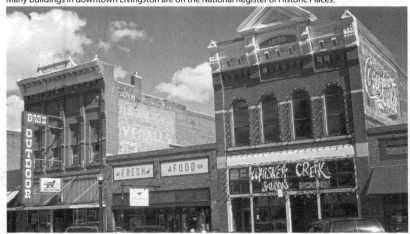

visage, and it does look splendid. Keep an eye open for elaborate brickwork and faded signs painted on the sides of the downtown buildings. Don't neglect the residential streets. Yellowstone Street, three blocks west of Main, was a tony address around the end of the 19th century. The east side of town, near G Street and Callender, was the figurative "other side of the tracks," where the blue-collar railroad workers lived. To round out the tour, visit the 300 block of South B Street. The four matching houses on the east side of the street were once Livingston's brothels.

Recreation

Fishing is Livingston's recreation of choice, and many locals make their living from guiding. **Dan Bailey's Fly Shop** (209 W. Park St., 406/222-1673 or 800/356-4052, http://dan-bailey.com) is a good first stop for any angler; the staff can also set you up with a guide. Guide services and a huge selection of flies are also available from **Anderson's Yellowstone Angler** (5256 Hwy. 89 S., 406/222-7130, www.yellowstoneangler.com), which has a shop just south of town on Highway 89.

Rent a raft, kayak, or float tube from **Rubber Ducky Rentals** (15 Mt. Baldy Dr., 406/222-3745, www.riverservices.com), near the I-90/Highway 89 junction; the folks here can also arrange a shuttle or send you off on a guided float trip.

The Absaroka Range rises up just south of Livingston. One convenient trailhead into the Absarokas is **Suce Creek,** about 10 miles south of Livingston off the East River Road. Trails beginning here provide access to Livingston Peak, the north fork of Deep Creek, Blacktail Lake, and Elephant Head Mountain. About three miles farther south on the East River Road, the **Deep Creek** trail heads to the Davis Creek Divide.

Timber Trails (309 W. Park, 406/222-9550, www.timbertrails.com) rents bicycles in the summer or cross-country skis and snowshoes in the winter.

The nine-hole **Livingston Golf Course** (406/222-1100, www.livingstongolfcourse.

com, $21 for nine holes) is a public course on View Vista Drive at the foot of Main Street.

The city **swimming pool** is near the foot of Main Street just east of Sacagawea Park.

Arts and Galleries

It may be a little surprising that a scrappy railroad town like Livingston has become something of an artists' colony. But the beautiful light and stunning scenery (not to mention the trout fishing) of the Paradise Valley work in counterpoint to Livingston's raucous edge to make this one of the state's most prestigious addresses.

Main Street is home to several high-quality galleries, including **Danforth Gallery and Park County Friends of the Arts** (106 N. Main St., 406/222-6510, www.pcfadanforth.com), a nonprofit gallery that focuses on contemporary Montana artists, and **Livingston Center for Art and Culture** (119 S. Main St., 406/222-5222, http://livingstoncenter.org), featuring regional artists and offering classes, workshops, and an open ceramic studio. Within the Center for Art and Culture is the **Parks Reece Gallery** (406/222-5724, http://parksreece.com), featuring Reece's whimsical paintings and prints. **Visions West** (108 S. Main St., 406/222-0337, www.visionswestgallery.com) is an elegant place with high-end contemporary Western art; it's always worth a visit.

The literary arts are represented at **Elk River Books** (120 N. Main St., 406/333-2330), a good bookstore with new and used books and regular events featuring authors who live nearby or are traveling in Montana. Step to the back of the store to find a juice bar.

Events

The **Livingston Roundup Rodeo** (http://livingstonroundup.com, 406/222-3199 to reserve seats at the rodeo) is on the Fourth of July weekend. It kicks off with a parade and segues into a lively Professional Rodeo Cowboys Association (PRCA) rodeo. An arts festival takes over Depot Square during this weekend.

The **Yellowstone Boat Float** (406/224-4414), a three-day mid-July event, runs 110 miles from Livingston to Columbus, following the route of Captain Clark and his party on their return from the Pacific. The float is open to all, any sort of boat is permitted, and like the river, it's "wet, wild, and dam free."

During the first week of August, Livingston hosts the **Park County Fair.**

Accommodations

The ★ **Murray Hotel** (201 W. Park St., 406/222-1350, www.murrayhotel.com, $139-359), across the street from the Depot Center, has enough character to hold its own in a lively, quirky town like Livingston. Like much of the rest of downtown, the Murray is listed in the National Register of Historic Places, and its interior architecture recalls the grander side of the Old West. The Murray has been restored with panache, retaining the eccentricities that have traditionally made it a haven for "writers, artists, and film people." (Film director Sam Peckinpah lived in a Murray Hotel suite in the 1970s and reputedly shot up the ceiling.) The hotel is very dog-friendly. Be sure to visit the rooftop hot tub.

Most of Livingston's motels are chains located west of downtown, near the intersection of I-90 and Highway 89, the road to Yellowstone. Behind its false-fronted faux-Western facade, **Livingston Inn Motel** (5 Rogers Ln., 406/222-3600, www.thelivingstoninn.com, $85) is a small family-owned place. Also near the I-90 exit on the west end of town, the **Quality Inn** (111 Rogers Ln., 406/222-0555 or 800/424-6423, $79-89) has an indoor pool and is one of the nicer places in this area.

Three miles south of town, the **Blue-Winged Olive** (5157 Hwy. 89, 406/222-8646, www.bluewingedolive.net, $110 single, $160 double) is a B&B catering mostly to anglers, who appreciate its proximity to the Yellowstone and to several spring creeks. (The big early-morning breakfasts are also a plus.)

Camping

Unless you're looking for RV camping, it's better to drive a ways up the Paradise Valley to find a site, but in a pinch there are private campgrounds in Livingston. Just south of I-90's motel strip, **Osens RV Park** (20 Merrill Ln., 406/222-0591, www.osensrvpark.com, tent $30, RV $39-44, cabin, $55) is convenient and quiet.

Food

Stop in for a drink or a meal at the **Sport Bar and Grill** (114 S. Main St., 406/222-3800, www.sportlivingston.com, dining 11am-9pm Mon.-Fri., 8am-9pm Sat.-Sun. $9-25), a local institution where the old-time Montana atmosphere comes with the burgers and beer. The food is good and goes well beyond pub grub; families are welcome to dine here.

★ **Rick's on Main** (116 S. Main, 406/222-3800, http://ricksonmainstreet.com, 5pm-9pm daily, $9-29) is a good bet for a fine-dining experience in Livingston. It's very much a chef-run restaurant; Rick is involved in nearly every detail, and his care shows in the dining room—with lots of gleaming wood, a brick wall, windows onto Main Street, and framed landscape paintings—and the food, which ranges from pasta or cioppino to slow-roasted steak. Most entrées are under $20, which adds to the appeal.

The specialties at the **Rib & Chop House** (307 E. Park, 406/222-9200, http://ribandchophouse.com, 11am-9:30pm Mon.-Thurs., 11am-10pm Fri.-Sat. 4pm-9:30pm Sun., $12-30) are ribs, hand-cut steaks, and Louisiana-style seafood. The atmosphere is casual and friendly, and its dining room is spacious and stylish, though more corporate than other places in town.

At the Murray Hotel in the **2nd Street Bistro** (201 W. Park St., 406/222-1350, www.secondsteetbistro.com, 5pm-9pm Mon.-Sat., $12-25), the simple wood tables and chairs and big windows allow diners to keep an eye on downtown Livingston. That is, if they lift their faces from their crab cakes and steak frites;

the food here is quite good, and the grass-fed beef comes from nearby ranches.

A great addition to downtown Livingston is the casual but classy ★ **Mustang Fresh Food & Catering** (112 N. Main St., 406/222-8884, www.mustangcatering.com, 10:30am-6pm Mon.-Fri., 11am-3pm Sat., $7-15), with prepared foods to go or to stay. The focus is on excellent sandwiches and salads, and you can pick up a sandwich to take on the road or hot dishes to go for dinner. The chef/owner has cooked for all the local celebrities, as well as Martha Stewart on her visit to Montana.

Chadz (104 N. Main St., 406/222-2247, http://chadzmt.com, 6:30am-2:30pm daily, $5-8) is a good place to spend the morning hanging out with the locals, who gather at the tables or sip coffee and read on the comfy couches. Stop in for coffee and a slice of breakfast pizza or lunch on a panini.

Stop for a burger and a shake at a local institution: **Mark's In and Out** (Park St. and 8th St., 406/222-7744, 11am-10pm daily Mar.-Oct., about $5) has been around since the 1950s and is a good place to sample shakes made from the locally made Wilcoxson's ice cream.

Just east of downtown, the microbrews at **Neptune's Brewery** (110 N. L St., 406/222-7837, http://neptunesbrewery.com, noon-8pm daily, $9-12) are quite tasty; food is good pub grub. Neptune's has a fun ocean theme inside; it's also very kid-friendly.

Information and Services

The **Livingston Chamber of Commerce** (303 E. Park St., 406/222-0850, www.livingston-chamber.com) is housed in a former railroad crew headquarters a couple of blocks east of the Depot Center.

For information on hiking, camping, Forest Service cabin rentals, and fishing, stop by the **ranger station** (5242 Hwy. 89 S., 406/222-1892) on Highway 89 about one mile south of Livingston.

Livingston Memorial Hospital (406/222-3541) is at 504 South 13th Street.

Mustang has fine food to eat in or to go.

Getting There and Around

Greyhound buses (1404 E. Park, 406/222-2231) stop in Livingston daily. **Rimrock Stage** uses the same terminal and provides daily service to Billings and Missoula.

PARADISE VALLEY

The never-dammed Yellowstone River flows through the Paradise Valley and separates the eastern Absaroka Range and the western Gallatin Range. The valley starts narrow, squeezing through Yankee Jim Canyon near Yellowstone National Park, then broadens enough for ranches to spread out on the valley floor. A few miles south of Livingston, the paved but potholed East River Road leaves Highway 89. Both roads along the Yellowstone are lovely, but East River Road gives a better view of the way people live in the valley.

Yellowstone's volcanoes spat out the Absaroka Range—a high lava field with relief etched by erosion from water and glacial ice. The Absarokas are lush wet mountains, more characteristic of western Montana than the dry peaks east of the Continental Divide. The same Yellowstone lava flows covered folded sedimentary rocks of the Gallatin Range.

Fishing

Summer and fall are the most popular seasons to fish the Yellowstone. In early summer, the salmon flies and caddis flies hatch, and around August, trout feed on grasshoppers near the river's edge. Numerous fishing-access sites dot this blue-ribbon trout stream along both Highway 89 and East River Road.

Besides the Yellowstone, a couple of "spring creeks" challenge the skillful angler. The two most notable of these, Nelson's and Armstrong's, are on private land, and a fee is charged for fishing them. For details, ask at **Dan Bailey's Fly Shop** (209 W. Park St., 406/222-1673 or 800/356-4052, http://dan-bailey.com) in Livingston or at any other local angler's shop. Another good source for advice, gear, or access to private fishing spots is **Angler's West** (406/333-4401, www.montanaflyfishers.com), just off Highway 89 at Emigrant.

Hiking

Mill Creek reaches into the Absaroka-Beartooth Wilderness Area. The lower stretches of Mill Creek Road, heading east from the town of Pray to the wilderness boundary, are good for mountain biking, and the foot trail continues into the wilderness area. **Thompson Lake, Elbow Lake, Mt. Cowan,** and **Passage Creek Falls** are some of the destinations for hikers. Snow Bank campground is a handy jumping-off point.

In the Gallatin Range, hike or cross-country ski just about any drainage: **Trail Creek** (there's cross-country skiing near the Forest Service cabin), **Big Creek** (28 miles south of Livingston, then west up Big Creek Road, trailhead is across from Mountain Sky Ranch), or **Rock Creek** (with access to a trail network).

The hike up **Tom Miner Basin** starts at the Tom Miner campground and includes an interpretive trail in the Gallatin Petrified

Forest. To reach the trailhead, turn west off Highway 89 between mile markers 16 and 17 onto Tom Miner Creek Road. Follow signs to the campground, approximately 12 miles from the highway. The petrified forest trail is about two miles round-trip.

Other Recreation

Even if you're not staying at the lodge, stop by **Chico Hot Springs** (163 Chico Rd., Pray, 406/333-4933, www.chicohotsprings.com, 8am-11pm daily, day pass $7.50 adults, $3.50 seniors, $3.50 children 3-6) for a swim. The pool is huge, and it's always a great place to people-watch.

The East River Road is a pleasant road ride for cyclists. Mountain bikers will want to turn off the main road and head up into the hills.

The upper stretches of the Yellowstone River, particularly through Yankee Jim Canyon, have some challenging white water. After the river leaves the canyon and enters the Paradise Valley, it calms down enough for novice floaters to navigate it without much difficulty. Gardiner's **Yellowstone Raft Company** (406/848-7777 or 800/858-7781, www.yellowstoneraft.com, half day $42 adults, $32 children, full day $82 adults, $62 children) runs raft trips on the Yellowstone.

During the winter, sign on with **Absaroka Dogsled Treks** (406/223-6440, www.absarokadogsledtreks.com, $125 and up) based at Chico Hot Springs. Trips range from a two-hour, six-mile introduction to a full-day trek ($330).

Horseback rides with **Rockin' HK** (406/333-4505, www.rockinhk.com, $45 for one hour) start from Chico Hot Springs's horse barn throughout the day and are suited to riders of all abilities. Rockin' HK also leads daylong trips into Yellowstone's backcountry ($200) and can combine multiday horse-packing trips with fishing.

Accommodations

★ **Chico Hot Springs** (406/333-4933, www.chicohotsprings.com, $59-239), halfway between Livingston and Gardiner in Pray, is the sort of spot you want all your friends to know about and everybody else to ignore. The lodge here is built around a large hot springs-fed swimming pool. The original rooms in the circa-1900 lodge are cramped and spartan, but the rooms aren't where most guests spend their time (and rooms in the lodge addition and the newer cabins and cottages are spacious and nicely furnished). Yellowstone National Park is right down the road, and there's plenty of hiking and fishing in the Paradise Valley, soaking and swimming in the pool, elegant dinners in the hotel dining room, and rowdy good times in the lively bar. An outfitter on the premises leads horseback trail rides. Rooms in the main lodge start at $59 for a very small room with shared bath and run to $98 (private bath); newer lodge buildings have rooms for $134-209; cabins, log houses, and a caboose are also available. Dogs are permitted in the rooms at Chico ($20 per stay).

Although Chico is the most renowned place to stay in the Paradise Valley, there are several other good spots between Livingston and Gardiner. **Pine Creek Store & Lodge** (2496 East River Rd., 406/222-3628, www.

pinecreeklodgemontana.com, $99-119), 12 miles south of Livingston, rents cabins built from shipping containers in a friendly community with easy fishing access to the Yellowstone. The nicely done-up cabins were built after a huge wildfire in 2012 burned the orginal rustic cabins. Cabins are heated, but share a bathhouse. Pets are allowed. The excellent **Pine Creek Café** (Wed.-Sun.) is also part of the complex.

Just up the road from the hot springs, find the **Homestead Cabin at Old Chico** (406/333-4772, www.homesteadcabin.com, $155-255, $1,085-1,645 per week). The tiny community of Old Chico consists of a scattering of old cabins; this one has been fixed up in a way that retains a sense of rusticity but adds a touch of elegance. The cabin sleeps four and has a full kitchen; pets are permitted with an extra charge.

At the **Yellowstone Valley Lodge** (38401 Hwy. 89 S., 406/333-4787 or 800/626-3526, www.yellowstonevalleyranch.com, $169-449), 14 miles south of Livingston, guests stay in tastefully decorated cabins perched just above the Yellowstone, affording wonderful river views and good fishing (fly-fishing packages are available). The lodge, which is known as much for its excellent restaurant as for its

Pine Creek Store & Lodge

comfortable accommodations, closes down from November through March.

Guest Ranches

The **63 Ranch** (184 Bruffey Ln., Livingston, 888/395-5151, www.63ranch.com, mid-June-mid-Sept., $2,040 per week adults double occupancy, $1,815 child 6-11, $300 child 5 and under), 12 miles southeast of Livingston, was founded in 1863 and has operated for many years as a dude ranch. Horseback riding is the main focus here, and guests often have the opportunity to help move cattle. Rates include all meals and riding; non-riders get a substantial discount, and shorter stays can be arranged.

Mountain Sky Guest Ranch (406/333-4911 or 800/548-3392, www.mtnsky.com, May-mid-Oct., $3,730-4,690 per adult for one week all inclusive, $4,160-4,040 per child age 7-12, $2,450-$2,960 per child 6 and under) is a family-oriented guest ranch set up in Big Creek with great views across the Paradise Valley of Emigrant Peak, in the Absaroka Range. Riding is one of the core activities here, but fishing, yoga, a golf course, tennis courts, a pool, and sauna are also available, and there's a well-developed program for kids, from infants to teens. Each guest is matched with a horse to ride for the week's stay, and either breakfast rides or 9am rides are scheduled daily. The food at Mountain Sky is first rate, and the "rustic" cabins are a far cry from the typical Montana rustic cabin (there are also modern cabins available). It's best to book far in advance. During the late spring and early fall, it's possible to arrange a three-night stay, at $370-380 per person per night.

Camping

Pine Creek campground (406/222-1892, www.fs.usda.gov/gallatin, Memorial Day-Labor Day, $14) is 10 miles south of Livingston, then 6 miles east of Highway 89 up Pine Creek Road (reservations at 877/444-6707, www.recreation.gov). This area was heavily burned by a 2012 fire, so the surrounding aren't quite as scenic as they once were.

Sites may also be reserved at **Snowbank** (406/222-1892, www.fs.usda.gov/gallatin, Memorial Day-Labor Day, $14), 20 miles south of Livingston on Highway 89, then another 15 miles east on Mill Creek Road.

Closer to Gardiner and Yellowstone National Park, **Tom Miner** Forest Service campground (406/848-7375, www.fs.usda.gov/gallatin, June-Oct., $7) is eight miles west of Highway 89 on Tom Miner Road (36 miles south of Livingston). The Gallatin Petrified Forest is a two-mile hike from the campground. The Forest Service has **cabins** for rent up Trail Creek, 20 miles southwest of Livingston, and Big Creek, 28 miles south of town, then 8 miles west on Big Creek Road. These cabins are rented year-round for $35 per night; winter visitors may need skis or a snowmobile to reach them. Contact the **Livingston ranger station** (406/222-1892) for reservations.

The **KOA** (163 Pine Creek Road, 406/222-0992, http://koa.com/campgrounds/Livingston, May-mid-Oct., RV $25-41, tent $18, cabin, $59-160) is right on the Yellowstone River in the community of Pine Creek. Although the sites can be a little cramped, the setting is excellent.

About 18 miles south of Livingston, the much-advertised **Yellowstone's Edge** (3502 Hwy. 89 S., 406/333-4036, www.mtrv.com, May-Oct., $48-53 RV) is a on a small strip of land between the river and the highway.

Food

The restaurant at ★ **Chico Hot Springs** (406/333-4933, www.chicohotsprings.com, 7am-10am Mon.-Sat., 8:30am-11:30am Sun., 5pm-9pm daily, $24-36; reservations strongly recommended) is known statewide for its gourmet fare. Penny-pinchers can eat salads, sandwiches, and burgers at the resort's **Poolside Grille** (lunch and dinner daily, $5-14).

Another place to find really good food in the Paradise Valley is the casual ★ **Pine Creek Café** (2496 East River Rd., 406/222-3628, www.pinecreeklodgemontana.com,

5:30pm-9pm Wed.-Fri., 9am-1pm and 5:30pm-9pm Sat.-Sun. summer, $13-25). It's worth the trip for the rainbow trout tacos or the ribs; in good weather there's deck seating.

Near the north end of the valley, **Yellowstone Valley Grill** (3840 Hwy. 89 S., 406/222-4815, 5:30pm-9:30pm Tues.-Sun. Apr.-Oct., $15-34), at the Yellowstone Valley Lodge, is a real gem. Food is locally sourced and expertly prepared; smoked trout comes from the local spring creek, and the lamb was raised in the Paradise Valley.

GARDINER

The only year-round route into Yellowstone National Park is at Gardiner (pop. 875, elev. 5,314 feet), where the park entrance is marked by the **Roosevelt Arch,** dedicated in 1903 by Theodore Roosevelt. The road along the northern tier of the park between Gardiner and Cooke City is plowed during the winter.

The **Yellowstone Association** (308 Park St., 406/848-2400, www.yellowstoneassociation.org) has its headquarters and a store just across from the Roosevelt Arch in downtown Gardiner; it's worth a visit.

Recreation

Boats aren't allowed on Yellowstone National Park's rivers, but **Yellowstone Raft Company** (406/848-7777 or 800/858-7781, www.yellowstoneraft.com, half day $42 adult) and **Flying Pig Raft Company** (406/848-7510 or 866/264-8448, www.flyingpigrafting.com, half day $42 adult), both headquartered in Gardiner, run trips on the Yellowstone River outside the park.

Local outfitters guide visitors on a wide variety of trail rides and fishing trips. **Hell's A Roarin' Outfitters** (406/848-7578, www.hellsaroarinoutfitters.com) is based in nearby Jardine and offers a wide range of activities, including horseback rides and fishing trips; **Parks' Fly Shop** (202 2nd St. S., 406/848-7314, www.parks-flyshop.com) is on Highway 89 in downtown Gardiner and can set you up with a guide. Richard Parks is author of a comprehensive fishing guide to Yellowstone National Park and is the local go-to guy on many conservation issues.

The Gallatin National Forest has a **ranger station** (406/848-7375) in Gardiner near the park entrance.

Accommodations

Not surprisingly, during the summer, many of the accommodations in Gardiner are booked

The town of Gardiner has an impressive setting right outside Yellowstone National Park.

full and on the expensive side. Parkgoers may prefer to reserve well in advance and stay in the lodge or cabins at Mammoth Hot Springs, which cost about the same. From mid-September through May, lodging prices drop significantly.

The riverside **North Yellowstone Lodge & Hostel** (1083 Hwy. 89 S., 406/823-9683, www.northyellowstonehostel.com, $30 per person dorm bed, $99-109 private room with shared bath) is friendly spot for visitors who don't need luxury or a high degree of privacy. All guests can use common areas, including the kitchen and rec room with table tennis and pool tables. The larger private rooms can accommodate a family. Tent sites go for $15 and include use of lodge facilities.

Another decent budget choice on Highway 89 is the **Hillcrest Cottages** (400 Scott St. W., 406/848-7353 or 800/970-7353, www.hillcrestcottages.com, mid-May-mid-Oct., $80-100, duplex $170); they're very old and very simple, but fine.

The **Absaroka Lodge** (406/848-7414 or 800/755-7414, www.yellowstonemotel.com, $135-150) is well-situated on the banks of the Yellowstone River. Kitchenettes are available at the higher rate. The **Best Western Plus by Mammoth Hot Springs** (406/848-7311, www.bestwesternmontana.com, $195-220) has an indoor pool and is set back off Highway 89 just north of Gardiner with views of the river.

At the **Yellowstone Village Inn** (1102 Scott St. W., 406/484-7417 or 800/228-8158, www.yellowstonevinn.com, $119-229), a nicely decorated place set up on a hill above the highway, there's an indoor pool and sauna, and a few suites with kitchens.

Just north of town, **Yellowstone Park Travelodge** (109 Hellroaring St., 406/848-7520, www.travelodge.com, $155-161) is well run and clean.

Four miles north of town, the **Yellowstone Basin Inn** (4 Maiden Basin Dr., 406/848-7080 or 800/624-3364, www.yellowstonebasininn.com, $195-445) has attractive standard rooms and suites on a hillside overlooking the highway and the river.

If you stay at the child- and pet-friendly **Gardiner Guest House** (112 Main St., 406/848-9414, www.gardinerguesthouse.com, $90-145 includes breakfast), run by guide Richard Parks and his wife, Nancy, you may come away from the breakfast table knowing just a bit more about the area, its critters, and its issues. There are four rooms in the Victorian house and a cabin out back.

Head out of town and up a steep dirt road to the **Crevice Mountain Lodge** (406/223-0148, www.crevicemountainlodge.com, $200 includes breakfast), where rustic wood-heated cabins are built on (and named for) old mining claims. The location is remote enough to feel a sense of reprieve from the crowds at Yellowstone, but close enough to allow a trip into the park.

Camping

Yellowstone RV Park (406/848-7496, $42-48) and **Rocky Mountain** (406/848-7251, $52-59) are RV campgrounds right in Gardiner. **Eagle Creek** (406/848-7375, $7) is the nearest Forest Service campground; it's four miles northeast of town on the road to Jardine.

Food

Take a break from the park and relax for a while with a tasty panini and a new book at **Tumbleweed Bookstore and Cafe** (501 Scott St., 406/848-2225, 7am-9pm daily summer, 7am-3pm Mon.-Fri., 8am-3pm Sat.-Sun. winter, $7-9).

For a surprisingly good dinner in an unpretentious setting, head to the tiny ★ **Raven Grill** (220 W. Park St., 406/848-7600, 11am-10pm Mon.-Fri., 5pm-10pm Sat.-Sun., $13-26). The menu features several pasta dishes, which are delicious, as are salads and the wild mushroom appetizer.

About eight miles up the road in Corwin Springs, **The Lighthouse** (752 Hwy. 89 S., 406/848-2138, www.lrmts.com, 5:30pm-11pm

Wed.-Mon. mid-May-mid-Sept., $10-26) has pasta and pan-Asian food, including spicy curries and vegetarian options. Bring your own beer or wine if you want alcohol.

Getting Around

Yellowstone National Park's main concessionaire, **Xanterra** (307/344-7311 or 866/439-7375, www.travelyellowstone.com), runs bus tours of the park. From late May through mid-September, buses leave Gardiner every morning at 7:30am, tour the Grand Loop of Yellowstone's roads, and return to Gardiner at 6:30pm. The fee is $86 adults, $43 kids 3-11.

Big Timber to Laurel

The Boulder River flows between the Absarokas and the Beartooths to Big Timber, passing ghost towns, church camps, and dude ranches on the way. Near Big Timber, the Boulder pours into the Yellowstone River, which around here changes from a cold-water trout stream to the broad warm home of paddlefish.

This whole area was Crow territory before eastern settlers moved in during the 1870s. When the railroad came through, a small settlement sprang up near the mouth of the Boulder River. This town, called Dornix (meaning "Rock Pile"), never made it as a railway station. In 1883 the town of Big Timber was founded just to the west. Ranching (especially sheep ranching), tourism, and recreation now support the local economy.

BIG TIMBER AND VICINITY

A mostly quiet and well-kept-up ranch town, Big Timber (pop. 1,653, elev. 4,072 feet) is not a forested spot. William Clark, who passed this way on the return from the Pacific, named Big Timber Creek for the stand of cottonwoods shading its confluence with the Yellowstone. Today it might be called "Big Wind" or "Crazy View" for the frequent gusts, and the nearby mountain ranges are far more noticeable than the trees.

Crazy Mountain Museum

A small garden at the entrance to the **Crazy Mountain Museum** (I-90 exit 367, Cemetery Rd., 406/932-5126, 10am-4:30pm Mon.-Sat., 1pm-4pm Sun., Memorial Day-Sept. 30, free) spotlights native plants collected by Lewis and Clark on their journey across Montana. Also outside, a Norwegian *stabbur,* a supposedly rodent-proof pantry building, has been built to acknowledge the area's Norwegian heritage. Indoors, historical photos are mixed with several striking modern photos, and one small room is filled with an impressive collection of chaps.

Greycliff Prairie Dog Town State Park

Pull off the interstate to visit the communal burrows of **Greycliff Prairie Dog Town State Park** (Greycliff exit from I-90, 406/446-2326, $5 per vehicle for non-Montana residents). It may not sound like much, but prairie dog behavior is kind of a kick to watch. They're very social animals, and also very vocal, giving sharp yelps or "barks" when alerted to possible danger. When this danger cry goes out, all the surrounding prairie dogs scuttle into their burrows.

Crazy Mountains

The Crazy Mountains, north of Big Timber, are a spectacular isolated range. To reach them from Big Timber, drive north on Highway 191 (the road to Harlowton) and follow signs for Big Timber Canyon. **Halfmoon Campground** and a trailhead into the mountains are about 15 miles from the pavement.

Recreation

Boulder River **fishing-access sites** include **Big Rock,** four miles south of Big Timber, and **Boulder Forks,** at the confluence of the Main Boulder and West Boulder Rivers in McLeod. Fish the Yellowstone from **Grey Bear,** six miles west of Big Timber on the frontage road, or **Pelican,** just east of the Greycliff exit on the frontage road.

Accommodations

The ★ **Grand Hotel** (139 McLeod St., 406/932-4459, www.thegrand-hotel.com, $69-169), built in 1890, has been restored as a bed-and-breakfast hotel. This is a great place to stay: The rooms are cozy, the breakfast is good, and the adjoining restaurant and bar are enjoyable places to while away an evening.

The **River Valley Inn** (600 W. 2nd St., 406/932-4943 or 877/899-1397, $80-140) is a newer motel and a good option if you can't stay at the Grand and want to be in town.

The **Buckin' Horse Bunkhouse** (361 Bridger Creek Rd., 406/932-6537, www.bunkhouse.biz, $145-200), southeast of Big Timber on Bridger Creek, rents a couple of B&B cabins that are rustic on the outside but nice on the inside. They permit well-behaved dogs.

Camping

Spring Creek Camp and Trout Ranch (257 Main Boulder Rd., 406/932-4387, www.springcreekcampground.com) has cabins ($54-62) and some tent sites ($20) but is essentially an RV park ($30-40) in a quiet spot two miles south of Big Timber along the Boulder River. Ponds here are stocked with rainbow trout.

Nineteen miles north of Big Timber, up Big Timber Canyon, **Halfmoon Campground** (406/932-5155, www.fs.usda.gov/gallatin, Memorial Day-Labor Day, $5) features hiking trails into the Crazy Mountains.

Food

Dinners at the ★ **Grand Hotel** (139 McLeod St., 406/932-4459, www.thegrand-hotel.com, 11am-2pm Mon.-Fri., 5pm-9pm nightly, $18-37) are just about the grandest thing going in this little town. Daily lunch specials are good reason to pull off the highway for a stop here. For a casual dinner ($7-30), eat in the attractive and friendly hotel bar.

Information

The **Sweetgrass County Chamber of Commerce** (406/932-5131, www.bigtimber.

the Crazy Mountains

com) runs the local visitors center at exit 367 on I-90. Find the **Forest Service** (406/932-5155) at 225 Big Timber Loop Road.

BOULDER VALLEY

It's hard to pick Montana's most beautiful river valley, but this one's a strong contender. Small wonder then that celebrities and novelists have become the modern-day homesteaders here.

Sights

Drive up the Boulder River Valley 25 miles south of Big Timber to the **Natural Bridge State Monument.** The limestone cliffs have been warped, lifted, dropped, and eaten away by weak river-water acids, leaving a spectacular gorge with a 100-foot waterfall. The eponymous natural bridge across the falls collapsed in 1988. Trails course the park, but there are no campsites.

Just down the road from the natural bridge, the **Main Boulder Ranger Station** dates from 1905. There are pictographs in the caves west of the ranger station.

Forty miles up the Boulder River from Big Timber, the ghost town of **Independence** recalls a past of gold mining and stock-promotion schemes. The final four miles to Independence are best driven in a high-clearance four-wheel-drive vehicle.

Recreation

When the Yellowstone River is brimful of muddy water, the rocky Boulder River usually runs clear. Upriver from Natural Bridge, the Boulder is populated with rainbow and cutthroat trout; below the tall falls at the bridge, browns and rainbows predominate.

Follow Boulder River Road to its end to pick up a trail into the **Absaroka-Beartooth Wilderness Area,** a remote high country studded with alpine lakes and covered with wildflowers late in the summer. It's a good spot for a week of backpacking.

In the winter, the Boulder River Road is maintained for snowmobiling starting about 30 miles south of Big Timber and continuing

to the wilderness boundary. Snowmobilers often spot the many elk and moose that winter in the Boulder Valley. For more information on snowmobiling, call the **Forest Service in Big Timber** (406/932-5155).

Accommodations

The Boulder Valley didn't support miners or farmers for long, but dude ranchers have done well by it. The **Hawley Mountain Guest Ranch** (45 miles south of Big Timber, 406/932-5791, www.hawleymountain.com, $1,895 weekly single guest, $1,498-$1,998 weekly per person for couple) offers reasonably priced weeklong (Sunday to Sunday) packages including cabin, meals, horseback riding, fly-fishing, and river floating. Accommodations are either in the lodge or in one of three cabins.

For less-expensive lodgings in a pretty setting, the tidy but rustic **McLeod Resort** (16 miles south of Big Timber, 406/932-6167, www.mcleodresort.com) has a campground ($20 tent, $28 RV), a few very simple cabins ($38-50), and a guest house ($1,000 a week for up to eight people) set alongside the West Boulder River. The cabins and the houses have cooking facilities, but cooking utensils are not provided in the cabins.

Camping

The **Gallatin National Forest** (406/932-5155, www.fs.usda.gov/gallatin, $5) is studded with campsites south of Big Timber, but you have to drive a ways to reach them. **Falls Creek Campground** is 30 miles south of town on Boulder River Road, with **Aspen, Chippy Park, and Hell's Canyon Campgrounds** all within the next 10 miles. **Hicks Park Campground** is 50 miles south of Big Timber on the same road. Turn right (west) at McLeod to reach the **West Boulder Campground,** 30 miles southwest of Big Timber, with a trail into the Absaroka-Beartooth Wilderness. The **McLeod Resort** (16 miles south of Big Timber, 406/932-6167, www.mcleodresort.com) also offers tent and RV camping.

Food

★ **Holly's Road Kill Saloon** (15 miles south of Big Timber, 406/932-6174, 11am-close daily summer, 11am-close Wed.-Sun. winter, $9-16) is a Boulder Valley landmark and de facto community center. During the summer, there's often a band—don't be shy about dancing, and don't forget to look up and admire the arched plank ceiling in the bar (behind the false front, the place is a Quonset hut).

REED POINT

Tiny Reed Point has barely changed from the early 20th century, when this was a booming trade center for local farmers and ranchers. In the 1920s, Reed Point was a major center for sheep ranchers; an estimated 48,000 sheep grazed in the mountains above the town.

This heritage is celebrated in the **Running of the Sheep.** Started in 1989 as a fundraiser for the tiny community's library, school, and other public facilities, the sheep drive has become an institution. Held on the Sunday of Labor Day weekend, the event consists of watching several thousand sheep scampering down Reed Point's main street, eating grilled lamb and sausages, and attending the parade and street dance that follow the drive. The Associated Press reports one local wag as stating: "It's like the running of the bulls in Spain, only a whole lot safer."

RAPELJE

In the late 1990s, Rapelje, 23 miles north of Columbus and surrounded by wide-open flatlands, was on the brink of becoming a ghost town when residents decided to stage a mountain bike race in order to raise funds to keep the local café in business. Area ranchers allowed the construction of trails on their private property and found a promoter to put on a small race. That race has grown to a 24-hour marathon, held on the June weekend closest to the summer solstice. The course follows county roads that wind through coulees and hills with spectacular mountain views. Shorter recreational rides are also offered. Mountain bike central in town is the

Rapelje Stockman Cafe (406/663-2231, http://stockmancafe.googlepages.com), collectively owned by a group of townspeople.

COLUMBUS AND THE STILLWATER RIVER

Thirty-seven miles east of Big Timber at the mouth of the Stillwater River, Columbus (pop. about 2,000) is renowned for the **New Atlas Bar.** But back before the New Atlas was the main thing people thought of when they thought of Columbus, the town was known for its frequent name changes. Previously it has been called Eagle's Nest, Sheep Dip, and Stillwater.

The jagged peaks of the Beartooth Range form the jawline of the horizon to the south. On the road down from Columbus, through Absarokee to Red Lodge, take in the fine views of former Crow country.

A lovely little town with one of the state's great names, Fishtail is worth a stop, if only for a soda at the mercantile. Of course, a brief stop will only make you wish you'd stayed longer, so plan on hanging out for a while.

If merely hanging around this lovely country sounds too unstructured, sign on with **Paintbrush Adventures** (86 N. Stillwater Rd., Absarokee, 406/328-4158, www.paintbrushadventures.com) for a trail ride ($30-165) or guided hike. They also offer working ranch vacations ($285 per person per day). Another outfitter, **Absaroka River Adventures** (113 Grove St., Absarokee, 406/328-7440 or 800/334-7238, www.absarokariver.com, half day $45 adults, $25 children), offers whitewater trips on the Stillwater River (not a contradiction!).

Accommodations

Although there are several chain motels, including a Super 8, up on I-90 at the Columbus exit, stay local in Absarokee, where the ★ **Stillwater Lodge** (28 Woodard Ave., 406/328-4899, http://stillwaterlodge.net, $84-102) is a small motel with comfortable, thoughtfully decorated rooms. Another pretty place in this little town is **The Big Yellow House**

(Main St., Absarokee, 406/328-7220, http://the-bigyellowhouse.biz, $80-150), which dates from about 1904; guests have use of the kitchen to make their own meals or they can pay an extra $10 for a full B&B-style breakfast. Guests can either stay in one of the house's three bedrooms (shared bath) or in cottages next door ($85).

Camp at **Pine Grove** or **Emerald Lake** campgrounds (406/446-2103, www.fs.usda.gov/custer, May-Sept., $9) out of Fishtail, or at **Jimmy Joe** or **East Rosebud Lake** out of Roscoe.

Food and Nightlife

In Roscoe, the **Grizzly Bar and Restaurant** (406/328-6789, www.wherethehellisroscoe.com, noon-10pm Mon.-Sat., $12-36), housed in a lovely log building along the East Rosebud River, offers a reason to linger in this attractive hamlet. Although the menu emphasizes burgers, steak, and prime rib, it also includes pasta and fish.

It's hard to find a bar that's as simultaneously stately and seedy as Columbus's ★ **New Atlas Bar** (522 E. Pike St., 406/322-4033)—it has a great back bar and more animal heads than most non-Montanans have seen in a lifetime. Don't expect anything here to be prettied up for refined sensibilities; spittoons help to keep the floor clean.

LAUREL

Located at a transportation crossroads, Laurel (pop. 7,000) is dominated by a large oil refinery. Although Laurel is not a particularly exciting place to spend the night, it's convenient to I-90 and not too far from the Beartooth Highway. The **Best Western Yellowstone Crossing** (205 S.E. 4th St., 406/628-6888, http://bestwesternmontana.com, $115-121) is a good place to bunk; it has a pool. Another good bet is the **Locomotive Inn** (310 S. 1st Ave., 406/628-8281 or 877/210-5626, www.locomotiveinn.com, $85), with a pool on the premises and a nice restaurant and health club next door.

Absaroka-Beartooth Wilderness

This is Montana's high country: Granite Peak, towering 12,799 feet in the Beartooth Range, is the state's highest point and a formidable climb. Geologically and ecologically different from one another, the Absaroka and Beartooth Ranges share a plateau and a wilderness area. The accommodating Beartooth Plateau tilts from a low northwestern Absaroka corner to the soaring Beartooths in the southeast.

The Beartooths were uplifted, eroded, partially blanketed with lava from Yellowstone's volcanoes, and covered with glaciers. The limestone cliffs of the Beartooth Range rise from high tundra cut through by steep canyons.

The weather in the Beartooths can change quickly and with arctic severity. Come prepared for a snowstorm, even in midsummer.

The Beartooths are largely above the timberline, and alpine meadows are the characteristic vegetation. The growing season here is about 45 days, and the plants and the soil are sensitive to trampling. During the late summer, snowbanks sometimes turn pink as microorganisms on the snow's surface die and turn red.

RED LODGE

Red Lodge (pop. 2,200, elev. 5,555 feet) is supposedly named for red clay-decorated Crow lodges. Once part of the Crow Reservation, this area was taken from them in 1882; coal mining commenced a few years later. The mines became the basis for the town, and many immigrants came to work in Red Lodge; Finns were particularly well-represented. Mining dropped off in the 1930s, and an explosion at the nearby Smith Creek Mine in 1943 halted large-scale coal mining in the area. Red Lodge is now a resort and jumping-off point for travelers on the Beartooth Highway and is also visited by many Montanans for its good spring skiing.

Sights

Red Lodge's **downtown** remains vital and is a showcase of historic preservation. Pick up a walking-tour map from the visitors center (or download it from www.redlodge.com/downloads/walktour.pdf) and ramble through the sandstone and brick edifices of the late 1800s. Red Lodge's Old Town, near the high school, was the town's business center from 1886 to 1893. Stroll along Broadway to visit several galleries and a number of Western-style home decor stores, but be prepared to pay the 3 percent local sales tax (most of Montana has no sales tax).

The **Carbon County Historical Museum** (224 N. Broadway, 406/446-3667, www.carboncountyhistory.com, 10am-5pm Mon.-Sat., 11am-3pm Memorial Day-Sept., 11am-4pm Thurs.-Sat., Oct.-Memorial Day, $5 adults, $3 students) has exhibits on rodeos, Native Americans, and mining. Another historical artifact, **Liver Eatin' Johnson's cabin,** is on the north end of town next to the visitors center. It's probably apocryphal, but Mr. Johnson was said to have avenged his Flathead wife's death by eating the livers he'd ripped from Crows.

Red Lodge's biggest attraction, besides its recreation and its many restaurants and shops, is the **Yellowstone Wildlife Sanctuary** (615 2nd St. E., 406/446-1133, www.yellowstonewildlifesanctuary.org, noon-4pm Tues.-Fri., 10am-4pm Sat.-Sun., $7 adults, $6 seniors, $3 children 3-12), a nonprofit organization that provides a home for native animals that can't be returned to the wild, including wolves, coyotes, elk, mountain lions, hawks, bears, and a porcupine.

Skiing

Red Lodge Mountain (406/446-2610 or 800/444-8977, www.redlodgemountain.com, $51 adults, $17-43 seniors, $41 teens, $21 children under 13) is a ski resort six miles west of town with a vertical drop of 2,400 feet and seven chairlifts, including two high-speed quads, to ferry skiers to the 70 trails. Ski season runs from early December through mid-April, sometimes later. Spring skiing is especially popular at Red Lodge.

near the West Fork of Rock Creek, in Absaroka-Beartooth Wilderness

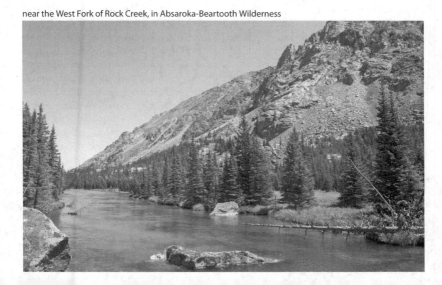

The **Red Lodge Nordic Center** (406/425-0698, www.beartoothtrails.org, $5 adults, seniors and children 12 and under free) has nine miles of groomed trails west of town on Highway 78. Rent skis in town at **Sylvan Peak** (9 S. Broadway, 406/446-1770).

Hiking and Other Recreation

Head up the **West Fork of Rock Creek** for hiking and fishing. The often-crowded **Wild Bill Lake,** six miles from Red Lodge on West Fork Road, is wheelchair-accessible and kid-friendly for fishing. Toward the end of the road, trailheads sprout up. Just out of Basin Campground, the 4.1-mile-long **Basin Lakes National Recreation Trail** is an easy day hike leading to two lakes (with some brook trout) and a few tumbledown prospectors' cabins. At the end of West Fork Rock Creek Road, the **West Fork Trail** puts you at the Absaroka-Beartooth Wilderness boundary, a 1-mile hike from a waterfall, 5 miles from a mountain lake, and 10 miles from Sundance Pass.

Many trails start from the area's Forest Service campgrounds, most of which are on roads heading off from the Beartooth Highway. The **Corral Creek Trail** starts near Sheridan Campground on East Side Road or pass Limber Pine Campground on the high winding Rock Creek Road to the trailhead for the **Hellroaring Plateau Trail,** which leads to a lovely chain of mountain lakes.

Golf at beautiful and challenging **Red Lodge Mountain Golf Club** (406/446-3344, $34-49 for 18 holes), southwest of town on Red Lodge Mountain Road.

Swim at the 25-yard-long mile-high **city pool** (14th and Hauser, daily June-Aug.).

Events

The **Red Lodge Music Festival** (www.redlodgemusicfestival.org) brings top high-school musicians to train with professionals. Both students and faculty perform over a nine-day span in mid-June.

The **Red Lodge Rodeo** is on Fourth of July weekend.

Mid-July brings the **Beartooth Rally** and a huge swarm of Harleys to town, making Red Lodge into the Sturgis of the Rockies.

Red Lodge's ethnic diversity is celebrated each August during the **Festival of Nations**. Lots of music, lots of food, and lots of people fill downtown. Be sure to book rooms in advance if you want to stay in Red Lodge during the first weekend of August.

Accommodations

Lodging can be pricey in Red Lodge in the summer. Expect prices to drop dramatically in the spring and fall, and to be somewhat lower in the winter.

If you're a fan of old downtown hotels, your best bet in Red Lodge is, without question, the ★ **Pollard Hotel** (2 N. Broadway, 406/446-0001 or 800/765-5273, www.pollardhotel.com, $110-270). Back when it was known as the Spofford, it hosted Calamity Jane and Buffalo Bill. Now after extensive renovation, there are even racquetball courts, a health club, and a sauna. Rooms are comfortable (though the least expensive ones are quite small), and many include in-room steam baths and whirlpool tubs.

A full-scale, full-service resort, the ★ **Rock Creek Resort** (406/446-1111 or 800/667-1119, www.rockcreekresort.com, $145-250 lodge) is four miles south of town on Highway 212. Accommodations range from single rooms to three-bedroom town houses ($390) and a log cabin ($355). A pool, tennis courts, volleyball, croquet, and nearby hiking and biking trails keep Rock Creek's guests occupied. The resort also features two restaurants.

Quite a bit less fancy but still comfortable is the alpine-looking and dog-friendly **Yodeler Motel** (601 S. Broadway, 406/446-1435 or 866/446-1435, www.yodelermotel.com, $89-135), which has half-basement rooms (not unpleasant) and, for a few dollars more, rooms that are fully above ground. Amenities here include an outdoor hot tub and in-shower steam baths, which although they initially seem improbable, are something to look forward to after a day of mountain biking or skiing.

The chaletlike **Chateau Rouge** (1501 S. Broadway, 406/446-1601 or 800/926-1601, www.chateaurouge.com, $119-149) is a good value, with rooms in studios with kitchenettes or two-bedroom condos. These rooms can be made up to sleep a crowd if necessary. There's an indoor pool and hot tub.

Book a vacation home through **Red Lodge Reservations** (406/446-4700 or 877/733-5634, www.redlodgereservations.com).

Camping

The **Red Lodge KOA** (406/446-2364 or 800/562-7540, http://koa.com/campgrounds/red-lodge, May-Sept., $32 tent, $42 RV, $46 cabin), four miles north of town on Highway 212, has a swimming pool, camping cabins, and sites for both RVs and tents. **Perry's RV Park and Campground** (406/446-2722, www.perrysrv.us, late May-Sept., $20 tent, $35 RV) is on Rock Creek 1.5 miles south of town.

To find **Forest Service campgrounds** (406/446-2103, www.fs.usda.gov/custer, May-Sept., $10-14), head south on Highway 212. Reach **Cascade** and **Basin** campgrounds via Red Lodge Mountain Road, which starts right near the ranger station. These are good spots for hikers heading into the Absaroka-Beartooth Wilderness. Farther south on Highway 212, find turnoffs for **Sheridan** and **Ratine. Parkside, Limber Pine, Greenough Lake,** and **M-K** are all part of the Rock Creek Recreation Area 11 miles south of Red Lodge and virtually at the foot of the Beartooth Highway. All of these spots except for Cascade have running water.

Food

It's not hard to find a meal in Red Lodge—the town boasts of having more restaurants per capita than any other place in Montana. One particularly pleasant spot is ★ **Bridge Creek Backcountry Kitchen & Wine Bar** (116 S. Broadway, 406/446-9900, www.eatfooddrink-wine.com, 11am-9pm Tues.-Sat., dinner $9-34), a lovely little place with sidewalk seating, a coffee bar, and a small gourmet market as well as a regular sit-down restaurant section. At lunch, a variety of wraps and sandwiches are offered ($6-9); dinners range from soba noodles with veggies to pan-seared trout with peach agrodolce and crabmeat. Wine pairings are suggested on the menu.

Another bright spot is **Hope's Artisan Foods** (113 N. Broadway, 406/446-0226, www.hopesartisanfoods.com, 11am-6pm

Red Lodge's Pollard Hotel has dining and a pub as well as lodging.

Fri.-Sat., Mon.-Tues., $6-13), with deli sandwiches on freshly baked bread (including a gluten-free option) and seasonal entrées that tend toward healthy (even vegan) comfort food.

The **Red Lodge Pizza Company** (115 S. Broadway, 406/446-3933, 11am-10pm Sun.-Thurs., 11am-11pm daily, $4 per slice) serves decent pizza, and it's available by the slice, making for a quick inexpensive lunch. It's also a good place to bring kids.

A bright spot for the bleary-eyed, **Coffee Factory Roasters** (6 S. Broadway, 406/446-3200, http://coffeefactoryroasters.com, 6:30am-6pm daily) roasts beans and serves coffee drinks and desserts. Find the other kind of brewing north of downtown at **Sam's Taproom** (1445 N. Broadway, 406/446-0243, http://redlodgeales.com, 11am-9pm daily, sandwiches $8-10), home of Red Lodge Ales, where the state's largest solar thermal array provides heat and hot water. Another good place to get a beer is **Natali's** (117 N. Broadway, 406/446-3333), though if you really want to kick up your heels, that's best done across the street at the **Snow Creek Saloon** (124 S. Broadway, 406/446-2542).

The Pollard Hotel's **Dining Room** (406/446-0001, www.thepollard.com, 7am-11am and 5pm-9pm daily, dinner $26-35) serves steaks from natural Angus beef from Montana; chops, fresh seafood, pasta, and game dishes also appear on the menu, and the wine list is extensive. **The Pub at the Pollard** (4pm-9pm, $12-27) is an easygoing place for a simple dinner or a cocktail.

Cafe Regis (501 S. Word, 406/446-1941, www.caferegis.com, 6am-2pm Wed.-Sun., $6-9), in a nicely renovated grocery store two blocks west of the main drag, has a less touristy feeling than most Red Lodge restaurants. The back doors open onto a patio that bumps up against town's community gardens. It's safe to say that the Regis has the best barbecued tofu in town (it really is good).

Head seven miles east of town to the **Bear Creek Saloon** (Hwy. 308, 406/446-3481, 5pm-10pm Thurs.-Sun., May-Sept. and Dec.-Mar., $8-30), known more for its **pig races** than its food (though the charbroiled steaks are tasty). Every 15 minutes, another group of porkers toes the line. Thanks to special state legislation, it is legal to bet on the pigs.

Information and Services

The chamber of commerce **visitors center** (601 N. Broadway, 406/855-4796, www.redlodge.com) has the expected brochures, plus an RV dump station. The **ranger station** (406/446-2103) is on Highway 212.

Beartooth Hospital (406/446-2345) is at 600 West 21st Street.

If you're setting out to drive the Beartooth Highway, be sure to gas up in Red Lodge.

Getting There

Fly into Billings; it's about 60 miles from Red Lodge. Also 60 miles away is the Cody, Wyoming, airport. Car rentals are available at the either airport.

★ BEARTOOTH HIGHWAY

Make sure there's gas in the tank, fresh batteries in the camera, an extra sweater in the back seat, and at least three hours to spare before setting out on the 68-mile-long Beartooth Highway. Built in 1936 and now a National Scenic Byway, this road climbs to 10,947 feet and crosses alpine meadows and snowfields. The Beartooth Highway is closed by snow a lot of the year—most years it's open from the end of May to mid-October.

The road climbs Rock Creek Canyon out of Red Lodge and switches back four times, crossing as many vegetation zones, starting in a valley of Douglas fir and lodgepole pine and topping out in alpine meadows strewn with boulders and wildflowers. Near Beartooth Pass, pink snow betrays the presence of high-elevation algae.

Watch for the Bear's Tooth, a tall spire left after a glacier devoured the rest of the peak. North of the summit of Beartooth Plateau, Granite Peak juts above the landscape.

Hiking

The high country around the Beartooth Highway is crossed by hiking trails and speckled with lakes. Hiking trails across fragile alpine terrain are rarely forged paths; rather, they're less precise routes marked by rock cairns. For a short hike through an alpine meadow, drive up to the fire lookout on **Clay Butte** and hike a little over a mile along the ridge.

For a longer trek, take **Trail 614** at the switchback in the road up to the lookout and hike about four miles (generally downhill) around Beartooth Butte to Beartooth Lake. There's a lovely campground at Beartooth Lake, and a loop hike around the butte passes several other lakes in its seven-mile course.

Fishing

Many of the alpine lakes on the Beartooth Plateau have been stocked with trout. The hikes in are lovely, the fishing's generally good, and Pat Marcuson details every fish-bearing Beartooth lake and stream in *Fishing the Beartooths*. Remember that the road dips down into Wyoming here—buy a Wyoming fishing license in Cooke City or at the Top of the World store before going after the rainbow, cutthroat, and brook trout in Beartooth Lake.

Skiing

Early in the season, it may seem more appropriate to ski than to hike. Find lifts at the **Beartooth Basin** (619/922-0726, www.beartoothbasin.com, 8am-1:30pm, $45) near Beartooth Pass from about Memorial Day through July 4, or however long the snow lasts. The Red Lodge International Summer Ski and Snowboard Camp uses this area; because the slopes are nearly vertical, skiers and boarders must be able to demonstrate expert abilities before getting on the lift.

Accommodations and Camping

The only motel along the road from Red Lodge to Cooke City is the tiny and extremely basic **Top of the World Resort** (307/587-5368, www.topoftheworldresort.com, $55-79), at 9,400 feet 38 miles from Red Lodge and 25 miles from Cooke City, but there are plenty of places to pitch a tent along the Wyoming stretch of the Beartooth Highway at **Forest Service campgrounds** (307/527-6921, www.fs.usda.gov/shoshone, June-Sept. depending on snowfall, $15). High on the Beartooth Plateau, **Island Lake** (Aug.-early Sept.), about 40 miles west of Red Lodge, and **Beartooth Lake,** 3 miles farther west, have trails leading to the many alpine lakes to the north. **Fox Creek,** 7 miles east of Cooke City, and **Crazy Creek,** about 3 miles farther east, don't have the alpine quality of the higher campgrounds, but they are convenient and attractive wooded riverside spots.

COOKE CITY AND SILVER GATE

John Colter, the first person of European descent in the area, led the 19th-century parade of mountain men, traders, prospectors, and speculators. Until 1882 this was still recognized as Crow land, and relatively few others intruded. By 1883, however, Cooke City, named after the son of a Northern Pacific financier, was a booming mine town. Gold, silver, and lead were extracted from the mountains, but because of the remoteness, the boom didn't last. Unmined lodes remain around Cooke City, but it's still hard to get to them, and until recently the mining costs were reckoned to be too high to maintain much of an operation.

Other than occasional mining speculation and attendant high-level wheeling and dealing, Cooke City (elev. 7,651 feet) is a tourist town. There's just one street to reckon with here, and it's easy to walk from one end of it to the other. Even in the summer, when drivers spill off the Beartooth Highway, there's an easygoing rustic flavor. During the winter, when the Beartooth Highway shuts down, Cooke City is open via the road through Yellowstone Park to Gardiner. Silver Gate, three miles west of Cooke City, was established as a resort town shortly after construction of the Beartooth Highway. Together the two towns have about 140 year-round residents.

Recreation

There is some gold in the hills around Cooke City, and fortune seekers may enjoy panning in the local streams.

Beartooth Plateau Outfitters (406/838-2328 or 800/253-8545, www.elkhuntin-montana.com) runs hunting, fishing, and horse-packing trips. **Skyline Guide Service** (406/838-2380 or 877/238-8885, www.fly-fishyellowstone.com) also leads trips into Yellowstone Park and the Absaroka-Beartooth Wilderness Area.

For a short forest hike to a waterfall, start at the Range Riders Lodge in Silver Gate.

Northeast of Cooke City, on the edge of the Absaroka-Beartooth Wilderness, the **"grasshopper glacier,"** has dark bands of grasshoppers frozen into it, which have been exposed as the climate warms. To reach the glacier, which is now classified just as a snowfield, drive a high-clearance four-wheel drive up the LuLu Pass-Goose Lake Road (near Colter Campground). The road stops at the Absaroka-Beartooth Wilderness border. Continue on foot (or horseback) along the old road to Goose Lake, then take the trail northeast to the saddle between Sawtooth Mountain and Iceberg Peak. Turn right at the saddle and climb the first rock ridge, from which the glacier is visible on the north side of Iceberg Peak. The hike from the road's end to this point is four miles. Topographical maps of the area are available at the Cooke City Store. Hikers should prepare for harsh weather any time of year.

Snowmobile rentals are readily available in town during the long winters.

Accommodations

Most accommodations in Cooke City are older but serviceable motels and cabins; they're neither fancy nor outrageously expensive. Unless noted otherwise, accommodations are along Highway 212 in the side-by-side towns of Cooke City and Silver Gate.

Some of the spacious 1950s-era log cabins at the **High Country Motel** (406/838-2272, www.highcountrymotelandcabins.com, year-round, $95-110) include kitchens, as do a few motel rooms; this is a very nice place to stay. The **Alpine Motel** (406/838-2262 or 888/838-1190, www.cookecityalpine.com, year-round, $87-145), also has well-kept rooms and a few suites. The cabins at **Antler's Lodge** (406/838-2432 or 866/738-2432, www.cooke-cityantlerslodge.com, $85-165) are older and pretty rustic, but have a certain homey charm. **Elk Horn Lodge** (406/838-2332, http://elk-hornlodgemt.com, $115-405), right along the main drag of Highway 212, also has both cute kitchenette cabins and motel rooms.

Down the road in Silver Gate, **Grizzly Lodge** (406/838-2219, www.yellowstonelo-dges.com, $110-160) has basic, but perfectly okay cabin-style rooms right near Soda Butte Creek. The other lodgings in Silver Gate are all owned by a group of people who are working to give this tiny town some vitality without destroying its woodsy laid-back beauty. **Pine Edge Cabins** (406/838-2371, www.pineedgecabins.com, $140-195) are open all year. The charming 1930s-era **Silver Gate Cabins** (406/838-2371, www.pineedgecab-ins.com, $140-165) all have kitchens; there are also some motel rooms here ($72).

The only real deviation from the small motel and cabin format in the area is the **Super 8** (406/838-2070, $99-143) in Cooke City. If you want to stay someplace a little more modern, this is it.

Camping

Chief Joseph, Soda Butte, and **Colter** are **Forest Service campgrounds** (406/848-7375, www.fs.usda.gov/gallatin, July-Sept., $8-9) just east of Cooke City on the Beartooth Highway.

Food

Unless otherwise noted, these restaurants are along Highway 212 in the side-by-side towns of Cooke City and Silver Gate. If you're dizzy from the elevation, sit on the porch of the ★ **Beartooth Cafe** (406/838-2475, www.beartoothcafe.com, 11am-10pm daily Memorial Day weekend-Sept., dinner $16-25) and gobble a burger or a sandwich ($8-11), stroke the town dogs, then order a beer from the impressive list of imports and microbrews. Stop for breakfast at the **Bearclaw Bakery** (406/835-2010, 5am-11am

Tues.-Sun., $4-11); breakfast burritos are a great way to start the day, but be sure to pick up a scone to eat as a mid-morning snack. Stop at the **Miner's Saloon** (406/838-2214, noon-2am daily year-round, $8-25) for either a beer or a meal (try the pizza). The saloon is loaded with historical touches, and the food is as fresh as you'll find in remote Cooke City, where it's nearly impossible to grow a vegetable.

Yellowstone National Park

There are many reasons why **Yellowstone National Park** (307/344-7381, www.nps.gov/yell, 3-day pass $30 per vehicle, $25 for motorcyclists and snowmobilers, $15 for hikers, bikers, and skiers, $60 annual pass for Yellowstone, $80 Interagency Annual Pass good for most federal recreation sites) is such a popular destination. First, its incredibly violent geological history left not only a giant caldera but also geysers, hot springs, and other geothermal oddities. Second, largely because it became protected as the country's first national park in 1872, the wildlife is abundant and diverse. Third, although it may not be as

visually stunning as Glacier National Park, the country is just plain beautiful.

Most of the park is in Wyoming, but three of its entrances—**West Yellowstone, Gardiner,** and **Cooke City**—are in Montana. For an excellent in-depth guide to the entire park, see *Moon Yellowstone & Grand Teton* by Don Pitcher (Avalon Travel).

Yellowstone Park closes for a couple of weeks early in December and from mid-March until May, but for those willing to make the effort to get in there during the winter, there's a wilder park to explore than most summertime visitors glimpse. Winter snows

The Roosevelt Arch marks the entrance to Yellowstone National Park at Gardiner.

Yellowstone National Park

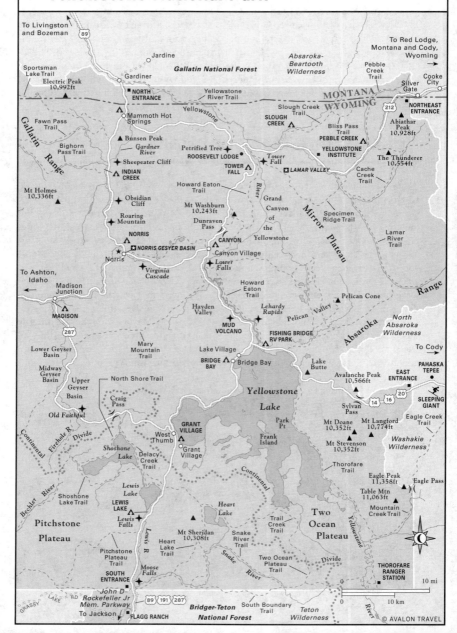

To Livingston
and Bozeman

Jardine

Absaroka-
Beartooth
Wilderness

To Red Lodge,
Montana and Cody,
Wyoming

Gallatin National Forest

Sportsman
Lake Trail

Electric Peak
10,992ft

Gardiner

Pebble
Creek
Trail

Silver
Gate

Cooke
City

NORTH
ENTRANCE

Yellowstone
River Trail

MONTANA

Fawn Pass
Trail

Mammoth Hot
Springs

Yellowstone

WYOMING

NORTHEAST
ENTRANCE

Slough Creek
Trail

SLOUGH
CREEK

Bighorn
Pass Trail

Bunsen Peak

Gardner
River

Bliss Pass
Trail

Abiathar
Peak
10,928ft

Petrified Tree

PEBBLE CREEK

Sheepeater Cliff

ROOSEVELT LODGE

Tower
Fall

YELLOWSTONE
INSTITUTE

The Thunderer
10,554ft

INDIAN
CREEK

TOWER
FALL

LAMAR VALLEY

Cache
Creek
Trail

Mt Holmes
10,336ft

Obsidian
Cliff

Howard Eaton
Trail

Mt Washburn
10,243ft

River

Grand
Canyon
of
the
Yellowstone

Mirror

Plateau

Specimen
Ridge Trail

Roaring
Mountain

Dunraven
Pass

Lamar
River
Trail

NORRIS

CANYON

To Ashton,
Idaho

NORRIS GEYSER BASIN

Canyon Village

Norris

Virginia
Cascade

Lower
Falls

Range

Madison
Junction

Hayden
Valley

Howard
Eaton
Trail

Lehardy
Rapids

Pelican Cone

North
Absaroka
Wilderness

MADISON

Pelican   Valley

To Cody

Lower Geyser
Basin

Mary
Mountain
Trail

MUD
VOLCANO

Absaroka

Midway
Geyser
Basin

Lake Village

FISHING BRIDGE
RV PARK

Lake
Butte

PAHASKA
TEPEE

Upper
Geyser
Basin

North Shore Trail

BRIDGE
BAY

Bridge Bay

Avalanche Peak
10,566ft

EAST
ENTRANCE

Old Faithful

Craig
Pass

Yellowstone
Lake

Sylvan
Pass

14   16

20

SLEEPING
GIANT

Continental

Firehole River

Divide

West
Thumb

GRANT
VILLAGE

Park
Pt

Mt Doane
10,352ft

Mt Langford
10,774ft

Eagle Creek
Trail

Shoshone
Lake

Delacy
Creek
Trail

Grant
Village

Frank
Island

Mt Stevenson
10,352ft

Washakie
Wilderness

Lewis
Lake

Continental

Thorofare
Trail

Eagle Peak
11,358ft

Eagle Pass

LEWIS
LAKE

Heart
Lake

Two
Ocean
Plateau

Table Mtn
11,063ft

Shoshone
Lake Trail

Bechler River

Pitchstone
Plateau

Lewis
Falls

Mountain
Creek Trail

Lewis R.

Mt Sheridan
10,308ft

Trail
Creek
Trail

Yellowstone

Pitchstone
Plateau
Trail

Heart
Lake
Trail

Snake River
Trail

Snake

Two Ocean
Plateau
Trail

Divide

Moose
Falls

River

THOROFARE
RANGER
STATION

10 mi

SOUTH
ENTRANCE

John D.
Rockefeller Jr
Mem. Parkway

89 191 287

Bridger-Teton
National Forest

South Boundary
Trail

Teton
Wilderness

River

10 km

GRASSY   LAKE   RD

To Jackson

FLAGG RANCH

© AVALON TRAVEL

drive the animals down to lower elevations, where they find easier winter grazing.

A 20-year road construction project designed to improve Yellowstone's notoriously potholed roads commenced in 2001. Much (though not all) of the work is done at night, causing regular nighttime road closures. Check with the park if you plan to drive through at night; recorded road information is available at 307/344-2117 and updates are posted on the park website.

THE LAND

Six hundred thousand years ago, a volcano erupted from the deep magma pocket underlying Yellowstone and left an immense hole, or caldera, gaping in the central part of what is now the park. Subsequent lava flows filled the caldera, and glaciers refined the landscape, carving out Yellowstone Lake.

The Madison and Gallatin Ranges are to the west and north of Yellowstone Park's high plateau; the Absaroka Range is off to the east. South of Yellowstone, in Wyoming, the Tetons shoot to 12,000 feet.

Plants and Animals

The wide range of habitats in Yellowstone can be broken down into ecological zones: The aquatic zone is home to trout, beavers, moose, eagles, ospreys, and otters. Low grasslands include rabbits, badgers, pronghorn, and in the winter, elk and bison. Forests contain elk, mule deer, mountain lions, and coyotes. The huge fires of 1988 have played a crucial part in the lodgepole pine's life cycle (their resinous cones require fire to release the seeds), and burned areas are now carpeted by midsummer wildflowers and a lush growth of trees. A climax forest of Engelmann spruce and subalpine fir and areas of alpine tundra top off the park's ecological zones. Elk, deer, and bears are attracted to the edges between high meadows and forests.

Yellowstone National Park cannot be thought of as a distinct entity. Surrounding areas are also part of the ecosystem, and the tendency of animals to naturally walk across unnatural park boundaries can be a source of conflict. The reintroduction of wolves into Yellowstone made area ranchers famously uneasy. Wolves were exterminated in the early 1900s because of their predatory nature. Without their predation, the population of other animals in the park, notably elk, burgeoned. The reintroduction of breeding wolf packs in the park met with everything from enthusiasm to fear that wolves would

elk in Yellowstone

make the park unsafe for children. However, the reintroduction has been a great success, and there has never been a serious wolf attack on humans in North America. The best wolf viewing is in the Lamar Valley, during the early morning hours.

INFORMATION

The **Yellowstone Association** (406/848-2400, www.yellowstoneassociation.org) sells books in park visitors centers, and it runs the **Yellowstone Association Institute,** a field school with classes ranging from Yellowstone history to wildlife photography to fly-fishing, including many day hikes and longer backpacking trips. The institute's field campus is based in the old "Buffalo Ranch" in the Lamar Valley.

For good information concerning issues affecting the entire Yellowstone ecosystem, contact the **Greater Yellowstone Coalition** (406/586-1593, www.greateryellowstone.org).

Within the park, **Xanterra** (307/344-7311 or 866/439-7375, www.travelyellowstone.com) is the sole concessionaire, providing all lodging and dining.

WEST YELLOWSTONE AND VICINITY

The site of a stiff competition between nature and motel space, West Yellowstone (pop. 1,300, elev. 6,666 feet) is the west entrance to the park. Here you'll find all the tourist schlock you'd ever want to see, and experience the out-of-doors purveyed as recreation, a commodity that'll bring people here and make them spend money. But never mind. It's great country, and if mass tourism gets you down, come in the off-season (spring) and share the place with buffalo grazing on south-facing hills, huge crows, relaxed locals, and false-fronted buildings shut down until the crowds return.

Sights

Trains once brought most visitors to Yellowstone National Park, and the **Yellowstone Historic Center** (104 Yellowstone Ave., 406/646-1100, www.yellowstonehistoriccenter.org, 9am-9pm daily Memorial Day-Labor Day, 9am-6pm daily Labor Day-early Oct. and mid-late May; $6 adults, $5 seniors, $3 teens and students, $2 children 12 and under) is housed in the old Union Pacific Railroad Depot and has exhibits on the park's history, from those railroad days up to the regeneration following the fires of 1988. The bookstore here is worth a browse; it has a strong regional section and a good selection of field guides.

Just outside the national park entrance, a huge statue of a bear heralds the entrance to the nonprofit **Grizzly and Wolf Discovery Center** (201 S. Canyon, 406/646-7001 or 800/257-2570, www.grizzlydiscoveryctr.org, 8:30am-dusk daily, $11.50 adults, $10.75 seniors, $6.50 children 5-12). The center has gathered orphaned or "problem" bears from all over the world and confined them with fences and moats to provide a walk-through wildlife-viewing experience. The center also houses a small gray wolf pack (all of the wolves were born in captivity) in a one-acre compound. The center really does put a strong focus on education, and the animals are fascinating to watch; although it's essentially an upscale zoo, it's worth a visit if you're not in a rush to get into the park.

The **Yellowstone IMAX theater** (101 S. Canyon St., 406/646-4100 or 888/854-5862, www.yellowstoneimax.com, 9am-9pm daily, call or check website for off-season hours, $9 adults, $8.50 seniors, $6.50 children) features an eye-popping presentation on Yellowstone's natural history on a six-story screen. Movies start on the hour. But remember not to let the just-like-being-there quality of IMAX keep you from actually *being* in the park.

Fishing

West Yellowstone is a good hub for fishing the area's trout streams. The Madison, both in and out of the park, is the most celebrated river, but there are smaller streams worth fishing: Grayling, Duck, and Cougar Creeks, and the South Fork of the Madison. Inside the park, the Firehole River is a favorite of many anglers. Venture into nearby Idaho and try Henry's Fork of the Snake River. Fishing season gets going on Memorial Day weekend (except on Yellowstone Lake and its tributary streams, where the season opens June 15) and runs through the first Sunday of November. State fishing licenses aren't needed inside the park, but a Yellowstone fishing permit, available from any park visitors center or ranger station ($15 for three days) is required.

If you need someone to initiate you into the mysteries of fly-fishing, find a guide to be your guru. Even experienced anglers can benefit from a guide's knowledge of local conditions. They don't come cheap, however; expect to pay at least $400 a day for a guided float or wading trip. **Bud Lilly's Trout Shop** (39 Madison Ave., 406/646-7801, www.budlillys.com) employs some of West Yellowstone's best guides. **Madison River Outfitters** (117 Canyon St., 406/646-9644, www.madisonriveroutfitters.com) is another good source of fishing expertise in West Yellowstone, as are **Jacklin's** (105 Yellowstone Ave., 406/646-7336, www.jacklinsflyshop.com) and **Arrick's** (37 Canyon St., 406/646-7290, www.arricks.com).

Other Summer Recreation

Rent bikes from **Freeheel and Wheel** (40 Yellowstone Ave., 406/646-7744, www.freeheelandwheel.com). The **Rendezvous Cross-Country Ski Trails** (www.rendezvousskitrails.com) are well suited to summer mountain biking. A bicycling and walking route runs along the old Union Pacific rail bed from West Yellowstone to Island Park, Idaho.

To find a horse for hire, head seven miles west of town on Highway 20 (the Targhee Pass Highway) toward the Idaho border. There you'll find guided rides at **Diamond P Ranch** (2865 Targhee Pass Hwy., 406/646-7246, www.thediamondpranch.com). Eight miles north of town, at the junction of Highways 191 and 287, **Yellowstone Mountain Guides**

(406/646-7230, www.yellowstone-guides.com) runs trail rides; they also offer overnight pack trips, photo trips, and fly-fishing.

Winter Recreation

During the winter, the only ways into the park from this direction are via cross-country skis, snowshoes, snowmobile, or snowcoach. Rent snowshoes or cross-country skis from **Freeheel and Wheel** (40 Yellowstone Ave., 406/646-7744, www.freeheelandwheel.com).

Snowcoaches—customized 10-passenger vans with treads—ferry passengers to Old Faithful and other thermal basins. **Yellowstone Alpen Guides** (555 Yellowstone Ave., 406/646-9591 or 800/858-3502, www.yellowstoneguides.com, $125 adults, $120 seniors, $115 children under 16, does not include park entrance fee) runs several snowcoach tours, including one with a bit of cross-country skiing worked in. **Yellowstone Expeditions** (406/646-9333 or 800/728-9333, www.yellowstoneexpeditions.com, snowcoach trips $100 adults, $80 children) runs cross-country ski, snowshoe, and snowcoach trips in the park, including multiday ski and snowshoe trips using comfy yurts as a base camp.

The **Rendezvous Cross-Country Ski Trails** (www.rendezvousskitrails.com) comprise 15 miles of trails groomed for both traditional cross-country and freestyle (skating) skiing. The trailhead is just off Yellowstone Avenue, about three blocks west of Canyon Street. Loops can be selected according to skill and stamina, and for that special Montana touch, there's a biathlon loop for gun-slinging skiers.

The **Riverside trails** start where Madison Avenue ends (at Boundary). These trails aren't as meticulously groomed as those at Rendezvous, but they offer a little more scenic punch. The trail network goes right into the park, where it runs along the Madison River. It's easy skiing, with a basic trip of about 2.5 miles. There's a good chance of seeing wildlife from these trails.

Snowmobiling has long been a major

wintertime activity in West Yellowstone. After years of hand-wringing about how to limit snowmobile use of Yellowstone, the park has imposed limits on the number of snowmobiles allowed in the park and requires snowmobilers to be part of guided trips, which run around $200. Join a tour with **Yellowstone Vacations** (415 Yellowstone Ave., 406/646-9564, www.yellowstonevacations.com), **Two Top Snowmobile Rentals** (645 Gibbon Ave., 406/646-7802 or 800/522-7802, www.two-topsnowmobile.com), or **Yellowstone Adventures** (131 Dunraven St., 406/646-7735 or 800/231-5991, www.yellowstoneadventures.com). Also, many hotels and motels rent snowmobiles; ask when you make reservations. Expect snowmobile rentals to run $115-150 per day, with an additional $45 or so guide fee.

Entertainment

The **Playmill Theater** (29 Madison Ave., 406/646-7757, www.playmill.com, $19.50 adults, reservations recommended) runs family-oriented shows on summer evenings.

Events

The early March **Rendezvous Marathon Ski Race** (http://rendezvousrace.com) brings hundreds of cross-country skiers to town. A winter festival has sprung up around this event, which is shortly followed by the **World Snowmobile Expo** (http://snowmobileexpo.com). The spring months, when the park is closed for road plowing, are relatively quiet in West Yellowstone. During the first two weeks of April, Yellowstone's roads are open to bicycle and pedestrian traffic but not to cars. Everything is usually up and going again by mid-April.

Accommodations

Most of West Yellowstone's "downtown" motels are family-run places that have been around for years. Some of the smaller places shut down in the winter; others have lower winter rates.

UNDER $100

The most distinctive budget rooms in town are the hostel rooms at the **Madison Hotel** (139 Yellowstone, 406/646-7745 or 800/838-7745, www.madisonhotelmotel.com, Memorial Day-mid-Oct., $36-159), a log-hewn cross between an old downtown hotel and a youth hostel built in 1912 and relatively little changed since then. Hostel rooms provide bunks at $36, while private rooms run $85 double, with a shared bath. The rooms at the adjacent Madison Motel are less charming but equipped with TVs and bathrooms, and run $99-159. (Check-in for both locations is in the gift shop.)

Moving up the scale a bit, the small and centrally located **Alpine Motel** (120 Madison Ave., 406/646-7544, www.alpinemotelwestyellowstone.com, May-Oct., $89-169) offers basic rooms (no phones) near the park entrance. The **Pony Express Motel** (at Firehole St. and Boundary St., 800/323-9708, www.yellowstonevacations.com, $79-189) is a simple budget motel on a side street close to the park; pets are accepted here.

The **Lazy G** (123 Hayden St., 406/646-7586, www.lazygmotel.com, $89-131), on a quiet street a few blocks off the main drag, has in-room refrigerators and an outdoor eating area with a gas grill and picnic tables.

Another small mom-and-pop courtyard motel is the **One Horse Motel** (216 Dunraven St., 406/646-7677, www.onehorsemotel.com, $79-145). Again, it's nothing fancy, but it's a convenient base.

OVER $100

Moose Creek Inn (220 Firehole Ave., 406/646-9546, www.moosecreekinn.com, $140-210) has both a newer inn and cute older log cabins with kitchenettes; larger units are available to house families.

Near the park entrance, **City Center Motel** (214 Madison Ave., 800/742-0665, www.yellowstonevacations.com, $109-149) is a older motel with a budget ambience.

Set just off a busy street, the **Yellowstone Inn** (601 Hwy. 20, 406/646-7633 or

800/858-9224, www.yellowstoneinn.net, $105-166) is a small inn with nicely decorated cabin-style units, many with full kitchens. Pets are allowed here.

For comfortable rooms in a newer motel, the **Yellowstone Lodge** (251 S. Electric St., 406/646-0200 or 877/239-9298, www.yellowstonelodge.com, $199-219) is a good bet. It's a few blocks from downtown, near the Rendezvous ski trails, and has an indoor pool.

The **Stage Coach Inn** (209 Madison Ave., 406/646-7381 or 800/842-2882, www.yellowstoneinn.com, $229-279) is a West Yellowstone classic with a historic lodge atmosphere and a great lobby. There's a hot tub and sauna here, and during the winter it's a hub for snowcoach tours.

Three Bear Lodge (217 Yellowstone Ave., 406/646-7353 or 800/646-7353, www.threebearlodge.com, $179-289) is a popular lodging, with both lodge and motel rooms and a pool. After the lodge sustained a fire several years ago, it was rebuilt using as many salvaged materials as possible, The lodge also runs snowmobile, snowcoach, and van tours of the park.

For more luxury, stay at the **Bar N Ranch** (890 Buttermilk Creek Rd., 406/646-0300, www.bar-n-ranch.com, $220-550), with lodge rooms, cabins, and a good restaurant in a pretty setting outside of town.

Camping

The campgrounds in the town of West Yellowstone are mostly for RVs, although **Rustic Wagon RV Park** (637 Hwy. 20 W., 406/646-7387, www.rusticwagonrv.com, $46-50 RV, $39 tent), **Wagon Wheel RV Park** (408 Gibbon Ave., 406/646-7872, www.wagonwheelrv.com, $46-50 RV, $39 tent), and **Hideaway RV Park** (320 Electric St., 406/646-9049, http://hideawayrv.com, $34-39 RV, $24 tent) reserve some space for tent campers. The Rustic Wagon and the Wagon Wheel also have cabins for rent (about $60).

Bakers Hole (Hebgen Lake Ranger Station, 406/823-6961, www.fs.usda.gov/gallatin, mid-May-mid-Sept., $14) is the closest public campground to West Yellowstone. It's just three miles north of town on Highway 191. Blue herons nest on the Madison River just across from the campground.

The **Gallatin National Forest** (406/823-6961, www.fs.usda.gov/gallatin) rents rustic (no electricity or bathrooms) cabins for $30-35 per night at **Beaver Creek, Cabin Creek,** and **Basin Station.**

Food

Start your day with the friendly folks at **Mocha Mamma's** (40 Yellowstone, 406/646-7744, 9am-7pm Sun.-Thurs., 9am-8pm Fri.-Sat.), a coffee bar inside the Freeheel and Wheel bike shop. If you want a full breakfast, the **Running Bear Pancake House** (538 Madison Ave., 406/646-7703, www.runningbearph.com, 6:30am-2pm daily, $6-11) is a longtime local favorite.

For a good to-go deli sandwich, swing by **Ernie's Deli** (406 Hwy. 20, 406/646-9467, www.erniesbakery.com, 7am-2pm daily, $7-12).

★ **Cafe Madriz** (311 Canyon St., 11am-2pm and 4pm-10pm Mon.-Sat. mid-May-Sept., tapas $7-19), a small and very popular restaurant toward the north edge of town, serves Spanish-style tapas, both hot and cold, as well as paella ($37 for two people).

Step out onto the main drag for the slowly cooked meats from **Beartooth Barbeque** (111 Canyon Ave., 406/646-4252, noon-10pm daily, $10-27).

Even when everything else is closed in town, you'll probably be able to get dinner at **Bullwinkle's** (115 Canyon St., 406/646-7974, http://yellowstonebullwinkles.com, 10am-2am daily, $10-29), a saloon and restaurant with a wide-ranging menu, a friendly atmosphere in the bar, a surprising number of good wines by the glass, and several Montana beers on tap.

Information and Services

The **chamber of commerce** (30 Yellowstone Ave., 406/646-7701, www.destinationyellowstone.com) has the expected array of brochures and a friendly staff. During the summer, rangers from **Yellowstone National Park** have an outpost in the chamber of commerce information center. The **Hebgen Lake Ranger Station** (406/646-7369, www.fs.usda.gov/gallatin), just north of West Yellowstone on Highway 191, can provide information on the nearby Gallatin National Forest. **Gallatin National Forest Avalanche Center** (406/587-6981, www.mtavalanche.com) posts daily avalanche reports outside the post office during the winter.

Find a **medical clinic** (406/646-9441) at 11 South Electric Street.

Getting There and Around

West Yellowstone Airport is open during the summer, but it's often easier (and cheaper) to fly into Bozeman and rent a car there. **Karst Stage** (406/388-6404 or 800/845-2778, www.karststage.com, $95 one-way, reservations required) runs a shuttle between the Bozeman airport and West Yellowstone. **Buffalo Bus Lines** (406/646-9564 or 800/426-7669, www.yellowstonenationalparktour.com, from $70 adult, $54 child) runs tours through the park.

To rent a car in West Yellowstone, contact **Big Sky Car Rental** (415 Yellowstone Ave., 406/646-9564, www.bigskycarrental.com).

Budget (406/646-5156) has an office at the airport.

MADISON JUNCTION

From West Yellowstone, follow the Madison River into the park. This is one of Yellowstone's premier fishing areas—the warm water of the Firehole River joins the cooler Gibbon River at Madison Junction, providing an ideal trout habitat.

Between Madison Junction and Norris Geyser Basin, the road follows the Gibbon River. Stop at 84-foot **Gibbon Falls.** Like Madison Junction, the falls perch on the edge of the main Yellowstone caldera.

★ NORRIS GEYSER BASIN

Yellowstone's most spectacular and changeable thermal area, Norris Geyser Basin may not be as well known as Old Faithful, but it's far more atmospheric and a better place to actually hike past numerous geysers and boiling pools.

Norris is situated over the junction of two major faults (one that runs down from Mammoth Hot Springs and another coming over from Hebgen Lake). These crustal cracks provide conduits for heat to rise to the earth's

visitors to Norris Geyser Basin

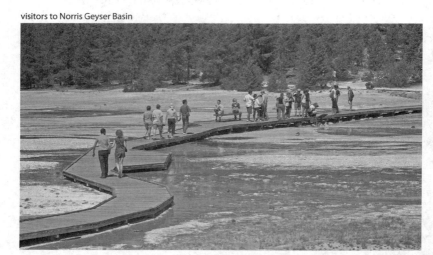

surface. Steam vents, hot springs, and geysers are all manifestations of this surface heat.

Sights

Between 1886 and 1916, when the army ran Yellowstone, some troops were based at the remote Norris outpost. The old Soldier Station has been renovated and now houses the **Museum of the National Park Ranger** (307/344-7353, 9am-5pm summer). History buffs and fans of rustic architecture will enjoy this stop, but for most people, time is better spent hiking around the geyser basin.

Stop in at the **Norris Geyser Basin Museum** (307/344-2812, 9am-6pm summer), located 0.25 mile east of Norris Junction to learn more about geothermal geology and ecology. Pick up a map of Norris's trail system and strike out through steam clouds, whiffs of sulfur, spurts of water, and brilliantly colored mineral deposits. Because the landscape here is relatively malleable, the map and signposts may not include all of the current thermal activity, but this unpredictability is part of Norris's charm. Be careful, stay on the trail, but do explore at least one of the two loops.

The path around **Porcelain Basin** is less than one mile long but has expansive pale (porcelain-hued) views of terraced hot springs and geysers. The more forested **Back Basin** loop is about 1.5 miles long and passes a near-boiling pure green spring that takes its color from the combination of the blue spring water and the yellow sulfur of the basin wall. **Steamboat Geyser,** which has rare 300-foot-high eruptions (and more frequent minor spurts), is also on the Back Basin loop.

Camping

Norris Campground (late May-late Sept., $20) is just across the road from the geyser basin and has a few walk-in tent sites. **Madison Campground** (reservations available at 866/439-7375, May-Oct., $21.50) is a large campground between Norris and West Yellowstone. Between Norris and Mammoth, there's camping at **Indian Creek** (mid-June-mid-Sept., $15, no flush toilets).

MAMMOTH HOT SPRINGS AND VICINITY

The grand arch leading into Yellowstone from Gardiner, dedicated by Theodore Roosevelt in 1903, was the original entrance to the park and is still the only entrance open to cars year-round.

Elk winter around Mammoth, spending much of their time, it seems, in the hotel parking lot.

Sights

Stop by the recently renovated **Albright visitors center** (307/344-2263, 8am-7pm May-Sept., 9am-5pm Oct.-Apr.) for general information and to view exhibits on the park's wildlife and cultural history. Pick up fishing or backcountry permits at the backcountry office here.

A boardwalk climbs the terraced hot pools. The pools are not static; as the flow of hot groundwater through limestone changes, so do the formations. Groundwater combines with burps of carbon dioxide from underground magma to form carbonic acid, which dissolves limestone. Limey carbonated water emerges from the ground at Mammoth Hot Springs, and the lime is deposited as travertine. Thermophilic bacteria and algae live in the hot water, tinting the white travertine with their brilliant colors. Pick up a brochure at the foot of the trail to take the self-guided tour of the springs. Take care to stay on the boardwalk; the hot pools are frequently boiling hot, and they may have very thin crusts around them. People and animals have died in these thermal pools.

The U.S. Army was the park's original overseer, and its old headquarters, Fort Yellowstone, is behind the visitors center. It has been used as the **National Park Service Headquarters** for the park since 1918.

During the summer, the Mammoth campground amphitheater is the site of nightly **talks by park rangers.**

For a roadside glimpse of the park, try Xanterra's **Yellowstone in a Day bus tour** (307/344-7311 or 866/439-7375, www.

travelyellowstone.com, $84 adults, $42 ages 3-11). Call ahead or sign up at the activities desk in the Mammoth Hotel; buses leave at 8am daily. Xanterra also offers tours in historic yellow buses (no, not school buses); from Mammoth they go on early morning wildlife-spotting trips in the **Lamar Valley** (6:15am-11:30am, $83 adults, $41.50 children 3-11).

Midway between Mammoth and Tower Junction, the **Blacktail Plateau** offers both a scenic drive and hiking trails. Follow the dirt road through grasslands and along a stretch of the old Bannock Trail, used by the Bannock tribe to cross from present-day Idaho to the eastern plains.

Mammoth's steaming pools and ghostly white terraces are particularly appealing in the winter, when it's not unusual to see elk lying in the hot pools. **Snowcoach tours** (307/344-7311, www.travelyellowstone. com, $93.50 adults, $46.75 children) leave Mammoth and head to Old Faithful.

Recreation

Hot springs empty into the Gardiner River at the 45th parallel, and this is one place where hot springs bathing is sanctioned. The parking lot is just over the state line in Montana. It's about a five-minute walk down the path to the springs, which are officially open 8am-6pm Remember to bring a bathing suit.

Register for **trail rides** at the Mammoth Hotel activities desk. A one-hour ride costs $42.

During the winter, the Mammoth Hotel opens an ice rink and rents **ice skates, cross-country skis,** and **snowshoes.** Guided ski tours are available, as is a **snowcoach shuttle service** ($21-31) to other areas of the park.

Accommodations

Mammoth Hot Springs Hotel (307/344-7311, www.travelyellowstone.com, May-early Oct. and mid-Dec.-early Mar.) has both hotel rooms ($129 with private bath, $90 shared bath, $479 suite) and cabins ($145-239 with bath, $89-172 without). As in all national park lodges, the rooms are fairly simple, with no TVs, telephones, or air-conditioning; there's a fee for Wi-Fi.

Camping

The campground at Mammoth is small by local standards—only 85 sites. It's open year-round and costs $20 per night; no reservations are taken. Showers are available for a couple of bucks at the Mammoth Hotel.

Travertine formations at Mammoth contain some very hot springs.

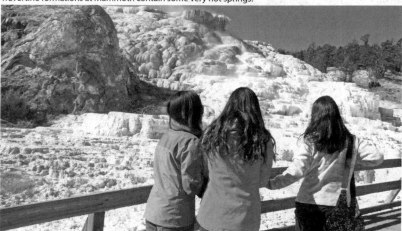

Food

Mammoth Hotel Dining Room (6:30am-
10am, 11:30am-2:30pm, 5pm-10pm daily, $14-
29) is open during the hotel's summer and
winter seasons (during winter, dinner service ends at 9pm and reservations are recommended). Dinners are pretty good, and small
plates such as bison or trout tacos are available for less than $15. Although many visi-
tors chow down on the breakfast buffet ($13),
the menu items are tastier. The **Terrace Grill**
(7am-9pm daily June-Sept., $4-7) offers burg-
ers, sandwiches, and ice cream in the same
complex, and the atmosphere is decidedly
casual. The grill shuts down from mid-October until the end of April; spring and fall
hours are shorter and somewhat variable. The
Mammoth General Store offers basic foodstuffs year-round. Remember, you didn't come
to Yellowstone for a culinary experience.

Information and Services

General park information is dispensed at
the **Albright Visitor Center** in Mammoth
(307/344-2263, 8am-7pm May-Sept., 9am-
5pm Oct.-Apr.).

The **Mammoth Hot Springs Clinic**
(307/344-7965) is near the visitors center.

The main Yellowstone **post office** is to the
side of the Park Service administration building in Mammoth. Foreign currency can be ex-
changed at the front desk of any Yellowstone
hotel.

TOWER JUNCTION AND VICINITY

Tower Junction is where the Mammoth-
Cooke City road is joined by the road to
Yellowstone Canyon. There's a small settle-
ment here: a ranger station, a lodge with cab-
ins, and a campground three miles south at
Tower Falls.

Tower Falls

The falls, nestled into a rocky gorge, are a popular sight. A more meditative viewing is often
afforded by taking the short but steep hike to
the bottom. Bannock Indians found a safe
place to cross the Yellowstone River just above
the falls; it's now referred to as Bannock Ford.

★ Lamar Valley

Elk and bison winter in the Lamar Valley,
east of Tower Junction. Coyotes are also commonly spotted jogging across the valley floor,
and this is usually the best place in the park
to see wolves. The wolves, which were reintroduced into Yellowstone in 1995, now number

THE MISSOURI HEADWATERS
YELLOWSTONE NATIONAL PARK

A mother bison nurses her calf in the middle of the road in Lamar Valley.

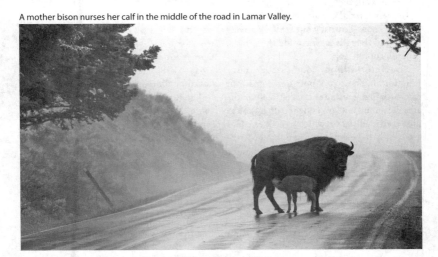

about 400-450 in the Greater Yellowstone Ecosystem, and several packs frequent the Lamar Valley. Get up *early* if you really want to see a wolf (dawn is the best viewing time) and be aware that the local wolves are way larger than the more common coyotes and range in color from almost blond to jet-black. Bring along a spotting scope or a good pair of binoculars and consider enrolling in a class with the **Yellowstone Association Institute** (406/848-2400, www.yellowstone-association.org), which bases its summertime field seminars on Yellowstone's wolves in the Lamar Valley; lodging is available for course participants in simple guest cabins.

Recreation

The **Buffalo Plateau Trail** swings north of the park into Montana on its 21-mile run from the trailhead three miles west of Tower Junction to Slough Creek Campground. It's best to wait until late July for this hike because the varied terrain includes Slough Creek, which can be difficult to cross when it's carrying lots of water. **Slough Creek Campground** is also the trailhead for an 11-mile hike (or wintertime cross-country ski trip) up Slough Creek to the northern edge of the park. Hikers should also check with park rangers to learn about current trail conditions.

In the winter, the road to Tower Falls becomes a **cross-country ski trail.** A private viewing of the falls is worth the three-mile, generally uphill slog.

Specimen Ridge, southeast of Tower Junction, is home to a petrified forest—in fact, petrified forests are stacked deep in this area. The mud and ash coughed up by volcanoes provided soil on which new trees could grow, only to be covered when the next volcano erupted. Erosion has uncovered some of the top layers; it's conjectured that 44 layers of forest exist. Naturalists lead daylong hikes on Specimen Ridge during July and August; details are available at any park visitors center.

Horseback rides leave from the Roosevelt corrals several times daily. One-hour rides cost $42; ride two hours for $63.

Accommodations

There's an emphasis on things Western at **Roosevelt Lodge** (307/344-7311, www.travelyellowstone.com, early June-Labor Day, $74 rustic cabin with a wood-burning stove but no bath, $124 cabin with bath). Stagecoach rides leave several times a day for a half-hour tour ($12 adults, $6 children 3-11), and cookouts at nearby Yancey's Hole involve a horseback or stagecoach journey.

Camping

Nearby campgrounds include **Tower Falls,** open late May-September; **Slough Creek,** open mid-June to early October; and **Pebble Creek,** open mid-June through September, $15, no reservations accepted.

Food

If you want a meal that's longer on experience than on cuisine, try the **Old West Dinner Cookout** (307/344-7311 or 866/439-7375). Jump on a horse or climb into a church wagon at Roosevelt Lodge and ride to Yancey's Hole for a slab of steak and other picnic fare. Dinner and an hour-long horseback ride cost $76 ($66 children 8-11). Wagon riders pay $57 ($46 for children).

The **Roosevelt Lodge** (307/344-7311 or 866/439-7375, 7am-10am, 11:30am-9:30pm, early June-Labor Day, dinner $10-26) prides itself on the barbecued ribs and baked beans served at its family-style restaurant.

Billings and Southeastern Montana

Look for ★ to find recommended sights, activities, dining, and lodging.

Highlights

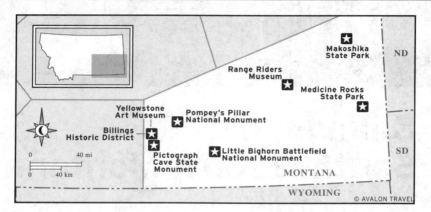

★ **Billings Historic District:** Once the center of Billings, the old hotels and storefronts on Montana Avenue were largely derelict until reborn as art galleries and upscale nightclubs (page 280).

★ **Yellowstone Art Museum:** This regional art museum features both historic and contemporary Western art, plus a shop for local crafts (page 281).

★ **Pictograph Cave State Monument:** Prehistoric Native Americans etched figures onto cave walls at this archaeological site overlooking Billings (page 283).

★ **Pompey's Pillar National Monument:** In 1806 the Corps of Discovery climbed this bluff, and William Clark carved his name in the rock (page 292).

★ **Range Riders Museum:** This museum tells the story of Miles City from Custer-era fort to cow capital of the West (page 295).

★ **Medicine Rocks State Park:** The eerie sandstone promontories at this park were sacred to the Native Americans of the prairies (page 297).

★ **Makoshika State Park:** This badlands park preserves a stark wilderness of gumbo buttes, eroded rock, and prehistoric fossils (page 301).

★ **Little Bighorn Battlefield National Monument:** One of the country's epochal battles, the Battle of the Little Bighorn is recounted here in chilling detail (page 310).

HERE
LIES
Lester Moore
FOUR SLUGS
FROM A 44
NO LES
NO MORE

Southeastern Montana is the most "Western" of Montana's regions. Historically, it is the West of the early trapper and hunter and of the clash between Native Americans and infantry. It was the Montana of the cattle drover and the

great cattle barons. Today, it is still home to thousands of American Indians, and it is still unashamedly cowboy country.

The Yellowstone River is the locus of the entire region. As the river moves eastward through the prairies, it picks up the waters of three major southerly tributaries: the Bighorn, the Tongue, and the Powder. As it discharges into the Missouri, the Yellowstone is the largest free-flowing river in the United States.

As the principal avenue of entry and exit in Montana during the pioneer days, the Yellowstone took out the region's wealth of furs, brought in soldiers, and transported cattle and sheep to eastern markets. Miles City, Glendive, and Billings grew up on its banks as railroads extended up the valley.

The dominant social unit in southeastern Montana today is still the working ranch and family farm, and the same Yellowstone Valley

towns are still the center of trade, shopping, and social life. This is about as real as the West gets, but it's not a Western theme park. Southeastern Montana is not a highly developed tourist destination, but for the traveler with patience, a sense of humor, and an interest in wildlife, pristine landscapes, Native America, and the lore of the West, this corner of Montana has few equals.

PLANNING YOUR TIME

Most travelers will explore southeast Montana along I-90 and I-94, which traverse the region. I-94 enters the state at **Wibaux,** a small ranch town with a rather splendid French-influenced stone church and a long history that brings together French nobility and Teddy Roosevelt. I-94 meets the Yellowstone River at Glendive, where scenic and austere badlands are preserved in **Makoshika State Park.** I-94 then follows

---

Previous: Billings skyline; bison. **Above:** Boothill Cemetery in Billings.

the Yellowstone through a badland-rimmed valley to **Miles City.** Founded as a military fort after the Battle of the Little Bighorn, Miles City became the center of the cattle trade for the entire northern Great Plains for many years, and it's still unabashedly a town where the Old West spirit lives on. The **Range Riders Museum** tells the story of the region's long and eventful history. The Wild West isn't all history in Miles City: Late May's **Bucking Horse Sale** is a cross between a rodeo and a bacchanal that truly brings the cowboy spirit to life. A clutch of newer hotels at I-94 exit 138 makes this a good spot to spend the night.

As I-94 passes west along the Yellowstone toward Billings, a flat-topped butte rises from the irrigated fields of corn and alfalfa. **Pompey's Pillar,** now a national monument, was a landmark noted by William Clark as he passed down the Yellowstone in 1806—he even carved his name on the hill's soft sandstone walls. Stop and explore the landscape and hike to view Clark's autograph—one of the few physical remnants of the Lewis and Clark Expedition.

Billings is Montana's largest city and a good base for exploring southeastern Montana. The downtown area has several good restaurants, busy watering holes, and cultural institutions like the **Yellowstone Art Museum** and the **Western Heritage Center.** Just outside of Billings is **Pictograph Caves State Park,** which preserves ancient Native American cave drawings.

I-90 enters southeastern Montana from the south and passes just below the **Little Bighorn Battlefield National Monument.** One of the most disturbing and resonant sites in all of Montana, the battlefield has a good visitors center and historic drives that interpret the calamitous events of June 1876. The actual battle site still feels profoundly haunted. If you visit in late June, consider attending **Custer's Last Stand Reenactment,** the centerpiece of a weekend's worth of events in and around Hardin called **Little Bighorn Days.**

HISTORY

The Yellowstone Valley was the ancient hunting grounds for Native Americans, especially the Crow Nation. The valleys of the Yellowstone and the rivers that feed it were rich with game and furs, and the prairies that adjoined the rivers teemed with buffalo. As the Sioux and Cheyenne were forced into this corner of Montana, fierce intertribal rivalries flared.

The Yellowstone was not explored by easterners until 1806, during Lewis and Clark's return voyage. Clark and his party floated most of the way down the river in dugout canoes. Upon reaching the confluence with the Missouri, he noted that because of the enormous abundance of game along the Yellowstone, the valley would be advantageous for a trading post.

Within a year, at the mouth of the Bighorn, near present-day Custer, traders erected the territory's first structures. Beginning with Fort Ramon, established by Manuel Lisa in 1807 and named after his infant son, and soon followed by other forts, this location drew adventurers and frontiersmen who came to trade, trap, and explore the wilderness.

Soon after, settlers moved in to exploit the rich Yellowstone country, and others, with gold prospecting in western Montana on their minds, followed the Bozeman Trail north to the Yellowstone Valley across Sioux and Cheyenne tribal land. The resulting conflicts with these tribes generated some of the most famous battles of the western Indian Wars, including the Battle of the Little Bighorn.

The eradication of the buffalo and the incarceration of the Native Americans left the prairies empty, but by 1880 huge herds of Texas cattle filled the "open range." The Northern Pacific Railway pressed up the Yellowstone Valley at the same time, bringing in settlers and establishing trade centers in Billings and Miles City. Homesteaders replaced cattle barons, but they made only a tentative impact on this vast and arid, almost hostile land. The coal and oil development of the last 40 years has done as much to change

Billings and Southeastern Montana

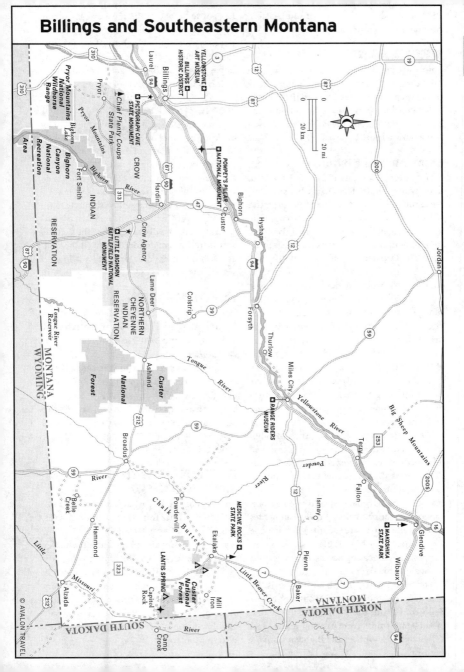

© AVALON TRAVEL

the landscape and character of southeastern Montana as a century of agriculture.

RECREATION

Southeastern Montana lacks the mountainous terrain of western Montana, but many outdoor enthusiasts return year after year to enjoy its wide-open spaces. In fact, in many smaller communities, the fall hunting season is the busiest tourist season.

Hunting and Fishing

Southeastern Montana is a hunter's dream. Trophy-size mule deer haunt brushy coulees, and game birds such as pheasant and wild turkeys are abundant. Elk, originally a prairie species, are increasingly common. Obtaining hunting access is relatively easy. The Department of Fish, Wildlife, and Parks's Region 7, which encompasses most of southeastern Montana, has the state's highest number of landowners signed up in the Block Management Program. The program opens and maintains access to 8.5 million acres of private land for recreational purposes. (A list of participating farmers and ranchers is available from the Department of Fish, Wildlife, and Parks office in Miles City or at http://fwp.mt.gov/hunting/hunterAccess/blockman/region7.) A number of ranchers run outfitting and guide services.

As the Yellowstone River winds through its wooded valley, it attracts anglers with its wealth of walleye, northern pike, smallmouth bass, ling, channel catfish, the occasional trout, and sauger. The river's lower reaches, especially near Glendive and Sidney, are home to the paddlefish. Public fishing sites on the Yellowstone are plentiful because the Department of Fish, Wildlife, and Parks is in the process of locating access areas every 12 miles along the river.

For trout fishers, the Bighorn River is the real news in southeastern Montana; below Yellowtail Dam, the Bighorn becomes one of the state's best trout-fishing areas, and Yellowtail Reservoir in the Bighorn Canyon has got to be one of the most awe-inspiring brown trout and walleye holes in the West. Because much of the Bighorn flows through the Crow Reservation, access is limited. The upper reaches of the Tongue River also provide good trout fishing.

Agate Hunting

The moss agates of the Yellowstone Valley are known around the world for their quality. Starting at the mouth of the Bighorn and continuing to its confluence with the Missouri, the Yellowstone passes through gravel beds rich with the semiprecious stones. It takes a trained eye to spot the yellowish matte exterior of an agate in the rough, but often the jostling of the river will have chipped the surface, and its translucent interior will be visible. Stop at a fishing-access area or along a bridge to search for agates.

INFORMATION

For general information on southeastern Montana, request the **Visit Southeast Montana guide** (800/346-1876, www.southeastmontana.com).

Find the **Custer National Forest offices** at 1310 Main Street in Billings (406/657-6361, www.fs.fed.us/r1/custer). Regional **Department of Fish, Wildlife, and Parks** offices are at 2300 Lake Elmo Drive in Billings (406/247-2940) and 352 I-94 Business Loop, Miles City (406/234-0900).

GETTING THERE AND AROUND

Billings has the largest airport in Montana (BIL), with service from Delta, United, Alaska, and Allegiant. **Cape Air** (800/227-3247, www.capeair.com) provides connections to smaller eastern Montana towns, including Miles City and Glendive. **Jefferson Lines** (800/255-7655, https://webstore.trailways.com) offers once-daily east-west service to the major towns along I-94 and I-90. You'll need an automobile to travel off the interstate in southeastern Montana.

Billings

Billings (elev. 3,117 feet) is Montana's largest city, with a population of nearly 165,000 in the greater urban area. Billings's physical setting is striking: The Rimrocks—sandstone cliffs several hundred feet high—ring the city; from them, five mountain ranges are visible. The Yellowstone Valley here is wide and green. Billings is primarily a sales and trade center, with oil refining and energy generation enlivening its economy.

Billings makes much of being the largest city in the vector north of Denver and between Spokane and Minneapolis, and boasts of being the capital of the "Midland Empire," a vague principality consisting of eastern Montana, northern Wyoming, the western Dakotas, and on an expansive day maybe even some of Canada's prairie provinces. Certainly, to judge by the license plates at the stockyards or at one

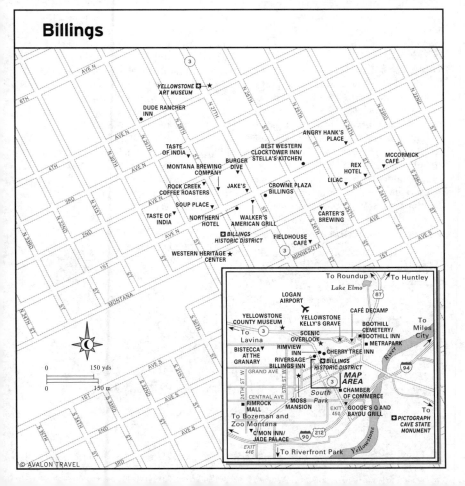

of the shopping malls, Billings is the service center for much of the northern plains. It's a city that is proud of its comparative wealth and growth, and as the center of a vast agricultural area, it has a strong sense of purpose and vitality.

Billings is also home to several institutions of higher learning including the state's oldest, Rocky Mountain College, founded in 1878. Rocky Mountain, affiliated with the United Methodist and Presbyterian Churches and the United Church of Christ, has 1,000 students. Montana State University at Billings, formerly Eastern Montana College, offers two- and four-year degrees to some 5,000 students.

SIGHTS
Tours of Billings

Get an entertaining overview of Billings's sights by taking the 1.5-hour **Montana Fun Adventure Bus** (406/254-7180 or 888/618-4386, www.montanafunadventures.com, 11:30am and 7pm Mon.-Fri., 2pm Sat.-Sun. June-Labor Day, 2pm daily Labor Day-May, $25 adult, $22 military, $15 children ages 7-15, 6 and under free). Stops include historic downtown Billings, Black Otter Trail on the Rimrocks, and Boothill. Tours begin at

the Moss Mansion at 914 Division Street. In addition to the standard introduction tour, daily van tours include options such as tours of local brewpubs, hat makers, and chocolatiers. In summer, guided tours are also offered to Little Bighorn Battlefield, Lewis and Clark sites, and other destinations in southeast Montana.

Downtown Billings
★ BILLINGS HISTORIC DISTRICT

The Billings Historic District stretches along **Montana Avenue** from 23rd to 26th Streets. Here, paralleling the old Northern Pacific tracks, is the heart of old Billings. Late-19th-century hotels and commercial buildings crowd in around themselves, and although the area is still filled with local color, so to speak, it's also filled with galleries, music clubs, and interesting restaurants. The bar and restaurant at the **Rex Hotel,** once frequented by Buffalo Bill Cody, is a major island of gentrification, as are the newly refurbished Northern Pacific Railway depot buildings. Other old hotels have been converted to art galleries, and others to jazz clubs and martini bars. This is one of the most diverse areas in Billings, which is otherwise a pretty conformist city.

Historic Montana Avenue is a hot spot for bars and restaurants.

WESTERN HERITAGE CENTER

The **Western Heritage Center** (2822 Montana Ave., 406/256-6809, www.ywhc.org, 10am-5pm Tues.-Sat., $5 adults, $3 students and seniors, $1 children under 12) is housed in the old Parmly Billings Library, built in 1901 by Frederick Billings in honor of his brother Parmly. The center is a museum of the history and culture of the Yellowstone Valley. Historical photos, period clothing, art, Western crafts, historic artifacts, and interpretive exhibits are featured.

★ YELLOWSTONE ART MUSEUM

The **Yellowstone Art Museum** (401 N. 27th Ave., 406/256-6804, www.artmuseum.org, 10am-5pm Tues.-Wed. and Sat., 10am-8pm Thurs.-Fri., 11am-4pm Sun., $6 adults, $3 students and children 6-18, under 6 free), housed in the old county jail, mounts up to 20 exhibits a year in its five galleries. Known by its acronym, YAM, the center is devoted to securing and displaying contemporary regional and Western art, although it houses international and historic pieces as well. Collections include photos of the Old West by L. A. Huffman and drawings and paintings by Will James and Charlie Russell; the collection

of contemporary Western art is significant. There's also a museum shop with local gifts and books.

MOSS MANSION

Just west of the downtown area is a district of beautiful old Victorian homes. Only one of these is open to the public, but for anyone interested in late-19th-century architecture, a walk along these streets (between Division and 3rd Streets, and Lewis and Yellowstone Streets) is a pleasant diversion.

The **Moss Mansion** (914 Division St., 406/256-5100, www.mossmansion.com, guided tours on the hour, 10am-4pm Tues.-Sat., Sun. 1pm-4pm Memorial Day-Labor Day [last tour at 3pm], 1pm-4 Tues.-Sun. Labor Day-Memorial Day [last tour at 3pm], $10 adults, $7 seniors and military, $6 ages 6-17, children 5 and under free) was built by an early Billings bank president who engaged Henry Hardenberg, the architect of the Waldorf-Astoria Hotel in New York City, to design his Billings home. Completed in 1903, the three-story sandstone mansion has pronounced European touches. In fact, each room seems to be designed to reflect a different European country, from the Moorish

The Western Heritage Center is in the 1901 Parmly Billings Library.

entry hall to the Tudor dining room. Most of the original furniture and fixtures remain.

The Rimrocks

The Rimrocks are worth a visit, if only for the views from the top. From **Black Otter Trail** off Airport Road, five mountain ranges are visible. To the southeast are the Bighorns, farther west are the Pryors, to the southwest are the Beartooths, and northwest are the Crazies and Snowies.

YELLOWSTONE KELLY'S GRAVE

On the Rimrocks along Black Otter Trail is **Yellowstone Kelly's Grave,** placed here at his request at a site overlooking the Yellowstone River. Luther Kelly was an adventurer of an old-fashioned sort, better suited to fiction than reality. He came west after the Civil War and found the rough-and-ready life here to his liking, despite his cultivated Eastern background. He learned both the Crow and Sioux languages and campaigned with General Miles when the U.S. Army forced the tribes onto reservations following the battle at Little Bighorn. Kelly later ventured to Alaska and later still became a

provincial governor in the Philippines. Back on this continent, he became an Indian agent in Nevada, where he also mined for gold. He died in California, and his body was returned to this site in 1928.

BOOTHILL CEMETERY

Follow Black Otter Trail to the eastern base of the Rimrocks to find **Boothill Cemetery.** At rest here are 52 early residents, many after meeting violent ends. An early sheriff, "Muggins" Taylor, is buried here, as is Henry Lump, the man who killed him. Taylor was the U.S. Army scout who brought news of the Custer massacre to the world via Fort Ellis in 1876.

YELLOWSTONE COUNTY MUSEUM

Also on the Rimrocks, near the airport, is the **Yellowstone County Museum** (1950 Terminal Cir., 406/256-6811, www.pyjrycm. org, 10:30am-5pm Tues.-Fri., 10:30am-3pm Sat., free). This community museum features an old steam engine from the Northern Pacific, a pioneer cabin, a sheepherder's wagon, a stuffed two-headed calf, a roundup wagon, and homesteader and Native

Moss Mansion

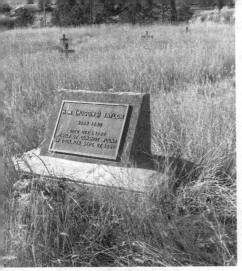

Boothill Cemetery contains the graves of many colorful characters from Billings's early years.

American artifacts. Diorama fans will be uplifted by its display of life in the early years of Yellowstone settlement, and outdoors near the picnic tables is a telescope for viewing Billings and vicinity.

★ PICTOGRAPH CAVE STATE MONUMENT

The most unusual of Billings's Rimrock attractions is the **Pictograph Cave State Park** (406/247-2940, http://stateparks.mt.gov/pictograph-cave, 9am-7pm daily Memorial Day-Labor Day, 10am-6pm daily Sept., Apr.-May, 10am-5pm daily Oct.-Mar., $5 per vehicle for non-Montana residents). Located southeast of Billings on the south side of the Yellowstone, the caves were inhabited for about 10,000 years. A succession of cultures has lived here, beginning with prehistoric hunters. Excavations have yielded almost 30,000 cultural artifacts of early Paleo-Indians, making this one of the richest archaeological sites in Montana.

However, don't come here expecting the vibrant Native American rock art of the American Southwest. The petroglyphs here are quite faded, and many have disappeared due to vandalism and deterioration since the site was documented in the 1930s. However, the visitors center and cave-side exhibits clarify what was once here, and the site itself—amidst the Rimrocks—is spectacular.

The road into the monument passes by

Pictograph Cave State Monument is in the Billings Rimrocks.

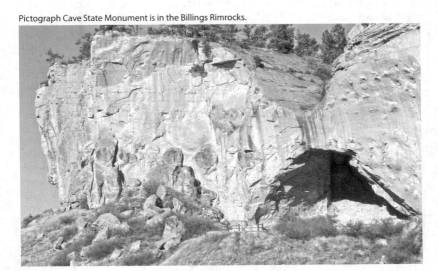

The Legend of Sacrifice Cliffs

Dominating the skyline south and east of Billings across the Yellowstone are the Sacrifice Cliffs. These 200-foot escarpments figure in a Crow legend. As recounted by Mark Brown in *The Plainsmen of the Yellowstone,* Crow storyteller Old Coyote told of two brothers, both warriors, who returned to their village to find it ravaged with smallpox.

They saw the dead on scaffolds. These brothers were courting two sisters. They saw many scaffolds on a cliff and climbed up there. One said to the other, "Take a look at these dead. What if they were the girls we were courting?" They recognized the sisters.

Their oldest brother was one of the chiefs. He was dead. There was no one to care for the people. They dug into their parfleches. They took out their best clothes and put them on. One had a grey horse. This was his best horse. They got on this horse, rode double. They rode through the camp and sang songs just like when there was no sickness, some lodge songs, and lastly their brothers' songs. After this ride, they went up to the cliff and rode along the rimrock singing their own songs. Then they blindfolded the horse and turned toward the edge of the cliff singing the Crazy Dog Lodge song. They were still singing when the horse went over the cliff.

spectacular cliffs and ponderosa pine forests. At the site, three caves have been cut into the sandstone by water erosion. The best-preserved cave paintings are in Pictograph Cave. Here, buffalo, elk, prehistoric animals, and figurative and abstract designs are just visible on the sandstone walls of the cave. That the paintings have survived at all is amazing, especially after repeated assaults by vandals with spray paint. However, nature eventually washed off the spray paint, and the colors of the painting, made from plant resins, cherry juice, animal fat, charcoal, and soil, once again show through. The other two caves, Ghost Cave and Middle Cave, were also inhabited by prehistoric Native Americans. A visitors center offers interpretive displays and a gift shop.

A hard-surface 1,000-foot trail links all of the caves from a central parking lot. A very nice picnic area (but no camping sites), water, and toilets make this a great place to stop and explore. The abundance of birdlife along the rims and the presence of typical prairie flora make the monument grounds a mini nature hike. To find Pictograph Cave State Monument, take exit 452 from I-90 and follow the signs south along Coburn Road for five miles.

ZooMontana

Billings's small **ZooMontana** (2100 Shiloh Rd., 406/652-8100, www.zoomontana.org, 10am-5pm daily May-Sept. 24, 10am-4pm winter, $7 adults, $5 seniors and military, $4 children 3-15) is devoted to Northern Hemisphere temperate species. It features native animals including river otters, owls, and ferrets, as well as more exotic species such as an Amur tiger and a pair of red pandas. In addition, there are a number of gardens and nature exhibits on the 70-acre property. The Discovery Center features hands-on exhibits and educational displays. To reach ZooMontana, take I-90 exit 446 and follow the signs west.

FOSSIL DIGS

The **Judith River Dinosaur Institute (JRDI)** (P.O. Box 80051, Billings, MT 59108, 406/696-5842, www.montanadinosaurdigs. com) is an independent paleontological research organization that, among other projects, sponsors fossil excavations involving serious and qualified lay participants. There are three five-day summer sessions, each of which takes on only up to 20 individuals; cost is around $1,700 per person.

Digs by the JRDI are noteworthy for their level of participation. Rather than being a grunt for researchers who have all the fun, as is commonly the case when the public pays to be part of an excavation, here participants get involved in all parts of the process, including learning field and extraction skills and helping with lab work. Note that from year to year the location of the digs will change; the current dig is in the Lewistown area.

Spaces go very quickly, so if you're serious about paleontology, inquire as soon as you start planning your Montana trip. Costs can change from year to year, depending on how remote the dig is. If the excavation is near a town, you have the option to camp or to rent a motel room; motel costs are not included in the rates. If the dig is remote and camping is mandatory, three meals daily and nonalcoholic drinks are provided; bring your own tent and sleeping bag. Participants must be 14 years of age or older.

In addition to the dino dig opportunities, the JRDI also offers four-day fossil preparation courses at their "Dino Lab" in Billings. During these courses, participants get hands-on experience preparing dinosaur remains for research or display. Cost is around $900; there are three courses offered yearly.

RECREATION

Head up to the Rimrocks to walk, run, or mountain bike. Highway 3 (aka Airport Road), which runs along the rim, gives access to miles of trails at **Swords Park** (near the east end of Airport Rd. near the Black Otter Trail) and **Zimmerman Park** (west of Zimmerman Trail on Hwy. 3).

Pioneer Park, between 3rd and 5th Streets on Grand Avenue, is a beautiful old park near the downtown area featuring tennis courts, jogging paths, and plenty of picnic space. The swimming pool is at **Athletic Park** (N. 27th at 9th Ave. N.). **Riverfront Park,** located along the Yellowstone River just off I-90, has picnic tables, jogging paths, fishing access, boat access for nonmotorized boats, and lots of room to romp. No overnight camping is

allowed. Take exit 446 north to King Avenue, follow it to South Billings Avenue, and follow South Billings Avenue to the park.

The **Billings Mustangs,** the rookie team for the Cincinnati Reds, train in Billings and draw enthusiastic crowds to their games at **Dehler Park** (2611 9th Ave.); call 406/252-1241 for a schedule.

Lake Elmo State Recreation Area (2400 Lake Elmo Rd., Billings Heights, 406/247-2940, http://stateparks.mt.gov/lake-elmo) offers swimming, fishing, nonmotorized boating, and picnic areas. Boat rentals are available. Non-Montana residents pay $5 per vehicle entrance fee. No overnight camping is allowed.

There are several public golf courses in Billings. **Briarwood Country Club** (3429 Briarwood Blvd., 406/248-2702) has 18 holes and is south of Billings along Blue Creek. **Eaglerock Golf Course** (5624 Larimer Ln., 406/655-4445) is a public 18-hole links-style course. The **Exchange City Golf Course** (19 S. 19th St. W., 406/656-2457, www.eaglerock-golfcourse.com) has 18 holes. The **Lake Hills Golf Course** (1930 Clubhouse Way, 406/252-9244, www.lakehillsgolf.com) is near Lake Elmo State Park in Billings Heights. Follow Lake Elmo Road past Lake Elmo and turn at Wickes Lane. The **Peter Yegen Golf Course** (1390 Zimmerman Trail, 406/656-8099) is an 18-hole course west of Billings.

BREWPUBS AND NIGHTLIFE

Like other Montana communities, Billings has a nightlife centered on bars and restaurants. **The Rex** (2401 Montana Ave., 406/245-7477) began as an experiment in urban renewal through drink. By putting a trendy bar in an old hotel in the dilapidated historic district along the tracks, the developers began the rejuvenation process of Billings's most historic district. This is still one of the most pleasant bars in the city, with a particularly attractive patio.

Jake's (2701 1st Ave. N., 406/259-9375) has one of the liveliest bar scenes downtown.

The Rex is king of nightlife along busy Montana Avenue.

Jake's is the kind of bar where, after a couple of drinks, everyone seems single. In a larger city this would seem threatening, but in Billings it seems endearing.

Check out the local brewing scene at these Billings brewpubs. **Yellowstone Valley Brewing Company** (2123 1st Ave. N., 406/245-0918, 4pm-8:30pm daily) hosts Saturday evening live music in its "garage pub." **Angry Hank's Place** (2405 1st Ave. N., 406/252-3370, 4pm-8pm Mon.-Sat.) offers microbrew ales in a converted filling station. **Carter's Brewing** (2526 Montana Ave., 406/252-0663, www.cartersbrewing.com, 4pm-8pm Mon.-Sat.) has a brewpub in an old railroad building right beside the tracks at the heart of Montana Avenue's nightclub district. Their Derailed IPA is a thing of beauty.

Popular brewpub Angry Hank's Place is in a converted filling station.

ENTERTAINMENT AND EVENTS

MetraPark (near the corner of 6th Ave. N. and Exhibition Dr., 406/256-2400, www. metrapark.com) is the major venue in Billings for concerts, rodeos, fairs, and just about any other event that requires extensive seating and exhibition space. Seasonal events include the **MontanaFair,** a large agricultural affair with a rodeo, carnival, and horse racing held during the middle of August. The **Northern International Livestock Exposition** is a large and prestigious livestock show held in October and featuring five nights of rodeo. Check the website for concert dates or sports engagements.

Live theater is presented in several venues. The **Alberta Bair Theatre** (2801 3rd Ave. N., 406/256-6052, www.albertabairtheater.org) hosts performance events, including theater by the Fox Committee for the Performing Arts, the Billings Symphony, and events featuring visiting artists. **Nova Theater** (2317 Montana Ave., 406/591-9535, www.novabillings.org) combines the talents of the Venture Theater, an ambitious acting troupe that mounts musicals, dramas, and comedies and also offers improv evenings several times each month, with Rimrock Opera, which produces a handful of operas and recitals each year. Both groups share a large theater space at the heart of Montana Avenue's nightlife scene. **Billings Studio Theatre** (1500 Rimrock Rd., 406/248-1141, www.billingsstudiotheatre. com) is a local community theater featuring old and new favorites of the popular stage.

SHOPPING

The downtown area of Billings hasn't fared so well as shoppers have deserted older businesses in favor of newer shopping centers with chain stores on the city's fringes. A few older businesses persist in their original locations.

Billings is a good place to get outfitted with Western goods. **Lou Taubert Ranch Outfitters** (123 N. Broadway, 406/245-2248) is an established Western store with a wide selection of boots, hats, and gear. **Al's Bootery** (1820 1st Ave. N., 406/245-4827) offers a wide selection of boots as well as silver jewelry.

Several art galleries in Billings emphasize Western and Montana art. **Catherine Louisa Gallery** (103 N. Broadway, 59101, www.catherinelouisagallery.com) represents some 30 Montana contemporary artists. **Toucan Gallery** (2505 Montana Ave., 406/252-0122, www.toucangallery.com) is located in the historic district and features contemporary local arts and crafts.

ACCOMMODATIONS

Generally speaking, Billings features two major centers for accommodations: downtown and the I-90 exits, where you'll find a great many chain hotels. Thanks to North Dakota's oil boom, eastern Montana hotels are often surprisingly booked up. Although Billings has many hotel rooms, it's not a bad idea to reserve in advance.

$50-100

The **Cherry Tree Inn** (823 N. Broadway, 406/252-5603 or 800/237-5882, $60-66) is just north of downtown. It features a complimentary continental breakfast, exercise room and sauna, and allows small pets. Just down the hill from the airport, the **Rimview Inn** (1025 N. 27th St., 406/248-2622 or 800/551-1418, www.rimviewinn.com, $79-86 and up) features large well-equipped rooms. Included is a complimentary continental breakfast; all rooms have refrigerators, and some have full kitchens. Two- and three-bedroom units are also available.

Across from Billings Clinic and an easy walk to downtown, the **Riversage Billings Inn** (880 N. 29th St., 406/252-6800 or 800/231-7782, www.riversageinns.com/billingsinn, $77-97) offers continental breakfast, a guest laundry, and nicely furnished rooms. Also close to downtown, the ★ **Dude Rancher Lodge** (415 N. 29th St., 406/259-5561 or 800/221-3302, www.duderancherlodge.com, $79-85) is a small and venerable motel with a pronounced Western atmosphere. The coffee shop here is a popular place for breakfast. Pets are allowed.

The Dude Rancher Lodge is a longtime favorite motel with a pronounced Western atmosphere.

Over $100

Right downtown, the **Best Western ClockTower Inn** (2511 1st Ave. N., 406/259-5511 or 800/628-9081, www.bwclocktowerinn.com, $99-125 and up) offers a pool, sauna, restaurant, exercise room, and a guest laundry; it's an easy walk to bars and restaurants on the trendy Montana Avenue strip.

At the center of downtown is the **Crowne Plaza Billings** (N. 27th St., 406/252-7400 or 877/270-1393, $190-208). The Crowne Plaza offers the service and amenities you'd expect in an executive hotel (such as an indoor pool, health club, and hot tub), but with the added privilege of doing so in Montana's second-tallest building (23 stories).

Billings's classic downtown hotel, the ★ **Northern Hotel** (19 N. Broadway, 406/867-6767, www.northernhotel.com, $170-190) has been beautifully updated to

the lobby of the Northern Hotel in downtown Billings

reflect the original hotel's art deco origins plus trendy New Western design. It's uncommonly handsome, and although the standard rooms aren't huge, they are very stylish and comfortable. Go for the suites if you need more room. The hotel also has two excellent restaurants (fine dining and a diner) and a hip cocktail bar.

The **Boothill Inn** (242 E. Airport Rd., 406/245-2000 or 866/266-8445, www.boothillinn.com, $113-185) is a well-run, locally owned motel just downhill from the airport with a pool and easy access to walking trails. The motel has a couple of preloaded GPS units that it will lend to guests who want to explore nearby geocaching sites.

At I-90 exit 447, **Hampton Inn Billings** (5110 Southgate Dr., 406/248-4949, $124-187) offers large comfortably furnished rooms convenient to the interstate. Facilities include a pool, fitness room, and complimentary breakfast.

Just north of I-90 exit 446, the **C'mon Inn** (2020 Overland Ave. S., 406/655-1100 or 800/665-1170, www.cmoninn.com, $119-184) is a good place to stay with kids; it has a relatively large pool and a baby pool, several hot tubs, exercise and video game rooms, and an indoor waterfall with a fish pond.

Camping
The **Billings Metro KOA** (3087 Garden Ave., 406/252-3104 or 800/562-8546) has 115 RV sites ($37-47), 60 tent-camping sites ($22-33), and a pool, playground, and minigolf course, all right next to the Yellowstone. The KOA is off exit 450. The Billings KOA has the honor of being the world's first KOA.

FOOD
The Billings restaurant scene is diverse, featuring several ethnic cuisines. The number of sophisticated restaurants here may surprise you, particularly if you've been traveling across the Montana outback for a few days.

Breakfast and Light Meals
A popular downtown spot for a breakfast or lunch is the **McCormick Café** (2419 Montana Ave., 406/255-9555, www.mccormickcafe.com, 7am-3pm Mon.-Fri., 8am-3pm Sat., 8am-2pm Sun., $3-10), housed in a historic hotel in the city's oldest district.

Stella's Kitchen and Bakery (2525 1st Ave. N., 406/248-3060, 5:30am-5pm Mon.-Sat., 7am-1pm Sun., $6-12) is the restaurant for a popular downtown motel, but it's also one of the locals' favorite spots for breakfast and lunch. Another good spot to know about is **The Soup Place** (106 N. Broadway, 406/294-7687, 11am-9pm Mon.-Sat., $5-13), a great spot for lunchtime soup, sandwiches, and salad, and at night you'll find pasta, fish-and-chips, and burgers plus sandwiches served on pretzel buns.

Harper and Madison Bakery Café (3115 10th Ave. N., 406/281-8550, 7am-6pm Mon.-Fri., 7am-1pm Sat., $5-11) is an excellent hybrid that joins the virtues of an upscale market, bakery, and café. The sandwiches here are remarkable and include variations on deli sandwiches, paninis, wraps, and quesadillas, as well as salads and daily quiche and soup specials. This is a special (and not exactly easy to find) spot that's definitely great for lunch.

The spot for coffee is **Rock Creek Coffee Roasters** (124 N. Broadway, 406-869-1600, 7am-6pm Mon.-Fri., 7am-3pm Sat., 8am-2pm Sun) for house-roasted, small-batch coffee, breakfast pastries, and lunchtime sandwiches.

American Fare and Pub Food
The Burger Dive (114 N. 27th St., 406/281-8292, www.theburgerdive.com, 10:30am-4pm Mon.-Fri., 11am-3pm Sat., $5-10) is a classic American diner with great burgers and hot dogs. For many fans, the burgers, while excellent, are surpassed by the sides, which are artery-clogging specialties like fresh-cut chili-cheese fries and beer-battered onion rings.

Billings has a number of brewpubs, but thanks to outdated state laws, only a few let you enjoy fresh brews and food at the same time. **Montana Brewing Company** (113 N. Broadway, 406/252-9200, www.montanabrewingcompany.com, 11am-11pm daily,

Yellowstone Moss Agates

Agates and sapphires are Montana's two official gemstones. Although agates occur worldwide, dendritic agates from the Yellowstone Valley are highly valued for their unusual figurations. Often called moss agates, the interiors of these stones reveal startlingly realistic mini-landscapes when correctly cut and polished.

Agates are made when gases form bubbles within cooling igneous strata. These cavities are slowly filled with water carrying a silica solution tinted with mineral traces, usually iron. As the silica hardens, it forms regular bands of color of varying intensity. Successive layers of colored silica are laid down within the cavity. As the overlying rock is eroded, the nodes of agate are freed from their setting.

Moss agates are different from banded, or riband, agates because of the presence of plume-like formations within the stone. Small fractures allow the penetration of minute amounts of waterborne minerals into the silica node, which forms treelike or featherlike apparitions in the translucent stone as it hardens. Combined with bands of color within the agate, these formations make landscape images of trees and sunsets, or trees along a lakeside. The verisimilitude of moss agates can be uncanny.

These agates, often called picture agates, occur almost exclusively in the Yellowstone Valley between the mouth of the Bighorn River and the confluence with the Missouri. Why this should be so is a matter of speculation. As the Bighorn, Tongue, and Powder Rivers drain a common area of Wyoming, some theories propose that the agates formed in volcanic ash and lava beds near the watersheds of these rivers and later washed downstream to the Yellowstone. This explanation seems rational, but no appropriate igneous formations have been found in Wyoming.

If you know what you are looking for, agates are not hard to find, but it takes a trained eye to spot them in the rough. Only if they are scuffed or broken do they reveal their translucent interior; otherwise they are a dirty yellow-white.

Agate hunting is a favorite pastime for many locals, and many shops carry baskets of cut agates or agate jewelry for those who are not willing to hunt for their own. The same locals and shop-keepers are usually willing to lend advice to novice agate hunters. The best agate-hunting seasons are early spring and midsummer, when snowpack runoff scours out the gravel beds. Inquire at the local chamber of commerce to find out if there are guided agate-hunting tours. Just be sure not to cross private property without permission.

$7-13) keeps things lively with good home-made beer and lots of local student activity. In addition to the burgers and nachos that you'd expect, you'll find a big selection of appetizers, pasta, salads, and a set of designer mac-n-cheese selections.

Goode's Q and Bayou Grill (2612 Belnap Ave., 406/259-9434, 6am-9pm daily, $8-22) is an outpost of Southern-style cooking, with tempting barbecue and such Cajun specialties as jambalaya and shrimp and crawfish étouffée.

Ethnic and Other Options

Billings is blessed with good Asian food; main courses at the following restaurants range $8-17. Near the hotels off I-90 exit 446 is **Jade**

Palace (2021 Overland, 406/656-8888, 11am-9:30pm daily), which mixes Cantonese and Szechuan cuisine in an attractive setting. If you're itching for sushi, you'll find it at **NaRa Oriental Restaurant** (3 Custer Ave., 406/245-8866, www.narabillings.com, 11am-3pm and 4:30pm-9:30pm Mon.-Fri., 3pm-9:30pm Sat., $6-16) near the corner of Division and Montana Avenues. NaRa also serves Korean dishes in addition to sushi and other Japanese specialties.

Taste of India (216 N. 28th St., 406/281-8001, www.tasteofindiabillings.com, 11am-2pm and 5pm-9pm Mon.-Sat., lunch buffet $11, dinner entrées $15-17) is perhaps the only Indian restaurant in eastern Montana; fortunately, it's good!

Less formal dining is available, of course: Grand Avenue is the strip where all of the fast-food places huddle.

Steaks and Fine Dining

Steaks share top billing with gourmet fare at several downtown restaurants. There's a good view of the city from the 20th-floor **Montana Sky** (27 N. 27th St., 406/252-7400, 6am-10am and 5pm-10pm daily) in the Crowne Plaza Billings, where steaks and seafood entrées average $28. **Jake's** (2701 1st Ave. N., 406/259-9375, 11am-10pm Mon.-Sat. $15-27) combines a lively bar scene with steaks, chops, and a selection of more internationally eclectic dishes.

Billings's dining hot spot is ★ **Walker's American Grill** (2700 1st Ave. N., 406/245-9291, www.walkersgrill.com, 5pm-10pm daily, $16-35). The stylish bar and dining room feature a large selection of tapas-style small plates ($6-14), medium plates (pasta, flatbread and burgers, $13-22), plus up-to-date New West cuisine ranging from steaks and buffalo to seafood ($27-37). Start with tamarind-glazed duck drumettes, followed by grilled lamb chops with roast cauliflower and black lentils. Walker's shares the block with the newly reopened Northern Hotel, making this the epicenter for Billings fine dining. Within the Northern Hotel, ★ **Ten** (19 North Broadway, 406/867-6767, 5pm-10pm daily) is a very handsome dining room (with adjacent cocktail bar) that serves one of Billings's most inventive menus. The steaks are impeccable, and there's a broad range of game dishes, plus fresh seafood, pasta, and pork. Top choices include pheasant breast pot pie with leeks and puff pastry, smoked pork chops with grits, and pumpkin risotto.

The old Billings Historic District on Montana Avenue has filled with excellent restaurants and beckoning bars and clubs. The **Rex** (2401 Montana Ave., 406/245-7477, www.therexbillings.com, 11am-10pm Mon.-Fri., 4pm-10pm Sat.-Sun., bar open until 2am, $16-38) combines excellent aged beef with pasta, game, smoked meats, and fresh fish in a refurbished and elegant old hotel.

★ **Lilac** (2515 Montana Ave., 406/969-4959, 5pm-9:30pm Tues.-Sat., 10am-2pm Sun, $13-26) offers modern American cooking in a small, handsome dining room. Lilac sources its food as close to home as feasible, and everything is as handmade as possible. Standouts include steak with local cherries and stuffed leg of lamb, served with ratatouille. Another outpost of seasonal and regional food is **The Fieldhouse Café** (2601 Minnesota Ave., www.thefieldhousemt.com, 10:30am-3pm and 5pm-9pm Tues.-Fri., 8am-3pm and 5pm-9pm Sat., $12-26), a made-from-scratch type restaurant that's also the Billings's only certified green restaurant. Top dishes include warm winter squash with kale, bing cherries, and spiced pepitas, and roast chicken with poached fig and tapenade. The city's top choice for Mediterranean-style cooking is ★ **Bistro Enzo** (1502 Rehberg, 406/651-0999,www.bistroenzobillings.com, 5pm-9pm Tues.-Sun., $13-24), in an unassuming strip-mall location. Main courses range from wood-fired pizza to couscous with beef, chicken, and shrimp brochettes. Fresh fish is a specialty; it's flown in daily.

Not far from downtown is the **Bistecca at the Granary** (1500 Poly Dr., 406/259-3488, www.bisteccagranary.com, 5pm-10pm nightly, $12-34), a light and airy restaurant in an old mill with a tap room, excellent prime rib, pasta, a selection of chicken dishes, and seafood. The outdoor deck here is a delightful spot in good weather.

INFORMATION AND SERVICES

The chamber of commerce **visitors center** (406/245-4111, www.visitbillings.com) is at 815 South 27th Street. The main **post office** is directly behind the chamber of commerce at South 26th Street and 9th Avenue South. The downtown branch is at 2602 1st Avenue North.

The **Department of Fish, Wildlife, and Parks** office (406/247-2940) is at 2300 Lake Elmo Drive. The **Custer National Forest headquarters** (406/657-6361) is at 1310 Main

Street. The **Bureau of Land Management** office can be reached at 406/896-5004.

Billings Clinic (406/238-2500) is at 801 North 29th Street. **St. Vincent's Hospital** (406/657-7000) is at 1233 North 30th Street.

Listen to **Yellowstone Public Radio** at 91.7 FM.

GETTING THERE AND AROUND

Billings is the largest air link in Montana. **Logan Field** sits atop the Rimrocks at the junction of Airport Road and North 27th Street, with service from Delta (SkyWest), United, Alaska/Horizon, Frontier, Allegiant, and Northwest. **Cape Air** (800/227-3247, www.capeair.com) provides connections to smaller Montana towns. **Hertz, Budget, Avis,** and **National** all operate car rental agencies at the airport.

Jefferson Lines (Billings depot at 19 N. 25th St., 800/255-7655, https://webstore.trail-ways.com) offers once-daily east-west service to the major towns along I-94 and I-90.

MET is the city's public transport system; call 406/657-8218 for information.

East Toward Miles City

Between Billings and Miles City lies an area of rich farmland and pastureland fed by the waters of the Yellowstone and shaded by cottonwoods. Irrigated farming is the mainstay of the local economy, with corn, sugar beets, and soybeans the most prevalent crops. Feedlots, where cattle are wintered or fattened, are also common.

Past the steep sandstone bluffs that rise out of the valley floor, beyond the reach of the center-pivot sprinklers, the badlands and prairies begin. Out here it's suddenly sagebrush and cactus, dusty roads, and cattle country. Small towns like **Forsyth** serve the needs of farmers, ranchers, and travelers alike.

When traveling the Yellowstone Valley, one is always following in someone's footsteps. The wide fertile valley cut by the river has been used for centuries as a thoroughfare, first on foot and horseback, then later by steamboat, railroad, and most recently by automobile along I-94.

Initially the wildlife brought people to the valley. Archaeological remains indicate that prehistoric Native Americans have lived here for thousands of years. Following William Clark (who left a signature at **Pompey's Pillar National Monument**) and other members of the Corps of Discovery, trappers exploited the region's abundance of fur-bearing animals and established trading forts at favorable points. By the end of the 19th century the range was being settled by big cattle and sheep outfits. Then the valley began to fall to the plow.

★ POMPEY'S PILLAR NATIONAL MONUMENT

Pompey's Pillar has always been a landmark. Native Americans used it as a lookout and for sending smoke signals, but the Corps of Discovery put Pompey's Pillar on the map. In July 1806, William Clark and his party were paddling down the Yellowstone when they sighted this 200-foot-high sandstone outcropping in the middle of the wide valley. Clark named the formation after Jean Baptiste, the son of Sacagawea and Charbonneau, the French trapper and adventurer who accompanied the corps. Clark had nicknamed Jean Baptiste "Little Pomp," meaning Little Chief. Clark wrote:

July 25th, 1806, at 4 P.M.: Arrived at a remarkable rock situated in an extensive bottom. This rock I ascended and from its top had a most extensive view in every direction. This rock, which I shall call Pompy's Tower, is 200 feet high and 400 paces in secumpherance and only axcessable on one side. The nativs have ingraved on the face of this rock the figures of animals &c near which I marked my name and the day of the month and year. From the top of this Tower I could discover two low Mountains and the Rocky Mts covered with snow one of them appeared to be extencive.

Some of the pillar's petroglyphs still remain and are reckoned to be the work of the Shoshone who lived in this area before the current Plains tribes moved west. But the real curiosity here is Clark's signature, carved in the rock and still legible after 200 years. Clark was not the last to sign Pompey's Pillar. A pair of crossed hatchets, insignia medallions worn by members of the corps, were probably carved by an enterprising corpsman while Clark finished his signature. Capt. Grant Marsh, pilot of the steamship *Josephine,* added his graffiti in 1875.

Climb the boardwalk staircase to see Clark's signature; continue on to a good vista of the Yellowstone Valley and surrounding

Elaborate boardwalks lead up the side of Pompey's Pillar.

rimrock hills. There are picnic tables near the river, but no overnight camping is allowed.

The Bureau of Land Management operates an excellent visitors center at **Pompey's Pillar National Monument** (406/875-2400, $7 per vehicle). The site is open 8am-8pm daily early May-Labor Day, and 8am-4pm daily Labor Day-mid-October. The rest of the year, vehicle access and the visitors center are closed, but visitors are free to park at the gates and walk in to the monument, about 0.75 mile.

FORSYTH

Forsyth (pop. 1,944, elev. 2,515 feet), nestled beneath a rim of rough gumbo badlands along the banks of the Yellowstone, is a pretty little town with lots of trees and Western character. For the traveler, Forsyth offers recreational opportunities and a friendly place to spend the night.

Forsyth is named for Gen. James Forsyth, a U.S. Army officer who first landed here in 1875, before the town existed. Steamers stopped here to refuel their engines from the abundant stands of cottonwood.

The town was established in 1880 and earned its own post office when the Northern Pacific arrived in 1882. The elaborate buildings along Main Street, including the imposing Rosebud County Courthouse, indicate the wealth of the young community during the early years of the 20th century.

Sights
The **Rosebud County Pioneer Museum** (1300 Main St., 406/356-7547, 9am-6pm Mon.-Sat., 1pm-6pm Sun., May-mid-Sept., free) houses artifacts from the area's early years of settlement and photographs of pioneer days.

Recreation
Forsyth is well-placed to serve as a center for hunters, as it is the hub of many country roads that quickly take the outdoors person into prime big-game territory. Pronghorn, mule deer, and white-tailed deer are the

usual quarry. Also, with the fields that line the river and the river itself both serving as habitat, bird hunters are rewarded with ample prey.

With fishing-access sites practically within city limits, Forsyth also welcomes anglers. The **Rosebud State Recreation Areas,** directly east and west of the city, offer fishing and boating access and camping. If you stop for a picnic, don't forget to look for agates.

The **Forsyth Golf and Country Club** (47 Smith Creek Rd., 406/356-7710, $15 for nine holes) has nine holes, rentals, and a clubhouse three miles west of town. The course winds up a steep gumbo canyon in the badlands just outside of town.

Accommodations

You'll find nicely furnished rooms at **The RestWel** (810 Front St., 406/356-2771, www. restwelmotel.com, $65-85). Convenient to interstate travelers, rates at the RestWel include continental breakfast; some rooms have kitchenettes.

The **Westwind Motor Inn** (225 Westwind Ln., 406/356-2038 or 800/346-2038, $80-90) has a pretty location near fishing access along the Yellowstone near I-90 exit 93. The inn provides a continental breakfast; pets are permitted in the rooms. The **Rails Inn** (3rd and Front, 406/356-2242 or 800/621-3754, $80-90) has a hot tub and lounge.

The **Sundowner Inn** (1018 Front St., 406/346-2115 or 877/356-2115, http://forsythsundownerinn.com, $92-100) is right in the center of this small town; all rooms are equipped with refrigerators and microwaves; pets are allowed.

Camping

There are campsites ($12) at both of the **Rosebud State Recreation Areas** on the east and west ends of town. **Wagon Wheel Campsites** (exit 95, 406/356-7982) welcomes both tent ($15) and RV ($22-29) campers.

Food

For home-style food 24 hours a day, go to the **Speedway Diner** (811 Main St., 406/356-7987) in downtown's vintage Howdy Hotel. The specialty is chicken fried steak ($8). **Fitzgerald's Restaurant** (109 S. 10th, 406/346-4444, 6am-9pm daily, $7-20) offers casino action in addition to quality steaks.

Miles City

Miles City (elev. 2,371 feet) is an attractive town at the confluence of the Tongue River and the Yellowstone. Gumbo buttes vaguely fringed with juniper ring the town. Miles City is the second-largest city in southeastern Montana, with about 8,600 inhabitants. It's a major trade center for farmers and ranchers who, in their pickup trucks, converge on the city for livestock sale days, during harvest for parts, or as often as an excuse can be found to "go to Miles."

HISTORY

Miles City was born in the aftermath of the Battle of the Little Bighorn. After the defeat of Custer's Seventh Cavalry, the army decided to establish a permanent military presence in eastern Montana to protect settlers and to drive the Sioux back onto reservations. In the fall of 1876, six companies of the Fifth Cavalry under the command of Gen. Nelson Miles established a military cantonment at the mouth of the Tongue River and arranged for the building of Fort Keogh. The civilian settlement that grew up downriver was initially known as Milestown. Fort Keogh, the largest military fort built in Montana, was finished in 1878, and Miles City reestablished itself on the Tongue River's opposite shore.

Miles City quickly became important as a trade center. The military payroll made for a relatively affluent citizenry, encouraging a stable base for the trades and mercantile.

Miles City

Steamboats were the vehicle for almost all transportation in the early days, and Miles City was an important port. The steamboats brought up goods for Fort Keogh and the young community of Miles City and took out a wealth of buffalo bones and hides.

After the U.S. Army had subdued the Sioux in 1877, and after the buffalo hunters had completed their own devastation, the vast prairies along the lower Yellowstone drainage were opened up for grazing. The first of the huge trail drives north from Texas was in 1879, and for the next 10 years Miles City was the center of a grazing region that summered tens of thousands of southern cattle. The Northern Pacific Railway arrived in 1881, providing a railhead to eastern slaughterhouses and markets. These boom years in the 1880s justified Miles City's swaggering boast of being the "Cow Capital of the West," for as its population and wealth grew, so did its reputation as a hard-drinking rough-and-tumble cow town.

SIGHTS
★ Range Riders Museum

Every community in eastern Montana has a local museum. If you see only one, make it the **Range Riders Museum** (W. Main St., 406/232-6146, www.rangeridersmuseum.org, 8am-5pm daily, Apr.-Oct., or by appointment, $7.50 adults, $5 seniors, $3 high school and college students, $1 grade school students). At the western edge of the city, near the confluence of the Tongue and Yellowstone Rivers on West Main Street, it contains enough items to impress even the most jaded of museum-goers.

A one-room school, a frontier cabin, tepees, and a sheep wagon have been moved onto the grounds and maintained in period condition with authentic furnishings. A building from Fort Keogh, officers' quarters, is open to visitors and is a vivid reminder of just how civilized life was on the Yellowstone in 1878.

Inside the museum are an excellent gun and weapon collection, artifacts and

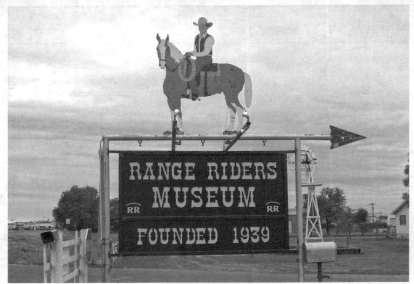

The Range Riders Museum commemorates the days of the open range.

memorabilia from the settling of the West, Native American art and artifacts, old photos, a southeastern Montana settlers "hall of fame," fossils, and more. There's also a reproduction of an 1890s Miles City street.

WaterWorks Art Museum

The **WaterWorks Art Museum** (85 Water Plant Rd., 406/232-0635, http://ccac.milescity.org, 9am-5pm Tues.-Sun. May-Sept., 1pm-5pm Tues.-Sun. Oct.-Apr., free) is in the historic Miles City Water Works building, a 1924 structure designed to filter and hold the city's water, and the galleries are inside the water-holding tanks. The center emphasizes Western art, not surprisingly, along with frequent talks, readings, and a "quick draw" contest. There's also a nice picnic ground around the museum, under some ancient cottonwoods. Turn north at the Fish and Wildlife office off Highway 10 one block west of the Range Riders Museum.

Downtown

Downtown Miles City is still intact enough,

despite the efforts of arsonists who plagued the city in the 1980s and another big fire in 2010, to look like the cattle-trading capital it was in times past. There's an undeniably Western flavor to the city, with its old bars, saddleries, cafés, and the clientele to appreciate them. Most of the downtown area is now listed on the National Register of Historic Places.

The Southeastern Corner

From Miles City, a network of paved roads head into Montana's far southeast corner, a remote area of ranchland and rugged pine-fringed uplands. **Broadus,** 79 miles southeast of Miles City on Highway 59, offers basic lodging and dining options from its position on the Powder River, once described as "Too thin to plow, too thick to drink." **Baker,** 79 miles east of Miles City on Highway 12 and just 12 miles west of the North Dakota border, offers motels, restaurants, and free camping on an in-town reservoir, Baker Lake.

The most interesting destination in this distant area is **Ekalaka,** known affectionately as "the town at the end of the road," for there is only one paved road to it. It is reached by first going to Baker (not exactly the center of the world itself) and turning south on Highway 7 for an additional 35 miles. No one just turns up in Ekalaka by mistake, but there are reasons to make the trip.

★ MEDICINE ROCKS STATE PARK

The **Medicine Rocks State Park** (11 miles north of Ekalaka on Hwy. 7, 406/234-0900, free) contains a series of sandstone outcroppings carved by the wind into weird and mysterious shapes. Some of the buttes tower 80 feet above the pine-clad countryside, and others wind along the hilltops like trains. The Sioux called the area *Inyan-oka-la-ka,* or "Rock with a hole in it," for the strange holes and tunnels in the stone. Legend maintains that the Sioux used the area for vision quests and other rituals, and they considered the rocks to be sacred and full of "medicine," or spirit power. Sitting Bull and his Sioux and Cheyenne warriors reportedly camped here before the Battle of the Little Bighorn, waiting for guidance from their medicine men. The mile-square park welcomes picnickers, campers, and sightseers.

CARTER COUNTY MUSEUM

Ekalaka also offers the **Carter County Museum** (306 N. Main St., 406/775-6886, http://cartercountymuseum.org, 9am-5pm Mon.-Fri., 1pm-5pm Sat.-Sun. Apr.-Nov., 9am-noon and 1pm-5pm Tues.-Fri., 1pm-5pm Sat.-Sun. Dec.-Mar., free). Ekalaka country is particularly rich in fossil remains, and Marshall Lambert, a science teacher at the local high school, was a keen amateur paleontologist. His discoveries of entire dinosaur skeletons, including the only remains of the pachycephalosaurus found in the world, allow the Carter County Museum to boast a collection of bones to rival the best private museums in the country. There's also a good selection of Native American artifacts, minerals, and exhibits on the early pioneer settlement of the area.

RECREATION

Riverside Park, on West Main at the Tongue River Bridge, has tennis courts and swimming in a natural lake. **Wibaux Park** has a good playground for kids and is easy to find from I-94 by following South Haynes Avenue from the Broadus exit toward town and turning south two blocks at South Strevell. The **Town and Country Golf Course** (Montana Ave. and S. 4th St., 406/232-1600) is a private nine-hole club open to the public.

White-tailed and mule deer are abundant in the countryside around Miles City, making it a good headquarters for hunters. Consider using an outfitter if you are new to the area. **Ray Perkins Outfitters Service** (1906 Main St., 406/232-1194, www.perkinsoutfitters.com) offers game-bird and big-game outfitting.

EVENTS

The **Miles City Bucking Horse Sale** (www.buckinghorsesale.com, rodeo $20 reserved seat, $15 general admission) is the one event that Miles City is known for throughout the West. On the third weekend in May, rodeo stock contractors and bacchants from just about everywhere gather in Miles City to watch young untamed horses buck. The most promising of these mounts are then sold at auction as rodeo broncs.

The Bucking Horse Sale is one of the biggest parties in the state, although the actual rodeo is now the central event in a weekend's worth of events that includes horse racing, a street dance, a barbecue, cowboy poetry readings, and the like. Don't let these more civilized pursuits fool you: This is a flat-out celebration of the Dionysian element of the Old West. For information, including tickets, contact the chamber of commerce or visit the website.

SHOPPING

Where better to buy your Western togs than in the Cow Capital of the West? The **Miles City Saddlery** (808 Main St., 406/232-2512, 9am-5pm Mon.-Sat.) will outfit you (and the horse you rode in on) with quality Western gear. Boots, cowboy hats, spurs, pearl-snap shirts, and handmade saddles: It's all here.

ACCOMMODATIONS

Because oil workers have settled into all of the available lodgings in nearby North Dakota, there's an increased demand for hotel rooms in eastern Montana, including Miles City. Be sure to reserve a room in advance (early on the day of your visit is usually okay).

The biggest concentration of lodgings is at I-94 exit 138. A top choice is the ★ **Sleep Inn & Suites** (1006 S. Haynes Ave., 406/232-3000, www.sleepinn.com, $112-129) with large, nicely decorated rooms plus a business center and an exercise room. Just down the street, the ★ **Guesthouse Inn and Suites** (3111 Steel St., 406/232-3661 or 800/214-8378, www.guesthouseintl.com, $99-130) has an indoor pool and hot tub, complimentary hot buffet breakfast, and a variety of large suites, including family suites with a separate bunk room for kids.

The **Econolodge** (1209 S. Haynes, 406/232-8880 or 800/456-5026, $80-90) has an indoor pool and complimentary continental breakfast. The **Best Western War Bonnet Inn** (1015 S. Haynes Ave., 406/232-4560 or 800/528-1234, $111-140) has an indoor pool and hot tub and a complimentary hot breakfast.

The **Holiday Inn Express** (1720 S. Haynes, 406/234-1000 or 888/700-0402, $114 and up) is a good place to stay right by the freeway, with complimentary breakfast, an indoor pool, and guest laundry.

Downtown is the **Olive Hotel** (501 Main St., 406/232-2450, www.historicolivehotel. com, $65-85), the only historic and original Miles City hotel in operation. The Olive is so well established that even fictional characters (such as Gus McCrae of *Lonesome Dove*) stay there. The Olive is a Montana institution, and its 1899 lobby is listed in the National Register of Historic Places. While rooms are not exactly opulent, they have been recently updated and are perfectly comfortable. It's a good choice if you plan to spend your evening in the downtown bars.

Camping

The **Miles City KOA** (1 Palmer St., 406/232-3991, $32-37 RVs, $20-25 tents) is near the Tongue-Yellowstone River juncture. It features a pool, tent sites, laundry, and hot showers from May to November. The **Big Sky Campground** (406/234-1511) is just off the Baker interchange

The Olive Hotel is one of Miles City's originals and is still in operation.

(exit 141) and is open to both RVs ($25) and tents ($15) from May to November. Not much shade is available, though.

FOOD AND NIGHTLIFE

There's a large concentration of fast-food restaurants, a 24-hour truck stop, and a dependable 24-hour **4-Bs** (1406 S. Haynes Ave., 406/232-5772) restaurant at the I-90 exit 138. Find good steaks and a casual but slightly upscale atmosphere at **Montana's Rib & Chop House** (3020 Stower, 406/234-9200, http://ribandchophouse.com, 11am-10pm Mon.-Sat., 10am-10pm Sun. $8-30). Another spot for excellent beef, much of it sourced from local ranches, is **Blackiron Grill and Rotisserie** (2901 Boutelle St., 406/234-4766, www.milescityrestaurant.com, 11am-10pm daily, $11-35). There's a lot going on in this attractive restaurant besides steaks, however: You'll also find pasta, seafood, rotisserie chicken and smoked meats. **Mexico Lindo** (717 S. Haynes, 406/234-3485, 11am-9:30pm Tues.-Thurs. and Sun., 11am-10pm Fri.-Sat., $8-12) is a local favorite.

A couple of downtown coffee shops are worth visiting. **Kafe Utza** (19 S. 9th St., 406/234-9821, 7:30am-2pm Mon.-Fri., 9am-2pm Sat.) has good coffee and pastries, and bills itself as a Basque coffee shop. In a newer building on Main Street, find ★ **Main Street Grind** (713 Main St., 406/234-4664, 7am-2pm, about $6), with some of the best bread you'll find in eastern Montana and good sandwiches.

A downtown landmark is the old diner-like **600 Cafe** (600 Main St., 406/232-3860, 6am-2am daily), full of character and characters, both local. It's a great place to catch the pulse of this old cow town. Immediately next door, and sharing the same kitchen, is the **Hole in the Wall** (602 Main St., 406/234-9887, $9-28), an old-fashioned steak house that's the best spot for a salad bar plus steak combo in downtown.

The ★ **Montana Bar** (612 Main St., 406/213-4002) is one of the greatest bars in the state, remarkably unchanged since it opened in 1902. You can imagine the many tall tales told and livestock trading that went on here. It's also a good spot for a burger or other simple meals.

INFORMATION AND SERVICES

The **Miles City Chamber of Commerce** (406/232-2890, www.milescitychamber.com) is located at 511 Pleasant Street.

The **Bureau of Land Management** office (406/233-4333) is across from the Miles City Sales Yards, about one mile west of the Tongue River Bridge. The **Department of Fish, Wildlife, and Parks** (406/232-0900) is just south of the BLM office.

The **post office** is at 106 North 7th Street. The **Holy Rosary Hospital** (406/232-2540) is at 2102 Clark Street.

Montana Public Radio is heard locally on KEEC 90.7 FM.

GETTING THERE

The **Jefferson Lines** bus station (406/232-6838) is at M&H Gas Station at 1019 Main Street.

The Lower Yellowstone

Between Miles City and its confluence with the Missouri, the Yellowstone becomes a languid prairie river flowing through increasingly arid badlands. The trees and the small towns thin out, and a kind of sullen barrenness grips the landscape.

This is ranch country, rugged and desolate. Since the days of the big cattle drives in the 1880s, the plains along the lower Yellowstone have been home to large holdings of livestock. Towns such as **Terry, Glendive,** and **Wibaux** had their beginnings as trade and rail centers in the early days of the West. Their economies are still largely tied to agriculture, although oil and gas production have bolstered them in recent years.

This area is also home to curious opportunities for the traveler. **Makoshika State Park** near Glendive offers startlingly rugged badlands filled with fossils, hiking trails, and wildlife. It also offers the chance to pull into old towns like Terry and Wibaux and experience the life of modern stockmen on their own turf.

GLENDIVE

Like other towns on the Yellowstone, Glendive (pop. 5,400, elev. 2,069 feet) seems like an oasis of green and trees after crossing the plains that surround it. Although agates are common all along the Yellowstone, Glendive probably has the best agate hunting in the state. The paddlefish lives in much of the lower Yellowstone, yet the Glendive area is the paddlefish capital of Montana. Makoshika State Park, a preserve of colorful and austere badlands at the southeastern edge of town, offers camping, hiking, wildlife viewing, and fossil hunting.

Glendive

Paddlefish and Montana Caviar

Paddlefish occur in only two places on earth: in the upper Missouri drainage and in the Yangtze River in China. No paddlefish had been seen in the United States since 1912, and the species was feared extinct. Then in 1962 a fisher near Intake landed a grotesque-looking specimen weighing 28 pounds, with no scales and a prominent snout. Since then, the sport of paddlefishing has become a popular early summer recreational pursuit in eastern Montana.

The paddlefish is a member of a primitive family that includes the sturgeon. Among its peculiarities are a three-chambered heart, a skeleton of cartilage instead of bone, a long life span (up to 30 years), and its snout, which can be up to two feet long on an adult. It eats only plankton, which it strains out of river water flowing through its gills. This means that the paddlefish won't rise to bait. Instead, it can only be snagged from the river depths where it lurks.

And thus, the *sport,* not art, of paddlefishing. Anglers use heavy rods and line as well as heavy weights (or even spark plugs) to drop the line to the bottom of the river. The line is jerked along the bottom, with the hopes of snagging a paddlefish from its muddy lair. Once on the hook, a tremendous battle ensues, because paddlefish frequently weigh upward of 80 pounds (the record paddlefish, apprehended in the Missouri, weighed 142.5 pounds).

The popularity of paddlefish snagging has begun to worry wildlife experts. In recent years, a disproportionate number of fish taken were huge and old. While exciting for the angler, the ages of the fish being taken has convinced the Fish and Wildlife Department that there aren't sufficient numbers of young fish surviving in the Yellowstone and Missouri. As a result, fewer paddlefish permits are available.

While not all paddlefish flesh is edible (much of it is ominously dark and strong-tasting), a large paddlefish yields an abundance of delicate white meat, which tastes like and shares texture with monkfish.

Since 1989 the Glendive Chamber of Commerce has been authorized to collect paddlefish roe to make into commercially processed caviar. (Actually, paddlefish anglers donate the roe to the chamber, in return for having their fish cleaned.) Although the caviar is not available in Glendive, or anywhere else in Montana (the Fish and Wildlife Department expressly forbids sale of the caviar in Montana to reduce the risks of a caviar black market), it fetches high prices on the international caviar market.

Glendive began as Fort Canby, a military camp built to protect railroad workers as they laid the track for the Northern Pacific up the Yellowstone Valley in the late 1870s. The train actually arrived in the settlement on July 4, 1881. The name Glendive is apparently a corruption of "Glendale," the name given to a nearby creek by Sir George Gore on his hunting trip in 1856. (A more colorful story maintains that the name is a reference to a particularly earthy bar on the site named Glen's.)

★ Makoshika State Park

The rugged beauty of 8,800 acres of heavily eroded badlands, as well as good facilities, makes **Makoshika State Park** (406/377-6256, http://stateparks.mt.gov/makoshika, $5 per vehicle for non-Montanans) the area's premier attraction. The same geologic buckling that forms the oil-rich anticlines of successive oil and natural gas booms raised these badlands hundreds of feet above the prairie. As water eroded the exposed land, it cut through the layers of the Fort Union Formation and revealed a lower, earlier stratum, the Hell Creek Formation. Embedded in the Fort Union Formation is a rich record of fossil life, including the enormous remains of such beasts as triceratops and tyrannosaurus. In 1990 a volunteer paleontologist sat down for a lunch break on what turned out to be a huge triceratops skull. The excavated skull is now on display at the park visitors center.

Today in Makoshika Park, deep ravines have been cut from ridgetops into box canyons whose walls contain fossils. Although fossil hunting is not encouraged in park lands, the park offers stunning overlooks onto the badlands and many opportunities for recreation.

As the road leaves Glendive it quickly climbs up a series of steep switchbacks onto a plateau. From here the road continues 12 miles along ridges and barren canyons with frequent viewpoints and picnic areas. Two maintained trails allow hikers access to the steep canyon walls and valley floors and to the fantastically sculpted formations carved by erosion.

The **Cap Rock Nature Trail** is an interpretive trail that drops 160 feet onto the canyon walls. It passes a short natural bridge, pedestal rocks, fossil beds, and a gumbo sinkhole. A brochure available at the trailhead relates geological history and explains how the formations occurred. About a half-mile farther in, the **Kinney Coulee Hiking Trail** winds down a canyon through juniper trees and eroded formations that take on fanciful shapes. This steep trail is about one mile long and puts you onto the valley floor. The brochure also identifies common plants and animals along the path.

Makoshika Park is also a good wildlife-viewing area. Most noteworthy is a summer population of turkey vultures. Golden eagles are common, as are hawks. Coyotes can be heard howling at night. Mule deer hide out here by day and descend to the valley floor by night.

At most overlooks there are picnic tables, and there is a visitors center at the park entrance. Overnight camping ($23 nonresident, $15 Montana resident) is allowed at the campsite one mile inside the park. Drinking water is available. Trailers are not allowed past the campground because the road becomes quite steep.

To reach Makoshika State Park, follow Merrill Avenue south from downtown and turn under the railroad tracks on Barry Street. Follow the signs right on Taylor Avenue to the park access road. The park is open all year, but heavy rain or snow may make the roads impassable.

Other Sights

The **Frontier Gateway Museum** (Belle Prairie Rd., 406/377-8168, www.frontier-gatewaymuseum.org, 9am-noon and 1pm-5pm Mon.-Sat., 1pm-5pm Sun. and holidays, Memorial Day-Labor Day, free) has several interesting exhibits. In addition to artifacts

The badlands of Makoshika State Park are rich in dinosaur fossils.

of local history, seven historic buildings have been moved to the site, as well as a collection of old fire engines. The museum basement houses a replica of old downtown Glendive. A unique exhibit here is a display of evidence from the area's past murder trials.

Don't let the humble storefront housing the **Makoshika Dinosaur Museum** (103 N. Merrill Ave., 406/377-1637, www.makoshika. com, 10am-5pm Mon.-Sat., $3) fool you. This museum offers a glimpse of Glendive's ancient life with fossils from local sites and around the world (including a *Tyrannosaurus rex* skull), full-size dinosaur replicas, fossil bed re-creations, and dioramas. Call ahead to confirm winter hours. The flashy 20,000-square-foot **Glendive Dinosaur and Fossil Museum** (139 State St., 406/377-1141, www.creationtruth.org, 10am-5pm Tues.-Sat. early May-Labor Day, 10am-5pm Fri.-Sat. Apr.-early May. and Sept.-Oct., $7 adults, $6 seniors and students, $5 children 2-12) presents a Christian view of the fossil record, linking dinosaur extinction with Noah's flood. Murals of local dinosaur life, 23 full-size models of dinosaurs, and exhibits corrective of evolution are featured. The museum is near I-94 exit 215.

Glendive's community art center, called **The Gallery** (109 N. Merrill, 406/377-6508, www.dcaugallery.org noon-4pm Mon.-Fri.), is in the West Plaza mall. The Gallery features works by local artists, including sculpture.

Glendive also has attractive parks. **Lloyd Square Park,** 1.5 blocks west of Merrill Avenue on Gresham Street, has an outdoor pool and tennis courts. On the west end of the Bell Street Bridge is **Eyer Park,** with a playground and picnic grounds. On the other side of the road is **Jaycee West Park** with more tennis courts.

Recreation

Intake, an irrigation diversion 16 miles northeast of Glendive, is the center for **paddlefishing,** although paddlefish are found south to Miles City and in the Missouri as well. The State Department of Fish, Wildlife, and Parks closely supervises paddlefishing areas to limit abuses and overfishing. The season runs May 15-June 30, and a special permit beyond the usual fishing license is necessary.

Spend a day searching for dinosaur fossils and petrified wood at **Baisch's Dinosaur Digs** (406/365-4122, www.dailydinosaurdigs.

The Glendive Dinosaur and Fossil Museum presents paleohistory with a creationist bent.

The Sights of Terry

The little ranch town of Terry sits along the Yellowstone, 40 miles east of Miles City and 37 miles west of Glendive, with prairies to the south and rugged badlands to the north. If you are traveling east, it's time to realize that you're well and truly on the plains of Montana.

Although the town doesn't offer many facilities for the traveler, it does have the **Prairie County Museum** (101 Logan, 406/635-4040, 9am-3pm Mon. and Wed.-Fri., 1pm-4pm weekends, Memorial Day-Labor Day), housed in an elegant late-19th-century bank building. Its exhibits include horse-drawn carriages, rebuilt offices and businesses, and historical photographs. The museum staff can direct travelers to several Native American tepee rings and buffalo jumps in the hills around Terry.

Evelyn Cameron, a pioneer photographer, took spectacular pictures of Terry and the surrounding area during the late 19th and early 20th centuries. Some of her photos hang in the **Cameron Gallery,** next door to the county museum, with the same hours and shared admission charges. A book, *Photographing Montana* by Donna Lucey, and a PBS special have each celebrated this remarkable pioneer photographer. If you'd like to spend the night in Terry, you can stay at the historic **Kempton Hotel** (204 Spring St., 406/635-5543, $55-65), which was built around 1902 and has hosted Teddy Roosevelt and Calamity Jane.

com, $100 per person per day, $75 half day) on a private ranch near Makoshika State Park. You'll be given guidance and tools; with a few exceptions, you can keep your finds.

The **Cottonwood Country Club** (406/365-8797), north after the Highway 16 exit to Highland Park Road, is a challenging nine-hole course.

Accommodations

As with all eastern Montana towns, hotels fill up quickly. Even in this small town, it pays to reserve a room in advance.

The oil boom in nearby North Dakota has led to a surge in new hotel construction in Glendive, most at I-94 exit 215. **La Quinta Inn & Suites** (1717 N. Merrill Ave, 406/377-7300, www.guesthouseglendive.com, $99-125) offers a complimentary hot breakfast, plus business center. The **Holiday Inn Express** (1919 N. Merrill Ave., 406/377-3300 or 877/859-5095, $103-120) offers in indoor pool and fitness center. The **Astoria Hotel and Suites** (201 California St., 406/377-6000, http://stayastoria.com, $139-179) has a pool, guest laundry, fitness center, and an outdoor patio and barbecue for guest use. The **Comfort Inn** (1918 N. Merrill Ave., 406/365-6000 or 800/228-5150, $109-125)

has an indoor pool, and offers a free continental breakfast.

If you're looking for inexpensive, head toward the old downtown area. The **El Centro** (112 S. Kendrick Ave., 406/377-5211, $50-55) is a block away from downtown on a quiet street, and rooms have refrigerators and microwaves.

Camping

The **Glendive RV Park and Campground** (206 1st St., Highland Park, 406/377-6721, $33) has both RV and tent facilities, plus a swimming pool and camping cabins with air-conditioning and TVs! The **Green Valley Campground,** 0.5 mile north on Highway 16 (124 Green Valley Lane, 406/377-1944, $17-24), has its own fishing pond. There's also a campground ($15) at **Makoshika State Park.**

Food

There's not a huge selection of dining options in Glendive. Amid the hotels out at I-94 exit 215 is **CC's Family Cafe** (1902 N. Merrill Ave., 406/377-8926, 6am-9pm daily, $6-13), with standard American fare. In town, **Mexico Lindo** (205 N. Merrill Ave., 406/377-5074, 11am-9pm Tues.-Sun., $8-13) serves satisfying Mexican food.

Information and Services

The **Glendive Medical Center** is at 202 Prospect Drive at Ames Street (406/377-3306). The **chamber of commerce** is at 808 North Merrill Avenue (406/377-5601).

Getting There

Glendive is 35 miles west of the North Dakota border on I-94. Glendive is served by the **Rimrock Stages** bus line.

WIBAUX

Wibaux (WEE-bo) is a quintessential cattle town that has seen some of the West's most colorful characters and was an actor in the region's most colorful periods. The fertile grasslands here along the Montana-North Dakota border were home to huge cattle ranches in the 1880s and 1890s, many owned by East Coast and European investors. Among them was a Frenchman, Pierre Wibaux, who arrived in Montana in 1883. He is rumored to have made it through the disastrous winter of 1886 by feeding his cattle cottonwood branches, and the following year bought up livestock at low prices from desperate fellow ranchers. By the mid-1890s there were 65,000 head of cattle bearing his brand, the W Bar.

Just over the border in North Dakota, the Marquis de Mores established the town of Medora. This French nobleman founded a huge cattle ranch and meatpacking plant in the middle of nowhere, built a manor house for his wife, and waited for fortune to come. He welcomed such visitors as Teddy Roosevelt, the future president, who had established a cattle ranch nearby after the deaths of both his mother and his wife. Pierre Wibaux was another fixture in this stylish set.

Pierre Wibaux left a legacy in Wibaux that seems very rich for such a small town. In 1884 Wibaux's father sent him money to build a church. **St. Peter's Catholic Church** was built the next summer out of native stone and lava rock. St. Peter's reveals its French background: Its quiet rootedness recalls a Normandy churchyard more than a pioneer parish eight miles from North Dakota. It is an imposing structure on the prairies, in summer covered with green ivy, rising above the town that Wibaux built.

Beyond the church is a statue of Pierre Wibaux looking north toward the location of his old ranch, which was 14 miles north of the present town. To conduct business in town, Wibaux built an office and bunkhouse. This small clapboard "town house" now houses the **Wibaux County Museum**

Wibaux's downtown boasts old bars and a new brewpub.

(112 Orgain St. at Wibaux St., 406/796-9969, 9am-7pm Mon.-Fri., 11am-7pm Sat., 1pm-6pm Sun., May-Sept., free). Tours are conducted daily at 1pm, 2pm, and 3pm Memorial Day-Labor Day. The town house has been returned to its original 1892 condition, including the grounds, which French gardeners had designed with a pond, flower beds, and a grotto. The museum houses personal belongings and furniture as well as items typical of the open range days.

In the same museum complex is the **Centennial Car Museum.** In 1964, during the New York City World's Fair, Montana sent a railcar containing promotional exhibits about the state, as it was celebrating its centennial as a territory in the same year. Today, the railcar contains Native American and pioneer relics, including the museum's pride, a human vertebra with an arrowhead imbedded in it, which has been unofficially dated to a period at least 2,000 years ago.

Also worth a stop: **Beaver Creek Brewery** (104 W. Orgain Ave., 406/795-2337, 2pm-8pm Thurs.-Sun.) is the most easterly brewpub in Montana. If you're not up for drinking the Paddlefish Stout or Redheaded IPA, have a glass of Beaver Creek's root beer.

Crow and Northern Cheyenne Reservations

The Crow and Northern Cheyenne Reservations are basically the upper drainages of Montana's Tongue and Bighorn Rivers. The landscape combines the lyricism of rough sandstone bluffs and uplands covered with ponderosa pine forest with the austerity of the high, barren prairies. And underlying everything here are the vast coal deposits of the Fort Union Formation.

Except for the river valleys and small reservation towns like **Hardin,** there is scarcely any development. Like the Custer National Forest to the east, the reservation lands seem to be maintained in a kind of ad hoc trust. While this has preserved the beauty and integrity of the area, it has hindered the economic development for the tribes.

This region has always been Native American land, first by tradition, later by decree. The Crow settled here 300 years ago. Later, other tribes vied for room on these rich hunting grounds south of the Yellowstone. When traders first sought to barter with the Native Americans for furs, they came here; when the U.S. Army needed to subdue the Native Americans, they came here as well. One of the most stirring events in Western history took place on these plains: the clash between the Seventh Cavalry under General George A. Custer and the assembled warriors of the Sioux and Northern Cheyenne, commemorated at **Little Bighorn Battlefield National Monument.**

HARDIN

Even though Hardin (pop. 3,470, elev. 2,966 feet) is not on the Crow Reservation, it serves as the primary trading center for residents of the reservation and the ranches to the north and west. It's a pleasant town, with a local museum that's worth a visit, and it is a good base for trips to the Little Bighorn Battlefield, Bighorn Canyon, and the Crow and Northern Cheyenne Reservations.

The confluence of the Little Bighorn and Bighorn Rivers was a strategic outpost during the Indian Wars. The steamboat *Far West* maneuvered up the Bighorn to the mouth of the Little Bighorn in June 1876 to pick up wounded soldiers after the Reno-Benteen battle. In 1877, the year after the Custer battle, Bighorn Post was built on the cliffs above the confluence. Renamed Fort Custer, it was apparently rather a grand fort, in the manner of Fort Keogh; it was abandoned in 1898.

By 1906 the Dawes Act opened the

reservation to outside settlement. The next year, only nine years after Fort Custer ceased its patrol of the Crow, the Chicago, Burlington, and Quincy Railroad built a spur line down to the present site of Hardin, both to bring in new settlers and to serve their needs.

During World War II, many Japanese American internees were brought into Montana to work sugar-beet fields because farmers were experiencing a labor shortage. A large number worked in the Hardin area; some settled here after the war.

Bighorn County Historical Museum

The **Bighorn County Historical Museum** (exit 497, 406/665-1671, www.bighorncountymuseum.org, 8am-6pm daily May-Sept., 9am-5pm Mon.-Fri. Oct.-Apr., $5 adult, $4 senior, $3 children 12 and over, 11 and under free) has 26 restored historic buildings open for viewing in summer, including a handsome 1917 German Lutheran church, an old post office and store, and old farm buildings, including a 1916 farmhouse that's never been renovated and particularly evokes early-20th-century rural life. (During the winter the historic buildings are closed.) The museum contains rotating exhibits and a good selection of books on local history and lore. The museum also has a visitors center, picnic tables, and bathrooms.

Other Sights and Recreation

Stop by the **Jailhouse Art Gallery** (218 N. Center, 406/665-3239) to see exhibits on Native American culture and art, and works by local artists.

Custer Park has a playground and picnic tables. Take exit 495 south on Crawford Street, but resist the urge to veer off to Yellowtail Dam, and instead follow Crawford until 3rd Avenue.

Hardin's community **pool** (621 W. 8th St., 406/665-2346) is Olympic-size and indoors.

Events

The Hardin Chamber of Commerce sponsors the annual **Little Bighorn Days,** whose main feature is the **Reenactment of Custer's Last Stand** (406/665-1672 or 888/450-3577, www.custerlaststand.org). The event is held on the Friday, Saturday, and Sunday closest to the anniversary of the battle on June 26. In addition to the battle, the actors stage the events that led up to the conflict. It's a huge swirl of horses, tepees, and warriors, with more than 200 participants, and the drama is matched by the dust. The reenactment is held six miles west of Hardin on old Highway 87, not at the battle site. Other events during Little Bighorn Days include a rodeo, an 1876 grand ball, Native American dancing, and special tours of the Little Bighorn Battlefield.

Tickets to the reenactment are $20 for adults and $8 for children. There are two shows on Saturday, and one each on Friday and Sunday. Tickets and information are available through the chamber of commerce or the website.

Accommodations

If you're looking for inexpensive, the **Lariat Motel** (709 N. Center, 406/665-2683, $55-70) is clean and basic, and allows pets.

The **Rodeway Inn** (1324 Crawford, 406/665-1870 or 800/582-8094, $70-119) has two guest laundries, a hot tub, pool, and 140-foot waterslide and pool. Also part of the complex is a lounge, restaurant, and casino, as well as a playground and barbecue area. The **Super 8** (201 W 14th St., 406/665-1700, www.hardinmontanasuper8.com, $83-95) offers a variety of room types, including two-room suites and a guest house with three bedrooms and full kitchen.

Camping

The **KOA** (406/665-1635) is one mile north of Hardin on Highway 47. **Grandview Campground** (406/665-2489) is south of Hardin on Highway 313.

Food

Hardin is not a place for cuisine. The fast-food outlets at exit 495 present one option. The **Lariat Country Kitchen** (721 N. Center, 406/665-1139) is where the locals go for well-prepared American fare, plus under new owners, a sampling of East Indian cooking. A locally owned place with good Mexican food, **La Chalupa** (317 N. Center Ave., 406/665-1175, 11am-9pm daily, $7-12), doesn't have liquor license.

Information and Services

The **chamber of commerce** (406/665-1672) can be found 10 East Railway Street. The **post office** is at 406 North Cheyenne. The **Big Horn County Memorial Hospital** (406/665-2310) is at 17 North Miles.

THE CROW INDIAN RESERVATION

The present-day Crow derive from Hidatsa tribes who originally lived along the Mississippi headwaters. Of Siouan linguistic stock, they were an agrarian people who lived in earth lodges and made pottery. Sometime during the 1600s the Crow left the larger Hidatsa tribe and began to move westward, first settling in the Black Hills area. Increasingly, lands as far west as the Powder, Tongue, and Bighorn River drainages were added to their hunting grounds, and by the 1770s the tribe had settled onto its historic homelands south of the Yellowstone.

Traditionally, the tribe was organized first by family, then by matrilineal clan. Known as the Absaroka in Hidatsan, or "children of the large-beaked bird," they were considered to be as crafty and enterprising as the raven, hence the English name Crow.

From their first contact with explorers and traders, the Crow have maintained mostly friendly relations with European settlers. Montana's first trading post, Fort Ramon, was built in 1807 at the juncture of the Bighorn and Yellowstone to serve the beaver-pelt trade with the Crow.

A complex relationship between the Crow and traders emerged: The traders provided tobacco, food, guns, manufactured goods, clothing, and liquor, while the Crow provided pelts and hides and protection from the hostile Blackfeet to the north. The traders and the Crow hunted together, sharing knowledge and cultures.

But the Crow became economically dependent on trade with the newcomers, a dependency served by plundering the riches of their homeland. While Native Americans like the Crow were instrumental in exterminating the vast herds of buffalo in the West, the buffalo remained their source of food and shelter. By the 1880s the buffalo had disappeared from its range on the Yellowstone.

It wasn't just political concerns that provided the bond between the Crow and the settlers. Their friendship lasted several generations and weathered many altercations. And while the U.S. government was not especially solicitous of the Crow (though they were treated somewhat less abjectly by the United States than some other tribes), the Crow remained faithful allies. Crow scouts accompanied Custer and his troops during his fateful Montana tour of June 1876.

The present Crow Reservation, much reduced from the 1868 land grant, contains over 3,000 square miles of rolling prairie and rugged foothills drained by the Bighorn River, making it Montana's largest reservation. There are about 11,000 tribal members, with about 7,900 living on the reservation. The Crow language, a cousin to Siouan and Assiniboine, is spoken by 85 percent of the tribe as a first language. The retention of their native language is a combination of tradition (no Crow addresses another Crow in English) and the fact that the federal government never mandated English-only boarding schools on the Crow Reservation. The **Crow Tribal Council** (406/638-3708, www.crow-nsn.gov) can be contacted at P.O. Box 129, Crow Agency, MT 59022.

Chief Plenty Coups State Park

Chief Plenty Coups, the last of the great Crow war chiefs, is credited for advocating

When the Buffalo Roamed

The buffalo, or the American bison (*Bison bison*), as it is properly known, once ranged over most of the North American continent. Between Pennsylvania and the Continental Divide, and from the lower Mississippi and the Arkansas River north to the northern Alberta border, these shaggy members of the cattle family roamed over 40 percent of the continent in herds of up to a million animals. They were migratory creatures, following the seasons north and south.

Eastern Montana was ideal buffalo country, no matter what season. Huge herds that summered on the Canadian plains moved south to winter on the Montana prairies, while equally numerous herds from the grasslands of Colorado and Wyoming migrated north to summer on the plains of Montana. Perhaps as many as 60 million of these animals once roamed the continent, and as many as four million lived in Montana alone.

As previously agricultural Native Americans entered Montana from the east, the vast herds of buffalo soon changed their lifestyle. Bison had always been an element of the Native American culture, but when these tribes were forced onto the plains, the buffalo's importance altered.

In ways that are difficult to imagine today, the buffalo provided the means of life for the early Plains Indians. The hide provided tepee coverings and leather for moccasins; the flesh was eaten fresh in season and also preserved for later consumption (steaks from the hump were delicacies). The bones were used to create tools, from bone-splinter awls (with buffalo sinew for thread) to shoulder-blade hoes. Dried manure was used in campfires. Even the dried tail was used—as a flyswatter.

Before the introduction of horses and firearms, Native Americans hunted buffalo with bow and arrow, often using buffalo "jumps" or *pishkuns*. The unsuspecting animals were stampeded off cliffs in large herds, after which the tribe harvested the dead and wounded. When the rifle and the horse met on the plains of Montana, the destruction of the vast herds began in earnest.

The development of new tanning techniques in the East allowed tanners to turn dried buffalo hides into soft marketable leather, changing forever the lives of the prairie Native Americans. In the 1840s most of the fur-bearing mammals of the West had been trapped out; by the 1860s and 1870s the great buffalo hunt was on. Waves of new settlers (many displaced by the Civil War) moved west and joined the slaughter. Entire herds were completely wiped out in the course of a summer, as sharpshooters picked off the animals while they grazed. The animals were skinned, the hides shipped east by steamboat or rail, and the carcasses left to rot. Areas of the northern plains were white with bleached bones where the large herds had been slaughtered, and as the buffalo became scarce, a trade developed in dried buffalo bones, used for fertilizers.

By 1884 the buffalo was effectively extinct in the United States. In 1908, when the government created the National Bison Range near Moiese in northwestern Montana, it was stocked mostly with animals from Canada.

As the buffalo passed, so did the life of the Plains Indian founded on the buffalo. The basis for a nomadic warrior society was gone, leaving Native Americans with no source of food, shelter, or support—except the U.S. government.

peaceful relations with the settlers and for being the first Crow leader to recognize the need to adapt to the new life of the reservation. When the U.S. government opened the Crow Reservation to individual allotments in 1887, the young chief applied for his 320 acres, just west of Pryor off Highway 416, along a pretty stretch of Pryor Creek. It had been revealed to Chief Plenty Coups in a vision quest almost 30 years before that he would live out his life there, "where the plums grow."

Chief Plenty Coups attempted to set an example of how the Crow might coexist with the settlers. He stressed education and mediated conflicts between his tribe and the settlers. He cultivated his holding and built a two-story log home and a store, symbolically forsaking the tepee and the hunting lifestyle of the prairie nomad. He and his wife lived there until his death in 1932.

The 40-acre **Chief Plenty Coups State Park** (406/252-1289, http://fwp.state.mt.gov/parks, free for Montana residents, $5 per vehicle for non-Montanans) houses a museum of Crow culture, Plenty Coups's home and store, his grave, and a gift shop featuring Crow crafts. The spacious grounds allow plenty of room to stretch your legs, and there is a well-developed picnic area (but no overnight camping). The park is open 8am-8pm daily, and the museum is open 10am-5pm May 1-September 30.

Events

The **Crow Fair** is the biggest event of the year and is perhaps the largest Native American gathering in North America. During the third weekend of August, the tribal campgrounds near Crow Agency become a sea of tepees, pickup trucks, and RVs as thousands of tribe members and visitors rendezvous to celebrate Crow heritage. Traditional games are played, including innocent-seeming "hand games," where money is gambled in a variation of the shell game. Some of the Crow dress in traditional garb, which shows off their complex and colorful beadwork. The costumes largely come off during the dance contests. There is also a parade, an all-Indian rodeo, and horse racing. Visitors are welcome, and bead goods and Native American food are for sale. Bring sunscreen and a hat, and be prepared to get dusty. For more information, contact the Crow Tribal Council or visit www.crow-nsn.gov.

★ LITTLE BIGHORN BATTLEFIELD NATIONAL MONUMENT

The Battle of the Little Bighorn was one of those epochal historical moments when individual strands of fate, personality, and history wove a whole that is larger and more meaningful than any sum of its parts. To stand on the sere slopes of the Wolf Mountains and ponder the events of 1876 is to sense that something much more than a battle between armies and cultures took place. The issues at stake continue to resonate as the historical march of culture confronting culture goes on.

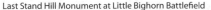
Last Stand Hill Monument at Little Bighorn Battlefield

The centerpiece of the monument is the battlefield, although the museum and interpretive center are also fascinating.

George Armstrong Custer

However hackneyed the observation, George Armstrong Custer was, and remains, an enigma. He graduated last in his class at West Point. He served the Union in the Civil War. He became the youngest general in the history of the U.S. Army after General Lee surrendered to him; he was later court-martialed for ordering the shooting of army deserters in Kansas.

Once reinstated, Custer—demoted to a lieutenant colonel—became commander of the Seventh Cavalry. His exploits made him and his wife colorful and frequent guests at New York society functions. He fell afoul of the Grant administration for allegations made in congressional hearings about corruption involving the president's brother and Native American trading licenses. Custer was arrested again.

A New York newspaper publisher who championed Custer as a future presidential candidate used his presses to mold opinion in Custer's favor. Released again, the 36-year-old Custer led 265 men to death on the Little Bighorn when he went on the offensive against a united war party with upward of 3,000 Sioux and Cheyenne warriors.

The Sioux and Cheyenne

This butterfly of a man confronted representatives of an ancient culture. The Sioux and Cheyenne were settled into one reservation in eastern Wyoming and the western Dakotas by the conditions of the Fort Laramie Treaty of 1868. However, the discovery of gold in 1874 in South Dakota's Black Hills immediately caused the treaty to be broken by gold hunters. Sioux and Cheyenne warriors, responding to these incursions onto their reservation and to the age-old need to hunt buffalo, began to leave their reservation. Under the leadership of such warriors as Sitting Bull and Crazy Horse, they camped in the drainages of the Powder, Tongue, and Rosebud Rivers, their numbers growing as more and more Sioux and Cheyenne became disenchanted with their treatment on the reservation. Here, for one last reprise, they practiced the centuries-old culture of the Plains Indian.

From here they also raided settlements and harassed travelers. The Commissioner of Indian Affairs ordered them back onto the reservation, threatening military action if they did not comply by January 31, 1875.

The Sioux and Cheyenne did not respond, and the U.S. Army was sent to force the issue.

The Battle of the Little Bighorn

Three separate expeditions were sent out to campaign against the hostiles. These troops were to move from three different directions into the southeastern corner of Montana, where the Native American forces were known to be encamped. Custer's Seventh Cavalry followed the Rosebud River up to its divide with the Little Bighorn, where he was to wait for the two other columns. Instead, he divided his own command into thirds, and on June 25, 1876, took the offensive against one of the largest Native American forces ever gathered.

The details of the engagement at the Little Bighorn are best left for the traveler to discover at the battle site. What actually happened is complex, far from certain, and compelling.

Perhaps we learn of Custer and the Sioux too early in life, when complex issues seem too simple. The battlefield is not merely a place for boys of all ages to gloat in the memory of battle. The site is as chilling as Civil War battlefields, where you sense the past and somehow recognize the end of a culture and an epoch with a tightened and hollow gut. This is Montana's most haunted ground.

Battlefield Sights

The battle site is 15 miles east of Hardin, one mile east of Highway 90. The **visitors center** (406/638-2621, www.nps.gov/libi, 8am-8pm daily Memorial Day-Labor Day, 8am-6pm daily Labor Day-Sept., and April-Memorial

Day, 8am-4:30pm daily Oct.-March, $10 per vehicle, $5 per pedestrian) is situated below the crest of the hill where the last stand took place. It contains some interesting exhibits, including a striking video presentation, and should be visited before going on to the battlefields. Exhibits explain the Native American background to the conflict, the military strategies, the contemporary lifestyles of both cultures, and also display artifacts of the battle. Interpretive information is also available via your cell phone at various viewpoints in the monument. Downhill from the visitors center is **Custer National Cemetery,** where some war dead from this and other conflicts are buried.

In 2003 the National Park Service unveiled the **Little Bighorn Battlefield Indian Memorial,** dedicated to Native American lives and perspectives on the conflict. The memorial consists of bronze spirit statues representing fallen warriors and a spirit gate for the dead army soldiers, plus story panels, petroglyphs, and plaques with writings of Native American leaders.

One-quarter mile up the hill is **Last Stand Hill Monument,** where the last of the Seventh Cavalry died. Grave markers stand where the bodies of soldiers were found.

They are interred in a common grave under the monument, which bears the names of the dead. Custer is buried at West Point.

To look down the grassy hillside at the markers, some standing alone, others huddled together, many clumped together around the swale where Custer's own body was found, is to vividly experience the full horror of the battle.

The paved road winds past the monument on a seven-mile loop road to the **Reno-Benteen Battlefield.** Maj. Marcus Reno and three of the Seventh Cavalry's companies were ordered by Custer to lead the first offensive against the Sioux and Cheyenne village on the Little Bighorn River. They retreated up to this ridge, where they took up defensive positions. During the melee, the main Native American attack was directed north to Custer's command. Reno was joined by Capt. Frederick Benteen and the cavalry's pack train, the last third of Custer's original unit. On this hill, behind the bodies of slaughtered pack horses, these soldiers withstood 48 hours of attack by the victorious Sioux and Cheyenne before the warriors, almost inexplicably, retreated. A self-guided walking tour of the battlefield begins at the parking lot. Park rangers and Native Americans give free tours

Custer National Cemetery at Little Bighorn

and programs relating to the battle, and a cell phone audio tour prompts visitors to call at stops on the walking and driving tours.

Down the road in Garryowen is the site of the Reno battle and the **Custer Battlefield Museum** (406/638-1876, www.custer-museum.org, 8am-7pm daily Memorial Day-Labor Day, 9am-5pm daily Labor Day-Memorial Day; $7.50 adults, children under 12 free). The privately owned museum has some superb Native American crafts, a collection of historic photos, a re-creation of Sitting Bull's campsite, and the tomb of an unknown soldier. There's also a gift shop and gallery.

Accommodations and Food

The Custer Battlefield is about as lonely and forlorn a place as you can imagine. However, some amenities have grown up nearby, and Hardin is only 15 miles away.

At the I-94 interchange at the battle-ground there's a restaurant and gift shop, the **Custer Battlefield Trading Post and Cafe** (406/638-2270, 8am-9pm daily summer, 9am-5pm daily winter). Indian tacos, actually a variety of fried bread, are featured ($8). The gift shop has a nice selection of Native American crafts and books.

BIGHORN CANYON NATIONAL RECREATION AREA-NORTH DISTRICT

Nothing in the prairies and valleys of the Crow Reservation prepares the traveler for the magnitude and sheer drama of Bighorn Canyon. The Bighorn River flows through a wide wooded valley from St. Xavier upstream to **Fort Smith** along Highway 313, where suddenly the land ends in upheaval, with bright red clinker stone topping gravel bluffs. The road climbs four miles up a series of steep switchbacks onto a plateau. At the base of the eroded face of the Pryor Mountains, an enormous canyon opens up, with the waters of **Yellowtail Reservoir** a ribbon of blue below thousand-foot cliffs.

In 1965 the Bighorn River was dammed near the site of Fort Smith. This beautiful

rugged landscape became the Bighorn Canyon National Recreation Area in 1968. By trapping sediment, cooling the water, and maintaining a steady flow, the dam changed the Bighorn from a slow-moving catfish river to a crystal-clear blue-ribbon trout stream, one of the best fisheries for trophy-size trout in the country.

Bighorn Canyon isn't particularly on the way to anywhere; you must really want to be there to get there at all. Much of the land around the canyon is Crow Reservation land and off-limits to most visitors. Despite the information on many road maps, non-Crow tribal members cannot get from the dam near Fort Smith in the Bighorn Canyon National Recreation Area's North District to the recreational access areas in the South District near Lovell, Wyoming (a distance of only 25 miles), by land, because the Crow do not allow non-tribe members to cross tribal land. This isn't a problem for locals with boats, as access to Yellowtail Reservoir is open to anyone, as long as boats land only at designated recreation area marinas. Lacking a boat, a visitor who wishes to see both halves of the recreation area will have to skirt the Crow Reservation by public highway—down into Wyoming and back up into Montana from the south—a one-way journey of at least three hours by car.

Contact the **Bighorn Canyon National Recreation Area** (406/666-2412, www.nps.gov/bica) at 5 Avenue B, P.O. Box 458, Fort Smith, MT 59035.

Fishing the Bighorn River

The Bighorn River below Yellowtail Dam has become one of the country's most famous trout fisheries since it opened to fishing in 1981. Though the Crow object to non-Crows on reservation land along the river, the state maintains four fishing-access sites within the reservation. Do not attempt to fish on private land without getting permission. Anglers should stay within high-water marks, in or on the river, to avoid trespassing on Crow land.

Because the Bighorn is both heavily fished and carefully monitored for access, anyone uncertain of the area and its conditions should consider using the services of a professional outfitter to guarantee fishing success and compliance with trespassing laws. Many outfitters, most based out of the tiny town of Fort Smith, also offer accommodations.

Bighorn Fly and Tackle Shoppe (406/666-2253, www.bighornfly.com) offers fishing gear rentals and sage advice with its guide service; lodging and guide packages are available. **Bighorn Angler** (577 Parkdale Ct., 406/666-2233 or 866/658-7688, www.bighornangler.com) offers boat rentals, accommodations ($100-175), a tackle shop, and full guide service.

The **Bighorn Trout Shop Motel** (7477 Parkdale Ct., 406/666-2375, www.bighorntroutshop.com, $145 double) offers gear and flies in addition to comfortable rooms. **Fort Smith Fly Shop and Cabins** (1.8 miles north of Fort Smith on Hwy 313, 406/666-2550, www.flyfishingthebighorn.com, cabins $60-150 per person per night) also provides boat rentals and guides.

Lodging and meals are provided for fishing clients at **Kingfisher Lodge** (406/666-2326 or 800/835-2529, www.bighornkingfisher.com, three nights lodging and two days fishing from $972 per person).

Camping is an economical means of staying over in Fort Smith. At **Afterbay,** the National Park Service maintains a free 30-site campground. A private campground in Fort Smith, **Cottonwood Camp** (406/666-2391, $25-30 RVs, $15 tents, $50-175 up cabins), offers all of the usual niceties plus a variety of cabin accommodations, boat rentals, and shuttle service to fishing-access sites.

While making motel reservations, check with your guide or outfitter because many offer room and board to their angling guests. **Hal's Cafe** (100 W. Main, 406/534-0149, 6:30am-11pm daily) is a full-service restaurant that sources its meat and produce as locally as possible.

Yellowtail Visitor Center and Ok-A-Beh Marina

The **Yellowtail Visitor Center** (406/666-9961, 9am-5pm daily Memorial Day-Labor Day, 9am-5pm Sat.-Wed. Labor Day-Sept. 30) offers a good museum exhibit of traditional Crow life in Bighorn Canyon, along with details about the dam's construction. However, tours of Yellowtail Dam, the tallest dam in the Missouri River drainage, are no longer offered because of security concerns. A very short jaunt, the **Beaver Pond Nature Trail,** leaves from the parking lot of the Yellowtail Visitor Center to overlooks of beaver ponds in Lime Kiln Creek.

To reach **Ok-A-Beh Marina** (406/629-9041), turn south at Fort Smith and ascend the steep face of the Bighorn Plateau, here burned to bright red clinker by the intense heat of ancient smoldering underground coal seams. Think twice about making this 11-mile trip if your brakes are poor or your vehicle pulls hard on hills. Otherwise, the road to Ok-A-Beh is a great vantage point from which to overlook the canyon, the Crow Reservation, and the Pryor and Bighorn Mountains.

Boat facilities at Ok-A-Beh include a landing, a fish-cleaning area, and gas, oil, and boating supplies. Pontoon boat rentals are also available at the marina. Shore fishing is almost impossible at public-access sites in the North District of Yellowtail Reservoir, but fishing by boat is good for brown trout and walleye. Remember to have the appropriate state fishing licenses, because the reservoir spans both Montana and Wyoming and there is no license reciprocity.

THE NORTHERN CHEYENNE RESERVATION

Located between the Crow Reservation and the Tongue River, the Northern Cheyenne Reservation was granted to the Cheyenne after a period of wandering and incarceration following the Battle of the Little Bighorn. The Northern Cheyenne Reservation contains 444,500 acres, almost 90 percent of which is controlled by tribal members. About 4,900 Cheyenne live on the reservation. Characterized by patches of dry prairie ringed by sandstone uplands covered with ponderosa pines, the area is rich in prairie wildlife and game birds, and the Tongue River affords the angler opportunities for walleye, smallmouth bass, and, south near the Tongue River Reservoir, trout.

Highway 212 cuts across the reservation on its way between the Little Bighorn Battlefield and the Black Hills of South Dakota, and it's an absolutely beautiful drive.

French traders first encountered the Cheyenne in 1680, when they were living in present-day Minnesota. At that time they were an agricultural people who lived in earth-and-log cabins. The pressure of settlements to the east forced all tribes to migrate west. Driven onto the plains, the Cheyenne lost their agricultural arts and divided into two federations: the Northern Cheyenne in Montana and the Dakotas, and the Southern Cheyenne in Colorado. By the time Lewis and Clark toured the West, the Northern Cheyenne tribe was living near the Black Hills. They lived in tepees and existed almost totally off the largesse of the buffalo. Their agricultural past had faded into tribal myth.

When gold was discovered in the Black Hills in the 1870s, treaties barring nonnatives from the area were promptly ignored, and the resulting gold rush and cavalry action forced the Cheyenne (and other Plains tribes) into greater confrontation with the settlers. In 1875, when all Western tribes were ordered onto reservations, the Northern Cheyenne refused, choosing to live their traditional life on the prairies. The victory of the Native Americans over Custer's forces in 1876 earned the Cheyenne brief freedom, but within a year of the Battle of the Little Bighorn, all tribe members were forced onto reservations.

The tiny town of Busby was the site of a historic and culturally significant **reburial** in 1993, when remains of Northern Cheyenne killed during the Indian Wars were retrieved from the Smithsonian and other East Coast museums and reburied in their homeland. The remains got to these museums as a result of an 1880s ballistics study commissioned by the U.S. Army—they wanted to see how effectively their new carbines were killing Native Americans. In 1990 a federal law permitted the remains to be returned to the reservation, where they were buried.

Sights

The **St. Labre Indian School** was established in Ashland in 1884, after a Catholic soldier stationed at Fort Keogh contacted his bishop to tell him of the woeful state of the Cheyenne, who were wandering, starving, and homeless on the Tongue River. The bishop bought land on the river, and in 1884 four nuns from Toledo, Ohio, established the school and mission.

The mission remains a center of Cheyenne cultural and educational life, currently schooling 700 students. The mission also operates alcohol treatment, employment counseling, and other social services. Its modern chapel, built from local stone in the shape of an enormous tepee, dominates the campus. Tours are available. On the mission grounds, the **Cheyenne Indian Museum and Ten Bears Gallery** (406/784-4500, 8:30am-4:30pm Mon.-Fri. Memorial Day-Labor Day, 9am-3pm Mon.-Fri. Labor Day-Memorial Day) displays and sells examples of the tribe's fabulous beadwork.

Events

There are two powwows, a large one in Lame Deer on the Fourth of July and another in Ashland over Labor Day. Cheyenne powwows feature dancing contests, singing, and lots of food.

Accommodations and Food

Although the tribal headquarters for the Northern Cheyenne is located at Lame Deer, Ashland is the reservation's primary trading town and has the reservation's only motel, the **Western 8** (406/784-2400, $55-75). Dining opportunities are rather perfunctory.

Information

Contact the **Northern Cheyenne Nation**

The St. Labre mission church was designed to resemble a traditional tepee.

(406/477-6284, www.cheyennenation.com) at P.O. Box 128, Lame Deer, MT 59043.

CUSTER NATIONAL FOREST, ASHLAND DIVISION

Across the Tongue River from the Northern Cheyenne Reservation is eastern Montana's largest block of national forest. Like other isolated islands of woodland within the vast archipelago of the Custer National Forest, the **Ashland Division** (406/784-2344, www. fs.usda.gov/custer) is largely overlooked by travelers, save the hunters who come to stalk trophy mule deer and wild turkeys.

As in the other forests of southeastern Montana, here ponderosa pine savannas are interspersed with short-grass prairie, and isolated sandstone bluffs rise up spookily from the plains. The entire area is rich in wildlife, especially birds.

Like the other Custer forests, this is largely an undeveloped destination for visitors. But before dismissing these remote areas, adventurous travelers should consider stopping to enjoy the vast and lonely expanses of these high-prairie grasslands and woodlands.

Three areas of the Ashland Division have been designated as riding and hiking areas. They are off-limits to motorized vehicles, making them ideal for nature study and wildlife viewing. While the Forest Service had horses in mind when they called it a riding area, the rough but open landscape is also ideal for mountain-bike exploration. There are no maintained hiking trails, but the nature of the landscape allows for considerable ambling and scrambling.

Red Shale Campground (no water, no fee) is six miles east of Ashland and has 14 units. Other campsites are remoter. The **Holiday Springs** campsite is of interest not only because it serves as a campground but also because the Forest Service maintains a rental cabin there. **Whitetail Cabin** (877/444-6777 reservations, $30) sleeps four and has electrical power (though no water). The cabin and campsite are about 18 miles east of Ashland, up the East Fork of Otter Creek.

The Judith Basin and Central Montana

Look for ★ to find recommended sights, activities, dining, and lodging.

Highlights

★ **Historic Lewistown:** Lewistown has one of the loveliest locations in the state, in a verdant valley below round-peaked mountains. The old town center is remarkably intact, showing the handiwork of immigrant stonemasons who quarried local sandstone (page 323).

★ **Lewistown Art Center:** You may be miles from the hubs of Montana art, but the Lewistown Art Center is an island of sophistication—and the gift shop is an excellent spot to pick up souvenirs (page 324).

★ **Big Springs:** A fish hatchery may not seem like a compelling destination on the surface, but the hatcheries are here due to Big Springs, the world's third-largest freshwater spring. More a

park than a hatchery, it's a lovely place for a stroll and a picnic (page 324).

★ **White Sulphur Springs:** Its hot mineral waters were popular with Native Americans for centuries. This old ranch town is still a fascinating destination for hot-springs enthusiasts. Successful cattle and sheep ranchers displayed their wealth by building prestigious homes here (page 332).

★ **Charles M. Bair Family Museum:** Tour the Bair family's rambling ranch house and experience a fascinating collection of European furniture, impressionist and cowboy paintings, silver, and Native American artifacts (page 339).

Central Montana is the state's hybrid province: Here, hundreds of miles from the Rocky Mountains' front range, isolated mountain peaks rise up like islands from the surrounding prairie. Called outliers, these ranges are literally habitat

"islands" to plants and wildlife otherwise found only in the fastness of the Rockies and represent some of Montana's most curious geologic history.

About 50 million years ago, vast amounts of magma began to rise randomly along faults and fractures in overlying rock. In some cases, as in the Highwood Mountains, volcanic eruptions occurred. Sometimes the magma pooled under existing sedimentary levels, bulging these strata up to mountain height (the Big Snowy Range). In other cases, magma flowed along fractures until lakes of lava formed at their ends. Erosion has eaten away the softer sedimentary casts, leaving spiny lava outcrops (like Square Butte).

The molten rock that hardened into mountains in central Montana is unusual. Not only has it proved to be rich in gold, silver, and lead, but it also contains minerals that are rare elsewhere. Some of the world's bluest and most valued sapphires are mined on Yogo Creek in the Little Belt Mountains.

Between the mountains are prairielike plateaus—the Judith Basin is the largest and most central of these—that were an ample home first to buffalo, and then, in the same pattern as the rest of eastern Montana, to livestock and farmers. But the mountains inevitably intrude, and nowhere on the central Montana prairies are they out of sight.

It seems odd that such a rich, central, and practical region should be one of the last settled in Montana. But the area's potent amalgam presents the traveler with a telescoped menu of the state's best offerings in hiking, hunting, fishing, wildlife viewing, scenery, and flat-out Western culture.

PLANNING YOUR TIME

The Judith Basin and central Montana are a place of quiet, uneventful beauty. While not a

---

Previous: downtown Roundup; in the Judith Basin near Stanford. **Above:** Lewis and Clark National Forest.

major destination, it's worth spending a day or two here to explore this agricultural heartland. If you're crossing the state, consider taking either Highway 12 or Highway 200, both of which transect this region. Each leads to plenty of worthy diversions for aficionados of history and recreation.

Spend a morning exploring **Lewistown's** handsome downtown, with stops at **Lewistown Art Center** and perhaps a picnic at the **Big Springs**, a lovely park and fish hatchery at the world's third-largest freshwater spring. Several gold-rush **ghost towns** in the surrounding mountains make a good excuse for an afternoon drive past grain fields and through lovely mountain meadows. If you plan to be in Lewistown in mid-August, consider taking in one of the many events at the **Montana Cowboy Poetry Gathering,** one of the West's largest Western poetry festivals.

Wind through the Little Belt Mountains to **White Sulphur Springs,** where you can unwind in the hot mineral pools at the **Spa Hot Springs.** Anglers should explore the **Smith River,** a blue-ribbon trout stream in a remote mountain canyon.

East on Highway 12, the drive follows the old tracks of the Milwaukee Road, which once brought farmers and ranchers to this isolated landscape of foothills and prairies. The old ranching towns of **Harlowton** and **Roundup** have well-preserved town centers that are little changed since the 1930s. A sleepy historicity is their main attraction today.

There's history of a different sort near Martinsdale at the **Charles M. Bair Family Museum,** a sprawling ranch house and art museum that preserves the paintings, furniture, and artifacts of one of Montana's most notable ranch families.

INFORMATION

For free travel information, contact the Montana Office of Tourism's **Central Montana** regional office at P.O. Box 3166, Great Falls, MT 59403, 406/761-5036 or 800/527-5348, http://centralmontana.com.

The **Bureau of Land Management office** (406/538-7461) is at 920 Northeast Main in Lewistown. Most of the mountains in the area are part of the **Lewis and Clark National Forest,** Jefferson Division. The Forest Supervisor's Office can be reached at P.O. Box 871, Great Falls, MT 59403, 406/791-7700.

GETTING THERE AND AROUND

Much of central Montana is within a couple of hours of Great Falls or Billings, both of whose airports are served by major air carriers. There is no public transportation through the area.

Auto Tours

If you're a fan of Charlie Russell paintings or Montana history, or just looking for a theme for your central Montana explorations, consider taking the **C. M. Russell Auto Tour.** Charlie Russell spent most of his life between Great Falls and the Judith Basin, and images of the unique landscape, as well as noted events from the area's early history, made their way onto his canvases.

Several private and public sponsors worked together to produce an interpretive guide to central Montana that brings the paintings and landscapes back together. The free guide, available from most tourism offices or directly from the Central Montana regional office, keys 25 of Russell's most famous paintings to the landscapes and stories that were part of their genesis. The interpretive points, marked by signs, stand mostly along Highway 200 between Great Falls and Lewistown, with a profusion around Russell's old stomping grounds at Utica. It's a great day trip through beautiful country—one that makes Russell's achievement even more meaningful.

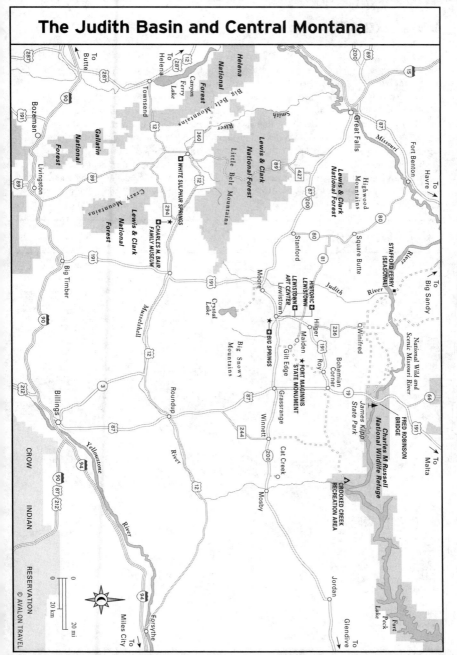

The Judith Basin and Central Montana

© AVALON TRAVEL

Lewistown

Nestled along Big Spring Creek at the foot of the Judith, Big Snowy, and Moccasin Mountains, is Lewistown (pop. 5,800, elev. 3,960 feet), the hub of central Montana (actually, the exact center of the state is located at 1105 W. Main St.). Lewistown is a lively trading center for farmers and ranchers in the fertile Judith Basin country and provides ample facilities and temptations for the traveler. Besides the city's many buildings of historic and architectural interest, within 30 miles are

hiking trails, mountain lakes, trout streams, wildlife viewing, and ghost towns.

For travelers heading east from Lewistown on Highway 200 toward Jordan, be sure to gas up before leaving town. Once the traveler descends from the pass of the Judith Mountains 10 miles east of Lewistown, unadulterated eastern Montana lies ahead. Between Lewistown and the North Dakota border on Highway 200—some 280 miles— you'll find only three small towns with gas stations and only two of these have motels. Plan accordingly.

HISTORY

Big Spring Creek Valley was strategically located for settlement and trade entering central Montana. Fort Sherman trading post, founded in 1873, served hunters, trappers, and the Crow. The Carroll Trail, a stage route connecting Missouri River steamboats with the gold camps at Helena, was established one year later and passed near the trading post. Camp Lewis, a temporary military post, was built to protect commerce along the trail in the same year.

The Métis

The first permanent settlement came in 1879, when Métis families settled along Big Spring Creek. The half-French, half-Chippewa Métis had lived on the prairies of the northern United States and southern Canada until the Riel Rebellion of 1870. Dislocated by the English, the Métis fragmented and drifted westward in search of a homeland. Louis Riel joined the Big Spring Creek Métis in the early 1880s, but in 1884 he returned to Canada with most of his people to organize and resist English Canadian incursions against the Canadian Métis.

After the second Riel Rebellion failed in 1885, the Métis drifted back into Montana as "landless Indians," most of whom were eventually settled on the Rocky Boys Reservation. Some Métis remained on Big Spring Creek and established homesteads. Francis Janeaux opened a store and laid out part of his land for the town that eventually became Lewistown.

Taming the Territory

Meanwhile, the Judith Basin was opening up to agriculture as ranchers moved in to graze the rich prairies in the 1880s. Prospectors discovered gold at Maiden in the Judith Mountains around the same time. The central Montana gold rush was on, and mining camps like Gilt Edge, Maiden, and Kendall boomed.

Lewistown remained a rough-and-ready

frontier town longer than comparable Montana communities. Rustlers preyed on local ranches, finding ample shelter in the rugged Missouri Breaks north of town. A shoot-out on Main Street in 1884 ended the careers of two suspected ringleaders, known to their contemporaries as Rattlesnake Jake and Longhair Owen.

Lewistown was incorporated in 1899, and in 1903 the Central Montana Railroad (bought in 1908 by the Milwaukee Road) reached this center of mining and ranch trade. What was taken out in cattle or gold was dwarfed by the numbers of homesteaders who came in. The Judith Gap and Lewistown area was quickly and heavily settled by hopeful farmers: Nearly 6.5 million acres of land were opened for homesteading. The hegemony of the open-range ranches was broken, and by 1920, mining had declined in importance. The fertile countryside of central Montana sheltered homesteaders from some of the vicissitudes encountered by settlers elsewhere, and the gracious homes and buildings of Lewistown bear testimony to the community's long-standing stability.

SIGHTS
★ Historic Lewistown

Lewistown has one of the prettiest physical settings in the state and almost matches its natural attributes with its graceful early-20th-century architecture. Three neighborhoods are listed as historic districts in the National Register of Historic Places. The **chamber of commerce** (408 N.E. Main St.) provides brochures with walking tours of Lewistown. Not to miss: The **Fergus County Courthouse,** at 8th Avenue and Main, built in 1907 mission style; behind it, on Broadway and 7th, is a wooden frame building that originally served as officers' quarters at Fort Maginnis, which was built in 1880 to protect ranchers from Indian attack; immediately next door is a wonderful example of a sandstone "four-square" home. The **Silk Stocking District,** an area bounded by Boulevard and Washington Streets at 2nd and 3rd Avenues, contains a

the Fergus County Courthouse

mix of arts-and-crafts style and neo-Georgian homes built by early haberdashers (hence the name). Dominant throughout, and especially downtown along Main Street, are buildings made of sandstone bricks carved by immigrant Croatian stone carvers.

Central Montana Museum

Located in the same complex as the chamber of commerce, the **Central Montana Museum** (408 N.E. Main St., 406/538-5436, 10am-4pm daily, Memorial Day-Labor Day, free) features Native American relics, homesteader memorabilia, and reminders of life on the open range.

★ Lewistown Art Center

Specializing in Montana art, the small gem of a gallery known as the **Lewistown Art Center** (323 W. Main St., 406/535-8278, www.lewistownartcenter.org, 11:30am-5:30pm Tues.-Fri., 10am-4pm Sat., free) mixes traveling shows of regional art with a good selection of local arts and crafts in its gallery shop. In addition to frequently changing exhibits, the center also offers art classes, workshops, and a variety of performing arts.

★ Big Springs

A scenic place for a picnic is the Big Springs, the source of Upper Big Spring Creek. Big Springs is the world's third-largest freshwater spring, discharging 62,700 gallons of water a minute—more than three million gallons per hour. Water from the spring is bottled and sold as drinking water throughout Montana. Some of the water is diverted into Big Springs Fish Hatchery, Montana's largest. Near the hatchery, along the stream and among trees, there's a lovely picnic area; tours of the hatchery are available. Follow 1st Avenue south to Country Club Road and then follow Highway 466 for two miles and watch signs for the hatchery. At the hatchery, take a sharp left turn and follow signs to the park. Big Springs is six miles south of Lewistown.

Ghost Towns

Note that most of the following ghost towns are on private land. Landowners have

Downtown Lewistown has a wealth of historic buildings.

reportedly been restricting access for several reasons, including liability and to keep people from packing everything off. If you're keen on actually investigating one of the following gold camps firsthand, call the chamber of commerce to find out what the current state of access is. Otherwise, just driving the public roads to the ghost towns makes for a nice afternoon drive.

Gold was discovered in 1880 in the Judith Mountains; by 1881 **Maiden** claimed a population of 6,000, making it larger than Lewistown, with which it vied for county seat when Fergus County was formed in 1882. To reach Maiden, take Highway 191 north from Lewistown for 10 miles, then turn east on a good secondary road, the Maiden Road, for nine miles. This gold camp burned in 1905, making the inevitable ghost town a bit more spectral.

The road up Warm Springs Creek in the Judith Mountains to Maiden is scenic, and it continues five miles over a steep pass (this is not a road for trailers) to **Gilt Edge,** another gold camp gone bust. Gilt Edge boomed when gold was discovered in the early 1890s. Calamity Jane Cannary claimed that Gilt Edge was her favorite town; she also claimed that she was the local law enforcement. A few intact brick buildings and more disintegrating plank buildings remain. Gilt Edge can also be reached by traveling Highway 200 east from Lewistown for 14 miles, then turn north another mile.

Farther west in the Moccasin Mountains is **Kendall,** a gold camp that reached its zenith in the first years of the 20th century. The foundations of the union hall and a bandstand are among the remains. Take Highway 191 north to Hilger, then turn west for about six miles.

Charlie Russell Chew-Choo

It's a real groaner of a pun, but this dinner train through farm and ranch land north of Lewistown has proved to be a popular summer weekend activity. The train, made up of historic dining cars, leaves from a boarding station about 40 minutes northwest of Lewistown, and travels to Denton, a 3.5-hour

Granville Stuart, Ambitious Prairie Pioneer

Granville Stuart—statesman, rancher, vigilante, writer, ambassador, and librarian—was among those early Montana settlers who thrived on challenge. Born to Scottish parents in West Virginia in 1834, Stuart accompanied his family to California during that state's gold rush. While returning east, he and his brother James detoured north through Montana. On Gold Creek, near Drummond, they discovered gold in 1858 and essentially started the Montana gold rush. But Granville was canny enough to realize that the real way to make money in a gold camp was to supply goods to miners, and he opened a store in Bannack in 1862. He also operated a small farm and soon ran a lumber company as well. He saved his money and began to dabble in ranching in the Deer Lodge Valley.

Stuart was elected to the Territorial Council in 1871 and to the lower house twice, in 1876 and 1879. By 1879 he moved cattle out of western Montana and onto the plains of the east. He helped found the DHS Ranch east of Lewistown, the first large ranch in this part of the state.

Entire towns of rustlers sprang up in the inaccessible Missouri Breaks to prey on these early ranches. At a meeting in Helena in 1884, the Montana Stockgrowers Association named Stuart—a founding member of the association—president. Stuart presented the cattlemen's concerns about rustling to the legislature and to the administrators of Fort Maginnis, which the U.S. Army had built in the hay yard of the DHS Ranch. When the branches of the government failed to adopt appropriate measures, Stuart and other fed-up ranchers founded "Stuart's Stranglers," a vigilante gang that broke the back of organized rustling. Estimates of the number of suspected rustlers killed in 1884 vary, but at least 25 died, and perhaps as many as 100.

The winter of 1886-1887 dealt with Stuart as sternly as others on the Montana prairies. He swore that he would never again winter an animal he couldn't shelter. In 1891 he became the state land agent, and he selected 600,000 acres of government land for lease, whose proceeds still support the state school system. In 1894 he was named envoy to Paraguay and Uruguay by President Cleveland. Stuart retired to Montana in 1899 and became the Butte public librarian until his death in 1918.

Although not formally educated, Stuart was an avid reader with a taste for Byron, Shakespeare, and the Bible. His memoir, *Forty Years on the Prairie,* is fascinating reading.

---

ride through some lovely country filled with wildlife, and over the vertigo-inducing Hanover Trestle.

A prime-rib dinner is included in the ticket price ($100 adult, $50 children 12 and under), along with Western entertainment. During Lewistown's Cowboy Poetry Gathering, the trip is accompanied by cowboy rhymes. The train has a somewhat erratic schedule, but generally runs most Saturdays from June through September, with several "polar express" runs in December. Contact 800/216-5436 or www.montanadinnertrain.comfor departure times and reservations.

RECREATION
Fishing
The Lewistown area offers great trout fishing.

Big Spring Creek issues forth from a spring seven miles south of town, and locals consider it one of the best fishing streams in the state. Turn south on 1st Avenue and follow signs to Heath or the State Fish Hatchery. Warm Springs Creek is also good trout fishing in a more rural setting. Take Highway 191 north 10 miles to the intersection of Warm Springs Creek Road.

Lake anglers are also in luck. **Crystal Lake,** high in the Big Snowy Mountains, affords excellent recreational opportunities, including good fishing for rainbows. No motorized boats are allowed. Good hiking trails, overnight camping, and picnicking make Crystal Lake a popular destination for locals. Crystal Lake is 35 miles south of Lewistown; follow Highway 200 west 7 miles, then follow well-signed gravel roads 28 miles south (or turn off at Moore; it's 21 miles to the lake from here).

Hiking

The gentle domed peaks of the Big Snowy Mountains provide surprisingly challenging and rewarding hikes. From the south end of Crystal Lake, **Uhlhorn Trail** leads up an initially steep grade to the Big Snowy Crest. High, moderately flat alpine meadows open out across the saddle of the mountains, with great views across the plains of eastern Montana. At the crest the trail divides. To the west a two-mile-long trail leads to Ice Cave, a cool and exciting place to explore with a flashlight. A longer hike involves following the crest trail to the east. The trail continues through meadows until, about six miles in, the ridge narrows to Knife Blade Ridge. The trail skirts abrupt drops on both sides before reaching Greathouse Peak, about 10 miles from the crest trailhead.

Parks

Symmes Park has a picnic area, tennis courts, and a playground, and is located right behind the chamber of commerce and museum at Highway 200 and Prospect Avenue. The city swimming pool and waterslide is in **Frank Day Park** (6th Ave. and Cook St., 12 blocks south of Main). Also at Day Park is Open Market, a farmers' and crafters' market held on summer Saturday mornings.

Golf

The **Pine Meadows Golf Course** (south of Lewistown on Spring Creek Rd., 406/538-7075) is a nine-hole course situated above a pastoral mountain stream. The **Judith Shadows Golf Course** (off Marcella Rd., 406/538-6062) is the town's new 18-hole course.

EVENTS

Lewistown's biggest summer festival is the **Montana Cowboy Poetry Gathering** (www.montanacowboypoetrygathering.com).

Every year the number and quality of the poets increase, with homespun artists coming from all over the western United States and Canada. Headquartered at the Yogo Inn, but with functions held in a variety of locations around Lewistown, the gathering happens in mid-August. It's a great time to visit Lewistown, as the festival has really taken off in popularity and reputation, with new functions and activities added every year. Be sure to make reservations well in advance.

ACCOMMODATIONS

The **Mountain View Motel** (1422 W. Main St., 406/535-3457 or 800/862-5786, www. mountainviewmontana.com, $65-85 and up) is located near restaurants and convenience stores and also has two two-bedroom houses and one two-bedroom suite, all fully furnished, for daily or weekly rent; pets are allowed.

The **Super 8** (102 Wendell, 406/538-2581, $76-85 and up) stands on the hill west of town. On the east edge of town is the well-maintained **B & B Motel** (520 E. Main St., 406/535-5496 or 877/538-3563, $75-85).

The ★ **Historic Calvert Hotel** (216 7th Ave. S., 406/535-5411 or 877/371-5411, www. thecalverthotel.com, $90-115) is a newly remodeled 1912 hotel that started out as the county's high school dormitory. The entire structure has been upgraded and renovated, and is lined with more than 12,000 square feet of granite, marble, and porcelain tile work (the new owner is a professional tile mason). The rooms are very comfortable and maintain a sense of history while offering modern conveniences. The restaurant here is one of Lewistown's best and most attractive.

The **Yogo Inn** (211 E. Main St., 406/538-8721 or 800/860-9646, $96-120) is Lewistown's most comfortable lodging. The Yogo was developed out of the old train station by a consortium of local citizens, and it caters to the small convention trade. The Yogo has the kinds of amenities (indoor and outdoor pools, a spa, good restaurant, lounge, meeting rooms) that dignify this class of motel.

Camping

Mountain Acres (406/538-7591, $32) is principally an RV park, located just north of Lewistown on Highway 191. Tent campers will prefer **Crystal Lake,** 35 miles south of town.

FOOD

For a treat, take the kids to the **Bon Ton** (312 W. Main St., 406/538-9650, 11am-8pm Mon.-Thurs., 10am-8pm Fri., 11am-8pm Sat.), an old-fashioned soda fountain that celebrated its 100th year in 2008. In addition to ice cream treats, the Bon Ton serves sandwiches and soup.

The **Stetson Restaurant** at the Yogo Inn (211 E. Main St., 406/535-8721, 6am-9pm daily, $12-28) has Lewistown's most varied menu, featuring local trout along with beef, pasta, and seafood.

The **Main Street Bistro** (122 W. Main St., 406/538-3666, 11am-8pm Mon.-Thurs., 11am-9pm Fri.-Sat., $10-18) adds continental flavors to the Lewistown dining scene, with pasta dishes, salads, and fresh vegetables. Although the decor is plain, someone in the kitchen clearly knows a thing or two about good cooking. Grilled pork chops are served with apple and red bell pepper compote. A pleasant addition to Main Street's dining scene is **Beans N Things** (319 W. Main St., 406/535-5720, 6:30am-5pm Mon., 6:30am-5pm Tues, Wed., and Fri., 6:30am-8pm Wed., 8am-5pm Sat.-Sun.), with espresso drinks, light meals, ice cream, desserts, and crepes. If you are looking for the area's best coffee, head to **Rising Trout Café** (217 W Main St., 406/535-4999, 7am-5:30pm Mon.-Sat., 8:30am-2pm Sun.), where you'll find house-roasted organic coffee plus fresh baked goods.

The **Onyx Bar and Grill** (in the Historic Calvert Hotel, 216 7th Ave. S., 406/535-5411 or 877/371-5411, $10-28) serves pizza, burgers, and such specialties as coq au vin and grilled rack of lamb with sun-dried tomato jam in an atmospheric dining room within Lewistown's oldest (and newly renovated) hotel.

The ★ **Mint Bar and Grill** (113 4th Ave.

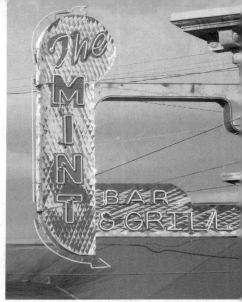

The Mint Bar and Grill is the area's top restaurant.

S., 406/538-9925, 5pm-9pm Mon.-Sat., $14-28) is a stylishly refurbished 1940s bar that's been updated with martinis and tempting New American-style cooking. Pork medallions with jalapeño cream sauce, prime rib, and lamb shanks are on the menu, and there's usually a long list of daily seafood specials too. This is the best cooking for miles around, so do stop in.

INFORMATION AND SERVICES

The **Lewistown Area Chamber of Commerce** (406/535-5436 or 800/216-5436, www.lewistownchamber.com) stands at 408 Northeast Main Street.

The **Carnegie Public Library** (406/538-5212) is at 701 West Main Street. The **Central Montana Medical Center** (406/538-7711) is at 408 Wendall Avenue. The **post office** (406/538-3439) is at 204 3rd Avenue North.

Winter storms can be intense in the local mountains. To check **local road conditions,** call 406/538-7445.

The Judith Basin

Bounded by the mountain ranges of central Montana, the broad basin of the Judith River contains some of the state's richest agricultural land. Streams course through fields and meadows; abundant crops and well-nourished livestock share this fecund domain.

For centuries, this open prairie supported hundreds of thousands of buffalo. After their decimation, the first open-range ranches of Montana prospered here. The Milwaukee Road and the Great Northern vied for supremacy in the Judith Basin, each luring settlers (and hence passengers and freight) by extensive advertising campaigns. The dryland farms were so successful that the Judith Basin became the poster child of the Montana homestead movement. Unfortunately, even here farmers could not survive on homestead allotments during cycles of bad years. Today,

small communities like **Stanford, Hobson, Utica,** and **Judith Gap** only just hang on as trade centers for local farmers and ranchers.

INFORMATION

For information about the Judith Basin area, contact the **Judith Ranger District, Lewis and Clark National Forest** (P.O. Box 434, Stanford, MT, 406/566-2292, www.fs.usda.gov/lcnf).

STANFORD AND VICINITY

Stanford (pop. 400, elev. 4,200 feet) was the Judith Basin's most important trade center for grain and livestock in the early 1900s. It has managed to survive the vicissitudes of drought and bad markets better than its neighbors, and the town's wide streets and

Stanford's Basin Trading Post is a good stop for coffee and gifts.

well-kept homes make it a handsome anomaly in central Montana.

If you're passing through Stanford on Highway 200, it's worth turning north from that road's shabby string of businesses and following Highway 80 north half a mile to the town's old center, where you'll find better restaurants and a couple interesting stops.

Stanford's **Judith Basin Museum** (93 3rd St. S., 406/566-2277, 10am-noon and 1pm-5pm Mon.-Fri., June-Aug., donation) features a collection of more than 2,000 salt and pepper shakers and frontier-era household items. Stop at the **Basin Trading Post** (94 Central Ave.), a large structure that houses a gift and housewares shop, a deli and café, an art gallery, and series of local history displays featuring vintage photos and an exhibit on a dastardly white wolf from homesteader days. It's no wonder that Stanford's top dining option (just across the street) is called the **Wolves Den** (99 Central Ave., 406/566-2451, 8am-10pm Mon.-Sat., $8-18), which specializes in pizza and burgers by day and steaks by night.

The **Sundown Motel** (west along Hwy. 200, 406/566-2316, $58-70) stands next to Stanford's steak house, the **Sundown Inn** (406/566-9911, $12-22).

HOBSON AND UTICA

The **Judith Basin Cattle Pool** was one of the earliest open-range outfits in the state. During the boom years of the 1880s, investors bought cattle and then pooled them together to be

Yogo Sapphires

Montana's most famous gemstones are Yogo sapphires, found in a small area of the Little Belt Mountains just south of Utica called Yogo Gulch. The primary rock in this mountain chain is Pre-cambrian limestone laid down more than 575 million years ago; however, the narrow vein of rock that holds precious Yogo sapphires is much younger.

About 50 million years ago, molten magma rose into the overlying limestone, where it slowly cooled to form a dike an average of eight feet in width but over five miles long. As the magma in the dike crystallized, atoms of oxygen combined with atoms of aluminum to form corundum, the mineral form of aluminum oxide. The corundum formed tiny, perfectly shaped transparent crystals rather than the usual blue-gray prisms. Moreover, virtually every crystal in this dike contained traces of iron and titanium that gave each crystal a beautiful cornflower-blue color, the signature hue that makes Yogo sapphires the most precious gemstone mined in the United States.

Although it is not known that Native Americans gathered sapphires in Yogo Gulch, in fact the word *yogo* means "blue sky" in the Piegan Blackfoot tongue. The discovery of sky-blue sapphires in the Little Belts awaited the Montana gold rush, when seemingly every drainage in Montana was explored by prospectors. Low-level gold deposits in Yogo Gulch were sufficient for a town site of nearly 1,000 miners to spring up in the early 1880s, but the lack of sustainable deposits caused the boomtown to go bust by the 1890s.

One hardened prospector named Jake Hoover persevered here despite the disappointing volume of gold nuggets. Over the years he had collected the small, brilliantly blue stones that appeared along the creek and in his gold pan. He sent a small cigar tin of these stones to Tiffany's in New York City for valuation in 1895 and in return received a check for $3,750, with the price set at a paltry $6 per carat for top-quality stones. Hoover and his business partners quickly staked claims along the dike and began sapphire mining in earnest. The mine later changed hands: By the time the British firm of Johnson, Walker, and Tolhurst ceased mining in 1929, more than 16 million carats' worth of sapphires had been extracted from Yogo Gulch.

The Yogo mines lay dormant until 1956, when production began again. New technology and run by hired cowboys. Calves were branded with the same brand as their mothers; in the fall they were sold, trailed to railheads, and shipped to feedlots for fattening.

Utica was the hub for open-range cowboys in the Judith Basin during the 1880s; here they gathered the immense herds of cattle to divide them according to brand. It was a raucous time: After a summer of sometimes lonely cattle herding, the cowboys had a chance to kick up their heels and celebrate being back in town. Painter Charlie Russell worked the ranges here, and many of his paintings feature the unique skyline of the Judith Basin.

Not much is left in Utica except a bar and a museum, both appropriate memorials to the ghosts of cowboys past. When the Great Northern line went through, Utica was bypassed for Hobson (pop. 244, elev. 3,940 feet), 10 miles down the Judith River.

The **Utica Museum** (406/423-5538, 10am-5pm Sat.-Sun., Memorial Day-Labor Day or by appointment, donation) preserves Utica's cowboy heritage with tools, saddles, and wagons.

Light meals are served at Utica's old bar, the **Oxen Yoke Inn** (406/423-5560, 11am-9pm daily, $7-14). At the junction of Highways 200 and 191 is **Eddie's Corner** (406/374-2471, $6-26), a popular truck stop with a café open 24 hours a day.

mining techniques have meant that miners can now follow the Yogo dike deeper and farther than before. Because of their intense blue color, Yogo sapphires have gained a loyal following among the world's royal and wealthy. Queen Elizabeth II's engagement ring from Prince Phillip featured a Montana Yogo sapphire. The largest cut Yogo sapphire is a 10.2-carat gem in the Smithsonian Institution in Washington DC.

The Little Belt Mountains are famed for silver and sapphires.

White Sulphur Springs and the Belt Mountains

The wide basin of the Shields and Smith Rivers stretches between the Missouri and Yellowstone drainages. Although hemmed in by five mountain ranges, the valleys are vast and flat.

White Sulphur Springs lies at the center of this valley network. The hot springs for which the town is named were first enjoyed by Native Americans; by the early 20th century, developers had started advertising them as America's answer to Europe's famous spas in Baden-Baden.

As elsewhere in central Montana, the mountains drew early settlers to mining camps. Diamond City in Confederate Gulch in the Big Belt Mountains, just west of White Sulphur Springs, was the site of one of the state's earliest and richest gold strikes. Three veterans of the Civil War found the deposits in 1864; by 1867 the town's population had swollen to 5,000, and it had a reputation for wildness and wealth.

The gravels were extraordinarily rich. Legends tell of single pans containing a thousand dollars' worth of gold; in one day miners claimed 700 pounds of gold from one strike. But the diggings were shallow; by 1870 the boom was over and the gold camp deserted, but not before prospectors extracted an estimated $16 million from the gulch. There's little left at Diamond City except ghosts; tiny former mining towns like **Monarch** and **Neihart** struggle on.

The basin offers unparalleled recreational opportunities. The Shields and Smith Rivers, and also Belt Creek, hold pedigrees as great trout streams. The Smith River passes through a deep limestone canyon, making it inaccessible to land vehicles for 61 miles; this section has become a favorite for river floaters.

★ WHITE SULPHUR SPRINGS

White Sulphur Springs (pop. 984, elev. 5,200 feet) was named for the white deposits left by the hot water that burbles up in the city's public park just off Highway 12. The 115°F waters only faintly smell of sulfur, but weary travelers have soaked in them for centuries. Today, the flow is tapped for use in the Spa Hot Springs Motel; it also heats the town bank.

White Sulphur Springs had long been a popular hot springs for local Native Americans; Crow chief Plenty Coups recalled pilgrimages by warriors to the medicinal mud baths. James Brewer chanced onto the area in 1866, as stagecoaches rumbled through along the Carroll Trail. Brewer developed the hot springs as a stage stop for travelers; the waters here are said to resemble the famous springs at Baden-Baden in Germany, and references to Baden-Baden dot his early promotional literature. However, the grand hotel and spa envisioned by early boosters never materialized.

Notoriety of another sort has clung to White Sulphur Springs. Two noted Montana writers, Walt Coburn and Ivan Doig, hail from local ranches. The latter's *This House of Sky* is autobiographical and is set hereabouts.

The Castle

The gracious homes built in White Sulphur Springs during the 1890s are testimony to the wealth of open-range ranchers who found the wide valleys hospitable for raising cattle and sheep.

The Castle, a mansion built in 1892 out of locally carved granite, now functions as the **Meagher County Historical Museum** (310 2nd Ave. N.E., 406/547-2324, 10am-5pm daily, Memorial Day-Labor Day, $5 adults, $3

The Judith Gap

These curious pear-shaped stones in Garneill were discovered by early settlers.

Named for the wide and desolate divide between the Big Snowy and Little Belt Mountains, the Judith Gap has been a transportation corridor for centuries. The Crow crossed the gap to hunt buffalo in the Judith Basin; Blackfeet warriors later pushed south across the area to menace the Crow along the Musselshell River. Traders used this notoriously windy pass to reach erstwhile settlements and gold camps in central Montana. Both the Great Northern and the Milwaukee lines laid track over the Judith Gap to reach homestead towns.

The first settlement in the area was the old crossroads of U-bet, which thrived as a stop on the old Carroll Trail stage line during the 1870s. U-bet was a well-loved watering hole for early cowboys. When Richard Harlow's Montana Railroad pushed through the Judith Gap in 1903, it too named its station U-bet.

During the homestead rush, a telling division of sentiment regarding alcohol led to the establishment of two communities. North Garneill was "dry," while nearby South Garneill (incorporating U-bet) had a guesthouse, saloon, and the accoutrements of an Old West town. In some kind of victory, today only North Garneill survives, if only diffidently and under the abridged name of Garneill.

The **U-bet and Central Montana Pioneers Monument** at Garneill is a huge block of granite on a concrete base. Embedded in the base is an array of local rocks. There are two large, nearly identical pear-shaped stones here, found by early settlers near Winnett. Apparently carved by Native Americans, their meaning has been lost.

Nowadays, the always windy Judith Gap area is noted for its wind turbines: with over 125 wind towers, this is Montana's largest wind farm. Each of the turbines is capable of producing 1,500 kilowatts of power at maximum generating strength (one kilowatt of power provides enough electricity for 240-300 homes). You can't miss the wind farm if you drive Highway 191 between Eddies Corner and Harlowtown—the highway passes beneath it.

seniors and children 5-12). It contains a selection of artifacts from the region's early history and some beautiful period furniture. The mansion is well restored, and the carved wood and moldings are to die for.

Floating and Fishing the Smith River

The Smith River gets off to an easygoing start in the wide basin around White Sulphur Springs but soon passes into a narrow canyon cut through extensive limestone formations. On the 61-mile stretch between old Camp Baker and Eden Bridge, the river can only be reached by boat. The extreme remoteness of this portion of the Smith, along with excellent wildlife viewing and old-fashioned excitement, make this float very popular.

The Smith also offers excellent fishing for brown and rainbow trout. The state maintains two fishing-access sites and campgrounds in otherwise inaccessible portions of the river north of White Sulphur Springs. Take Highway 360 west and follow signs to Smith River (18 miles) or Fort Baker (26 miles).

Because of increased traffic on the river, **Montana State Parks** (406/454-5840, http://stateparks.mt.gov/smith-river) has begun to limit the number of **float trips** down the Smith. Only 73 commercial launches are allowed during the summer, and permits for public float trips not run by outfitters are now distributed in a lottery. Even the campsites are available by reservation only. For up-to-date information on Smith River float trip regulations, including a list of sanctioned outfitters, check out http://fwp.mt.gov/recreation/activities/boating/smithRiver.

Most outfitters will offer four-, five-, and six-day trips down the Smith; the difference in the length of trips is the pace. Four days is breakneck and exhausting, whereas six days is leisurely and suited to anglers. A full Smith River trip costs around $3,750-4,300.

The following outfitters are among the best and most environmentally sensitive. Try **Pro Outfitters** (P.O. Box 621, Helena, MT 59601, 406/442-5489 or 800/858-3497, www.

The Castle houses White Sulphur Springs's local museum.

prooutfitters.com), or contact **Smith River Flyfishing Expeditions** (406/370-2868, www.smithriverflyfishing.com).

Winter Recreation

The **Showdown Ski Area** (406/236-5522 or 800/433-0022; 24-hour snow line 406/771-1300, http://showdownmontana.com), high in the Little Belts, holds the state's record for snowfall—33 feet in one winter. For your $42 lift ticket, you get access to 34 runs with a vertical drop of 1,400 feet, plus a terrain park. Facilities include a cafeteria, a bar, ski rentals, and a pro shop. Showdown is 30 miles north of White Sulphur Springs.

Accommodations

The new **All Seasons Inn and Suites** (808 3rd Ave. S.W., 406/547-8888 or 877/314-0241, www.allseasonsinnandsuites.net, $77-95) has a pool and a complimentary continental breakfast.

The ★ **Spa Hot Springs Motel** (202 W. Main St., 406/547-3366 or 800/898-3303,

John Ringling, Showman and Rancher

John Ringling was born in 1866 to a Wisconsin family seemingly predestined for big times in the big top. One of seven siblings who formed the Ringling Brothers Circus in 1884, John was perhaps the most entrepreneurial of the brothers. After years of touring the Midwest with its signature big tent (the tent could seat 4,000 and still had room for three rings of activities), Ringling led his brothers toward consolidation with the Barnum and Bailey Circus in 1907 to form "The Greatest Show on Earth."

With the world's largest circus in his back pocket, Ringling decided he needed another hobby. He purchased 100,000 acres of prime ranch land on the Shields River, not far from the town now called Ringling, 20 miles south of White Sulphur Springs. He had major dreams for his Montana holdings: Not only would the ranch serve as a training camp for circus performers, but Ringling would also lead the tourist development of this part of Montana, basing his plans on the hot mineral springs at White Sulphur Springs.

Ringling was the chief financier and driving force behind the grandly named White Sulphur Springs and Yellowstone Park Railroad, an 18-mile-long line that linked the town of White Sulphur Springs with the mainline Milwaukee Road rail service at Ringling. This transportation link would bring travelers to White Sulphur Springs. Here, Ringling and other developers planned to build a grand spa hotel and resort based on the European style, where wealthy customers could come to "take the waters" in scenic splendor.

The rail line was built in 1910, but before the rest of Ringling's dreams of the spa lifestyle came into being, World War I broke out in Europe, causing worldwide recession and displacement. Managing the circus throughout this period of intense labor shortage and financial crisis preempted Ringling's Montana vision, and plans for the spa were soon abandoned. However, the Ringling family continued to own and operate their ranch until 1949.

www.spahotsprings.com, $77-105) has White Sulphur Springs's trademark hot water piped into indoor and outdoor pools. Nonguests can drop by for a swim and soak for $5. The mineral pools are drained and cleaned nightly, making this a very clean spa.

Camping

Consider free camping lakeside at **Newlan Creek Reservoir,** 10 miles north of White Sulphur Springs, or along **Sutherlin Reservoir,** 12 miles east on Highway 12.

Food

The **Stockman's Bar and Steakhouse** (117 Main St., 406/547-9985, 11:30am-9pm daily, $7-24) offers burgers and steaks; for the restaurant, go in the green door on the side street. **Montana K&L Roadhouse** (904 3rd Ave. SW, 406/547-3638, $9-21), just south of town, serves barbecued chicken and beef and more steaks.

Information

The **Meagher County Chamber of Commerce** can be reached at P.O. Box 365, White Sulphur Springs, MT 59645, 406/547-3366. The **Lewis and Clark National Forest** office's address is P.O. Box A, White Sulphur Springs, MT 59645, 406/547-3361.

Highway 12 and the Musselshell Valley

The Musselshell River rises in the peaks of the Crazy, Castle, and Little Belt Mountains and flows east through a wide, wooded valley lined with farms and ranches. Here is some of the gentlest beauty in Montana; shaded by majestic cottonwoods, cattle graze along a rushing river flanked by steep sandstone cliffs. As everywhere in central Montana, mountains loom in the distance like ramparts.

Almost nowhere else in Montana have a region and a railroad been so closely linked as the Musselshell River Valley and the Milwaukee Road; the solid towns built alongside the railroad reflect the confident dreams of the settlers that it brought west. **Roundup** and **Harlowton** have endured as trade centers; however, the scope and solid stylishness of their old town centers contrast oddly with their present chastened realities. They wear their pasts awkwardly, like ill-fitting clothes—modest communities occupying towns built for larger purposes.

Other settlements—Shawmut, Twodot, Ryegate—didn't fare as well. Today all but ghost towns, these old communities are stone and brick monuments to the poignant and mostly unrealized dreams of an entire generation of Montanans. One exception to the rule of hard-luck agriculture was Charles Bair, an early and very successful sheep rancher. The rambling ranch house occupied by Bair and his daughters and their collection of fine art and furniture from around the world are preserved as the **Charles M. Bair Family Museum.** It's one of the true must-sees in central Montana.

Highway 12 parallels the old Milwaukee Road tracks and serves the farming, ranching, and mining communities that sprawl across this piece of Montana. This is one of the most beautiful drives in the state; east to west, it's more direct than the freeway.

HISTORY

The Musselshell Valley provided a rich hunting ground for early Native Americans, but it didn't historically belong to any single tribe; it was either shared or battled for.

By the 1870s, open-range cattle companies grazed the valleys of central Montana. The U.S. Army established a trail linking Fort Custer on the Bighorn and Fort Maginnis near Lewistown; it crossed the river near the present town of Musselshell. Texas drovers considered this ford to be the last stop in the long trail from the south; thereafter, cattle fanned out to graze the rich prairies to the north. Uncharacteristically, the big cattle outfits here shared the range with enormous sheep ranches, especially near Martinsdale and Sumatra.

The Chicago, Milwaukee, St. Paul, and Pacific Railroad, on its way to Seattle, laid tracks up the Musselshell in 1908. Coal deposits at Roundup were developed to fuel the Milwaukee's engines.

Ad campaigns from the railroad convinced prospective settlers of the richness of central Montana. Towns sprang up along sidings, and farmers claimed the bottomland, half section by half section, signaling the end of the open range. The media trumpeted the bumper crops raised by these first-time farmers, and many immigrants responded, choosing new and seemingly secure lives and opportunities on the Montana prairies.

In 1915 the Milwaukee announced that it would electrify its engines between Harlowton and Avery, Idaho, which made it the longest stretch of electric railroad in North America at the time. The engines that pushed the trains uphill ran backward downhill, working both as brakes and as generators to recharge up to 60 percent of the electricity expended on the inclines.

The decline of central Montana began with the droughts of the late 1910s and continued

Ingomar's Jersey Lilly is perhaps the most authentic Old West bar in Montana.

to vast nearby stretches of open prairie that needed a railhead for shipping livestock to outside markets.

Within the Musselshell Valley, irrigated farmland replaces the arid plains. Little towns like **Melstone** (pop. 160, elev. 2,897 feet) and **Musselshell,** once centers for homesteaders, are today crossroads and gas stations for travelers and local farmers. West of Melstone, the sandstone cliffs and bluffs of the Fort Union Formation shelter the valley; their rich coal veins enriched the local economy when the steam engines of the Milwaukee Road crossed the West.

Food and Drink

One of the most famous bars in Montana is the ★ **Jersey Lilly** (406/358-2278, 8am-11pm Mon.-Sat., 8am-9pm Sun.) in the little community of Ingomar. The bean soup here is the pièce de résistance and enjoys statewide fame. The Jersey Lilly is the only business left in town, and only local ranchers and the occasional traveler keep the bar from going the way of the rest of the town. Plank sidewalks, hitching posts, and tumbleweeds in the street aren't added for effect: They're real. Enthusiasts of Western lore can test their mettle at the authentic outdoor privies.

ROUNDUP

The Milwaukee Road railroad put Roundup (pop. 1,931, elev. 3,184 feet) on the map, though it had been the center of cattle round-ups (hence its name) since the 1880s. In 1908, the railroad's steam engines arrived to create a demand for cheap coal in central Montana. The Bull Mountains, an uplift of sedimentary sandstone containing significant amounts of coal, are south of Roundup. Mines here became the Milwaukee's fuel source.

Highway 87 intersects Roundup north to south. Klein, a largely defunct community just across the Musselshell River from Roundup, was once a vibrant mining community. Early immigrants solved the housing problem by building lodgings into the cliff side. Some of these cave homes are now used for livestock;

as later droughts combined with the Great Depression of the 1930s. Nature in Montana proved to be cruel; of the tens of thousands who moved to central Montana during the homestead era, only the frugal, driven, and lucky endured until the 1940s. The rural population decamped; coal mining at Roundup ended in the 1950s, and the Milwaukee Road, struggling since the 1940s, ended its central Montana rail service in 1980.

Today, agriculture nevertheless remains the backbone of local economies. Although large farms and ranches have replaced homesteads, rural life for many in central Montana is as unsure nowadays as it was for earlier, perhaps more naive, settlers.

FORSYTH TO ROUNDUP

Highway 12 climbs out of the Yellowstone Valley and across an arid plain before it drops into the Musselshell River Valley. This is historically sheep and cattle country, and the early prosperity of now-flagging communities like **Ingomar** and **Sumatra** was linked some still house people. Watch for electric lines and TV antennas protruding from stone cliff-side dwellings.

Sights

The **Musselshell Valley Historical Museum** (524 1st St. W., 406/323-1403, 9am-6pm daily, Memorial Day-Labor Day, donations) contains reminders of Roundup's dual heritage as pioneer cow town and mining camp.

Accommodations

Autumn's Inn (740 Main St., 406/323-1000 or 888/422-1224, $64-80) offers air-conditioned rooms with cable TV. Nonsmoking rooms are available, and dogs are allowed. The **Big Sky Motel** (740 Main St., 406/323-2303, $50-75) has rooms in traditional motel units and also a newer motor lodge; all are clean and comfortably furnished. Dogs are allowed.

At **Cowbell Park,** off Highway 12 south of town, there is free overnight camping along the Musselshell River.

Food

Good for a quick bite in Roundup is the **Busy Bee** (south on Hwy. 87, 406/323-2204, $7-26). It's principally a diner that's open 24 hours a day; the large parking lot explains its popularity with truckers. Along the town's handsome old Main Street, try the **Pioneer Café** (229 Main St., 406/323-2622, 7am-7pm Mon.-Sat., 7am-3pm Sun.) for Western home-cooking.

Information

Contact the **Roundup Chamber of Commerce** (P.O. Box 751, Roundup, MT 59072, 406/323-1966) for more information.

HARLOWTON

Between Roundup and Harlowton, the traveler is rarely out of sight of ponderosa pines on sandstone buttes or the cottonwood-lined Musselshell on this length of Highway 12. As elsewhere on the early Milwaukee Road, community hopes ran high: The huge now-defunct hotel at bypassed Lavina testifies

to the ambitions of homestead-era settlers. At Barber, among the deserted storefronts, is Grace Lutheran Church. Built in 1917 by German homesteaders, it could be the prototype for the Little White Church in the Vale; it is also the smallest active Lutheran congregation in the nation.

The original settlement at Harlowton was called Merino, indicating the importance of sheep and wool production in the area. When Richard Harlow's Montana Railroad reached the village in 1900, the jubilant citizens renamed their town in his honor.

Harlowton (pop. 1,000, elev. 4,167 feet) was a division station for the old Milwaukee line; this and a flour mill provided a suitable basis for substantial early growth.

At Harlowton, Highway 191 cuts through north to south. Access to the Judith Basin and the Yellowstone Valley make Harlowton a hub of local travel.

Historic Harlowton

Harlo (as it is known to locals) has one of the best-preserved early-20th-century town centers in Montana, a perhaps unwelcome benefit of limited recent growth. Immigrant stonemasons cut sandstone from nearby quarries to build storefronts. Three blocks of the downtown area, now a historic district, are built of this handsome native stone. Especially notable is the grand **Graves Hotel** (106 S. Central Ave.), a lovely old stone building with wraparound porches and a third-story turret. Built in 1908, for many years the Graves was a beacon of hospitality in this remote part of Montana. It is currently closed.

Other Sights

The **Upper Musselshell Historical Society Museum** (11 S. Central Ave., 406/632-5519, 10am-5pm Tues.-Sat., 1pm-5pm Sun., May 1-Nov. 1, donations) offers two different locations in downtown, both containing local memorabilia, such as the requisite pioneer schoolroom re-creation, old conveyances, and an interesting display of serving vessels carved from 200 different kinds of wood.

On the corner of Central Avenue and Highway 12 is a circa-1915 Milwaukee Road Electric Locomotive. Trains pushed by engines like this were the first to climb the Rockies under electric, not steam, power. The old Milwaukee depot has been restored and is now the **Milwaukee Depot Museum** (noon-4pm Fri.-Mon. Memorial Day-Labor Day, by donation; call 406/632-4720 to request tours outside of season).

Accommodations

The **Country Side Inn** (309 3rd Ave. N.E., 406/632-4119 or 800/632-4120, $65-75) is a handsome log motel with a new hot tub, sauna, and exercise room. It's the top place to stay in Harlo, with clean and simple rooms. In addition to nonsmoking rooms and king-bed rooms, there's also one room that's wheelchair accessible; pets are allowed.

The **Corral Motel** (406/632-4331 or 800/392-4723, $63-70) is 0.25 mile east of town at the junction of Highways 12 and 191. There are three kitchenette rooms, plus three units with suite-style separate bedrooms.

Food

Food choices are very limited in Harlowton. The only place serving food currently is the **Sportsman's Bar & Steakhouse** (406/632-4848, 7am-9pm daily, $8-22), just east of Harlowton. Don't let the shabby exterior put you off—the weird unpainted edifice on the end of the bar is the remnants of the original round dancehall that stood here in pioneer days.

Information

Contact the **Harlowton Chamber of Commerce** (P.O. Box 694, Harlowton, MT 59036, 406/632-4694, www.harlowtonchamber.com) for more information. The **Musselshell Ranger District Office** (809 2nd Street Northwest, Harlowton, MT 59306, 406/632-4391) is just west of town off Highway 12.

HARLOWTON TO THE CRAZY MOUNTAINS

West of Harlowton, the horizon is punctuated by the rugged peaks of the Crazy Mountains, the most dramatic of central Montana's ranges. Highway 191 cuts south along the eastern face of the Crazies to Big Timber and the Yellowstone Valley.

The Musselshell River skirts the northern edge of the Crazies; its headwaters are in the more modest peaks of the Castle and Little Belt Mountains. Highway 12 follows the Musselshell until it divides; it then follows the North Fork through a canyon and past Checkerboard, a pretty community sadly turned into a trailer court. Highway 294 follows the South Fork of the Musselshell and the old Milwaukee tracks, between the Castle and Crazy Mountains.

This is rich agricultural land: The wide green valleys provide open winter pasture, while nearby mountain slopes afford rich summer grazing, especially for sheep. In 1910 Charles Bair, the local sheep baron, shipped 44 railcar loads of wool out of Martinsdale, the largest single shipment of wool in the state's history. At the tiny community of **Lennep,** one of the Milwaukee's electric powerhouses sits idly beside the road, a remnant of that railroad's early electrified service. Along a gravel road seven miles north of Lennep is the ghost of Castle, a silver-mining town that ran its boom-to-bust cycle in the last decades of the 1800s. Lennep was the site of the first Lutheran church service held in Montana, in 1891; the present church, built in 1910, commands a broad view over the valley.

★ Charles M. Bair Family Museum

The Bairs were one of Montana's wealthiest and most unusual ranch families, and their home was opened in 1996 as a museum. One mile south of Highway 12 at Martinsdale, the **Charles M. Bair Family Museum** (406/572-3314, http://bairfamilymuseum.org, 10am-5pm daily Memorial Day-Labor Day, 10am-5pm Wed.-Sun. Labor Day-Oct., $5 adults, $3 seniors, $2 children 6-16, children 5 and under free) is easily one of Montana's most intriguing sites.

To say that the museum is in the family ranch house is to become involved in the kind of understatement that makes describing this collection so difficult. Certainly this house started out as a ranch house, but by the time the Bairs were through with it, the house had been added to sporadically until it was several hundred feet long and contained 26 rooms, many built just to house the family's art and furniture collections. In 2004, Sotheby's estimated the value of the Bair collections at $55 million.

Bair's clout with the rich and powerful at the beginning of the 20th century in Montana made it easy for him to amass his astonishingly wide collection of Native American artifacts, including headdresses, beaded clothing, and parfleches from the last of the Montana tribes' great chiefs. He also accumulated an impressive collection of Western paintings by Charlie Russell, J. K. Ralston, and J. H. Sharp, as well as a gallery of inscribed photos of presidents and celebrities.

Charles Bair's penchant for collecting paled beside his daughters' enthusiasm for it. In their 20 trips to Europe, Marguerite and Alberta indulged in a passion for Louis XV furniture, Scottish china, Sevres pottery, antique textiles, and English silver—and that's just for starters. The Bair daughters were also smart enough to buy up a collection of late French impressionist paintings by Edouard Cortes. When they couldn't find upholstery fabric opulent enough (or one could opine, sufficiently gaudy), they hired French mills to custom-weave designs to their specifications.

This is not your average Montana sheep ranch, and no matter what your preconceptions, you will be bowled over by the collection.

Alberta Bair left the ranch buildings and art collection to the people of Montana, stipulating that the Bair home be operated as a museum. However, the aging ranch house was finally judged to be unsafe to be the home to the art collection and in 2011, a new Bair Museum opened just south of the original ranch buildings. This $3.1 million, 7,300-square-foot museum now houses the Bairs' unique collection. The new museum sensibly groups the art and artifacts into galleries and showcases works that were never on display in the cramped ranch house.

However, anyone who visits the museum must also take time to tour the original ranch

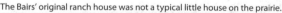
The Bairs' original ranch house was not a typical little house on the prairie.

house, which must be seen to be believed. Though the original artworks have been moved to the new museum, reproductions take their place, so the wildly eclectic spirit of the Bairs' original collection is still there to be experienced. It's not just the sheer abundance of priceless antiques and fine art from all over the world; it's also that in the Bairs' democratizing artistic vision, a Charlie Russell oil painting of cowboys hangs over an 18th-century marble commode that once graced Versailles, or that a Crow vest embroidered with porcupine quills, feathers, and beads belongs next to an impressionist masterpiece. And when you think you've seen it all, there's always the White Bathroom.

Recreation

The Crazy Mountains' heavily glaciated peaks loom miragelike above the surrounding plains; isolated and spectacular, they are among Montana's undiscovered gems for hiking and high-mountain lake fishing. Legends abound as to how they got their name, but they all have to do with women gone crazy with grief.

Hiking trails into the east side of the Crazies depart from the U.S. Forest Service's **Halfmoon Campground,** 15 miles west of Highway 191 on a good gravel road. There are several steep ascents, and the snow lasts well into June at higher elevations, so plan your hikes carefully. A short day hike of five miles round-trip from the campground takes in views of jagged peaks rising impertinently from deep-blue lakes; there's even good trout fishing in the lakes, although not all are easily accessible. Mountain goats were transplanted here in the 1940s and have flourished.

To reach Halfmoon Campground, travel eight miles south of Melville on Highway 191. The road passes through bucolic ranch lands before entering Big Timber Canyon on its way to the trailhead.

Accommodations and Food

The highly atmospheric ★ **Crazy Mountain Inn** (110 Main St., 406/572-3307, www. crazymountaininn.com, $50-58) is an enchanting relict, a turn-of-the-20th-century hotel-slash-former-brothel that's just about the only business left in the near ghost town of Martinsdale. This hotel isn't for everyone, but it's clean and cheerful and totally authentic. If you're fine sharing a bathroom and don't mind ghosts, this hotel might be one of your best Montana memories. The hotel bar and café is open Wednesday through Sunday, but

South of the original ranch buildings, a new museum now houses the Bairs' art collection.

Montana's Late Great Bair Family

Charles Bair came to Montana in 1883 as a conductor on the Northern Pacific Railway and went into ranching in 1891. At the time the land in central and southern Montana was just opening up to agriculture. Bair was able to acquire a sizable holding in the Musselshell River Valley—and grazing rights to acreage on the Crow Reservation. On these properties he amassed one of the largest herds of sheep in the world. At one point in the 1910s, he owned 300,000 head.

A large part of the Bair fortune was made in the Yukon. In 1898 Bair sold 25,000 head of sheep and invested in a company that developed a machine to heat and pressurize water. This hot water was then pumped into the gold-bearing permafrost along the Klondike River, freeing the gold from the frozen earth. Bair came back from the Yukon a much richer man. As befitted a man of power and influence, Bair was friends with many of the celebrities and politicians of his era, including many of the U.S. presidents of his time. He also cultivated friendships with artists, including Charlie Russell and J. K. Ralston (whose works he began to collect), Will James, and several early film stars. While operating on the Crow Reservation, Bair became acquainted with Chief Plenty Coups, the great chieftain who led the Crow toward a more agrarian life. Bair began to collect Crow artifacts, many of which were gifts from the chief.

Bair had two daughters, Marguerite and Alberta, who were educated at Bryn Mawr College. On their grand tours of Europe, the women began collecting the fine furniture and art that distinguish the Bair collection today. In time the art and furniture collection outgrew the family's original ranch house, so the daughters simply added more rooms. Eighteenth-century French furniture was a particular passion of the Bairs, as was Paul Storr silver.

Charles Bair died in 1943. Marguerite married the ranch foreman, Scotsman Dave Lamb, in 1938, and they continued to live at the ranch until their deaths in the 1970s. Alberta, who never married, also continued to live in the family mansion. She was a well-known and colorful character, equally at home sealing a lamb sale in a Miles City bar as dining with royalty in an English country manor. Alberta was known for her proclivity for red hats, fine automobiles, vodka, and outspoken views on nearly everything. She was 98 when she died in 1993.

By the end of her life, Alberta had become a fixture on the Montana cultural scene. The Bairs were one of the most philanthropic families in the state, funding museums, hospitals, libraries, colleges, and charitable organizations. The Alberta Bair Theater in Billings, the city's performing arts center, was one of their gifts. Each year, four students from each of four rural Montana counties are given full-ride four-year academic scholarships, also courtesy of the Bair family.

Alberta's will stipulated that the Bair family home be left as a museum for the people of Montana.

if you're staying at the hotel on days when the café is closed, the owners will make sure that you get fed.

Guest Ranches

With the Crazy Mountains as a backdrop, it's no wonder that some of Montana's best guest ranches have developed such devoted audiences.

The ★ **Sweet Grass Ranch** (Box 161, Melville Rte., Big Timber, MT 59011, 406/537-4477 summer, 406/537-4497 winter, www.sweetgrassranch.com, seven-day, all-inclusive $1,750-1,900 and up) welcomes guests

to live the good life at the base of the Crazy Mountains; it has been in the same family for five generations and still operates as a cattle ranch. Horseback riding is the principal activity, with daily trail rides on the ranch's mountain trails or out onto the high plains. This is a working ranch, so when the Angus need to be moved or checked on, guests are invited to go along to help. The ranch provides a variety of other real-life activities as well, including milking the cows and riding the fence line. Guests are welcome to fish local streams and lakes or hike in the Crazies; cookouts and rodeos are featured, and outfitted trips into the

Crazy Mountain backcountry can also be arranged. The original lodge, where meals are served, is listed on the National Register of Historic Places. Lodging is either in the lodge (bathrooms down the hall), in secluded cabins with wood-burning stoves and private baths, or in small cabins à la frontier. There is a seven-day minimum stay; children's rates are available.

Bonanza Creek Guest Ranch (Lennep Rte., Martinsdale, MT 59053, 800/476-6045, fax 406/572-3366, www.bonanzacreekcountry. com) is a large longtime working cattle ranch with a new focus on guest ranching. If your idea of a guest ranch stay is horseback riding by day and lounging in a private log cabin by night, Bonanza Creek is a good bet. Unlimited horseback riding is the main activity here, and as the ranch maintains a herd of 1,500 cattle, you'll probably have the chance to use a horse as God intended—to push cows around. Guests are also free to explore the ranch on mountain bikes, to head out fishing, or simply to kick back and relax. Lodging is in four new family-size log cabins, each with a full bath, or you can opt for the tepee and the kids can camp out in the sheep wagon. Meals are served in the cathedral-ceilinged main lodge. Sunday-Saturday six-night stays only are offered ($2,100 adult, $1,800 ages 8-12). In May and October, single-night stays are $125 (meals not included; horseback riding not available).

Camping

Free lakeside camping is available at **Martinsdale Reservoir,** two miles east of town on a local access road, and at **Bair Reservoir,** 11 miles west on Highway 12.

Information

For information on the Crazy Mountain area, contact the **Gallatin National Forest, Big Timber Ranger District** (P.O. Box A, Big Timber, MT 59011, 406/932-5155).

The Big Open and Northeastern Montana

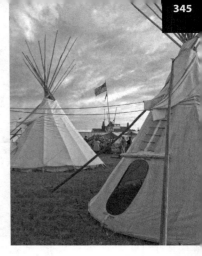

One of the state's least-visited areas, northeastern Montana is usually dismissed as an unwieldy piece of real estate that must be crossed to reach more verdant or populated destinations. But this vast region contains enormous

reserves of wildlife, the homelands of three Native American tribes, and some of the state's best hunting and fishing. Some of the wildest rodeos in the state are permitted out here. At Fort Union, would-be frontiersmen in buckskins gather to shoot muskets. Local tribes look for new reasons to throw powwows. Memories of the Old West—of the open range, cattle rustlers, and the homestead movement—drift in and out of conversations.

Even though you probably won't plan your vacation around it, what you're likely to remember about this part of the state is the people. In some kind of contrast to the rugged terrain and remorseless weather, the inhabitants of this lonesome corner of Montana are genuinely friendly, if haughtily independent, and they are probably some of the most inveterate socializers you'll ever meet.

PLANNING YOUR TIME

Although the long straight asphalt ribbons of Highways 200 and 2 tempt the traveler to

shoot across this isolated corner of Montana, in fact the region offers several unusual destinations that reward the road-tripper willing to take a day or two and get off the main highway.

Off Highway 2 at the North Dakota border, **Fort Union** is a re-creation of the trading fort founded in the 1820s at the confluence of the Yellowstone and Missouri Rivers. More than just an open-air museum, the rebuilt fort evokes both the sweep of history and of the landscape. Come here in late June for the **Fort Union Rendezvous,** a reenactment of a fur-trader's rendezvous.

Fort Peck Reservoir is one of the world's largest, and even if dams aren't usually your favorite destination, there's plenty of reason to make the detour to Fort Peck. The town boomed during the New Deal 1930s and has some massive buildings, including a 1,100-seat theater still in operation as an excellent **summer stock theater** with a five-play season. Near the power-generation towers is

---

Previous: Fort Union; deer at Fort Peck. **Above:** Fort Union Trading Post National Historic Site.

Look for ★ to find recommended sights, activities, dining, and lodging.

Highlights

Plentywood

St. Marie

Fort Peck Interpretive
Center and Museum

Medicine Lake
National Wildlife Refuge

Ft Peck ★ Fort Peck Public
Works Buildings

★ Fort Union Trading
Post National
Historic Site

Sidney

★ Charles M. Russell
National Wildlife Refuge

0   25 mi

0   25 km

© AVALON TRAVEL

★ **Fort Peck Interpretive Center and Museum:** One of the world's largest dams, Fort Peck Dam spans the Missouri River, creating a vast body of water 134 miles long. The Fort Peck Interpretive Center and Museum displays the fossils discovered during the building of the dam and retells the area's history (page 354).

★ **Fort Peck Public Works Buildings:** Fort Peck Dam was built at the height of the 1930s New Deal, so the town center features many massive old Public Works Administration buildings that exemplify the monumental lodge-style architecture of the period (page 354).

★ **Medicine Lake National Wildlife Refuge:** Long lake beds in abandoned channels

of the ancient Missouri River form this refuge, an unlikely migratory bird stopover in the midst of the prairies (page 359).

★ **Fort Union Trading Post National Historic Site:** At the junction of the Yellowstone and Missouri Rivers, Fort Union recreates an 1840s fur-trading fort in fascinating detail (page 361).

★ **Charles M. Russell National Wildlife Refuge:** This refuge preserves the wildlife ecosystem that Lewis and Clark experienced as they journeyed across the prairies in the 1800s. Its most popular site is the water-sport destination Hell Creek State Park on Fort Peck Dam, famous for fossil excavations (page 367).

The Big Open and Northeastern Montana

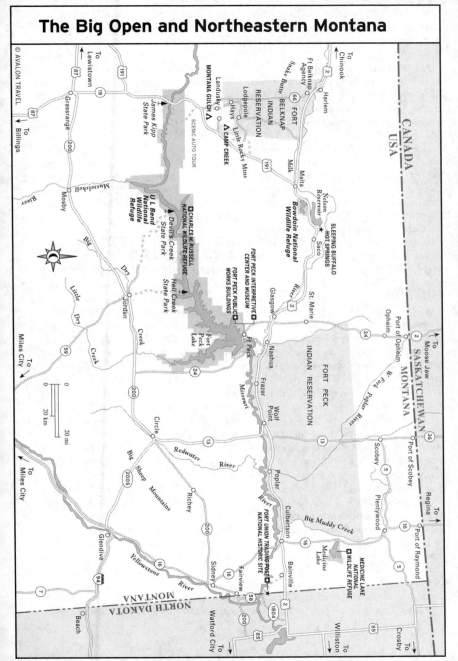

To Lewistown
To Billings
To Chinook
CANADA
USA
To Moose Jaw
SASKATCHEWAN
MONTANA
To Regina
To Port of Raymond
To Williston
To Crosby
To Miles City
To Miles City
Glendive
NORTH DAKOTA
MONTANA
Beach
To Watford City

Grassrange
Mosby
Musselshell River
James Kipp State Park
MONTANA GULCH
Landusky
Hays
Lodgepole
Little Rocky Mtns
CAMP CREEK
SCENIC AUTO TOUR
Snake Butte
BELKNAP
FORT
INDIAN RESERVATION
Ft Belknap Agency
Harlem
Milk
Malta
Nelson Reservoir
Saco
Bowdoin National Wildlife Refuge
SLEEPING BUFFALO HOT SPRINGS
Milk River
St. Marie
Glasgow
Ophiem
Port of Ophiem
Port of Scobey
Scobey
Plentywood
Big Muddy Creek
Medicine Lake
MEDICINE LAKE NATIONAL WILDLIFE REFUGE

U L Bend National Wildlife Refuge
CHARLES M. RUSSELL NATIONAL WILDLIFE REFUGE
Devil's Creek State Park
Hell Creek State Park
Fort Peck Lake
FORT PECK INTERPRETIVE CENTER AND MUSEUM
FORT PECK PUBLIC WORKS BUILDINGS
Ft Peck
Nashua
Frazer
Wolf Point
FORT PECK INDIAN RESERVATION
Poplar
Culbertson
Bainville
Fairview
FORT UNION TRADING POST NATIONAL HISTORIC SITE
Sidney

Big Dry Creek
Little Dry Creek
Jordan
Circle
Redwater River
Big Sheep Mountains
Richey
Yellowstone River
Missouri River

To Miles City

0   20 mi
0   20 km

a new **interpretive center** offering Native American and frontier history plus a rich collection of fossils discovered during the dam-building.

On the edge of the Fort Peck Indian Reservation, Wolf Point isn't really a tourist town, but in late July the **Wolf Point Wild Horse Stampede** brings lots of top-notch cattle wranglers to town for one of Montana's best rodeos.

Along Highway 200, the remoteness of the countryside is the main reason to make the trip. Isolated ranches fill the vast landscape of the **Big Open** between Sidney and the Musselshell River. At the center of this uncrowded region is **Jordan,** gateway to the **Charles M. Russell National Wildlife Refuge** and to recreation on the southern shores of Fort Peck Reservoir at **Hell Creek State Park.**

HISTORY

The Sioux, Assiniboine, and Blackfeet shared these buffalo-rich plains in shifting, suspicious alliances. The development of transportation corridors reaching across Montana's northern tier—first with steamboats on the Missouri River in the 1830s, then with the Great Northern Railway up the Milk River Valley in the 1880s—set the stage for the tribes' removal to reservations.

The homestead era from 1900 to 1930 brought the greatest changes to northeastern Montana. With a farm family on every half section, these arid plains were forced momentarily to yield a bounty of grain. Scandinavians and other Northern Europeans were especially attracted to this unsettled area, and many small villages dominated by a Lutheran or Methodist church spire were settled with vague utopian aspirations. The varying climate, leagued with Great Depression-era drought and insect infestations, brought an end to most homesteads.

Many of the unemployed farmers and tradespeople did find local work, however. The greatest of all Public Works Administration projects was Fort Peck Dam on the Missouri River, built between 1933 and 1940. Employing tens of thousands of workers and flooding 250,000 acres of riverbottom, Fort Peck is one of the world's largest dams and an important source of hydroelectricity.

INFORMATION

Travel Montana's **Missouri River Country** region covers much of northeastern Montana. Write for the free travel information at P.O. Box 118, Fort Peck, MT 59223, or call 800/653-1319. The website is www.missouririver.visitmt.com.

GETTING THERE AND AROUND

Amtrak's *Empire Builder* (800/872-7245, www.amtrak.com) traverses northern Montana, with service east from Portland and Seattle and west from Chicago. There are daily stops in each direction at Wolf Point, Malta, and Glasgow. **Cape Air** (800/227-3247, www.capeair.com) provides twice daily air service to/from Glasgow or Wolf Point to Billings.

Automobile travelers need to be especially aware that parts of northeastern Montana are very isolated: Not every dot on the map has a gas station, nor in fact does every dot exist in a form that's helpful to travelers. Along Highways 2 and 200, gas up whenever possible. Don't count on 24-hour service stations to help you cross the area at night.

If you are thinking of driving through this region in winter, make sure you're ready for it. Winter winds hit nothing between the Arctic Circle and here to halt their chilling advance. While winters are not particularly snowy, cold temperatures—Glasgow's average reading in January is 10°F—combine with these winds to produce even more intense chill factors. Make sure your vehicle is winterized, and travel with plenty of warm clothing and a sleeping bag.

The Milk River Valley

Between Chinook and Glasgow, Highway 2 unrolls between cottonwoods and willows and the green thread of the Milk River. The prairies of northern Montana continue their expansive monotonous rhythm. Occasionally a ridge of uplands infringes—the lumpy Little Rockies and outriders from the wild Missouri Breaks just south—causing the horizon to hike up its skirts.

Ice age glaciers covered this part of Montana, homogenizing the prairie surface and obstructing the old Missouri River course. When the ice sheets retreated about 10,000 years ago, the Missouri found a more southerly valley to its liking. The sluggish Milk River, so named by Lewis and Clark, who thought its waters resembled "a cup of tea with the admixture of a tablespoonful of milk," has borrowed the old channel.

Eastern Montana's only hot-springs resort, a wildlife refuge dense with birdlife, and some of the state's best big-game hunting make a virtue out of these implacable prairies.

MALTA AND VICINITY

Yes, Malta (pop. 2,120, elev. 2,254 feet) was named for the Mediterranean island. No,

Malta was not named for or by Maltese immigrants. As the Great Northern built across unpopulated northern Montana in 1887, enterprising employees spun the globe and then stopped it with a jab of the finger. Thus were deserted sidings along the Great Northern saddled with exotic names (Glasgow, Inverness, Kremlin, Havre).

The siding at Malta jump-started the town. Ranchers whose herds of cattle ranged the unfenced prairies needed a railhead, and thirsty cowboys needed a town to carouse in. Irrigated farms along the Milk River notwithstanding, this is still cattle country: Malta is a rancher's, not a farmer's, town.

Sights

The **Phillips County Museum** (431 Hwy. 2, 406-654-1037, www.phillipscountymuseum. org, 10am-5pm Mon.-Sat. and 12:30pm-5 Sun. mid-May-Sept. 30, 10am-5pm Tues.-Sat. the rest of the year, $5 adult, $ children). With displays of cowboy gear, Native American beadwork, and homesteader-era artifacts, it commemorates the area's history and also its

Malta's museums are filled with the remains of prehistoric life.

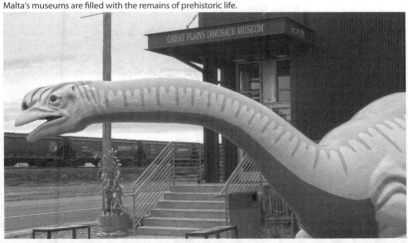

The Little Rockies

On the horizon south of Malta, the Little Rockies are the easternmost of central Montana's volcanic outlier mountains. The core of the range, blanketed by displaced tilted layers of limestone, contains significant deposits of gold. Even though the Little Rockies were in the Fort Belnap Indian Reservation and off-limits to mining exploration by non-Indians, prospectors found the gold in 1884; by the 1890s, in contravention of treaties, miners overran the narrow gulches of these low mountains. The federal Indian agent for the reservation was unable to stop the influx, and he urged the Assiniboine and Gros Ventre tribes to sell a strip of land four miles wide and seven miles long to the Bureau of Land Management. The tribes received $350,000 for the land in 1895; in the early 1990s, the mines were producing $25 million a year in gold and silver.

Even for mining camps, the towns of **Landusky** and **Zortman** drew more than their quota of rough characters. Pike Landusky was no milquetoast: In 1868 he went to the mouth of the Musselshell to trap and trade with Native Americans; instead he was ambushed by a party of Sioux. The irascible Landusky seized his frying pan and started beating one of the warriors with it. Startled, the Sioux braves ceased their advance, and Landusky jerked the breechcloth off another and commenced lashing him in the face with the frying pan. Sensing a demonic presence, the Sioux withdrew, leaving this dervish two ponies as an offering.

Landusky was representative of other rough-and-tough characters in this neighborhood: This was not a delicate society. Jew Jake was the local barkeeper. His leg had been shot off by a lawman in Great Falls, and he used a Winchester rifle for a crutch. The Curry Gang, three brothers who sidestepped civility and the law, owned a ranch just south of town. Landusky fell afoul of the Curry Gang when he objected to the wooing of his daughter by the youngest of the Curry boys, Lonnie. Sensing a slight, the eldest Curry, Kid, rode to town and shot Landusky dead at Jew Jake's bar. As a final humiliation, the third Curry brother, Johnny, moved in with Mrs. Landusky. The Currys gained national prominence after they formed the Wild Bunch with Butch Cassidy and the Sundance Kid and went on a spree of bank and train robberies.

Mining in Landusky and Zortman peaked in the 1910s. The second-largest cyanide mill in the world was erected in Zortman to leach gold out of quartz ore. By 1940 almost all activity had ceased, but in the 1980s the price of gold was high enough to justify reopening the mines at Zortman. Both Zortman and Landusky have preserved the flavor of old gold camps and are protected as national historic sites. Although nominally considered ghost towns, neither has developed its old buildings as a tourist attraction.

prehistory. The museum features local dinosaur finds, including a 33-foot-long skeleton of "Elvis" the brachylophosaurus, a complete *T. rex* skull, and a 28-foot Albertosaurus skeleton.

Fossil diggers have recovered so many fossils locally that the Phillips County Museum ran out of room to display them. And thus was born the **Great Plains Dinosaur Museum** (405 N 1st Ave. E., 406/654-5300, 10am-5pm Tues.-Sat., May-Oct., $5 adults, $3 youth 6-12), which preserves even more of the area's ancient megafauna, including the remains of a stegosaurus, sauropod, and triceratops.

Just two miles east of Malta is the **Bowdoin**

National Wildlife Refuge (406/654-2863). Founded in 1936, this marshy lake is a major stopover for both migrating and nesting waterfowl. White pelicans are commonly seen (there are more than 800 nesting pairs), as are rarer white-faced ibises and night herons. In the spring, watch male sharp-tailed grouse as they drum their chests to impress the females. Access is by canoe or along a six-mile auto tour.

Accommodations

The **Sportsman Motel** (231 N. 1st St. E., 406/654-2300, $55-65) has comfortable older units, some with kitchenettes. The Sportsman also rents RV spaces, and restaurants are within easy walking distance.

The nicest place to stay in Malta is the **Great Northern Motor Hotel** (2 S. 1st Ave. E., 406/654-2100 or 888/234-0935, $72-80), with updated rooms, a bar, restaurant, casino, and steak house. The hotel also offers inside parking—just the thing if you're visiting in winter. The pleasant **Maltana Motel** (138 S. 1st Ave. W., 406/654-2610, $62-70) is a very well-maintained older motel just one block from downtown on a quiet street.

Out on Highway 2, the **Edgewater Motel** (101 W. Hwy. 2, 406/654-1302 or 800/821-7475, $85-90) offers an indoor pool, sauna, exercise facilities, and campsites. A restaurant is adjacent.

Food

For steaks, try the **Great Northern Motor Hotel** (2 S. 1st Ave. E., 406/654-2100, 7am-9pm daily, $12-24). The **Hitchin' Post** (east of Malta, 406/654-1882, 6am-9pm daily, $6-14) is the place for breakfast or light meal.

Information and Services

Contact the **Malta Chamber of Commerce** at P.O. Box GG, Malta, MT 59538 (406/654-1776 or 800/704-1776, www.maltachamber.com). The **Phillips County Hospital** is at 417 South 4th Street East (406/654-1100).

For emergencies, call the **sheriff** at 406/654-1211.

For a local **road report,** phone 406/265-1416.

SLEEPING BUFFALO RESORT

Unique along the northern tier, this rustic—some might say funky—hot-springs spa combines inexpensive accommodations, waterskiing, and aquatherapy. Named for large glacial rocks half buried in the prairies, the hot springs were tapped in 1924 when oil drillers struck a pool of hot, highly mineralized water at a depth of 3,200 feet. When the water reached the surface, the mineral gases ignited. The spring burned for six years.

Initially developed as an old-fashioned health spa, the hot springs at Sleeping Buffalo have been somewhat modernized and converted into a family recreational facility. Presently, the resort, which once included both indoor and outdoor hot pools (106°F), a waterslide, two bars, a restaurant, a nine-hole golf course, and lodging, has new owners who are in the process of restoring the facilities. Stop by and see how it's progressing. **Sleeping Buffalo Resort** (Box 13, Star Rte. 3, Saco, MT 59621, 406/527-3370) lies 10 miles west of Saco on Highway 2, then a mile north along a good gravel road.

Glasgow and Fort Peck

The largest Public Works Administration project of the 1930s New Deal era, Fort Peck Dam—holding one of the world's largest reservoirs—is an enormous tribute to the spirit that overcame the Great Depression. The old rail town of Glasgow, now the largest city in northeastern Montana, was the stepping-off point for the dam project and is now the farm and ranch trading center of the region. Vivid history and unparalleled recreational opportunities, as well as tours of the enormous hydroelectric facilities and a new paleontology museum, make this northeastern Montana's most enticing stopover.

GLASGOW

The Great Northern established a wide spot along the rails called Siding 45 in 1887. The town, originally just a series of tents, became Glasgow in 1889. Glasgow (pop. 3,300, elev. 2,216 feet) grew fitfully as homesteaders and ranchers used the rail connections.

During the 1930s, Glasgow boomed as it became the primary trade and transport center for the shifting population of workers at Fort Peck Lake. The city has a cache of handsome art deco-style buildings; check out the New Deal mural in the post office, 605 2nd Avenue South. This period of growth lasted less than a decade, and although few dam workers permanently settled in the area, Glasgow remains the focus for anglers and holidaymakers at the reservoir.

More problematic for the city was the Glasgow Air Force Base. During the mid-1960s the population of Valley County nearly doubled with base personnel and their families. Glasgow built new schools, redesigned the old downtown for more traffic, and prepared for sustained growth. When the air force pulled out in 1969, the city planners were left with a facility that, unlike Fort Peck, had no apparent afterlife. Currently, Boeing rents the base for flight training and equipment testing. The 1,200 living units on the base are being marketed as St. Marie's, a retirement community for military personnel.

Sights
The **Valley County Museum** (816 Hwy. 2, 406/228-8692, www.valleycountymuseum. com, 10am-5pm daily Memorial Day-Labor Day, $3 adults, $2 children 7-12) is one of eastern Montana's best museums. It presents a Lewis and Clark exhibit focusing on the natural history they documented while traveling up the Missouri River. Local history is presented in a series of dioramas. An authentic tepee and other artifacts are the focus of the Assiniboine exhibit, while a sheep wagon and chuck wagon commemorate the life of the early stockman; there's also a re-creation of a frontier town.

Accommodations
The **Campbell Lodge** (534 3rd Ave. S., 406/228-9328, www.campbelllodge.com, $85-95 and up) is within easy walking distance of downtown shopping and offers discounts for AAA, AARP, and commercial travelers. The Campbell Lodge is two blocks from the city pool and recreation center.

Glasgow's largest motel complex is the **Cottonwood Inn** (406/228-8213 or 800/321-8213, www.cottonwoodinn.net, $96-102 and up), east on Highway 2, on the edge of town. There's a good restaurant, pool, sauna, hot

Glasgow's small downtown has a number of art deco-style buildings.

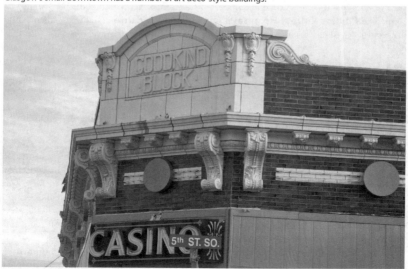

tub, guest laundry, meeting and small convention facilities, and over 100 rooms. A newer wing offers a number of parlor suites. Adjacent, the hotel also operates an RV park.

Camping

For a campsite, consider driving the 17 miles to Fort Peck.

Food

If you like a good steak and a Western bar atmosphere, then you'll treasure ★ **Sam's Supper Club** (307 1st Ave. N., 406/228-4614, 4:30pm-10pm Tues. and Sat, 11am-2pm and 4:30pm-10pm Wed.-Fri.). The clientele, a mix of cowhands, anglers, and businesspeople, converge here for the outstanding charbroiled beef (steaks $14-24) and good salad bar. ★ **Durum** (1015 Hwy. 2, 406/228-2236, 11am-2pm and 5pm-9pm Tues.-Sat., $10-22) is quite a find in northeast Montana. A culinary institute-trained chef prepares food of a quality and selection not often experienced in this corner of the state. House-made pasta, hand-cut aged beef from local ranches, homemade soups, and such main courses as apple walnut-stuffed pork chops with honey balsamic glaze make this a welcome stop for food lovers.

The 24-hour dining room at the Cottonwood Inn's **Willows Restaurant** (east on Hwy. 2, 406/228-8213, $8-18) offers chicken and pork dishes in addition to the compulsory steaks. **Eugene's Pizza** (193 Klein, 406/228-8552, 4pm-midnight daily, $12-20) serves Glasgow's best pizza.

Information

Contact the **Glasgow Chamber of Commerce** (406/228-2222, www.glasgowmt.net) at 110 5th Street South.

Getting There

Amtrak (424 1st Ave. S., 800/872-7245) passes through Glasgow daily each way. The depot is operated by Burlington Northern and endures Amtrak traffic without promoting it.

Budget Rent-A-Car (626 2nd Ave. S., 406/228-9325) is part of Newton Motors.

FORT PECK

Early traders built the original Fort Peck as a trading post in 1867. Located right on the banks of the Missouri River for ease in loading and unloading steamboats, the trading post did a bang-up business with the Sioux and Assiniboine. The Great Northern Railway in 1887 chose to build through the gentle Milk River Valley rather than traverse the intemperate badlands of the Missouri River, thereby bypassing the old fort.

Fort Peck Dam

In the fall of 1933, workers began to clear brush in preparation for the building of Fort Peck Dam. The largest and most ambitious of Franklin Roosevelt's Public Works Administration projects, construction of the dam created jobs for tens of thousands of people during the Great Depression and altered the face of Montana. At the time of its completion, Fort Peck was the world's largest reservoir. At 150 miles long, with a shoreline longer than California's, it is still the planet's second-largest earth-fill reservoir.

The Army Corps of Engineers justified the expense of Fort Peck ($150 million) by promising better river navigation, flood control, hydroelectric generation, and irrigation possibilities. But Fort Peck's biggest impact on Montana was the amount of jobs it provided. During the seven years of construction, at one time or another 50,000 people worked at the dam.

The Corps of Engineers built a showpiece town to house its personnel and serve as the dam headquarters. Named after the old trading post, Fort Peck also contained an enormous theater and a grand hotel, each built in the arts-and-crafts style characteristic of New Deal architecture.

But handsome, well-planned Fort Peck was not where the workers lived or played. The towns that grew up to serve this largely young, energetic, and migratory workforce quickly accrued reputations for wild times that would have made Dodge City jealous. Shanty boomtowns like Wheeler, New Deal, and Park Grove shot up, invigorated with government cash and hard-won 1930s jouissance. For its first issue (November 23, 1936), *Life* magazine sent Margaret Bourke-White to Fort Peck to chronicle life on this new frontier. Little remains of this short and incandescent moment of Montana's development except the landmark New Deal structures at the heart of Fort Peck.

★ Fort Peck Interpretive Center and Museum

Adjacent to the power plants, the **Fort Peck Interpretive Center and Museum** (406/526-3421, 9am-5pm daily Memorial Day-Sept. 30, free) presents the region's rich paleontological, natural, and human history. When the dam was built in the 1930s, workers found a wealth of fossils in the Missouri River badlands, and these specimens form the backbone of the center's impressive collection of ancient species. More recently, the Fort Peck area has become known as prime hunting ground for *Tyrannosaurus rex* specimens—three full skeletons have been unearthed in just the last decade and a cast of one of these is also on display here. In addition, the interpretive center contains exhibits on the native Sioux and Assiniboine and also details Lewis and Clark's journey along this stretch of the Missouri, an adventure-filled episode often neglected in popular histories. Kids will love the exhibits on local wildlife, including tanks filled with mammoth fish—including paddlefish and sturgeon—found in the deep waters behind Fort Peck Dam.

Tours of the **Fort Peck Power Plants** originate in the interpretive center. The hourlong tours are free (9am, 11am, 1pm, and 3pm weekdays, on the hour 9am-5pm weekends and holidays Memorial Day-Labor Day). All adults must have photo ID to take the tour.

★ Fort Peck Public Works Buildings

While the town of Fort Peck will not overwhelm the visitor with its sheer size, some

Fort Peck Facts

- Construction crews at Fort Peck Dam moved 130 million cubic yards of dirt and replaced it with four million cubic yards of gravel and 1.6 million cubic yards of riprap.

- The reservoir has the capacity to store 19 million acre-feet of water (the runoff from one-third of Montana).

- The maximum depth of the lake is 220 feet.

- The dam stretches from bluff to bluff across the Missouri, a distance of 3.5 miles.

- The construction technique that built Fort Peck Dam is called "hydraulic fill." The sediment from the Missouri River bottom was pumped to the dam face as slurry, where it was drained into rock structures that trapped the mud and let the water pass through. More rock was then layered on top of this earth embankment.

of the old Public Works Administration buildings are astonishing relics. The **Fort Peck Theatre** (201 Missouri St.) was built in 1934 as a cinema in an imposing and somewhat squatty chalet style, all the better to accommodate its 1,100-patron capacity. It's hard to imagine a grander example of rustic New Deal architecture. For more than 40 years the theater has been home to one of the state's best **summer theater companies** (406/526-9943, www.fortpecktheatre.org, $17 adults and seniors, $12 students, $5 preschool), staging five shows each summer, from late May through August. Reserved seating is available for an additional $5 per seat.

The **Fort Peck Hotel** on Missouri Avenue and the dam's **administration building** on Kansas Avenue were built at the same time, and share the grandiose architectural vision of the 1930s.

Other Sights

There's excellent wildlife viewing just downstream from the dam. Starting at the Downstream Campground, the **Beaver Creek Nature Trail** winds along brushy streams and ponds; interpretive signs point out habitat and help identify species. Larger mammals, like deer, pronghorn, and buffalo, can be seen along an auto trail at the **Leo B. Coleman Wildlife Exhibit,** which begins on Big Horn Street, just across from the Fort Peck Theatre.

If there's any question in your mind about the meaning of the term "badlands," then continue south of Fort Peck on Highway 24 toward Highway 200. Like a boat cresting waves, the road peaks and troughs through sandstone uplands and spectacular badland ridges and valleys. This land is adjacent to the C. M. Russell National Wildlife Refuge and offers opportunities for viewing pronghorn, mule deer, coyote, and other prairie residents.

Recreation

The Fort Peck area offers the best recreational opportunities in eastern Montana. The 245,000-acre reservoir contains sturgeon, northern pike, walleye, paddlefish, sauger, channel catfish, and lake trout. Locals also use the lake for waterskiing, sailing, parasailing, and windsurfing. There are six recreation areas within four miles of the dam and a dozen others farther afield. The best and most accessible fishing spots are south along Highway 24, along the Big Dry Arm.

If you're a compulsive walleye fisher, consider entering the **Montana Governor's Cup,** a very popular walleye fishing tournament held the second weekend of July at Fort Peck Lake. Hundreds of people from all over the West converge on Fort Peck to compete for nearly $40,000 in prizes. Contact the Glasgow Chamber of Commerce for information.

For boat rentals, contact the **Fort Peck Marina** (406/526-3442). Boaters need to pay attention to storm and wind warnings: Intense thunderstorms build quickly along the prairies, and strong winds can create waves high enough to endanger small boats.

Fossil Hunting

From the mouth of the Musselshell River on, the Missouri River cuts down through the Hell Creek Formation, a geologic layer containing one of the richest records of prehistoric life in the world. Few anglers or boaters go to Fort Peck Lake without keeping an eye open for fossils, and others, taken by the area's Cretaceous-era

THE BIG OPEN AND NORTHEASTERN MONTANA
GLASGOW AND FORT PECK

The Fort Peck Theatre seats 1,100 people.

outcroppings, come to the lake expressly to hunt fossils. Although vertebrate fossil excavation isn't allowed on the C. M. Russell National Wildlife Refuge without a permit, nonvertebrate plant or shell fossils can be removed from public land. Banks of sandstone and shale often offer up fossils for viewing, particularly petrified fish, mollusks, and leaf imprints.

A word of warning: If you are exploring Fort Peck environs on back roads, head back to pavement at *the first sign* of rain; the gumbo hills quickly become impassably slick.

Accommodations

The ★ **Fort Peck Hotel** (175 Missouri Ave., 406/526-3266 or 800/560-4931, http://thefortpeckhotel.com, $69 bathroom down the hall, $81-117 in-room bathroom), built to house visitors during Fort Peck Dam's heyday, is one of Montana's most unusual lodgings. This venerable three-story hotel is on the National Register of Historic Places and contains 47 guest rooms, a bar, and a dining room. The spirit of the hotel hasn't changed much since the 1930s, but that is all the more draw for anyone who hankers for a taste of bygone days. The hotel closes in winter; it's dependably open May through December, but it's worth calling to confirm spring and fall opening and closing dates.

Camping

Numerous campgrounds are scattered around Fort Peck Dam, all with access to fishing. Just under the bluff from the Fort Peck town site on Highway 117 is the **Downstream Campground;** it's in a great location, but bring the insect repellent. Likewise, the **Rainbow Campground** is three miles north of Fort Peck on Highway 117, where there's good fishing for walleye and northern pike. On the lake is **West End Campground,** three miles west of Fort Peck off Highway 24.

Food

The **Fort Peck Hotel** (175 Missouri Ave., 406/526-3266, 6:30am-9pm daily May-Oct., $10-26) offers tasty and imaginative food in a great dining room that's reminiscent of summer camp.

Information

The Fort Peck office for the **C. M. Russell National Wildlife Refuge** (406/526-3464) is north along Highway 117. For information on the history of Fort Peck, visit www.fortpeckdam.com, with a great collection of vintage photos.

The Fort Peck Hotel was built for dignitaries during the 1930s.

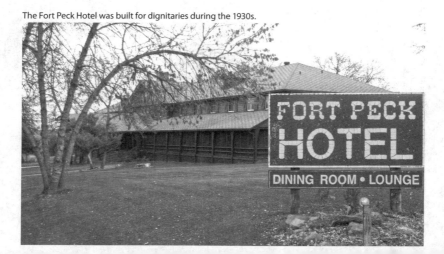

The Missouri River Valley

East of Fort Peck Dam, the Missouri River flows down a wide fertile valley lined by cottonwood trees. Extending north and south of the river are the relentless and austere plains. Also north of the river is the Fort Peck Indian Reservation, the state's second largest, home to the Yanktonai Sioux and Assiniboine. Highway 2 follows the Missouri, linking old river-freighting centers and ranch towns like Wolf Point and Poplar.

WOLF POINT

Wolf Point (pop. 2,600, elev. 2,004 feet) began as a trading post on the Missouri. The thick groves of shady cottonwoods were home to early "wood hawks," who made a rugged living felling trees to feed the engines of steamboats that trundled the river between St. Louis and Fort Benton.

The name Wolf Point apparently derives from an event in the fur-trading days. During an especially harsh winter, trappers had good luck trapping and poisoning wolves. However, the wolves froze solid before they could be skinned, so the trappers piled the carcasses along the river's edge, to be skinned in the spring. But when the trappers returned, Native Americans had taken control of the landing, and the trappers were forced to abandon their booty. The putrefying wolves became a landmark for steamboat crews.

Wolf Point is now a trade town for local farmers and ranchers and a center for the Sioux and Assiniboine. Grain-storage facilities here can warehouse 1.5 million bushels, making Wolf Point one of the state's most important terminals. The Wolf Point Wild Horse Stampede is the state's oldest organized rodeo and one of the best.

Sights

The **Wolf Point Area Museum** (203 Hwy. 2, 406/653-1912, 9am-5pm Mon.-Fri. May 15-Sept. 15, free) contains artifacts from its early frontier and homesteading days, plus a reliquary devoted to native-son trick roper Montie Montana and his horse Rex.

Events

The **Wolf Point Wild Horse Stampede** began as a Native American celebration of horse racing and horsemanship. Early cowboys found the event to their liking and joined in. The Stampede became a full-blown rodeo in 1915, after it was sanctioned by the Professional Rodeo Cowboy Association. Today, it is the oldest and one of the most prestigious rodeos in Montana, where rodeo events alternate with Native American dancers in a mutual celebration of shared culture. The Wolf Point Stampede is held the second weekend in July, with three separate rodeos and parades. Contact the chamber of commerce for further details.

The Assiniboine celebrate **Red Bottom Day** west of Wolf Point at Frazer the third weekend of June. The powwow involves singing, traditional dancing, a giveaway, and a display of handmade wares.

Accommodations

The **Homestead Inn** (101 Hwy. 2 E., 406/653-1300 or 800/231-0986, www.homesteadinnmotel.com, $93-105) has clean and comfortable rooms, complimentary coffee and doughnuts in the morning, microwaves, fridges, queen-size beds, guest laundry, cable TV, and free wireless Internet access; pets are permitted.

In downtown Wolf Point, the **Sherman Inn** (200 E. Main St., 406/653-1100 or 800/952-1100, www.shermaninn.com, $88-93) offers a good restaurant, a lounge and casino, a fitness center, and meeting facilities on-site.

Camping

Rancho Campground (406/653-1940) is one mile west on Highway 2.

Food

Several drive-ins and fast-food parlors are strung along Highway 2, but it's worth driving downtown to find better atmosphere. A real surprise is **Missouri Breaks Brewing and Doc Z Coffee Shop** (326 Main St., 406/653-1467, 5pm-8pm Mon., 4pm-8pm Tues.-Thurs., 7:30am-noon and 4pm-8pm Fri., 9am-noon and 2pm-8pm Sat.). Though the food selection is pretty much limited to breakfast items (it's the coffee shop that serves food), it's worth a stop just to sample the ales. The restaurant at the **Sherman Inn** (200 E. Main St., 406/653-1100, 6am-9pm daily, $9-19) is the nicest in town, with a menu that offers ribs, steaks, and daily dinner specials that present alternatives to the beef pervasive in most eastern Montana eateries. For Wolf Point's best steak ($14-18), go to the **Elk's Club Dining Room** (302 Main St., 406/653-1920, 5am-9pm Wed.-Sat., $12-22).

Information

Contact the **Wolf Point Chamber of Commerce** (201 4th Ave. S., 406/653-2012) for more details.

Getting There and Around

Amtrak's Western District ends (or begins) in Wolf Point, and one train daily passes through in each direction. The depot (406/653-2350) is on Front Street.

CULBERTSON AND VICINITY

As the valleys of the Yellowstone and Missouri prepare to meet, a ridge of high gray badland buttes rises to the south. To the north the prairies begin their flat sweep to Canada.

The land here is rich, and grain production has dominated the local economy since the Great Northern Railway brought homesteaders here to plow. If good soil wasn't enough in itself, nature also found time to bury a wealth of oil here. A new crop for the region is wine: **Rolling Hills Winery** (220 6th St. W., Culbertson, 406/787-5787, 10am-6pm daily June-Aug., 2pm-6pm daily the rest of the year) is eastern Montana's only winery, with a tasting room right along Highway 2. Most of the wines produced are based on locally grown fruit, not grapes, and include rhubarb, plum, raspberry, and blueberry. This may be your only chance to taste wines made from wild chokecherries, the sour but full-flavored fruit that local tribes and pioneers both used for sustenance.

Culbertson (pop. 710, elev. 1,921 feet) has come a long way since the day in 1892 when a young woman stepped from the train at Culbertson station and spent some time looking for the town. Where she came from, two buildings did not constitute one. Early ranchers engaged in horse breeding. The many military forts along this length of the Missouri demanded a large number of mounts. Now a pleasant farming town, Culbertson sits at the crossroads between northern Montana and Saskatchewan.

If you are planning on crossing into Canada, the **Port of Raymond** (406/765-1852) is 62 miles north of Culbertson and open 24 hours daily.

Just shy of the Saskatchewan border are two of Montana's remotest rural towns, Scobey and Plentywood. Though not tourist towns—these communities are noted for grain and cattle production—each have welcoming lodging and dining options.

Accommodations

The **King's Inn** (408 E. 6th, 406/787-6277 or 800/823-4407, $85-95 and up) is an attractive modern motel with all queen beds along Highway 2. There's free camping in the city's **Bicentennial Park** (off 3rd Ave. E.), where you'll also find a playground and picnic area.

Food

The **Wild West Diner** (20 E. 6th, 406/787-5374, 7am-8pm Mon.-Sat., $8-12) is a classic roadside café with a pleasingly unassuming menu. **Stagecoach Casino** (602 2nd Ave. E., 406/787-6181, 11am-9pm daily, $8-21) has a full-service restaurant near the junction of Highways 2 and 16.

Information and Services

Contact the **Culbertson Chamber of Commerce** (P.O. Box 639, Culbertson, MT 59218, 406/787-5275) for all your travel needs. **Roosevelt Memorial Hospital** (406/787-6281) is at 818 2nd Avenue East.

★ MEDICINE LAKE NATIONAL WILDLIFE REFUGE

Medicine Lake lies in an old channel of the Missouri River. Before the ice ages, the Missouri flowed north from near Culbertson along this watercourse, eventually to empty into Hudson's Bay. Ice sheets blocked this channel about 15,000 years ago, and the Missouri sought more southerly outlets. Now the broad valley through which the river once flowed holds a series of shallow lakes.

Established in 1935, the **Medicine Lake National Wildlife Refuge** (406/789-2305, www.fws.gov/medicinelake) is a superior example of a prairie lake ecosystem. Containing 31,000 acres of lake, wetlands, and prairie, the refuge is home to enormous numbers of ducks (10 different species) and geese, as well as pelicans, herons, grebes, and cranes. Pronghorn and white-tailed deer are common along brushy coulees. In an area called the Sandhills are stands of chokecherry, buffalo berry, and native prairie grasses; hiking trails cross the rolling hills.

In 1976, a wilderness area was designated of 11,360 acres of the refuge. No motorized boats are allowed on the lake. On the 18-mile auto tour around the lake, one of the 10 stops is the **Tepee Hills Site.** Here, rings of stone indicate the sites of ancient Native American lodges perhaps 4,000 years old.

Medicine Lake National Wildlife Refuge is 22 miles north of Culbertson on Highway 16.

Fort Union and Vicinity

"A judicious position for the purpose of trade" is what Capt. William Clark recorded at the confluence of Montana's two mighty east-flowing rivers, the Missouri and the Yellowstone. Traders quickly agreed. The American Fur Company built the region's grandest fur-trading post here in 1828, overlooking the juncture of the two rivers. Fort Union prospered in the 1830s and 1840s as it became the undisputed focus of the Montana fur trade.

Today, the site is administered by the National Park Service, which is in the process of reconstructing the fort as it stood in 1851.

FORT UNION

Lewis and Clark camped at the confluence of the Missouri and Yellowstone Rivers on their way into Montana and again as they exited a year later. Upon arriving in late April 1805, they were glad to have made it to this famous landmark, where the forks of the Missouri divide. The captains allotted each member of the Corps of Discovery a dram of whiskey in celebration; the fiddle came out, and the evening was spent in song and dance. The expedition continued up the Missouri River.

Although overwhelmed with mosquitoes, Clark recognized the strategic nature of this site on his return trip. These two enormous, easily navigable rivers drained a vast region rich in wildlife. Whoever controlled the Missouri and Yellowstone confluence controlled the wealth of the two river basins.

During the early 1800s the Americans controlled trade on the Yellowstone and had made friends with the Crow; however, the Missouri River all the way to Three Forks dominated by the Blackfeet, who, through trade for firearms, were allied to the British in what is now Canada. The Americans repeatedly attempted to establish trade with the Blackfeet, with uniformly bloody results.

In 1828, John Jacob Astor of the American

Fur Company ordered Kenneth McKenzie to build a trading fort at the confluence and to break the British hegemony over trade on the Missouri. McKenzie dispatched a trapper who spoke the Blackfeet language to induce warriors to accompany him back to Fort Union. Showered with gifts, the Blackfeet shortly entered into trade at Fort Union. With the Blackfeet suddenly compliant, and with steamboat service (starting in 1832) to Fort Union, all of Montana was open for exploitation. Until the 1850s, Fort Union reigned undisputed over Montana trade.

McKenzie—powerful, unscrupulous, and vain—built up Fort Union to be the most elegant habitation west of St. Louis. Liveried servants poured French wines into crystal goblets at his table; bagpipers piped as he entered his dining room; Native American chiefs were sometimes greeted by McKenzie in full chain mail. The list of guests at Fort Union reads like a *Who's Who* of the American West: painters Karl Bodmer, George Catlin, and J. J. Audubon, Germany's Prince Maximilian, Father De Smet, Jim Bridger, and Washington territorial governor Isaac Stevens.

The enormous success of Fort Union was not based solely on geography. Although it was illegal to sell alcohol to the Native Americans, McKenzie established a still at Fort Union and used alcohol to cement tribal loyalty to his trading post and the United States. This was not a fine single malt that he traded for furs: An early recipe for "Indian whiskey" cut McKenzie's homemade liquor with river water, cayenne pepper, tobacco, sagebrush, and a dash of strychnine.

The damage to the Plains Indians begun by alcohol at Fort Union was hastened by the arrival of the steamboat *Saint Peter* in 1837. The Assiniboine camped at Fort Union contracted smallpox from the crew; from here it spread quickly among the Native Americans in northern Montana. An estimated 15,000 of them—two-thirds of the tribe—died from the disease that year.

As fur-bearing animals in Montana approached extinction, Fort Union waned. By 1867 it had fallen into disrepair. Some buildings were dismantled to build Fort Buford two miles downstream, and the remainder was sold by wood hawkers as steamboat fuel.

Fort Union was the region's grandest fur-trading post.

★ Fort Union Trading Post National Historic Site

Behind 20-foot-high palisades situated on the high banks of the Missouri River, the reconstructed **Fort Union Trading Post National Historic Site** (Buford Rte., Williston, ND 58801, 701/572-9083, www.nps.gov/fous, 8am-6:30pm central time daily Memorial Day through Labor Day and 9am-5:30pm central time daily otherwise, free) is located only yards east of the Montana border in North Dakota and is again the focus of traffic at the Yellowstone and Missouri confluence. The **Bourgeois House** was the home of the fort's factor, or governor. The building was reconstructed as an exact replica of the surprisingly elegant 1851 house seen in paintings of the time; it now shelters the visitors center and a good museum detailing the history of trade and early frontier life on the Missouri. The **Indian Trade House,** where natives swapped beaver, mink, and marten skins for rifles, trinkets, and whiskey, has also been reconstructed, as has a native village of tepees and earth lodges.

From the palisades, the Missouri and Yellowstone confluence can be seen, and it's easy to imagine steamboats pulling up to the embankment to load up with furs.

On the third week of June, the **Fort Union Rendezvous** takes place. At this re-creation of an 1800s trappers' gathering, hundreds of buckskin-clad, musket-bearing, tepee-dwelling reenactors gather to celebrate frontier-era skills and fortitude. There are hatchet-throwing contests, food cooked à la frontier, and black-powder rifle shooting. On Labor Day weekend, the fort is the site of a living-history program, with actors and history buffs playing the parts of early traders, trappers, and natives, all in period garb.

It's important to note that Fort Union Trading Post National Historic Site is not a commercial reconstruction: This isn't a theme park, and it's not just for kids. The fort is one of the most informative and satisfying stops in this part of Montana and definitely worth a detour.

FORT BUFORD AND THE MISSOURI-YELLOWSTONE CONFLUENCE

Two miles farther into North Dakota are the remains of Fort Buford. Built in 1866 in the midst of hostile Sioux territory, the fort was conceived less as a military staging site than as a thorn in the side of the Sioux. It was at Fort Buford that Sioux leader Sitting Bull surrendered in 1881.

The old fort is now preserved as North Dakota's **Fort Buford State Historic Site** (15349 39th Ln. N.W., 701/572-9034, http://history.nd.gov/historicsites/Buford, 10am-6pm central time daily mid-May-mid-Sept., weekdays by appointment the rest of the year, $5 adults, $2.50 children). Although about half of the buildings at old Fort Union were dismantled and brought here to be rebuilt, currently just three original buildings stand at Fort Buford State Historic Site: the stone powder magazine, a wood-frame officer of the guard building, and a wood-frame officers' quarters, which contains a museum exhibit and interpretive center featuring artifacts and displays about the frontier military and Fort Buford's role in the history of the West. The fort's 1860s graveyard is definitely worth a visit: Reading the tombstones gives a fascinating glimpse of what life—and death—was like at this frontier outpost.

Just east of the ruins of Fort Buford along the same road is the confluence of the Yellowstone and Missouri Rivers. A nice picnic area on a broad embankment overlooks this historic crossroads. A respectful stillness seems to encroach: These two prodigious rivers, meeting beneath yellow bluffs in a tangle of cottonwoods, willows, and a crisp dialogue of waters, have embraced almost all of Montana. During the heyday of Fort Union, the confluence was farther upstream near today's fort replica, but in accordance with some fluvial law, their junction has drifted eastward.

Half a mile east of Fort Buford is the new **Missouri-Yellowstone Confluence**

Interpretive Center (701/572-9034, http://history.nd.gov/historicsites/mycic, 9am-7pm central time daily mid-May-mid-Sept., 9am-4pm central time Wed.-Sat, 1pm-5pm Sun. the rest of the year, $5 adults, $2.50 children), which focuses on the natural and human history of the area, with an emphasis on the Lewis and Clark Expedition.

Note that Fort Buford and the interpretive center share admissions—one ticket gets you into both facilities.

Highway 200: Fairview to Circle

The highway system in Montana almost exclusively follows river valleys or old rail lines, but there's one marked departure from the general rule. Highway 200 enters eastern Montana near the Yellowstone-Missouri confluence and, like a sensible highway, follows the Yellowstone Valley to Sidney. Then, perversely, it lights off west across the prairie toward nowhere in particular.

Between Sidney and Lewistown—a distance of almost 300 miles—Highway 200 passes through only three towns with gas pumps (Circle, Jordan, and Grassrange); their *combined* population approaches 1,500 people. As it connects these remote enclaves of humanity, Highway 200 intersects a part of Montana often called the Big Open or the Big Lonely. Unpopulated, marginally productive, and often starkly beautiful, this is one of the last vast frontiers left in the state.

FAIRVIEW

Squat on the Montana-Dakota state line and 11 miles east of Sidney is Fairview, a small farming town in the heart of sugar beet country. Fairview's principal claim to fame is that half the town is in North Dakota. There's camping in **Fairview City Park,** complete with RV hookups, a playground, a swimming pool, and picnic facilities.

SIDNEY AND VICINITY

Although stockmen had begun to establish ranches along this stretch of the Yellowstone Valley in the 1880s, it took the Lower Yellowstone Project, a federally funded irrigation program begun in 1904, to put Sidney (pop. 6,200, elev. 1,928 feet) on the map. The wide fertile valley fell to the plow and hip waders. Sugar beets became the principal crop, inducing Holly Sugar to build a refinery here.

Sidney finds itself on the western edge of the massive Bakken oil basin in North Dakota, and with its new hotels and busy bars, it has the feel of a boomtown.

Mondak Heritage Center

One of the largest community museums in this part of the state, the **Mondak Heritage Center** (120 3rd Ave. S.E., 406/433-3500, www.mondakheritagecenter.org, 10am-4pm Tues.-Fri., 1pm-5pm Sat.-Sun., free) combines the function of a regional art center and local history museum. In addition to displays of area history, the basement houses a re-creation of an old-time Sidney street.

Accommodations

The oil boom has had an ameliorative effect on the quality of lodging in Sidney; be sure to reserve in advance as rooms are in short supply. The **Best Western Golden Prairie Inn** (820 S. Central Ave., 406/433-4560, $143-199) has a pool and a fitness center with a workout room. The **Microtel Inn** (1500 S. Central Ave., 406/482-9011, $159-189) offers free breakfast and has a pool. The **Richland Inn** (1200 S. Central Ave., 406/433-6400, $119-139) is pet-friendly and offers free breakfast.

Camping

Six miles east of Sidney on Highway 200 is **Richland Park.** This fishing-access area with campground is shaded by cottonwood

Sidney's county courthouse reflects the region's wealth from oil revenue.

and elm trees, and it provides latrines, potable water, picnic facilities, and a playground. If you plan to camp overnight, don't leave Sidney until you get permission and buy a $1 ticket from the **Richland County Sheriff's Department** (110 2nd Ave. N.W., 406/433-2919).

Food

Meadowlark Brewing Company (117 S. Central Ave., 406/433-2337, 7am-11am Mon., 7am-11am and 4pm-10pm Tues.-Sat., dinner $8-17) is open in the mornings as a coffee shop and in the evenings as a brewpub with burgers and other simple American fare. For lunchtime burgers and sandwiches and dining featuring steaks or seafood, go to the **South 40** (207 2nd Ave., 406/433-4999, 11am-10pm Mon.-Thurs., 11am-11pm Fri.-Sat., 9am-10pm Sun., $14-32). The **Cattle-Ac Niteclub, Casino, and Steakhouse** (119 N. Central Ave., 406/433-7174, 11am-10pm daily, $14-32) has an ambitious menu that covers the bases from pasta and Mexican food on to steaks and specialty sandwiches.

Information and Services

For more information you can contact the **Sidney Chamber of Commerce** (909 S. Central Ave., 406/433-1916, www.sidneymt. com). **Community Memorial Hospital** is at 216 14th Avenue Southwest (406/433-7700).

CIRCLE

Circle (pop. 644, elev. 2,450 feet) got its start as a cattle town during the open-range years. The biggest outfit hereabouts had a simple circle for its cattle brand, hence the name for the settlement that grew up beside it. Both the Northern Pacific and the Great Northern schemed about extending into Circle; this alone was sufficient to bring in grain-farming homesteaders who had plans for the flat grazing lands of the Redwater River Valley.

South of Circle are the **Big Sheep Mountains,** obviously named by people who hadn't seen a mountain recently. Actually little more than a series of high sandstone ridges, they mark the watershed between the Yellowstone and Missouri drainages. At one time, Audubon mountain sheep grazed along

The Big Sheep Mountains mark the watershed between the Yellowstone and Missouri drainages.

these chokecherry-laden bluffs. They live on in the name of the mountains only: Like the buffalo, early frontiersmen found them an easy, tasty prey and hunted them to extinction.

Sights

The **McCone County Museum** (west of town on Hwy. 200, 406/485-2414, 9am-5pm Mon.-Fri. May-Sept., $2 adult, children 12 and under free) contains displays commemorating Circle's frontier history. On the museum grounds are a restored country schoolhouse, an old church, and a caboose from the Northern Pacific.

Accommodations

The **Traveler's Inn** (at the junction of Hwy. 13 and Hwy. 200, 406/485-3323, $58-70) is Circle's sole lodging option.

Food

The **Wooden Nickel** (204 Main St., 406/485-2575, 11am-9pm Mon.-Sat., $10-16) features local beef in burgers and steaks. **Round Towne Tavern and Casino** (217 Main St., 406/485-7868, $8-19) offers pizza, homemade chili, salads, sandwiches and steaks in an attractive, newly refurbished downtown storefront.

Information and Services

Contact the **Circle Chamber of Commerce** at 406/485-2414. For emergencies, the **sheriff's office** can be reached at 406/485-3405.

There is one service station, open until 9pm. For **road conditions,** call 406/365-2314.

The Big Open

West of Circle, the farms thin out, the fields coarsen into badlands, and signs of human habitation grow scarcer. From here to the banks of the Musselshell River 150 miles west, Highway 200 traverses a vaguely defined region of ranches, gumbo buttes, sagebrush, coyotes, and cowboys. It's known by many names: Big Dry Country, the North Side, Jordan Country, the Big Empty, the Big Lonesome, and the Big Open.

The last of these gained currency a few years ago when environmental activists proposed turning the area into an enormous wildlife park; it's hard to imagine how much more of a wilderness this forlorn and lonesome land could be. Garfield County, nearly the size of Connecticut, encompasses much of this area; it has the lowest population density in the Lower 48, with just 0.27 people per square mile.

But if you asked one of the locals, you'd be told there's not much room left. Out here, under a trademark big sky, where single farms and ranches engulf a whole township's worth of land, people get used to taking up space.

For better or worse, this is one of the last outposts of the frontier spirit: Cowboy hats are mandatory, the bar doubles as the community hall, and the rodeo club is the biggest extracurricular activity at the high school. Here more than anywhere else in the state, there is still some wild left in the West.

JORDAN AND VICINITY

No one comes to Jordan (pop. 364, elev. 2,800 feet) because of its interesting history or architecture. Like other late-germinating communities, many of its first settlers were outlaws. Homesteaders drifted through desultorily, recoiling when they discovered what a nasty piece of business the Big Dry Country was. Big ranches and big families have always ruled the rangelands. Now what makes Jordan exceptional is that it never bothered to change.

Jordan is remote. In 1931 only eight households had running water. Rural homes didn't

Big Dry Creek drains most of the Big Open, a region of prairies and badlands the size of Connecticut.

have electrical service until 1952, and ranches didn't get telephones until 1956. Public transportation? Never had it, probably never will. The most isolated county seat in the continental United States, Jordan is 175 miles from the nearest major airport, 85 miles from the nearest bus line, and 115 miles from the nearest train line. The local high school serves such a vast area that until the 1990s it maintained a public coed dormitory.

All this remoteness suits some people: In the 1990s, Jordan was the site of the siege of the Montana Freemen, the militia-like group that attempted to set up its own self-governing state. The 81-day standoff ended when the 20-odd Freemen surrendered to the awaiting army of FBI agents (at its peak, Jordan was hosting nearly 600 FBI operatives and over 200 journalists).

Sights

Despite its reputation as the last stronghold of the Old West, Jordan is a friendly town with adequate facilities for the traveler. It is central to great hunting and to recreation and wildlife viewing on the C. M. Russell National Wildlife Refuge and Fort Peck Lake.

The **Garfield County Museum** (406/557-2517, 1pm-5pm daily June 1-Sept. 1, free), just east of town, offers both historic and prehistoric overviews of the locality. A replica of a triceratops found north of town, an actual triceratops head, and other fossil remains are the highlights here. Also on display are homesteader memorabilia, early photos, and a restored one-room school.

About eight miles west of Jordan is a curious landmark known as **Smokey Butte.** This promontory, which rises a thousand feet above the surrounding prairie, is the easternmost of the many igneous intrusions that rose into mountains in central Montana. More curiously, the mineral that makes up Smokey Butte, armalcolite, has never been found elsewhere except in rocks collected on the moon.

Accommodations

One of Jordan's original hotels, the **Garfield** (corner of Main St. and Hwy. 200, 406/557-6215, $60-75), is still in business and offers updated rooms in the hotel or in newer motel units. **Fellman's Motel** (Hwy. 200, 406/557-2209 or 800/337-1863, $65-75) is Jordan's other option.

The Garfield County Museum includes the old jail.

Dinosaur Country

The dun-colored badlands that rise along the Missouri River, fantastically carved by erosion into sharp canyons and buttes, contain one of the world's richest chronicles of early life on earth. Paleontologists discovered some of the first and most important remains of dinosaurs in these desiccated hills. Today, the annual arrival of the summer "bone diggers" is almost an institution in Jordan.

In 1902, Dr. Barnum Brown of the American Museum of Natural History journeyed to the Jordan area to search for dinosaur remains. Brown cut quite a figure: He reported to the digs in a starched white collar and polished knee boots, popping his gold pince-nez on and off. The existence of large dinosaurs was still a matter of conjecture in scientific circles—the giant reptiles certainly didn't yet form part of the popular imagination.

What attracted Brown to this area was its Cretaceous-era badlands. Laid down by shallow marshy seas about 70 million years ago, these layers of mudstone, shale, and sandstone were normally covered by thick layers of more recent sediment. When the Missouri River cut its way through the badlands, it opened up a gorge through millions of years of geologic history. Here, in the arid bluffs of Garfield County, the earth had stored its memories of vanished life. In the stratified layers of sediment revealed by erosion, Brown reasoned, one should be able to find the band corresponding to the "Age of the Dinosaurs."

In a gumbo escarpment on Hell Creek, Brown found much more than he was looking for: two skeletons of *Tyrannosaurus rex*. The fossil-rich Cretaceous sediments, now called the Hell Creek Formation in honor of Garfield County's dinosaur haven, have continued to yield specimens. In 1988 a Jordan couple found the most complete tyrannosaurus skeleton to date (the 11th discovered in the area) along the shore of Fort Peck Lake. Triceratops has almost become Jordan's dinosaur mascot. Aquatic duck-billed dinosaurs and the mosasaur—a sea serpent-like dinosaur—have also been found in the Hell Creek Formation. Smaller finds—dinosaur eggs, petrified mollusks, and fish—are common.

Camping

Campers should go to **Kamp Katie** (406/557-2851), just west of the bridge, a pleasant enough campground on the banks of Big Dry Creek.

Food

The **Hilltop** (406/557-6287, 6am-9pm daily, $8-19), west of Jordan on Highway 200, is Jordan's only full-service restaurant.

Information and Services

For emergencies, call the **sheriff's office** at 406/557-2882. The **C. M. Russell National Wildlife Refuge** (406/557-6145) maintains a wildlife station in Jordan along Highway 200. The **Bureau of Land Management** (406/557-2376) has an office on Main Street. There is one service station, open until 9pm.

For local **road conditions**, call 406/365-2314.

★ CHARLES M. RUSSELL NATIONAL WILDLIFE REFUGE

Known to locals, with widely varying degrees of affection, as the C.M.R., the 1.2-million-acre Charles M. Russell National Wildlife Refuge flanks the entire northern edge of Garfield County along the Missouri River. One of the largest refuges in the nation, the C.M.R. is home to an abundance of wildlife, including elk and bighorn sheep, which were once common on the prairies. Recently, ranchers have reported sightings of wolves and cougars, although it's not clear if these animals were passing through or if there are sustainable populations in the refuge.

Garfield County contains more of the C.M.R. than any other Montana county; feelings run high here about having such a huge wilderness area (and its champion, the federal government) for a neighbor—to say nothing

Charles M. Russell National Wildlife Refuge

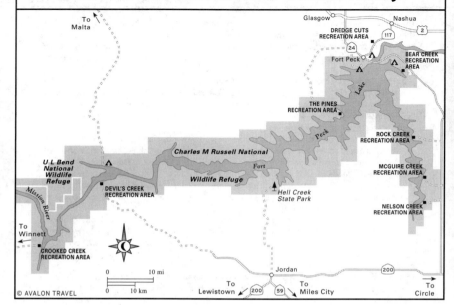

of errant herds of deer, pronghorn, elk, and worst of all, hungry coyotes and wolves.

Quite apart from the incredible wealth of wildlife—lacking only grizzly bears to replicate the Missouri River flora and fauna experienced by Lewis and Clark—the Missouri Breaks are dramatic and austere badlands that are still full of outlaw lore. At the center of the refuge is Fort Peck Lake, one of the largest artificial lakes in the world, important as a migratory waterfowl stopover and famed for its stellar fishing and recreational possibilities.

There is public access to the refuge and Fort Peck Lake at two sites in Garfield County: Hell Creek State Park and Devil's Creek Recreation Area. Both sites offer good scouting for fossils.

Hell Creek State Park

The most popular site in the C.M.R. is **Hell Creek State Park** (26 miles north of Jordan, 406/232-0900). Developed as a recreation area for local anglers and boaters, Hell Creek offers

a campground, marina (406/557-2345), store, and cabins. The road in, best attempted in dry weather, passes through rugged badlands. Elk, deer, waterfowl, eagles, foxes, and coyotes are pervasive. Entrance is $5 per vehicle for non-Montana residents, and camping is $15-20 (Montana resident), $23-28 (nonresident) per night. Yurts and cabins are $45 (Montana resident) or $55-60 (nonresident).

Devil's Creek Recreation Area

Farther afield, along a dodgier road, is Devil's Creek Recreation Area, with undeveloped campsites (free), about 40 miles northwest of Jordan. Here the gumbo buttes fringed with ponderosa pines drop away in canyons to the lake's shore.

Information

A regional office for the **C. M. Russell National Wildlife Refuge** (P.O. Box 110, Lewistown, MT 59597, 406/538-8706, www.fws.gov/cmr) is in Lewistown.

The Hi-Line and North-Central Montana

Look for ★ to find recommended sights, activities, dining, and lodging.

Highlights

Lewis and Clark National Historic Trail Interpretive Center

Two Medicine Dinosaur Center

Old Trail Museum

Giant Springs State Park

C. M. Russell Museum

Havre Historical Underground Tours

Upper Missouri River Breaks National Monument

Fort Benton

First Peoples Buffalo Jump State Park

Square Butte Natural Area

0   50 mi
0   50 km

© AVALON TRAVEL

★ **Lewis and Clark National Historic Trail Interpretive Center:** In a fantastic structure overlooking the Missouri River at Great Falls, the state's premier Lewis and Clark site encapsulates the Corps of Discovery's journey across Montana (page 376).

★ **C. M. Russell Museum:** The patron artist of Montana is Charlie Russell. This museum offers the largest collection of his subtle and arresting Western art (page 377).

★ **First Peoples Buffalo Jump State Park:** Ancient Native Americans stampeded bison off the cliffs here—today a new interpretive center relates the history and culture of the plains tribes (page 378).

★ **Giant Springs State Park:** Underground aquifers burst from the cliffs above the Missouri River at this park, creating a unique ecosystem and a wonderful spot for picnicking (page 379).

★ **Square Butte Natural Area:** An isolated volcanic plug capped with virgin prairie flowers and grasses, Square Butte rises 2,400 feet above the prairies. Bring a picnic and enjoy the views from one of Montana's most enchanted destinations (page 383).

★ **Fort Benton:** Montana's oldest settlement, Fort Benton was the head of Missouri River boat traffic from the 1840s to the 1880s, making it a one-stop Montana history lesson (page 384).

★ **Upper Missouri River Breaks National Monument:** From Virgelle to the backwaters of Fort Peck Lake, the monument preserves 150 miles of the Missouri River's prairie canyon as a near pristine wilderness (page 386).

★ **Havre Historical Underground Tours:** Havre was once such a party town that some of its downtown businesses had to go underground—literally. Tours lead visitors to a circa-1900 business district that included brothels, barber shops, and bars (page 390).

★ **Old Trail Museum:** Known nationally for its fossil collection, this Choteau museum is one of the state's top paleontology centers (page 398).

★ **Two Medicine Dinosaur Center:** Visit the fossil gallery at this paleontology outpost to watch scientists prepare ancient dino bones, or schedule a hands-on encounter at a real fossil dig (page 399).

From the dramatic eastern front of the Rocky Mountains to the long views of the Hi-Line, this agricultural heart of Montana has more for the visitor than a look at a topographic map would imply. This is the country where the Nez Perce were finally run down by U.S. Army troops and where Chief Joseph gave his remarkable surrender speech. It's where dinosaur nests have revised scientific opinion on the ancient reptiles, transforming their image from flesh-ripping brutes into loving parents. It's where the Blackfeet have held fast to a small part of the land they used to race across with their horses and where they now host a big annual powwow. And it's where cowboy artist Charlie Russell settled down to work in his log-cabin studio.

The Hi-Line was built by the Great Northern Railway—in fact, its name refers to its being the state's northernmost railroad line. Thousands of hardworking homesteaders, many of them European immigrants, took the train to the Hi-Line, stepped off onto the windswept plain, and plowed into the short-grass prairie.

PLANNING YOUR TIME

This is road-trip territory. While there's enough quiet history here to keep a buff occupied for days, for most travelers the Hi-Line and the Rocky Mountain Front will be experienced in transversal—on the way to elsewhere. Don't just blow through. **Great Falls** deserves a day, with the excellent **Lewis and Clark National Historic Trail Interpretive Center** and the **C. M. Russell Museum.** If you're here in late June, the **Lewis and Clark Festival** is a colorful event. Hundreds of living history reenactors gather in buckskins and moccasins to relive frontier times.

Take back roads through **Shonkin Sag,** a weird landscape centered on an abandoned ice age channel of the Missouri, to reach **Fort Benton,** Montana's oldest town. Once the furthest upstream landing for Missouri riverboats, Fort Benton preserves many remnants of its trading post past—the trading fort is in the process of being reconstructed. The highlight of a Fort Benton visit will be a night at the **Union Hotel.** Built in 1882, this beauty is totally renovated and back in business.

Previous: Square Butte; Great Northern steam locomotive in Havre. **Above:** early morning at Great Falls.

East of Fort Benton, the Missouri River drops into a series of badlands canyons. Now preserved as part of the **Upper Missouri River Breaks National Monument,** the river and the landscapes remain much as Lewis and Clark saw them some 200 years ago. Much of this territory can only be seen on multiday float trips, although travelers with high-clearance vehicles and a bit of time can explore the landscape on secondary roads.

Havre is now at the center of Montana's wheat-growing region, although a century ago the community found itself at a crossroads as both the United States and Canada began expansion onto the northern Great Plains. This rowdy, hell's-a-popping era is preserved in Havre's "underground" commercial district, which served the needs of thirsty cowboys, opium addicts, and love-starved plainsmen. **Havre Historical Underground Tours** offer a glimpse of this forgotten world.

The plains roll right up to the base of the **Rocky Mountain Front.** This strikingly dramatic landscape was once the grazing land for open-range cattle outfits, and the Western spirit lives on in the region's **guest ranches**—some of the state's most famous dude ranches are here. If you don't have time to spend a week in the saddle, at least plan a stop at one of the area's splendid **rural B&Bs.** Amateur paleontologists should plan an outing at one of Choteau's many dino sites. The new **Two Medicine Dinosaur Center** offers both day trips to fossil digs and multiday get-your-hands-dirty field excavation programs.

HISTORY

The Great Northern Railway defined the development of the Hi-Line. James J. Hill had rails laid across northern Montana after Montanans such as Marcus Daly and Paris Gibson convinced him that it was worth taking the trouble to compete with the Northern Pacific, whose line already ran across the southern part of the state. In order to keep the railcars filled, settlers were recruited for Gibson's town, Great Falls, and for the prairies along Montana's northern tier, which would be coaxed into producing grain.

Hill and Professor Thomas Shaw were proponents of dryland farming. Shaw developed a theory that called for deep plowing and unrelenting cultivation of the land, a method that was practiced widely and led to widespread erosion. Precious topsoil, catching a windy ride, blew completely out of the state.

Between 1910 and 1918, homesteaders, sometimes derogatorily called "honyockers," swarmed to Montana for free land. Typically, a family would get off the train, which had a boxcar full of their possessions, pay a "finder" $20 to lead them to their homestead, and start plowing. During the middle of the 1910s, the homesteader's life looked good. Wet weather helped crops flourish, and World War I inflated the price of grain. But when drought began in 1918 and didn't let up for years, homesteaders scattered almost as fast as the dry topsoil.

Wheat farming has remained a major part of the local economy, and one way of dealing with the dry windy climate is the strip agriculture you'll see wherever wheat's been planted, in which one strip of land is cultivated and the adjoining strip lies fallow.

INFORMATION

Travel Montana provides excellent free travel information. Most of the Hi-Line falls within their **Central Montana division** (P.O. Box 3166, Great Falls, MT 59403, 406/761-5036, http://centralmontana.com). Ask for a free travel guide of the region.

GETTING THERE AND AROUND

Amtrak's *Empire Builder* (800/872-7245), taking its name from James J. Hill's sobriquet, crosses northern Montana daily in each direction traveling between Chicago and the West Coast, with stops in Havre, Shelby, Cut Bank, and Browning. Five major airlines serve Great Falls, but beyond that, there's little other public transport. Notably, there is no longer bus service between Great Falls and Havre, or along I-15 to Canada.

The Hi-Line and North-Central Montana

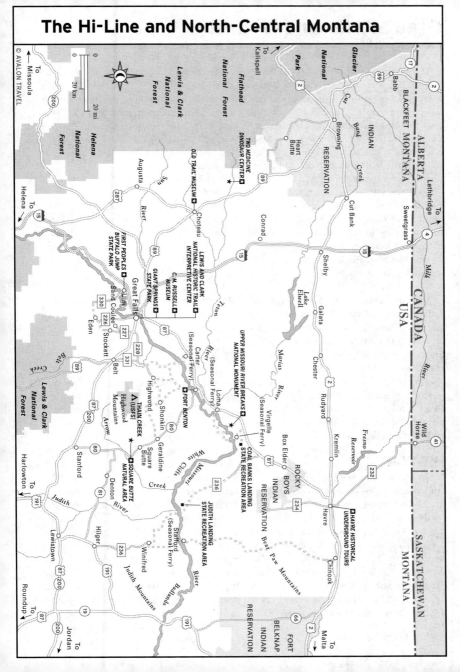

© AVALON TRAVEL

Solid, wholesome, and prosperous, Great Falls (pop. 59,000, elev. 3,333 feet) suffers if compared to Montana's more dynamic and cosmopolitan cities. It's the kind of uneventful place that feels like a good spot to raise a family. The casual explorer who doesn't venture off the long bleak 10th Avenue South commercial strip may well think that there's little reason to stop for more than a fill-up and a soda.

Look again, though: To start with, there's rich Lewis and Clark history here, albeit mostly obliterated by the hydroelectric dams that now rope in the once-awesome Great Falls of the Missouri. There's also the C. M. Russell Museum, and the unexpected: contemporary art at the Paris Gibson Square Museum of Art.

The Sun River flows into the Missouri at 10th Avenue South in Great Falls. The Highwood, Little Belt, and Big Belt Mountains crop up to the east, southeast, and south of town, while the main spine of the Rockies runs 50 miles west. But the Missouri River has always defined Great Falls—the falls themselves, remembered in the city's name; the Giant Springs, which now nourish hatchery trout; and the riverside parks beckoning bicyclists and anglers.

HISTORY

When sheets of glacial ice covered the northern Montana plains 15,000 years ago, present-day Great Falls was under 600 feet of water. Ice dams backed up glacial Lake Great Falls between Great Falls and Cut Bank, spilling out into the Shonkin Sag. Blackfeet controlled the area when Lewis and Clark spent June 15 through July 15, 1805, negotiating the Great Falls of the Missouri, actually portaging 18 miles in 13 days. A grizzly bear chased Lewis into the Missouri at one point; he was also impressed that there were "not less than 10,000 buffalo in a circle of two miles."

Paris Gibson first visited the river-bend site of present-day Great Falls in 1880 and quickly set to building a city there. He conferred with James J. Hill, of the Great Northern Railway, and in 1887 the Montana Central Railroad was built through Great Falls, connecting the Great Northern line to the mining centers farther south.

The Anaconda Company came into town in 1908 and built a copper-reduction plant, powered by a dam on Black Eagle Falls. The cheap electricity generated by the Black Eagle Dam and the others that followed on other falls spurred Great Falls to an industrial economy early on, with attendant labor union and political imbroglios.

Immediately east of Great Falls is **Malmstrom Air Force Base,** established in 1939. It is now home of the 341st Missile Wing of the Air Force Global Strike Command.

SIGHTS

Be warned that street addresses are a little confusing in Great Falls. Avenues run east-west, streets run north-south, and both are named almost exclusively with numbers. Central Avenue divides north from south; most of the city lies east of the Missouri River; streets west of the river wear a W as part of their names.

For an introduction to Great Falls sights, take a tour on the **Great Falls Historic Trolley** (406/771-1100, www.greatfallshistorictrolley.com). Two tours are available: an hour-long "Urban Adventure Tour" ($13 adults, $5 children 2-12), and a two-hour "Historic Tour" ($22 adults, $5 children 2-12). Tours originate at the **Visitor Information Center** (15 Upper River Rd., daily June-Sept. and year-round by appointment). Both narrated tours visit downtown, the C. M. Russell Museum, and the historic homes district, while the longer Historic

Great Falls

© AVALON TRAVEL

To Helena and Butte

To Choteau, Glacier Park, and Shelby

0   1 mi
0   1 km

HILTON GARDEN INN

BEST WESTERN HERITAGE INN

FOX   FARM   RD

Sun River

6TH ST NW

CENTRAL AVE W

15 BUS.

STAYBRIDGE SUITES

CHILDREN'S MUSEUM OF MONTANA

MACKENZIE RIVER PIZZA

CITY POOL

LA QUINTA INN

RIVER DR

GIBSON PARK

SMELTER AVE

3RD ST NW

MOTEL 6

VISITORS CENTER

UPPER RIVER RD

2ND ST S

5TH ST S

6TH ST S

7TH ST S

TOWNHOUSE INN

SUPER 8 LODGE

13TH AVE S

17TH AVE S

21ST AVE S

13TH ST S

14TH ST S

15TH ST S

10TH AVE S

24TH AVE S

JAKER'S STEAK, RIBS AND FISH HOUSE

26TH ST S

To Lewistown and Billings

CENTRAL AVE

1ST AVE N

2ND AVE N

8TH AVE N

SEE DETAIL

BORRIE'S

BLACK EAGLE FALLS AND DAM

Missouri River

EDDIE'S SUPPER CLUB

38TH ST S

3RD AVE S

56TH ST

87

To Fort Benton and Havre

87

LEWIS AND CLARK NATIONAL HISTORIC TRAIL INTERPRETIVE CENTER

GIANT SPRINGS RD

GIANT SPRINGS STATE PARK

RAINBOW FALLS AND DAM

MALMSTROM AFB MAIN GATE

Detail:

THE HISTORY MUSEUM

QUALITY INN PONDEROSA

TRACY'S

Riverside Park

RIVER DR N

BERT AND ERNIE'S

DAILY GRIND

MID-TOWN MOTEL

CENTRAL AVE N

O'HAIRE MOTOR INN

BRIAN'S

MORONY NATATORIUM

TOP NOTCH CAFE

C.M. RUSSELL MUSEUM

PARIS GIBSON SQUARE MUSEUM OF ART

DANTE'S CREATIVE CUISINE

1ST AVE N

2ND AVE N

3RD AVE N

4TH AVE N

5TH AVE N

6TH AVE N

7TH AVE N

8TH AVE N

1ST AVE S

2ND AVE S

3RD AVE S

4TH AVE S

5TH AVE S

6TH AVE S

5TH ST S

6TH ST S

7TH ST S

10TH ST S

12TH ST S

13TH ST S

14TH ST S

15TH ST S

Missiles on the Prairie

Scattered among 23,000 acres of prairie surrounding Great Falls, tucked away in fields or meadows, are some 200 unremarkable enclosures of chain-link fencing and cement, more or less perfectly innocuous in appearance. But each of these facilities is home to a Minuteman intercontinental ballistic missile. Malmstrom Air Force Base in Great Falls is the headquarters for the Minuteman defenses.

The missiles were located in Montana for several reasons. Their fuel is sensitive to humidity, making the arid prairies a natural habitat. Also, the average elevation of 3,500 feet gives the missiles a head start, yielding a 6 percent fuel savings. And the fact that not many people live hereabouts probably didn't hurt either.

Each subterranean silo consists of an 80-foot-deep tube, launch equipment, and missile. The silo door *alone* weighs 108 tons. The launch facilities are controlled from a nearby underground chamber. Launch-control chambers have walls 4.5 feet thick and dangle in a 90-foot-deep pit, suspended by cables that allow the chamber to swing three feet in any direction.

Since the end of the Cold War, the Minutemen have been deactivated. Once staffed 24 hours a day in readiness for enemy attack, the sites now slumber, awaiting the arrival of another strategic threat. A flick of a switch would bring the system back to full readiness.

Tour adds on Giant Springs, the Lewis and Clark Interpretive Center, and Malmstrom Air Force Base. Call or check the website for departure times. The tour company also offers longer and more customized sightseeing tours through its sister organization **Tour de Great Falls** (406/771-1100); destinations include the buffalo jump and specialized Lewis and Clark tours.

★ Lewis and Clark National Historic Trail Interpretive Center

In 1998 the 25,500-square-foot **Lewis and Clark National Historic Trail Interpretive Center** (4201 Giant Springs Rd., 406/727-8733, www.fs.fed.us/r1/lewisclark/lcic, 9am-6pm daily Memorial Day-Sept. 30, 9am-5pm Tues.-Sat. and noon-5pm Sun. Oct.-Memorial

the Missouri River in Great Falls

The mazelike exhibits follow the expedition's journey across the Rockies, to the Pacific, and then back down the Missouri through Montana and back to St. Louis. Along the way, the center features a Mandan earth lodge, a Shoshone tepee, replicas of boats used by the expedition, and a display illustrating the difficulty of translating Lewis and Clark's English into local languages and back. The center does an especially good job of illustrating the contribution and cultures of the various Native American tribes the corps encountered along its route. A 158-seat theater shows a free 20-minute film covering the highlights of the expedition.

The interpretive center is located just off River Drive on Giant Springs Road, about three miles northeast of downtown Great Falls. From either Highway 87 or 10th Avenue South, just follow River Road west. If you're coming in from the east on Highway 200, turn north on the 57th Street bypass and follow the signs.

★ C. M. Russell Museum

One of the finest museums in Montana, and a must-see for anyone interested in Western art, is the **C. M. Russell Museum** (400 13th St. N., 406/727-8787, http://cmrussell.org, 10am-5pm Tues.-Sun. late May-early Nov., 10am-5pm Tues.-Sat. early Nov.-late May, $9 adults, $7 seniors, $4 students). Charlie Russell's brilliant colors are astounding and complex—if you're familiar with these paintings only from reproductions, then seeing the originals is a real treat. In addition to Russell's own paintings, the museum displays painting and sculpture from other artists of Old West-themed art, plus occasional shows of more contemporary art—in 2011, the museum hosted a show of Andy Warhol silk screen prints. The museum complex includes Russell's log-cabin studio and house; there's also a good bookshop and reproduction gallery.

diorama in the Lewis and Clark National Historic Trail Interpretive Center

Day, $8 adult, children 15 and under free) opened on a cliff overlooking the Missouri's Great Falls. This $6 million facility instantly transformed Great Falls into a major Montana destination.

The exhibits follow the course of the journey, from St. Louis up the Missouri, into Montana, and to the Great Falls, which the explorers reached in June 1805. The corps spent a hellacious month portaging their boats around the falls of the Missouri River, which is lined by cliffs here. The two-story diorama of corps members pulling canoes up the cliff is an especially vivid illustration of the fortitude of these early explorers. Try your hand at pulling a specially weighted rope meant to reproduce the effort required in the portages, and let your thoughts marvel that these men— dressed in just moccasins and buckskins, and living on rations—had the strength to pull these boats for 18 miles, filled with a total of about a ton of gear.

Paris Gibson Square Museum of Art

A few blocks from the Russell Museum, the **Paris Gibson Square Museum of Art** (1400 1st Ave. N., 406/727-8255, www.the-square. org, 10am-5pm Mon.-Fri., 7pm-9pm Tues., noon-5pm Sat., free) mounts some surprisingly forward-thinking art exhibits housed in a handsome old school.

The History Museum

The Cascade County Historical Society administers **The History Museum** (422 2nd St. S., 406/452-3462, www.thehistorymuseum.org, 10am-5pm Tues.-Fri., free) in the High Plains Heritage Center. The museum, which has over 95,000 objects in its permanent collection, offers changing interpretive exhibits that tell the story of central Montana with intriguing exhibits on Great Falls's early industrial history.

Children's Museum of Montana

The **Children's Museum of Montana** (22 Railroad Sq., right behind the Civic Center, 406/452-6661, www.childrensmuseumofmontana.org, 9:30am-5pm Mon.-Sat., $4 per person, children under 2 free) is just the thing if you're traveling with kids. Hands-on exhibits teach about Montana history and wildlife and feature science, math, and cultural activities, all while making sure kids are amused.

★ First Peoples Buffalo Jump State Park

Turn off I-15 at the Ulm exit, 15 miles south of Great Falls, and follow the state park signs 6 miles to the **First Peoples Buffalo Jump State Park** (406/866-2217, http://fwp.mt.gov/parks, 8am-6pm daily Apr.-Sept., 10am-4pm Wed.-Sat., noon-4pm Sun. Oct.-Mar., $5 per vehicle for non-Montana residents), formerly called the Ulm Pishkun State Park. Tepee rings abound near the 30-foot-high buffalo jump, and there are supposed to be some pictographs there too. Poke around the base of the cliff for decaying buffalo bones, but wear boots to guard against the prickly pear and rattlesnakes, and don't carry off any souvenirs—the area is protected by the State Antiquities Act. The visitors center is open year-round and does an excellent job of interpreting the past uses of the jump and how Native Americans used the bison they slaughtered here. A prairie-dog town and picnic area share the *pishkun* site.

Buffalo were driven off the cliff at this *pishkun,* or buffalo jump.

SPRINGS, RIVERS, AND DAMS

Everywhere you turn in Great Falls there's a park, and the pathway that links them all—the River's Edge Trail, a greenway along the Missouri and River Drive—is worth a special visit.

★ Giant Springs State Park

The **Giant Springs State Park** (4803 Giant Springs Rd., http://stateparks.mt.gov/giant-springs, free) is three miles from downtown on River Road, and the Department of Fish, Wildlife, and Parks Visitor Center provides a vivid description of Lewis and Clark's portage of the falls, as well as information and exhibits on fishing and hunting.

Giant Springs itself is a gushing natural spring that captured the attention of Lewis and Clark. The genesis of this 134,000-gallon-per-minute fountain is in the Little Belt Mountains southeast of Great Falls. Exposed Madison limestone absorbs mountain snowmelt and rain, which then drains and flows underground through fissures to Great Falls, where it surges up and spews into the Missouri River. The mineral-rich water has proved to be a good fish-breeding medium, and there's a trout hatchery a stone's throw away from the springs. This is an enchanting place to picnic or just relax amid leafy lawns and the sounds of rushing water.

Black Eagle and Rainbow Dams

Downstream from the springs are overlooks onto the dams that harness Black Eagle and Rainbow Falls. Both of these dams have preserved the essential nature of the waterfalls. From the roadside overlook, look across the Missouri to the town of **Black Eagle,** a company town that was built up around the beginning of the 20th century to serve the copper-reduction works.

Ryan Dam

Head north on Highway 87 to visit the Ryan Dam, which marks the site of the Great Falls of the Missouri, described by Meriwether Lewis as "the grandest sight I ever beheld," with its roily cascades, foamy spray, and spiky rock projections.

Benton Lake Wildlife Refuge

Twelve miles north of town on Highway 87, the 12,300-acre **Benton Lake Wildlife Refuge** (www.fws.gov/refuge/benton_lake, daylight hours Apr. 1-Oct. 31) harbors nearly 200 bird species, including shorebirds, snow geese, tundra swans, burrowing and short-eared owls, and mammals such as rabbits, deer, and long-tailed weasels.

RECREATION

Bike or jog along the Missouri River on the **River's Edge Trail,** stretching from the 10th Avenue Bridge to Giant Springs State Park and past Crooked Falls. This rails-to-trails path has more than 60 miles of paved, gravel and dirt pathways. The River's Edge Trail is a great recreational asset to the city and a good place for travelers to take in both the urban and natural history of the area.

Swim outdoors (or take one of the waterslides) at **Electric City Water Park** (100 River Dr. S., 406/771-1265, noon-6pm daily, early June-Labor Day, $5 adults, $3 children ages 3-17, additional charges for the waterslides and wave pool), just south of the 1st Avenue Bridge on River Drive. The city has also installed a Flow Rider, which lets hearty souls boogie board the artificial waves. Kids will enjoy the state's largest children's water-play structure. Serious lap swimmers may prefer the beautifully named, carefully maintained **Morony Natatorium** (111 12th St. N. 406/452-3733).

The Great Falls **Voyagers** are the Pioneer League farm team of the Chicago White Sox. Minor-league baseball fans can catch them throughout the summer at **Centene Stadium** (406/452-5311 for schedule and ticket information).

The **Eagle Falls Golf Club** (1025 25th St. N.,

406/761-1078, greens fees $30-33) is a busy 18-hole public course on River Road next door to Legion Park.

Across the river in Black Eagle, the **Anaconda Hills Golf Course** (2400 Smelter Ave., 406/761-8459, greens fees $26-30) has expanded to 18 holes.

EVENTS

The **C. M. Russell Auction of Original Western Art** (406/727-8787, http://cmrussell.org) is an annual March event benefiting the C. M. Russell Museum, and bidders descend from all over the country to participate. If you are in Great Falls in March, you'll find a week's worth of arty events associated with the sale; contact the museum for details.

With tons of Lewis and Clark history in the area, it's natural for Great Falls to host the **Lewis and Clark Festival** (P.O. Box 2848, Great Falls, MT 59403, 406/452-5661) in late June. Frontier cooking, flintlock demonstrations, and fire-making are some of the things you'll see at the living-history encampment at Gibson Park, where actors and docents in period dress re-create the daily life of the expedition's soldiers. Mini float trips and longer dinner float trips down the Missouri take in some of the river's historic sites, while other guided tours visit more out-of-the-way Lewis and Clark and naturalist destinations. Other festival events include dramatic readings, academic lectures on the Corps of Discovery, children's events, a buffalo barbecue, and a Western art show and sale. This is quickly becoming a major event in Great Falls. Many of the events are free.

Beginning the last Saturday of July and lasting eight days, the **Montana State Fair** (www.montanastatefair.com) takes over the town and the fairgrounds, located just west of downtown across the Missouri. Throughout the summer, the fairgrounds also host **horse races.**

ACCOMMODATIONS

Great Falls lodgings are found basically in two areas. Several older, well-maintained hotels and motels are downtown and provide the best value for money, while along the 10th Avenue strip, amid the casinos, car lots, and malls, you'll find many inexpensive older motels, as well as several newer motel complexes. All of the usual chain hotels have properties along 10th Avenue South. On all but the busiest weekends, you'll have no trouble finding a room without reservations. Just remember that most of 10th Avenue South is a busy six-lane highway.

$50-100

Downtown, the pleasant **Mid-Town Motel** (526 2nd Ave. N., 406/453-2411 or 800/457-2411, www.midtownmotelgf.com, $75-80) has clean and simple rooms, a favorite locals' restaurant, and an on-site bakery; pets are allowed.

The **O'Haire Motor Inn** (17 7th St. S., 406/454-2141 or 800/332-9819, www.ohairemotorinn.com, $75-99) features an indoor pool, restaurant, and indoor parking. Some two-bedroom suites are available. The O'Haire's ★ **Sip 'N' Dip** lounge was named by *Condé Nast Traveler* as one of the world's top watering holes—the authentic tiki bar shares a glass wall with the hotel's swimming pool, affording drinkers a voyeuristic view onto the underwater frolics of the swimmers (and occasional mermaid). The inn's restaurant, **Clark & Lewie's,** is also good.

The **Quality Inn Ponderosa** (220 Central Ave., 406/761-3410 or 877/424-6423, $69-99) is right downtown and has an outdoor pool, sauna, restaurant, lounge, and casino; microwaves and refrigerators are included in all rooms. Small dogs are permitted.

The **Super 8 Lodge** (1214 13th St. S., 406/727-7600, $73-87) sits back off the 10th Avenue South strip and offers a continental breakfast. This is a good midprice choice along the 10th Ave S. strip.

The **Town House Inn** (1411 10th Ave. S., 406/761-4600 or 800/442-4667, $83-99) has stylish rooms (including some that are in effect efficiency apartments), plus a casino, pool, sauna, hot tub, and restaurant. The

Town House is near Holiday Village Mall, the area's largest shopping center.

Over $100

The **Best Western Heritage Inn** (1700 Fox Farm Rd., 406/761-1900 or 800/548-8256, $110-130) is 0.25 mile off busy 10th Avenue South and is the city's largest hotel. The recreational facilities are noteworthy, with two indoor pools, hot tubs, saunas, and a game room. Also on-site are a restaurant and a lounge/casino. Rooms are nicely furnished; executive suites with kitchenettes are available.

On a lovely spot right on the Missouri River, a few blocks south of downtown, the ★ **La Quinta Inn and Suites** (600 River Dr. S., 406/761-2600 or 800/531-5900, $94-125) is faced with stone and logs and offers great views west toward the distant Rockies. Rooms are large and nicely furnished; facilities include an indoor pool and sauna. Continental breakfast is included in room rates.

The **Hilton Garden Inn Great Falls** (2520 14th St. S.W., 406/452-1000, www.hiltongardeninn.com, $159-179) is near I-15 exit 278 and has large, well-equipped rooms plus a restaurant and fitness center. On the west back of the Missouri, across from downtown, the **Staybridge Suites** (201 3rd St. N.W., 406/761-4903 or 877/834-3613, www.staybridge.com, $127-154 and up) is a large, distinctive hotel focused on upper-end business trade but has plenty of amenities for travelers, with an indoor pool, fitness and business centers, and a restaurant.

FOOD

Order breakfast 24 hours a day at **Tracy's** (127 Central Ave., 406/453-6108, $6-14), a downtown Great Falls institution. Another favorite spot for an old-fashioned and bountiful breakfast is **Brian's Top Notch Café** (718 Central Ave., 406/727-4255, 7am-3pm daily, $6-12).

At night downtown, dining choices are limited. **Bert and Ernie's** (300 1st Ave. S., 406/453-0601, www.bertandernies.com,

11am-9pm Mon.-Wed., 11am-10pm Thurs.-Sat., $10-25) offers burgers, pastas, light entrées, and regional microbrews in an old brick storefront. **Dante's Creative Cuisine** (1325 8th Ave. N., 406/453-9599, 11am-9pm Mon.-Thurs., 11am-10pm Fri.-Sat., $15-29) is a Great Falls's hot spot for stylish international cooking. In addition to steaks and seafood, Dante's specializes in creative Italian, Mexican, and Southwestern cooking.

A few blocks south of downtown, right along the Missouri River, is the **Mackenzie River Pizza Company** (500 River Dr. S., 406/761-0085, 11am-9pm Sun.-Thurs., 11am-10pm Fri.-Sat. $8-22), with gourmet pizza, burgers, and sandwiches.

Great Falls's unflappable sense of tradition extends to its favorite restaurants. Up in Black Eagle, the old union town on the north bank of the Missouri, ★ **Borrie's** (1800 Smelter Ave., 406/761-0300, 5pm-10pm nightly, $16-28), has been the place for massive servings of Montana steaks and traditional Italian pastas laden with the hearty sauces of our immigrant forebears. The menu at Borrie's says a lot about the early labor currents in industrial Great Falls, and besides that, the food is quite good.

Not as fancy, **Eddie's Supper Club** (3725 2nd Ave. N., 406/453-1616, 3pm-11pm Mon.-Thurs., 3pm-midnight Fri.-Sat., $16-28) has been the steakhouse choice for meat lovers since 1944: More care is taken in the kitchen than on stylish redecoration. Expect cracked red vinyl booths, equestrian decor, and "cowboy-style steaks," which means fire-charred and enormous. For a more contemporary experience, **Jaker's Steak, Ribs, and Fish House** (1500 10th Ave., 406/727-1033, 11am-10pm Mon.-Thurs., 11:30am-10pm Fri.-Sat., 11am-9pm Sun., main courses $10-30) just about says it all, except that Jaker's is also a casino.

INFORMATION AND SERVICES

The **Great Falls Chamber of Commerce** (406/761-4434, www.greatfallschamber.org) is at 710 1st Avenue North. The **visitors center** is located just east of the 10th Avenue Bridge, beneath the "big flag" on Upper River Road.

The **public library** (406/453-0349) is at 301 2nd Avenue North. Listen to **Montana Public Radio** at 89.9 FM.

GETTING THERE AND AROUND

Southwest of town, **Great Falls International Airport,** the region's largest, is served by Alaska, United, Delta, Frontier, and Allegiant airlines.

Salt Lake Express buses (www.saltlakeexpress.com), with connections to Helena and Butte, which has links to the national Greyhound network, stop at 326 1st Avenue South.

Great Falls Transit System (406/727-0382) runs buses in and around town. Hail a **Diamond Cab** by calling 406/453-3241.

Fort Benton and Big Sag Country

East of Great Falls, the Rockies fade from view, the buttes and peaks of central Montana loom, and the Missouri leaves its wide valley to plunge into a badlands gorge. This transitional landscape between the prairies of eastern Montana and the foothills of the Rockies contains some of the most interesting history, geology, and scenery in the state.

The region is also home to the oldest town in Montana—**Fort Benton.** Steamboats from St. Louis docked here in the 1840s (it was known as "the innermost port"), making it the stepping-off point for thousands of settlers and their chattel.

THE BIG SAG AREA

For travelers who like side roads and exploring the oddities of geology, there's no better detour than the byways of the Big Sag, or as it's more officially called, the Shonkin Sag. Part of this route is on unpaved roads, but except in extremely wet weather, these graded gravel roads present no challenges for cars and low-clearance vehicles.

The Shonkin Sag

Geologically speaking, relatively recent events created the distinctive landscapes of the Big Sag area. About 20 million years after the Rockies formed, a vast surge of volcanic activity forced molten rock to the surface in many parts of central Montana. Not all lava erupted; some

molten rock squeezed up through fissures and faults or fed into underground reservoirs, called laccoliths. Erosion has exposed these formations—steep vertical ridges of volcanic stone, called dikes, running in straight lines across the landscape. One of the most prominent laccoliths in Montana, Square Butte, rises spectacularly from the plains near Geraldine.

Edging down from the north, ice age glaciers reached the Great Falls area and then stopped. The leading edge of the glaciers trapped river flow from Missouri River tributaries that were south of the ice sheets and that would have normally flowed north and east along the ancestral Missouri drainage. Even though this was the ice age, the leading edge of the glacial advance saw seasonal thawing, which also created lots of fresh water. The result was the glacial Lake Great Falls. About 15,000 years ago, the present site of Great Falls was flooded by 600 feet of meltwater; water stretched from the Highwood Mountains to the Rocky Mountain foothills. As the lake grew and the glaciers receded, this vast body of water eventually cut a new spillway. About 10,000 years ago, the overflow of Lake Great Falls began to course through this channel, until the melting glaciers revealed a lower watercourse. The glacial lake spillway, called the Shonkin Sag by geologists and the Big Sag by locals, remains a deep U-shaped valley, 500 feet deep and one mile wide, along the base of the Highwood Mountains and Square Butte. All that's left of the huge river that once flowed here are the awesome canyon that it cut and a few shallow lakes.

Today, the Shonkin Sag is home to the small community of **Highwood** and scattered farms and ranches. To reach the Shonkin Sag, follow Highway 228 east from Great Falls or Highway 331 north from Belt. Highwood sits at the mouth of the sag. From here, gravel roads continue on to Geraldine or Fort Benton—both are well signed and in good condition.

The more scenic choice is the Geraldine road. It continues up the Shonkin Sag to the little crossroads of Shonkin and then cuts south into a steep valley in the Highwood Mountains. The road leaves the mountains and again crosses the Shonkin Sag; Square Butte looms to the south across several marshy lakes, and a spiky palisade of igneous rock (a volcanic dike) marches across the valley. The county road ends at Geraldine and Highway 80. The landscape is curiously spare and beautiful. This is one of the most compelling side trips in the state.

★ Square Butte Natural Area

The **Square Butte Natural Area** is a 2,000-acre preserve along the butte's high plateau and peaks, 2,400 feet above the prairies. Maintained by the Bureau of Land Management, this is one of the most unusual destinations in Montana. The steep sides of the butte have protected the native grasses and plants from overgrazing; Lewis and Clark saw such stands of grasses when they crossed the prairies 200 years ago. In a good year the plants reach waist level. Some varieties here are no longer found on rangeland. The wildflower display in May and June is astonishing, and deer, pronghorn, and birds are abundant.

The views are also spectacular. The core of the laccolith rises hundreds of feet above the plateau in cliffs and ridges of shonkinite and syenite. The Shonkin Sag runs along the north side of Square Butte (look for the escarpment of an ancient waterfall in the watercourse). Here, as at few other places, one can truly grasp the expanse of the plains. The mountains of central Montana perforate the otherwise limitless prairie horizon stretching outward for hundreds of miles.

Although ascending to the Square Butte Plateau is relatively easy (given a high-clearance vehicle and a little chutzpah), getting to the top of the volcanic plug requires a rigorous scramble up rough terrain. Square Butte

Square Butte is a fixture along the northern Montana skyline.

is much more rugged than it looks from a distance. Don't attempt to climb it alone, and don't feel as if you have to. Heroism isn't required to enjoy the plant and animal life; a good picnic will do just as well.

Square Butte is accessible only through private land. The landowners ask that you check in with them before starting up the butte (this just means signing in at the parking area). The road is a four-wheel-drive track, and although adequately maintained, it is quite rocky. Cars with narrower axles than pickup trucks will need to straddle the tracks, as the trademark shonkinite can easily puncture the oil pan of a low-bellied car. Although a high-clearance vehicle is preferable for this road, at least one Honda Accord has made it up and back.

To reach Square Butte Natural Area, turn at the community of Square Butte and follow the signs along Square Butte Road. The road passes through a ranch yard. From here to the top of the plateau is about three miles.

Accommodations and Food

The Big Sag area is within easy driving distance of Great Falls, Lewistown, Stanford, and Fort Benton, each of which offers a full range of lodgings and amenities.

★ FORT BENTON

Once the bustling head of Missouri River navigation, Fort Benton (pop. 1,600, elev. 2,600 feet) is now a quiet, even sleepy, town. When the fur trade boomed, steamboats struggled up the narrow sandbar-filled waters of the Missouri to discharge fortune-seeking trappers and prospectors and load up with furs. The Great Falls of the Missouri, 25 miles upstream, barred farther river travel.

Fort Benton was built in 1846 and served primarily as a fur-trading post. By 1859 the Mullan Road linked Fort Benton with Walla Walla, Washington, the easternmost outpost on the Columbia River system. The Whoop-up Trail led from Fort Benton to Alberta and was used to supply western Canada with illegal Indian whiskey. Incongruously, the fort was also a supply depot for Canadian Mounties charged with bringing order to the wild whiskey-sodden western territories.

Of all the trading forts built in mid-19th-century Montana, only Fort Benton survives as a town today. History is well displayed in Fort Benton's long green riverside park. And the Missouri River still flows by, as wide and muddy as ever, headed for an area that's still barely touched by roads.

the Missouri River at Fort Benton

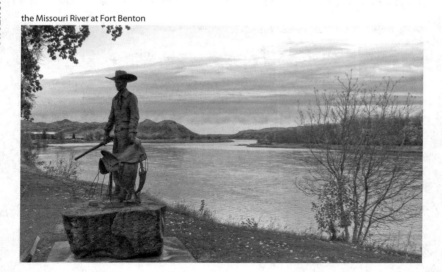

Sights

The **Fort Benton Heritage Complex** (20th and Washington, 406/622-5316, www.fortbenton.com/museums, 10:30am-4:30pm Mon.-Sat., noon-4pm Sun., Memorial Day-Sept., $10 adults, $1 children under 12) is the overall name given to a multiblock complex that features the Museum of the Northern Great Plains, the Museum of the Upper Missouri, Hornaday Buffalo and Art Museum, a homestead village, the Upper Missouri River Breaks National Monument Interpretive Center, and historic archives with fantastic photos of Fort Benton in its heyday. One admission price gets you into all these sites plus tours of the restored old Fort Benton, which has largely been rebuilt by volunteers to resemble the original 30,000-square-foot trading post from the 1860s.

Walk down the river levee to find a statue of Lewis, Clark, and Sacagawea, sculpted by artist Bob Scriver from Browning, Montana; a keelboat replica built in the early 1950s for the movie *The Big Sky*; and the 15th Street Bridge, which has spanned the Missouri since 1888. Historical signs along the grassy riverside strip discuss riverboats, the fur trade, and wild times in the streets of 19th-century Fort Benton.

Facing the river at 1718 Front Street, the **Wild and Scenic Upper Missouri Visitor Center** has wildlife and archaeological exhibits and a Lewis and Clark slide show.

Among the town's historic buildings, the **Grand Union Hotel** (1 Grand Union Sq.) stands out. It was indeed grand when it was built in 1882—just as the railroad was poised to eclipse the steamboat as a means of transportation. The hotel has been magnificently refurbished and has reopened to overnight guests and diners.

In front of the hotel is a bronze statue of **Shep,** Fort Benton's most famous canine denizen and an object of near-obsessive veneration for some (a web search reveals some surprising websites). Shep was the faithful workmate of a local sheepherder. The herder died, and his body was ferried away by rail.

Shep, however, kept vigil. The dog met every train into town for over five years. Shep's story became known across the country, and he became the darling of travelers and locals alike. However, Shep was eventually run over by a train and buried on a hill overlooking the depot. Read his story and weep.

Accommodations

You may drive right by the **Pioneer Lodge** (1700 Front St., 406/622-5441, www.pioneerlodgemt.com, $65-85) the first pass through, and maybe even the second time. The building used to be a general store. The rooms are comfortable and full of character, and they have TVs and wireless but no telephones. Some rooms have an additional loft sleeping area.

The ★ **Grand Union Hotel** (1 Grand Union Sq., 406/622-1882 or 888/838-1882, www.grandunionhotel.com, $128-198) reopened as a lodging in 1998. When it was built in 1882, the resplendent Grand Union was probably the finest hotel in the entire Montana territory. This beautiful Historic Register building adds a real touch of class to any stay in Fort Benton. Rooms are beautifully refurbished with tasteful period decor, and the restaurant serves perhaps the best meals in central Montana. In addition to standard guest rooms ($128-148), the hotel also offers suites with private sitting rooms ($158-198).

Camping

RV campers can pull up and spend the night for free in the city park, but there are no amenities. Tent campers are *not* encouraged to do the same.

Food

For morning coffee and breakfast, or lunchtime soup and sandwiches, go to **Wake Up Coffee House** (1714 Front St., 406/622-5400, 7am-5pm Mon.-Fri., 8am-3pm Sat. $6-11). ★ **The Union Grille** (406/622-1882, 5pm-9pm daily June-Aug., 5pm-9pm Tues.-Sun. Sept., 5pm-9pm Wed.-Sun. Oct.-Dec. and Feb.-May, entrées $19-29), in the beautiful dining room at the Grand Union Hotel, serves

Fort Benton's 1882 Grand Union Hotel is totally refurbished.

an eclectic regional menu with such dishes as pan-roasted duck breast with huckleberry sauce, local trout crusted with pine nuts and citrus, and buffalo rib eye steak with whiskey cream sauce. Outdoor riverside seating is available.

Information

Contact the **Fort Benton Chamber of Commerce** (1500 Front St., 406/622-3864, www.fortbenton.com) for more information.

★ UPPER MISSOURI RIVER BREAKS NATIONAL MONUMENT

East of Great Falls, the Missouri River leaves its valley and begins to cut down through the prairie surface. In 1976, the now slow-flowing river and the deep badland canyon it cuts were designated a Wild and Scenic River; 149 miles of river and 131,840 acres of adjacent land are preserved much as Lewis and Clark encountered them. Today, this makes for one of the great float trips in the nation, with tons of wildlife viewing enhancing the historic and

scenic value of this last remnant of free-flowing Missouri River.

The Land

The austere gorge cut by the Missouri between Fort Benton and Fort Peck Dam is a relatively recent accomplishment. Until the most recent ice ages, the Missouri flowed north from this point until it debouched into Hudson's Bay. But when ice sheets blocked that outlet, huge ice age dams—filled with the Missouri's flow and glacial melt—spilled over the plains. Almost surreptitiously the Missouri began to flow along the southernmost face of the glaciers, slowly cutting a new series of east-flowing channels all the way to the Mississippi. When the ice sheets began their last retreat 10,000 years ago, the Missouri remained in this new channel.

The precipitous and highly eroded walls of much of the Wild and Scenic Missouri's canyon are known locally as breaks or badlands. These strata, sedimentary remains of ancient seas, began to wash up in eastern Montana 80 million years ago. The 1,000-foot-deep gorge cuts through most of this geologic history.

The White Cliffs and the Missouri Breaks

Downriver from Virgelle, the Wild and Scenic Missouri River passes beneath the **White Cliffs,** escarpments of white limestone looming above the river. Passing through the limestone are dikes of volcanic rock radiating from mountain ranges in central Montana.

Erosion has dealt harshly but creatively with these formations, incising them into landmarks for river travelers. The White Cliffs are often compared to the fortifications of ruined cities, with isolated towers and spires emerging in bas-relief from the canyon. Imaginative minds have accorded the formations fanciful names: Eye of the Needle, Citadel Rock, Steamboat Rock, Hole in the Wall.

Once past the PN Bridge, the river enters the **Missouri Breaks.** Here in a badlands gorge hemmed by outcrops of sandstone, erosion has segregated colorful but barren gumbo soil into buttes, bluffs, and canyons. Gangs of rustlers menaced early stockmen from these inaccessible ravines. Today, the fringe of pine and juniper shelters elk, deer, mountain sheep, and birds of prey.

In 1805, Lewis and Clark paddled upriver along this same expanse of the Missouri River. The beauty and monumentality of the canyon overwhelmed them. No self-respecting travel writer would dare attempt to match Meriwether Lewis's elegiac prose (or his spelling):

> May 31st, 1805: The hills and river Clifts which we passed today exhibit a most romantic appearance. The water in the course of time has trickled down the soft sand clifts and woarn it into a thousand grotesque figures, which with the help of a little immagination and an oblique view are made to represent eligant ranges of lofty freestone buildings, having their parapets well stocked with statuary; columns of various sculpture both groved and plain, in other places with the help of less immagination we see the remains or ruins of eligant buildings; some collumns standing and almost entire with their pedestals and capitals; As we passed on it seemed as if those seens of visionary inchantment would never have an end; for here it is too that nature present to the view of the traveler vast ranges of walls of tolerable workmanship.

Erosion has isolated monoliths of sandstone, craggy outbursts of rock, and sheer cliffs of startlingly white limestone.

The soils are extremely infertile—rich in alkali and salt, they support little plant life except for occasional junipers and ponderosa pines. Along the river, however, there are beautiful groves of shade-giving cottonwoods.

In its lower reaches, the Wild and Scenic Missouri merges with the C. M. Russell National Wildlife Refuge. Here elk, bighorn sheep, deer, beavers, mink, coyotes, and birds in abundance live along the riverbanks.

Exploring the Wild and Scenic Missouri by Boat

Only one road crosses the Missouri between Fort Benton and the Fred Robinson Bridge, north of Grassrange, 150 miles away. Only remote ranch-access dirt roads even come close to it. Without any doubt, the best way to see the Wild and Scenic Missouri is by boat. A float trip on the Missouri takes two forms: a trip with a guide and outfitter or a well-planned float on your own. Each has its advantages.

While a traveler's independent streak might initially value a go-it-alone attitude, consider the following: There are no towns along the river, no shops, no restaurants, and no motels. You have to bring your own water—even boiled, the water of the Missouri, while potable, is far too muddy to be appealing for drinking. Portable toilets are now mandatory. There are no telephones or ambulances waiting if accidents occur (actually, heat stroke and sunburn are the greatest dangers). The Missouri is not a fast shoot-the-rapids river; it takes seven days to float all the way from Fort Benton to the Fred Robinson Bridge. When it's all over, you still have to get back to your vehicle, several hundred road miles back upstream.

If you do decide to float on your own, remember to sign in at the **Upper Missouri Breaks Interpretive Center** (701 7th St., 406/622-4000 or 877/256-3252, 8am-5pm daily Memorial Day-Sept., 8am-5pm the rest of the year) in Fort Benton before putting into the river. The stretch of the Missouri between Fort Benton and Loma is an easy one-day trip and is the most heavily used segment of the Wild and Scenic Missouri. For more information, contact the **Upper Missouri River Breaks National Monument** (920 N.E. Main, Lewistown, 406/538-7461, www.blm.gov/mt).

Outfitters

The following outfitters are among the best for guided trips on the Missouri. Each offers different packages involving trips of varying lengths (a minimum number of floaters is also usually required), and both rent canoes. Expect to pay $225-500 per person per day for completely guided and outfitted trips. Outfitted trips (they supply the canoe and food, but no guide) are roughly $200 per day. Canoe rentals are roughly $25-45 per day. The BLM provides a complete list of permit-holding outfitters on its website.

Missouri River Outfitters (P.O. Box 762, Fort Benton, MT 59442, 866/282-3295, www.mroutfitters.com) was one of the first to offer trips down the Missouri; this company has been in business for more than 35 years. There are several choices of destinations, and depending on your schedule and interests, you'll choose from a three-, four-, or six-day trip. The outfitters provide all food, wall tents, cots, and camping gear, and you'll be expected to bring appropriate clothing. This outfitter also operates a canoe and kayak rental service for those who wish to plan their own trip.

Missouri River Canoe Company (Box 50, H.C. 67, Loma, MT 59460, 406/378-3110 or 800/426-2926, www.canoemontana.com) is a unique operation based out of the almost ghost town of Virgelle, once a railhead for Missouri River traffic. The old general store is now an antiques store and the headquarters for this canoe outfitting and rental

operation. The four boarding rooms ($140-250, includes breakfast) above the store plus six homesteaders' shacks and a sheep wagon ($70 per person per night, includes continental breakfast, shared modern bath house and toilets) are scattered around the old town site. As you might guess, any B&B operated by an antiques dealer is well done and beautifully authentic; the as-was homesteaders' homes are especially evocative of bygone days.

Canoe trips are available in three forms. Guided and outfitted trips range 1-12 days, including all transportation, food, and gear except a sleeping bag and personal effects. Outfitted but unguided trips are also available, including canoes, food, camp gear, and shuttle. Simple canoe rentals are also available.

Exploring the Wild and Scenic Missouri by Car

While there's no substitute for a float trip down the Missouri, travelers who are on a tight schedule or fearful of water have interesting options. On this section of the Missouri, only one gravel road bridges the river; other less-traveled roads cross the river on ferries.

The **Missouri River ferries** are among the last river ferries in the country. Licensed by the U.S. Coast Guard, these cable-drawn ferries connect obscure county roads for ranchers and farmers who live in this lonesome stretch of Montana.

The ferries are free during the day; simply pull up to the landing and drive onto the small plank barge. If the ferry is on the other side, the operator will cross to pick you up. If there is no sign of life, honk your horn. Out of consideration, plan to use the ferries within normal waking hours (also, there's sometimes a fee for late-night crossings). The ferries normally operate April to Thanksgiving; the rest of the year the river freezes over.

Ferries operate at Carter, Virgelle, and Stafford. The **Carter Ferry** links up with a network of country dirt roads in the Fort Benton-Highwood area, making a loop trip easy (if dusty).

The **Virgelle Ferry** crosses the Missouri near the frontier community of Virgelle, home of the **Missouri River Canoe Company.** Just downstream from Virgelle is the **Coal Banks Landing State Recreation Area,** a popular departure point for float trips. The **Stafford (or McClelland) Ferry** is the remotest of the Missouri River ferries, linking dirt roads north of Winifred with a gravel road south of Chinook. It's a long road—about 80 miles—but it passes through breathtaking badlands, along the trail of Chief Joseph's last flight and battle, and through the lonesome and lovely Bear Paw Mountains. It's countryside not often seen by travelers. Note, however, that you should *not* attempt to drive on this road if rain threatens.

Practicalities

There aren't many lodging options in this remote stretch of badlands. You can call and ask for one of the charmingly authentic rooms at the ★ **Virgelle Mercantile,** now operated by **Missouri River Canoe Company** (406/378-3110 or 800/426-2926, www.canoemontana.com), although their canoe clientele have first dibs. They offer a variety of lodgings—including homesteaders' homes and sheep wagons ($70 per person per night) plus pioneer hotel rooms ($140-250, includes breakfast)—that are some of the most unique accommodations in Montana.

Otherwise, the closest lodgings are in Fort Benton. Great Falls and Havre are close enough to serve as bases for day trips.

There are undeveloped campgrounds at the ranger stations at **Coal Banks Landing** near Virgelle and at Judith Landing north of Winifred.

The Hi-Line

More than any other part of Montana, this is the country the railroad built. James J. Hill, head of the Great Northern Railway, mounted an aggressive campaign to bring European immigrants to the Hi-Line—by train, of course. Towns named Zurich, Malta, Inverness, and Kremlin were supposed to welcome them.

Today, this is the Montana known by Amtrak passengers, wheat farmers, and few others. Almost nobody comes here on vacation, unless it's to help their parents out with the harvest. Glacier National Park-bound Easterners zip past the grain elevators and filling stations, seldom turning from Highway 2 to explore the old downtowns.

However, the area does warrant a second glance. **Havre** offers tours of its "underground" city and its Native American buffalo jump—definitely worth taking in—and the Bear Paw Battleground has been elevated to national monument status, with a visitors center and better facilities hopefully on the way.

Other small grain-belt towns like **Chinook, Chester, Shelby,** and **Conrad** offer basic facilities for the traveler.

HAVRE

You wouldn't know it by the pronunciation, but Havre (HAV-er, pop. 9,621, elev. 4,167 feet) takes its name from the French city Le Havre. Originally it was called Bull Hook Siding, but James J. Hill pleaded for a name befitting the dignity of a Great Northern town. The locals complied, because Hill was ensuring the town's prosperity by making it a railway division point.

Raucous boom times came to town with the railroad and with cowboys in the 1890s. Gambling and prostitution both swelled to legendary proportions, some of which took place "underground" in Havre's below-street-level carousing and shopping district. By 1910 homesteaders were piling into the land office at Havre to claim their 160-acre plots. They were, as a whole, a much more serious bunch than the railroad workers, cowboys, bartenders, card sharks, and prostitutes who had gathered around Hill's esteemed division point, but Havre did its best to resist the new morality imposed by farmers and prohibitionists.

Traces of this heritage linger in the drive-up bars and the gambling joints that are still thriving in downtown Havre. And why Havre's high school teams are called the Blue Ponies is anyone's guess.

★ Havre Historical Underground Tours

A century ago, some of Havre's pioneer businesses, including brothels, bars, and opium dens (as well as bakeries, butchers, laundries, and pharmacies) were located beneath the city streets. The tunnels that run through downtown Havre have been partially restored and opened as **Havre Historical Underground Tours** (120 3rd Ave., 406/265-8888, www.havremt.com/attractions, $14 adults, $12 seniors, $8 children 6-12), or "Havre Beneath the Streets," one of the state's most interesting history lessons. Many of the businesses are re-created with the exact fixtures and objects that were originally used in the underground district at the beginning of the 20th century, making this a fascinating snapshot of a bygone era. Access to the underground area is by tour only. Hour-long tours are offered throughout the year: on the half hour 9:30am-3:30pm daily Memorial Day-mid-October, and 10am-4pm Monday-Saturday mid-October-late May. Call ahead to confirm schedule times and for reservations. You'll need to be able to negotiate steep stairs to access the tour, although wheelchairs are available once underground.

Other Sights

The **H. Earl Clack Museum** (1753 Hwy. 2, in the Holiday Village Shopping Center, 406/265-4000, www.hearlclackmuseum.org, 10am-6pm Mon.-Sat., noon-5pm Sun. Memorial Day-Labor Day, 1pm-5pm Tues.-Sat. Labor Day-Memorial Day, free) presents the region's colorful history. The **Wahpka**

Havre's downtown is a mix of old bars and ranch supply stores.

Chu'gn Buffalo Jump (406/265-6417 for reservations, tours 9am-4pm daily Memorial Day-Labor Day, $9 adults, $8 seniors, $5 students) provides the fodder for the museum's most interesting exhibits. At this archaeological site, which is directly behind the Holiday Village Shopping Center in Havre, Native Americans from three different prehistoric cultures, dating from 2,000 to 600 years ago, drove herds of bison off a cliff and then processed the slain animals for meat, hides, and tools. Excavations of the *pishkun* have uncovered campsites, stone tools, and piles of buffalo bones. The site is open for tours only, which are operated by Clack Museum.

The remains of **Fort Assiniboine** are south of the intersection of Highways 2 and 87. The Clack Museum leads tours out to the old fort, built in 1879 to protect U.S. citizens from both the Blackfeet and the feared return of Sitting Bull from his exile in Canada. The fort was converted to an agricultural research station in 1913 and was used to house transients during the Depression.

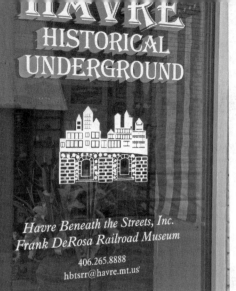

The Havre Historical Underground Tour is an eye-opening experience.

Montana State University-Northern, formerly Northern Montana College, has a well-tended campus south of downtown and is a good place to sit in the shade. The Math-Science Building houses natural-history displays, including a stuffed specimen of the extinct Audubon mountain sheep once displayed above the bar of one of Havre's bygone high-class joints.

Ten miles south of Havre on Highway 234 is **Beaver Creek Park,** the nation's largest county park. With 10,000 acres of rolling hills and streams, the park is a popular place for picnics, camping, and for getting a sense of the lovely and remote Bear Paw Mountains. These low mountains are 50-million-year-old volcanic humps that rise just enough above the surrounding prairies to provide welcome relief from the heat and to sustain plants, wildlife, and streams otherwise absent from the plains.

From the park, follow back roads to the Chief Joseph Battleground, or to the Rocky Boys Reservation, home to about 2,000 Chippewa and Cree.

Accommodations

The **Siesta Motel** (600 1st St., 406/265-5863, $75-90 and up) is a good, clean, and comfortable budget choice. It's convenient for downtown shopping and dining options.

On the west end of town, near the fairgrounds and buffalo jump, is the **Havre Super 8 Motel** (166 19th Ave. W., 406/265-1411 or 800/800-8000, $70-95); pets are allowed with permission.

The **Townhouse Inns of Havre** (601 1st St. W., 406/265-6711 or 800/442-4667, www.townhouseinnhavre.com, $100-115) is a large motel complex with an adjoining casino and lounge. There's an indoor pool, sauna, and fitness room, and convention rooms are also available. The **Best Western Great Northern Inn** (1345 1st St., 406/265-4200 or 800/530-4100, $97-125) is one of Havre's newest lodgings, with nicely furnished rooms, an indoor pool and fitness room, and a complimentary breakfast bar. Also recently built, the **AmericInn Lodge** (2520 Hwy. 2 W., 406/395-5000 or 800/634-3444, $95-125) has an indoor pool and complimentary breakfast. The only downside is that the lodge is about five miles west of downtown dining and shopping.

Camping

The **Lions Campground** (west on Hwy. 2, 406/265-7121 or 888/265-7121, $10) is fine for RVs, but tent campers are better off heading toward the Bear Paw Mountains. It's only about 15 miles south on Highway 234 to the campgrounds at **Beaver Creek County Park** (406/395-4565), a huge park with 250 sites in several discrete campgrounds. Purchase a $10 camping permit at the park office, 10 miles south of Havre on Highway 234.

Food

Pizza Hut, McDonald's, and Kentucky Fried Chicken all rear their heads on the west end of town, but there are a few alternatives. **Nalivka's Original Pizza Kitchen** (1032 1st St., 406/265-4050, 11am-9pm Tues.-Thurs. and Sun., 11am-10pm Fri.-Sat., $7-14) is the locals' favorite for pizza, sandwiches, and pasta. **Grateful Bread** (220 3rd Ave., #102, in the lower level of the Atrium Mall, 7am-2pm Mon.-Sat., $6-10) is a marvelous little bakery café where you can load up on fresh bread and baked goods or order freshly made sandwiches and soup. It's very popular so come early if you don't want to wait in line.

Andy's Supper Club (658 1st St. W., 406/265-9963, 4:30pm-10pm daily, $15-25) is Havre's top old-fashioned steakhouse. You won't need to spend much time studying the menu, because it's basically just a list of steaks. At the Duck Inn's **Mediterranean Room** (1300 1st St., 406/265-6111, 5pm-10pm Tues.-Sat., $15-29), classical statues gaze at you as you ponder the admirably extensive (for northern Montana) menu of steaks, seafood, and pasta.

For a casual meal and a good selection of microbrews, go to **Murphy's Pub** (1465 Hwy. 2 N.W., 406/265-4700, 11am-9pm Sun.-Thurs., 11am-10pm Fri.-Sat., $8-10), where you'll find a few traditional Irish dishes hidden among the burgers. For a less nutritious view of Havre, stop by the **Oxford Bar** (329 1st St.), where drinks are swallowed unnoticed when the gambling gets hot. Across the street at the **Palace Bar** (281 1st Ave.), there's a wonderful back bar and generous drinks. Food is served at both these bars, but that's not why you're there.

Information and Services

You'll notice that the streets in Havre run parallel to the railroad tracks (Highway 2 is 1st Street); avenues are perpendicular to the tracks. Names for both rely principally on numbers, leading to maximum confusion.

For more information, contact the **chamber of commerce** (518 1st St., 406/265-4383, www.havremt.com). Find the **post office** at 306 3rd Avenue, just across from the lovely courthouse. The public **library** is just a couple of blocks away at the corner of 3rd Street and 4th Avenue.

Getting There and Around

Amtrak's *Empire Builder* makes a brief layover in Havre, which is a restocking point. Trains arrive once daily in each direction; contact the station (235 Main St., 406/265-5381 or 800/872-7245) for schedule information. **Cape Air** (800/227-3247, www.capeair.com) provides twice daily air service to Billings.

Budget Rent-A-Car (Hwy. 2 W., 406/265-1156) is located at Tilleman Motor Company.

BEAR PAW BATTLEGROUND

To reach the site of the Bear Paw Battleground, drive east 22 miles on Highway 2 to Chinook, and turn south 16 miles on paved Highway 240.

This is where Gen. Nelson Miles overtook the Nez Perce, who were less than 40 miles from sanctuary in Canada. And it was here that Chief Joseph gave the speech for which he is most remembered:

It is cold and we have no blankets. The little children are freezing to death. My people, some of them, have run away to the hills, and have no blankets, no food; no one knows where they are—perhaps freezing to death. I want to have time to look for my children and see how many I can find. Maybe I shall find them among the dead.

Hear me, my chiefs. I am tired; my heart is sick and sad.

From where the sun now stands, I will fight no more forever.

The windswept patch of prairie has a few plaques and a trail through the grass that leads to small markers strewn over the battlefield, marking the sites of deaths and camps. The battlefield is now managed by the National Park Service as part of the Nez Perce National Historical Park.

In Chinook, the **Blaine County Museum** (501 Indiana, 406/357-2590, 8am-noon and 1pm-5pm Mon.-Sat., noon-5pm Sun., Memorial Day-Labor Day, donation) can provide information about the battlefield. The museum also offers an audio-visual

The Nez Perce and the Battle at Bear Paw

After the Nez Perce crossed the Missouri on their 1877 flight to Canada, they changed command and slowed down. They'd been on the run for four months and were tiring. Poker Joe, who'd proven himself to be a strong strategic leader, let Looking Glass, who pressed for a more relaxed pace, take over.

This pause gave Gen. Nelson Miles and his battalion from eastern Montana the opportunity to attack the Nez Perce while they were still in U.S. territory. The Nez Perce were caught off guard, but they fought hard on the cold snowy prairie for six days before finally agreeing to lay down their arms.

Chief Joseph negotiated a ceasefire with Miles in which the Nez Perce would surrender their weapons but would see the return of their horses and their homeland in eastern Oregon. That night, White Bird—the only other Nez Perce chief still alive following the Bear Paw battle—led a band of Nez Perce toward Canada. More than 200 escapees made it to Canada, where they joined Sitting Bull and his Lakota followers.

Those who remained with Joseph were sent to Miles City, then to Kansas, and then to Oklahoma. Not until 1885 were they allowed to return to reservations in the Northwest.

presentation called *40 Miles to Freedom,* which depicts the battle and siege at Bear Paw.

WEST OF HAVRE

Every six miles or so, Highway 2 passes through yet another tiny town dominated by grain elevators and Lutheran church spires. Many are fancifully named (by the Great Northern), and most are just hanging on to existence. This is marvelous farmland for high-protein wheat, which fetches premium prices from bread and pasta makers.

Small towns like Joplin, Hingham, Rudyard, Chester, and Gilford don't have much in the way of facilities for travelers, but invariably there's a bar, a grocery store, and a coffee-klatch café in each town that would be glad to see a stranger.

Shelby

A boxcar was thrown from a Great Northern train here in 1891, and the site was named after Montana's general manager of the Great Northern, who swore the place would never amount to much. Shelby (pop. 3,200, elev. 3,283 feet) developed into a trade center, supplying cowboys and sheepherders with food and wild times. Oil was discovered north of town in 1921, and though the town's population swelled, it didn't quite live up to its own expectations. In 1923, Shelby hosted a prizefight between Jack Dempsey and Tommy Gibbons. A 45,000-seat arena was erected for this occasion; unfortunately, only 7,000 seats were filled for the fight.

The **Marias Museum of History and Art** (206 12th Ave., 406/434-2551, 1pm-5pm and 7pm-9pm Mon.-Fri., 1pm-4pm Sat., free) has memorabilia from the big fight and displays concerning the region's oil wealth.

The **Sweet Grass border crossing,** 24 miles north of Shelby on I-15, is open 24 hours and is the state's busiest Canadian port of entry.

Shelby is a stop on Amtrak's *Empire Builder,* which passes through once daily in each direction.

ACCOMMODATIONS

Shelby has several motels and sees a lot of Canadian travelers. The **Crossroads Inn** (1200 Hwy. 2, 406/434-5134, $65-80) offers clean basic rooms plus a heated pool.

The **Comfort Inn** (455 McKinley, 406/434-2212 or 800/442-4667, $95-120 and up), at the junction of I-15 and Highway 200, has a lounge and casino, exercise room and hot tub, and allows pets. The **Best Western Shelby**

Inn (1948 W. Roosevelt Hwy., 406/424-4560, $99-125) is Shelby's newest motel, with a pool, fitness center, and free hot breakfast.

CAMPING

Campers may want to swing seven miles south of town to **Williamson Park** on the Marias River.

FOOD

Country Skillet (406/434-2175, open 24 hours, $6-20) is the spot for a hearty breakfast—it's in Shelby Travel Plaza truck stop just west of town. **Dixie's Inn & Dining Room** (406/434-5817, 11am-10pm daily, $12-24), west of Shelby, is a good choice for a night out on the town, with steaks and seafood.

Blackfeet Indian Reservation

Just east of Glacier National Park and the Rocky Mountains, short-grass prairie rolls across the Blackfeet Reservation, a high plain cut through by creeks and dotted with lakes. Strong winds from the west, long and cold winters, and short hot summers make it difficult to ignore the weather here.

Among the reservation communities, **Heart Butte** is the most traditional; **East Glacier, St. Mary,** and **Babb** cater to tourists, with many businesses owned by non-Indians. **Cut Bank,** on the reservation's eastern border, has more in common with the Hi-Line towns to the east. **Browning** is home to the fascinating **Museum of the Plains Indian.**

The Blackfeet, originally from north of the Great Lakes, moved west in the 1600s and established southern Alberta as their territory. What is now known as the Blackfeet Nation is composed of three distinct tribes: the Northern Piegan (Pikuni), the Southern Piegan or Blackfeet (Siksika), and the Blood (Kainai). By the 1700s, bands of Blackfeet had settled in what is now Montana. The Northern Piegan and the Blood mostly remained in Canada.

When early explorers and mountain men arrived in the 1800s, the Blackfeet controlled the northern plains. Settlers feared the Blackfeet's raids as much as they vied for their business at trading posts. Early trading posts in Blackfeet country included Fort Piegan on the Missouri River near present-day Loma.

The U.S. government was eager to confine the Blackfeet, and in order to start the process along, marked the land north of the Yellowstone and south of Canada's Saskatchewan River, east of the Continental Divide and west of the confluence of the Missouri and Yellowstone Rivers, for a reservation. Pressure from settlers wanting the land for their own uses resulted in an incredible shrinking reservation. The Blackfeet Reservation now comprises 1.5 million acres, with more than one-third of that owned by non-Indians.

CUT BANK

This foothills oil and gas town of 3,100 souls was named by the Blackfeet for "the river that cuts into the white clay bank," or Cut Bank Creek. There was an initial burst of development when the Great Northern Railway came through in the 1890s and another big spurt in the 1930s when oil and gas were discovered nearby. Cut Bank is just east of the Blackfeet Reservation, and unlike Browning, it's not a thoroughly Native American town.

Accommodations

The **Glacier Gateway Plaza** (1130 E. Main, 406/873-2566 or 800/851-5541, www.glacier-gateway.com, $69-75) has an indoor pool, hot tub, complimentary continental breakfast, and free high-speed Internet service. Owned by the same hoteliers, the **Glacier Gateway Inn** (1121 E. Railroad St., 406/873-5544 or 800/851-5541, $63-75) is also comfortable, with well-appointed rooms. You can't miss it—it's next to the 27-foot penguin. There are

How the Blackfeet Got Their Name

Two legends tell of how the Blackfeet got their tribal name.

The first, and oldest, is a story about a man and his three sons. Obeying a vision, the man sent his sons west to hunt buffalo. The buffalo were where they were supposed to be, by the thousands, but they were difficult to approach. The sun appeared in a second vision and provided the father with black medicine with which to paint his oldest son's feet. It worked, and the son was able to run down the buffalo. His descendants are called Blackfeet. The man's other two sons weren't ignored. One became a warrior—his painted red lips earned his descendants the name "Bloods." And the third son returned home with clothes of distant tribes; his descendants became the Pikuni, or "Far-Off Clothing." English-speakers transformed this into "Piegan."

The less visionary explanation points to the fact that the tribe's long travels across scorched prairies to reach what is today Montana probably blackened their moccasins.

three themed rooms, one with a two-story tepee inside! The **Super 8** (609 W. Main, 406/873-5662, $90-101) is adjacent to a shopping mall and restaurants and has an indoor pool and hot tub.

Food

The **Cut Bank Cafe** (13 W. Main, 406/873-4010, 6am-9pm daily, $5-12) is the spot for big breakfasts and good homecooked American fare. Get sandwiches at the **Smokehouse Deli** (5 N. Central Ave., 406/873-4747, 11am-3pm Mon.-Sat.). For dinner, look to the **Village Dining and Lounge** (601 W. Main, 406/873-5005, 11am-10pm daily, $8-22), in the North Village Shopping Center, for sandwiches, steaks, pasta, and seafood.

BROWNING

Browning (pop. 1,065, elev. 4,462 feet) is the headquarters of the Blackfeet Nation. It's 18 miles east of Glacier National Park, and many parkgoers zip through in a hurry to get to the mountains. Although Browning is not a fancy place—the café fare is no more compelling than the highway motel rooms—there is a certain spirit to the place, and there are reasons to stop here.

Sights

Browning's main attraction is the **Museum of the Plains Indian** (124 2nd Ave. N.W., 406/338-2230, www.browningmontana.

com/museum, 9am-4:30pm daily June-Sept., 10am-4:30pm Mon.-Fri. Oct.-May, admission charged in summer only, $5 adults, $1 children 6-12), near the intersection of Highways 2 and 89. The exhibits of cultural artifacts are well curated and professionally displayed, the slide show is vivid, and the gift shop is a good place to buy Native American art and jewelry without fear of getting inferior or inauthentic goods and with the assurance that the artist is being fairly compensated.

At the same highway intersection, the **Blackfeet Heritage Center and Art Gallery** (333 Central Ave. W., 406/338-5425, www.blackfeetnationstore.com, 9am-6pm daily June-Oct.) exhibits and sells art, jewelry, and crafts from a number of Native American tribes.

The back roads of the reservation pass homes (with an occasional tepee pitched out back), lakes, oil and gas rigs, and a ceremonial sun lodge (a polygonal log-limbed structure). While common manners dictate that one shouldn't trespass, it is especially important not to enter tribal religious sites, such as a sun lodge.

Events

North American Indian Days are held the second week of July at the powwow grounds behind the Museum of the Plains Indian. Dancing and drumming are the highlights of the weekend activities. Teams of drummers come from all over the West to compete at this powwow, and their drumming is frequently rhapsodic. Stick games, jewelry peddlers, and the bustling encampment of tepees, tents, and pickups round out the scene. Spectators will quickly realize that this is *real,* not something trotted out for tourists, and while non-Indians are welcome, events aren't geared toward them.

Accommodations

The new **Holiday Inn Express Browning** (50 Museum Loop, 406/338-2400 or 877/859-5095, $86-115) is by far the nicest spot to stay in Browning, with a pool, fitness center, and complimentary breakfast buffet. Another comfortable and engaging place to stay in the Browning area is the slightly over-named ★ **Aspenwood Resort** (10 miles east of Browning on Hwy. 89, 406/338-3009, www. aspenwoodresort.com, $95-115), a rural B&B with three guest suites in a log lodge. The setting is astonishing, with the Rockies rising up from groves of aspen directly west of the

resort. The suites are very comfortable, with quality furniture and rustic warmth. There are also RV ($30 and up) and tenting ($18) sites among the aspens and near the beaver ponds. The resort restaurant, the Outlaw Grill, is the best place to eat for miles around.

Food

Browning is no culinary mecca, but the **Jackpot Restaurant** at the Glacier Peaks Casino (Junction of Hwy. 2 and Hwy. 89 W., 406/338-2274, 10am-9pm daily, $7-18) offers a broad menu.

The **Outlaw Grill** (10 miles east of Browning on Hwy. 89, 406/338-3009, www. aspenwoodresort.com, 7am-9pm daily, $10-26) is a small dining room at a B&B lodge and serves burgers, steaks, and seasonal specialties.

Information

Information is available from the **Blackfeet Nation** (P.O. Box 850, Browning, MT 59417, 406/338-7276, www.blackfoot.org).

Rocky Mountain Front

The Rocky Mountains hoist themselves off the plains just west of Choteau and Augusta. It's as dramatic a transition as you'll find in any landscape: flat rangeland to the east, and wilderness mountains rising abruptly to the west. In winter, chinook winds blow down off the mountains to warm the plains; the rest of the year, the wind just plain blows.

In this spectacular setting, near **Choteau** and **Augusta,** are found some of the state's best-loved and longstanding **guest ranches.** Many also operate as outfitters for fishing and hunting trips and lead pack trips into the Bob Marshall Wilderness.

Natural-gas pumps and missile sites dot the fields stretching out from the Rocky Mountain Front. Controversy has erupted between those who want to develop natural gas (and feel that it can be balanced with wilderness) and those

who fear such gas exploration and mining will harm the Front's environment.

There's compelling ancient history here too: Near Choteau is **Egg Mountain,** where paleontologists discovered nests of egg-laying dinosaurs that may be the missing link between birds and reptiles. Although tours of the fossil beds are no longer offered, Choteau's **Old Trail Museum** has exhibits on these and other local dinosaurs, and the **Two Medicine Dinosaur Center** offers a gallery of dinosaur fossils and a variety of hands-on fossil dig programs for amateur paleontologists.

HIGHWAY 89: BROWNING TO CHOTEAU

Edging along the face of the Rocky Mountain Front, Highway 89 passes through bucolic ranching communities—the cattle and horses here have it very lucky, at least in summer. The scenery, with verdant pastures and wooded streams serving as foreground to the massive, near-vertical rise of the Rockies, is as dramatic as any in Montana.

While there aren't many developed tourist sites along this route—this remains first and last ranch country—there are two exceptional bed-and-breakfasts in this rural area that warrant a stop.

Accommodations

If you're looking for historic character, then you'll love the ★ **Inn Dupuyer** (406/472-3241, www.inndupuyer.com, year-round, $85 double), 34 miles north of Choteau in the little community of Dupuyer—the setting for several Ivan Doig novels. The original inn is a century-old two-story log home that the owners carefully refurbished by constructing a modern house around the older building, largely encasing the log structure. While the dining room, kitchen, and a parlor area are new and commodious, the bedrooms and the common room are all in the historic log home. All four rooms have private baths and are carefully decorated with local period furnishings; the antique beds all have down comforters. The upstairs

common room, with an old wood-burning stove, saddle tack, and rustic furniture, will make you feel as if you've just settled into a stylish 1890s ranch house. Off the back is a deck with great views onto the Front Range. Rates include a Western-style breakfast. In summer, ask about staying in a sheep wagon, tepee, or one-room log cabin.

In Valier, the ★ **Stone School Inn B&B** (820 3rd St., 406/279-3796, http://stoneschoolinn.com, $105-115, breakfast is additional $10 pp) preserves a handsome three-story stone school building from 1911. The five large guest rooms, which take up the entire second floor, are beautifully furnished and each has a private bathroom. Guests share a library and game room; free Wi-Fi is available throughout. This is quite an enterprise, and definitely worth the detour.

Food

A local favorite for excellent steaks and refined preparations of local meats and produce, the **Lighthouse Restaurant** (1162 Valier Hwy., 406/279-3798, 11am-10pm daily May-Sept., 11am-10pm Wed.-Sat. and 1pm-8pm Sun. Oct.-Apr., $12-26) is right on the shores of Lake Frances in the center of Valier.

the Inn Dupuyer

Maiasaura, Montana's State Fossil

As far as dinosaurs go, maiasaura are practically heart-warming—enough so that Montana school-children spearheaded a drive in 1985 to have this recently discovered reptile named as Montana's state fossil.

Maiasaura lived during the late Cretaceous period, about 80 to 65 million years ago, when this part of Montana was at the edge of vast saltwater swamps. Maiasaura grew to about 30 feet in length and were distinguished by duckbills, which enabled them to dredge coastal marshes for leaves, berries, and seeds. Although they walked on four feet, when they ran—and they were relatively fast for dinosaurs, sprinting at 12-18 miles per hour—they ran upright on their hind legs.

Maiasaura were the first dinosaurs to be found with their eggs, leading to new theories about saurian maternal instincts and a kinder, gentler reputation for ancient reptiles. At Egg Mountain, just outside Choteau, researchers found maiasaura fossil skeletons alongside scooped-out holes in the ground about six or seven feet across. These holes were filled with up to 25 grapefruit-size eggs. Nests were 25-30 feet across, roughly the size of a maiasaura, which suggests that the dinosaurs lived and nested in colonies in order to protect and nurture their young.

Researchers estimate that Egg Mountain was home to roughly 10,000 maiasaura; these individuals died when ancient volcanoes carpeted the area with volcanic ash. Because of this great population concentration, scientists also speculate that maiasaura were migratory, returning to the rocky outcrop now known as Egg Mountain at nesting season.

Since their extinction, maiasaura have traveled quite a distance from Egg Mountain. A maiasaura bone fragment and a piece of egg shell flew on an eight-day Spacelab 2 mission with astronaut Loren Acton, making the "good mother lizard" the first dinosaur in space.

CHOTEAU

Choteau (pop. 1,791, elev. 3,800 feet), at the feet of the Rocky Mountains, is not in Chouteau County; it's the county seat of Teton County. The town is built around the county courthouse, smack where Highway 287 crosses Highway 89.

The town has become known as a paleontological hot spot. Dinosaurs used this area as a breeding ground, and paleontologists (led by Jack Horner, based in Bozeman at the Museum of the Rockies) have pieced together revolutionary dinosaur life theories based on bones and fossilized eggshells excavated at nearby Egg Mountain.

The Old North Trail, running from the Arctic to Mexico more than 8,000 years ago, was an important migratory trail for proto-Indians. Traces of it are still visible at the Pine Butte Preserve just west of present-day Choteau.

Catholic missionaries preceded the fur traders who started settlements here. The town was named after Pierre Chouteau,

who was associated with the American Fur Company. (The first *u* in the name was dropped to distinguish the town from Chouteau County.) When fur trading died out, the economic mantle was picked up by cattle ranchers.

Choteau was home to novelist A. B. Guthrie until his death in 1991. Guthrie, best known for *The Big Sky*, was an environmentalist in this land of ranchers and natural-gas speculators.

★ Old Trail Museum

When you're standing on Choteau's main street, Teton Trail Village, a cluster of old re-furbished cabins loaded with period artifacts, is hard to miss, and you shouldn't. The biggest draw (besides the ice-cream shop) is the **Old Trail Museum** (823 N. Main, 406/466-5332, http://theoldtrailmuseum.org, 9am-5pm daily Memorial Day-Labor Day, $5 adult, $3 children 6-18, 5 and under free).

The paleontology gallery features discoveries from the area's Two Medicine Formation, including a maiasaura and an einosaurus skull along with nestling, hatchling, and teenage maiasaura skeletons and bones. It's no longer possible to visit the Egg Mountain site, but you can visit the museum's tribute to the 1978 Egg Mountain fossil bed discovery by Marion Branvold.

Other displays focus on more recent Choteau history, such as the Old North Trail and the story behind a contentious trial and hanging in the 1920s.

★ Two Medicine Dinosaur Center

Ten miles north of Choteau in the tiny community of Bynum is **Two Medicine Dinosaur Center** (406/469-2211 or 800/238-6873, www.tmdinosaur.org, 10am-5pm Wed.-Sun. May and Sept. 16-Oct., 9am-6pm June-Sept. 15, $5 adults, $4 military and seniors 55 and up, $3 for children 4-12, free for kids 3 and under), a recent addition to the area's dinosaur culture. The center is worth a stop to view the skeletal model of a seismosaurus, the longest dinosaur every discovered; the first baby dinosaur remains found in North America; and Bob, or "block of bones" (hence the "bob" acronym). Bob is over 11 feet in length, weighs 5.5 tons, and contains over 100 dinosaur bones and fragments from at least three individuals and two separate species. Visitors can usually watch professional paleontologists extract and prepare fossils in the lab. The center also offers an array of hands-on programs that offer keen amateur paleontologists a chance to participate in a dig. A three-hour program ($75) offers an introduction to basic fossil recognition, area history, and geology. One-, two-, five-, and ten-day programs offer a chance to help out in fossil excavations (visit the website for details and dates). There's a lot going on here, so check online to find the latest on dig opportunities across the state. Prior reservations are required for all programs.

The Nature Conservancy's Pine Butte Swamp Preserve

Nestled between the Front Range and a former MX missile silo, this preserve stretches from the mountains to the plains across a rare (for this area) wetland. (More precisely, it's a fen, which means that the water actually flows.) Grizzly bears forage here and have historically used the brushy swamp as a corridor to the plains. This is now one of the easternmost outposts of the grizzly, which was formerly native to the plains.

While access to the preserve is limited,

Two Medicine Dinosaur Center

there is one area open to visitors. Drive past the old Bellview schoolhouse (five miles west of Egg Mountain, along the same road) and turn right on a cut-across road (there's a sign). Drive northwest on this road for about two miles to an information kiosk. Park here, read the posted information, and take the trail starting at the kiosk. It's a short easy hike up a flower-strewn ridge to a view of glacier-carved Pine Butte, wetlands, glacial moraines, faint traces of the Old North Trail, and the Rocky Mountain Front.

Contact the **Pine Butte Swamp Preserve** (26 Meltwater Rd., Choteau, 406/466-5526) for more information regarding access and natural history programs offered through Pine Butte Guest Ranch.

Another good wildlife area, southeast of Choteau, is **Freezout Lake,** a waterfowl area and wetlands that migrating birds use as a rest stop. Pelicans, blue-winged teal, and marsh hawks reside here, as do snow geese in the spring and tundra swans each fall. Access to the refuge is at multiple pullouts along Hwy. 89 between Choteau and Fairfield. Nearby Priest Butte was the site of a Catholic mission for the Blackfeet.

Recreation

Take your pick of trails on the South Fork of the Teton River—many of them lead into the Bob Marshall Wilderness. **Our Lake** (called Hidden Lake on the trailhead sign) is three miles up and in. Mountain goats are often visible above the lake. The hike to **Headquarters Pass** starts at the same trailhead (near the Mill Falls Campground) and passes a high waterfall on the Sun River on the way to expansive views. Grizzly bears are sometimes spotted in the area, so take precautions. It's not unusual to run into snowfields on the higher trails even in July.

Teton Pass Ski Area (406/466-2209, www.tetonpassresort.com) has cross-country and downhill trails at Teton Pass. The relatively small downhill area has lift tickets for $39. Cross-country skiers headed for the Bob Marshall Wilderness Area often start from

Choteau, because roads are plowed all the way to the mountains.

Fish **Pishkun Reservoir,** southwest of town, for kokanee salmon, northern pike, and rainbow trout.

Events

The **Choteau rodeo** takes place on the Fourth of July.

Accommodations

The **Stage Stop Inn** (1005 Main Ave. N., 406/466-5900 or 888/466-5900, www.stages-topinn.com, $104-109) has handsomely furnished rooms and a pool and hot tub. Complimentary continental breakfast is included.

Guest Ranches

Two of Montana's best guest ranches are tucked in behind the Rocky Mountain Front, west of Choteau.

For an old-fashioned horse-based guest ranch, it's hard to beat the ★ **Seven Lazy P Deep Canyon Guest Ranch** (P.O. Box 178, Choteau, MT 59422, 406/466-2044, www.sevenlazyp.com, closed in winter, daily $268 per person double occupancy with 4-day minimum, weekly $1,720 per person double occupancy). In operation since 1958, this beautifully located ranch offers lodging in comfortable log cabins large enough to sleep an entire family; each has a private bath and toilets. Meals are served in the gracious lodge headquarters, reached by a short bridge across a stream. The lodge common room, dominated by a stone fireplace and filled with comfortable rustic furniture, is an atmospheric place to hole up with a book or talk about the day's adventures. Activities include daily organized horseback riding, hiking, and fishing trips—or plain old relaxing. If you're considering a long-distance pack trip into the Bob Marshall Wilderness, the Seven Lazy P offers 7- to 10-day backcountry excursions. Pack trips run $385 per day for a five-day trip, or $3,250 for 10 days.

Visitors are in for a slightly different

experience at the ★ **Pine Butte Guest Ranch** (351 South Fork Rd., Choteau, MT 59422, 406/466-2158, http://pinebutte-guestranch.com, $2,250 per week for adults, $1,750 for youths 13-18 and $1,550 6-12, one-week minimum, Sun.-Sun. stays only). Stunningly located on the South Fork of the Teton River, with steep escarpments rising on all sides, Pine Butte has been a dude ranch since 1930. The original owners sold it to the Nature Conservancy, which is dedicated to preserving plants, animals, and natural communities by protecting the land and waters they need to survive. Consequently, in addition to traditional dude-ranch activities like trail rides, the ranch also sponsors daily naturalist hikes and programs along the Front Range, focusing on the area's unique natural history. During the spring and fall, the ranch sponsors a series of longer, hands-on workshops on topics such as grizzly bears, the local dinosaur digs, or nature photography. You'll leave the Pine Butte Ranch not only saddle sore but also wiser about the natural world of Montana.

Lodging is in very comfortable single or duplex cabins, each with private bathrooms and fireplaces; there's even a swimming pool. Meals are served in the lodge, which is filled with handmade furniture made by the ranch's original owner. Room, board, naturalist tours, and horseback riding are included in the fee, as is Sunday transportation to and from the Great Falls airport.

Camping

The free **Choteau city park campground** is right in town; turn off Highway 89 at the blinking light and follow the KOA signs. The city park is closer in than the **KOA** (one mile east on Hwy. 221, 406/446-2615), which is farther east. Choose the city park if flush toilets and running water are amenities enough; for hookups, showers, and campground fees, continue on to the KOA.

Mill Falls Campground is small, free, and well situated for hikers. Follow Highway 89 north out of Choteau and turn down the road to Teton Canyon.

Food

Summers heat up east of the Rockies, and Choteau is a good place to cool off with an ice-cream cone. There's an ice-cream parlor in the **Teton Trail Village** and another one right across the street at the **OutPost Deli** (819 7th Ave. N., 406/466-5330, 6am-3pm Mon.-Sat., 6am-2pm Sun.), which is also a good spot for a breakfast or a lunchtime sandwich. The **Elk Country Grill** (925 N. Main Ave., 406/466-3311, www.elkcountrygrill.com, 11am-8pm Mon.-Thurs., 11am-9pm Fri.-Sat., $6-23) serves homemade soup and sandwiches for lunch and hand-carved steaks and authentic Dutch oven meals for dinner.

Information

The **Forest Service ranger station** (406/466-5341) is on Highway 89 at the northern edge of town, and the **Old Trail Museum** (823 N. Main, 406/466-5332, http://theoldtrailmuseum.org, 9am-5pm daily Memorial Day-Labor Day) is another good source of information, especially for dinosaur details.

AUGUSTA

Even more so than Choteau, Augusta (pop. 284) is spectacularly located and a good way to access the Bob Marshall Wilderness Area. As you head south on Highway 287 from Choteau, past mounded glacial moraines, the east face of the Rockies becomes closer and more dramatic. The road crosses the Sun River seven miles north of Augusta as it flows from the Rockies to the Missouri. The Blackfeet referred to the Sun as the Medicine River because they used mineral deposits from a side gulch medicinally. Gibson Reservoir, named after Paris Gibson, the founder of Great Falls and initiator of hydroelectric power on the Missouri, is on the Sun River right where the Rockies jut up from the plains. The dam was built in 1913 primarily to store and divert water for irrigation.

Augusta is home to the American Legion Rodeo, the state's oldest. It's also one of the best regarded, and people drive hundreds of miles to attend. The rodeo is held on the last Sunday of June.

Sights

Gibson Reservoir is 26 miles northwest of Augusta. Reach it via the road toward the south end of town with the sign to Willow Creek fishing-access area (Rd. 1081). On the way to the Rocky Mountain Front, the road crosses a moraine strewn with glacial erratics—boulders carried in glacial ice and then dropped where the ice melted. Once the road meets up with the Sun River, you come right up against the rocks, and the whole geologic idea of overthrust becomes startlingly clear.

The road ends just past the dam, and trails continue the length of the reservoir, past medicine springs and Native American pictographs, into the Bob Marshall Wilderness. Bighorn sheep, elk, and deer winter north of the reservoir.

The state bought land for **Sun River Wildlife Management Area** in the 1940s to provide wintering ground for the Sun River elk herd. Previous to that, the elk had competed with cattle on the plains and with bighorn sheep in the mountains. Thousands of elk now winter on the moraine between the Gibson Reservoir and Augusta. Hunting is permitted here, although it's prohibited in the Sun River Game Preserve, which is part of the Bob Marshall Wilderness Area. The range is closed in the winter (although elk are often visible from nearby roads) and open in the summer to bird-watchers, hikers, and mountain bikers.

Recreation

The trail from Mortimer Campground on Gibson Reservoir goes into the Bob Marshall Wilderness Area. Other trails into the Bob Marshall and Scapegoat Wilderness Areas start from Benchmark and South Fork Campgrounds, south of the reservoir. A trail starts at the South Fork Campground and

passes through the Sun River Game Preserve on its way to the spectacular Chinese Wall, a 13-mile-long 1,000-foot-tall escarpment on the Continental Divide.

Accommodations

The place to stay in Augusta is the **Bunkhouse Inn** (122 Main St., 406/562-3387 or 800/553-4016, $49-55), a 1912 hotel that started out in Gilman, which is now a ghost town. The old hotel was moved to Augusta, then renovated into a unique rustic inn. It has 10 rooms, all with shared baths (the owners point out that this is an improvement over the outhouses of the original hotel).

Camping

Settle in and contemplate geology at **Home Gulch Campground,** below Gibson Reservoir on the Sun River, 21 miles from Augusta. Five miles down the road, **Mortimer Campground** perches above the reservoir. A trail leads from Mortimer into the Bob Marshall Wilderness Area.

Three campgrounds south of Gibson Reservoir are on Road 234 (Benchmark Rd.) west of Augusta. **Wood Lake** is 25 miles from Augusta, **Benchmark** is another 5 miles down the road, and **South Fork** is yet another mile on, at the end of the road. For information on these campgrounds, call the ranger station at 406/562-3247.

Guest Ranches

The mountains behind Augusta harbor a clutch of excellent guest ranches. For a real outback Montana ranch experience, try the **Benchmark Wilderness Ranch** (422 County Line Rd., Fairfield, 406/467-3110, www.benchmarkwildernessranch.com). The Benchmark Ranch is located deep in the Lewis and Clark National Forest, so far back that there are still no phones and no electricity (the otherwise modern comfortable cabins and lodge are powered with propane appliances and lights). You can drive to the ranch, or if you're traveling by plane, the ranch has its own airstrip. The advantage of this remote site is that you don't have to go far from your cabin to arrive in real wilderness. Benchmark specializes in backcountry horse pack trips, which involve overnight camping trips to remote lakes and streams teeming with trout; a four-day backcountry fishing trip is $1,000 per person. Five- to seven-day hunting and adventure trips are also available. Cabins (with kitchens) are located near a modern bathhouse and are available on a per-day basis ($75 for up to four guests). If you'd prefer to eat your meals in the main lodge dining room, lodging packages are available that include all meals, lodging, and horseback riding, starting at $200 per person per day. À la carte horseback riding is $110 per day. You'll get a friendly welcome at the Benchmark—the ranch has been in operation since 1928, and you can rest assured that the stock and the hands here are some of the best in the state.

The **JJJ Wilderness Ranch** (P.O. Box 310, Augusta, MT 59410, 406/562-3653, www.triplejranch.com, 6-day Sun.-Sat. $2,040 per person adult double occupancy), on Gibson Reservoir, operates a full-fledged dude ranch with horseback riding, nature photography, swimming in the heated pool, and fishing. Exploring the Front Range on horseback is the specialty of the Triple J, and you'll get plenty of hands-on instruction from the wranglers. Kids get a special welcome—there's even a special wrangler for kids who supervises rides and games. Lodging is in cabins, all with modern bathrooms and ample sitting room. Four- and five-day programs are also available in June and September, and include all meals (including steak barbecues) and activities. The Triple J also runs five-, six-, and seven-day pack trips into the Bob Marshall Wilderness ($375 per day all-inclusive).

Food

Restaurant choices are pretty much limited to the dining room at the **Buckhorn Bar** (120 Main St., 406/562-3344, 11am-9pm daily, $7-18), with burgers, chicken, and steaks, and **Mel's Diner** (121 Main St., 406/562-3408,

6am-7pm daily May-Nov., 6am-5:30pm Dec.-Apr., $6-12), a friendly café with good breakfasts and a famed buffalo burger.

Information

The Forest Service operates a **ranger station** (406/562-3247) just down Willow Creek Road.

BOB MARSHALL WILDERNESS AREA

This wilderness area was created in 1940, when three national forest primitive areas were combined and named for a New Yorker who was a strong advocate for wilderness and an inveterate hiker.

The Land

The eastern face of the Bob Marshall is characterized by overthrust—old rocks on young. The Sawtooth Range, which forms the Rocky Mountain Front, shows off faults, folds, and overthrusts in the layers of limestone jutting into the prairie. The rocks here are generally younger than those to their west. Oil and gas speculators have been petitioning the Forest Service since the 1940s for the right to drill in the Bob Marshall and Great Bear Wilderness Areas.

The eastern Sawtooth side of the Bob Marshall is, as expected, drier, windier, and more sparsely vegetated than the western Swan Range side. Bears, mountain goats (native, not transplants), elk, and bighorn sheep all thrive in this wilderness area.

Getting In

Despite its imposing appearance, the Rocky Mountain Front offers several entrances to the Bob Marshall Wilderness Area. Roads west from Choteau and Augusta end at trailheads, some near the wilderness boundary. There's a real visual punch gained by entering over the Front Range, where escarpments are pronounced, rather than from the west, across the trailing ends of the propped-up rocks.

The Benchmark trailhead west of Augusta is a particularly popular one, especially with horse packers. Just to the north, trails from Gibson Reservoir lead right into the wilderness.

From the Headquarters Pass Trail, west of Choteau, continue on to Rocky Mountain Peak, the Bob's highest peak at 9,392 feet. This trail can also be followed to the Chinese Wall.

Backpackers should plan to spend a minimum of five days to a week—distances are great. The Forest Service puts out a topographical map of the Bob Marshall, Great Bear, and Scapegoat Wilderness Complex. Use this map or U.S. Geological Survey (USGS) topos to select a route.

Destinations

Hikers and packers can start at virtually any trailhead and reach the **Chinese Wall.** This 1,000-foot-high escarpment near the Continental Divide is the hallmark of the Bob and can see a surprising amount of traffic during the summer. For solitude, it's worth studying the maps and consulting with rangers to pick a less-traveled area.

West of the Divide, the South Fork of the Flathead River cuts through the Bob and is a favorite with floaters and anglers, who usually come in from Holland Lake on the western border. East of the Bob Marshall's divide, anglers go after rainbow, brown, lake, golden, and cutthroat trout. Grayling are here too, but they must be released when caught.

The **Sun River Game Preserve** was established in 1912 to protect and develop big-game herds. It now covers much of the eastern half of the Bob Marshall Wilderness Area—the only part of the Bob where hunting is prohibited.

Information

Contact the **Forest Service at the Choteau Ranger Station** (Rocky Mountain National Forest, Choteau, MT 59422, 406/466-5341) for detailed information.

Background

The Landscape

Montana's borders rope in just over 147,000 square miles, making it the fourth-largest state behind Alaska, Texas, and California. The northern edge of the state spans the Canadian province of Alberta and catches two-thirds of Saskatchewan and the eastern part of British Columbia to boot. North and South Dakota lie off to the east, Wyoming flanks much of the south, and the Idaho state line rims the Bitterroot Mountains at the western and southwestern borders.

Western Montana is where the state's name (from the Spanish word for mountainous) rings particularly true: Steep pitches and narrow north-south valleys line up from the Idaho border to I-15. The Continental Divide enters from Canada in Glacier National Park, twists through the western mountains, and exits on a high flat stretch of land just west of Yellowstone National Park. Central Montana is particularly varied, with high plateaus and isolated mountain ranges running in no set direction. The eastern part of the state, where the landscape gradually flattens out into the Great Plains, is coursed by the Missouri and Yellowstone Rivers and a host of smaller valleys. Contorted badlands, eroded terraces, and steep rimrocks fringe river valleys and dot the plains. Minerals, coal, and oil are concealed throughout the state, giving rise to the nickname "Treasure State."

GEOGRAPHY

More than 570 million years ago—before the supercontinent of Pangaea broke up into Europe, Africa, and the Americas—Precambrian sand and mud deposits blanketed the land that would become western Montana. Traces of blue-green algae are the only fossils found in Precambrian-era rocks, which can still be seen in western and central Montana, where later movements forced them to the surface. Glacier National Park is almost entirely Precambrian in origin.

Toward the end of the Mesozoic era, tectonic plates were scudding all over the earth. As the Atlantic Ocean widened, the North American Plate was shoved into the Pacific Ocean Plate, which slipped under the western edge of the continent. The crust of western Montana, then at the leading edge of the continental plate, crumpled, cracked, and faulted as it rammed into the Pacific plate. The crust of Montana eventually overrode the Pacific plate and was then lifted high above sea level. About 70 million years ago, the Rocky Mountains were produced by this collision of tectonic plates.

Some sedimentary layers, laid down with older strata topped by younger, were scrambled during these crustal collisions, and in some places older rocks were forced up from the geologic basement and slipped on top of younger ones. This is especially apparent in Glacier National Park. As the Rockies lifted, older layers of rocks skidded eastward from what are now the Flathead and North Fork Valleys, ending up as the Lewis Overthrust on the eastern front of the Rockies. Volcanic intrusions further developed the Rockies and formed separate mountain ranges to the east of them.

As western Montana lifted, ancient seas rolled back off the eastern part of the state for the final time. Swamps and floodplains stretched across eastern Montana by the end of the Mesozoic era, about 65 million years ago. Many plants and animals lived on these sedimentary flats, and their remains, as oil, go into our gas tanks today. Peat swamps were

---

Previous: wild mustangs; rural Montana mailboxes.

prevalent; eventually they crumbled and rotted into thick veins of coal.

Volcanoes began erupting in present-day Yellowstone National Park about 50 million years ago. A monumental eruption 600,000 years ago shot magma over the West, leaving a large crater, or caldera. Recurrent outpourings of lava formed the high plateau that's there now.

Alternating wet and dry periods over the past 40 million years modified terrain all over the state. During dry spells, river valleys filled with sediments, nearly burying many mountain peaks. When the climate dampened, rivers washed away the fill to reexpose underlying structures. This deposit-erosion cycle has made eastern Montana a paleontologist's dream. One of the largest complete tyrannosaurus skeletons on record was unearthed in remote Garfield County.

Cenozoic glaciers advanced south about 15,000 years ago. Valley glaciers ran down from northwestern Montana mountaintops and scoured out broad U-shaped valleys along their route. East of the divide, glaciers plowed the land flat as far south as the Missouri River. The Beartooth Plateau, just north of Yellowstone National Park, was glacier-covered at much the same time lava was flowing over it. An ice dam in Idaho backed up the Clark Fork River until most of the valleys in western Montana were covered by glacial Lake Missoula. When the ice dam gave way, which it did repeatedly, torrents of water barreled across the Northwest, scouring topsoil and carving river gorges all the way to the Pacific coast.

East of the Rockies, glacial Lake Great Falls formed at the southern edge of the glacial sheet and reached from Great Falls to Cut Bank. Glacial ice forced the Missouri River, which originally emptied into Hudson's Bay, to alter its course southward to the Mississippi; the Milk River now flows in a section of the Missouri's original bed.

The Plains

Erosion and uplifts formed the prairie landscape. Water, frost, and wind have cut gullies and gulches into the plains and sculpted benches or terraces along river valleys. Northeastern Montana prairie is broad, flat, and underlain by gravel beds. These high plains were formed 3-15 million years ago in a dry climate. The gravel layer allows efficient surface drainage, avoiding erosion and the channels and gullies of the badlands. Glacial debris has further enriched the soil, making this some of the state's best agricultural land.

Montana's badlands, desolate and vegetation-poor, tend to be found south of the Missouri, where glaciers did not deposit thick layers of good soil. Soft bedrock just beneath the surface of bare ground is easily eroded by rain; gullies form, with sediment outwashes spreading from their mouths. The bare, rain-pounded soil develops a hard crust, which exacerbates the runoff and makes it all the more difficult for any vegetation to take hold. The barrenness of the badlands perpetuates itself.

The Mountains

The ranges of the Rockies have different geologic histories and compositions. The Boulder Batholith, a mass of intrusive granite between Butte and Helena, is filled with mineral veins, especially copper and silver. The Absarokas and the Gallatin Range in south-central Montana are blanketed with volcanic rocks from eruptions in and around Yellowstone National Park.

In the far northwestern part of the state, glaciers shrouded the mountains, leaving them relatively rolling and softly shaped. Where glaciers ran down from high cirques into mountain valleys, there is a characteristic straightening of the valley's path and a U shape to its floor, unlike the V-shaped river valleys. Glaciers also pushed along piles of gravel and soil; these moraines are still visible to the geologically savvy.

The isolated mountain ranges of central Montana are not part of the Rockies. Many of them were formed at the end of the Mesozoic

Trailing *T. Rex*: Fossil Stops

Montana may be a ways from the center of life in the modern United States, but 70 million years ago, Montana was a happening place. At the time, Montana was at the rim of a vast shallow sea, where ancient dinosaurs prowled the shoreline forests. These plants and animals eventually met their fates and are preserved in Montana's incredibly rich fossil beds. If you have a fossil or dinosaur enthusiast in your family, you might want to visit a few of these sites.

SOUTHEASTERN MONTANA

- **Ekalaka:** It's one of the most isolated towns in all of Montana, but this Old West community is home to the **Carter County Museum,** which contains the only known remains of *Pachycephalosaurus,* discovered locally by the high school science teacher, a noted amateur paleontologist.

- **Billings:** The **Judith River Dinosaur Institute** offers a variety of hands-on programs at fossil excavations along the Missouri. While these multiday camps can't accommodate drop-in enthusiasts, with a little planning they would be the perfect focus for a family or group excited to learn extraction techniques and lab skills.

NORTHEASTERN MONTANA

- **Jordan:** In the Missouri River badlands north of Jordan are some of the richest fossil beds in the nation: A full-size *T. rex* cast from the original fossil is in the small community museum in this remote capital of the Big Open.

- **Hell Creek State Park:** As you drive to this park on the banks of Fort Peck Reservoir, you'll drop through geologic time; the Hell Creek Formation is the geologic layer with the greatest concentration of Cretaceous-era remains.

- **Fort Peck:** The **Fort Peck Interpretive Center** displays the fossil remains of ancient life uncovered while this enormous Missouri River dam was constructed in the 1930s.

NORTH-CENTRAL MONTANA

- **Choteau**: The dinosaur nests of **Egg Mountain,** where paleontologists unearthed the ancient nesting grounds of maiasaura aren't open to the public, but displays of fossilized maiasaura eggs are found at the excellent **Old Trail Museum** in Choteau.

- **Bynum:** The **Two Medicine Dinosaur Center** leads tours and offers dino dig programs to the local fossil beds. Multiday paleontology workshops are also offered through the center.

SOUTH-CENTRAL MONTANA

- **Bozeman:** Jack Horner, from Montana State University in Bozeman, has been the driving force behind the surge in Montana dinosaur excavation and interpretation in recent years, and the fossil highlights of his long career can be seen at the **Museum of the Rockies** in Bozeman.

era, about 20 million years after the Rockies rose, when molten granite shot up from the depths of the earth and bowed up the overlying sedimentary formations. Other areas of central Montana were lifted along faults to form high plateaus and buttes.

The Rivers

The Missouri and Yellowstone Rivers look on the map like a big crab's pincer, joined to the leg just over the North Dakota border and grasping a big chunk of eastern Montana. Western rivers such as the Clark Fork of the

Columbia, the Flathead, and the Kootenai are tucked into mountain valleys. Rivers provided the way into Montana for the first European explorers, who were hoping to sail out on the Columbia. Trappers and traders also used the rivers as thoroughfares. Steamboats made the difficult trip up the Missouri from St. Louis through sandbars, rapids, and fallen trees to Fort Benton—until railroads took over the transportation business. Towns sprang up in the river valleys, and highways were built on their banks.

The dams that now harness water power and create reservoirs across the state have altered Montana's geography. Every large river but the Yellowstone has been dammed at some point, and millions of gallons of water are backed up in Fort Peck Reservoir on the Missouri and in Lake Koocanusa on the Kootenai River. The Great Falls of the Missouri, which took Lewis and Clark 22 backbreaking days to portage in 1805, are now a series of hydroelectric dams.

CLIMATE

There's as much variety in Montana's weather as there is in the state's topography. The Continental Divide splits Montana into two broad climatic regions. West of the divide, the climate is influenced strongly by mild marine air from the Pacific; to the east, harsher continental patterns prevail.

Stories of extreme weather abound in Montana. It can get *cold*; the lowest temperature in the lower 48 states was recorded at Rogers Pass, northwest of Helena, in 1954: -70°F. Hot summers are common, with temperatures of 117°F recorded in both Glendive and Medicine Lake.

During the spring, the winds shift, and moisture comes up from the Gulf of Mexico. These storms sweep through the Midwest and hit the east slopes of the Rockies. May and June are the wettest months over most of the state; the exception is in the northwest, which gets most of its moisture from wintertime Pacific storms.

July and August are usually the warmest months. It does rain during the summer, but brief thunderstorms are the norm. By September, the weather may start to change for the colder and wetter, but there is frequently a lovely Indian summer in October. Winter storms can begin anytime, but roads are often clear through early November.

Chinooks

Warm, dry winter winds coming off the

Yellowstone River at Miles City

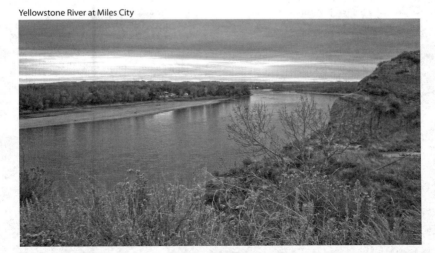

Montana Weather Lore

Back before the Weather Channel, Native Americans and early settlers needed to know the weather forecast. As they spent the majority of the day outdoors, they came to recognize the signs that preceded or produced a change in the weather. Many of these signs of changing weather are still a part of the rural Montana folklore.

- At sunset, watch for small rainbowlike reflections beside the sun. Called **sundogs,** these luminous spots indicate increasing moisture in the atmosphere. Old-timers predict rain or snow when sundogs appear. In the fall, a sundog to the north of the sun indicates impending snow; to the south, a warm rain.

- When the moon is high in the sky, look for a wide reflective ring around it. A **ring around the moon** is also predictive of moisture; the number of stars within the ring equals the number of days before the rain or snow arrives.

- **Three days of east wind** means a storm is imminent.

- Expect rain 90 days after a **heavy fog.**

- **Animal activities** are often thought to indicate weather changes. Skittish, rambunctious animal behavior precedes a storm. Horses standing stock still on a high hill during the heat of the day indicate an approaching thunderstorm.

- Expect a **rainstorm** to continue as long as raindrops are still hanging from tree leaves; the rain is over as soon as birds begin to sing.

east slopes of the Rockies and across the plains are called "Chinooks." As the Pacific air passes over the mountains, it unloads its moisture and is warmed on its eastern downslope run. Chinook winds carry an almost mythological force. They can bring incredibly rapid relief from frigid weather; in Great Falls, the temperature once rose from -32°F to 15°F in seven minutes, almost seven degrees a minute.

Droughts

Montana's dry spells can be as striking as its extremes in heat and cold. Average rainfall for the western part of the state is 18 inches per year, 13 inches for the east. Studies of almost 300 years' worth of tree rings have shown that, every 20-some years, the western United States experiences a drought. A five-year drought that started in 1917 in eastern Montana drove many homesteaders away from agriculture. This drought was coupled with particularly harsh winters. The 1930s saw not only economic depression, but (according to tree rings) the most severe drought since 1700. The 1980s proved to be another era of drought for much of the state. When it's too dry for prairie grasses to survive, ranchers are forced to buy expensive feed or sell their herds and wait for rain.

Plants

Montana's geography dictates its habitats, and the flora and fauna can be considered in two broad categories: prairie and mountain. Precipitation and elevation are the major factors determining what grows where. The state's varied ecosystems provide a home to more than 2,400 types of vascular plants.

THE PRAIRIES

Nineteenth-century atlases called the plains the Great American Desert, an undeserved name that ignores the subtle variety of the grasses and plants found here. While the prairie is not known for its trees, the savannas of eastern Montana offer more than sagebrush and prickly pear landscapes. Willows take root in the river valleys, and Lewis and Clark noted a "scattering of pine and cedar" on the hills, and chokecherries and currants on lower ground. The cottonwoods that grow near riverbottoms were prized for firewood and for dugout canoes.

Eastern Montana is mostly short-grass prairie—that is, a dry grassland supporting perennial grasses such as bluestem, bluejoint, bluegrama, June, wheat, and pine grass. Cheat grass grows in overgrazed areas; it starts strong but can't last through the summer. Other "nuisances" are feather grass and needle grass, which irritate the skin and eyes of sheep and cattle. Russian thistle, or tumbleweed, arrived with European immigrants and is almost universally reviled for its uselessness and prolific nature.

Prairie flowers include the buttercup, yellowbell, crocus, shooting star, bluebell, blanketflower, golden aster, and daisy. Blue camas and death camas grow in moist areas. Prickly pear and three other species of cactus still dog those who try to walk across the prairie. Milkweed, a common roadside plant, was variously used as eye medicine, gravy stock, and chewing gum by the Cheyenne. The deep thick roots of the Indian breadroot plant were an important food for eastern Montana Indians.

Chokecherry bushes are widespread on the northern plains and into the Rockies. Chokecherries were pounded, dried, and stored for the winter by Plains Indians. Native Americans also brewed a tea from the bark to relieve stomach ailments; unripe chokecherry puree was used by both Native Americans and settlers to treat diarrhea.

Prairie sage is a traditional sacred and medicinal plant to many Montana Indians.

CONIFEROUS FORESTS

Most of western Montana supports lush growth, dominated by coniferous forests. Although there are some western Montana prairies (especially around the Mission Valley and Dillon), timbered hillsides are the rule. This category is usually broken down into at least two separate habitats: lower montane and higher subalpine. The highest peaks of Montana also support small areas of alpine tundra.

Ponderosa pine predominates low on the slopes. A little higher, Douglas fir takes over, and above that, lodgepole pine (a species that depends on fire for its propagation) may form dense stands. Western larch, western red cedar, western white pine, grand fir, aspen, and birch can also be found. Willows and alders sprout up along streambeds, and kinnikinnick, Oregon grape, and serviceberries are common elements of the understory.

Subalpine forests are rooted in subalpine fir and Engelmann spruce. Tasty huckleberries are the best-loved subalpine understory shrub. Alpine larch is another hardy high-elevation conifer. An autumn hillside of reddish-gold "evergreens" doesn't necessarily mean a lot of dead trees. Rather, it's probably a stand of larch, one of the few conifer species that drops its needles in the winter.

Wildflower meadows of glacier lilies,

alpine poppies, columbine, Indian paint-brush, asters, arnica, globeflowers, white dryads, and bear grass color the midsummer hillsides. Dogtooth violets and mariposa lilies grow a little farther down the slopes. In the valleys and low on the hills, the state flower, the bitterroot, blossoms in early June. Serviceberry bushes turn white with flowers early in May and bear purplish berries late in July. This member of the rose family

grows on the slopes and canyons of the Rocky Mountains.

ALPINE TUNDRA

Alpine conditions exist in a few places in Montana. Above the timberline (9,000-10,000 feet), the gray-green ground cover includes small low-lying vegetation: grasses, mosses, lichens, sedges, and krummholz (small, twisted trees pruned by the wind) of whitebark pine.

Animals

Montana's wildlife is varied and abundant. Lewis and Clark's journals, the first written account of the region's flora and fauna, are filled with wonder at the vast numbers of animals they had never encountered in the eastern states.

THE PRAIRIES

Lewis and Clark found the plains fairly swarming with wildlife, and not just with "musquetoes," either. Just upstream from the confluence of the Missouri and Yellowstone Rivers, Lewis noted:

> The whole face of the country was covered with herds of Buffaloe, Elk & Antelopes; deer are also abundant, but keep themselves more concealed in the woodland. the buffaloe Elk and Antelope are so gentle that we pass near them while feeding, without appearing to excite any alarm among them; and when we attract their attention, they frequently approach us more nearly to discover what we are, and in some instances pursue us to a considerable distance apparently with that view.

They also reported encounters with rattlesnakes, wolves, black bears, grizzlies, beavers (one of which gave Lewis's dog a nasty bite), bighorn sheep (whose meat was reportedly a delicacy), a "polecat" (skunk), mule deer, and prairie dogs. On their trip up the Missouri, Lewis provided the first descriptions of the

sage grouse, the western meadowlark, and the cutthroat trout.

The buffalo, bears, and wolves may be mostly gone from the prairies, but what Lewis called "our trio of pests"—mosquitoes, gnats, and prickly pear—remain.

Prairie life calls for adaptation, and many animals that live here dig burrows. Witness the **prairie dog.** It can metabolize its own waste water and survive for years without drinking anything else. The black-tailed prairie dogs of Montana live in "towns" of burrows, which are occasionally sublet by burrowing owls.

Another burrowing animal is the **pocket gopher,** a long-clawed, small-eyed rodent that comes aboveground only for quick passes at mating. Pocket gophers get their nutrition—both food and water—from plants they suck, roots first, into their burrows.

While burrows may provide defense for many rodents and birds, the **pronghorn** relies on fleetness. Individuals have been clocked at 70 miles per hour. Their horn is part of a sheath composed of keratin (a fingernail-like protein) and fused hairs covering a core of bone. Pronghorns (which despite the common appellation are not antelopes) shed their horn sheaths annually and pass the winter and spring sporting the bare bony horn core. They are the only mammals that shed their horns (as opposed to antlers, which are, as a rule, dropped annually).

Deer, both white-tailed and the large-eared mule deer, roam the breaks of the big eastern Montana rivers. **Coyotes** still prey on both wild and stock animals. **Gray wolves,** edging in from Canada and Minnesota, have returned to the badlands of the Missouri River in recent years.

Rattlesnakes can turn up just about anywhere in eastern Montana, and it pays to watch where you put your hands and feet. Wear sturdy shoes for hiking. Although healthy adults rarely die from a rattlesnake's venom, a bite does warrant prompt medical attention.

There's abundant **insect** life on the prairie. Most everyone who's read a Western novel can conjure an image of grasshoppers scouring the grasslands and swarming around cattle, cowboys, and horses.

Although magpies seem to control Montana's airways, the sharp-tailed grouse, mourning dove, killdeer, bobolink, long-billed curlew, horned lark, western mead-owlark, goldfinch, Brewer's blackbird, and sparrow hawk are all **birds** to be spotted above the eastern Montana plains.

Warm-water species of fish, such as paddlefish, walleye, northern pike, and channel catfish, inhabit the Yellowstone and the Missouri as they cross the plains.

CONIFEROUS FORESTS

Both **black bears** and **grizzlies** live in and around western Montana's forests. **Elk,** sometimes called wapiti, live high in the summer, low in the winter. **Moose** are common but private. **Mule deer** negotiate rough forest terrain; **white-tailed deer** run across more open areas. Transition areas between two types of habitat (such as the edges of a meadow or clear-cut) are usually good places to look for all sorts of wildlife. **Bighorn sheep, mountain goats,** and grizzly bears are all more likely to be seen high on the slopes of the Rockies.

Mountain lions have been showing up in some unlikely places, like the streets of Columbia Falls, the parks of Missoula, and the campgrounds of Glacier National Park. Big people can usually frighten them off with shouting and menacing gestures, but children and small adults have been attacked. Youngsters should hike within sight of adults.

Because of its predatory instincts, the **gray wolf** has been trapped, hunted, and poisoned

white-tailed deer in Glacier National Park

to near extinction. Since receiving protection as an endangered species, wolf populations have made a comeback, mostly near Glacier National Park and in the far reaches of northwestern Montana. Even before wolves were introduced to Yellowstone National Park, some seemed to have slipped in unescorted. Montana's wolf population grew to over 420 before wolves were delisted as endangered species in 2009. Responsibility for wolf population management has passed to individual states, and Montana has started up a limited wolf hunt.

The wolf's smaller relative, the **coyote,** has managed not only to survive the abuses given to predator species but to actually thrive in human-inhabited areas.

Birds such as dippers, Clark's nutcrackers, spruce grouse, owls, woodpeckers, jays, chickadees, wrens, sparrows, flycatchers, mountain bluebirds, western tanagers, warblers, rufous hummingbirds, waterfowl, bald eagles, ospreys, and hawks all find niches in the varied habitats provided by western Montana's forests.

Westslope cutthroat trout, the state fish, is native to Montana's streams and lakes. First described by Meriwether Lewis, its Latin name, *Salmo clarki,* remembers William Clark. The name cutthroat is just as revealing: These black-specked fish sport two red slashes under their jaws. Because of their tendency to hybridize with rainbow trout, cutthroat are becoming rarer.

Bull trout live mostly in northwestern Montana, especially in their native Clark Fork and Flathead drainages, although stream degradation from overlogging has severely damaged their habitat and reduced their numbers. They're olive green with orange or yellow spots on their sides and can run up to 30 pounds.

Brown trout were imported from Europe in the 1880s, and their numbers have now surpassed many native species. Browns have a reputation for being wily and tough to hook. Another introduced species, the **brook trout,** comes from the eastern United States. The backs of these fish have light-colored "worm tracks" on their otherwise dark olive backs.

Whitefish are silver-sided with olive-green backs and small mouths. They are usually five pounds or less and live in the western part of the state.

Arctic grayling are trout cousins; they're not common, but they can be caught in southwestern and south-central Montana. These small copper-colored or bluish fish are usually less than a foot long, with large dorsal fins.

Until recently, **kokanee salmon,** landlocked salmon with small dark spots on a blue-tinted body, thrived in Flathead Lake, where they'd been planted in the 1920s. Although changes in the lake's ecology have not favored the Flathead kokanee, they are still abundant in other parts of northwestern Montana.

ALPINE TUNDRA

Plants and animals pack as much as possible into the short cool summers of the high country. **Hoary marmots, ground squirrels, pikas,** and **mountain goats** are commonly spotted around Logan Pass (6,680 feet), one of Glacier National Park's alpine communities. The **white-tailed ptarmigan** is the only bird living year-round on the tundra, although other species, such as **water pipits** and **finches,** summer here.

Environmental Issues

THE FUTURE OF MONTANA'S WOLVES

When Lewis and Clark crossed Montana in the early 1800s, gray wolves (*Canis lupus*) were commonly seen on the plains and were, along with grizzly bears (also originally a prairie animal), the dominant predator of the plains wilderness ecosystem. But with the advent of the fur trade, and then agriculture based on livestock, the native wolf populations were gradually exterminated. By the 1930s, no gray wolves remained in Montana.

The rise of environmentalism and the passage of the Endangered Species Act (ESA) in 1973 created a new atmosphere of advocacy for reintroducing the wolf to the western United States. Organizations including Defenders of Wildlife and the National Wildlife Federation spearheaded a successful effort to have wolves listed as "endangered" under the ESA's provisions. "Bounty" programs, which paid hunters to kill wolves, were discontinued, and it became illegal to kill wolves in the United States. In addition, provisions of the ESA called on the federal government to implement a plan for the recovery of the gray wolf population.

In the early 1980s, wolves from Canada began to move into northwest Montana, and by 1995 there were six wolf packs in that region. Advocates for wolves proposed boosting the recovery of wolf populations by actively restoring wolves to suitable areas in the Northern Rockies. Objections arose from livestock ranchers, hunters worried about the impact of wolves on game populations, and other concerned people, while environmentalists and wildlife advocates cheered on the reintroduction.

Eventually, the U.S. Congress held hearings and ultimately ordered the U.S. Fish and Wildlife Service (USFWS) to prepare an Environmental Impact Statement on the reintroduction of wolves to Yellowstone National Park and central Idaho. In 1995 and 1996, as part of its wolf recovery plan, the USFWS trapped 66 wolves in southwestern Canada and transplanted them to Yellowstone National Park and central Idaho.

The wolves quickly made themselves at

wolf in Glacier National Park

home, reproducing and expanding their range faster than any of the experts had predicted.

One major objection to the reintroduction of wolves to the West was that wolves would devastate livestock herds. Even fans of reintroducing wolves acknowledged that wolves are highly efficient predators. To help address this concern, Defenders of Wildlife launched a program to compensate livestock producers when the reintroduced wolves preyed on their stock. By the end of 2002 the fund had paid out more than $270,000 to ranchers in the Northern Rockies.

In general, predation on livestock has been lower than predicted when the wolf reintroduction was first proposed, though it has still been significant. Many wolves have been killed by the state and federal agencies when it has been impossible to deter them from further predation.

By the mid-2000s, approximately 900-1,250 wolves were living in the Northern Rockies in about 100 packs. While most of the population was in the Yellowstone Park area, some packs and individuals—the archetypal lone wolf—dispersed across other parts of Montana.

In 2011, citing the successful reintroduction of the gray wolf, the USFWS delisted the wolf as an endangered species, passing responsibility for wolf population management from the federal government to the individual states of Montana, Idaho, and Wyoming. Each state was required to come up with a wolf management plan that will allow for a population of at least 300 wolves, which is the minimum number for maintaining a stable population. In 2012, Montana had over 600 wolves. As part of its wolf management program, Montana has instituted a limited hunting season for wolves.

POWER GENERATION ON THE GO

Coal-based power generation has been a political and environmental issue in Montana since the 1970s, starting with Colstrip's enormous coal-fired plants. Now the development of coal bed methane gas is the principal topic of contention between energy developers and environmentalists.

Vast reserves of methane gas occur naturally in the coal beds that underlie much of southeastern Montana. Record high prices for natural gas have led energy companies to develop plans to tap into the coal seams and extract the gas, which would then be used for electric power generation.

However, extracting the coal bed methane may have serious consequences for ranchers and farmers who depend on groundwater for wells and springs. Underground coal is a natural aquifer for groundwater—it's a porous layer of rock that allows the water to percolate below the landscape. Water is also what holds the methane gas in the coal beds. To extract the methane, wells are drilled into the coal seam and the water is pumped out. Methane gathers in the recesses formerly occupied by the water and is drawn to the surface and piped to power plants to be burned.

Pumping coal seams dry to extract methane also risks that wells drilled into the same coal aquifers will cease to provide water for rural residents of the region, meaning that longtime farms and ranches may suddenly have no access to water.

Methane gas development stalled until environmentalists and power-generation companies agreed on a plan to reinject the groundwater back into the coal seams after extracting the gas. Although this is costly for the power producers, it seems to address the concerns of ranchers and environmentalists.

THE GIFTS OF MINING PAST

One of Montana's founding industries was mining. The history of the huge mines at Butte—to say nothing of the 1860s gold rush, the sapphire mines, the silver and lead mines, and on and on—have all contributed mightily to the spunk and character of the state. However, recent years have revealed just what enormous environmental damage is now being exacted by the state's mining past.

Even though copper mining has ceased in

Butte, the Berkeley Pit remains a mile-deep reservoir of toxic water. In the 1980s, investigations revealed that many homes in the Butte area, built on foundations made from mining tailings, were highly radioactive. The Butte-Anaconda area is the nation's single largest Superfund site. (The Environmental Protection Agency's Superfund allows for cleanup of particularly toxic areas.)

Downstream from Butte, in the drainage of the Clark Fork, recent restoration programs have been largely successful in reintroducing trout to this magnificent river. By the 1950s the river's chemical load was so high that it had become essentially sterile. However, the arsenic and heavy metals that flowed in the river for nearly a century haven't disappeared; many of these deposits are merely coated in mud.

Most of these toxic sediments lie behind the Milltown Dam, just upriver from Missoula, which corrals the waters of the Clark Fork and Blackfoot Rivers at their confluence. The dam, an increasingly unstable log structure that was built in 1907 to generate electricity for an adjacent lumber mill, now serves primarily as a repository for sediment and mining wastes.

After years of debate about how to address the issues presented by the Milltown Dam, NorthWestern Energy, the dam's owner, and Arco, which is liable for the contamination, agreed to an EPA recommendation to remove the structure and restore the rivers by extracting the toxic sediments from the riverbottom—all without harming downstream fish populations.

The scope of the project was enormous: The price tag for removing the dam and the sediment was $120 million and involved taking out the 500-foot-wide wooden dam and 2.6 million cubic yards of sediment. In 2008 the last of the dam and sediments were extracted, and the rivers were rejoined as free-flowing streams of water.

However, by far the greatest human tragedy related to past Montana mining involves the small northwest Montana community of Libby, site of a vermiculite (used in planting soil and kitty litter) mine. Libby residents discovered in the late 1990s that mixed in with the vermiculite, which many residents had spent their lives mining and that stood in piles around the town, was a mineral called tremolite, a rare and toxic form of asbestos. The miners and many townspeople are now suffering from the effects of asbestos poisoning. Many have died from asbestos-related cancers, and even more are ill. Although the W. R. Grace Company (which owned the mine) *and* the government knew about the asbestos, nothing had been done to stop the dust that contaminated the town. In 2000, after the *Seattle Post-Intelligencer* and other news sources began running stories on the asbestosis, W. R. Grace bought back the mine (which they'd sold years before), banned EPA officials from it, and backed off from promises to clean it up. In 2001 W. R. Grace filed for bankruptcy, claiming it could not handle the deluge of personal-injury lawsuits. By the summer of 2001 about 5,500 Libby residents had been tested for asbestos, and nearly 20 percent of those had lung abnormalities. Many homes were contaminated, thanks to the free vermiculite insulation that was available for years in big piles outside the processing site. The EPA has cleaned up most of the town's biggest sources of asbestos and continues to work on smaller sites around town.

History

EARLY INHABITANTS AND EXPLORATION
The First Settlers

Proto-Indians first arrived in Montana from Asia about 10,000-15,000 years ago. After crossing the Bering Sea causeway, they traveled along the Great North Trail, the rift that opened up along the east face of the Rocky Mountains when the ice fields of the last ice age retreated into the mountains.

These people hunted big game and used tools made of chipped stone. Between 8000 and 6000 BC, these early inhabitants lived principally on the plains and foothills. Around 5000 BC, a desert climate developed, and game animals and the people who hunted them left.

Buffalo again spread across the region as a more moderate climate developed about AD 500. The hunters returned, probably from the south and west, bringing with them new techniques and cultural practices. These early dwellers were probably the ancestors of the Salish. Before the introduction of horses, hunting techniques such as using a buffalo jump, or *pishkun,* were developed. Entire herds of buffalo would be stampeded off precipices and slaughtered for meat. The use of the tepee, or movable skin tent, was introduced. Pictographs and petroglyphs (rock paintings and carvings) were first made during this period.

Historic Tribes

When European traders and settlers arrived in the region in the early 1800s, they did not find a land peopled with indigenous tribes. Instead, the Native Americans of Montana were only recent immigrants, attempting to establish homelands and work out the cultural changes that their recent uprooting had caused. These tribes had been displaced as European settlement along the East Coast and in the Southwest increasingly forced Native

American inhabitants from their traditional homelands, and they in turn displaced other tribes as all were forced north and west.

Some of the tribes that migrated to Montana during this period were not traditionally nomadic. Most came from woodlands in the Great Lakes-Mississippi Basin region, where they had been sedentary, sometimes agricultural people who lived in permanent earthen dwellings. During the process of dislocation to the West, agriculture was left behind and a hunting culture developed. The earth lodge was abandoned for the tepee. For these people, the buffalo became more than a food source: It was the central assumption on which their entire cultural life was predicated. Social organization was structured by warrior societies, and in some cases, by clan. Women were responsible for most of the daily work, save hunting and fighting. The Plains Indians shared an animistic religion.

The first tribe to enter Montana during the historic period was the Shoshone, who began to move into the southwestern corner of the state from the Great Basin area about 1600. They drove the resident Salish tribes (who had migrated from the Pacific Northwest several centuries earlier) farther north into the mountains. The Shoshone were fearsome warriors and the first Montana tribe to ride horses, which they had procured from the Spanish colonies.

The Crow arrived in Montana shortly thereafter and settled along the Yellowstone River drainages, the first tribe to actually reside on the Montana prairies. The Blackfeet entered Montana from the north and east about a century later, around 1730, and brought the rifle. The Blackfeet, and their allies the Gros Ventre and the Assiniboine, soon established dominance over the northern Montana plains.

Further pressure from European settlements forced the Sioux and Northern

Cheyenne into eastern Montana. The Cree and Chippewa tribes entered Montana in the 1870s as they were displaced from the Canadian prairies. As more and more tribes were squeezed into the area that would later become Montana, intertribal rivalries intensified. The Crow were hated enemies of the Blackfeet. The Blackfeet slaughtered the Salish or Kootenai who dared to leave the safety of the mountains. As the Sioux entered Montana, they too became enemies of the Crow.

The Salish and Kootenai retained some traditions of the Northwest Indian tribes. Although these tribes once traveled over the Rockies to hunt buffalo, the presence of the fierce Blackfeet confederation on the prairies soon made these expeditions too dangerous.

The Corps of Discovery

In 1803, President Thomas Jefferson purchased the Louisiana Territory from France for $11.25 million. The territory was understood to be the land west of the Mississippi to its Missouri headwaters, and north of the Arkansas River to the 49th parallel. Jefferson engaged his personal secretary, Meriwether Lewis, to head an expedition to explore this new U.S. territory and to search for a passage from the Missouri River to the headwaters of the Columbia River. Lewis in turn chose William Clark to be the cocommander of what Jefferson called the Corps of Discovery.

The two captains, three sergeants, 23 enlisted men, and Clark's black slave, York, left St. Louis in May 1804. In North Dakota they were joined by French trader Toussaint Charbonneau, who had traveled widely on the upper Missouri and spoke several Native American languages. One of Charbonneau's wives, a 15-year-old Shoshone girl named Sacagawea, gave birth during the spring. Lewis and Clark hired Charbonneau as interpreter and allowed the young mother and baby to accompany the corps, as they later expected to travel through Shoshone territory.

The corps entered Montana on April 26, 1805, passing the confluence of the Missouri and Yellowstone Rivers. They wound their way up the Missouri, traveling in pirogues, huge French-Canadian dugout canoes. By July 25 they were at the Three Forks of the Missouri and were heartened by Sacagawea's claim that they were near her homeland. Nineteen days later, near Lemhi Pass, Lewis encountered the expedition's first Montana Native American (a Shoshone, who led them to Sacagawea's brother). They beached their pirogues, traded for horses, and proceeded down the Bitterroot Valley. On September 13 they crossed Lolo Pass out of Montana toward the Pacific Coast.

After a hungry and flea-ridden winter on the Oregon coast, the corps started back up the Columbia. They backtracked to Lolo Pass and crossed into Montana on June 27, 1806. On July 1, at the point where Lolo Creek meets the Bitterroot River, the expedition divided. Clark took part of the corps and retraced the previous journey to the Missouri headwaters, but this time followed the Gallatin River over the Bozeman Pass in order to explore the Yellowstone River Valley. Lewis took the rest of the men and followed old Native American trails up the Blackfoot River and then over the Rockies to the Great Falls in order to scout a more direct passage over the Continental Divide. While Clark had an uneventful journey down the Yellowstone, Lewis had a confrontation with a group of Blackfeet that left two warriors dead.

The two parties met at the confluence of the Yellowstone and the Missouri on August 12. By September 23, 1806, they were in St. Louis. This amazing journey had an almost immediate impact on the history of Montana. Members of the corps retold stories of vast amounts of wildlife, especially fur-bearing mammals. Within a year, the first fur-trading fort was built in Montana.

Trading Posts

The first fur-trading post, Fort Ramon, was founded in 1807 by Manuel Lisa at the confluence of the Bighorn and Yellowstone Rivers, between present-day Billings and Miles City. Beaver, much sought for European fashions, was the major item of trade. Some tribes, notably the Salish and Crow, maintained friendly relations with the incoming traders and trappers. The Blackfeet, who controlled the Missouri River area, were hostile to the Salish, Crow, and new arrivals.

John Jacob Astor's American Fur Company built Fort Union at the confluence of the Yellowstone and Missouri in 1829 and finally induced the Blackfeet to trade peacefully by dispatching a Blackfeet-speaking trapper to bring them to the fort for a conference. The Blackfeet complied. Four thousand beaver pelts were taken from the heart of the heavily defended Blackfeet territory by Astor's trappers in 1838.

Fort Union and the American Fur Company soon ruled the Montana fur trade. As beavers were increasingly trapped out (and European fashion changed), trade continued in buffalo hides. By 1840 when the era of the trapper and mountain man was over, almost three dozen trading forts had been built in Montana, and the beaver had been trapped to near extinction.

The Black Robes

Iroquois accompanied French trappers to western Montana in the early 1800s. While the Iroquois were to teach the local Flathead and Nez Perce how to trap, they also passed on information about Christianity. The Montana Native Americans heard of "Black Robes" who possessed a Book of Heaven, whose "medicine" or power was great. The Flathead were greatly intrigued and sent four delegations to St. Louis to ask for a Black Robe to come and visit the tribe.

Finally, in 1840, Father Pierre Jean De Smet, a Belgian-born Jesuit, came west. Although the Native Americans' spiritual demands had more to do with the search for powerful medicine to protect them from the hostile Blackfeet than with traditional salvation, the Flathead and Nez Perce seemed genuinely friendly and anxious to learn the way of the Catholic fathers.

In 1841, St. Mary's Mission was established in the Bitterroot Valley near Stevensville. Here the Jesuits taught the them agriculture, music, milling, and, of course, religion. The original mission was abandoned in 1850 after De Smet made the mistake of starting missionary work with the Blackfeet. The Flathead were not eager to share their "medicine" with their enemies and lost interest in De Smet's projects. Another influential early church, St. Ignatius Mission, was established in 1854 in the Mission Valley among the Pend d'Oreille.

Little effort was made to bring Christianity to the Plains Indians until they were on reservations. Most of the early missionary work was done by the Catholic Church. Protestant missionaries entered the state only after settlement had begun, when gold ore and high living induced the kind of bad doings best corrected by regular churchgoing.

SETTLEMENT AND THE INDIAN WARS
Gold

The trappers and traders of the early 19th century left little behind them except endangered species. There were no roads, no communications networks, and almost no settlements (from this era, only Fort Benton still exists as a community).

James and Granville Stuart discovered gold on Gold Creek near Deer Lodge in 1860. In 1862 gold was found on Grasshopper Creek near Bannack, and the next year saw prospecting along Alder Gulch near Virginia City. Last Chance Gulch, which was to become Helena, boomed in 1864.

These large strikes and many smaller mines attracted people of varied character to Montana. In 1860 fewer than 100 Caucasians were in the state, but by 1870 there were more than 20,000. Some men came to Montana to prospect for gold and get rich; others came to get rich by stealing and killing. Travel between the settlements of Virginia City, Bannack, and other mining camps became increasingly dangerous as "road agents" preyed on stagecoaches and miners.

For its protection, Virginia City elected

Henry Plummer as sheriff. Plummer, however, doubled as leader of the principal gang of road agents, called the "Innocents." More than 100 people were killed by the Innocents during 1862-1863. In response, committees of vigilantes formed, which reached summary judgment and hanged the Innocents.

By 1870, approximately $100 million in gold had been extracted from Montana claims. The advent of great wealth and private property soon made firm government and community lawfulness imperative. In 1864, Montana became a territory, with Bannack its capital. Schools, churches, and other civic institutions were established in Virginia City. Miners began bringing their families out to the frontier to settle.

Treaties Made and Broken

While the Native Americans of the western mountains accommodated the arrival of miners, trappers, and missionaries, the Plains Indians largely maintained their traditional ways during the first years of ingress.

The first trail across the northern United States was the Oregon Trail. To protect travelers along its passage through Wyoming, the U.S. government produced the Fort Laramie Treaty in 1851, which was signed by the Crow, Gros Ventre, and Assiniboine. These tribes were assigned reservations in eastern Montana, as were the Blackfeet, who did not attend the meeting or sign the treaty, but were assigned a reservation in absentia.

The discovery of gold in the Rocky Mountains increased the demand for transportation routes across treaty Indian country. The Bozeman Trail, blazed during the 1860s, cut across Sioux tribal land to reach Montana's goldfields. Three military forts were built to protect the trail. Gold was also discovered in the Black Hills of South Dakota, country considered sacred by the Sioux, and prospectors flooded in.

These infractions infuriated the Native Americans. The U.S. government responded by unilaterally diminishing the size of the original reservations. The Sioux and

Cheyenne, among the last of the tribes to be forced into Montana by western expansion, were especially angry at the ongoing incursions. After the gold rush in the Black Hills, the Sioux quit the reservation completely and resumed their traditional plains lifestyle on the prairies of eastern Montana.

Army Versus Native Americans

The U.S. government in 1876 ordered the Sioux and the Cheyenne back onto the reservation. They refused, and the army was dispatched to compel them to return. Three columns of infantry set out. The first column to arrive in Indian country divided, sending Gen. George Custer and the Seventh Cavalry on ahead to seek the hostiles. They found the combined Cheyenne and Sioux force (perhaps 3,000 warriors) on June 26, 1876. Custer rashly decided to do battle alone, and his entire command (265 men) was destroyed.

The next year, the Nez Perce under Chief Joseph fled from their Oregon homeland across Idaho and Montana, attempting to reach sanctuary in Canada. After a battle with the U.S. Army at the Big Hole in western Montana, the Nez Perce fled south to the Yellowstone Park area and then veered north, hoping to escape into Canada near Havre. Thirty miles from the border, Gen. Nelson Miles overtook the fleeing tribe. The Nez Perce, of Northwest origins, were sent to reservations in Oklahoma.

Custer's annihilation notwithstanding, by 1877 all of the tribes in Montana had been incarcerated on reservations. In fact, many forces besides the army had worked to weaken and inevitably subjugate them. Diseases introduced from settlements of Easterners devastated Native American populations. An outbreak of smallpox among the Blackfeet in 1837 is reckoned to have killed three-quarters of the tribe. Alcohol, illegally traded to the Native Americans, corrupted and debilitated the traditional warrior societies.

As trade evolved from peltry to buffalo robes, the Native Americans were unwittingly involved in exterminating the animal that provided the cornerstone of their entire traditional culture. Before settlers reached the plains, 60 million buffalo lived in North America. By 1870, that number was down to 10-20 million. By 1883, after railroads crossed the West and settlers were streaming in after the Civil War, there were only 100-200 buffalo left in the United States.

With the buffalo largely exterminated, Native Americans were reduced to complete dependence on handouts from the government's Indian agents. By the mid-1880s the U.S. federal government spent $7 per year per person on a reservation, while it spent $1,000 per year on a soldier stationed in Montana's tribal land.

The Railroad Arrives

Riverboats were the only form of transportation linking Montana and the rest of the nation until the 1880s. Boats could reach as far inland as Fort Benton on the Missouri and to Pompey's Pillar on the Yellowstone, but real economic growth and settlement awaited the coming of the railroad.

The Union Pacific built a spur line north from Utah to Butte in 1881. The Northern Pacific crossed the length of Montana, linking Portland and Chicago in 1883. In return for opening the northern transcontinental line, the Northern Pacific was given a land grant: For every mile of track laid, the railroad received 40 sections (40 square miles) of land. In Montana alone, this amounted to 17 million acres.

The Great Northern stretched its service along the Montana-Canada border, joining Minneapolis and Seattle in 1893. The Milwaukee Road crossed central Montana on its way to Seattle in 1909. With access to coastal markets, Montana opened up to further development and immigration.

Cattle Country

Montana had had a cattle trade in the western valleys and foothills since the 1860s as ranches grew up to feed the mining camps, and Texas

longhorns had been trailed into Montana as early as 1866. But the era of the cattle rancher didn't really begin until the 1880s, when longhorn cattle were brought north from Texas in great numbers.

Typically, the large "outfits" running cattle were owned by a group of investors who bought shares in herds often numbering in the tens of thousands. Cowboys would bring these longhorns north from Texas, summer them free on the grassy unfenced prairies of Montana, and then round them up, sort them by brand, and sell them to eastern markets. This get-rich-quick scheme worked for many, because with a small investment in the startup animal, low labor costs with the cowboys, and no feed bills to pay, the profitability was great.

Initially, the fattened steers were trailed south into Wyoming to railheads on the Union Pacific. With the construction of the Northern Pacific along the course of the Yellowstone River in 1881-1882, railheads such as Wibaux, Miles City, and Billings became centers for the livestock trade and turned into full-blooded Old West cattle towns. In 1870 there were 48,000 head of cattle in Montana. By 1886, the height of the open-range period, there were 675,000 head.

Butte

In 1864, two miners staked a claim for gold on a lonely bluff near the Continental Divide at the headwaters of the Clark Fork River. The gold soon played out, but miners discovered something else: silver.

As a source of wealth, silver was as good as gold, but the mining techniques were quite different. Gold can be panned from streams by individuals working alone and sold as powder or lumps. Silver, however, requires underground mining to extract the ore, which then must be refined by smelters. As mining at Butte developed in the 1870s, the era of the independent prospector passed and corporate mining began. Then, as silver ran out, copper became the lodestone of Butte mining.

The transcontinental railroads vied for lucrative contracts to take the refined metal to world markets. The railroads also brought in immigrants to work the deep veins. Railroads were built between Butte and Anaconda and between Butte and Great Falls to take the ore to smelters.

Butte, soon to be known as "the richest hill on earth," was dominated by smokestacks, peopled by immigrants, and undercut with 10,000 miles of mineshafts. It quickly became Montana's largest and wealthiest city. The city never slept: Miners worked the veins 24 hours a day, and bars, restaurants, and other businesses were always open to serve their customers. The huge influx of immigrants that poured into Butte during this period from Central Europe, Italy, Cornwall, Ireland, and China gave Butte its cosmopolitan flavor and ethnic neighborhoods.

Other factors were not so positive. Butte was an environmental disaster. The pollution from the smelters soon killed all the vegetation within a 20-mile radius. The trees that weren't killed by smoke were cut for mine supports or to fuel the smelters. Smelting also used vast amounts of water, which was simply returned to streams laden with toxic chemicals and minerals. The mining process produced mountains of tailings, some of which were radioactive. Entire communities were built on these tailings.

EMPIRES GAINED AND LOST
The End of the Open Range

While Butte was booming during the 1880s and 1890s, events conspired to end the Old West cattle days on the eastern prairies. The winter of 1886-1887 has been made most famous by the grim drawing of the *Last of the 5,000* by artist Charlie Russell. A very dry summer led to a long, extremely cold winter. The warm-weather longhorn, summered on the drought-stricken plains, died in huge numbers as temperatures remained below zero for weeks. One-half to three-quarters of the cattle in Montana reportedly froze or starved to death. A single winter ended the era of the great cattle drives.

Sheep had played a part in Montana agriculture since the days of De Smet's St. Mary's Mission, but now the number of sheep on the plains increased considerably as ranchers realized that the hardy sheep were a good hedge against losses of the more temperate cattle. In 1870 there were just 2,000 head of sheep in the state, one for every 10 settlers; by 1900, with six million head, and sheep outnumbered people 24 to one.

While the railroads opened up the growth of the cattle trade in Montana, they also brought in settlements. The open range was increasingly privately owned. The various homesteading acts of the late 1800s and early 1900s freed up public land for settlement. With the hegemony of the big cattle outfits broken after 1886, homesteaders set up along the fertile valley bottoms, fencing off some of the best range and water access.

Homesteaders

Rail entrepreneurs like James Hill of the Great Northern quickly realized the benefits of establishing settlements all along his rail lines. Huge advertising campaigns were launched to tempt the homesteader to the plains of Montana. Rural European communities received advice from experts regarding the fertility of the Great Plains, and immigrants were given pamphlets as they disembarked onto U.S. soil.

Much of the promotional material presented by the railroads was fanciful, and some of it was flat wrong. It promised, for example, plenty of rain, fertile soil, and opportunities for all. Nonetheless, the advertising worked. The population of Montana grew 60 percent during the first decade of the 20th century, and the number of farms doubled.

While homesteading acts allotted 320 acres of "free land" per individual (a husband and wife qualified for two allotments), even this quantity of land was insufficient to make a living in Montana. During good years with plenty of rain, the prairies provided adequate grazing, but most new settlers did not come to raise livestock (stockmen were seen as an

The Kings of Copper

During the boom years of copper and silver mining in Butte—in the 1870s and 1880s—the mines, the city, and the whole state were dominated by three men, called the Copper Kings.

William Clark made his first fortune mining and smelting silver, and extended his empire into banking and politics. Marcus Daly cannily bought up depleted silver mines in order to exploit the mines' rich veins of copper (electrical power created a market for copper wire, which turned copper from a junk metal to one of Montana's most precious commodities). Daly also had large business holdings in the lumber industry: His Butte-area mines used 40,000 board-feet of timber a day. Fritz Augustus Heinze cleverly manipulated the "Apex Law," which states that if a vein of ore surfaces on one person's claim, then that person has the right to the rest of the vein, no matter where it goes when underground. Because he owned the apex of mines controlled by large mining interests, Heinze was able to thumb his nose at big business while becoming very wealthy.

Each of these men led an almost raucously public life. Heinze's wealth and reputation had less to do with his mining knowledge than with his control of the courtrooms. He courted public affection by publicly taking on the giant companies, such as Standard Oil, that were swallowing up Butte mining. Daly and Clark engaged in a fiercely contested rivalry involving wealth, political influence, and popular opinion. Each controlled newspapers, bought judges, and paid off legislators. A classic battle was fought in 1889 as Montana became a state. Daly favored Anaconda as state capital, while Clark lobbied for and triumphed with his choice of Helena. Daly got revenge by denying Clark a long-sought-after seat in the U.S. Senate. These and other battles were chronicled in the state press and were the stuff of public gossip and debate.

Butte was not the only area influenced by the era of the Copper Kings. Missoula and Hamilton were largely built by the Daly logging empire. Anaconda was essentially a Daly company town, built around his Washoe smelter, but with great pretensions. The growth of Great Falls was assured when smelters were built on the banks of the Missouri to refine Butte ore.

The political complexion of early Montana was largely established by events centered in Butte. Many of the early miners and prospectors who were attracted to the gold strikes of the 1860s and the boom of the 1870s were Southerners dislocated by the Civil War. They brought to Montana a strong hatred of Yankee Republicanism; most Irish immigrants were dependably Democratic. Both Daly and Clark fought their political battles from within the Democratic Party. Butte was the largest city in the state by far, and its population of workers, when unionized, voted unswervingly Democratic. To this day, Montana has a stronger Democratic Party than many western states.

anachronism). Farmers represented progress and the evolution of the West: They came to turn the soil over and raise grain.

Communities sprang up along the rail lines, particularly along the Great Northern's track through the Hi-Line and along the Milwaukee Road through central Montana. Towns were established near the rail sidings and usually consisted of a grain elevator, bank, hotel, and bar. Farms were "improved on" according to Homestead Act requirements, but were often little more than a tar paper or sod shack with ad hoc outbuildings for livestock. Eastern Montana has never been more populated than it was in 1918, with at least one homestead per square mile of arable land.

The Company

In the first years of the 20th century the Copper Kings Fritz Augustus Heinze, Marcus Daly, and William Clark, largely to spite each other, each sold out to the buyer that was least likely to benefit the others. In each case it was Standard Oil. By 1906, Standard Oil, soon to reconfigure its holdings as the Anaconda Company, controlled almost everything in Butte. It became known simply as "The Company." Then, in the 1910s, when the Anaconda Company became yoked with the Montana Power Company, these two corporations controlled practically the whole state.

The Copper Kings had been largely beneficent to their workers and even suffered the unions gladly. Not so The Company. During the 1910s, Butte was a battlefield of labor-management disputes. Conditions in the mines worsened. The presence of "Wobblies" from the International Workers of the World (IWW), a labor union that propounded revolutionary struggle during World War I, led to the Anaconda Company's targeting of "communist" influences that resulted in lynchings. The Great Depression further darkened conditions in Butte as the world price of copper fell 80 percent. Production of copper in 1933 was 10 percent of what it had been in 1929. The Company shifted much of its operations to Chile and Mexico, where copper was mined in open pits, involving lower labor costs. Butte, once one of the richest cities in the West, now faced massive unemployment problems.

The Dust Bowl Years

For a time the weather cooperated with the homesteaders in eastern Montana. Then, from the late 1910s to the mid-1920s, nature shifted gears. In 1916, Shelby, on the Hi-Line, received more than 15 inches of rain; in 1919, the third year of intense drought, the town received less than seven inches. Drought continued, coupled with high winds and grasshoppers. Range fires ruined crops and destroyed communities. Sixty thousand people had left Montana by 1925, representing 11,000 abandoned farms; 214 state banks failed, and Montana led the nation in bankruptcies. A few years later, disaster struck again. The stock market crash, combined with a second severe drought during the Dust Bowl years of the 1930s, eliminated many more farmers and ranchers.

The New Deal

As elsewhere in the United States, in Montana the Great Depression of the 1930s was followed by the spending programs of the New Deal. The works projects had a great impact on the state. Not only did programs like the Civilian Conservation Corps (CCC) and the Works Progress Administration (WPA) give employment and training to people who were out of jobs, but they produced monumental results. One of the largest public works projects in the country was Fort Peck Dam, completed in 1940 to dam the Missouri. Going-to-the-Sun Highway in Glacier Park was a CCC project. Dozens of roads, parks, fairgrounds, and other landmarks of public infrastructure were also built.

After the end of the New Deal era, government spending in Montana ceased to be a civilian affair and was given over to the military. Malmstrom Air Force Base was built in Great Falls in 1942 as a transit base for war materials shipped to the United States' then-ally the Soviet Union. By the 1950s it became a strategic air base that was assigned fighter jets to defend against the then-enemy Soviet Union. In the 1960s Malmstrom became the first center for the Minuteman missile system. Two hundred Minuteman missiles were buried in silos under 23,000 acres of central Montana prairie by 1970, pointed at equivalent missiles in Russia. Glasgow Air Force Base brought population and business to that eastern Montana town until the base was closed in 1969.

Decline of the West

While the 19th century saw the buildup of wealth and influence in western Montana, the 20th century brought decline to the mining and logging industries that had fueled early growth.

Butte struggled on until 1955, when open-pit mining began, diminishing overhead and overburden at the same time. The old Butte communities were ripped apart as steam shovels tore into the soil. The huge Berkeley Pit swallowed up Meaderville, which was once a lively Italian neighborhood sitting on a vein of low-grade copper ore. Although Berkeley Pit revived industry in Butte for about 20 years, by the 1980s the Anaconda Company had sold all of its holdings in Butte. A mile high and a mile deep, Butte contained just a century's worth of riches.

Likewise, centralized ownership and

overproduction have crippled the timber-products industry. Huge companies control much of the timber production in Montana and have put local lumber mills and logging companies out of business. Much of the good timber on easily accessible private and state lands has already been harvested. With the old-growth trees gone, local loggers and mills have had to bear the expense of retooling machinery to accommodate smaller trees. Even though the loss of jobs and revenue in logging towns is a result of market forces, environmentalists usually receive the blame.

Coal and Oil

The 20th century saw other mineral development come to the eastern prairies. Coal had been mined in Montana since the early days of settlement, but large-scale exploitation of the incredible reserves of fossil fuels waited until the railroads arrived. The Northern Pacific developed Red Lodge, and later Colstrip, as sources of fuel for its steam trains, and the Milwaukee built up Roundup as its source. After trains were converted to electricity, coal mining ceased for several years. However, as machinery and technology refined the techniques of strip mining, the vast reserves of coal in the Fort Union Formation in southeastern Montana became more attractive.

In the 1970s, energy companies proposed building four electric generators in Colstrip, with the power to be sold to markets on the West Coast. Battles erupted in courtrooms and communities as the breadth of the mining and environmental damage became clear. The issues surrounding development sundered many communities as the benefits of conservation and economic opportunity were debated. Despite grassroots opposition from ranchers, Native Americans, and environmentalists, the generators went in.

Oil and gas exploration also brought wealth to some eastern Montana communities. Refineries helped Billings boom during the 1970s, and towns such as Sidney, Broadus, and Baker escaped the worst of recent agricultural

downturns because of the presence of large nearby oil reserves.

Farming and Ranching

Bad years still follow good in Montana agriculture. A series of good years in the 1960s and early 1970s brought prosperity and high land prices. The family ranch and farm began to modernize after borrowing against the inflated real estate values of the land. Then drought hit again, and land values fell. Farmers and ranchers found themselves with unsecured loans. The drought, bad markets, and financial breakdown of the 1970s and 1980s became known as the Farm-Ranch Crisis, an echo of earlier times and of an ongoing cycle.

Government programs in the 1970s and 1980s were designed to help the family farm and ranch but were too easily manipulated by unscrupulous investors. Huge tracts of cheap drought-stricken grazing land were bought up solely for the government payments available for plowing it. The broken land, plowed but not planted, simply drifted on the wind across the prairies while the investment "farmers" pocketed the payments.

Farms and ranches are large and far between in Montana. Those that remain have long histories and many experiences of lean times. Most are still operated as family businesses, with the work and pleasures shared by several generations living together on one farm or ranch site. While during much of the 20th century agriculture became more specialized and reliant on production of only one commodity (usually cattle or wheat), rural Montana is taking on the future with its eyes cast backward. A ranch that raises cattle, sheep, hay, and wheat and keeps chickens and a milk cow not only has diversified products to sell but also goes a long way toward being self-sufficient. The repeated cycle of boom and bust, rain and drought will continue, but after surviving four generations in eastern Montana, farmers and ranchers don't pretend to be in it for the money.

Government and Economy

GOVERNMENT

Montana became a territory in 1864 and a state in 1889. The original state constitution of 1889 reflected the mining and timber interests that dominated the early days of the state. Partly because of that document's datedness and partly because of the climate of political reform in the late 1960s, Montanans voted to draft a new constitution. The results of the second Constitutional Convention in 1972 were a reformist, populist set of laws that affirms that the state government exists by consent of the people and for their benefit. The privileges of business and industry were diminished accordingly.

Montana granted women's suffrage in 1916, four years before the passage of the 19th Amendment. Jeannette Rankin, the first woman representative in the U.S. Congress, was elected from Montana in the same year.

The Montana Legislature is a bicameral, biennial body. There are 56 counties. Since the 1990 census there is only one federal House member (down from two). One particularity of the Montana primary system is its open ballot. Voters are not asked to identify party affiliation to receive a primary ballot; instead, they receive a voting form from both the Democratic and Republican parties. In the voting booth the voter marks only one form, and both are deposited in the ballot box. The system has been both hailed as the truest form of democratic voting and denounced as the most open to political hanky-panky.

Reservation Self-Government

Native American reservations make up 9 percent of Montana and, even though a substantial amount of this land may be owned by non-Indians, tribal law prevails within reservation boundaries. Reservations are recognized by the federal government as independent political units. Legal jurisdiction is therefore something of a puzzle on reservations.

Tribes have certain inherent sovereign rights. Tribes can run their own schools, regulate transport and trade, and have their own constitutions, legislative councils, and tribal court and police systems. The state cannot tax reservation land or transactions that occur on reservations. While such legal considerations may not seem crucial to the traveler, Montana has in effect seven independent political entities within its borders. Visitors need to be aware that certain state laws do not apply on reservations.

Those cheap gas stations advertising cheap cigarettes aren't found just inside reservations by chance. State fuel and cigarette taxes aren't levied on those products sold by tribal members within reservations. Some local roads on reservation land are maintained by the tribes. Do not automatically assume that there is public access; sometimes use is reserved for tribal members. For instance, some of the Crow Reservation is off-limits to non-Indians.

Not all areas are open for recreation. The state does not have authority to regulate hunting, fishing, and recreation on reservations. Tribes can issue their own licenses for hunting and fishing, and may levy a user fee for hikers and campers. If you are not a tribe member, always check with tribal authorities before crossing reservation land.

ECONOMY

Montana is a rural state. Agriculture, mining, and the timber industry were among the founding trades of Montana and remain among its most important. Tourism is increasingly lucrative, and service industries like trucking and medical-treatment centers are major employers. Because it is so far from coastal markets or other significant population centers, it is unlikely that Montana will quickly become anything but a source of raw materials. Transport costs make industry unprofitable in so remote a state.

Agriculture

Montanans make strict differentiations between farms and ranches: Farms raise grain, and ranches raise livestock. To the purist, any amount of cultivation degrades a ranch to a farm. Even though most people think of Montana as primarily an agricultural state, less than 10 percent of the population makes a living from farming and ranching. Still, recent census figures indicate that the number of farms and ranches in Montana is increasing slightly (there are more than 15,000). Beef cattle production is the most common form of ranching, with sheep production remaining a steady alternative. Spring and winter wheat are by far the most common crops, with barley a significant third. Along the Yellowstone River, corn, soybeans, and sugar beets grow in irrigated fields. In the Flathead Lake region, sweet cherry orchards augment the local tourist economy.

Mining

The state of Montana was born of prospecting and mining camps. However, the copper, silver, and gold that established the Montana economy are largely depleted. Traditional centers of mining, such as Butte and Anaconda, have fallen on hard times as the world market has moved elsewhere to find cheaper, more easily mined minerals. But it's not that Montana has given up mining; copper, silver, and gold are still produced, but with modern techniques that don't demand an entire city's workforce.

Montana remains rich in other mineral wealth: from the unpronounceable molybdenum to the sublime Yogo sapphire to ordinary talcum powder. Thirty-foot-thick veins of bituminous coal lie under much of southeastern Montana and are unearthed by modern strip-mining techniques at places like Colstrip. The Stillwater Mine is the only U.S. source for valuable platinum. Oil and gas wells dot the eastern prairies.

Timber

About half of Montana's open land is forested. However, early overcutting and slow regrowth have limited the state's competitiveness in the world timber market. Many locally owned independent mills have been forced to close when they can't compete against large corporate "timber product" conglomerates, whose efficient automated factories have transformed logging from a lifestyle to a job, and which have largely practiced extractive "cut and run" logging with little concern for the forests' future. The forests still provide a living for enterprising Montanans, though: Christmas tree farms are found in northwestern Montana, and log-home manufacturers have moved Montana into the first ranks of home-kit producers in the nation. More log homes are shipped each year to Japan than remain in Montana.

People and Culture

MONTANA'S PEOPLE

The first residents of Montana arrived from Asia via the Bering Strait land bridge more than 14,000 years ago, at the end of the last ice age. These prehistoric people were the ancestors of the North American Indians. However, the tribes who now live in Montana were not native to the area: They were forced westward after being displaced by other tribes and European settlers from the east.

Montana was one of the last states to be settled. Only after gold was discovered in the 1860s did people start to build communities and settle in the state permanently. In addition to the gold diggers from other western states, like California, where gold had already played out, the first towns were peopled by Southerners who had been displaced by the Civil War. Railroads and the Homestead Act made Montana's free acreage tempting to the thousands of immigrants who poured into the United States in the early 20th century. Many communities still retain their strong European heritage.

Native Americans

There are approximately 56,000 Native Americans, representing 11 different tribes, living in Montana today (nearly 14 percent of the state's total population). The majority live on reservations, which make up 9 percent of Montana's total land area.

Native Americans are often lumped together as "Indians," with the assumption that one culture, language, and history link these people. However, the tribes that now live in Montana come from very different traditions, speak different languages, and have not always been friendly toward each other.

KOOTENAI

The Kootenai tribe had settled in the Kootenai River area by 1500, and there is evidence that they are descended from the area's prehistoric inhabitants. Their original range included the northwestern corner of Montana and adjacent areas of Alberta and British Columbia. As a people, the Kootenai are closely related to peoples of the Columbia Basin, although they speak a language seemingly unrelated to other languages of the area.

The Kootenai share the Flathead Reservation with the Flathead and Pend d'Oreille. Approximately 1,500 Kootenai presently live on the reservation.

PEND D'OREILLE

These Salish-speaking people are closely related to tribes of the Pacific Coast, but they moved up the Columbia drainages into Montana many thousands of years ago. The Salish tribes were the first to welcome Christian missionaries to Montana, and St. Ignatius Mission was built in 1854 to minister to the Pend d'Oreille tribe's spiritual needs. The Pend d'Oreille largely retained the culture of Northwest Coast Indians, although Plains Indians' influence was evident in some aspects.

FLATHEAD

There is no satisfactory explanation for the term "Flathead," for these Salish-speaking people never practiced head flattening (though other Salish tribes did). The Flathead also differed from their Salish kinfolk by leaving the river valleys of the Columbia drainage and moving onto the plains of central Montana. Here they evolved a culture based largely on the buffalo while maintaining the religious and social traditions of the Northwest Coast.

Like other Salish tribes, the Flathead were generally friendly to settlers as they entered Montana. The tribe was moved from the Bitterroot Valley and settled on the Flathead Reservation in the Mission Valley.

CROW

The Crow were the first of the contemporary Native American residents to enter Montana from the east, arriving as early as 1600 in response to dislocations farther east. The Crow, or the Absarokee, originally lived in the Great Lakes region, where they built earthen lodges and practiced agriculture.

Having arrived first onto the Montana plains, the Crow had the most to lose as other tribes crowded into the state. They became sworn enemies of the Blackfeet and later the Sioux.

BLACKFEET

Like other Plains tribes, the Blackfeet originally lived farther east, in the forests north of the Great Lakes. As they drifted westward across the Canadian prairies, the various Blackfeet tribes evolved into a loose confederation of entities sharing a common language (an Algonquian dialect) and mutual defense of their hunting lands. These groups, later known as the Piegan, the Blood, and the Northern Blackfeet, combined to form the Blackfeet Nation, one of the largest and most feared Native American tribes.

The Piegan ventured farthest south, taking control of much of northern Montana by 1800. The Blackfeet were celebrated horsemen and warriors, and their social order was structured by membership in military societies. Men who were not militarily inclined were treated as women; first reported by French trappers, this cultural practice, called the *berdache*, was later found to be common in other aboriginal societies. Religious practice centered on the ritual Sun Dance and shamanistic powers derived from dreams and visions.

GROS VENTRE

Meaning literally "Big Belly," Gros Ventre is a misnomer for a tribe more properly known as the Atsina. The Gros Ventre represent the northernmost tribe of the Arapaho and belong to the Algonquian linguistic family. After moving to the Montana plains from their Minnesota homeland in the late 1700s, they allied with the Blackfeet, sharing in their dominance over the prairies. The Fort Belknap Reservation was established in 1888 for the Gros Ventre and Assiniboine. The Gros Ventre tribe now claims nearly 4,000 members.

ASSINIBOINE

The Assiniboine are a Siouan-speaking people who historically represented the most northerly of the Yanktonai Sioux in their original homeland north of Lake Superior. They were traditionally allied with the Cree against their common enemy, the Blackfeet. By the 1700s the Assiniboine had crossed into the present-day United States, where they established a territory in the northeastern corner of Montana where the state meets North Dakota. The 2,000-member tribe is today divided onto two reservations, Fort Belknap and Fort Peck.

SIOUX

The Sioux, one of the largest tribal nations in North America, divides into three large linguistic groups: the Dakota, the Lakota, and the Nakota. All originally came from Canada and were pushed westward as settlers from the East displaced other tribes along the eastern seaboard. They arrived on the northern plains comparatively late, around 1800,

when they settled in the Dakotas, southern Saskatchewan, and eastern Montana. They were regarded as a noble but fearsome people, skilled in battle and famed hunters of buffalo.

The Yanktonai Sioux settled around Fort Peck, and along with some Assiniboine kinfolk, became residents of that reservation when it was created in 1888. Today almost 10,000 individuals belong to the tribe.

NORTHERN CHEYENNE

The Cheyenne are a tribe of Algonquian linguistic ancestry who lived largely agrarian lives in the Minnesota area. Pressures from other tribes forced the Cheyenne westward, and in about a 25-year period they evolved from a people who cultivated corn and other grains and made pottery into a nomadic Plains culture predicated on buffalo hunting. About 1830, after reaching the Black Hills, the tribe divided, with one group moving south to Colorado and the other moving farther westward into traditional Crow territory. Today there are about 9,900 members of the Northern Cheyenne tribe.

CHIPPEWA AND CREE

The Chippewa and Cree originally lived in northern Michigan and southern Manitoba. On these northern prairies, the tribes lived close to French trappers and settlers. Intermarriage produced a culture and a people known as Métis. Like so many other native peoples around this time, they moved west in the mid-1700s in response to displacement in the east.

By 1818, when the U.S. border was established, there were estimated to be about 10,000-12,000 Métis people living on the prairies. In 1868 a Métis leader named Louis Riel declared the Métis land a separate province of Canada. His rebellion against English-Canadian authorities failed, and the Chippewa under their chief Rocky Boy along with some of the Métis moved south to Spring Creek, near Lewistown, Montana. In the following years, as the United States evacuated the Métis to Canada and the Canadians deported them back south, they were part of the "landless Indians" (those without a reservation) who wandered the West after the United States decided to forgo its policy of granting reservations. The Métis, Chippewa, and the Cree were given a part of old Fort Assiniboine as a reservation in 1910.

The Immigrants

The establishment of the huge silver and copper mines in western Montana in the 1880s called for a large and stable workforce, supplied mostly by immigrants. The mines demanded workers, and Europe had workers to spare. The population of Montana grew 365 percent from 1880 to 1890, largely as a result of immigration into Butte and Anaconda. Great numbers of Irish, Germans, Slavs, Italians, Finns, and "Cousin Jack" miners from Cornwall poured into Butte to work the mines. These foreign workers settled into separate ethnic neighborhoods, where traditional food, customs, and languages prevailed. Some Jewish immigrants moved to the thriving mining centers and set up retail establishments. In 1910 African American settlers in Montana, most of whom lived in mining towns, numbered almost 2,000. Only after the establishment of U.S. Air Force bases near Glasgow and Great Falls in the 1960s did this number increase. Chinese immigrants were also attracted to Butte, where they set up laundries and restaurants. Although Butte's preeminence in Montana has dimmed, the early growth of immigrant populations in the mining communities established Roman Catholicism as the state's dominant religion, and Butte set a standard of openness to immigrants that is still observed by Montanans.

The railroads brought settlers to the plains of eastern Montana. Ambitious campaigns by the Great Northern and the Milwaukee Road succeeded in luring thousands of farmers to cultivate the dry prairie. Between 1900 and 1910 the number of farms and ranches in Montana doubled, and while many American-born homesteaders settled in Montana during

this time, immigrants had an especially strong influence in eastern Montana. By 1910 one-quarter of all Montanans were foreign-born. Entire communities of Germans, Russians, and Scandinavians were founded as farms, and towns sprang up alongside rail sidings, as did the telltale Lutheran church. Scots and Irish continued to settle the plains as ranchers and herders. Today in northern and central Montana the names in small-town phone books read like similar directories in Norway, Sweden, or Scotland.

Even though droughts and the Great Depression worked to depopulate the Montana plains, the foreign character remains in communities founded by immigrant farmers and ranchers. Fifty thousand foreign-born settlers moved to the state from 1900 to 1920, while 120,000 American-born settlers did so. But during the droughts and bad markets of the 1920s, 10 times more American-born homesteaders than immigrants gave up and moved on. By 1930, people of foreign birth or first-generation Montanans made up 45 percent of the population.

Some foreign settlers moved to Montana expressly to form communities. Mennonite groups settled in Montana during the homesteading years, but many left after the state legislature, urged on by an organization called the Montana Council of Defense, drafted laws during World War I that forbade speaking the German language. Hutterites maintain 22 communities in Montana and currently number more than 2,000 adherents.

War policies have not always driven Montanans from the state. During World War II, Japanese internees from California were shipped to the state to work in sugar beet fields. Some found Montana to their liking; farming communities along the Yellowstone are still home to Japanese families.

Like other western states, Montana is now home to a growing population of Hispanics, many of whom work on farms and ranches. Hispanics now make up more than 2 percent of the state's population.

THE ARTS

If there is a Western culture, a lack of snobbery lies at its heart. Even in the literature it shows: A rancher's memoirs share a bookshelf with poems that don't rhyme. Both writers are from Montana, and natives brag on them both. Rural cafés often sell local arts and crafts, whether homemade pottery or country scenes painted on old saws—and locals will buy both. Montanans respect people who are creative; rare is the rural community that doesn't have a resident poet, painter, or musician. *L'art naïf* or kitsch? In Montana, as often as not, it's the urge to express that's admired; it's not polite to question the quality of the expression.

From pioneers who kept journals and sent letters back east, to fifth-generation ranchers, to established novelists who have found a home in the state, Montana's literary tradition is a source of pride to Montanans, who generally read a lot and who positively devour the work of regional writers. It's not surprising that Montana should harbor such a dynamic writing community. It's a small step to go from respecting the work of a local rhymester to welcoming a nationally known author to the farm next door.

Literature

Any state that can fill a 1,150-page anthology with its literature is impressive. To have that become a regional best-seller points to a phenomenon. *The Last Best Place* chronicles the literary history of Montana, from Native American stories to modern cowboy poetry. Those who are unfamiliar with Montana's place in the literary firmament will be surprised at the number of writers who have had Montana addresses.

EARLY WRITERS

Montana literary history begins with the diaries and memoirs of early settlers and the transliteration of Native American tales. Teddy Blue Abbott trailed cattle up from Texas to Montana during the 1870s and 1880s and wrote *We Pointed Them North*. Andrew

Say It Right!

- Absaroka: ab-SOR-ka
- Absarokee: ab-SOR-kee
- Charlo: SHAR-lo
- Choteau: SHOW-toe
- creek: CRIK (almost always)
- Ekalaka: EEK-a-lak-a
- Garnet: gar-NET
- Havre: HAV-er
- Helena: HEL-en-a
- Hysham: HI-sham
- Kootenai: KOOT-nee
- Laurin: law-RAY
- Lima: LI-ma
- Makoshika: ma-KOE-shi-ka
- Marias: ma-RI-us
- Meagher: MAR
- Missoula: ma-ZOO-la
- Ronan: ro-NAN
- Rudyard: RUD-yerd
- Spokane: spo-KAN
- Winnett: WIN-et

Garcia was a novice mountain man when he married a Nez Perce woman who just escaped after Chief Joseph's surrender at Bear Paw. In *Tough Trip through Paradise*, Garcia gives his version of the Nez Perce flight in the 1870s and describes what it was like for him to be an innocent among mountain men and Native Americans. Frank Bird Linderman got to know Crow chief Plenty Coups and Pretty Shield, a Crow medicine woman, and recorded their stories. *Indian Why Stories* and *How It Came About Stories* are his versions of fireside tales.

Frontier photographer L. A. Huffman

brought his camera to early eastern Montana; *Before Barbed Wire* by Mark Brown and W. R. Felton features his photographs and recounts Huffman's life. Evelyn Cameron was an English immigrant whose passion for photographing the early settlement of remote Terry, Montana, resulted in the book *Photographing Montana: 1894-1928* by Donna Lucey. Charlie Russell, whose greatest fame derives from his paintings of frontier Montana, also wrote books. His life straddled the open range and the homesteading eras. His book, *Trails Plowed Under,* recounts this period. Will James had a ranch south of Billings. Books like *Cow Country* were popular adolescent reading during the 1930s.

THE MISSOULA SCHOOL

The University of Montana at Missoula has had a seminal effect on serious writing in the state. In 1919 a writing program was established by Professor H. G. Merriam at the university, only the second such program in the nation. Merriam, who had left Colorado to attend Oxford University in England, returned west determined to promote regional Montana writing. He began the literary journal *Frontier and Midland.* His writing program flourished, soon growing to offer a Master of Fine Arts degree. Students have included A. B. Guthrie Jr., author of *The Big Sky,* and Dorothy Johnson, author of *The Man Who Shot Liberty Valance* and other popular Western stories.

The program has continued to attract many talented students and nationally recognized faculty. Poet Richard Hugo inherited the directorship of the writing program from Leslie Fielder in 1964 and remained until his death in 1982. Hugo had a tremendous influence on the development of Northwest regional literature. His poems speak of disappointment and abandonment in both life and the physical world, sometimes ending with a wry glimmer of hope. Joining Hugo at the U of M at one time or another were Madeline DeFrees, Patricia Goedicke, William Kittredge (who with Annick Smith

edited *The Last Best Place*), William Pitt Root, and Tess Gallagher.

Missoula has also attracted writers whose connections with the writing program are more tenuous. Rick DeMarinis (*Under the Wheat*) did a stint as a mathematician before becoming a full-time writer. James Crumley, whose hard-boiled detective novels are frequently placed in the Northwest, still lives in Missoula. Norman Maclean, who wrote *A River Runs Through It,* an idyll to fly-fishing and the spirit, grew up in Missoula. James Welch, who spent his youth on the Blackfeet and Fort Belknap Reservations, studied with Hugo. Welch wrote several fine contemporary and historic novels of Native American life, including *Winter in the Blood.* Another Missoulian by way of the Hi-Line is Deirdre McNamer, whose novel *Rima in the Weeds* is set among the missile silos of northern Montana. Malta-area native Judy Blunt has written *Breaking Clean,* a vivid memoir of growing up female on a traditional cattle ranch. Debra Magpie Earling writes of her upbringing on the Flathead Reservation in *Perma Red.*

NATIVES AND NEWCOMERS

Although there are writers scattered across the expanse of Montana, a principality of established authors has grown up around the town of Livingston, north of Yellowstone National Park. Thomas McGuane's novels, including *Keep the Change,* are Westerns filled with modern neuroses. McGuane lives in the area, as has Richard Ford (*Rock Springs*). Ford's *Wildlife* is set in Great Falls, and many of his stories are set in small Montana towns. Richard Brautigan, famous for *Trout Fishing in America,* was also a resident. Jamie Harrison writes Montana-based detective novels (*Going Local, Unfortunate Prairie Occurrence*) from her Livingston home.

In the Internet age, writers can live just about anywhere, and Rick Bass's book *Winter: Notes from Montana* chronicles the author's first winter in remote northwestern Montana. Bass has also written *The Ninemile Wolves,* a passionate book about wolves reestablishing themselves in Montana.

Not all Montana authors are imported. Joseph Kinsey Howard, a journalist and lightning rod for progressive politics in the 1940s, wrote a classic Montana history in *Montana: High, Wide and Handsome*. Ivan Doig's memoirs of his Montana boyhood (*This House of Sky*) and his fictional trilogy about Scottish ranchers in Montana (*Dancing at the Rascal Fair, English Creek*, and *Ride with Me Mariah Montana*) have garnered a wide readership.

Wallace Stegner, although not strictly a Montana writer, spent part of his boyhood in Montana and has written Western novels and memoirs such as *Big Rock Candy Mountain*. Wally McRae, eastern Montana rancher and conservationist, is admired on the cowboy-poet circuit. Another rancher-writer was Spike Van Cleve, who wrote with wit of the changing West in *A Day Late and a Dollar Short*.

To catch the latest-breaking literary movements in Montana, check out *Cutbank* at www.cutbankonline.org.

Art

Montana was visited in its earliest days of settlement by noted artists, who left a rich legacy of landscape and wildlife art. Early artist-explorers Karl Bodmer and John James Audubon passed through Fort Union and up the Missouri; their journals and paintings portray Montana before settlement.

Charlie Russell is the quintessential Montana painter. He knew the West from the inside, having lived the life of a cowhand for many years. A native of St. Louis, Russell came west during the days of the great cattle ranches and lived in the Judith Basin area of central Montana. He began by sketching in bars and around campfires. The lives of the Native Americans and cowboys that he encountered daily became his subject matter. He often traded his sketches for drinks, and after his death some of the best collections of his works were in bars. His studio in Great Falls is now the Charles M. Russell Museum.

His works are also on display in the Montana Historical Society Museum in Helena.

The regional and Western tradition is still strong in Montana art. Ace Powell of Great Falls inherited the mantle of Charlie Russell and painted fine tableaus of the emerging West. A contemporary master of reproducing the light and shade of the Montana landscape is Russell Chatham. His carefully balanced scenes capture the expanse and intimacy of the Montana countryside. Gary Carter paints wildlife and Western scenes, while Clyde Aspevig concentrates on landscapes.

The Montana arts scene doesn't end with Western-themed painting and sculpture. The universities and the Montana Arts Council foster more experimental artists. In Missoula, Rudy Autio produced nationally recognized ceramic sculpture. Another former U of M professor was Walter Hook, a math professor turned painter. Hook developed a wry syntax of images, including buffalo, kites, and Easter eggs, that recur like visitants across his canvases.

John Buck and Debbie Butterfield are Bozeman-area artists whose work flirts with Western icons. Butterfield sculpts horses out of old signs or commercial media to achieve a haunting dissonance. Buck confounds Western art images, ready-mades, and methods—such as whittling—by incorporating them in aggressively modern constructions.

While the mountains allure writers, the prairies seem to attract—and inspire—visual artists. Far-flung ranches and small towns in eastern Montana harbor conceptual artists. Pat Zentz and Dennis Voss are ranchers who each employ quirky and experimental sculpture and assemblages to convey a sense of Montanan ritual and whimsy. Ted Waddell employs modern expressionistic techniques to paint the cows on his ranch, imbuing them with near-totemic presence. Gary Hornick's installations juxtapose isolation and a rich historicity.

A Missoulian who garnered fame as a poster illustrator is Monte Dolack. His easily recognizable movie and commercial poster paintings are avidly collected. Dolack's Missoula gallery markets his stylish and whimsical fine-art paintings and prints.

REGIONAL ART CENTERS

Several Montana communities, some of them quite small, have community art centers. These host touring shows of regional art and frequently feature the works of local artists; the gift shop is often a great place to buy that special souvenir. You may be surprised at the sophistication of work turned out by a ranch wife or a retired railroad worker. Look for regional art centers in Glendive, Miles City, Kalispell, Anaconda, Bigfork, Billings, Colstrip, Great Falls, Hardin, Helena, Lewistown, and Missoula.

Additionally, some towns have developed reputations as visual arts centers, and privately owned galleries proliferate. If you're planning a visual arts tour across Montana, you'll want to check out the private galleries at Bigfork, Livingston, Bozeman, Big Timber, Missoula, Billings, and Red Lodge.

Theater

While the most vital theaters in Montana are associated with the universities in Missoula and Bozeman, other community theaters are of note. Billings has two theater venues, and the Missoula Children's Theater has an excellent reputation throughout the Northwest.

Summer-stock theater is especially good in Montana. Bigfork's summer theater recruits many of its actors from the University of Montana. The Fort Peck summer theater also draws heavily from the Montana universities; the theater building is a lovely relic from the CCC days of the 1930s. Virginia City presents summer melodramas in a frontier opera house; West Yellowstone also has a summer family theater. Montana's "newest" summer theater is in Philipsburg—the Opera House Theater, built in 1891 but newly reopened.

Montana State University presents an ambitious Shakespeare in the Parks series. During summers, the troupe tours the entire state, including remote towns in eastern Montana, with its productions.

FESTIVALS AND EVENTS

Here is a selective list of some of the most notable annual events in Montana.

January

- Last weekend—**Montana Winter Fair,** Lewistown (406/535-4520 or 406/366-2607, www.montanawinterfair.com). Just like a state fair, but no tomatoes.

February

- Midmonth—**C. M. Russell Western Art Auction,** Great Falls (406/727-8787, http://cmrussell.org). This huge event has become a full-fledged arts festival.

- March 17—**St. Patrick's Day Parade,** Butte (406/723-3177 or 800/735-6814, www.buttecvb.com). Experience Irish Montana at its wildest.

April

- Late—**International Wildlife Film Festival,** Missoula (406/728-9380, www.wildlifefilms.org). The whole community gets involved in this highly regarded festival.

May

- Third weekend—**Miles City Bucking Horse Sale,** Miles City (406/234-2890, www.buckinghorsesale.com). Unvarnished cowboy culture prevails when rodeo representatives shop for the West's wildest horses.

June

- Third weekend—**Custer's Last Stand Reenactment,** Hardin (www.custers-laststand.org). The central event of Little

Bighorn Days, which also includes an arts festival, a dance, and a book fair.

July

- July 4—**Terry Rodeo,** Terry (www.visitterrymontana.com). Local cowboys and cowgirls come in off the range for this rodeo, one of the state's oldest and most authentic, held in a real Old West town.

- Second weekend—**North American Indian Days,** Browning (406/338-7406, www.blackfeetcountry.com). A long weekend of drumming and dancing hosted by the Blackfeet Nation.

August

- First weekend—**Sweet Pea Festival,** Bozeman (406/586-4003, www.sweetpeafestival.org). Food, art, and entertainment take over downtown Bozeman.

- Second week—**Festival of Nations,** Red Lodge (www.redlodgefestivalofnations. com). Celebrate the town's ethnic diversity.

- Midmonth—**Montana Cowboy Poetry Gathering,** Lewistown (www.montanacowboypoetrygathering.com). Not just poetry, but music and storytelling.

- Third weekend—**Crow Fair,** Crow Reservation (406/665-7120, www.crowfair.com). This powwow draws participants from across the country.

September

- Second weekend—**Nordicfest,** Libby (www.libbynordicfest.org). Celebrate the area's rich Scandinavian heritage.

October

- Fourth Sunday—**General big-game season opens** (http://fwp.mt.gov/hunting). Be sure to dress in blaze-orange before taking a walk in the woods.

November

- November 8—**Anniversary of Montana's statehood** (1889).

December

- First Saturday—**Christmas parade,** Bigfork (www.bigfork.org). Bigfork glitters as the whole town decorates for the holidays.

Essentials

Transportation

GETTING THERE

Montana is a long way from just about any-where, and once you get there, it's a long way between stops. Although Montana has fine airline and bus service, and Amtrak's *Empire Builder* rolls along Montana's 550-mile border with Canada, the best way to visit the state is with your own vehicle. With so much terri-tory to move around in, you'll want to wan-der freely.

Air

There are no international airports in Montana with direct service to foreign desti-nations, except for regional flights to Alberta. The closest international airports are Seattle to the west, Denver and Salt Lake City to the south, Minneapolis to the east, and Calgary to the north. Billings is the major air hub in Montana, served by most major western air-lines. Missoula, Bozeman, Butte, Helena, Kalispell, and Great Falls are also served by major carriers.

Train

Amtrak's *Empire Builder* (800/872-7245), which travels daily between Chicago and Seattle and Portland, provides rail service to extreme northern Montana. Unfortunately, most of Montana's population and many of its popular tourist destinations are farther to the south (with the exception of Glacier National Park). Public transport linking these north-ern-tier cities to the rest of the state is sketchy, partly because Amtrak has trouble keeping its trains close to their schedule. If you are dependent on public transportation or rental cars, make sure that your Amtrak destina-tion at least offers bus service to other parts of Montana or has vehicles for rent.

Bus

Greyhound buses (800/231-2222) travel along the interstate system, linking Montana to other regional centers.

Jefferson Bus Lines (800/451-5333, www. jeffersonlines.com) also serves towns on the I-90 corridor as well as some smaller towns in eastern Montana.

Car

Montana's most traveled roads cross the state east to west. It's no coincidence that these roads parallel early explorer routes; then as now, most travelers come to Montana to get across it as expeditiously as possible. The I-94/I-90 corridor follows the Yellowstone and Clark Fork Rivers and is the most per-functory route across the state. Dawdlers will prefer to cross the state along more northerly routes. Highway 12 follows the old Milwaukee Road line across central Montana; Highway 2 parallels the Canadian border on Montana's Hi-Line along the old Great Northern rail line. Highway 200 connects the dots between the two. The only major highway cutting north to south is I-15, which links Canada with Great Falls, Helena, and Butte, and extends to Salt Lake City.

GETTING AROUND

There's no question that the best way to see Montana is by automobile. Traveling by pub-lic transport is certainly possible, as buses, trains, and planes traverse the state. But the population centers that serve as public trans-portation hubs are few in number, and who re-ally goes to Montana to see the cities anyway?

Air

There's very little regional air service.

Previous: a welcome to Montana; bison on a road in Yellowstone National Park.

Weather and Road Reports

National Weather Service: Check the website at www.wrh.noaa.gov or call the regional offices:

- Billings: 406/652-1916
- Glasgow: 406/228-4042
- Great Falls: 406/453-2081
- Helena: 406/449-5204
- Missoula: 406/329-4840

Statewide recording: Call 511 or 800/226-7623, or check the website at www.mdt.mt.gov/travinfo.

Delta-associated **SkyWest** (800/453-9417) links Billings, Bozeman, Butte, and Helena, with seasonal summer flights to West Yellowstone.

Train

Amtrak's *Empire Builder* (800/872-7245) crosses Montana's northern extreme along the old Great Northern rail line. By doing so, it offers service to none of Montana's major population centers. Unless you simply want to traverse Montana, or have friends or rental cars lined up to ferry you southward (bus links at Whitefish aren't designed to meet the train), Amtrak isn't a very meaningful way to visit the state: You can't get there from here. The good news is that the *Empire Builder* skirts the southern edge of Glacier National Park and is reckoned to be one of the most scenic Amtrak routes. The independent traveler bent on kicking loose in Montana is best advised to hop off the train at either Spokane, Washington, or Williston, North Dakota, and rent a car.

Bus

Jefferson Bus Lines (800/451-5333, www.jeffersonlines.com) provides more extensive bus service between eastern Montana's

smaller towns. **Flathead Valley Eagle Transit** (406/758-5728, https://flathead.mt.gov/eagle) runs between Missoula and Whitefish.

Car

A few considerations apply when you are planning a road trip to Montana. It's not that there are any real tricks involved in driving Montana, but those who are used to city and freeway driving may need some reassurance and a pointer or two.

If you are planning to rent a car, be sure to reserve one well in advance. Just about any regular car will serve you fine most of the time, but some remote dirt roads get pretty dodgy without a high-clearance vehicle. Likewise, a two-wheel drive will handle most situations, but it's not a bad idea to throw a tow rope in the trunk, and except in the dead of summer, it makes sense to carry tire chains.

Distances are great in Montana: Fill your tank frequently, especially in eastern Montana. Along Highway 200, hundreds of miles separate gas stations. Plan ahead. Don't assume that every little dot on the map will have gas; many are merely pioneer post offices that mapmakers haven't bothered to delete from base maps. Ask gas station attendants how far the next gas station is, if you are in doubt. Make sure your vehicle is in reasonable shape. Check tires, oil, and radiator water. Carry extra oil and water.

A less apparent consideration involves foreign cars. By and large, Montana is Ford and Chevy country. If, by Montana standards, you are driving a moderately obscure foreign vehicle, don't anticipate that parts will be readily available should a breakdown occur. If you know that the alternator is failing on your Citroën, don't head into rural Montana assuming that repairs will be easy.

If cattle are in the road, just drive slowly toward them, and more often than not they'll grudgingly move out of the way. Sheep will rarely give way in any logical fashion.

Logging trucks rule the roads in the western forests. It's wise not to be stubborn about

Mileage in Montana

© AVALON TRAVEL

keeping your piece of the roadbed when one bears down on you.

The speed limit in Montana is 75 mph on freeways, 65 mph on two-lane roads.

The white crosses that you occasionally see standing beside state highways do indeed mark the sites of fatal automobile accidents.

The state **highway information number** is 800/226-7623, TTY 800/335-7592, or check the website at www.mdt.mt.gov/travinfo. During the winter, call this number to find out which passes are closed and what the driving conditions are like. Recordings are updated two to three times daily.

Recreation

PUBLIC LANDS

Public lands, state and national forests, and Bureau of Land Management (BLM) land constitute roughly 35 percent of the state, opening much of the state up for recreation and a plethora of other uses.

State Parks

Montana operates more than 50 **state parks** (406/444-3750, http://stateparks.mt.gov) focusing on both recreation and history. Many of the parks include campgrounds, which are open mid-May to mid-September. Day-use fees for non-Montanans are $5 per vehicle at most state parks, and it is $23-28 for overnight campers. Some parks feature yurts, tepees, and cabins for rent. The state's parks are diverse, including historic ghost towns, Native American museums, and lakeside campgrounds.

U.S. Forest Service Lands

Much of the public land in Montana's western and southern mountains is administered by the **U.S. Forest Service** (406/329-3511, www.fs.usda.gov/r1). Forest Service ranger stations are good places to get information on camping and recreation. All national forests contain developed hiking trails, and Forest Service roads in winter become de facto cross-country skiing trails. Most national forests also have developed trail systems for mountain bikers and can provide maps highlighting roads and areas best suited for backcountry cycling. Much of this land is also open to hunting in season—usually late September through November.

Forest Service campgrounds are widespread in western Montana. Fees range from free to $20, depending on the amenities (free campgrounds are those with a pit toilet and no running water—they're usually remote and rarely crowded). The Forest Service also rents out some rustic cabins and fire lookouts, usually for about $30 per night. Check the individual national forest's website for cabin descriptions, accessibility, information about what supplies you'll need to bring along, and details about reserving a cabin.

Wilderness Areas

Montana has 17 federally managed wilderness areas, roadless and closed to mechanized use, including mountain bikes. Designated wilderness areas are sometimes more heavily used than remote nonwilderness areas. Stop in at a Forest Service ranger station and ask which local trails they favor. In addition to the wilderness areas that fall under the jurisdiction of the Forest Service, there are several tribal wilderness areas in Montana. Before hiking or fishing on tribal land, be sure you have the necessary permits.

National Parks

Glacier National Park (www.nps.gov/glac) falls entirely within Montana, and its Canadian counterpart, **Waterton Lakes National Park** (www.watertoninfo.ab.ca), is directly above the border. Although the bulk of **Yellowstone National Park** (www.nps.gov/yell) is in Wyoming, three of the park's entrances, as well as its northern edge, are in Montana. Entrance fees are $30 for either Glacier or Yellowstone (or $80 for a year-long pass to any national park). This pays for a week's unlimited entrance into the specified park. An extra fee is charged to stay in park campgrounds.

PRIVATE LAND

Even though much of Montana is publicly owned, you sometimes need to cross privately owned land to *reach* public land. This is an issue especially for anglers and hunters, because access to the best streams and hunting grounds is often across private land.

Always ask permission to cross private land, especially when it's fenced and *always* if there is a No Trespassing sign. Don't be surprised if you are asked to pay a small fee to cross private lands, especially in popular fishing areas such as the Madison Valley. In parts of eastern Montana, the state has agreements with private landowners to allow access to private lands for hunting purposes. However, you must have written permission to hunt on these lands and must report in to the landowner.

Most landowners are tolerant of people who ask permission to enter their land, but don't be surprised if permission is not granted. If a pasture is filled with cows and young calves, a rancher probably won't want people trooping through to fly-fish and certainly wouldn't allow someone in to start shooting rifles. Be considerate and polite and you'll usually get the permission you want. You may even make a friendly acquaintance with a real Montanan.

Tribal Lands

Each of Montana's seven Native American reservations is self-governing, and the state does not have authority to regulate fishing, hunting, or other recreational activities on tribal land. In fact, most reservation land is off-limits to all but tribe members. Remember that for many tribes, the land contains sacred sites and possesses a deeper significance to them than it may to you—it's perhaps more

than just a cool place to race a mountain bike, in other words. Some tribes are more open to multiuse recreation than others; the Flathead Reservation is generally open to nonmembers (as long as they have tribal permits), while the Crow Reservation is generally off-limits to the public.

As you would for any privately owned land, always ask permission before trespassing. Tribal permits for hiking or fishing, if necessary, are generally available from most businesses on the reservation for a small fee. When in doubt, call the tribal office to inquire about access and permits.

None of this information is intended to give the impression that reservations are closed to visitors or that tourism isn't welcome. Respectful visitors are welcome at powwows and other cultural and sporting events (rodeos are especially enjoyable).

OUTDOOR PURSUITS
Hiking and Backpacking

In a state that's as big as all outdoors, don't be surprised to find that hiking and backpacking are the preferred outdoor activities. Long backpacking trips through national forests and wilderness areas are something of a rite of passage for many Montanans.

The most famous hiking area in the state is **Glacier National Park.** Even more so than Yellowstone, Glacier yields its wonders only to those who get out of the car and hike up its trails. However, in high summer the trails can be very busy and may therefore not deliver the wilderness experience you're looking for. Other areas to consider for longer backpacking trips are the **Bob Marshall Wilderness,** south of Glacier Park; the **Bitterroot Mountains,** south of Missoula; and the **Absaroka-Beartooth Wilderness,** north of Yellowstone.

The national forests are all laced with hiking trails, and the staff at any ranger station can help you put together a hiking trip that suits your interests, time limitations, and endurance.

Cycle Touring and Mountain Biking

There are plenty of opportunities for touring and mountain biking, from Glacier Park to the Pryor Mountains. Missoula is home to the **Adventure Cycling Association** (150 E. Pine, 800/755-2453, www.adventurecycling.org), a touring organization and advocacy group for cyclists. They provide great maps and can answer questions regarding routes and conditions. Bozeman is another center for biking, especially mountain biking.

Leading local bike shops can offer plenty of good advice and route ideas. Many shops carry route maps showing local trails. Most national forests have developed information and maps for mountain bikers, and ranger stations are another good place to seek advice.

In general, cyclists need to remember two things: Montana is a very big place, and it's a long way between towns, especially in eastern and central Montana. Weather is another consideration. Summer can be a short season, and inclement weather can blow in quickly. Also, much of Montana is windy.

The **Montana Department of Transportation** (406/444-9273, www.mdt.mt.gov/travinfo/bikeped) offers information for cyclists. It can provide information on the suitability of specific roads and on road-repair schedules.

Hunting

Hunters flock to Montana in the fall for elk, pronghorn, pheasants, deer, bear, and the occasional mountain lion or bighorn sheep. To hunt for certain animals—including moose, mountain sheep, and mountain goats—hunters need to enter special drawings. Nonresidents also need permits to hunt for antelope. For more information, contact the **Montana Department of Fish, Wildlife, and Parks** (406/444-2535, http://fwp.mt.gov). If you'd like to enlist the aid of a hunting guide, check the website for recommendations on established outfitters, or contact the **Montana Outfitters and Guides Association** (406/449-3578, www.montanaoutfitters.org) for a list of licensed outfitters.

Fishing

Montana's streams and rivers are famous for their plentiful but wily trout. Although it's theoretically possible to fish year-round in lakes and large rivers, late June through October are the most popular months for fishing. The state maintains more than 300

mountain biking in Montana

fishing-access areas across the state. The basic fee for a fishing license, including the required conservation license, is $16 for adult Montana residents and $70 for a nonresident year-long license (or $25 for a two-day license).

The list of blue-ribbon fishing streams in Montana is lengthy and includes such well-known (and now crowded) rivers as the Yellowstone, Bighorn, Madison, and Big Hole. However, these are just the famous fisheries; many other rivers and streams provide ample sport and fishing pleasure. Lake fishing is also popular, especially in northwestern Montana, with such bodies as Flathead Lake.

Even arid eastern Montana is a fishing destination, with famed walleye fishing in Fort Peck Reservoir and paddlefishing in the Yellowstone River near Glendive.

You don't have to hire a fishing guide or outfitter to fish in Montana, but if you're new to angling or would like to gain more skill as a fly-fisher, it's a good idea to enlist the aid of an outfitter. Also, access to fishing holes can be a problem, and a local outfitter can remove potential hassles that could otherwise complicate a quick fishing trip to Montana. Each chapter of this book includes the names of reputable fishing guides and fly shops.

Contact the **Montana Department of Fish, Wildlife, and Parks** (406/444-2535, http://fwp.mt.gov) for up-to-date information on licensing and season dates.

River Rafting and Floating

Montana's many rivers are popular for white-water rafting and more leisurely float trips. The most famous white-water rivers are the branches of the Flathead near Glacier National Park and the Gallatin and Yellowstone near Yellowstone National Park. These rivers are also popular with kayakers. Other river trips will take you to remote areas of wilderness reached only on multi-day float trips. The Wild and Scenic designated portion of the Missouri, downstream from Fort Benton, is a favorite for naturalists and devotees of Lewis and Clark. The Smith River takes anglers through limestone canyons to otherwise unreachable fishing holes.

River trips are offered by many guide services, and boats can be rented in most river towns. For most multiday trips, advance reservations are required; in fact, for popular rivers such as the Smith, you'll need reservations many months in advance. Most white-water guide services offer day and part-day trips that require only a day's advance reservations.

Dependable and experienced guides are listed in each chapter. For a complete list of guides, contact the **Montana Outfitters and Guides Association** (406/449-3578, www.montanaoutfitters.org).

Horseback Riding and Cattle Drives

Resorts and guest ranches all generally offer horseback riding. Guided trail rides are the norm, although longer pack trips into the mountains are also scheduled. **Cattle drives** remain popular, with several Montana ranches offering guests the chance to trail cattle from pasture to pasture or ranch to town. These trips usually involve several days of horseback riding, camping out on the prairie, and eating meals from chuck wagons.

Again, the **Montana Outfitters and Guides Association** (406/449-3578, www.montanaoutfitters.org) is a good place to start.

Skiing

Whitefish Mountain Resort, just outside of Whitefish, and **Big Sky,** some 30 miles south of Bozeman, are Montana's two big destination ski resorts. If you'd rather avoid the development but still can't resist the thrills of downhill, try one of the smaller ski areas outside Libby, Missoula, Bozeman, Anaconda, Darby, Dillon, Neihart, Red Lodge, or Choteau. The ski season generally runs from Thanksgiving through mid-March.

Once the back roads of national forests are covered with snow, many of them become **cross-country** ski trails. The Forest Service distributes a list of ski trails, and local ranger stations have specific maps for their areas.

Trails groomed for both standard cross-country skiing and "freestyle," or "skating," are maintained by lodges, such as the Izaak Walton Inn in Essex, and by individual communities, like the Rendezvous Trails in West Yellowstone. There may be a fee to ski on groomed trails.

For an overview of downhill and cross-country ski areas, as well as information on snowmobiling, contact **Winter Montana** (800/847-4868, www.wintermt.com).

Rockhounding and Prospecting

Explore the Treasure State with a pan or a bucket. Prospect for gold near Libby, or buy a bucket of dirt outside Helena or Philipsburg and pick through it in search of sapphires. Hunt for garnets in southwestern Montana, agates along the Yellowstone, and petrified wood in the Gallatin National Forest.

GAMBLING IN MONTANA

Several forms of gambling are legal in Montana, as any visitor to the state will instantly notice—many old-time bars, taverns, clubs, and lounges have all become casinos. Gambling is regulated by the state, which takes 10-15 percent of the proceeds from the various games—and makes about $300 million a year in the process.

While card rooms have always been legal—or at least tolerated—in Montana, electronic gambling has been legalized comparatively recently. Other forms of gambling, such as pari-mutuel and video-link horse racing, calcuttas, and shake-a-day dice games, are legal as well. Montana also participates in three multistate lotteries.

Card Room Games

In the back room of many an old-time bar is a well-burnished green felt table, usually watched over—with hawklike vigilance—by sharp-eyed denizens. At some cue—perhaps the arrival of a newcomer with fresh money or the advent of a lucky omen—the game begins, often lasting long into the early hours of the morning.

All traditional forms of poker are legal; stud and draw are the favored games. There's a $300 pot limit. To play, you need to buy chips from the house; if you're lucky and win, you cash out your chips from the house. The house will keep its—and the state's—share.

Blackjack, pan, pitch, and other card games in which the players bet against the house are *not* legal in Montana. Neither are most dice

skiing at Whitefish Mountain Resort

games—including craps—or "beat-the-house" games, such as roulette.

Keno, a hopped-up version of bingo, is legal, both as an electronic game and in its original form—as a barroom diversion. If you've ever wondered what that large checkered game board on the wall of an old bar is, you're probably looking at a lighted keno display.

While it's permissible to watch strangers play poker in the back rooms of bars, remember that there is frequently a lot of money at risk, tempers can be short, and often liquor has flowed liberally. Keep your mouth shut and act reverential. Don't do anything that might break the concentration of the players or that may be interpreted as interaction.

Electronic Games

Video poker is by far the most popular of the various kinds of electronic gambling in Montana. The whirring, ringing, and beeping of the machines have all but eliminated the gentle buzz of conversation in Montana watering holes.

To play video poker, you put a coin—usually a quarter—in the slot. A random five-card hand appears on the screen, and you decide which, if any, of the cards you want to keep. Press the corresponding buttons, then press a different button to receive replacement cards. The machine will let you know if you have any combination of winning cards. Should you win, don't expect a cascade of small change. Winning combinations earn points (which usually equal quarters). You decide whether to use your points to play more hands or to cash them out by contacting the bartender or game-room manager.

Other Legal Gambling

Pari-mutuel **horse racing** is popular at summer fairs. Some bars and clubs offer a more cutting-edge method of betting on horseflesh—video broadcasts of live horse races. You get racing forms, track conditions, lines at the betting booth—everything but the dust and the smell of horse sweat.

A more distinctly Montana form of legal betting is the **calcutta.** Usually held as a charity event, a calcutta involves auctioning off the performance of a sportsman, usually a rodeo contestant or golfer. If the cowboy you "buy" wins his event, then you get a share of his prize money, while the majority of the money raised from the auction goes to the charity.

As in other states, Native Americans on federal reservations have opened **casinos** that feature games not otherwise allowed by Montana state law. Under the confusing laws that govern activities on reservations, Native Americans can bypass restrictive state laws by invoking federal laws that recognize reservations as sovereign entities. Nevada-style casinos are present in several locations on Montana reservations.

SPECTATOR SPORTS
Rodeos

Most communities in Montana have rodeos at least once each summer, often on the Fourth of July, during the county fair, or sometimes just whenever enough interested parties come together in one place. "Little Britches" rodeos are held for grade-school children. High-school rodeo clubs are often the largest extracurricular groups in small towns. Intercollegiate rodeo is also popular—and a source of scholarships for Montana students. Bozeman hosts the national finals for intercollegiate rodeo.

Make an attempt to attend *some* rodeo. Rodeos are quintessentially Western but haven't yet become heavily commercialized. Be prepared to get hot and dusty, and be friendly. Summer rodeos are a community's way to visit with friends and family. Dates of rodeos are available from local chambers of commerce or from publications available from regional tourism bureaus.

Rodeos can be confusing to the first-time spectator. **Saddle-bronc riding** involves a cowboy staying on a saddled bucking horse for eight seconds. Similarly, in **bareback bronc riding,** the rider tries to stay aboard a bucking horse for eight seconds, but the rider has only a "rigging" (a very small seatless leather saddle) for assistance. **Bull riding** pitches an enormous bull, usually a Brahma, against a cowboy, who must ride the bull for eight seconds. The bulls and the horses in these events are strapped around their lower abdomen with a "flank cinch," which annoys the animals into greater bucking fits. In all events, the cowboy must make the ride using only one hand to hang on (using two hands, even briefly, results in disqualification). The cowboys are not judged on the length of their ride. If they make it the necessary eight seconds, the ride is then judged on its particular merits, including amount and quality of spurring (which further annoys the animal, increasing the bucking), the general comportment of the cowboy on the animal, and the fierceness of the animal's bucking.

In **bulldogging,** a steer emerges at full lope from the chute. A cowboy gives chase aboard a galloping horse, jumps from the horse to the steer, and wrestles the steer to the ground. Winners are determined by speed. **Calf roping** begins similarly, but the cowboy must lasso the calf, leap from his horse (while the horse keeps the rope taut), and tie three of the calf's legs to immobilize it for five seconds. Some rodeos also include **team roping,** where one of a pair of cowboys ropes the head and the other the hind legs of a steer.

In most rodeos, the sole cow*girl* event is **barrel racing,** in which cowgirls zip in a cloverleaf pattern around three barrels. If the horse knocks over a barrel, five seconds are added to the contestant's time.

Other rodeo events include the **grand entry** at the beginning of the rodeo, wherein two young cowgirls "present the colors" (United States and state) while galloping around the arena on horseback. Every entrant who has brought a horse to the event immediately joins the flag bearers in the arena for a horseback national anthem.

Clowns are also a part of the rodeo. During the bull-riding event, irate bulls can turn on thrown addled riders and gore them. Clowns draw the bull's attention to themselves by teasing or throwing tractor inner tubes at the bull, while the dazed cowboy makes a safe escape.

Some rodeos also include **novelty events** such as wild-cow milking (first team with any milk at all wins), various kinds of racing, or some children's events such as greased pig contests or wild-sheep riding.

Montana Minor League Baseball

The only other spectator sport in Montana is professional baseball's **Pioneer League** (www.pioneerleague.com), which has been a crowd-pleaser here since 1939. Most of the players are recent draft picks, and the Pioneer League is their first real baseball job.

The Billings Mustangs (a farm team for the Cincinnati Reds), the Missoula Osprey (associated with the Arizona Diamondbacks), the Helena Brewers (Milwaukee Brewers), and the Great Falls Voyagers (Chicago White Sox) play in the Pioneer League's northern division.

Each team plays 70 games between mid-June and the end of August. Games are taken seriously, and fans often develop a rapport with the young players.

Accommodations and Food

ACCOMMODATIONS
Traditional Lodging

A wide variety of lodging options exist in Montana. Generally speaking, rooms in hotels and motels are rather expensive in the summer season and are often in short supply. Reserve rooms several days in advance, especially if you want a specific type of room or a special hotel. Especially around the national parks, but anywhere on a summer weekend, expect the lodging situation to be tight.

Prices in this guide reflect summer high-season rack rates. Room prices will often change according to the night of the week (weekends may be more expensive in tourist areas; weeknights are pricier in eastern Montana's towns that house oil-field workers). If you're traveling outside high season, expect to find cheaper room rates, especially in tourist areas.

Chain motels cluster around interstate highway off-ramps on the edges of towns. Better deals on lodgings are often found away from these developments, along the old arterials. Also, don't dismiss staying at old downtown hotels. Some are renovated and reflect the splendor of yore; others, for the more daring, have survived as residential hotels. Chances are you'll have a unique experience.

Historic Hotels

Travelers have been journeying to Montana for a couple of centuries, and if you count the Native Americans who traveled to the plains to hunt, for quite a bit longer. Though the native hunters didn't build hotels, the travelers who came after Lewis and Clark became increasingly used to comfortable accommodations, and by the early 1900s most towns had hotels—and many of these historic hotels are still in operation. Visits to these historic hotels and B&Bs in historic homes will bring you close to the history of the Old West and take you to out-of-the-way destinations that were once important travel centers.

NORTHWESTERN MONTANA

South of Bigfork (a good spot for lunch), the **Double Arrow Resort** is a well-loved lakeside lodge and cabin resort from the 1930s, stretching along the shores of beautiful Seeley Lake. The old resort has just the right degree of rustic homeyness, and food in the lodge restaurant is notable.

GLACIER NATIONAL PARK

Glacier National Park has many famous lodges, but savvy travelers and railroad die-hards make their way to Essex (on the southern border of the park) to spend the night at the **Izaak Walton Inn,** built as a railway workers' hotel in the 1930s. This old lodging is wonderfully atmospheric and is a magical destination in winter for cross-country skiing—and the fishing ain't bad either.

SOUTHWESTERN MONTANA

The biggest news in Philipsburg in, well, 120 years is the reopening of the **Broadway Hotel.** This handsome old lodging reopened its doors after a complete updating and refurbishing of its rooms and is a fun and comfortable place to begin exploration of the region's rich mining history.

In Boulder, history of a different kind is on display at **Boulder Hot Springs.** For centuries, Native Americans came for R&R in these hot mineral waters, and when entrepreneurial settlers moved in during the 1880s, a glamorous European-style hot-springs spa and hotel sprang up—one of the earliest tourist destinations in the state. If you're looking for a unique and colorful spot to soak away travel aches and pains, this is it.

SOUTH-CENTRAL MONTANA

In Three Forks, where the three branches of the Missouri join, the imposing **Sacajawea Hotel** offers very comfortable lodgings and fine dining in a beautifully renovated lodge.

The **Grand Hotel** in Big Timber, while not exactly big-city grand, is pretty special for this little town. The handsome brick building has comfortable rooms upstairs and the town's best restaurant downstairs. Naturally, there's also a good bar where you can get to know the mix of locals and travelers who end up here at the end of the day.

SOUTHEASTERN MONTANA

Miles City once boasted fine hotels where ranchers and livestock buyers met to trade stories and cattle, but only one of these old hotels is still in business. The **Olive Hotel** is no longer the gem it once was—'round about 1890—but it's still a pretty interesting place to stay, and there's no better spot to use as base camp to explore the fantastic old bars of downtown Miles City.

NORTHEASTERN MONTANA

The **Fort Peck Hotel,** about 120 miles from the state line, was built in the 1930s to house guests at one of the nation's largest New Deal projects, the Fort Peck Dam. The old hotel has been upgraded in recent years, but the rambling old structure perfectly captures the spirit of the 1930s.

NORTH-CENTRAL MONTANA

Some of the most unique accommodations in Montana are the homesteaders' homes, pioneer hotel rooms, and sheep wagons at Virgelle, a ghost town that has come back to life as a departure point for canoe trips down the Wild and Scenic Missouri River. A variety of lodgings are offered by the **Virgelle Mercantile;** the owner has collected deserted homes from the prairies and brought them here, rebuilding them in all their frontier glory.

If homesteading isn't in your blood, then the **Grand Union Hotel** in Fort Benton, south of Virgelle, might be more your style.

When it was built as one of the most luxurious hotels in Montana in 1882, Fort Benton was the uppermost point of navigation on the Missouri River, and the Grand Union Hotel welcomed guests off steamboats from St. Louis. This opulent hotel has been completely updated and refurbished and offers excellent meals.

On the way to Glacier National Park, stop by the tiny community of Dupuyer to stay at **Inn Dupuyer.** This bed-and-breakfast has built a larger structure around a century-old two-story log cabin. Guests have the benefit of a modern dining room and bathroom facilities while spending the night in the homey comfort of a historic log home.

Guest Ranches and Resorts

High-end resorts have sprung up across the state, many with the ambience of a country lodge or guest ranch. More traditional dude and guest ranches and hot-springs resorts, many with a lengthy pedigree, abound. There's scarcely a community in Montana now that does not offer some form of guest ranch accommodation. Some of these can be wonderfully rustic and located in beautiful rural settings, and most offer unlimited horseback riding in addition to other recreational activities. Some small guest ranches enjoy a quiet fame with a long-standing bluechip (and even royal!) clientele. Hot-springs resorts vary from the full-blown convention-sized facilities, such as Fairmont Hot Springs, to modest mom-and-pop affairs. Some ski resorts like Big Sky and Whitefish Mountain Resort have reputations that precede them. They are open year-round for hiking, fishing, and other summer activities.

Other guest ranches and resorts can be much more modest. Your rustic farm vacation might call for you to sleep in the sheep wagon. When you're deciding on a guest ranch vacation, ask plenty of questions on the phone before booking, and make sure that you're comfortable with the accommodations and facilities.

The **Montana Dude Ranchers' Association** (1627 W. Main, Ste. 434,

Bozeman, MT 59715, www.montanadra. com) can provide information on its member ranches.

Bed-and-Breakfasts

Bed-and-breakfasts are found across Montana. Some are newly built and luxurious, with swimming pools, trendy New West decor, and hot tubs; others are located in historic homes or buildings and provide a wonderfully evocative insight into the Old West.

If you are among those people leery of B&Bs or have had bad experiences at homestays where it was too much like staying in the back bedroom under Aunt Lulu's watchful eye, rest assured that the B&Bs listed in this guide have been personally inspected and are heartily recommended. Another good source for information on quality B&Bs is the **Montana Bed and Breakfast Association** (www.mtbba.com), a self-policing membership organization whose accommodations are inspected and approved according to a rigorous standard of requirements. These standards provide for the highest degree of cleanliness, convenience, and comfort for the traveler and are regulated with regular inspections by the association.

Camping and RV Parks

If you're at all inclined toward camping, bring along your gear and head out to the wilds of Montana. Western Montana is especially well-endowed with public campgrounds in national forests and state parks. Tent campers need to plan ahead in other parts of the state if they want formal campsites, because public campgrounds thin out on the prairies. Ask to camp in town parks; the locals may be glad to have their parks appreciated. RV campers will find campgrounds in most towns. Fees in public campgrounds usually range from free to $20; privately owned campgrounds charge $15-50 per night (most have rudimentary facilities for tent campers).

In between a motel and a campground are Forest Service cabins and lookouts, which are rustic accommodations generally with outhouses and without bedding or cooking utensils. They normally rent for about $30 per night. Contact the **USDA Forest Service, Northern Region Office** (200 E. Broadway, Missoula, MT 59802, 406/329-3511, www. fs.usda.gov/r1, for a cabin directory).

FOOD

Here's the stereotype, mostly true: Steaks are standard and usually good. Vegetarians manage to make do with iceberg lettuce salads. Although espresso is served in all corners of the state, be prepared for plenty of thin, often bitter coffee laden with sugar and powdered creamer.

There really isn't anything to justify the label "Montana cuisine." Dishes peculiar to the region usually bring changes to established entrées, which is not to say they're bad. Adding huckleberries to every dish does not a cuisine make. However, local beef and fresh Montana trout give even a teenage fry cook a chance for greatness.

Buffalo burgers are simply hamburgers made with ground buffalo meat; promoters claim buffalo is a leaner, more flavorful alternative to beef. Indian tacos load taco ingredients onto fry bread. Rocky Mountain oysters are more often threatened than served; served correctly, lamb or calf testicles are the quintessential offal meat, surprisingly palatable.

But even when restaurant fare seems unimaginative compared to cuisine on the coasts, the general quality of the food is quite good. Home cooking sets the standard, and simple unprepossessing food is often the best.

There are happy exceptions to the rule, however. Chefs have mastered sauces in some pretty out-of-the-way places: Where you least expect it—Chico, Broadus, Essex—you will find that isolated but enterprising cooks have established restaurants with sophisticated dining.

Montanans like to eat out. Cafés and restaurants are social centers, and eating out is a way of combating isolation. The bar is another meeting place, and not just for adults. Entire families meet up at bars, where it's perfectly normal to stick to soft drinks.

Shopping

Montana has no sales tax, so you may want to provision for the holidays while on vacation.

GIFTS AND SOUVENIRS

There aren't many places that evoke the Wild West as clearly as Montana, and a gift or souvenir that recalls the Western past makes a good keepsake. Almost every town will have a clothing store and saddlery featuring Western clothes. Pearl-snap shirts, tooled leather belts, and other leather goods make nice and functional gifts. If you're wondering why cowboys and cowgirls look so good in their jeans, it's because the pants are Wrangler brand. Look for the Cowboy Cut jeans if you want to squeeze into something that's bound to get attention when you get back home. Likewise, Montana is a good place to buy a pair of cowboy boots. Several saddleries make boots to order; be ready to mortgage your house to pay for them.

Although none of Montana's Native American tribes has a long tradition of commercial arts or crafts, gift shops and galleries now feature the works of Native American artists. Look for silver or beaded jewelry and leather goods, as well as paintings on hide.

Other local artists and artisans show their works in craft shops and galleries. Most of the larger towns across Montana—including Sidney, Miles City, Lewistown, Kalispell, Billings, and Glendive—have community art centers that feature the works of local people.

Montana is also a major center for Western art, especially for blue-chip bronze statuary and wildlife art. Bozeman, Livingston, Kalispell, Whitefish, Big Fork, and even such unlikely towns as Wisdom and Big Timber all feature world-class galleries.

Another good gift or souvenir idea is Montana food products. Native fruits and berries make up into delicious jams and jellies. Huckleberry and chokecherry products will make nice remembrances. Local honey is also common and easy to find. Local cherries and wild huckleberries find their way into a wide selection of candies and confections. On the other end of the food scale, dried jerkies and smoked fish are produced by small local companies.

SPORTING GOODS

Montana is a real mecca of recreation and sports, and several excellent manufacturers and stores have sprung up to serve the market. Again, without a sales tax, Montana may be a tempting place to buy these items.

Almost every little town in western Montana has a fly-fishing shop, complete with hand-tied flies and fancy rods and reels. The R. L. Winston fly rod company in Twin Bridges is especially famous, a place many anglers approach almost with the reverence of religious supplicants on a pilgrimage to a holy site.

Many ski shops turn into mountain bike shops by summer, and vice versa, and you can often get really good prices on skis or bikes if you visit Montana in the right season. Likewise, canoes and kayaks can get pretty cheap at the end of the season, when proprietors need to make room for snowboards.

While it's not a piece of sporting gear that the average visitor will use often, nothing says Montana quite like a handmade saddle. The state is home to several famous saddlers, who make saddles to order for professional cowboys, celebrity ranchers, and anyone else capable of paying for them. Expect a handmade saddle to start at around $2,500.

Travel Tips

CROSSING TO AND FROM CANADA

Of the 15 roads that cross from Montana into Canada, only three are open around the clock. Highways 93 and 15 and Road 16 (in the state's far northeastern corner) have 24-hour ports of entry. U.S. and Canadian citizens should carry their passports to cross the border—even if you can get across the border in one direction with a driver's license and a birth certificate, there's no guarantee that you'll get back across in the other direction. Everyone has stories of stranded travelers caught on the wrong side of the line.

Citizens of any other nation should be prepared to show a passport and the appropriate visas. Citizens of any country may be asked to provide proof that they have sufficient funds for their intended length of stay.

U.S. Customs

Customs allows each person over the age of 21 to bring 34 ounces of liquor and 200 cigarettes into the United States without paying duty. U.S. citizens are allowed to import, duty-free, $400 worth of gifts from abroad, and non-U.S. citizens are allowed to bring in $100 worth. Should you be carrying more than $10,000—in U.S. or foreign cash, traveler's checks, money orders, or the like—you need to declare the excess amount. There is no legal restriction on the amount that may be imported, but undeclared sums in excess of $10,000 may be subject to confiscation.

Canadian Customs

Adults (age varies by province but is generally 19 years) can take 40 ounces of liquor or a case of 24 beers as well as 200 cigarettes, 50 cigars, and 14 ounces of tobacco into Canada. You can bring in gifts totaling up to C$60 in value. Pistols or handguns cannot be taken into Canada, although hunting rifles can be.

TRAVELERS WITH DISABILITIES

For the most part, Montana complies with federal and state guidelines for access. State and national parks feature accessible trails when possible, and most modern hotels provide barrier-free lodgings. However, Montana is a rural state, and you may find that facilities are less accessible off the beaten path.

WOMEN TRAVELERS

Although it's not the expected thing, there's little reason for a woman to feel uneasy about traveling alone around Montana. If you're not up to being outgoing, people will generally leave you alone. But if you get to feeling chatty or flirtatious, you're in real luck. You'll be a curiosity, and men and women alike will sit you down and spin tales, feed you, and make you grin. You do have to look out for weirdos, but they're usually about as much of a threat to the average female traveler as grizzly bears, and easier to deflect. If a place makes you nervous, do the smart thing and leave. On the whole, travel in Montana is exhilarating and ego-boosting for a woman on her own.

GAY AND LESBIAN TRAVELERS

Like much of the mountainous West, Montana is socially conservative, and open displays of affection by gay people won't be found endearing by the majority of natives. While there's no reason to anticipate open discrimination or hostility if you're openly gay, it's good to remember that Matthew Shepard was murdered in neighboring Wyoming—especially in bars, don't assume that everyone is going to think it's cool that you're gay. Don't ask, don't tell is still a reasonable rule for gay people traveling in Montana. As of 2014, same-sex couples cannot marry in Montana.

That said, both Missoula and Bozeman

Montana Fashion

While fashion may not appear to be much of a preoccupation in Montana, even this low-key style has its system. Here are a few clues to understanding the dictates of Montana chic.

In general, fashion is dictated by function. Ranchers dress the way they do because it's effective. Levi's are eschewed in favor of **Wrangler jeans,** for example. One cowboy claimed that Wranglers fit better over boot tops, but a more understandable reason is the seam: On Wrangler jeans, the double seam runs down the outside of the leg; the seam running along the *inside* of a pair of Levi's can get pretty uncomfortable for a cowpoke on horseback.

Boots are still mandatory footwear. They provide necessary protection for the feet and calves while riding on horseback, and their high tops are prophylactic against snakebite. Boot-making is still a custom trade in several Montana towns.

Neck scarves are not just colorful accessories: They insulate against cold drafts in winter and dust and chaff the rest of the year.

Cowboy hats are still a popular hedge against the sun and wind: straw for summer and felt for winter. The hegemony of the cowboy hat, though, has been somewhat shaken by the rise of the baseball cap, although no one in Montana would consider calling a head covering by that name. Rather, net caps are known by the brand names they feature—call it a "Cat Cap" or a "King Rope Cap"—and they are both identified and justified within Montana fashion.

The prevalence of **pearl snaps** over buttons is as real as it is, sadly, inexplicable.

As in certain ornithological species, the male's attire is often more engaging than the female's. It is probably a judgment on Montana couture that women's fashion generally reaches its apex in the menswear department. Women often look their best when they dress in the same clothes as men: jeans, plaid shirts, and boots.

Warning: *Do not try to duplicate Montana fashion.* Most attempts look as staged as they are. Getting yourself up in full Western regalia is probably not going to win you any extra points. While in Montana, just dress comfortably and—especially if you want to win the confidence or friendship of native Montanans—observe a few simple rules:

- Don't wear anything really trendy or goofy. This will put an extra barrier between you and the residents.

- Hot summer weather doesn't necessarily mean shorts for men.

- Shirtlessness is almost taboo.

- Err on the side of comfortable modesty. In Montana, this is considered an element of style.

have active but somewhat underground gay networks, largely because of their large student populations. Montana may seem on the surface more hospitable to lesbians than to gay men—to the untrained eye, there's not a lot of style and fashion differentiation between young lesbians and young straight women out in the backcountry.

MONEY

Almost all Montana banks have ATMs, making it easy to travel without the hassle of traveler's checks. Credit cards are widely—although not universally—accepted.

Foreign Exchange

In short, don't depend on exchanging foreign currency or traveler's checks in Montana. While banks in the larger cities supposedly offer exchange services, the transaction is so out of the ordinary that you may be told to come back another day after they figure out how to do it. Save yourself time and hassle and change your money before getting to Montana. Or just use ATMs to draw money out of your foreign account.

Sales Tax

There is no sales tax or value-added tax (VAT)

in Montana. It is one of three U.S. states that do not levy a tax on products at the register (the others are Oregon and New Hampshire). Taxes on property and income, however, are steep.

The frequently dire financial condition of the Montana state government makes the sales tax a tempting revenue enhancer to some politicians, landowners, and advocates of public education. However, voters have repeatedly turned down the sales tax by referendum.

COMMUNICATIONS AND MEDIA

Montana may be remote, but you can use your cellular phone in most of the state, though service may be spotty in some mountain valleys. Public libraries usually have computers for public use, including Internet connections. Most motels and coffee shops, have wireless access.

Media

The only national newspapers you can count on finding in Montana are *USA Today* and (to a more limited extent) the *Wall Street Journal*. Regional daily papers include the Billings *Gazette,* the Great Falls *Tribune,* the Butte *Standard,* and the *Missoulian.*

Regional newspapers do a poor job of reporting national and international news. If you don't want to lose touch with the outside world, your best bet is the various **National Public Radio affiliates** across the state. Translator stations carry public radio to pretty remote parts of Montana, so if you are hungry for *Morning Edition* or *All Things Considered,* try scrolling around the bottom end of the FM radio dial.

If you want to read up on Montana on a monthly basis, check out *Montana Magazine,* a high-quality monthly devoted to history, travel, and culture in the state. If you can't find it on your newsstand, contact the magazine for a subscription at 888/666-8624, www.montanamagazine.com.

MAPS

The state highway department puts out a free road map that will suffice if you stick to paved roads. Request a copy from **Travel Montana** (301 S. Park Ave., Helena, MT 59520-0533, 406/841-2870 or 800/847-4868, www.visitmt.com), the official Montana travel information source.

For a more detailed look, the *Benchmark Montana Road & Recreation Atlas* is a handy book of topographic maps covering the entire state. It's $22.95 and is available at most bookstores in Montana.

National forest maps are invaluable for off-the-beaten-path travel in the western part of the state. Day hikers sticking to established trails will usually be able to navigate nicely with these maps, available at local ranger stations or from the **U.S. Forest Service Northern Region Headquarters** (406/329-3024, www.nationalforeststore.com, $10 each).

Serious backpackers and hunters will want U.S. Geological Survey quadrangle maps. Many sporting-goods stores carry these maps for the more popular areas; they can also be ordered directly from the **USGS** (303/236-5953, www.usgs.gov, $8-15). It pays to do a little research before contacting the USGS; they'll want to know the exact names of the maps you're ordering.

INFORMATION AND SERVICES

The **area code** throughout Montana is **406.** The entire state is on Mountain Time.

Liquor stores are operated by the state and are closed on Sunday. However, most bars are also licensed to sell liquor, beer, and wine, so you should have no trouble keeping in alcohol while in Montana. Wine is also for sale in grocery stores.

Most businesses are open from 9am-6pm Monday-Saturday. In smaller towns, don't count on stores being open on Sunday.

- **Southeast Montana:** 406/346-1876 or 800/346-1876, www.custer.visitmt.com

- **Glacier Country:** 406/873-6211 or 800/338-5072, http://glaciermt.com

- **Southwest Montana:** 406/846-1943 or 800/879-1159, http://southwestmt.com

- **Missouri River Country:** 406/653-1319 or 800/653-1319, www.missouririver.visitmt.com

- **Yellowstone Country:** 406/556-8680 or 800/736-5276, http://visityellowstonecountry.com

Governmental Organizations

The following federal, state, and regional services can provide detailed information on Montana:

- **U.S. Forest Service (Northern Region):** P.O. Box 7669, Missoula, MT 59807, 406/329-3511, www.fs.usda.gov/r1

- **Bureau of Land Management:** 222 N. 32nd Ave., Billings, MT 59101, 406/255-2888, www.mt.blm.gov/bifo

- **Department of Fish, Wildlife, and Parks:** 1420 6th Ave., Helena, MT 59620, 406/444-2535, http://fwp.mt.gov

- **Glacier National Park:** West Glacier, MT 59936, 406/888-7800, www.nps.gov/glac

- **Yellowstone National Park:** Yellowstone National Park, WY 82190, 307/344-7381, www.nps.gov/yell

- **Montana Historical Society:** 225 N. Roberts, Helena, MT 59620, 406/444-2694, http://mhs.mt.gov

- **Montana Outfitters and Guides Association:** P.O. Box 1248, Helena, MT 59624, 406/449-3578, www.montanaoutfitters.org

- For **road conditions,** call 800/226-7623.

Liquor stores are closed on Sunday.

Travel Montana

The state's tourism bureau can answer most questions about travel in Montana. Some of their brochures are invaluable. Contact the **Montana Office of Tourism** at 301 South Park Ave., Helena, MT 59520-0533, 406/841-2870 or 800/847-4868, www.visitmt.com.

In addition, **Travel Montana** has divided the state into six regions. Each local unit also produces brochures about sites, history, and amenities.

Regional Montana Tourism Information

Contact the following regional tourist offices for information about Montana.

- **Central Montana:** 406/761-5036 or 800/527-5348, http://centralmontana.com

ESSENTIALS
TRAVEL TIPS

Health and Safety

MEDICAL CARE

In Montana, you'll find no unexpected health dangers, and excellent medical attention is readily available. However, in rural parts of the state, doctors and hospitals can be quite far apart, so it's a good idea to begin your journey in good health and to take no unreasonable risks while traveling the state. Throughout the state, call 911 in an emergency.

PRECAUTIONS

Montana is not a particularly menacing place; however, a few considerations may save the traveler unpleasant experiences. The greatest risks most travelers will face are related to weather and insect bites.

Animals

Grizzly bears are found in Glacier and Yellowstone National Parks and in smaller populations in wilderness areas in much of the Rockies. When provoked—and it doesn't take much to rile them—grizzlies are vicious. Every year, it seems, someone is mauled by a grizzly, with deaths not infrequent. If you are traveling through grizzly country, check with local rangers for bear updates; areas in Glacier are often closed to hikers because of grizzly problems. If possible, hike in a large group. Make noise as you hike to forewarn nearby bears; small "bear bells" hooked on packs are common noisemakers, but are generally scorned by park rangers, who say that talking or singing is better. Don't sleep near smelly food, such as bacon; hang food from branches away from tents or in bear-proof containers available in many campgrounds.

Mountain lions are not as aggressive as grizzlies, but as their territory is progressively whittled away, there is more lion-human contact. Mountain lions live in most of the Rocky Mountain region. While human adults are in little danger from mountain lions, small children—especially if unattended—can attract them. Montana newspapers report regularly on mountain lion attacks and sightings of lions stalking people. Again, safety lies in numbers.

Not all threats come from carnivores. **Moose** are great hulking animals given to

Strong boots can help protect against a rattlesnake bite.

Getting Along with Bears

When a bear is spotted in western Montana, there's always the question: grizzly or black? Grizzly bears are huge; adults commonly weigh 600-800 pounds and stand four feet tall at their muscular shoulder humps. A grizzly's dish-shaped profile contrasts with the black bear's straight Roman nose. Black bears are also smaller (about 200 pounds and about three feet tall) and lack a shoulder hump.

Color is not a reliable distinguishing trait. No shade of brown is unusual for either bear; black bears can be honey-colored and are commonly cinnamon, while grizzlies are not always silver-tipped and grizzled looking.

But perhaps the ability to tell bears apart is not the most important thing to know when confronted by any ursine specimen.

Take precautions when traveling in bear country.

SAFETY CONSIDERATIONS

- Find out where bears, especially grizzlies, live, and take precautions. In Montana, grizzlies live in Glacier and Yellowstone National Parks and in wilderness areas throughout the Rockies. Rangers will usually know if bears have been spotted locally, and trails are sometimes closed because of bear activity.

- Try not to surprise a bear. Stay alert and make some noise while hiking; many hikers wear bells. Keep strong odors down. Don't wear a fragrance, and don't cook strong-smelling foods (freeze-dried foods are almost odor-free). At night, keep food and smelly clothing inside a car or strung high in a tree. Sleep well away from the cooking area. Women are frequently cautioned to avoid bear country while menstruating.

- Montana hikers are frequently advised to carry bear spray. If you purchase spray, make sure it is actual bear spray and not self-defense pepper spray. Also be sure that you know how to use it.

- If you do see a bear, give it plenty of room. Try to stay upwind of the bear so it can get your scent. If the bear becomes aggressive, drop something that may absorb its attention and climb the nearest tall tree. If this isn't possible, the next best bet is probably to curl up into a ball, clasp your hands behind your neck, and play dead, even if the bear begins to bat you around.

Bears can, and occasionally do, kill people, but most people who enter bear country have few problems. In fact, it is a special thing to see a grizzly. They are as impressive as they are rare. Precautions and respect for bears will ensure not only your continued survival, but theirs as well.

spontaneous charges if surprised. **Buffalo,** either at Yellowstone National Park or on private land, can be short-tempered if provoked. These animals are not vicious, but they are territorial and easily surprised. Be careful.

Rattlesnakes are common over the eastern two-thirds of the state. While a rattlesnake bite is rarely fatal these days, it's no fun either. If you are hiking anywhere in eastern Montana, it is imperative to wear strong boots with high tops. Watch where you step. Be especially careful around rocky promontories: Snakes like to sun themselves on exposed rocks. Rattlesnakes are not aggressive to humans; given their druthers, they will slink away, rattling. If you have never heard a rattlesnake rattle, don't worry that you might mistake it for something else. It is an instinctive human reaction to leap backward and shriek when you hear the rattle. When angered, however, rattlesnakes will coil and strike. If you are bitten, immobilize the affected area and seek immediate medical attention.

Be suspicious of overly friendly small mammals. Rabies is, as elsewhere, a real problem. If you are hiking in the vicinity of stock animals, especially cattle, it is wise to remember that bulls can be threatened by the presence of humans. Give them a wide berth.

Insects and Parasites

If you have insect bite allergies, don't mislead yourself into thinking that Montana's dry climate might be bug-free; it's not. An abundance of fierce insects awaits, and mosquito repellent is definitely recommended. Montana mosquitoes do not carry diseases, but they can be annoying, and an infected bite can be both unsightly and painful.

Ticks pose some slight risk of diseases such as Rocky Mountain fever and Lyme disease. If practical, wear light-colored clothing so you can spot ticks more easily. When you're hiking through underbrush, wear long-sleeved shirts and long pants tucked into your shoes or boots. Apply an insect repellent containing DEET. Be sure to check your body for ticks after walking in the woods or grassy meadows—and look *everywhere* on your skin—especially in patches of body hair (also be sure to check pets for ticks). If you find a tick with its head imbedded, don't panic. Using tweezers or your fingers, pull gently and steadily on its body until the tick disengages. Do *not* crush the tick, burn it with a match, douse it in alcohol, or any other home remedy, because these actions can cause the tick to regurgitate bacteria into its bite, increasing your chance of infection.

Under no circumstances should you drink unfiltered or untreated water straight from streams, springs, rivers, or lakes. The microscopic parasite **giardia** lives in mountain streams and will happily take up residence in your lower intestinal tract. Giardia enters streams through the fecal remains of animals—especially beavers (which gives the condition its common nickname, "beaver fever")—and is prevalent throughout Montana.

Symptoms of giardia infection include stomach cramps, nausea, a bloated stomach, watery foul-smelling diarrhea, and frequent gas. Giardia can appear several weeks after exposure to the parasite. Symptoms may disappear for a few days and then return, a pattern which may continue. Tinidazole, known as Fasigyn, or metronidazole (Flagyl) are the recommended drugs for treatment; both are prescription drugs. Either can be used in a single treatment dose. Antibiotics are not effective as a treatment.

Giardia is a fairly common summer affliction in the region. It has even been known to enter the water supply of entire mountain towns.

Weather

Weather extremes are common in Montana. Listen for weather forecasts: Sudden storms can blow in, causing rapid changes in temperature and wind conditions. Certain parts of Montana are known for their windiness: Great Falls ("the Windy City"), Livingston, and Cut Bank each deserve their reputation. If you are driving a high-profile vehicle, listen for wind warnings.

Too much summer sun can lead to sunburn, especially at Montana's higher altitudes. Wear sunscreen. Heat exhaustion can also be a problem if you're struggling up a hot hiking trail in full sun. Be sure to drink plenty of water and slow down if you feel yourself overheating.

Winter cold is the greatest weather concern. Roads can be treacherous if snow-covered, and incremental melting leaves small, invisible patches of ice on the road. If you travel by automobile in Montana in the winter, make sure you have tire chains, and know how to put them on. Make sure you also have blankets or a sleeping bag, plenty of warm clothing, gloves, a shovel, a flashlight (days aren't long in the winter), and maybe even a paraffin heater. Carrying extra food and water is a good idea. Again, pay attention to weather and road reports, and don't take chances.

Resources

Suggested Reading

DESCRIPTION AND TRAVEL

Federal Writers' Project of the Work Projects Administration for the State of Montana. *Montana: A State Guide Book*. State of Montana: Department of Agriculture, Labor, and Industry, 1939. New York: Hastings House, 1949. Long out of print, but it's worth snaring a copy at a used-book store. Also reprinted as The WPA Guide to 1930s Montana.

Melcher, Joan. *Montana Watering Holes: The Big Sky's Best Bars*. Guilford, Conn.: Globe Pequot Press, 2009. Find and enjoy Montana's top historic bars.

Mullan, John. *Miners and Travelers' Guide to Oregon, Washington, Idaho, Montana, Wyoming, and Colorado via the Missouri and Columbia Rivers*. 1865. New York: Arno Press, reprinted 1991. One of the earliest travel guides to the region, filled with colorful stories of the opening of the West.

Therriault, Ednor. *Montana Curiosities: Quirky Characters, Roadside Oddities, & Other Offbeat Stuff*. Guilford, Conn.: Globe Pequot Press, 2010. A guide to the wacky and unusual in Montana.

HISTORY

Brown, Mark H., and W. R. Felton. *Before Barbed Wire*. New York: Bramhall House, 1956. A commemoration of the life of L. A. Huffman, the frontier photographer who captured on film the era of the Native Americans and the open range.

Connell, Evan S. *Son of the Morning Star*. New York: Harper Collins, 1984. Story of the Battle of Little Bighorn.

Fritz, Harry, Mary Murphy, and Robert Swartout. *Montana Legacy: Essays on History, People, and Place*. Helena: Montana Historical Society Press, 2002. A lively compendium of essays on Montana history and culture.

Howard, Joseph Kinsey. *Montana: High, Wide, and Handsome*. Lincoln: University of Nebraska Press, 1943. A lively and opinionated history; a classic and still controversial Montana history.

Malone, Michael P., and Richard B. Roeder. *Montana: A History of Two Centuries*. Seattle: University of Washington, 2003. Now the accepted text on Montana's history, it is authoritative, rich in vignettes, and almost punchy.

Spitzer, Donald E. *Roadside History of Montana*. Missoula: Mountain Press, 1999. Learn the fascinating history of Montana as you motor across the state.

West, Carroll Van. *A Traveler's Companion to Montana History*. Helena: Montana Historical Society Press, 1986. An excellent roadside historical companion.

NATIVE AMERICANS

Bryan Jr., William L. *Montana's Indians.* Montana Geographic Series, no. 11. Helena: *Montana* magazine, 2003. Historical and contemporary sketches.

Eagle/Walking Turtle. *Indian America.* Santa Fe, N. Mex.: John Muir Press, 1991. Tribal histories and cultural information for visitors.

Hungry Wolf, Adolf and Beverly, compilers. *Indian Tribes of the Northern Rockies.* Skookumchuck, B.C.: Good Medicine Books, 1989. Tribal histories from Indian and non-Indian sources.

Miller, David Humphreys. *Custer's Fall: The Indian Side of the Story.* Lincoln: University of Nebraska Press, 1957. An enthralling retelling of the familiar Custer story based on Indian documentation.

Morgan, R. Kent. *Our Hallowed Ground: Guide to Indian War Battlefield Locations in Eastern Montana.* Bloomington, Ind.: Authorhouse, 2004. A guide to sites of battles and skirmishes between Native Americans and U.S. forces.

Wilfong, Cheryl. *Following the Nez Perce Trail.* Corvallis: Oregon State University Press, 2005. An absolutely wonderful, well-thought-out, and moving book that will enhance any trip intersecting with the Nez Perce Trail.

LEWIS AND CLARK

Ambrose, Stephen. *Undaunted Courage.* New York: Simon & Schuster, 1996. Scholarly, readable account of the Corps of Discovery, focusing on Lewis.

De Voto, Bernard, ed. *The Journals of Lewis and Clark.* Boston: Houghton Mifflin, 1953. Of the one-volume versions of the journals, this is the best.

Duncan, Dayton. *Out West.* New York: Viking Penguin, 1987. Along the Lewis and Clark Trail in the 1980s.

Lavender, David. *The Way to the Western Sea.* New York: Harper and Row, 1988. One of the West's most noted historians gives the fascinating details of the Lewis and Clark story.

NATURAL SCIENCES AND THE ENVIRONMENT

Alt, David, and Donald W. Hyndman. *Roadside Geology of Montana.* Missoula: Mountain Press, 1986. A comprehensive road-by-road guide to Montana's unique geology. For those willing to read slowly, there's a wealth of information.

Bass, Rick. *The Ninemile Wolves.* Livingston: Clark City Press, 1992. Passionate book-length essay chronicling wolves' return to northwestern Montana.

Chronic, Halka. *Pages of Stone: Geology of Western National Parks and Monuments, Vol. 1: Rocky Mountains and Western Great Plains.* Seattle: The Mountaineers, 1988. A clearly written and untechnical geology of the West, including Yellowstone and Glacier National Parks.

Dingus, Lowell. *Hell Creek, Montana: America's Key to the Prehistoric Past.* New York: St. Martin's Press, 2004. The story of rich fossil digs in eastern Montana overlain by a tableau of Jordan-area personalities and politics.

Kavanagh, James. *Montana Trees and Wildflowers.* Phoenix: Waterford Press, 2005. A pocket-size guide to Montana's flora, good for young naturalists.

McEneaney, Terry. *Birding Montana.* Helena: Falcon Press, 1998. Montana's best birding sites and tips on planning a birding trip.

Van Bruggen, Theodore. *Wildflowers, Grasses, and Other Plants of the Northern Plains and Black Hills.* Interior, S. Dak.: Badlands Natural History Association, 1971. A good guide to the plantlife of Montana's arid plains, with photographs.

RECREATION

Bach, Orville. *Exploring the Yellowstone Backcountry.* San Francisco: Sierra Club Books, 1998. Pick a trail and leave the crowded roads of Yellowstone National Park. Contains backcountry information for hikers, mountain bikers, canoeists, and cross-country skiers.

Birkby, Jeff. *Touring Hot Springs Montana and Wyoming: A Guide to the States' Best Hot Springs.* Billings and Helena: Falcon Guides 2013. A comprehensive guide to hot springs, including developed resorts and remote mountain pools.

Feldman, Robert, and Montana Hodges. *Rockhounding Montana.* Billings and Helena: Falcon Press, 2006. Feldman breaks the state into over 50 rock-hunting regions, complete with maps.

Fischer, Hank. *Paddling Montana.* Billings and Helena: Falcon Press, 2008. A comprehensive guide to floating 26 Montana rivers.

Grossenbacher, Brian and Jenny. *Fly-fishing Montana: A No-Nonsense Guide to Top Waters.* Tucson: No Nonsense Fly Fishing Guidebooks, 2007. A good guide for first-time Montana fly fishers.

Holt, John. *Flyfishing Adventures Montana.* Belgrade, Mont.: Wilderness Adventures Press, 2010. Holt is one of the state's top fishing writers, who includes frank discussions about ecology and culture in this book that's more than just a how-to guide.

Romans, Ben. *Montana's Best Fly Fishing: Flies, Access, and Guide's Advice for the*

State's Premier Rivers. Mechanicsburg, Pa.: Stackpole, 2010. Know before you go . . . lots of detailed advice and great photos.

Schneider, Bill and Russ. *Hiking Montana.* Billings and Helena: Falcon Press, 2004. Descriptions and maps of 100 hikes, mostly in western Montana.

Spomer, Ron. *Big Game Hunter's Guide to Montana.* Belgrade, Mont.: Wilderness Adventures Press, 2011. Information on all of Montana's game animals, where to find them, and where to find meat processors once you've had a successful hunt.

Wilderness Adventure Press. *Montana's Best Fishing Waters: 170 Detailed Maps of 34 of the Best Rivers, Streams, and Lakes.* Belgrade, Mont.: Wilderness Adventure Press, 2006. In-depth maps of top Montana fishing holes.

LITERATURE

Bass, Rick. *Winter: Notes from Montana.* Boston: Houghton Mifflin Company, 1992. Journals of the author's first winter in far northwestern Montana.

Bevis, William W. *Ten Tough Trips: Montana Writers and the West.* Seattle: University of Washington Press, 1990. One of the first works of literary criticism solely on Montana writers.

Blew, Mary Clearman. *All But the Waltz.* New York: Viking Penguin, 1991. Blew's family came to Montana in 1882. These affecting essays trace their lives in the Judith Basin country. Also look for her collections of short stories *Runaway, Lambing Out, Sister Coyote,* and a memoir, *Balsamroot.*

Crumley, James. *The Last Good Kiss.* New York: Random House, 1978. Follow hard-boiled Montana detectives around the seedy sides of the West in this book—and in *Dancing Bear* and *The Wrong Case.*

Ford, Richard. *Wildlife*. New York: Atlantic Monthly Press, 1990. A Great Falls teenager watches his father go off to fight fires and his mother take up with another man.

Frazier, Ian. *Great Plains*. New York: Farrar, Straus, Giroux, 1989. A wonderful conglomeration of Frazier's rambles across the historical and contemporary plains.

Fromm, Pete. *Indian Creek Chronicles: A Winter in the Bitterroot*. New York: Lyons and Burford, 1993. Good memoir to read by a toasty fireplace. Fromm has also written the novels *How All This Started* and *As Cool As I Am*.

Garcia, Andrew. *Tough Trip Through Paradise*. Sausalito, Calif.: Comstock Editions, 1967. Discovered in 1948, this is the powerfully written chronicle of the 1878 Montana frontier penned by a Caucasian who lived with Native Americans.

Guthrie Jr., A. B. *The Big Sky*. Boston: Houghton Mifflin Company, 1947. Classic, unvarnished tale of a young man living the Western life.

Hugo, Richard. *Making Certain It Goes On*. New York: W. W. Norton, 1984. Hugo's collected poems. For a change of pace, try Hugo's detective novel, *Death and the Good Life*, which hopscotches between the lower Flathead River and Portland, Oregon.

Jawort, Adrian and Cinnamon Spear. *Off the Path: An Anthology of 21st Century Montana American Writers*. Billings: Off the Pass Press, 2014. The best of contemporary Native American writing.

Kittredge, William, ed. *Montana Spaces*. New York: Nick Lyons Books, 1988. Evocative essays by the likes of Thomas McGuane and Gretel Ehrlich with perfect black-and-white photos by John Smart.

Kittredge, William, and Annick Smith, eds. *The Last Best Place*. Helena: Montana Historical Society Press, 1988. This 1,158-page compendium anchors down every Montanan's bedside table. From Native American myths to Paul Zarzyski's modern cowboy poems, it's all here.

Krakel, Dean. *Downriver: A Yellowstone Journey*. San Francisco: Sierra Club Press, 1987. The eclectic chronicle of a float trip down the full length of the Yellowstone River.

Maclean, Norman. *A River Runs Through It*. Chicago: University of Chicago Press, 1976. The classic novella of fly-fishing and two brothers' love and doomed relationship.

McGuane, Thomas. *Driving on the Rim*. New York: Vintage, 2011. Tough, sensitive guy tries to set his life straight in a town that's a lot like Livingston.

McMurtry, Larry. *Lonesome Dove*. New York: Pocket Books, 1985. A masterfully written epic of the last days of the great Texas cattle drives, told from the point of view of faded but wisecracking cowboys. Also from McMurtry, *Buffalo Girls* is an engaging saga of Calamity Jane and her gang.

Raban, Jonathan. *Badlands*. New York: Vintage Books, 1996. Rambling narrative that examines the homesteading movement on the eastern Montana plains.

Stegner, Wallace. *Wolf Willow*. New York: Viking Press, 1962. Stegner spent his youth on a homestead just north of Montana, in Saskatchewan.

Stockton, Bill. *Today I Baled Some Hay to Feed the Sheep the Coyotes Eat*. Billings and Helena: Falcon Press, 1983. Vignettes by a Montana-raised, Paris-educated writer and illustrator on the vicissitudes of sheep ranching.

Van Cleve, Spike. *A Day Late and a Dollar Short.* Kansas City: Lowell Press, 1982. The full-spirited reminiscences of one of Montana's foremost dude ranchers and storytellers.

Welch, James. *The Indian Lawyer.* New York: W. W. Norton, 1990. A Blackfeet lawyer in Helena finds his life suddenly very complicated . . . It's a page-turner with good insights. Welch's other novels include *Fools Crow, Winter in the Blood,* and *The Death of Jim Loney.*

MAGAZINES

Montana magazine is published in Helena and is a good collage of history, photography, travel information, discussion of current issues, and whatnot. You're warned: It can become addictive reading. Call 800/821-3874 in Montana or 800/654-1105 out of state for subscription information.

Montana Outdoors is published by the Montana Department of Fish, Wildlife, and Parks and contains the latest information on fishing, hunting, and recreation, and of course, great photography. Call 800/678-6668 for subscription information.

ATLAS

Montana Road & Recreation Atlas. Medford, Oreg.: Benchmark Maps, 2008. A handy collection of topographic maps and recreational information covering the entire state.

Internet Resources

www.visitmt.com
The website of the **Montana Office of Tourism,** with lodging, destinations, events, and much, much more.

www.montanakids.com
Games and resources for kids.

www.wintermt.com
Information on Montana ski areas and winter recreation.

http://fwp.mt.gov
The **Montana Fish, Wildlife, and Parks** site, with information on state parks, wildlife, and recreation.

www.fs.usda.gov/r1
The **U.S. Forest Service Region 1** encompasses Montana, and this site provides information on recreation and camping in Montana's public forests.

www.blm.gov/mt/st/en.html
The **U.S. Bureau of Land Management (BLM)** office for Montana provides information on national monuments and hunting on public lands.

www.montanaoutfitters.org
Start here with the **Montana Outfitters and Guides Association** site if you are planning a hunting, fishing, or guided backcountry vacation.

www.mtpr.org
The **Montana Public Radio** site, with information on public radio programming in the state.

www.umt.edu
www.montana.edu
In addition to enrollment information for the **University of Montana** and **Montana State University** and links to various departments, you can also reach each university library through these addresses.

www.montanamuseums.org
A listing of contact information for Montana museums from the **Museums Association of Montana.**

http://mhs.mt.gov
The state's best museum, the **Montana Historical Society,** also has an excellent online book and gift shop.

http://hotelstravel.com/usmt.html
Listings of all of the major hotels, motels, and B&Bs in Montana.

www.mtbba.com
Comprehensive listing from the **Montana B&B Association** of member bed-and-breakfasts.

www.mdt.mt.gov/travinfo
Check the **Montana Department of Transportation** site for Montana road conditions.

Index

List of Maps

Photo Credits

MAP SYMBOLS

▨▨▨	Expressway	★	Highlight	✈	Airfield	⛳	Golf Course
──	Primary Road	○	City/Town	✈	Airport	🅿	Parking Area
──	Secondary Road	◉	State Capital	▲	Mountain	🔺	Archaeological Site
─ ─ ─	Unpaved Road	⊛	National Capital	✚	Unique Natural Feature	⛪	Church
─ ─ ─	Trail	★	Point of Interest			⛽	Gas Station
⋯⋯	Ferry	•	Accommodation	⚑	Waterfall	🌀	Glacier
┅┅	Railroad	▼	Restaurant/Bar	▲	Park		Mangrove
▨▨▨	Pedestrian Walkway	▪	Other Location	🚩	Trailhead		Reef
▥▥▥	Stairs	ᴧ	Campground	⛷	Skiing Area		Swamp

CONVERSION TABLES

$°C = (°F - 32) / 1.8$
$°F = (°C \times 1.8) + 32$
1 inch = 2.54 centimeters (cm)
1 foot = 0.304 meters (m)
1 yard = 0.914 meters
1 mile = 1.6093 kilometers (km)
1 km = 0.6214 miles
1 fathom = 1.8288 m
1 chain = 20.1168 m
1 furlong = 201.168 m
1 acre = 0.4047 hectares
1 sq km = 100 hectares
1 sq mile = 2.59 square km
1 ounce = 28.35 grams
1 pound = 0.4536 kilograms
1 short ton = 0.90718 metric ton
1 short ton = 2,000 pounds
1 long ton = 1.016 metric tons
1 long ton = 2,240 pounds
1 metric ton = 1,000 kilograms
1 quart = 0.94635 liters
1 US gallon = 3.7854 liters
1 Imperial gallon = 4.5459 liters
1 nautical mile = 1.852 km

MOON MONTANA
Avalon Travel
a member of the Perseus Books Group
1700 Fourth Street
Berkeley, CA 94710, USA
www.moon.com

Editor and Series Manager: Kathryn Ettinger
Copy Editor: Ashley Benning
Graphics Coordinator: Elizabeth Jang
Production Coordinator: Elizabeth Jang
Cover Design: Faceout Studios, Charles Brock
Moon Logo: Tim McGrath
Map Editor: Albert Angulo
Cartographer: Brian Shotwell
Indexer: Greg Jewett

ISBN-13: 978-1-63121-017-4
ISSN: 1537-579X

Printing History
1st Edition — 1992
9th Edition — June 2015
5 4 3 2 1

Front cover photo: Swiftcurrent Lake at sunset,
Glacier National Park © Tom Schwabel, Tandemstock

Back cover photo: © Sherry Yates/123rf.com

Printed in Canada by Friesens

KEEPING CURRENT

If you have a favorite gem you'd like to see included in the next edition, or see
anything that needs updating, clarification, or correction, please drop us a
line. Send your comments via email to feedback@moon.com, or use the address above.